International Marketing

Third edition

Stanley J. Paliwoda
Michael J. Thomas

Published on behalf of
The Chartered Institute of Marketing

OXFORD AUCKLAND BOSTON JOHANNESBURG MELBOURNE NEW DELHI

Butterworth-Heinemann
Linacre House, Jordan Hill, Oxford OX2 8DP
225 Wildwood Avenue, Woburn, MA 01801-2041
A division of Reed Educational and Professional Publishing Ltd

A member of the Reed Elsevier plc group

First published 1986
Reprinted 1988, 1989, 1990, 1991
Second edition 1993
Reprinted 1993, 1994, 1995, 1997
Third edition 1998
Reprinted 1999

British Library Cataloguing in Publication Data
A catalogue record for this book is available from the British Library

ISBN 0 7506 2241 5

Typeset by Jayvee, Trivandrum, India
Printed and bound in Great Britain by The Bath Press, Bath

Contents

Foreword

This is my second preface to this book. In this, the Third Edition of a book which has found its own niche on the market, the authors, two well-respected professors in their own right, have produced a volume which is both comprehensive and readable.

Make no mistake, international marketing should not be just an elective or just one paper en route to a further or higher qualification. It will prove to be one of the most challenging and sustaining subjects which you will study. For the 'world's favourite airline' – yes, you have deduced that I am referring to British Airways – survival in the new global marketplace would not be possible without the implementation of the precepts of international marketing. To have achieved consistent success faced with the volume of changes and opportunities that we continually confront, requires knowledge. No business can exist, never mind succeed, without knowledge. That knowledge is corporate knowledge and it comes down to the very individuals who work for our airline in no matter what capacity. Your perception of us as an airline is formed by how you view our activities as a passenger. This means that in all we do besides getting you to your destination, we have to be considerate of your needs. All our staff are first carefully selected then well trained to appreciate our customers. We understand the needs of our business and we know that when passengers arrive at an airport, they are generally tired, stressed and often very anxious. We want to be able to offer you, our customer, a comfortable flight in whatever class you travel so we seek to ensure that you are welcomed at check-in without undue delay and that any special needs such as vegetarian meals or perhaps wheelchair assistance are properly recorded. Similarly, boarding should be a task that is expedited efficiently by our ground staff at the gate. We wish to offer assistance wherever we can and like to demonstrate to other passengers BA's passenger care in action. Once on board the aircraft you are in the hands of our cabin crew who are trained not just to serve you but to deal with emergencies when they occur. Many times per minute there are customers boarding BA flights throughout the network across the globe so the scenario just described is a familiar one and has to be standardized while seeking to offer maximum added value to each of our customers in terms of care and attention. Each and every member of our staff bears a responsibility towards our customers.

The travelling public appreciate us for our service and so we are careful to seek to replicate that level of service in all markets in which we operate. This means we have to train staff to meet our standard for world-class service. However, there is more to being a world-class airline. The image which we have formed in your mind is created through our advertising and our ability to fulfil the promise of our advertising. We are undisputed as the 'world's favourite airline' because we fulfil our promise to each passenger each second of the day throughout the BA network. That service package which we have to provide includes customer reception and enquiries, check-in, baggage handling, seating and by means of the provision of food, entertainment and reading matter for every flight we offer and to the same exacting standard in each case.

We have enforced a standardization policy with regard to service and as to how we look and are seen, by means of uniforms and livery. We have also to be careful to meet individual needs and also be culturally sensitive and aware so as not to offend. The knowledge of our marketing and advertising professionals allows us to gain the benefits of international standardization where applicable and to create customization where appropriate. On all our flights worldwide we are travelling with people of many cultures and of many nations. That they choose to fly with us repeatedly is testimony to our customer care programme. We deploy our resources as a large and successful airline to pamper you as a customer. We undertake research and development in all aspects of our operations including seating, into the provision of in-flight entertainment and communications which we build into your chair seat. Few airlines are able to offer you individual television screens in your own armrest, satellite telephone sets which are also built into your armrest and, in front of you, our own in-house publications such as In Flight and Executive Life.

The story never ends. Success creates the challenge to stay on top. We are mindful of our position and respectful of our customers who put us there so as an organization we endeavour always to make continuous improvements wherever possible. We not only welcome the competition which we face in every country in which we operate, but we seek to drive it further and higher by continually reviewing what we offer our customers, so setting in train increasingly demanding standards for our competitors to achieve. We are a global business by matching the needs of individual customers across all the nations we serve. Each and every one of them is important to us. We never allow ourselves to be complacent about what we offer our customers.

The challenge for you then is to gain an understanding of what is required to compete in the new global marketplace for what was once an option for large firms is today a requirement for all companies irrespective of size.

I wish you success in your studies. As a global business, we continually need globally aware and educated people. No nation and certainly no business can afford to be ignorant of the challenge of this new global marketplace in which we all live today; it is our future.

Sir Colin Marshall
Chairman
British Airways

Introduction

As President of the Chartered Institute of Marketing, it is a pleasure for me to be asked to write an introduction to this book by two of our distinguished Fellows.

The Chartered Institute of Marketing has many students around the world taking its certificate and postgraduate diploma examinations. International Marketing has a rightful place on our postgraduate diploma programme to ensure that people receive the knowledge and skills set which they require to function effectively in business.

Many of you will be familiar with the name Cadbury, which is to be found today in many markets around the world. Certain of our products are international success stories and so you will see, for example, the familiar purple and white colours and the glass and a half of milk symbol in the advertising of our dairy milk chocolate which is as important as the colours. Today, this advertising is being replicated in many countries. Tastes differ, languages differ and so we have to exercise caution but today, how often are you able to stop and actually read a billboard or newspaper advertisement? We function more and more today by standardizing our advertising and by repeating the same colours, patterns and symbols which you associate with Cadbury and its products, so that when you see our advertising, you immediately recognize it as Cadbury without necessarily reading it. You recognize the images and you do not need to read the words to know it is Cadbury.

Bringing a product to market today is more expensive and more risky than ever before. In our line of business, we have to be mindful of ensuring product quality and freshness and that means partly packaging, sometimes using tins, but we also need guaranteed cool storage and as we look at our distribution channels, we seek this in turn of our distributors and retailers. It used to be the case that a manufacturer only produced things, but no more. Today, manufacturers are involved in advertising, often collaborative advertising, in promotions such as our current sponsorship with Granada Television's *Coronation Street*, where we also had the familiar introductory scene with the buildings, people, shops and vans all represented in a chocolate tableau. Cadbury is a major manufacturer and a world name in the chocolate industry. That translates into market power and some of that same power behind the name is being sought by retailers seeking the Cadbury signage for their sales outlets.

You know us for what we produce but we really need to know everyone's business as well. To provide you the consumer with a better product, we need to continually monitor all of our operations including those of our intermediaries to ensure that what reaches you is a fresh product. Perishability is a problem common to our industry so good distribution is essential. Now it helps production if we can supply the same package to, say, Britain and France, but that is not the case. We have national labelling requirements that necessitate special labelling. For example, we are bound by language requirements as well as by local labelling laws. The one common element which we retain is the logo, which we wish to be instantly recognizable.

We pride ourselves on the quality of our production and we like to consider ourselves as one of the world's best producers. However, if ever there was a time when you could simply produce and then hope to sell, it is not today. There has been a perceptible shift in power from manufacturer to retailer over the last ten years. Producers today cannot afford to fall out with retailers for there is keen competition for shelf space and no matter the quality of our product, substitutability has to be acknowledged. Companies such as ours have to consider collaborative business ventures which were unknown to my predecessors who certainly knew and built the family business. From collaborative advertising to shop signage, Cadbury is becoming visibly and financially involved in order to heighten market positioning. While such market entanglements are increasing so, too, are market competition and market regulation.

There can hardly be anyone alive today either in Europe or outside who is unaware of the European Union. We are dealing with new market realities and if the needs of the industry are to be reflected in training, then these problems have to be confronted. Professors Paliwoda and Thomas have done well to encapsulate so succinctly the diversity of market environments and the tools, techniques and skills required to master them. This is a very useful book with important lessons to be learned for business, for as the saying goes: 'If you do not learn from your mistakes you are condemned to relive them.' Professors Paliwoda and Thomas have produced a very comprehensive treatment of an essential subject. This book should be on everyone's reading list, whether a practitioner, who believes that he or she has ten or twenty years' experience and little to learn, perhaps even in my firm, or a student. There are eight chapters which bring together very well the international marketing operating environment and how to deal with it, then a ninth chapter which deals more with monitoring, planning and reviewing operations and then finally, the last two chapters which deal with Europe and the Pacific Rim respectively. It is interesting to see Europe being treated here as a focus on European Union while still acknowledging the diversity of Europe West and Europe East and Central, notably the former communist countries. The last chapter is noteworthy for its treatment of developing the contrasts in a region of tremendous economic growth and cultural diversity: China, Japan and the Mini Dragons (formerly 'Tigers') need to be better understood by us all.

This book has many strengths, from the use of anecdotes, exhibits and illustrations from the trade and business press to innovations such as the use of the Internet. There are perhaps many sources we could turn to for information but this book presents analysis and discussion and identifies further sources of information including Web sites. Professors Paliwoda and Thomas have to be congratulated on a job well done. They have produced an excellent book for the Chartered Institute of Marketing series. The marketing challenge before us now is to make everyone aware of this.

Sir Dominic Cadbury
Chairman, Cadbury Schweppes plc and
President, Chartered Institute of Marketing

Preface

There is one major difference between writing a book and writing a textbook on international marketing and that is that the subject of international marketing is forever changing. The world has changed enormously for this present generation now studying. Our mindset has had to change with the fall of communism and the opening up not just of new markets but of membership of our economic and strategic defence alliances of countries perceived previously to be our enemies. Elsewhere, South Africa ended apartheid, held free elections with universal suffrage and joined the rest of the free world, although perhaps this term 'free' remains open to question. Technology has introduced many innovations including the Internet, a source now of hitherto inaccessible and difficult to find market data. Communications have changed so that we are able to correspond not just by phone or mail but by fax and by e-mail which offers a potential also for international payments transactions just as Web sites offer internationally accessible shop windows for products and services.

This third edition is a marked departure from the first two. It was redesigned to meet the new global market situation and appraise students of actualities. The Chartered Institute of Marketing allows us the leeway to focus on actual practice as well as theory. We have sought to produce a comprehensible synthesis. We do not believe that national identities are under threat. Quite the reverse: as we learn more about each other, the perceived risk of foreign travel and of doing business abroad lessens greatly. As international marketing becomes more of the norm than a luxury, services to exporters small and large increase, there emerges a larger pool of expertise and knowledge, and gains are shared by all.

To those lecturers who have loyally used this book, our apologies for such drastic revision, but in this new edition we seek to offer your students many new things not previously available. We have inserted interesting anecdotes and stories from the business press wherever we have considered them to be useful illustrations of points covered in the text. This time, working closely with the publisher, we have sought to ensure that in production, illustrations are kept separate in box panels from the main text and that tables are not bunched together away from the text that introduces and explains their meaning. We have incorporated several photographic illustrations and new material on the Pacific Rim and on Europe, bringing together East and West. While we have sought to present and to discuss trends which we consider to have a lasting future presence, we can never hope to be able to publish the most recent statistics nor easily update them in reprinting. It is a perennial problem that the publication of international statistics seems to occur only years after national statistics have appeared. We have sought to address this question by citing useful Internet addresses for further updates and information. Where appropriate we have also sounded a note of caution for, as Shakespeare phrased it: 'all that glisters is not gold'. We have endeavoured not just to present material but to make students think more about its meaning and significance. Our responsibility as educators is to seek to prepare our students for the markets of today and tomorrow.

What is becoming increasingly clear is that international marketing ought really to be a required course. The reality of the European Union today is known to present-day importers in the UK, if not to would-be exporters. If we seek to ignore these present-day market challenges we may well witness the loss of our markets tomorrow both at home and abroad. Speed to market has increased enormously in recent years and consequently market dynamism in all markets exhibiting the least economic growth has increased accordingly. The stakes are now much higher which means that both the potential gains and potential losses are consequently greater.

International marketing has passed from the stage of the enthusiast to that of a professional in a virtual regional office. The boundaries, whether national, regional or international no longer exist; they have been superseded and made obsolete by communications technology. International marketing is no longer a subject which we may choose to learn but one which everyone should know and be able to operationalize. We acknowledge the Chartered Institute of Marketing which has long had the foresight in this respect to recognize the importance of international marketing in its postgraduate diploma syllabus.

Finally, to those who may be wondering about the intricacies and complexities of communications across the Atlantic, it may be revealed that this book was written with both authors sitting cheek by jowl in Professor Thomas's office at Strathclyde University. That is, on the days when they were not both travelling to distant parts of the world. Professor Paliwoda would like to receive all compliments with regard to redesign and suggests that all errors of omission and commission are best addressed to Professor Thomas! In fact, it has really been a pleasure to work together and share our thoughts on this book, so do not take such comments too seriously . . .

Best wishes from us both for success in your studies and please let us have your feedback. We may now both be reached by e-mail.

Stanley J. Paliwoda	*Michael J. Thomas*
Professor of Marketing	*Professor of Marketing*
University of Calgary	*University of Strathclyde*
Canada	*Scotland*
E-mail: spaliwoda@msn.com	E-mail: michaelt@market.strath.ac.uk

Acknowledgements

Every effort has been made to locate the copyright holders of material used and the authors would like to thank the following for granting permission to include material copyrighted to them in the book: Table 10.10 – Reprinted by permission of Addison Wesley Longman Ltd; Figure 1.8, 1.10, 5.7, 10.4, Table 1.7, 2.11, 5.14, 8.1, 9.2, 10.2, Exhibit 9.1 – Reproduced by permission of the American Marketing Association; Figure 1.13, 1.14, 9.8, 9.9, 9.10 – Copyright © 1972 by Basic Books, Inc. Reprinted by permission of BasicBooks, a subsidiary of Perseus Books Groups, LLC; Exhibit 3.7 – Reproduced by kind permission of Clyde & Forth Press Group; Table 2.3 – Copyright © 1945 by Columbia University Press. Reprinted with permission of Columbia University Press; Figure 1.2, Table 1.3 – © Crown copyright 1996; Figure 4.3 – Copyright © 1994 by The Dryden Press, reproduced by permission of the publisher; Exhibit 2.2, 4.2, 6.3, 8.6 – © The Economist; Table 10.9 – First published in *Business Central Europe* © 1994 The Economist Newspaper Limited; Table 2.15, Figure 4.15 – Permission for this material has been granted by ESOMAR (European Society for Opinion and Marketing Research), J. J. Viottastraat 29, 1071 JP Amsterdam, The Netherlands. E-mail: publications@esomar.nl; Table 5.8 – Copyright © 1983. Reproduced with permission of Greenwood Publishing Group Inc., Westport, CT, USA; Figure 6.1 – Copyright © 1987 by Kenton W. Elderkin and Warren E. Norquist. Reprinted by permission of HarperCollins Publishers, Inc; Figure 5.5, Table 5.6 – Copyright © 1987, The Hawarth Press; Table 7.3 – Copyright © 1990, International Chamber of Commerce (ICC); Figure 4.5, Table 4.16 – Reproduced with kind permission of Kluwer Law International; Figure 1.12, 1.15, 1.16 – Reproduced by permission of the McGraw-Hill Companies; Figure 1.5, 1.6, 2.6, 2.8, 4.6, 4.7; Table 1.8 – Reproduced by permission of Macmillan Press Ltd; Table 3.5 – Reproduced by kind permission of Keith Monk; Figure 1.1, Table 1.1, 1.2, 6.4 – © OECD. Reproduced by permission of the OECD; Figure 5.4 – Reproduced by kind permission of Pinter Publishing, Cassell Academic, Wellington House, 125 Strand, London, UK; Exhibit 1.3 – © 1996 Time Inc., all rights reserved; Figure 10.5 – Copyright © 1990 by Nicholas Colchester and David Buchan. Reprinted by permission of Times Books, a division of Random House, Inc. Exhibit 5.14 – © Times Newspapers Ltd, 1996; Table 9.3 – Copyright © 1979, by the Regents of the University of California. Reprinted from the *California Management Review*, **22**(2). By permission of the Regents; Table 2.2, 9.4 – Copyright © John Wiley & Sons Ltd. Reproduced with permission; Table 3.1, Exhibit 4.1 – Copyright © *World Trade* magazine, 1997.

CHAPTER 1

Internationalization: a necessity not a luxury, but does corporate behaviour reflect it?

The concept of advantage

The starting point begins with international trade, something which has been practised by many civilizations over many thousands of years. A visit to any museum will reveal some of the artefacts of ancient daily life which were traded across vast distances, as with the Roman treasures still being found in Britain today. These ancient goods represent what today we might call standardized products. The urns, bowls, vases and pottery ware, which are all identified as indisputably Roman, conformed to a certain specification of manufacture and were then transported.

The Roman garrisons in Britain in 44AD were captive markets for products known to the Romans. Their situation was similar to that of the US army divisions in the Second World War which simply by taking overseas with them certain products or more importantly brands, which US soldiers regarded as being from 'home', created a multinational product and presence for products such as Coca-Cola.

Today, we have moved one step further from Ricardo's Theory of Comparative Advantage to the point where in some sections of industrial activity, the competition which exists is global rather than national, as in computers or automobiles where the sourcing of components and assemblies is another multinational activity. Size and the well-understood principle of economics of scale have given rise to highly dynamic competition. The critical mass that a company requires to cover breakeven costs is also forever increasing, partly because of technological push, partly also because of market-driven forces which create demand for new or improved products. The so-called 'Green Revolution', which has swept Europe and North America, has given rise to new car specifications and to engines able to burn unleaded fuel; and to soaps, detergents and products generally that are biodegradable and will not pollute the environment. These products in turn offer new advantages which are passed on to the consumer. However, if the customer does not value these new product advantages, which have been created at a cost that has been passed on to the customer, then the customer will avoid this particular brand in future in favour of a cheaper, more basic variant. In this case the manufacturer will only add to overhead costs and have lost certain of his customers.

With the passage of time, it is noticeable how these changes sweep through different countries almost simultaneously. Countries at approximately the same level of economic advancement may be expected to have environmentally aware consumers able and willing to do something about caring for the environment involving changing their behaviour, perhaps changing their product purchases, even if it does mean finding an extra few pence outlay on a shopping bill. This differential can be labelled 'conscience money', and the psychological benefit of doing something positive for the environment may well compensate those consumers for this additional outlay. The problem is in establishing the critical threshold as to how much people are prepared to pay. It does create marketing segmentation opportunities for companies to explore across nations, so spreading the costs of product development further, and across more than one market. The Green Revolution is a good example of social change that has led to segmentation strategies for specially formulated, environmentally friendly products.

Where is the nation state?

Absolute advantage, which is traced back to Adam Smith, stated that trade would take place

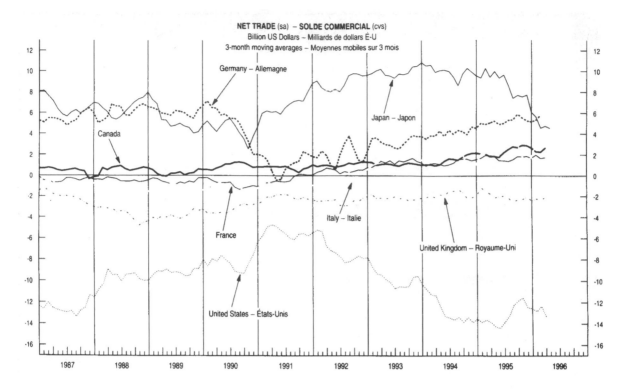

NET TRADE (sa) – **SOLDE COMMERCIAL** (cvs)
Billion US Dollars – Milliards de dollars É-U
3-month moving averages – Moyennes mobiles sur 3 mois

Source: OECD (1996) *Main Economic Indicators*, Paris, August

Figure 1.1   Foreign trade

between two nations, each having something the other wanted to buy, but could not produce for itself. The instances of absolute advantage were few and so the Ricardo Theory of Comparative Advantage then took hold. This said that it made sense still to trade when there was no absolute advantage; prices may be similar to those at which you could produce yourself. However, what the Theory of Comparative Advantage then went on to say was that this offered the nation the opportunity for specialization in a certain sphere of activity. Depending on a nation's factor endowment, it could choose to focus and specialize in a particular area in which it then could create an advantage. Minerals and raw materials might give an advantage but cheap labour was only a very short-term advantage.

Yet to Porter, the key to whether a nation is competitive in an industry is not whether it trades, but whether it has a combination of trade and investment that reflects advantages and skills that have been created at home. Porter (1990) sees classical economic theory as deficient in explaining trade and investment in advanced nations for three reasons:

1.   **Globalization** which decouples the firm from the factor endowment of its home nation.
2.   **Factor pools** of many nations reaching a certain comparability. Comparative advantage in terms of factor costs is only temporary.

3.   **Technology**. Where labour content is too high, automation can be introduced. Similarly with raw materials, if these prove to be scarce, new synthetic ones can be created.

Porter (1990) then argues for the sources of advantage to be 'relentlessly broadened and upgraded'. Where home customers are demanding, and seek quality and sophistication, this in turn forces the firm to improve; but, where home customers are merely accepting of variable quality offerings, this then can place the firm at a disadvantage in international markets. Demanding customers and strong competition move companies away from dependence on the lowest common denominator.

In the same way, many new products today have arisen from technologies related to mature industries. Examples of internationally competitive-related industries include Denmark in dairy products and brewing, giving rise to industrial enzymes; Switzerland with its strength in pharmaceuticals, giving rise to flavourings; and the UK with a strength in engines, giving rise to a related industry in lubricants and 'anti-knock' preparations.

Governments are generally eager to help national companies but Porter does not find this governmental help to have been an advantage. Instead, it is better to have firms which are self-sustaining and able to compete independently.

Table I.I Exports less imports

EXPORTS less IMPORTS (f.o.b.-c.i.f.)–EXPORTATIONS moins IMPORTATIONS (f.a.b.-c.a.f)
Billions US dollars; monthly averages, sa—Milliards de dollars E-U; moyennes mensuelles, cvs

	1993	1994	1995	1995 Q3	1995 Q4	1996 Q1	1996 Q2	1995 Oct	1995 Nov	1995 Dec	1996 Jan	1996 Feb	1996 Mar	1996 Apr	1996 May	1996 Jun
Canada[1]	1.13	1.45	2.34	2.52	2.91	2.30		2.75	2.50	3.48	2.68	1.81	2.41	2.56	3.01	
United States – États-Unis[1]	-9.63	-12.55	-13.23	-13.25	-11.56	-12.82		-11.89	-11.22	-11.59	-14.53	-11.61	-12.33	-13.09	-14.48	
Japan – Japon	10.03	10.10	8.84	8.58	7.53	5.62	4.54	5.18	9.28	8.14	5.72	4.28	6.87	2.51	4.81	6.30
Australia – Australie[1]	0.02	-0.21	-0.37	-0.23	-0.17	-0.01	-0.11	-0.23	-0.41	0.12	-0.03	-0.29	0.29	-0.25	-0.23	0.15
New Zealand – Nouvelle-Zélande	0.08	0.03	-0.02	-0.01	-0.01	-0.11	-0.04	0.05	-0.01	-0.07	-0.14	-0.08	-0.11	-0.01	0.08	-0.19
Austria – Autriche	-0.70	-0.85														
Belgium – Belgique[2]	0.41	0.84	1.17	1.43	0.84			0.95	0.80	0.78	0.94	0.54				
Denmark – Danemark	0.55	0.49	0.45	0.43	0.34	0.55		0.38	0.30	0.33	0.54	0.54	0.57	0.54	0.70	
Finland – Finlande	0.45	0.54	0.92	0.76	0.99			0.91	0.98	1.09	0.48	0.85				
France[1]	1.30	1.23	1.71	1.38	1.81	1.97		1.48	2.48	1.46	1.59	2.01	2.29	0.67	2.23	
Germany – Allemagne	3.04	3.68	5.30	5.30	5.53	5.31		5.16	6.35	4.58	4.31	6.55	5.08	5.78		
Greece – Grèce	-1.13	-1.04	0.00													
Iceland – Islande	0.00	0.01	0.00	0.00	0.01	0.00		0.00	0.01	0.01	-0.02	0.03	-0.01	-0.01	-0.04	
Ireland – Irlande	0.59	0.67	0.95	1.03	0.91			1.12	0.78	0.84	1.28	1.25				
Italy – Italie	1.73	1.84	2.30	2.82	1.78	3.13		2.20	3.85	-0.70	1.43	4.44	3.51	3.59	0.15	
Netherlands – Pays-Bas	1.22	1.42	1.62	1.98	1.58	1.71		1.15	0.70	2.87	0.71	2.21	2.23	2.77	0.91	
Norway – Norvège	0.65	0.61	0.72	0.70	0.73	1.20		0.56	0.68	0.95	1.12	1.13	1.33	1.12		
Portugal	-0.72	-0.74	-0.82	-0.74	-0.89	-0.76		-1.03	-0.74	-0.90	-0.73	-0.88	-0.68	-0.71		
Spain – Espagne	-1.59	-1.59	-1.93	-2.05	-1.95	-2.07		-2.19	-2.10	-1.57	-1.93	-2.61	-1.68	-1.51	-1.68	
Sweden – Suède	0.58	0.78	1.23	1.27	1.37	1.38	1.73	1.56	1.49	1.06	1.65	1.17	1.34	1.61	2.04	1.53
Switzerland – Suisse	0.19	0.19	0.11	0.20	0.10	-0.12	0.15	-0.03	0.06	0.28	-0.53	0.02	0.16	0.23	0.12	0.11
Turkey – Turquie	-1.20	-0.38	-1.8	-1.31	-1.42			-1.52	-1.35	-1.40						
United Kingdom – Royaume-Uni	-2.13	-1.87	-1.92	-2.15	-2.27	-2.22		-3.10	-1.36	-2.36	-2.45	-2.41	-1.79	-2.54	-2.04	
OECD-Total – OCDE-Total	4.98	4.90	5.13	5.49	5.24	3.54		0.42	10.84	4.46	-3.15	5.48	8.30	1.60		
Major seven – Sept grands	5.49	4.17	5.29	5.19	5.73	3.28		1.79	12.37	3.02	-1.23	5.05	6.03	-0.52		
OECD-Europe – OCDE-Europe	3.48	6.09	7.54	7.89	6.54	8.57		4.56	10.70	4.38	3.14	11.38	11.17	9.89		
EU15 – UE15	3.81	5.70	7.36	8.29	7.13	9.95		5.55	11.31	4.54	5.08	12.62	12.15	10.84		

Note: Data presented in the foreign trade tables may differ from those shown in OECD, *Monthly Statistics of Foreign Trade (Series A)*. Generally, national statistical institutes are the source for data in these tables while customs offices provide data for certain countries published in *Series A*. The conversion to US dollars and the timing of the introduction of revisions may also account for differences with the data in *Series A*. As the figures shown here refer only to total trade (without breakdown by product or country of origin or consumption), they may be available more quickly than the detailed data published in *Series A*.

Source: OECD (1996) *Main Economic Indicators*, Paris, August

Note: Les données présentées dans les tableaux Commerce extérieur peuvent être différentes de celles publiées dans OCDE, *Statistiques mensuelles du Commerce extérieur (Série A)*. En général, les offices nationaux de statistiques sont la source des séries présentées ici; tandis que les offices de douane fournissent les données de la *Série A* pour certains pays. D'autre part, la conversion en dollars des États-Unis et la date de mise à jour des révisions peuvent également expliquer des différences entre ces séries et celles de la *Série A*. Les tableaux ci-dessus ne présentant que le commerce total (sans ventilation par produit ni par pays d'origine ou de consommation), les chiffres sont quelquefois disponibles plus rapidement que les chiffres publiés dans la *Série A*.

Principaux Indicateurs Économiques OECD
OCDE, © août 1996 OCDE

Table 1.2   Gross debt load 1993–6

(% of GDP)					
Fig. 7	*Country*	*1993*	*1994*	*1995*	*1996*
AUT	Austria	63.0	65.7	69.2	72.3
BEL	Belgium	137.5	135.0	134.6	132.7
DEU	Germany	**52.0**	**51.5**	**60.0**	**59.9**
DNK	Denmark	86.1	81.1	80.9	79.7
ESP	Spain	65.7	68.2	70.8	72.8
FIN	Finland	**59.8**	62.3	69.0	71.1
FRA	France	**52.6**	**54.7**	**57.5**	**59.1**
GBR	United Kingdom	**56.9**	**54.5**	**56.8**	**58.1**
GRC	Greece	117.1	119.0	117.5	115.8
IRL	Ireland	97.5	92.3	87.9	84.9
ITA	Italy	118.4	123.9	124.4	124.0
NLD	Netherlands	81.3	79.1	78.8	78.5
PRT	Portugal	67.6	70.5	71.2	70.9
SWE	Sweden	76.0	79.5	80.8	80.8
Maastricht	Treaty Convergence Criteria	60.0	60.0	60.0	60.0

1995 and 1996 figures: forecasts
Figures in **bold type**: Maastricht Treaty Convergence Criteria respected
Source: OECD, December 1995

The UK share of world trade has decreased from around 25 per cent at the end of the nineteenth century to approximately 6.5 per cent of global exports and imports today. Nevertheless, the UK still earns a greater, although declining, percentage of its GDP from exports than many other major industrial countries. At the same time the need to import raw materials plus half

first in volume then in price. This is emphasized in the last column, 'Terms of Trade', and is depicted in Figure 1.2.

Britain has had a balance of trade deficit on manufactured goods since 1983. It is worth bearing this point in mind also when we come to discuss the product life cycle and its applications to international marketing.

Table 1.3 Trade in goods (on a balance of payments basis)

	Volume indices (SA)		Price indices (NSA)		
	Exports	*Imports*	*Exports*	*Imports*	*Terms of trade*[1]
Annual					
1991	101.2	94.7	101.4	101.2	100.2
1992	103.7	100.9	103.5	102.1	101.4
1993	107.4	104.8	116.2	112.3	103.5
1994	118.5	109.2	118.6	116.1	102.2
1995	127.1	113.8	126.4	127.8	98.9

1990 = 100
[1] Price index for exports expressed as a percentage of price index for imports.
Source: Office for National Statistics, *Economic Trends* (1996), Office for National Statistics, London (517), November

its food needs, underlines Britain's dependency on foreign trade. Table 1.3 shows that if we focus particularly on the export sector, we find that exports indexed over 1990 levels have been increasing in both volume and value.

It is interesting to note, from Table 1.3, that imports are now down and overtaken by exports

Analysing national competitiveness

An analysis of international competitiveness is the annual IMD World Competitiveness Report which uses a questionnaire survey assessing 326 criteria divided into ten categories and

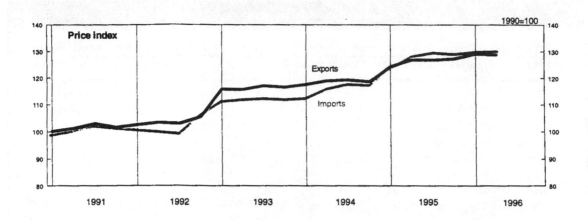

Source: Office for National Statistics, *Economic Trends* (1996), Office for National Statistics, London

Figure 1.2 UK visible trade: unit values of exports and imports

mailed to 10,000 selected executives in the 34 countries covered by the report. Eight of the criteria are:

1. domestic economy
2. internationalization
3. government
4. finance
5. infrastructure
6. management
7. science and technology
8. people.

IMD maintain that a nation's competitiveness can only be tested in the international marketplace. Some nations act as host to foreign direct investment, others are investors. However the means by which value added is created is behind the IMD survey. They adopt a matrix approach to try to present a balanced picture of an economy and to represent where investment is taking place. Nations are compared within the groups, OECD and non-OECD. Interestingly, Poland joined the OECD in June 1996 and so is categorized here as non-OECD but is ranked alongside other non-OECD countries. It is not possible therefore just to transfer the scores into the other grouping.

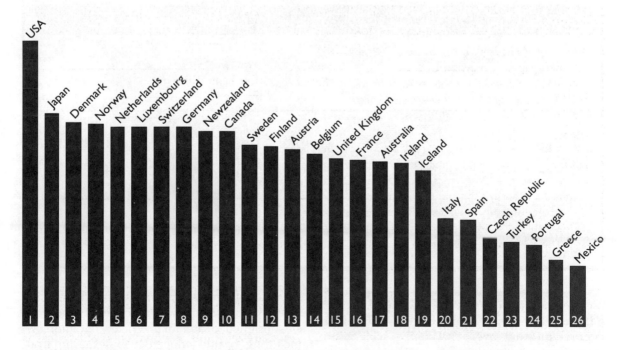

Source: *The World Competitiveness Yearbook* (1996) IMD/World Economic Forum, Lausanne, Switzerland

Figure 1.3 The OECD scoreboard: developed nations

Exhibit 1.1   Surveys agree to disagree

A rift between co-authors of the annual World Competitiveness Report has led to a second international survey on wealth creation in less than a week – with radically different results.

While the United States topped the charts of the Lausanne-based International Institute for Management Development, the country slips to fourth place when judged by the Geneva-based World Economic Forum.

Germany, ranked 10th by the IMD earlier this week, plummets to 22nd place on the latest list compiled by the Forum.

Canada was listed 12th by the IMD but is eighth on the Forum's report.

Singapore, Hong Kong and New Zealand, small, open economies with relatively small governments and low tax rates, steal the top three rankings in the Forum's report.

Macha Levinson, a director of the World Economic Forum, calls it a reflection of the growing debate over just what competitiveness is.

'There is no way this is meant to be a definitive answer to the whole question of competitiveness. There is a very heated discussion going on right now. Our methodology will evolve,' she said.

The World Competitiveness Report has been published for 17 years by the World Economic Forum, an independent, non-profit organization. Half of the reports have been compiled jointly with the IMD.

The two organizations parted ways last year after a dispute over research methods.

The Forum says its latest report offers a new way of judging competitiveness, which it defines as the ability of a nation's economy to make rapid and sustained gains in living standards.

The survey analyses the characteristics of 49 economies that are 'likely to determine prospects for economic growth over the next five to ten years.'

While the United States and Canada score in the top 10, Europe lags behind with Britain the top scorer, ranked 15th, Austria 19th, Sweden 21st, France 23rd, Spain 32nd and Italy 41st.

Japan, long the world leader in the competitiveness stakes, scores a poor 13th.

The two reports did agree on at least one point. Both put Russia at the bottom of their lists.

'Russia is isolated from world markets, taxation is high and unstable and there is a general disdain for the infrastructure, technology and management,' the Forum said.

Competitiveness ranking

The competitiveness of top countries as ranked in The Global Competitiveness Report 1996 by the World Economic Forum (rankings given by rival competitiveness compiler the International Institute for Management Development in parentheses):

1.   Singapore (2)
2.   Hong Kong (3)
3.   New Zealand (11)
4.   United States (1)
5.   Luxembourg (8)
6.   Switzerland (9)
7.   Norway (6)
8.   Canada (12)
9.   Taiwan (18)
10. Malaysia (23)
11. Denmark (5)
12. Australia (21)
13. Japan (4)
14. Thailand (30)
15. United Kingdom (19)
16. Finland (15)
17. Netherlands (7)
18. Chile (13)
19. Austria (16)
20. Korea (27)
21. Sweden (14)
22. Germany (10)
23. France (20)
24. Israel (24)
25. Belgium (17)
26. Ireland (22)
27. Iceland (25)
28. Jordan (not ranked)
29. Egypt (not ranked)
30. Indonesia (41)
31. Philippines (31)

Source: *Calgary Herald*, 30 May 1996

Governments and national comparative advantage

Government intervention may include monopoly or antitrust control: in terms of public procurement, it can have a decisive effect in stimulating industry; taxation and regional incentives for green field investment; and policies designed to cater for the society of tomorrow, including health, education and the environment. These may help create or upgrade an advantage, but so too does the role of chance itself. Porter points out, that across nations, it is

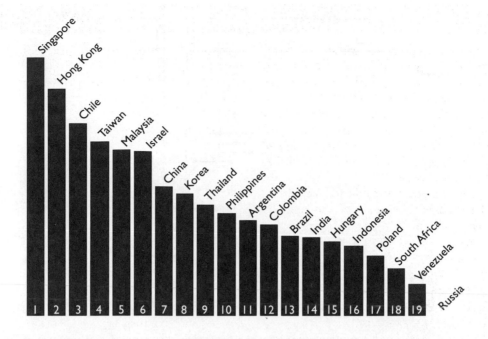

Source: *The World Competitiveness Yearbook* (1996) IMD/World Economic Forum, Lausanne, Switzerland

Figure 1.4   The non-OECD scoreboard

those industries in which government has been most heavily involved that have for the most part been unsuccessful in international terms.

In Figure 1.5, in what has become known as the 'Porter Diamond', the four determinants are clearly stated: factor conditions; demand conditions; related and supporting industries; and firm strategy, structure and rivalry. Governments can influence, and be influenced by, each of these four determinants, either positively or negatively. Porter's research shows that the perception of buyer needs is most often strongly defined by the home customer. Although foreign demand may give rise to product modifications, the essential core product is designed according to home market perceptions.

This process or cycle, which Porter then depicts in Figure 1.6, is one of a need to move

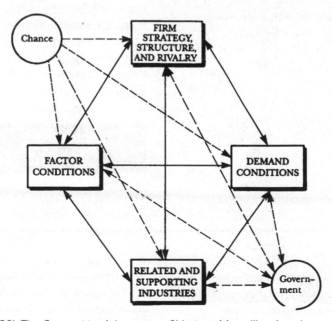

Source: Porter, M. E. (1990) *The Competitive Advantages of Nations*, Macmillan, London

Figure 1.5   The Porter Diamond: determinants of national advance

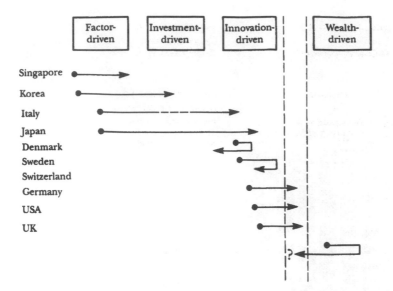

Source: Porter, M. E. (1990) *The Competitive Advantages of Nations*, Macmillan, London

Figure 1.6   Porter's estimated evolution of national competitive development during the postwar period

as quickly as possible from a factor-driven to an investment-driven economy, where nations compete in the price sensitive or standardized segments of more advanced industries. The next stage is innovation-driven, where firms are able to attain the state of the art in technology. Finally, in the last stage, the wealth-driven economy, which is one of decline, companies exhibit different signs of complacency, one of which is unrest; and industrial decay continues while income per head still continues to rise.

Porter (1990) states clearly that while government policy plays a significant role with regard to national advantage, it is only partial, and that government policy should take heed of the following:

1.   Firms compete in industries, not nations.
2.   A nation's competitive advantage in industry is relative. With generally rising standards, some companies may not be improving fast enough to keep up with their buying public.
3.   Dynamism leads to competitive advantage, not short-term cash advantages.
4.   National economic prosperity demands that industries upgrade.
5.   A nation's competitive advantage in industries is often geographically concentrated.
6.   Competitive advantage in a nation's industries is created over a decade or more, not over three- or four-year business cycles.
7.   Nations gain advantage because of differences, not similarities.
8.   Many categorizations used to distinguish or

prioritize industries have little relevance, e.g. labels such as 'sunrise' and 'sunset' industries.
9.   The process of sustaining advantage may be intensely uncomfortable for firms and those who work in them because of the never-ending pressures for improvements, which also requires new investment.

Governments, then, cannot create advantage, but can influence the four determinants in the diamond. Education and skills training are seen as a nationally important area in which it is the responsibility of government to act, but government intervenes also in other areas, including national currency markets; industrial research and development; safety and product standards; deregulation and privatization; and foreign investment.

The hierarchy of free trade and integration

There are important differences in what is meant by a free trade area, customs union and common market with monetary and political union.

1.   Free Trade Area (To reduce trading barriers)
2.   Customs Union (A common trading policy; creator of a common external tariff or trade barrier)
3.   Common Market (Harmonization and integration of trade relations to ensure free movement of capital and labour)

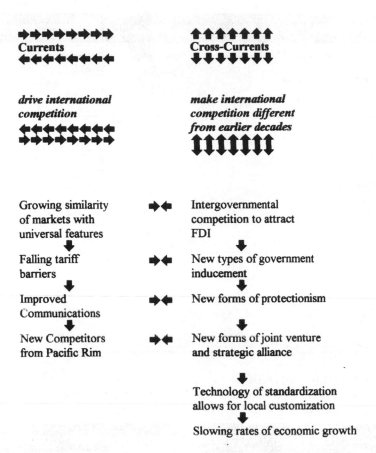

Source:　Porter, M. E. (1986), 'Competition in Global Industries: A Conceptual Framework', in *Competition in Global Industries*, Harvard Business School Press, Boston, Mass.

Figure 1.7　The forces of internationalization

4.　Monetary and Political Union (Common currency and legal system, shared economic and political goals in a full monetary and political union).

The new trading regions of the world

The European Union is the major force in global trade today, accounting for approximately 39 per cent of world exports and imports, with 15 members. In this new Europe, three tiers will emerge: the strong economies who will direct and influence strategy; the question marks, including Britain and Denmark; and the third group, those with weak currencies such as Italy, Spain, Portugal and Greece.

Further changes on the world scene are likely; with the North American Free Trade Agreement comprising of Canada, the USA and Mexico; which if it goes ahead will effectively transform the nature of trading within the North American sub-continent as well as have major implications for traders outside.

As one bloc becomes successful, a 'demon-stration' effect creates pressures in other parts of the world to develop similar structures. It transforms the stability of the particular trading bloc. The only impartial arbiter of free trade is the WTO (World Trade Organization) which succeeded GATT in 1995 (the United Nations organization formed around the General Agreement on Tariffs and Trade of 1948). WTO now takes it upon itself to investigate the trade restrictive implications of these new international trading alliances and customs unions.

From economic advantage to marketing advantage

The first difficulty is in defining 'international marketing'. Too often, attention is devoted only to those activities conducted by companies which constitute in their aggregated total, a foreign trade balance for individual countries. Here we are studying not just trade between nations. Instead we are studying the companies at home and abroad who are the buyers and sellers, and in so doing, international marketing as a network of relationships between firms engaged in

Table 1.4   Four largest trading blocs in world trade

		Pop.	GDP total US$ millions	Number of member countries	Country members	Intra-trade	Stage of integration
EU	European Union			15			
NAFTA	North American Free Trade Area	381.5	7676	3	USA Canada Mexico	42	1
Mercosur	Spanish for 'Southern Common Market'	198.4	984.8	4	Argentina Brazil Paraguay Uruguay	31	2
APEC	Asia Pacific Economic Cooperation			15			

Exhibit 1.2   Global competitiveness observed from an unfamiliar angle

The competitive advantage of nations is a topic dear to the heart of economists. Year by year, bodies such as the World Economic Forum rank countries by their competitiveness. The listings contain the usual suspects: the US, naturally: and – in varying order – Singapore, Hong Kong, Switzerland and so forth.

There is a snag to this. Countries do not compete for business, companies do. And while a company's origin obviously has some bearing on its effectiveness, most of the world's leading corporations are now transnational.

One answer is to look at the problem not top down, as an economist, but bottom up, as an industry analyst. This is the approach of a study from the US investment bank Morgan Stanley.

The study asked Morgan Stanley analysts around the world to identify companies with a sustainable competitive edge worldwide. It then arrived at a map of global competitiveness.

The results are in one sense familiar. The US advantage is overwhelming: of 238 companies identified as world leaders, over half – 125 – are American.

Thereafter, the picture is more surprising. Second in terms of the number of world leaders is the UK, with 21. Japan comes third with 19, Germany fourth with only 10. Singapore, Hong Kong and Taiwan are nowhere.

There is arguably a bias here. The study is aimed at Morgan Stanley's investment clients. It therefore looks only at quoted companies, mostly large and easily traded. The UK economy, like that of the US, is unusually reliant on big quoted companies.

According to Mr Richard Davidson, of Morgan Stanley's London office, there is more to it than that. 'On a macro and micro basis', he says, 'we think the UK has a fairly bright future. The macro reforms of the past 15 years have made it one of the most competitive countries in the world.'

More so than Japan? Well, Mr Davidson says, the Japanese findings came as a surprise. 'The gap has opened up because around the world, the advantages which the Japanese had in the mid-1980s, like just-in-time management, are now owned by everybody.'

The next leap forward has been a matter of new technology and downsizing, where the lead has been taken by the US, followed by the UK. 'The culture in Japan has not shifted to allow that. We found very few Japanese companies which had made the right structural changes.'

The study's methodology can be summed up by looking at the car industry. Only three carmakers make the list: BMW, Toyota and Honda. The Americans, for once, do not qualify.

→

➤ **Exhibit 1.2** *continued*

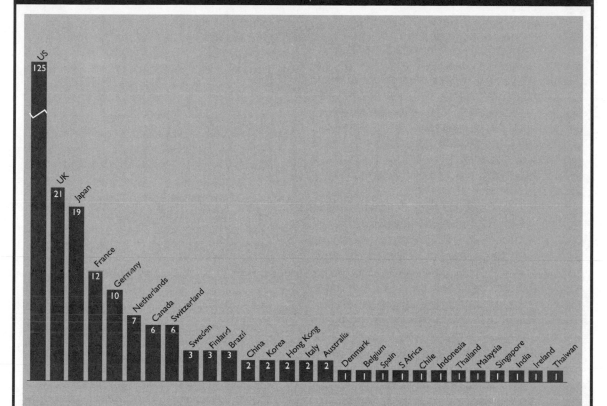

In accordance with the teaching of Professor Michael Porter of Harvard, Morgan Stanley's analysts argue that competitiveness comes down to either of two things – differentiation, or low-cost production. BMW has the first, the Japanese the second. The Americans have neither. Nor, as a corollary do they practise true globalisation, merely 'localisation across markets.'

Among UK companies thrown up by this approach, some are unsurprising: Glaxo Wellcome, British Airways, Unilever, Reuter and RTZ. Others are less obvious: Spirax Sarco, for instance, or Bass.

Spirax Sarco, an engineering company which makes steam controls, is there because it has a world market share of 30 per cent, half again as big as its nearest competitor. This advantage is reckoned to be sustainable – a key aspect of the study – for 10–20 years: that is, it would take that long for a new entrant to overhaul it.

Bass is included not because it is the UK's biggest brewer, but because its Holiday Inn chain is the world's biggest hotel operator by number of properties. It is global in reach; and Bass, the study says, has the financial muscle to push that forward.

If the UK ranks high collectively, individual companies may find the study less encouraging.

ICI does not qualify, though its erstwhile daughter company Zeneca does. British Steel, once claimed as the world's most profitable steel company, does not make it into a list of eight steel makers from such as China, Korea and India. Among technology companies, GEC does not qualify, though General Electric of the US does. Nor do British Aerospace or Rolls-Royce, or any of the British banks.

Worldwide, less familiar names in the lists include AES Corp, Kurita Water, Cone Mills and Nan Ya Plastics. They are, respectively: a US power plant operator: a Japanese maker of ultra-pure water systems for the semiconductor industry: a US denim maker: and a Taiwan polyester producer.

As a means of describing whole economies, the Morgan Stanley approach is obviously rough and ready. Its great advantage is to approach the issue from an unfamiliar angle. If not a substitute for the top-down method, it is at least a useful addition.

Source: Financial Times, 21 November 1996

Table 1.5 Government and business relations

	Corporate headquarters	Corporate subsidiary	Intermediary	Home government	Host government	Supranational authority	International organization
Dumping	√	√	√		√	√√	WTO
Parallel exports	√		√		√	√√	–
Parallel imports	√		√	√		√√	–
Counter trade	√	√	√		√		IMF World Bank
Transfer pricing	√	√	√	√	√	√	–
Pricing within a joint venture	√	√	√		√		UNECE
Duties and tariffs	√			√√	√	√√	WTO
Non-tariff barriers	√			√√	√	√	WTO
Questionable payments related to orders received	√		√	√		√	OECD; UN Centre for research on Transnational
Counterfeiting	√		√	√		√	International Chamber of Commerce IACC; ACG

Note: Where a supranational authority is involved, eg EC, it has signatory powers rather than its individual members. This is emphasized by a double √√. Elsewhere, the Commissioner will take an interest in activities 'in restraint of trade.'

buying and selling through to the final consumer. We examine separately the variables with which they have to deal, so as to arrive at a proper understanding of international marketing as a truly dynamic force.

International marketing is seen as a relatively new adjunct to marketing itself. Even so, the meaning of the word 'marketing' has come to be devalued during the relatively short post-war period that it has been among us. It has come increasingly to be used, quite wrongly, as a synonym, or more upmarket word, for 'selling' rather than as in the words of the Chartered Institute of Marketing 'the management process which seeks to identify, anticipate and satisfy customer requirements profitably'. Or, turning to the American Marketing Association: 'the process of planning and executing the conception, pricing, promotion and distribution of ideas, goods and services to create exchanges that satisfy individual and organizational objectives'. Either or both of these definitions will serve our purpose as there is much in common between them.

Implementing the four Ps of marketing (for the six Ps, including the two new Ps of marketing, see below) – product, place, promotion and price – involves interactions with variables which will be different for the domestic and international markets. In domestic marketing, one is familiar with the extent of political risk: the nature and extent of government policy towards business; with the quality of skilled human resources and of natural resources; and with the ramifications of existing and likely legislation on such areas as safety, hygiene, employment, and ownership of capital. International marketing, on the other hand, involves dealing with societies where politics, beliefs and values may be very different from those held in the home market and, yet, legislation abroad will have important ramifications for international marketing – there may, for example, be legislation requiring the majority employment of local nationals, or of majority equity ownership by local nationals in joint ventures, restrictions on sourcing, labelling and on the use of certain product ingredients, including flavourings, preservatives and sweeteners, to name but a few.

In this context, it is useful to consider alternative views of the marketing function. Some, such as Baker (1994), see marketing as somewhere between an art and a science. Bartels (1968), however, viewed international marketing quite differently from domestic marketing, seeing marketing as having two facets: technical and social. The technical facet or the 'science' consists of the application of principles, rules or knowledge relating to the non-human elements of marketing. It is these concepts and generalizations which are held to have a universality transcending national boundaries and culture differences.

On the technical level, we are dealing with universals without regard to time and space. We are dealing with concepts which have applications across natural boundaries and language barriers, such as economies of scale, distribution channels, etc. Table 1.6 reflects a list of products successful in their own domestic market but which may not have the unique global transferability of a brand name such as Coca-Cola or Pepsi. On the social level, we deal with interactions among individuals acting in role positions in the various systems involved in the distribution of goods and services. This facet emphasizes the human element, the individual acting under the full range of influences, both economic and non-economic, which affiliation with the social institutions of his society imposes on him.

As a social process, marketing in two nations may differ quite markedly. While the roles in which individuals interact may be identical, their expectations and behavioural patterns within two societies may be quite different. Interactions affect the societal environment, and in turn, shape marketing policies within that environment. Greater environmental differences may be found within a country than between countries, if, for example, we were to compare two cities. Yet, this is not to forget either that foreign companies by virtue of their foreign ownership will often be constrained by governments from engaging in free trade across their borders. Arguments, such as protecting national interests, are frequently raised on such occasions. This is one of the differences which Bartels points to as an 'international difference' between what may otherwise have been two identical market structures with similar levels of demand. Bartels depicts this influence in Figure 1.8 by the interactions: B, C, D, E and F.

Governments relate to their own citizens (B and C), and may give encouragement to export and invest abroad through research, assistance, trade fairs, export credit insurance and investment guarantees. Equally, it may choose to discourage foreign companies through export and investment restrictions, and monopoly or antitrust legislation. In the same way each national government may affect the way in which foreign nationals trade with their own citizens (interactions D and E). Then there are, too, the interactions of government (F) which affect international marketing as through the creation of common markets and free trade areas, consummation of commercial treaties,

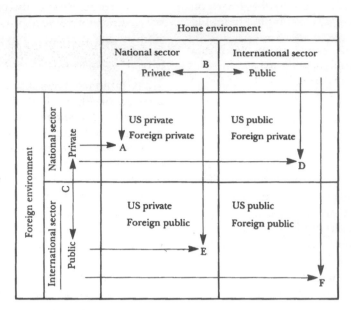

Source: Bartels, R. (1968) Are domestic and international marketing similar? *Journal of Marketing*, **32** (July), 55–61

Figure 1.8   Bartels: relations of private and public sectors in the international environment

agreements or tariffs, or the inspection of antitrust and monopoly laws (Bartels, 1968).

Kotler (1984), recognizing the political nature of the marketing environment, introduced a further two Ps to the existing four Ps of marketing, coining the term 'megamarketing'. This was now to include political power and public opinion formation. This meant that the environment had to be managed as well as the traditional marketing mix. To cite Kotler:

Table 1.6   Ill-fated foreign products

1.   Ass Glue (blood tonic from donkey parts: China)
2.   Blue Peter (canned fish: Norway)
3.   Colon Plus (liquid detergent, Spain)
4.   Fockink (liqueur: Netherlands)
5.   Green Piles (lawn fertilizer: Japan)
6.   Homo Sausage (beek jerky: Japan)
7.   Hornyphon (video recorder: Austria)
8.   Krapp (toilet paper: Sweden)
9.   Last Climax (paper tissues: Japan)
10. Mucos (soft drink: Japan)
11. Pansy (men's underwear: China)
12. Pipi (orangeade: Yugoslavia)
13. Plopp (chocolate bar: Sweden)
14. Polio (detergent: Czech Republic)
15. Pschitt! (soft drink: France)
16. Shitto (hot spiced pepper sauce: Ghana)
17. Skinababe (baby cleanser: Japan)
18. Superglans (car wax: Netherlands)
19. Trim Pecker (trousers: Japan)
20. Zit (lemon/lime soft drink: Greece)

Sources: Compiled by Charles Brymer of Interbrand Corporation (14 E.60th Street, New York, NY 10022) and by Reinhold Aman, the Editor of *Maledicta*, the irregular 'Journal of Verbal Aggression' *Maledicta* can be purchased through PO Box 14123, Santa Rosa CA95402–6123, USA. Published in Wallechinsky D. and Wallace, A. (1993), *The Book of Lists*, Little, Brown and Company, Boston, Mass., p. 170

Marketers are always looking at economic factors and national factors, but they fail to study political science. They should examine the conflicts, the special interest and pressure groups, the vested interests, the political realities and create appeals in those arenas. Marketers can no longer sit back and adopt a defensive posture when power is being used against them.

The implications to be drawn from mega-marketing (Kotler, 1996) are then:

1. Enlarging the multiparty marketing concept. Marketers spend much time analysing how to create preferences and satisfaction in target buyers. Because other parties – governments, labour unions, banks, reform groups – can block the path to the target buyers, marketers must closely study the obstacles these parties create and develop strategies for attracting their support or at least neutralizing their opposition.
2. Blurring the distinction between environmental and controllable variables. Marketers have traditionally defined the environment as those outside forces that cannot be controlled by the business. But megamarketing argues that some environmental forces can be changed through lobbying, legal action, negotiation, issue advertising, public relations and strategic partnering.
3. Broadening the understanding of how markets work. Most market thinkers assume that demand creates its own supply. Ideally, companies discover a market need and rush to satisfy that need. But real markets are often blocked, and the best marketer doesn't always win. We have seen that foreign competitors with offers comparable or superior to those of local companies cannot always enter the market. The result is a lower level of consumer satisfaction and producer innovation than would otherwise result.

How companies 'go international'

To paraphrase Paul Fifield and Keith Lewis, authors of the *CIM Workbook for International Marketing Strategy*, the biggest problem in international marketing is often not the foreign customer but the international marketer. The single most important problem any organization faces within its international setting often comes not from the environment but from its own reactions to the environment.

It is regrettable that the rationale offered is no more sophisticated than the following:

1. Product maturity. The product life cycle stage at home may be one of maturity, whereas there may be a new embryonic market abroad enabling the product to start a new life cycle from introduction where quantities available are low but the price commanded is high. The Intermediate Technology Development Group (ITDG) is a lobby group based in London, who are championing for mature technology product exports to the LDCs rather than the sophisticated Western products demanded of Western markets, which in turn require Western levels of maintenance and after-sales care. Increasingly, however, this argument is becoming less and less convincing. Many of Western society's more advanced products are made in Pacific Basin countries with economies least able to afford them. A further paradox is contained in the fact that these production countries are capital intensive rather than perhaps relying solely on cheaper factor costs such as labour or raw materials.

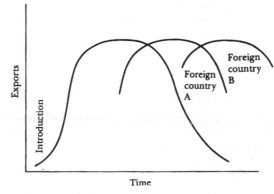

Note: The product life cycle explanation here would require an infinite number of markets accepting of mature technologies to be viable. It assumes that technology is held only by a few countries and that other markets are undemanding. Neither assumption is accurate. Chapter 2 will deal with further implications of the product life cycle and international trade.

Figure 1.9   Product maturity and the international product life cycle

2.   Competition. Competition may be less intense abroad than at home. This area has been the subject of study for many international economists, but suffice it to say that there may be significant differences in factor costs between the home country and other countries. Other countries may, for example, have cheaper raw material or labour costs, or they may have gained 'experience curve' cost advantages through experience of volume productivity, so that it becomes advantageous to operate abroad. Also, the market structure of other countries may reveal advantages like centralized buying, and perhaps state-buying, where market access may be assured in return for guarantees on investment, employment, etc. There may also be a certain element of attempting to start a

---

Table 1.7

Environmental management strategies to control conditions previously thought uncontrollable

1 *Competitive aggression.* The company exploits a distinctive competence or improves internal efficiency of resources for competitive advantage. Examples: product differentiation, aggressive pricing, comparative advertising.

2 *Competitive pacification.* Company takes independent actions to improve relations with competitors. Examples: helping competitors find raw materials, advertising campaigns which promote entire industry, price umbrellas.

3 *Public relations.* Establish and maintain favourable images in the minds of those making up the environment. Example: corporate ad campaign.

4 *Voluntary action.* Company tries to manage and becomes committed to various special-interest groups, causes, and social problems. Examples: McGraw-Hill's efforts to prevent sexist stereotypes and 3M's energy-conservation program.

5 *Dependence development.* Create or modify relationships with external groups so they become dependent on the company. Examples: raising switching costs for suppliers, production of critical defence-related commodities, providing vital information to regulators.

6 *Legal action.* Company engages in private legal battle with competitor on antitrust, deceptive advertising, or other grounds.

7 *Political action.* Company tries to influence elected representatives to create a more favourable business environment or limit competition. Examples: corporate constituency programmes, issue advertising, direct lobbying.

8 *Smoothing.* Company attempts to resolve irregular demand. Examples: telephone company lowers weekend rates, airline offers inexpensive fares during off-peak times.

9 *Demarketing.* Firm attempts to discourage customers in general or a certain class of customers in particular, on either a temporary or permanent basis. Example: petrol filling stations adopt shorter hours of operation.

10 *Implicit cooperation.* Firm adopts patterned, predictable, and coordinated behaviours. Example: price leadership.

11 *Contracting.* Company negotiates an agreement with another group to exchange goods, services, information, patents, etc. Example: contractual vertical and horizontal marketing systems.

12 *Co-optation.* Firm absorbs new elements into its leadership or policy-making structure as a means of averting threats to its stability or existence. Example: consumer representatives, women, and bankers on boards of directors.

13 *Coalition.* Two or more groups coalesce and act jointly with respect to some set of issues for some period of time. Examples: industry associations, political initiatives of the Business Roundtable and the US Chamber of Commerce.

14 *Domain selection.* Firm enters industries or markets with limited competition or regulation and ample suppliers and customers, or enters high-growth markets. Examples: IBM's entry into the personal-computer market and Miller Brewing Co.'s entry into the light-beer market.

15 *Diversification.* Company invests in different types of businesses, manufactures different types of products, integrates vertically, or expands geographically to reduce dependence on a single product, service, market, or technology.

16 *Merger and acquisition.* Two or more firms form a single enterprise or one company gains possession of another. Examples: merger between Pan American and National Airlines, Phillip Morris' acquisition of Miller Brewing Co.

Source: Zeithaml, C. P. and Zeithaml, V. A. (1984), Environmental management: strategic options, examples. *Marketing News*, American Marketing Association, 14 September

march on a competitor by foreign market entry where that foreign market is also the home base of a major competitor. Such an act can help define competitive behaviour in other markets.

3. Excess capacity utilization. This concept is drawn also from economics, whereon a given manufactured item, which has been on sale in the domestic market for sufficiently long to have recouped its original research and development costs, may find new profitable export markets, costed only at its actual production costs, plus overhead; its original research development costs being regarded now as 'sunk' costs. However, this in effect means that the export item will be sold abroad for less than its recommended price in the domestic market of its country of origin and this leaves the company open to charges of 'dumping'. Western industrialized markets may react swiftly to what they see as the destructive effects of 'dumping' while less developed countries may actually welcome the importation of Western goods at low cost, particularly where they do not have production of their own. For domestic producers, 'dumping' may have several advantages. Since 'dumping' is seen as a short-term strategy, it may solve an immediate excess supply problem for a company unable to reduce its prices to a correspondingly low figure for domestic clients without creating embarrassing precedents for future price negotiations.

4. Geographical diversification. Geographical diversification may be preferable to product-line diversification. It is commonsense for a company to stick to producing what it is good at. This is one of the main themes of Peters ' and Waterman (1982) in their *In Search of Excellence* and also in Igor Ansoff's strategic portfolio matrix of new and existing products and new and existing markets, a four-cell matrix. Finding new markets for existing products or modified products does not expose the company to the attendant risks of expanding the product range simultaneously with foreign market entry. In terms of corporate strategy, it makes sense to focus on the strengths of the company and not to depart too greatly from these strengths whether in product innovation, adaptation or service. Elsewhere, rival companies seem to be uniting together in sharing research and development on parts, components, subassemblies and product range extension as will be seen later, when we discuss strategic business alliances.

5. Potential of a population and purchasing

power. Markets may be local, regional, national, international or even global. Generally, the more specialized the end-use application of any product or process, the larger the geographical market that needs then to be found. Depending on a company's technology, its place in domestic industry and resources, a company 'footprint' in foreign markets may be found which is either long and narrow (spread over many markets) or short and wide (concentrated in only a few markets). Generally, where there is a need, a willingness to find a solution to that need, plus an ability to pay for it, a market will be created. Assessing market potential requires data. Not all countries produce data with the frequency or detail of the British Central Statistical Office. Very often, and particularly with developing countries, there will be significantly large gaps between the publications of national economic data. Even when data exist they may be of questionable value, they may be collected for different reasons on a quite different statistical base, and, therefore, may not be directly comparable to the exporter's known domestic situation. For these reasons, more is said later of the techniques of foreign country selection where economic indicators are poor or non-existent.

Porter's prescription for competitiveness

1. Create the climate for upgrading advantage.
2. Sell to the most demanding customers.
3. Find the right location at the centre of the greatest concentration of forces making for competitiveness.
4. Do not overdo globalization. The home base counts most when it comes to creation of competitive advantage.
5. Get involved in factor creation, including training.
6. Consider a base move.
7. Competition and alliances assure growth and manage competition, but do not overdo it.
8. Role of leaders is important.

The dilemma of the multinational – a force for good or evil?

The case of the multinational is frequently stated in strong terms both for and against it. Livingstone (1989) stated some of the accusations against as including:

1. That they interfere politically in the affairs of the host nation.

2. That they destroy local jobs.
3. That by exporting its knowhow and national technology, multinationals destroy their home country's technical leadership.
4. That they destroy local culture.

Yet, all in all, Livingstone states that the multinational can be seen as 'the modern metamorphosis of free trade'. It is simply resorting to a vast oversimplification to try to resort to a single element in a very complex trade equation. Singling out the multinational for undue attention in this way avoids looking at the real and highly complex world (Livingstone, 1989). The love-hate relationship with the multinational continues, however, and was well summarized by the *Economist*:

It fiddles with its accounts. It avoids or evades its taxes. It rigs its intra-company transfer prices. It is run by foreigners, from decision centres thousands of miles away. It imports foreign labour practices. It overpays. It underpays. It competes unfairly with local firms. It is in cahoots with local firms. It exports jobs from rich countries. It is an instrument of rich countries' imperialism. The technologies it brings to the third world are old fashioned. No, they are too modern. It meddles. It bribes. Nobody can control it. It wrecks balances of payments. It overturns economic

policies. It plays off governments against each other to get the biggest investment incentives. Won't it please come and invest? Let it bloody well go home.

The arguments for and against the multinational are shown in Table 1.8, where Kinsey (1988) has listed the positive and negative impacts of the multinational against seven criteria.

Globally, competition is dynamic and forever changing. It is no longer possible to compete solely with the competitive tools that rightly belonged to the past, but to innovate. In the past, it was enough for former colonial powers to offer aid to former dependencies that was in some way 'tied' to certain goods. However, in the search for trade, other countries have willingly stepped in, offering loans and credits. This has been one of the major changes to world trade, together with the new forms of financing, including countertrade (CT), which have emerged postwar and have introduced new institutions, including the World Bank, IMF, Bank for International Settlements, European Bank for Reconstruction and Development, and Euromoney markets.

Meanwhile, other newer, industrial, countries have been aggressively establishing themselves on the international scene, and it was also seen to be politically important for them to

Table 1.8

Positive impact of the multinational in relation to:	Negative impact of the multinational in relation to:
1 *Technology* Industrialization initiated and promoted. Knowledge and skills transferred.	1 *Technology* Inappropriate technology. Key sector domination. R & D remains in home country. Knowledge and skills transfer limited.
2 *Jobs* Directly created in the multinational. Indirectly created by stimulating entrepreneurship and efficiency.	2 *Jobs* Wrong type of jobs provided. Economic and social inequalities promoted. Jobs destroyed now through local competition.
3 *Competition and complementary activity* Competition stimulated to improve. Entrepreneurship in complementary activity promoted. Overall efficiency improved.	3 *Competition and complementary activity* Local competition eliminated. Oligopolistic industrial structure promoted.
4 *Management* Effective management promoted.	4 *Management* Inappropriate management techniques introduced. Destruction of local culture.
5 *Foreign exchange* Earned or saved by host nation.	5 *Foreign exchange* Lost through transfer pricing and other means.
6 *Attitudes* 'Modernizing' attitudes promoted.	6 *Attitudes* Materialistic attitudes stimulated and local culture destroyed.
7 *Demand* Increased consumer and industrial demand.	7 *Demand* Demand distorted. Social inequalities promoted.
	8 *Politics* Interference by the multinational in the host nation's politics.

Source: Kinsey, J. (1988) *Marketing in Developing Countries*, Macmillan, London

develop trade, and, through trade, a relationship and understanding with the developing countries which also enhanced their own power and prestige.

The multinational phenomenon of the twenty-first century trades more within itself and its subsidiaries and affiliates than just between nations. With multinationals responsible for 30 per cent of global product and 70 per cent of global trade, the multinationals have created in effect their own internal markets. This internalization theory contained within Dunning's Eclectic Approach (see Chapter 2) is one explanation of the growth of the multinational. The multinational corporation escapes an internationally agreed definition, being referred to as an international corporation by some, as a transnational by the United Nations, and a multinational enterprise or 'megacorp' by yet others. While it is impossible to agree on a definition, the multinational may be said to meet two important criteria, with the emphasis being laid particularly on the second:

1. Foreign direct investments either in manufacturing or service industries in more than two countries.
2. Corporate planning which employs a worldwide perspective and impartially allocates resources such as management, other personnel, company-specific technology, business expertise and funds on a global basis.

The working definition of a multinational offered here states that:

A multinational enterprise is a corporation which owns (in whole or in part), controls and manages income-generating assets in more than one country. In so doing, it engages in international production, sales and distribution of goods and services across national boundaries financed by foreign direct investment.

The multinationals have been active in dismantling psychological as well as geographical frontiers. Yet, here we touch on another very important point. The multinationals as such, in terms often of ownership as well as management style, owe allegiance to no one particular country. Consequently, the term 'national' should not appear in their title. More correctly, the largest of these are truly global companies and so the term 'global company' will be found used in this text more frequently than the term 'multinational'. An increasing number of truly global brands, such as Pepsi-Cola or Coca-Cola, underline this point. Language may change with the country concerned, there may be quite different environmental conditions of use, but still perhaps the bottle, the logo and all that is normally associated with the product, including taste, flavour,

fragrance and lifestyle association, will usually remain intact and instantly recognizable worldwide. For others, such as IBM who produce and sell what are essentially industrial products worldwide, this requires a different form of co-ordination, integrating multinational sourcing of components and division of labour. With IBM's degree of integration, 'foreignness' is relatively meaningless as the company needs to know as much about its operations in say, Britain, and its market situation there, as it does of its home base, the USA. With business becoming more international in a search for markets, new competitive pressures are created which result in a greater dynamism. Technological change, societal change, increasing protectionism internationally (despite the existence of a General Agreement on Tariffs and Trade), and creeping nationalism on a regional, as opposed to national, scale in purchasing, as still practised within the EU, are only a few of the challenges placed before business corporations seeking to do business in world markets today.

Benjamin Barber, author of *Jihad vs McWorld*, has opened an interesting debate on the conditions which are shaping our present trading environment whether we are trading nationally or globally:

Gillette's Chairman Alfred M. Zeien has said: 'I do not find foreign countries foreign'. Welcome to McWorld. There is no activity more intrinsically globalizing than trade, no ideology less interested in nations than capitalism, no challenge to frontiers more audacious than the market. By many measures, corporations are today more central players in global affairs than nations. We call them multinational but they are more accurately understood as transnational or postnational or even antinational. For they abjure the very idea of nations or any other parochialism that limits them in time or space. Their customers are not citizens of a particular nation or members of a parochial clan: they belong to the universal tribe of consumers defined by needs and wants that are ubiquitous, if not by nature then by the cunning of advertising. A consumer is a consumer is a consumer.

International marketing mythology

- The traditional marketing mix of 4Ps is of no validity either in domestic or international marketing.
- Totally standardized products will succeed, customers basically have the same needs everywhere. Although needs may be shared across national frontiers, this may result in demand only for competitive products. Attention has to be paid to all aspects of the marketing interface and to the concept of adding value to the customer. This is where the uniqueness and competitive advantage is often created.

Exhibit 1.3 Fortune's Global 500 – The world's largest corporations

RANK 1996	RANK 1995			REVENUES $ mil.	REVENUES % change from 1995	PROFITS $ mil.	PROFITS % change from 1995	PROFITS Rank	ASSETS $ mil.	ASSETS Rank	STOCK-HOLDERS' EQUITY $ mil.	STOCK-HOLDERS' EQUITY Rank	EMPLOYEES Number	EMPLOYEES Rank	Industry table number
1	4	GENERAL MOTORS	U.S.	168,369.0	(0.3)	4,963.0	(27.9)	8	222,142.0	42	23,418.0	20	647,000	3	29
2	7	FORD MOTOR	U.S.	146,991.0	7.2	4,446.0	7.4	11	262,867.0	33	26,762.0	14	371,702	7	29
3	2	MITSUI[1]	JAPAN	144,942.8[2]	–	321.9	2.3	292	61,144.5	135	5,391.5	236	41,694	276	41
4	1	MITSUBISHI[1]	JAPAN	140,203.7[2]	–	394.1	13.8	271	77,871.5	121	8,864.0	129	35,000	308	41
5	3	ITOCHU[1]	JAPAN	135,542.1[2]	–	110.9	(8.5)	411	59,179.6	140	3,961.3	308	6,995	470	41
6	10	ROYAL DUTCH/SHELL GROUP	BRIT./NETH.	128,174.5[E]	16.7	8,887.1	28.7	1	124,373.4	80	63,126.6	2	101,000	98	30
7	6	MARUBENI[1]	JAPAN	124,026.9[2]	–	178.6	14.0	370	60,865.4	136	4,134.9	300	65,000	175	41
8	9	EXXON	U.S.	119,434.0[E]	8.6	7,510.0	16.1	2	95,527.0	102	43,542.0	4	79,000	141	30
9	5	SUMITOMO[1]	JAPAN	119,281.3[2]	–	(1,292.8)	(714.2)	491	43,506.3	173	4,500.3	281	26,200	354	41
10	8	TOYOTA MOTOR[1]	JAPAN	108,702.0	(2.1)	3,426.2	28.7	18	102,417.0	95	45,762.4	3	150,736	51	29
11	12	WAL-MART STORES[3]	U.S.	106,147.0	12.0	3,056.0	11.5	22	39,501.0	186	17,143.0	38	675,000	2	17
12	20	GENERAL ELECTRIC	U.S.	79,179.0	13.1	7,280.0	10.8	3	272,402.0	31	31,125.0	9	239,000	22	9
13	11	NISSHO IWAI[1]	JAPAN	78,921.2[2]	–	136.9	–	395	43,647.6	172	2,184.1	395	17,497	407	41
14	15	NIPPON TELEGRAPH & TELEPHONE[G,1]	JAPAN	78,320.7	(4.4)	1,330.3	(39.8)	100	115,864.5	84	36,997.5	6	230,300	25	39
15	18	INTL BUSINESS MACHINES	U.S.	75,947.0	5.6	5,429.0	29.9	6	81,132.0	115	21,628.0	23	268,648	19	7
16	13	HITACHI[1]	JAPAN	75,669.0	(10.1)	784.2	(46.6)	186	80,328.2	116	26,472.3	16	330,152	10	9
17	16	AT&T	U.S.	74,525.0[1]	(6.4)	5,908.0	4,150.4	5	55,552.0	148	20,295.0	28	130,400	65	39
18	14	NIPPON LIFE INSURANCE[1]	JAPAN	72,575.0	(12.8)	2,799.1	15.3	33	322,759.2	20	4,822.0	262	86,695	126	21
19	22	MOBIL	U.S.	72,267.0[E]	8.3	2,964.0	24.7	24	46,408.0	166	19,072.0	35	43,000	272	30
20	17	DAIMLER-BENZ[4]	GERMANY	71,589.3	(0.9)	1,776.1	–	73	72,331.5	126	16,975.2	39	290,029	12	29
21	27	BRITISH PETROLEUM	BRITAIN	69,851.9[E]	22.6	3,985.2	125.1	12	55,307.3	149	21,725.9	22	53,150	218	30
22	19	MATSUSHITA ELECTRIC INDUSTRIAL[1]	JAPAN	68,147.5	(3.2)	1,223.9	–	112	70,100.0	129	29,792.1	12	270,651	18	9
23	24	VOLKSWAGEN	GERMANY	66,527.5	8.2	437.9	77.3	257	60,823.3	137	7,375.2	170	260,811	21	29
24	34	DAEWOO	SOUTH KOREA	65,160.2	27.2	468.3	–	250	73,091.6	125	10,432.2	104	186,314	38	29
25	25	SIEMENS[5]	GERMANY	63,704.7	5.0	1,877.1	48.0	66	57,310.1	143	15,431.0	50	379,000	6	9
26	30	CHRYSLER	U.S.	61,397.0	15.4	3,529.0	74.3	16	56,184.0	146	11,571.0	83	126,000	67	29
27	23	NISSAN MOTOR[1]	JAPAN	59,118.2	(5.5)	690.2	–	203	60,248.1	138	10,931.8	91	135,331	61	29
28	44	ALLIANZ	GERMANY	56,577.2	1.9	1,096.3	3.7	131	200,361.9	51	9,884.7	112	65,836	171	24
29	29	U.S. POSTAL SERVICE[G,5]	U.S.	56,402.0	3.9	1,567.2	(11.5)	82	51,603.5	153	(2,623.5)	497	887,546	1	25

30	31	PHILIP MORRIS	U.S.	54,553.0[E]	2.7	6,303.0	4	15.7	54,871.0	150	14,218.0	57	154,000	48	40
31	38	UNILEVER	BRITAIN/NETHERLANDS	52,067.4	4.7	2,499.7	42	7.5	30,993.3	219	8,803.6	130	306,000	11	13
32	41	FIAT	ITALY	50,509.0	10.0	1,470.1	88	11.5	70,111.8	128	15,166.2	53	237,865	23	29
33	40	SONY[1]	JAPAN	50,277.9	5.7	1,238.1	109	120.3	45,790.7	170	11,764.8	81	163,000	46	9
34	26	DAI-ICHI MUTUAL LIFE INSURANCE[1]	JAPAN	49,144.7	(15.3)	1,941.3	59	12.1	225,977.4	40	2,696.5	364	66,953	166	21
35	50	IRI[G]	ITALY	49,055.7	17.1	279.4	313	(28.7)	66,392.9	131	4,617.9	274	132,489	64	39
36	39	NESTLÉ	SWITZERLAND	48,932.5	2.4	2,751.2	35	11.5	37,905.5	191	16,293.8	44	221,144	26	13
37	32	TOSHIBA[1]	JAPAN	48,415.8	(8.7)	595.5	222	(36.4)	46,830.2	164	10,195.7	106	186,000	39	9
38	46	HONDA MOTOR[1]	JAPAN	46,994.5	6.7	1,963.6	57	167.7	33,787.1	203	11,192.5	87	101,100	97	29
39	47	ELF AQUITAINE	FRANCE	46,818.0[E]	7.6	1,363.7	97	35.1	47,143.4	162	15,287.8	51	85,400	129	30
40	21	TOMEN[1]	JAPAN	46,506.3[2]	–	42.2	448	(8.7)	19,363.2	287	898.8	466	11,500	455	41
41	75	BANK OF TOKYO-MITSUBISHI[1,6]	JAPAN	46,451.0	42.0	361.6	281	136.6	696,477.8	1	23,994.0	18	19,304	398	3
42	42	VEBA GROUP	GERMANY	45,246.2[E]	(2.2)	1,633.2	75	22.2	46,254.8	167	12,535.4	72	122,110	69	41
43	33	TOKYO ELECTRIC POWER[1]	JAPAN	44,735.0	(14.6)	724.5	201	34.9	114,738.5	86	12,049.7	76	43,166[7]	268	42
44	61	TEXACO	U.S.	44,561.0[E]	21.1	2,018.0	55	232.5	26,963.0	242	10,372.0	105	28,957	336	30
45	36	SUMITOMO LIFE INSURANCE[1]	JAPAN	44,063.3	(13.1)	1,858.4	69	(0.7)	188,553.7	55	2,295.6	390	67,027	164	21
46	118	SUNKYONG	SOUTH KOREA	44,031.0	–	313.0	294	–	30,171.0	223	5,876.0	220	33,299	320	30
47	45	NEC[1]	JAPAN	43,932.7	(3.6)	813.1	180	1.7	38,687.3	187	8,088.4	149	151,966	50	9
48	48	ÉLECTRICITÉ DE FRANCE[G]	FRANCE	43,658.7	0.3	209.4	351	(15.1)	132,978.0	75	32,434.5	7	116,919	77	42
49	52	STATE FARM INSURANCE COS.	U.S.	42,781.2	4.8	2,567.9	40	102.0	93,245.1	104	30,078.4	11	71,612	154	23
50	43	DEUTSCHE TELEKOM[G]	GERMANY	41,910.7	(9.2)	1,168.1	123	(68.2)	112,120.5	89	29,203.8	13	201,000	32	39

Source: Fortune (1997), 136 (3)

- Use of the English language is a prerequisite for success. Examples such as the successful international launch of *Ultra Doux* by Laboratoires Garnier illustrates how uniqueness and exclusivity can be enhanced by the use of a foreign language, in this case, French.
- Doing business in an English-speaking country does not mean that your trading partner necessarily shares the same view of legal responsibilities or outlook. There may be major differences of opinion relating to profit sharing within a joint venture resulting from differences in outlook.
- Payments and even credit status checking need not be a problem. The agencies responsible for credit status checking are international and all banks have good international correspondent arrangements with overseas banks. Information technology has created the opportunities for instantaneous electronic transfers where necessary. Credit cards internationally have increased their share of sales to the point where in developed countries, purchases are seldom made with cash. On the supply side there are companies which offer the ATMs at no cost to the banks and fees are charged only on a transaction basis.

International marketing reality

- Money has no nationality and follows good market opportunity. Capital can be easily transferred across national boundaries.
- Highly dynamic competition is present in all markets exhibiting any degree of economic growth.
- The marketplace is global for all specialized products or products containing high value added.
- Investment can take two forms, portfolio investment and foreign direct investment. FDI is much more conspicuous but portfolio investment is equally sizeable and should not be overlooked.
- Product adaptation is required if not ostensibly by customers then by the needs of local competition to create product differentiation. The costs of adaptation are falling and the costs of not doing so are increasing making it easier for competitors to make inroads against a standardized product which can be as easily transferred to other markets. Levi's offer through their own retail outlets, for an additional premium, customized jeans which will fit exactly.
- Diffusion of new products is occurring simultaneously today across markets. A pan-European launch for a new car is fairly common. The media after all, are now common and accessible to people living in many different nations. Opportunities for product life cycle extensions are greatly curtailed over previous years.
- Trade intermediaries are not the final consumers! The relationship should not end with the sale and transfer of goods. Learning about the product and final consumer has to continue to better define the product in the future. Marketing is about planning, exporting is about adventuring.
- Instant international communications have eliminated many problems of geographical distance an d dismantled many previously existing barriers associated with distance and therefore perceived risk. Fax and e-mail mean instantaneous message transfers. There does not need to be anyone present at the other end to receive the communication as with a telephone call. A printed message will be left behind waiting for the attention of the recipient. In other words, a hard copy of the message is left behind which improves upon a verbal communication. It is also possible to circumvent the difficulties of different time zones by leaving a hard copy of a message.
- Industrial property rights which include patents, licences and trademark protection are becoming increasingly important as large companies produce today for a global market.
- Patience is required as building a market presence requires both time and money.
- The importance of new trading regions cannot be overemphasized as this often provides a rationale for investment within an particular country. As Ohmae points out, the nation state is increasingly being seen to be dysfunctional as nationalist sentiments combined with ignorance of global trading conditions produce conditions inappropriate to the needs of functioning within a global economy.

Issues surrounding management control

- First are issues relative to size and resource allocation. Investments have to be viewed relative to the company's position, not in isolation. The rationale for market entry and perceptions of risk, payback and anticipated payback period are important as time dependence forces strategic choice of market entry.
- Use of a financial intermediary such as an export factor or countertrade house can allow the company to focus on building its competitive advantage without concern for payment problems.

- Where there is a high quality image associated with the product then there should be concern about the conditions of sale and servicing in the foreign market even if production is not taking place. The same applies with services such as in higher education where offshore MBA programmes are now commonly being made available and so standards require to be maintained.
- Motivation is necessary throughout an organization yet what creates motivation in employees, agents, associates is difficult to determine once monetary incentives fail to work. For example, agents and distributors in the Middle East have been found upon occasion to deliberately sub-optimize on their operations. In other words, they do not achieve their full potential because to do so would require a higher degree of effort whose reward is marginal to their present lifestyle.
- Power should not be divorced from responsibility. Anyone can delegate authority but empowerment is insufficient unless there is also accountability. This is the problem often of using consultants: they have power without responsibility so they do not have to live with the consequence of their decisions, unlike company employees.

Network explanations for internationalization

Johanson and Mattson view international trade as a series of networks between firms involved in production, distribution and use of goods. Each firm in the network has different relationships at different levels with customers, distributors and suppliers and then with the suppliers' suppliers, customers' customers etc. Exchange is therefore taking place within established relationships and so ongoing efforts should be made to maintain, develop, change, even break these relationships so as to secure the long-term profitability and development of the firm.

Random walk approach

In approaching foreign market entry, Cavusgil and Li argue that companies will pursue either a sequential process or a random process. In the random process, firms will bypass or leap over certain stages. It does not mean that their actions are without justification or unplanned. If we accept that the best market entry form is contingent upon market conditions, then it is easy to accept this suggestion.

Export marketing and international marketing

The exchange process, which is the basis of international marketing, is different from that found in domestic markets and yet more than just exporting. Exporting would require the use of only four Ps, whereas international marketing requires the six Ps, of megamarketing. To export means simply to send or carry abroad, especially for trade or sale. Marketing goes beyond that, introducing the concept of the end-user, moving the orientation away from finding sales for a company's existing products to analysing the market and assessing whether the company is able to produce a product or service for which there is either current or potential demand, given that other factors can be controlled, such as price, promotion and distribution (Paliwoda, 1991). International marketing requires greater commitment, and that may mean executive time and resources, much more than does exporting.

Exporting may be simply a short-term solution to an immediate problem of under-capacity of production or over-capacity of stocks. Marketing identifies market needs, either current, potential or latent. Marketing helps to bridge the information gap between the company and the final consumer of its product. Exporting, on the other hand, is deemed to be successful whenever a sale is concluded. That sale will usually be with a trade intermediary. The company doing the exporting has achieved a profitable sale, but knows little or nothing about the final market for his product, nor will he receive any ongoing communication about how his product is received and what customers think of it. It may be a very bad product or may simply not be selling through the distribution system to the final consumer, but just gathering dust because trade margins are too low. In any event the final consequence will be known but not the reasons. International marketing offers then a reasoned management approach to international markets whereas exporting is more of an adventure in realizing short-term gains.

Root (1987) lists out a number of characteristics between what we may term an export sales approach and an international marketing approach. The objectives and the criteria by which they are defined are incredibly far apart (see Table 1.9)

Exporting behaviour reviewed

There have been a number of attempts to research the export decision process since the

Table 1.9   Export sales approach versus international marketing approach

	Export sales	*International marketing*
Time horizons	Short run	Long run (say three to five years)
Target markets	No systematic selection	Selection based on analysis of market/sales potential
Dominant objective	Immediate sales	Build permanent market position
Resource commitment	Only enough to get immediate sales	What is necessary to gain permanent market position
Entry mode	No systematic choice	Systematic choice of most appropriate mode
New-product development	Exclusively for home market	For both home and foreign markets
Product adaptation	Only mandatory adaptations (to meet legal/technical requirements) of domestic products	Adaptation of domestic products to foreign buyers' preferences, incomes and use conditions
Channels	No effort to control	Effort to control in support of market objectives/goals
Price	Determined by domestic full cost with some ad hoc adjustments to specific sales situations	Determined by demand, competition, objectives and other marketing policies, as well as cost
Promotion	Mainly confined to personal selling or left to middlemen	Advertising, sales promotion and personal selling mix to achieve market objectives goals

Source: Root, F. R. (Second Edition 1994) *Entry Strategies for International Markets*, Lexington Books, Lexington, MA.

study undertaken by Johanson and Wieder-sheim-Paul (1975). Based on empirical research of four actual Swedish exporters, their findings pointed to a 'gradual process occurring in stages', rather than large spectacular investments. They found that some expansion, immediately outside of the national market but within the immediate geographical region, preceded internationalization and so they were able to state that it was reasonable to assume that the same held true for many firms in other countries with small domestic markets. By expanding first out of the nation state into, for example, the immediate neighbouring regional market of Scandinavia, a Swedish firm could reduce its perceived risk and the overall uncertainty of exporting. It was exporting, but within a region where language and cultural values were consistent with one's own. What was interesting to note from their research was that the nature of pre-export activity influences the likelihood of a firm becoming an exporter. The firm will have first a natural preference for operations in the nearby geographic areas. Again, the question of regional expansion is affected by the personal perception, individual characteristics and experience of the decision maker. Within the context of the firm, this involvement in international

marketing could be viewed as an innovation, but this would be to deny the economic necessity that often prevails on companies to export when faced with stagnation or extinction.

The Uppsala school 'model', as devised by Weidersheim-Paul, influenced subsequent writings on the subject and identified four stages. A further study by Bilkey and Tesar (1977) (see Table 1.10) among Wisconsin exporters identified six stages:

1. Management is not interested and would not even fill an unsolicited export order.
2. Management is willing to fill solicited export orders but makes no effort to explore the feasibility of actively exporting to that country or region.
3. Management actively explores the feasibility of exporting to that foreign market.
4. The firm exports experimentally to some psychologically close country.
5. The firm is an experienced exporter to that country.
6. Management explores the feasibility of exporting to additional countries, psychologically more distant.

Table 1.10 Comparison of the four export development models			
Johanson and Wiedersheim-Paul (1975)	Bilkey and Tesar (1977)	Cavusgil (1980)	Czinkota (1982)
	Stage 1 Management is not interested in exporting	Stage 1 Domestic marketing: the firm sells only to the home market	Stage 1 The completely uninterested firm
Stage 1 No regular export activities	Stage 2 Management is willing to fill unsolicited orders, but makes no effort to explore the feasibility of active exporting	Stage 2 Pre-export stage: the firm searches for information and evaluates the feasibililty of undertaking exporting	Stage 2 The partially interested firm
	Stage 3 Management actively explores feasibility of active exporting		Stage 3 The exploring firm
Stage 2 Export via overseas agents	Stage 4 The firm exports on an experimental basis to some psychologically close country	Stage 3 Experimental involvement: the firm starts exporting on a limited basis to some psychologically close countries	Stage 4 The experimental exporter
	Stage 5 The firm is an experienced exporter	Stage 4 Active involvement: exporting to more new countries—direct exporting —increase in export volume	Stage 5 The experienced small exporter
Stage 3 Establishment of an overseas sales subsidiary	Stage 6 Management explores the feasibility of exporting to other more psychologically distant countries	Stage 5 Committed involvement: management constantly makes choices in allocating limited resources between domestic and foreign markets	Stage 6 The experienced large exporter
Stage 4 Overseas production manufacturing			

Source: Ford, D., Leonidou, L. (1991) Research developments in international marketing: A European perspective. In Stanley J. Paliwoda *New Perspectives on International Marketing.* Routledge, London

Psychological commitment and resource allocation

The concept of psychological closeness of one market to another was to prove an important and useful finding. This model was subsequently refined by Cavusgil and Nevin who went on to identify yet further characteristics, finding that the internal company factors explaining export marketing behaviour fell into four groups as in Figure 1.10:

1. Expectations of management, as a result of the impact of exports on growth.
2. Level of commitment.
3. Differential advantages to the firm.

4. Managerial aspirations, often related to security.

This incremental model identified three states of internationalization:

1. *Stimuli for experimental international involvement.* Non-exporters need stimuli to enter exporting. Cavusgil and Nevin identified external and internal stimuli. External stimuli often take the form of unsolicited orders from buyers or distributors abroad or domestic export agents. Banks, trade associations, and middlemen also serve as change agents. External stimuli clearly exceed the number of internal stimuli received. In eight separate studies, external stimuli (Cavusgil, 1976) accounted for 54–84 per cent of all

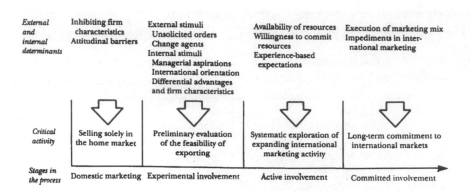

Source: Cavusgil, S. T., and Nevin, J. R. (1980) Conceptualizations of the initial involvement in international marketing. In *Theoretical Developments in Marketing* (eds Lamb, C. W., and Dunne, P. M.) American Marketing Association, Phoenix, April

Figure 1.10   A model of the incremental internationalization process of the firm

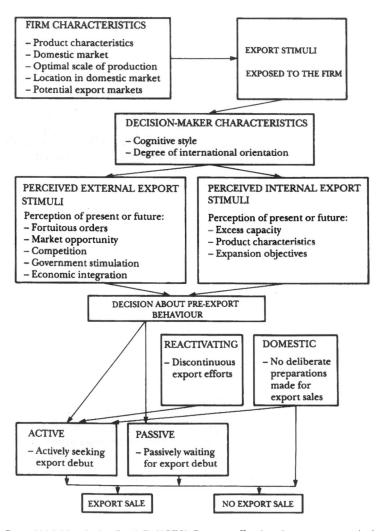

Source: Olson, H.C., and Weidersheim-Paul, F. (1978) Factors affecting the pre-export behaviour of non-exporting firms. In *European Research in International Business* (eds Ghertman, M., and Leontiades, J.), North-Holland Publishing Co., New York, p. 285

Figure 1.11   Model of export propensity

stimuli. Firms which start exporting as a result of external inquiries exemplify a passive approach in international marketing, with an involvement which was fortuitous, marginal and intermittent, with short-run profits being likely to be the motivating force, rather than clearly formulated long-term objectives.

2. *Active international involvement.* This involves a systematic exploration of marketing opportunities imposing demands on the resources of the firm – physical, financial, and managerial which will test the willingness of management to allocate these resources. Smaller firms face an obvious disadvantage in not being able to commit resources, financial incentives do not immediately change matters. Another major determinant of active involvement in international marketing is management's experience-based expectations of the attractiveness of exporting for the firm.

3. *Committed international involvement.* The firm moves into the position of committed participants in international marketing. Now managers are constantly making choices in the allocation of resources between foreign and domestic markets.

Taken all in all, the internationalization approach does not appear to be a sequence of deliberate planning, beginning with a clearly defined problem and proceeding through a rational analysis of behaviourial alternatives. Personal characteristics of the decision makers, lack of information, and perception of risk and presence of uncertainty seem to be especially valuable in understanding a firm's involvement in international marketing.

There are aspects of the internationalization process as having both a learning sequence as well as export stages. Czinkota's six-stage model overlaps with the previous models discussed but emphasizes the experimentation aspect and the differences that may be introduced by company size, small as opposed to large.

Incremental internationalization

The sequential process of internationalization is similar then to the process of an adolescent growing up. It implies that there is only one way to go and that is to proceed further along the continuum. Rugman depicts this graphically in Figure 1.12.

Although depicting what is said to be a 'typi-cal' process by which a firm producing a stand-ardized product will seek to involve itself in a foreign market, it emphasizes the learning aspect of internationalization and the acquisition of market knowledge, which reduces both risk and perceived risk. It does show that companies will change their form of market representation over time, and that this can happen only in one direction with the ultimate aim of foreign direct investment. The experienced company entering into FDI will be in a much better placed situation than is the case at either the licensing stage or the stage that still uses agents or distributors.

Organization for internationalization

Stopford and Wells (1972) suggested that multinational companies manage their international operations through an international division at the early stage of foreign expansion, when both foreign sales and the diversity of products sold abroad are limited. Different organizational structures are adopted at different stages of international expansion. Foreign product diversity is measured by the number of products sold

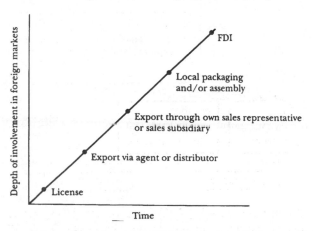

Source: Rugman, A. R., Lecraw, D. J., and Booth, L. D. (1986) *International Business – Firm and Environment,* McGraw-Hill, New York

Figure 1.12   Entry into foreign markets: the internationalization process

internationally, while the importance of international sales to the company is implicit on the axis 'foreign sales as a percentage of total sales'. Stopford and Wells, therefore, saw the international division as an intermediate phase, as seen in Figure 1.13.

The international division is outlined in more detail in Figure 1.14. This division is characterized by a staff group duplicating most of the functions of the corporate staff, which assists the general manager of the division. Later this duplication is lessened with the divisional staff group concerned primarily with the control of the foreign subsidiaries. It provides an illustration of how management procedures will change as further experience of international business is gained.

However, in other respects, this is not a working model. Companies, irrespective of size, will not actively follow this continuum. Instead, there will be within each company a portfolio of overseas opportunities being exploited simultaneously by a number of different modes of market entry across different markets. There is no one 'right' or 'best' strategy other than the one which achieves the highest degree of situational fit at that given moment in time. This means then that international modes of operation, once selected, have to be constantly monitored for effectiveness rather than institutionally accepted. Some multinationals use the full range of market entry modes across their different markets in Europe, for example, but a Single European Market creates further opportunities for rationalization of production and distribution. Thus, political and economic realities tend to diminish the effectiveness of the 'stages' theory as a viable policy option.

Life cycle for international trade: beyond its sell-by date?

The work of Louis T. Wells, has held an important place in the international marketing literature since its first publication in 1968.

Essentially, the trade cycle, which used the same bell-shaped curve as the product life cycle,

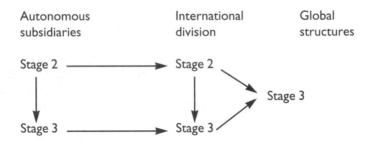

Note: The term 'global structures' includes all the area division, worldwide product division, mixed and grid forms.
Source: Stopford, J. M., and Wells, L. T., Jr (1972) *Managing the Multinational Enterprise*, Basic Books, New York

Figure 1.13   Sequences of structural change

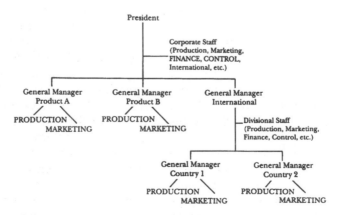

Note: The functions in capital letters indicate operating responsibility; those in lower case indicate advisory and co-ordinating roles.
Source: Stopford J. M., and Wells, L. T., Jr (1972) *Managing the Multinational Enterprise*, Basic Books, New York

Figure 1.14   Internal structure of the international division

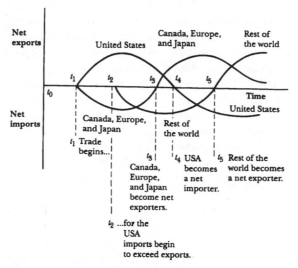

Source: Rugman, A. M., Lecraw, D. J., and Booth, L. D. (1986) International Business: Firms and the Environment, McGraw-Hill, New York

Figure 1.15   Trade flows over the product cycle

identified four stages in international trade, mirroring in fact the domestic PLC stages:

1.   US export strength,
2.   Foreign production starts,
3.   Foreign production becomes competitive in US export markets,
4.   Import competition begins.

As the domestic market demand peaked products would be moved internationally and as sales in secondary markets peaked, those products moved to tertiary markets thereby utilizing the full potential of global markets for good product management. The trade cycle model was built uniquely around the US market, not that US entrepreneurs have ever had any monopoly over scientific invention but because of its sheer market size and so importance in terms of product innovation, bringing the scientific breakthrough to market. The US market, however, is important in terms of both size and affluence. Wells made a statement that Porter would agree with, though, when he says: that 'It is also likely that the final product development leading to commercial production will be achieved by an entrepreneur responding to his own national demand.'

There is consensus in the argument that a manufacturer ought to be close to his market, to be attuned to it and design for it. This means here a US base. When the product is in the early stage of the PLC, and it is not of major importance, quality is more important. Any foreign demand in the form of unsolicited orders (arising from the demonstration effect) is met by exports from the USA. As the demonstration effect continues,

product familiarity abroad increases and foreign production starts. The foreign producer will have to cover factor costs, e.g., labour, which is expensive in the USA, but little or no product development costs. Imports from the USA give some guidance as to the market potential in the country concerned. The foreign producer may even be a US subsidiary realizing that if it does not start production abroad, someone else will. There are problems of scale economies, freight and tariffs. So, although foreign production has started, US exports still supply most of world demand.

In phase 3, the foreign manufacturer becomes larger and more experienced, so these costs should fall. With a different cost structure, they may be competitive with US-made goods in their markets. US exports must soon start to decline as foreign production becomes more and more competitive. The cost savings may be sufficient to enable him to pay ocean freight and US duty, and still compete with US producers on their own market as there is high value added in the product to cushion against such costs. For the US producer in this situation, the only strategy is their exit and future sourcing from abroad. This points to the phenomenon of 'runaway industry', whereby multinationals manufacturing products which are mature, and therefore labour-intensive and more price-sensitive, may continually move their bases of production around the world in a never-ending search for lower operational costs.

In phase 4, the foreign manufacturer reaches mass production and may have lower costs than his US counterpart, enabling him to pay freight and duty, and still compete favourably in the US market. A marginal pricing policy will bring forward the confrontation with US producers. US exports meanwhile have been slowed down to supplying only special customers abroad, while import competition is making inroads into the domestic market. Early foreign producers were seen to be most probably the West Europeans, who would then face a similar cycle. Manufacturers would then move down to lower income countries in a pecking order across continents.

The cycle was not standard for all products but was seen to exhibit three main characteristics:

1. appeal of the product to the US market,
2. reduction in unit costs as the scale of production increases,
3. cost of tariffs and freight.

The product was classified in terms of the US consumer. The US market reflected a particularly unique demand for products that fell into the following categories:

1. luxury function,
2. expensive to buy,
3. expensive to own,
4. labour saving.

Wells did say, however, that not all products could be expected to follow the cycle as they may be tied to a certain local national resource as with American cigarettes. The model did open the way, though, for market segmentation to play a role both in increasing exports and protecting against imports. Product differentiation can be advanced through a number of means, including price and design changes. Product appeal may be changed with a design change, reflecting the needs of the home market, and new product versions may be brought out for the wealthy consumer at home.

Raymond Vernon, also from the Harvard Business School, started with the premise that enterprises in any one of the advanced countries are not distinguishably different from those in any other advanced country, in terms of their access to scientific knowledge and their capacity to comprehend scientific principles. The ability to turn inventions into commercially successful innovations is not, however, equal among nations. Vernon moves away from the notion that knowledge is a universal free good, and introduces it as an independent variable in the decisions to trade or invest.

Attention is then turned towards the US market which, because of high individual disposable incomes, is an excellent market in which to introduce innovations aimed at high-level income earners. The US has high unit labour costs but relatively unrationed capital relative to other countries. This, too, conditions demand. Logically, then, goods which conserve labour would find a ready market in the USA. Because of the market potential, US manufacturers will invest more heavily in new product development than their counterparts in other countries, particularly with regard to products which substitute capital for labour, and are associated with high levels of income. In a similar way, Vernon argues that Germany's comparative disadvantage, in her lack of a raw materials base, led Germany to develop a world position in plastics.

Vernon's hypothesis is that US producers are closer to their market than producers elsewhere, and so they will be the first to identify an opportunity for high-income or labour-saving sources, and, consequently, the first production facilities for these products will be in the USA. The attractiveness of a US location can only be explained by forces that are stronger than relative factor-cost and transport considerations.

*   In the early stages, the product may be quite unstandardized for a time and thus, this carries with it a number of locational implications.
*   Price elasticity of demand for the output of individual forms is comparatively low. This follows from the high degree of production differentiation, or the existence of a monopoly in the early stages.
*   Need for swift effective communication, on the part of the producer with customers, suppliers and even competitors, is especially high at this stage. A considerable amount of uncertainty still remains regarding the market, its ultimate dimensions, competition, specifications of inputs needed for production, and the specifications of products likely to be most successful.

As demand expands, a certain degree of standardization usually takes place. Variety may appear as a result of specialization. While this product differentiation increases, a growing acceptance of certain general standards becomes established. This, too, has locational implications. The need for flexibility declines. Economies of scale, through mass production, become more important and this leads to long-term commitments to some given process and fixed set of facilities.

Concern about production cost replaces concern about product characteristics, even if increased price competition is not yet present. Although the first plant may be in the USA, demand also begins to appear elsewhere. If the product has a high income elasticity of demand or it is a satisfactory substitute for high-cost labour, demand in turn will begin to grow in Western Europe. As the market expands, the question arises as to whether the time has come to establish a local production facility. While the marginal cost of production, together with the freight costs of exporting from the USA, is lower than the average cost of prospective producers in the market of import, US producers will delay investment. If economies of scale are being fully exploited, the principal differences between any two locations are likely to be factor costs. Thus, the servicing of third markets may take place from the new location, and if labour costs offset the cost of freight, the servicing of the US market as well. Vernon does not find rationality in the decision-making relating to lower cost locations abroad, but generally finds threat to be more of a stimulus to action than opportunity. Investment may, therefore, be a defensive measure. US manufacturers fear losing global market share while unaware of the production cost structure of their foreign competitors.

The Vernon Hypothesis would have the USA exporting high-income labour-saving products in the early stages of their existence; and importing them later on. Labour cost, which is high in the early stage, is high because the product is still as yet relatively unstandardized, and so with standardization comes a shift from labour intensive to capital intensive production.

With standardized products, the LDCs may offer competitive advantages as production locations, yet as Vernon points out, this leaves marketing considerations out of the reckoning. Information is not free but comes at a cost. If these products are selling on price, then the sources of market information become much less important. Significant inputs of labour, high price elasticity of demand for the output, are necessary characteristics as is production of standardized specifications for inventory without fear of obsolescence and the high value of items capable of absorbing freight costs. Vernon finds little evidence of corroboration apart from Taiwan's foreign-owned electronics plants. Japanese exports then (in 1966) were more capital intensive than the Japanese productions displaced by imports.

A reason for the lack of corroborative evidence may be that the process has not advanced far enough: due to export constraints and overvalued exchange rates. Capital costs are not a barrier to production in the LDCs.

1. Investments will occur in industries which require significant labour inputs in production.

2. Production will be concentrated in sectors capable of producing highly standardized products in self-contained production centres.

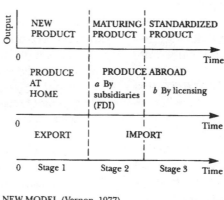

NEW MODEL (Vernon, 1977)

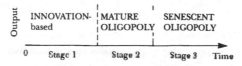

Note: In stage 1 of Vernon's product cycle model the new product is produced and consumed in the home nation. Exports take place. In stage 2 the maturing product can be produced abroad, perhaps in subsidiaries of the MNE. Some of the goods may start to be imported by the home nation. In stage 3 the now standardized product is entirely produced abroad, even by licensing. The home nation imports all of the good that it needs. In Vernon's later model the stages are the same; only the terminology changes.
Source: Rugman A. H., Lecraw, D. J., and Booth, L. D. (1986) *International Business: Firms and the Environment*, McGraw-Hill, New York

Figure 1.16 Product cycle model – Vernon 1966

Capital costs have to be weighed against the opportunity costs, and so, this ability to compare rates internationally will not present any problems for multinational companies. The kind of investor here is not vulnerable to the limitations of only domestic capital in the LDCs themselves. Their access to capital becomes a direct function of their capacity to propose plausible projects to public international lenders. Vernon is aware of the imperfections, but is not afraid to challenge existing thought and literature.

In 1979, Vernon revisited his earlier work, recognizing that the world had changed since 1966. Firstly, in the geographical reach of many of the enterprises involved in the introduction of new products; there was now found to be a network of overseas subsidiaries. Secondly, the differences between the markets of the advanced industrialized countries had much diminished. Consequently, Vernon now stated that the product cycle concept 'can no longer be relied on to provide as powerful an explanation of the behaviour of US firms as in decades past'.

Nevertheless, some interesting points emerge. The assumption that the stimulus to innovation is provided by some threat or promise in the market is still there. The home market is still seen as the source of stimulus for the innovating firm and as the preferred location for the actual development of the innovation. Innovations reflect the characteristics of their market: USA with products responding to labour-saving or high-income wants; continental Europe with products and processes that were material saving and capital saving; and Japan with products that conserve not only material and capital but also space.

The home market is still likely to be the first production site as the movement from research to development to production follows imperceptible stages. There will be minimal transportation costs. The specifications and manufacturing procedures are still undetermined; and there is, too, the characteristic inelasticity in the demand of the earliest users of many new products. Foreign demand is met from the home production plant although now Vernon is saying that the firm may consider other alternatives, such as licensing a foreign producer or establishing a subsidiary, balancing the delivered cost of exports against the costs of overseas production.

The decision to create a foreign producing facility is usually triggered by a threatened loss of market monopoly position due to foreign producers now ready to manufacture the product at lower costs.

Vernon points to the spread of the multinational's network of subsidiaries and affiliates, stating that innovating firms that are limited to their own home markets are no longer very common. In a study of 180 US firms, Vernon found that they typically set up their subsidiaries' product lines and new products, in a sequence that began with the geographical area with which they were most familiar, such as Canada and the UK, and eventually spread to those that had originally been least familiar, such as Asia and Africa. With time, the unfamiliar became less so and the disposition to move first into the traditional areas visibly declined (Vernon, 1979(b)). Experience was another important variable. Firms that had experienced a number of prior transfers to their foreign producing subsidiaries were consistently quicker off the mark with any new product, than were firms with fewer prior transfers. This change appears to be unaffected by changes in exchange rates or in price-adjusted exchange rates, so Vernon concludes that we are dealing with a basic change in the institutional structure of the multinationals concerned.

The descriptive power of the product cycle model was enhanced by the special post-war characteristics of the US market, then not only the largest single market in the world but by far the most affluent. Convergence has since taken place with many other countries approaching US income levels, and developing similar market needs and wants. This development weakened a critical assumption of the product cycle, namely, that the entrepreneurs of large enterprises confronted markedly different conditions in their respective home markets. The rise of the EU has been an important factor in creating new standard conditions within Europe. Other assumptions of the product cycle are therefore now questioned:

- it cannot be assumed that innovating firms are uninformed about conditions in foreign markets,
- it cannot be claimed that US firms are exposed to a very different home environment than their European or Japanese counterparts and,
- differences among the advanced industrialized countries are reduced to trivial dimensions.

Vernon then classifies multinationals into three types to explore their likely behaviour as regards innovation:

1. The global scanner – the MNC with a powerful capacity for global scanning. Communication is virtually costless between any two points in the world; information storage and retrieval on a worldwide scale is used to diminish risk and properly evaluate market opportunity. Innovations in response to market promise or threat can still be expected.

Once the product was developed, all markets that had been identified by global scanning could then be served. As incomes rise, new markets emerge in a largely predictable pattern. New global producers might, over time, perceive an opportunity to expand, but lack now the size and the information resources of the multinationals. Whatever the original source of the exports might be, the hold of the exporting country would be tenuous, as the global scanner continuously recalculates the parameters that determine the optimal production location.

2.   Producers of standardized products for homogeneous world demand, e.g. oil and chemicals. They are hoping for two benefits: to reduce or avoid the costs of processing and interpreting the information relative to the distinctive needs of individual markets; and to capture the scale economies of production and marketing on a global scale. Such firms are likely to perform consistently with the product cycle pattern. With ease of communication and transportation, the more routine aspects of product development can be directed to more distant locations. They may be able to respond to local host government demands in this manner, but they need to be integrated. The cross-hauling of components between various plants in advanced industrialized and developing countries is at odds with the product cycle. Not all companies will commit themselves to the development of standard global products even if they have the resources to do so. Different firms will make different decisions on strategies for products that are essentially seen as closely competing products.

3.   Myopic innovation and home-oriented production remain while all analyses of foreign markets are left to individual foreign producing subsidiaries. The foreign subsidiaries may be allowed to select which home-based innovations they wish to transfer for production in their plant abroad. As long as this does not conflict with the activities of subsidiaries in other countries, local managers are given their independence. Explanations are seen in the costs of processing the necessary information for a centralized policy of production and marketing exceeding the likely benefits. Alternatively, the firm may not have the means to absorb, interpret and act on information from the subsidiaries. The product cycle is still valid here, but the active role of the parent in serving foreign markets is lessened.

The global scanning explanation is limited and is not costless, as gathering information from the network of subsidiaries may not prove worthwhile. Flexibility is endangered. The conditions necessary for the product cycle are gone as regards the multinationals, but as regards smaller companies that have not as yet developed the resources for a global scanning activity, the assumptions of the product cycle may still apply. Even multinationals with global scanning are unlikely to make use of this facility in the siting of their first production facility, but as US home

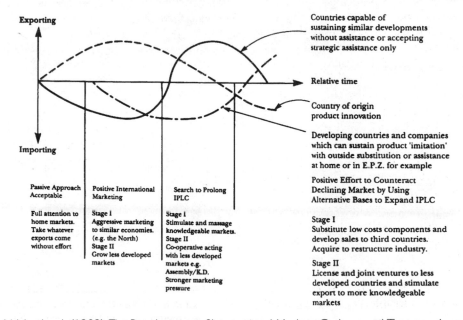

Source: Walmsley, J. (1989) *The Development of International Markets,* Graham and Trotman, London

Figure 1.17   Positive relationships between international product life cycle (IPLC) and international commitment

Table 1.11   The eclectic theory of international production*

1 *Ownership-specific advantages* (of enterprises of one nationality, or affiliates of same, over those of another).

    (a) Which need not arise due to multinationality.

        Those due mainly to size and established position, product or process diversification, ability to take advantage of division of labour and specialization; monopoly power, better resource capacity and usage.

        Proprietary technology, trade marks (protected by patent, etc., legislation).

        Production management, organizational, marketing systems; R & D capacity; 'bank' of human capital and experience.

        Exclusive or favoured access to inputs, e.g. labour, natural resources, finance, information.

        Ability to obtain inputs on favoured terms (due e.g. to size or monopsonistic influence).

        Exclusive or favoured access to product markets.

        Government protection (e.g. control on market entry).

    (b) Which those branch plants of established enterprises may enjoy over *de novo* firms.

        Access to capacity (administrative, managerial, R & D, marketing, etc.) of parent company at favoured prices.

        Economies of joint supply (not only in production, but in purchasing, marketing, finance, etc., arrangements).

    (c) Which specifically arise because of multinationality.

        Multinationality enhances above advantages by offering wider opportunities.

        More favoured access to and/or better knowledge about information, inputs, markets.

        Ability to take advantage of international differences in factor endowments, markets.

        Ability to diversify risks, e.g. in different currency areas, and to exploit differences in capitalization ratios.

2 *Internalization incentive advantages* (i.e. to protect against or exploit market failure).

    Reduction of costs (e.g. search, negotiation, monitoring) associated with market transactions.

    To avoid costs of enforcing property rights.

    Buyer uncertainty (about nature and value of inputs, e.g. technology, being sold).

    Where market does not permit price discrimination.

    Need of seller to protect quality of products.

    To capture economies of externalities and interdependent activities (see 1(b) above).

    To compensate for absence of futures markets.

    To avoid or exploit government intervention (e.g. quotas, tariffs, price controls, tax differences, etc.)

    To control supplies and conditions of sale of inputs (including technology).

    To control market outlets (including those which might be used by competitors).

    To be able to engage in practices, e.g. cross-subsidization, predatory pricing, etc., as a competitive (or anti-competitive) strategy.

3 *Location-specific advantages*

    Spatial distribution of inputs and markets.

    Input prices, quality and productivity, e.g. labour, energy, materials, components, semi-finished goods.

    Transport and communications costs.

    Government intervention.

    Control on imports (including tariff barriers), tax rates, incentives, climate for investment, political stability, etc.)

    Infrastructure [commercial, legal, transportation].

    Psychic distance (language, cultural, business, customs, etc. differences)

    Economies of R & D production and marketing (e.g. extent to which scale economies make for centralization of production).

*These advantages are not independent of each other. For example, those listed in (2) may be partially dependent on how MNEs exploit those listed in (1).

Source: Dunning, J. H. (1988) The eclectic paradigm of international production: A restatement and some possible extensions. *Journal of International Business Studies*, **19**, (1), 1–32

conditions are now found to be replicated abroad, only a 'shadow' of the hypothesized behaviour may well remain. Examples such as the utilization of national market characteristics

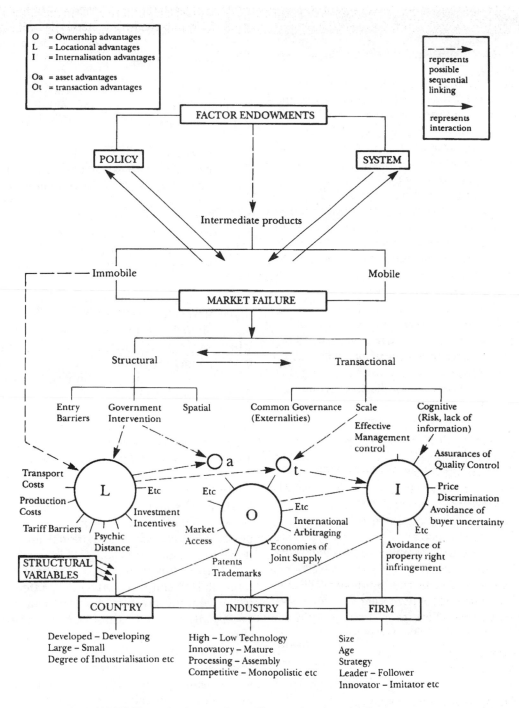

O = Ownership advantages
L = Locational advantages
I = Internalisation advantages

Oa = asset advantages
Ot = transaction advantages

------→ represents possible sequential linking

——→ represents interaction

FACTOR ENDOWMENTS

POLICY

SYSTEM

Intermediate products

Immobile

Mobile

MARKET FAILURE

Structural

Transactional

Entry Barriers   Government Intervention   Spatial

Common Governance (Externalities)   Scale   Cognitive (Risk, lack of information)

Effective Management control

Assurances of Quality Control

Transport Costs

Production Costs

Tariff Barriers

Psychic Distance

L   Etc

Investment Incentives

Market Access

Etc

O

Patents Trademarks

Etc

International Arbitraging

Economies of Joint Supply

Price Discrimination

Avoidance of buyer uncertainty

I   Etc

Avoidance of property right infringement

STRUCTURAL VARIABLES

COUNTRY   INDUSTRY   FIRM

Developed – Developing
Large – Small
Degree of Industrialisation etc

High – Low Technology
Innovatory – Mature
Processing – Assembly
Competitive – Monopolistic etc

Size
Age
Strategy
Leader – Follower
Innovator – Imitator etc

Source: Dunning, J. H. (1988) The eclectic paradigm of international production: a restatement and some possible extensions. *Journal of International Business Studies,* **19** (1), 1–32

Figure 1.18   The endowment/market failure paradigm of international production

in creating advantage, e.g., European and Japanese small car technology, fit within the product cycle, but would not be expected to remain with it for long.

Another aspect of this product cycle would be to expect that the industrializing countries, e.g., Brazil, Mexico, India, would start to initiate their own cycle of exportation and eventual direct investment in other developing countries.

This, though, has only been reported among multinational subsidiaries. The product cycle model, while it can no longer be relied on to provide as powerful an explanation of the behaviour of US firms as before, will continue to provide a guide to the motivations and responses of some enterprises in all countries of the world. The link with just the USA, or the industrialized countries, has now been totally broken.

Dunning's eclectic approach and later revision

The word 'eclectic' was deliberately chosen to convey the idea that a full explanation of the transnational activities of enterprises needs to draw on several strands of economic theory: foreign direct investment, being only one of several possible channels of international economic involvement, yet the one most closely identified with the eclectic approach.

The eclectic theory brings together three strands of economic theory: internalization advantages; ownership advantages; and locational advantages. The propensity of a firm to engage in international production depends on three conditions being satisfied:

1.   Ownership advantages relative to firms of other nationalities in the same foreign market. These may comprise of intangible assets (Ownership).
2.   It must be profitable for the firm to continue these assets with factor endowments located in the foreign markets; otherwise, the foreign markets would be served by exports (Location).
3.   It must be more beneficial to the enterprise possessing these advantages to use them itself rather than sell them, or the right to use them, to a foreign firm (Internalization).

The eclectic approach suggests that all forms of international production by all countries can be explained with reference to the conditions in Table 1.11. These advantages are not static, but will change over time. A firm possessing an advantage can either use the advantage itself, or can sell or lease the advantage to other firms. Dunning points to the existence of multinationals as proof that some ownership advantages are transferable across national boundaries. An illustration of the eclectic approach as applied to the international hotel industry is provided by Dunning and McQueen in Rugman (1982).

In a 1980 revision, Dunning concedes that the eclectic approach has only limited power to explain or predict particular kinds of international production or the behaviour of individual enterprises.

A country's propensity to engage in outward direct investment, or else receive foreign direct investment, will vary according to:

1.   its stage of economic development,
2.   the structure of its factor endowments and markets,
3.   its political and economic systems, and
4.   the nature and extent of market failure in the transaction of intermediate products across national boundaries.

Dunning also draws the distinction between structural and transactional market imperfections. Market failure results from:

1.   risk and uncertainty,
2.   ability of firms to exploit the economies of large-scale production, but only in an imperfect market situation,
3.   where the transaction of a good or service yields costs and benefits external to that transaction, but that are not reflected in the terms agreed to by the transacting parties.

The greater the perceived costs of transactional market failure, the more MNEs are likely to exploit their competitive advantages through international production rather than by contractual agreements with foreign firms.

In the restatement, Dunning makes two qualifications to the earlier version of the eclectic approach. Firstly, he is now drawing on the neoclassical theory of factor endowments to include intermediate products and the transferability of these endowments across national boundaries. Secondly, Dunning draws on the theory of market failure to explain, not only the location of some kinds of economic activity across national boundaries, but also the division of activity between multinational and uninational (domestic) firms.

The more multinational a firm becomes, the more it is inclined to engage in internalized trade. Dunning, however, holds that internalization is only one of the three parts of the eclectic approach. It is one part not the sum of the parts, although it appears increasingly to be taken by some researchers for the whole.

Looking to the future, Dunning sees the increasing complexity of foreign direct investment, and this modelling of transactional market failure requiring the fusion of a number of disparate approaches, pointing for example to the network approach developed by the Swedish researchers, Johansson and Mattson. Collaborative ventures between multinationals, their buyers and suppliers internationally will have important implications for all.

International marketing and the Internet

In spite of all the hyperbole, the Internet has to be recognized not for what it is at present but for the potential which it presents. For the first time location is not important, only good communications. A business can operate literally anywhere, far distant even from the majority of its customers, provided all important parts of what we may call customer service are fulfilled. The Internet has produced at the moment a few isolated success stories of small companies in remote areas, now finding that they are prospering through being able to offer their specialized services to a much greater and wider customer base than ever before, and that has come around simply because of the Internet. Customers learn about products and services on the Internet through the home pages which companies create and through word of mouth. This is equal to a shop window in the traditional sense, but with one with a very important difference. It is possible for a very small company to have a more professional home page than a much larger company and so instead of size or surrounding, customer perception focuses simply on those elements which are visible to the customer.

The last edition of this book contained a case study about Minitel, an early videotext system developed by France Telecom, which certainly predated the Internet. France Telecom achieved their pre-eminence in the field by giving their regular telephone customers free terminals which integrated the telephone with a small screen and thus created access for up to 16,000 additional services including directory enquiries. The strategy was successful in that France Telecom quickly acquired a mass market for its new range of services, and although the terminal was free, the services had to be paid for and were invoiced together with the regular telephone bill. This created an illusion at least of freedom to use. Minitel in France was an instant success with 6.5m users creating a $2 billion source of revenue for France Telecom. As a result of the market penetration strategy pursued by France Telecom, advertisers soon had to integrate Minitel into their advertising strategies and all their advertising messages. In France, 15 per cent of all direct marketing sales are channelled through Minitel, but yet there is hardly an advertisement to be seen anywhere which fails to display a Minitel address for enquiries.

The situation is quite different in the USA and elsewhere. The USA has the highest computer penetration but still does not as yet have the penetration of online services to be found in France and this is reflected clearly in statistics for direct marketing. In the USA, all online services together add up to less than 1 per cent of the $58 billion sales generated by direct marketing, so if sales were to rise to the levels found in France, this would constitute an $8.7 billion market. The

potential therefore is enormous and the displacement effect will be equally large as this new technology begins to usurp existing channels and fails to recognize traditional borders. Neil Barrett in his book titled *The State of the Cybernation* stated:

The Internet allows services, correspondence and trading to take place in a non-physical realm. The term 'Cyberspace' was coined to describe this domain of computer communication; a world in which physical, national boundaries become irrelevant; a world in which tiny, back-street shops can market and sell to customers throughout the globe. And a place in which the laws and regulation painstakingly devised over centuries become difficult, impossible or irrelevant to apply; a place which might evolve its own nationhood: a Cybernation.

The developed nations of the world have had a temporary advantage only. Initially, the Internet was available only in English but most of the world's major languages can now be accommodated and it is now possible to compose a message in one language and transmit it via the Internet so that what arrives will be translated into the language of the recipient. This may sound like science fiction but is science fact and is being used in practice by the police and customs officers at either end of the Channel Tunnel, so simultaneous machine translation is available. It is also within the reach of companies small, medium and large as the systems can now be bought outright or else obtained through a service provider such as CompuServe on a need basis. As with everything else, the more you are willing to pay the better the product, but there is now a new and important tool available to us today and we have to acknowledge that at a time when international markets are a necessity. A small specialized company today has no option but to go global and to chase those prospects wherever they may be found within its industry, which may span continents. Some industries such as oil and gas learned that lesson many years ago, others are just waking up to the fact.

To encourage usage of the Internet and develop an awareness of useful Web sites, we have suggested a number of them at the end of each chapter in this book. The sites have been chosen to complement the material in the chapter.

Revision questions

1. Explain the difference between Absolute Advantage and Comparative Advantage.
2. How does international marketing relate to the concept of Comparative Advantage?
3. What is the role of the nation state in world

trade? Is it doomed always to be reactive and a hostage to the decisions of multinational corporations? Can the nation state be proactive in international trade?

4. What is the meaning of globalization and how does it differ from 'going international'?

5. What do the tables of competitiveness actually tell us, if we are considering foreign market entry? What good advice is to be learned?

6. With regard to any industry of your choice, illustrate how Porter's Diamond helps the intending international marketer to prepare for local conditions in the target foreign market.

7. The region is said by Kenichi Ohmae to have replaced the nation state. Illustrate the differences between a region such as the EU and any of its member states and NAFTA and its member states.

8. Explain what is meant by extraterritorial reach of foreign domestic legislation.

9. Citing two examples, show how international trade organizations have undergone change to remain current with global practices.

10. Having explained economic advantage, what then is a marketing advantage?

11. Do the traditional 4 Ps transfer equally well to international marketing? Any shortcomings? Does Kotler's 6 Ps fill a void then, or not?

12. What common factors do you identify in the reasons put forward by companies for 'going international'?

13. How might flexibility be important to the success of a firm wishing to enter foreign markets? What might this then involve?

14. Is the debate over the multinational corporation a dead one? Who won?

15. How does marketing differ if we talk of a small exporter as opposed to an international company, or a multinational corporation against a truly global corporation? What factors change?

16. Networking theory goes back to the early market relationships of major companies to form a theory. It is based upon the evolution of a few major companies. Can it help us predict which companies should go international and when?

17. With regard to the product life cycle for international trade, take three examples of your choice to illustrate whether or not you believe this theory to have current relevance.

18. Why is Dunning's theory called an 'eclectic approach'? What does it tell us essentially?

19. Is internationalization a process which is best approached in stages or not? Give one or two examples.

20. What advantages and disadvantages do you perceive in the Internet as a means of extending your company operations outside of your domestic market? What present difficulties do you perceive? How might these difficulties be resolved?

Note: The term *European Economic Area* (or EEA) refers to the combined market size of EFTA (European Free Trade Area) and European Union

References

Baker, M. J. (1994) One more time – what is marketing? In *The Marketing Book* (ed. M. J. Baker), Butterworth–Heinemann, Oxford.

Barber, B. R. (1996) *Jihad vs. McWorld*, Ballantine Books, New York

Barrett, N. (1996) *The State of the Cybernation: Cultural, Political and Economic Implications of the Internet*, Kogan Page, London.

Bartels, R. (1968) Are domestic and international marketing dissimilar? *Journal of Marketing, Vol* 32, 56–61.

Bartlett, C. A. and Ghoshal S. (1989) *Managing Across Borders: The Transnational Solution*, Hutchinson Business Books, London.

Bilkey, W. J., and Tesar, G. (1977) The export behaviour of smaller sized Wisconsin manufacturing firms. *Journal of International Business Studies*, Spring, 93–98.

Bryan, L., Farrell, D. (1996) *Market Unbound: Unleashing Global Capitalism*, John Wiley & Sons, New York.

Cavusgil, S. T., and Nevin, J. R. (1980) Conceptualisations of the initial involvement in international marketing. In *Theoretical Developments in Marketing*, (eds C. W. Lamb and P. M. Dunne), American Marketing Association, Theory Conference, Phoenix, April.

Dunning, J. H. (1981) *International Production and the Multinational Enterprise*, George Allen and Unwin, London.

Dunning, J. H., and McQueen, M. (1982) The eclectic theory of the multinational enterprise and the international hotel industry. In *New Theories of the Multinational Enterprise*, (A. M. Rugman) St. Martin's Press, New York.

Dunning, J. H. (1988) The eclectic paradigm of international production: A restatement and some possible extensions. *Journal of International Business Studies*, **19**, (1), 1–32.

The Economist Pocket World in Figures, 1997 Edition, London.

Fifield, P. and Lewis, K. (1996) *CIM Workbook: International Marketing Strategy 1996–97*, Butterworth–Heinemann, Oxford.

Gibson, R. ed. (1997) *Rethinking the Future*, Nicholas Brealey Publishing, London.

Gillespie, K. and Arden, D. (1989) Consumer product export opportunities to liberalising LDCs: A life cycle approach, *Journal of International Business Studies*, Spring, 93–112.

Hood, N., and Young, S. (1979) *The Economics of Multinational Enterprise*, Longmans, London.

Johanson, J. and Mattson, L. G. (1995) International marketing and internationalization processes: a network approach. In *International Marketing Reader* (eds S. J. Paliwoda and J. K. Ryans Jr), Routledge, London.

Johanson, J., and Wiedersheim–Paul, P. (1975) The internationalisation of the firm: Four Swedish cases. *Journal of Management Studies*, 12(3), 305–322.

Kotler, P. (1986) Megamarketing. *Harvard Business Review*, March–April, 117–124.

Levitt, T. (1983) *The Marketing Imagination*, Macmillan – The Free Press, New York.

Livingstone, J. M. (1989) *The Internationalisation of Business*, Macmillan, London.

Marketing News (1987) Marketing milestones of four decades reviewed, July 31.

Marketing News (1984) Kotler: rethink the marketing concept – there are 6 Ps' not 4. September 13.

Naisbitt, J. (1996) *Megatrends Asia: The Eight Asian Megatrends that are Changing the World*, Nicholas Brealey Publishing, London.

Noonan, C. (1996) *The CIM Handbook of Export Marketing*, Butterworth-Heinemann, Oxford.

Ohmae, K. (1985) *Triad Power: The Coming Shape of Global Competition*, Macmillan – The Free Press, New York.

Ohmae, K. (1995a) *The Evolving Global Economy: Making Sense of the New World Order*, Harvard Business School Press, Boston, Mass.

Ohmae, K. (1995b) *The End of the Nation State*, The Free Press, New York.

Paliwoda, S. J. (1991) *New Perspectives in International Marketing*, Routledge, London.

Paliwoda, S. J. (1994) International marketing – Getting started. In *The Marketing Book*, (Baker M. J.) 3rd ed, Heinemann, Oxford.

Perlemutter H. V. (1969) Some management problems on spaceship Earth: The megafirm in the global industrial estate. *Academy of Management Proceedings*, New York, August.

Peters, T. J., and Waterman, R. H. (1982) *In Search of Excellence*, Harper and Row, London.

Porter, M. E. (1986) Competition in global industries: A conceptual framework. In *Competition in Global Industries*, Harvard Business School Press.

Porter, M. E. (1990) *The Competitive Advantage of Nations*, Macmillan, London.

Root, F. R. (1987) 2nd ed *Entry Strategies for International Markets*, Lexington Books, Lexington, MA.

Rugman, A. M., Lecraw, D. J., and Booth, L. D. (1986) *International Business: Firms and the Environment*, McGraw-Hill, New York.

Stopford, J. M. (1980) *Growth and Organizational Change in the Multinational Firm*, Arno Press, New York.

Stopford, J. M., and Louis, L. T. Wells (1972) *Managing the Multinational Enterprise*, Basic Books Inc., New York.

Turnbull, P. W. (1987) A challenge to the stages theory of the internationalisation process. In *Managing Export Entry and Expansion*, (Rosson, P. J., and Reid, S. D.) Praeger, New York.

Turnbull, P. W., and Paliwoda, S. J. (1986) *Research in International Marketing*, Croom-Helm, London.

Vernon, R. (1979a) *Product cycle hypothesis in a new international environment*. Oxford Statistical and Economic Papers, November, pp. 255–267.

Vernon, R., and Davidson, W. H. (1979b) *Foreign production of technology-intensive products by US-based multinational enterprises*. Working Paper 79–5, Harvard Business School, Cambridge, MA.

Vernon, R. (1966) International investment and international trade in the product cycle, *Quarterly Journal of Economics*, May, 190–207.

Wells, L. T. Jr. (1968) A product life cycle for international trade? *Journal of Marketing*, 32, 1–6.

Walmsley, J. (1989) *The Development of International Markets*, Graham and Trotman, London.

Web sites

Asia Pacific Business and Marketing Resources gopher: hoshi.cic.sffu.ca
Choose: David See_Chai Lam Centre for International Communication–Asia Pacific Business & Marketing Resources

Bank of England
http://www.bankofengland.co.uk

BBC
http://www.bbc.co.uk

British Chamber of Commerce
http://www.brainstorm.co.uk/BCC/Welcome.html

Businesses on the Internet
http://www.yahoo.com/Business_and_Economy/Corporations/

Business to Business Marketing Exchange
www.btob.wfu.edu/b2b.html

Chartered Institute of Marketing
http://www.cim.co.uk

CNN Interactive
http://www.cnn.com/

Commerce Business Daily
gopher:cscns.com
Choose: Internet Express Gopher by Subject
         Business–Commerce Business Daily-
         Softshare

Commercenet
www.commerce.net

Currency Converter
http://bin.gnn.com/cgi-bin/gnn/currency

Department of Trade and Industry
http://www.dti.gov.uk/

Europa
http://www.europa.eu.int/welcome.html

EWR (Early Warning Report): Chokepoints for
    World Trade
http://www.subscriptions.com/beacon/
    mapchokepoints.html

EXPOguide – trade shows and conferences
    worldwide
http://www.expoguide.com

Financial Times
http://wwwft.com/

Foreign Exchange Rates
http://www.dna.Ith.se/cgi-bin/kurt/rates/

Global Internet News Agency
www.gina.com

Global Trade Center
http://wwwtradezone.com/tz/

Importing and Exporting
Usenet: alt.business.import-export

Information Market Europe – European
    Commission
http://www.echo.lu/

Institute of Export
http://www.export.co.uk

International Business Forum
http://wwwibf.com/

International Chambers of Commerce Business
    Opportunities
http://www.icc.ibcc.org/gbxhp.html

International Chamber of Commerce, Paris
http://wwwl.usal.com/~ibnet/icchp.html

International Trademark Classes
http://www.naming.com/naming/
    icclasses.html

Internet Address Finder
www.iaf.net

International Internet Marketing
www.clark.net/pub/granered/iim.html

Irish Times
http://www.ieunet.ie/ois/irishtimes/
    inde.shtml

Microsoft/NBC
http://www.msnbc.com

Minitel
http://www.minitel.fr

Moneyworld UK
http://www.moneyworld.co.uk

NAFTANET – North American Free Trade
    Agreement
http://www.nafta.net/

News from Reuters On-Line
http://beta.yahoo.com/headlines/current/
    business/

St. Petersburg Business Journal
http://www.spb.su.sppress/

Sunday Times
http://www.delphi.co.uk/innov/News.html

The British Council
http://www.britcoun.org/

The Economist
http://www.economist.com

The European Business Directory
http://www.europages.com/g/home.html

The Times
http://www.the-times.co.uk

Trade Statistics
http://www.census.gov/ftp/pub/
    foreign-trade/www/

UN Documents
http://www.un.org/Docs/index/html

UNCTAD (UN Conference on Trade and
    Development)
http://www.unicc.org/unctad/en/
    enhome.html

United Nations Homepage
http:///www.unicc.org/

Dept. of Commerce
http://www.doc.gov/
    CommerceHomePage.html

US Fedworld
www.fedworld.gov

US National Trade Data Bank
http://www.stat-usa.gov/BEN/Services/
ntdb-home.html

USA – Economic Bulletin Board
gopher://una.hh.lib.umich.edu/11/ebb

Wall Street Journal
http://wsj.com

Wall Street Net
http://www.netresource.com/wsn/

World Bank
http://www.worldbank.org/

World Health Organization
http://www.who.ch/

World Wide Web Virtual Library
http://W3.org

WTO (World Trade Organization): Agreement
Establishing the WTO
http://www.soton.ac.uk/~nukop/data/
fullrecs/1660.htm

WTO
http://www.unicc.org//wto/Welcome.html

WWW Yellow Pages
www.cba.uh.edu/ylowpges/ylowpges.html.

Yahoo Reuters
http://www.yahoo.co.uk/News

Yellow Pages UK
http://www.yell.co.uk

CHAPTER 2

Environmental market scanning: the 'SLEPT' and 'C' factors

Nations differ in their dependence on trade. For example the US, while accounting for 13.95 per cent of total world exports (visible and invisible), is also listed as no. 11 in the ranking of countries least dependent on trade, measuring trade as a percentage of GDP. In this case, the US accounts for 8.7 per cent of its GDP as being derived from trade. Contrast this with Canada where almost 40 per cent of all Canadian-made goods and services in 1996 were sold as exports, which put it top among the G7 countries. The ramifications of trade dependency, or not, are to be seen in the legislature where a less trade-dependent country such as the US is able to pass more easily legislation controlling trade activities.

In this chapter we will be studying the international environment from the SLEPT perspective: social and cultural, legal, economic, political and technological dimensions as well as the 4'C' factors: corporation, countries, currency and competitors. Before doing so, it may be useful to consider eight new directions of international business and two megatrends which have been pointed out by Paliwoda and Ryans and shown in Table 2.1.

Special attention ought equally to be given to a few trends which could prove to influence the way in which international marketing is conducted, namely:

*   **The Eurobrand**, the product or service developed specifically to meet the needs of the EU-wide consumer or business–business market. The economies of scale afforded by the new European market for a Europe-wide product make it highly probable that we shall

Table 2.1 Eight new directions of international business

1. The full impact of the EU and its partners, NAFTA and economic integration in general are just beginning to be recognized by marketers. For example, Eurobrands are just beginning to gain importance.
2. The increased number of strategic alliances, especially marketing alliances, have dramatically altered new product strategy and development, especially in high technology firms.
3. More and more firms are testing the use or moving directly to standardized (or global) marketing, particularly promotion. This has increased dramatically the segmentation and pre-testing work in overseas markets.
4. Time-to-market and product differentiation (physical and psychological) are becoming even more significant in the second half of the 1990s.
5. The importance to the firm of getting immediate awareness, image and preference data from the EU etc. has led to new types of marketing research, such as the use of omnibus tracking studies.
6. Regulation is becoming an increasingly important factor in marketing planning; the developments in GATT and the new World Trade Organization highlight this importance.
7. Greater concentration in retailing and the total channel for consumer products is underway, as is the growth of the international retailer. Business-to-business marketers are finding it increasingly difficult to identify exclusive agents and reps, as concentration is becoming stronger in most European middlemen categories.
8. Consumers in virtually all markets have shown more price sensitivity, as evidenced by the success of private brands. To date, market concentration in most industries has failed to lead to price increases.

Source: Paliwoda, S. J. and Ryans Jr, J. K. (1995), *International Marketing Reader*, Routledge, London

see a large increase in Eurobrands, aided and abetted by pan-European and global advertising agencies.

- **Centralization and standardization.** With the increase in regional economic integration in Europe, Pacific Rim and South America, companies are realizing that they have to reconsider the way in which they do business in these national as opposed to regional markets. This poses a challenge to the 4 Ps traditionally held sacred as being within the power only of the company to alter, not publics, competitors, suppliers nor customers.

The social environment (S)

The costs of international competition: costs of research, product development, market launch and the necessary market size to recover these costs, has meant that products need to be international from conception. International marketing has moved from being a marginal activity to becoming the nerve centre of the company's operations. In so doing, brands have become international rather than national, but, as we shall see in Chapter 6 we have still a long way to go before reaching global branding. What is still happening is that the promotion for a brand can often be more easily standardized than the brand itself. Certainly, some brands have become universally recognized 'family' brands, e.g. Kellogg's and Ford Motor Co. always have their name prominently displayed before the brand in question whether Kellogg's Corn Flakes or Ford Escort. In some instances, and this happens more on a country-by-country basis, brand names may have taken the place of the product class as is the case in Britain with Sellotape, Formica, Hoover and Thermos. We shall examined this question later in relation to industrial property rights in Chapter 6.

As regards global products, they are perhaps fewer in number but they are increasing (see also Chapter 10) Global products are stateless; they are products without frontiers and so benefit from international exposure whether it is an American Express card, Visa or Mastercard; McDonalds or Burger King; Coca-Cola or Pepsi-Cola.

The social environment shapes the collective attitude of the buying public to foreign companies, their product line and management orientation. A strong home country or ethnocentric approach by the company may produce an extreme reaction, positive or negative. It must be said that products which capitalize on their home origins may fall from favour quickly whenever political climates change. This has happened on occasion to US multinationals such as Coca-Cola and American Express and to a lesser degree to British Airways. A highly conspicuous foreign presence may become a conduit for negative as well as positive feelings towards the home country in question. Some companies regularly suffer more than others as a result of a political backlash against the home country in question. Conspicuous links with the parent home country are to blame. To some observers it is simply the law of colonial ingratitude in that countries given independence, for example, retain only what may be called a 'love – hate' relationship with their former colonial master due to a grudging acknowledgement of political independence but not of total self-sufficiency.

Given that the product or service has to be acceptable to the society in the foreign market for which it is intended, there are three levels, as Terpstra and Sarathy (1994) have pointed out, at which the marketing mix operates as a possible agent of change within society:

1. *Folkways or conventions*, where social behaviour is learned and accepted, and followed habitually and does not require rationalizing. If someone, for example, devises a better way of doing things, the new method may very well be adopted, otherwise things will very likely stay as they are, and the status quo will remain. Persuading people to buy requires first selling them the product concept and making them aware of it, and then moving towards an understanding not only of the product class, but also of the particular advantages and benefits of the particular brand in question. Having arrived at this stage, it is relatively easy then to move consumers to a trial stage. Electronic cash registers are to be found everywhere in Britain today not just because they are more dependable than their electric forerunners but because they also incorporate a stock control and sales tax function as well and may also include an electronic funds transfer at point of sale (EFTPOS) terminal which with one simple pass of the customer's personal bank card will automatically debit his or her bank account with the sum in question. To succeed, though, an innovation such as an EFTPOS terminal requires acceptance both by retailers and by their customers.

2. *Morals* are the more strongly held and less easily assailable custom of a nation or subculture within the nation. A country may be composed of many nations, many peoples, many languages. It is unwise to give offence in the promotion of a product, particularly

where it may offend the religion of people in the target market in question. The moral here is that it is neither easy nor particularly wise to try to change the *mores* of a country; it is much easier and wiser, perhaps, not to try.

3. *Laws* are the embodiment of the *mores* or the social norms of a country, but laws are constantly under review and pressure can be brought to bear by lobbying the legislature to make them aware of a given situation and to try to motivate them towards changing it. Laws are seldom more than a 'freeze frame' of society's views or wishes on a specific topic at a specific moment in time. In a dynamic world, the relevance of laws must be steadily challenged. This is a rearguard action faced with technological change and changing social attitudes of a society which has itself changed, becoming more affluent and less religious than its predecessors.

The cultural dimension

Culture is an extrapolation of the past. It is learned behaviour rather than innate, a characteristic emphasized in the *Oxford English Dictionary* definition which defines culture as the: 'Improvement or refinement of mind, tastes and manners; the condition of being thus trained and refined: the intellectual side of civilisation'.

It is ironic therefore to consider how the Nazi general Hermann Goering was once quoted as saying, 'When I hear anyone talk of culture, I reach for my revolver.' Culture is popularly used as a loose term to embody what is in effect a syndrome, as when we refer to the whole set of social norms and responses which condition society's behaviour. More than that, we tend to measure other cultures by our own (a self-reference criterion – SRC). A self-reference criterion always comes into play in the assessment of a foreign culture, and this shapes our evaluation. When visiting foreign countries, a British salesman may find it unusual that the standard working day may start at 6.30–7.30 a.m. and continue without a lunch break until approximately 3 p.m. Unless

prepared to expect it, he may find it difficult to adjust to a working pattern so different from the 'normal' British pattern of one meeting in the morning and one in the afternoon. There may well be no one around when he wants to do business! The same occurs with the length of the working week in the Middle East where Friday is not a working day but Sunday is. Again we could introduce, too, the further difficulty encountered with the multiplicity of local holidays worldwide as in trying to find a week in May when France does not have at least one public holiday. The obvious we can prepare for, e.g. local time differences are published and easily quantifiable, but local resistance to change and innovation and the degree of psychological distance between two countries are many times more difficult to quantify and have to be experienced.

Maslow's Hierarchy of Needs (1954) depicting a pyramid hierarchy of needs would imply that lower-order needs must first be satisfied before higher-order needs can initiate or influence behaviour (see Figure 2.1). As each important need is satisfied, the next most important need will come into play. It is interesting to note how many of our so-called global products, e.g. Kellogg's Corn Flakes, Coca-Cola, Pepsi-Cola, are intrinsically US products with global acceptance and so global demand creates availability. Their corporate approach is definitely ethnocentric, but on this Hierarchy of Needs is it a physiological or a higher need – e.g., esteem and social acceptance – which they satisfy? In many less developed countries, Coca-Cola and Pepsi are available at a premium. Other local products would suffice to quench the physiological need of thirst. Perhaps then there is more to these US products in terms of benefits brought to the consumer, of which some kudos, a taste perhaps of luxury, of merely being able to afford and have ready access to a Western product, are often the main motivations themselves. Actualization may arise from being able to have access to Western goods or goods that are otherwise scarce.

Again, what people say they drink at home, what they in fact drink at home, and what they

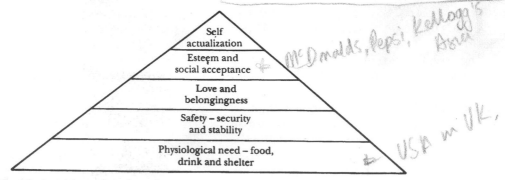

Figure 2.1   The Maslow hierarchy of needs

will drink in company, are subject to a number of peer-group influences. This is society at work. The marketer's task is to try to understand the persona or personae, achieved by an understanding of the culture or cultures prevailing. According to Freud (1955) the real motives guiding behaviour were shaped in early childhood, where gratification was not always satisfied; and this led to frustration, which led to the development of more subtle means of gratification. Frustration and denial of need gratification led to repression, and feelings of guilt and shame with regard to that particular need.

According to Herzberg (1966) human motivation is more readily understood when studied in terms of what he called 'hygiene' and 'motivator' factors. Firstly, there were those factors which did not in themselves create satisfaction but whose very absence may well cause dissatisfaction. Expectations of a particular product may be such that although a first-time purchaser, we nevertheless expect this product to be equipped or to perform to a certain specification. Cars, for example, are supplied with wheels and an engine as standard, although airbags and air conditioning may be included as 'extras', depending on the sophistication of the market segment at which it is aimed. Now, these features which are supplied as standard are not motivators. Motivator factors are the second category according to Herzberg. These are the factors which do influence behaviour. To identify these factors precisely involves researching each individual situation, but the potential rewards from doing so are great. When the Japanese first started shipping cars to Britain around 1972 they met with instant success because their cars contained many features traditionally only found as 'extras' on other makes of car, and so would otherwise involve paying extra. In 1996 Daewoo started to use this strategy of offering many extras at low price by selling direct to the customer.

Defining the meaning of culture

An alternative definition from the one cited earlier in the *Oxford English Dictionary* is that of *Webster's Third International Dictionary* which adds certain insights.

The act of developing by education, discipline, social experience: the training or refining of the moral and intellectual faculties . . . The state of being cultivated especially the enlightenment and excellence of taste acquired by intellectual and aesthetic training; the intellectual and artistic content of civilization; refinement in manners, taste, thought . . . The total pattern of human behaviour and its products embodied in thought, speech, actions and artefacts and dependent upon man's capacity for learning and transmitting

knowledge to succeeding generations through the use of tools, language and systems of abstract thought . . . The body of customary beliefs, social forms and material traits constituting a distinct complex of tradition of a racial, religious or social group . . . A complex of typical behaviour or standardized social characteristics peculiar to a specific group, occupation or profession, sex, age grade or social class.

Webster's Third International Dictionary 1976

Matthew Arnold summarized much of this thought when he wrote:

Culture, the acquainting ourselves with the best that has been known and said in the world, and thus with the history of the human spirit.

Literature and Dogma, Preface to the 1873 edition

This brings out the learning and transference of knowledge and of values from one generation to the next but it also brings out the thought that we can learn from others and also from other cultures around the world towards the betterment of mankind. Not all countries are linguistically or culturally homogeneous but may, to take the example of India or Nigeria, comprise a few hundred subcultures each proud of their tribal or caste allegiance and each with their own language or dialect but communicating at a national level only by means of English. This reduction of population demographics into homogeneous units has been termed as 'clans', whereby members share a common set of values or objectives plus beliefs about how to coordin-ate efforts in order to reach common objectives. This is a basis for marketing segmentation, which is discussed more fully later.

Cultural sensitivity is vitally important in international business. It is essential for the manager to be as aware of the similarities as the dissimilarities between the foreign market and his own. Too often, attention is paid solely to that which is different rather than that which unites. Yet it is through focusing on similarities we are able to practise segmentation. The Americans in the 1960s provoked a political response from the French ('Le défs américain' (the American Challenge) when they profited from a vision of Europe as one market, while Europeans of diverse nationalities still continued to see it as more of a patchwork quilt with too many languages and local differences to allow for any standardization. This is where part of the difference lies. It is possible to have a standardized product with a localized approach. The Japanese are no more culturally sensitive than other world traders, but by targeting consumers with good, well-researched products and locally · adapted promotion, have been able to make inroads into Europe despite tariff and non-tariff

Exhibit 2.1

Original and native speaker translations

Jemand musste Josef K. verleumdet haben, denn ohne daß er etwas Böses getan hätte, wurde er eines Morgens verhaftet. Die Köchin der Frau Grubach, seiner Zimmervermieterin, die ihm jeden Tag gegen acht Uhr früh das Frühstück brachte, kam diesmal nicht.

Somebody must have bad-mouthed Josef K. because one morning, without having done anything wrong, he was arrested. His landlady Frau Grubach had a cook, who brought him his breakfast every day at about eight o'clock, but she did not appear this time.

Quelqu'un avait dû dire du mal de Joseph K., car un matin et sans qu'il eût rien à se reprocher, il fut arrêté. La cuisinière de madame Grubach, sa logeuse, lui apportait son petit déjeuner chaque matin vers huit heures, mais ce matin-là elle ne vint pas.

Machine translations

Someone had to have slandered Josef K. for without that it would have done something bad, became it a Mo Rgens arrests. The cook of the woman Grubach, its room landlord, the it every day about eight o'clock early the breakfast brought, came this time not.

Quelqu'un doit avoir le mauvais-mouthed Josef K. parce qu'un matin, sans avoir a fait n'importe quoi incorrectement, il wa S a arrêté. Sa propriétaire Frau Grubach a eu un cuisinier, qui a apporté lui son petit déjeuner tous les jours à environ huit l'heure, mais elle n'est pas apparue cette fois.

Jemand hätte Übel von K Joseph sagen sollen, für einen Morgen und ohne, daB es eût nichts zu Tadel selbst, es Aufgehalten Wurde. Der madam Grubach Bereich, sein logeuse, haben ihm sein Frühstück, aber jenen Morgen sie nicht vint nein jeden Morgen ungefähr acht Stunden gebracht T.

Kafka loses something in translation

Students of literature have laboured over the nuances of language and subtleties of meaning in Franz Kafka's *Der Prozess* (The Trial) ever since this German work appeared in 1925. Translating the words of a writer into a foreign language is difficult. And along with translations for technical and commercial purposes, it is a time-consuming occupation.

Technology, however, offers some relief. A variety of software programs have been developed which can produce a version of a text in another language. *The European* set a computer the task of translating the opening of Kafka's work (above). The first lines appear in the original German at top left. Below it, there is a version in English and French, translated by native speakers. On the right is a reproduction of each paragraph translated electronically with a service offered by US online company CompuServe.

It takes about ten minutes after inputting the text for a translation to appear in the user's electronic mailbox. So far CompuServe only offers the service with English as either the original or translated language. The version from French into German was therefore first translated into English from the French before the German version was produced.

Kafka's poetic style raised some difficulties for the computer, which is designed for straightforward technical prose. For the moment it seems human translators need not fear for their jobs.

Source: The European, 2–8 January 1997, p. 19

---

barriers, including voluntary export restraint agreements.

When communication necessitates translation, a message becomes vulnerable to distortion by means of various idioms used that are peculiar to that foreign language. Ruthstrom and Matejka (1990) pointed to four different meanings of 'yes' in the Far East due partly to culture, and partly to a weak understanding of the language, namely:

1.   *Recognition.* The first level acknowledges that

you are talking to me, but I don't necessarily understand what you are saying. In many societies politeness demands that we recognize the words of the speaker either through a nodding of the head or uttering the word 'yes' more out of instinct and focusing on the conversation than any real affirmation.

2.   *Understanding.* The second level acknowledges that you are talking to me and adds that I understand you perfectly, but I may have no intention of doing what you propose. This is

Table 2.2   McCall and Warrington: Language and compliance gaining strategies

Compliance-gaining message strategies: The examples are drawn from a situation in which a manufacturer, because of appreciation of his country's currency in relation to that of the agent's country, is seeking to become more price competitive there. He is asking the agent to accept a reduced commission in line with his own reduction in margin in the belief that his business will be increased and that the agent will obtain a greater aggregate commission than under the previously agreed rate. The agent feels that there is a matter of principle involved and that his rate of commission should remain inviolate.

Message strategy	What the strategy implies	Persuasive message strategies Manufacturer	Agent
1 Promise	If you comply, I will reward you	If you agree to reduce your rate of commission, we will revoke the annual renewal of the agreement and replace it with one for five years.	
2 Threat	If you do not comply, I will punish you	If you feel you can't reduce your rate of commission, we feel the market demand will be negligible and perhaps we should discontinue our relationship with immediate effect	
3 Positive expertise	If you comply, you will be rewarded because of the order of things	If you reduce your rate of commission, the stimulation of demand will result in a greater aggregate commission	
4 Negative expertise	If you do not comply, you will be punished because of the nature of things	If you don't reduce your rate of commission, our market share will fall even further and so will your annual commission	
5 Pre-giving	You reward target before requesting compliance		
6 Aversive stimulation	You continuously punish target to obtain compliance by making cessation contingent on compliance	We would certainly consider some way of speeding up commission payments on extended credit contracts if you were to reduce your rate of commission	
7 Debt	You owe me compliance because of past favours I have done you	We have regularly reduced our price under pressure from you, but have paid you full commission. We would hope that you will now reduce your rate of commission to . . .	We have built up your business here as a result of our hard work and expertise. Surely you're not going to punish us for . . .
8 Liking	You are friendly and helpful to get target in good frame of mind so that compliance will be achieved		
9 Moral appeal	A moral person would comply		You must agree a principle is a principle and not for negotiation
10 Positive self-feeling	You will feel better about yourself if you comply		If you accede to our request, you will live in the realization you have acted in an honourable way
11 Negative self-feeling	You will feel worse about yourself if you do not comply		If you were to insist on going back on your word, do you think you could live with yourself?
12 Positive altercasting	A person with 'good' qualities would comply	You are experienced and professional businessmen who, I'm sure will agree to the proposal in our mutual interest	
13 Negative altercasting	Only a person with 'bad' qualities would not comply	We know that when the chips are down your commercial judgement wouldn't let you make an ill-advised decision	
14 Altruism	I need your compliance very badly, so do it for me	It's important for you *and* us that we get the price down. I need your help and I'm asking for . . .	It's important for you and us that our relationship is maintained. I need your help and I'm asking for . . .
15 Positive esteem	People will think highly of you if you comply	If you agree to this reduction in commission, your associates will respect your judgement in the light of subsequent events	
16 Negative esteem	People you value will think worse of you if you don't comply	If you don't agree to this reduction, events may well lose you the professional respect of your associates	

Source: McCall, J. B., and Warrington, M. B. (1989), *Marketing by Agreement: A Cross-Cultural Approach to Business Negotiations*, 2nd edn, John Wiley and Sons, Chichester

similar to 'tacit agreement' in our US culture. The 'yes' means that your words and meaning are clear to me. Whether I agree with what you are saying cannot be determined unless it is specifically asked.

3. *Responsibility*. The next level of 'yes' conveys that I understand your proposal, but I must consult with others and secure their agreement before your proposal can be accepted.

4. *Agreement*. The final level of 'yes' means that I understand, we are in total agreement, and your proposal is accepted.

Similarly, McCall and Warrington (1989) point to the use of language in compliance-gaining strategies as may be seen in Table 2.2. A standardized global advertising campaign is therefore most vulnerable to distortion, as a result not only of language but local slang, or regional dialect or 'patois' where this exists. Differences will be found also (Hall, 1960) relative to other aspects of culture, e.g.:

• Material culture, e.g. attitudes towards acquisition of goods and services.
• Aesthetics, e.g. attitudes towards colour, brand names, design, music.
• Education, degree of national literacy, opportunities for university education, and employment of graduates.
• Mores – religion, beliefs and attitudes.
• Social organization whether hierarchical or not; role of women in society; etc.
• Political life – period of time it has been a sovereign independent nation; characteristics of its political life, whether democratic, one party state; etc.

On a comparative basis, attitudes may be expected to differ towards work and achievement; towards management; towards the concept of profit. Indeed the role of the consumer is clearly seen to be much more influential in the developed countries where he or she is deemed to be sovereign than in the developing countries where some Western companies continue to sell products which have already been banned or voluntarily removed from their home market for some years. This applies to certain pharmaceuticals as well as high tar cigarettes to take but two examples. Poverty, general lack of education, low levels of literacy, poor communication and low levels of general awareness, together with political opposition, prevent consumerism from becoming a popular movement in the developing countries.

Table 2.3   Murdock's Cultural Universals

Age grading	Food taboos	Music
Athletic sports	Funeral rites	Mythology
Bodily adornment	Games	Numerals
Calendar	Gestures	Obstetrics
Cleanliness training	Gift giving	Penal sanctions
Community organization	Government	Personal names
Cooking	Greetings	Population policy
Cooperative labour	Hairstyles	Postnatal care
Cosmology	Hospitality	Pregnancy usages
Courtship	Housing hygiene	Property rights
Dancing	Incest taboos	Propitiation of supernatural
Decorative art	Inheritance rules	beings
Divination	Joking	Puberty customs
Division of labour	Kin groups	Religious rituals
Dream interpretation	Kinship nomenclature	Residence rules
Education	Language	Sexual restrictions
Eschatology	Law	Soul concepts
Ethics	Luck superstitions	Status differentiation
Ethnobotany	Magic	Surgery
Etiquette	Marriage	Tool making
Faith healing	Mealtimes	Trade
Family	Medicine	Visiting
Feasting	Modesty concerning	Weaning
Fire making	natural functions	Weather control
Folklore	Mourning	

Source: Murdock G. P. (1945), The common denominator of cultures. In *The Science of Man in the World Crisis*, (ed. Linton, R.), Columbia University Press, pp. 123–42

Assessing the cultural environment

Many attempts have been made over the years to devise a means of testing for cultural significance across countries. The all-pervasive effect of culture to be found in all aspects of life is reflected in the fact that Murdock (1945) composed a list of 72 cultural 'universals' (see list below). These could be found in all societies and encompassed amongst them courtship, dancing, incest, taboos, and sexual restrictions, although not necessarily in that order. These cultural 'universals' were to be found in every society known to man, and formed the essential social infrastructure.

Basis of comparisons would be drawn more easily now by identifying differences in attitudes with regard to any of these 72 universals. Hall (1960) went further with his *Map of Culture* which listed ten aspects of human activity which he referred to as primary message systems. Some things such as different languages could be compensated for by translation and interpretation but not so with differences relating to the language of time; space; things; friendship; and agreements. If we were interested in attitudes to learning we could not only examine responses to

moved abroad, factors which were previously held constant – e.g. labour law or contract law – became variable as the firm found itself working within an individual framework in each country in which it was represented. Such differences could have an important effect on relative costs, influencing sourcing of inputs; forcing changes in production, marketing or financial processes; or by restricting price changes of outputs. These variables could be identified as falling within four categories:

*   economic
*   political-legal
*   sociological-cultural
*   educational.

Farmer and Richman define an environmental constraint as

some factor which prevents a firm from performing in a given way. The term 'constraint' implies some limitation of action, usually in the negative sense ... In one sense, every environmental factor is a constraint. One cannot have everything, and the limiting factors are the constraints referred to here.

Some of these variables have a direct effect as when there is a law relating to the employment

Table 2.4   Hall's Map of Culture

*   Interaction, i.e. interaction with the environment through language or any of the five human senses.
*   Association, i.e. grouping and structuring of society.
*   Subsistence, i.e. feeding, working, making a living.
*   Bisexuality, i.e. differentiation of roles along the lines of sex.
*   Territoriality, i.e. possession, use and defence of space and territory.
*   Temporality, i.e. use, allocation, and division of time.
*   Learning, i.e. adoptive process of learning and instruction.
*   Play, i.e. relaxation, leisure.
*   Defence, i.e. protection to include medicine, welfare, and law.
*   Exploitation, i.e. turning the environment to man's use through technology, construction and extraction of minerals.

each of these ten variables separately but cross-refer also, to check what kind of interaction was at work between play and association or play or subsistence.

Eighteen possibilities would provide us with a more structured view of that particular culture. Looking then to each of his ten primary message systems, we have Table 2.4.

An understanding of any civilization could therefore be attained through a study of the interaction of any single variable on this list with any other.

This attempt at using matrices to explain culture was developed further by Farmer and Richman (1971) who expanded the number of variables examined to seventy-seven. As a firm

of women or children. The second kind of impact which these variables have is in relation to the decisions and activities of managers. Managers are a product of their own culture, they argue, and their attitudes and perceptions are based on prior experience which, in turn, is in large part determined by the educational and sociological setting in which they have lived. This is the Self-Reference Criterion, or set of criteria, we mentioned earlier. These research findings help us to understand and appreciate differences and to put parameters on culture, but culture still does not help us understand the functioning of markets and whether it is possible to differentiate between markets as between cultures. To some extent, this has been answered by

Kay (1990) – whose work on identifying the strategic market we shall review in the next section – and by Barnhill and Lawson (1980) who developed a theory of modern markets characterizing markets as follows:

1. *Markets are purposive.* Exchange transactions are entered into and consummated primarily because participants to the exchange are seeking to achieve some purpose or self-interest. Exchanges are made to gain value whether in the form of personal, family or tribal sustenance; individual or corporate wealth; sales; market share; profits or some other purpose or desired condition.
2. *Markets are allocative.* Markets are initiated by the desire of bodies to reallocate their value, e.g., goods for other goods, goods for services, goods for money, etc. Markets provide means and stimulate activities that distribute goods, services, money, and other media of exchange.
3. *Markets are active.* While market potential and other latent conditions are ascribed to markets, interactive exchanges involving co-operation, competition, and conflict provide the overt characteristics of markets. These overt characteristics are necessary for classifying, organizing systematically, expressing quantitatively, and for predicting and controlling marketing.
4. *Markets involve operative activities or functions.* While an extensive list of functions characteristic of exchange transactions can be developed, four fundamental functions are production, finance, distribution and promotion.
5. *Markets tend to function in the form of exchange flows at various levels of complexity, e.g.* dyads, processes, and systems. In a single dyadic transaction there is a two-way flow of value, typically manifested by the movement of goods, services, money or other items of value between the two participants. Except where ultimate consumption occurs, exchanges seldom are limited to a single dyadic transaction. The flows inherent in market transactions continue as an on-going process that, in total or in aggregate, take on the attributes of more complex systems. Again, this ties in well with the IMP Group's Interaction Model which identifies the long-term nature of relationships between buyer and sellers in an industrial context, and the institutionalization and adaptations which will take place between them over time.
6. *Markets are dynamic.* Markets reflect the dynamics and complexity of exchange transactions and the conditions surrounding those transactions. The source of these dynamics can be identified as: (a) environmental, i.e. those forces and conditions that influence market participants but are outside their control; (b) transactional, i.e. those influences resulting from the exchange between and/or among the participants or a mega-body to the transaction; and (c) participant, i.e. those influences emanating, from time to time, from the parties involved in exchange transactions. Each of these sources may have a direct or indirect dynamic influence on exchange transaction(s) or the market(s) functions.
7. *Markets are constrained or inhibited.* Markets are not free or unfettered. They are constrained or inhibited by various forces and influences – among them being the ecology; resources; socio-cultural conditions; technology; economy; competition; and political, governmental, legal, and participant influences.

A set of ten inhibitors have been identified:

*   ecology
*   resources
*   economy
*   technology
*   competition
*   socio-cultural forces
*   political influences
*   legal influences
*   governmental influences
*   organizational influences

These ten are related to three stages of market activity – namely, entry, performance, and exit – in addition to four market functions – namely production, finance, distribution, and promotion as per the matrix shown in Table 2.5.

Rokeach value survey

There are five basic assumptions behind the Rokeach Value System:

1. The total number of values that a person possesses is relatively small.
2. All men everywhere possess the same values to different degrees.
3. Values are organized into value systems.
4. The antecedents of human values can be traced to culture, society and into institutions, and personality.
5. The consequences of human values will be manifested in virtually all phenomena that social scientists might consider worth investigating and understanding.

Table 2.5	Barnhill and Lawson: Market Inhibitors – a three dimensional matrix			
Market activity stage:	Entry	Performance	Exit	
Ecology				
Resources				
Economy				
Technology				
Competition				
Socio-cultural forces				
Political influences				
Legal influences				
Governmental influences				
Organizational influences				
	Production Finance Distribution Promotion	Production Finance Distribution Promotion	Production Finance Distribution Promotion	Production Finance Distribution Promotion

Rokeach then goes onto define 'value' and 'value system' in the following terms:

- A value is an enduring belief that a specific mode of conduct or end-state of existence is personally or socially preferable to an opposite or converse mode of conduct or end-state of existence.
- A value system is an enduring organization of beliefs concerning preferable modes of conduct or end-states of existence along a continuum of relative importance.

Rokeach recognizes that values cannot be completely stable or else change would be impossible, nor, on the other hand, can they be unstable or else there would be no continuity. Thus, any model has to be able to incorporate both change and continuity. Citing Allport (1961) 'A value is a belief upon which a man acts by preference', Rokeach then goes on to differentiate further in that an individual may have beliefs concerning desirable modes of conduct (which he refers to as instrumental values which may be either moral values or competence values) or desirable end-states of existence (which he refers to as terminal values, which may be self-centred or society-centred). Moral values relate to modes of behaviour which may give rise to feelings of conscience. Competence values relate to feelings of personal adequacy. Rokeach points out that an individual may experience conflict between two moral values (e.g., behaving honestly and lovingly), between two competence values (e.g., imaginatively and logically) or between a moral and a competence value (e.g., to act politely and

to offer intellectual criticism). The more widely shared a value, the greater the societal demands placed on us. Nevertheless, Rokeach points out that man possesses far fewer terminal than instrumental values, perhaps eighteen as against sixty or seventy. Yet values and attitudes differ:

An attitude differs from a value in that an attitude refers to an organization of several beliefs around a specific object or situation. A value on the other hand, refers to a single belief of a very specific kind. It concerns a desirable mode of behaviour or end-state that has a transcendental quality to it, guarding actions, attitudes, judgements, and comparisons across specific objects and situations and beyond immediate goods to more ultimate goals.

Values, it is argued, occupy a more central position and are determinants of attitudes as well as behaviour.

The Rokeach Value Survey (RVS) comprises two lists of eighteen alphabetically arranged instrumental and terminal values, each with a brief definition. The respondent is asked to rank them for importance. The value which is least important is then number eighteen. There are no prompted answers with this survey, the respondent has to fall back on his own internalized system of values to help him rank order the thirty-six values which Rokeach has distilled from a literature review and empirical research. Various tests have been conducted with different national samples as to reliability and validity measures. It has also been claimed by Brown (1976) that the RVS is the best values instrument available for management and organizational research given its design simplicity,

Table 2.6   Test–retest reliabilities of 18 terminal and 18 instrumental values, Rokeach (N = 250)

Terminal value	r	Instrumental value	r
A comfortable life (a prosperous life)	.70	Ambitious (hard-working, aspiring)	.70
An exciting life (a stimulating, active life)	.73	Broadminded (open-minded)	.57
A sense of accomplishment (lasting contribution)	.51	Capable (competent, effective)	.51
A world at peace (free of war and conflict)	.67	Cheerful (lighthearted, joyful)	.65
A world of beauty (beauty of nature and the arts)	.66	Clean (neat, tidy)	.66
Equality (brotherhood, equal opportunity for all)	.71	Courageous (standing up for your beliefs)	.52
Family security (taking care of loved ones)	.64	Forgiving (willing to pardon others)	.62
Freedom (independence, free choice)	.61	Helpful (working for the welfare of others)	.66
Happiness (contentedness)	.62	Honest (sincere, truthful)	.62
Inner harmony (freedom from inner conflict)	.65	Imaginative (daring, creative)	.69
Mature love (sexual and spiritual intimacy)	.68	Independent (self-reliant, self-sufficient)	.60
National security (protection from attack)	.67	Intellectual (intelligent, reflective)	.67
Pleasure (an enjoyable, leisurely life)	.57	Logical (consistent, rational)	.57
Salvation (saved, eternal life)	.88	Loving (affectionate, tender)	.65
Self-respect (self-esteem)	.58	Obedient (dutiful, respectful)	.53
Social recognition (respect, admiration)	.65	Polite (courteous, well-mannered)	.53
True friendship (close companionship)	.59	Responsible (dependable, reliable)	.45
Wisdom (a mature understanding of life)	.60	Self-controlled (restrained, self-disciplined)	.52

administration convenience, reasonable measures of reliability and validity, ease of understanding by literate respondents and its self-involving, thought-provoking challenge of completion.

However, Payne (1988) points to a few of the criticisms of the RVS as being:

1. The ranking procedure used; normative or rating evaluations for each value may be more appropriate when investigating value perception.
2. Respondents are constrained to a standard set of values that may not effectively describe values that they recognize and view as important.
3. Values are suggested to respondents which may not actually be part of their cognitive worlds.
4. There can be questions involving respondent agreement concerning definitions, connotations or meanings of terms used in the RVS.
5. Interpretations of high- and low-value rankings must be made carefully. Rokeach poses several explanations for high and low values. A value may be ranked high either due to wanting something strongly that has been missing before or valuing something that has proved rewarding. Weakly held values may be the result of either not being mature enough to appreciate their importance or

having a characteristic and over time taking it for granted.

Semiotics and the science of meaning of signs

The notion that all the seemingly disparate products of society work together to create a cultural framework has given rise to a new area of interdisciplinary research which business is turning to, and has been termed semiotics.

Semiotics, as a sub-discipline in philosophy, has been in existence since at least the early Middle Ages (Clarke, 1987). The term semiotics can be traced back to John Locke (1690) and is from the Greek *semeiotikos*, meaning an observer of signs, one who interprets or derives their meaning. Smoke as a sign of fire; clouds as sign of an impending storm for the sailor at sea. One natural object or event which can be directly observed in the present standing for another which cannot. For example, as Hamlet picks up Yorick's skull it is a sign and a symbol. Language is enhanced by the addition of signs making the

one-dimensional, three-dimensional. Similarly, the medical symptom as a means of diagnosing a patient's condition. Associative signs are signs as smoke/fire which stand for what is observable and for which there is a correlation in past experience between the sign and what it signifies. The Stoics used certain signs such as a torch signifying an approaching enemy or a bell signifying the selling of meat. St Augustine is on record as stating 'A sign is something which is itself sensed and which indicates to the mind something beyond the sign itself.' Later developments linked conventional signs with linguistic expressions and looked at the relation between them and the thoughts or conceptions they express. Lange-Seidl (1977) recommended that signs should be easy to represent, free from secondary notions and clearly distinguishable. The sign may be linguistic or non-linguistic, e.g. the causal effect of the object it is found to represent – bullet hole as sign of a bullet.

Locke's notion of semiotics as put forward in 1690 divided knowledge into speculative and practical (see Figure 2.2).

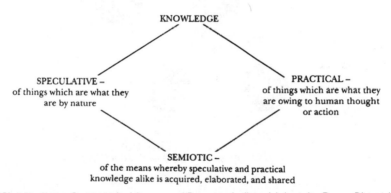

Source: Deely, J. (1982) *Introducing Semiotic: Its History and Doctrine*, Indiana University Press, Bloomington, Indiana

Figure 2.2

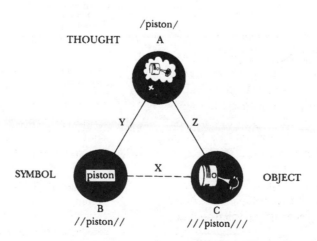

Source: Bunn, J. H. (1981) *The Dimensionality of Signs, Tools and Models*, Indiana University Press, Bloomington, Indiana

Figure 2.3   A semiotic triangle

From this arose the concept of the semiotic triangle where there is an imputed relation between the symbol and referent. Symbolism arose from the need to give perceptible form to the imperceptible (see Figure 2.3). Yet further dimensions could be added with the mix of words and signs, although in Figure 2.4 the word 'sphere' has many possible connotations and so has not been as fully or as clearly understood as might a graphical depiction. Language and experience are important in the interpretation of signs and symbols. Man is a thinking being but in terms of trying to make sense of what he sees around himself he will fall back on himself and his own thoughts and experience to help determine exactly what he perceives.

Through language, experiences and perceptions may be shared. In Figure 2.5 language passes through different layers or groups of the social structure as a unifying process. The languages and signs of each of these groups or seg-

ments will differ. There is recognition here of society at work, of a mass public but of important differential groups or segments.

Semiotics is said to have come to prominence following the English translation of Roland Barthes' *Mythologies*. In essence, every positive trend will eventually give rise to a negative trend and so to take one example, the problems of inner-city living will create an interest in small-town and rural life. Pursuing this line of thought further, according to semiotics there can be no creativity in advertising as we are simply borrowing themes from our everyday experience, e.g., nostalgia and togetherness, and so we are not creating them. The semiotician (the practitioner of semiotics) and the advertising executive differ in that the semiotician believes that one must relate to more than one cultural sign. It is indeed likely that in future years, more will be heard about semiotics in international business activity. For the moment,

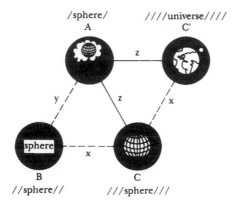

Source: Bunn, J. H. (1987) *The Dimensionality of Signs, Tools and Models*, Indiana University Press, Bloomington, Indiana

Figure 2.4

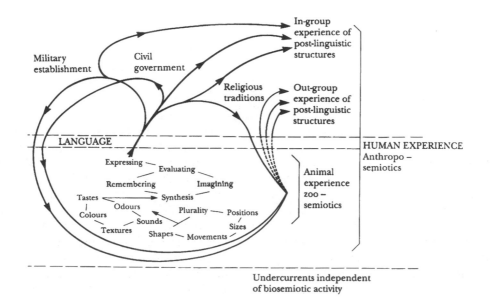

Figure 2.5

much empirical and intellectual work has still to be done to develop this area as Lange-Seidl (1977) pointed out that methods which had proved useful heuristically were still not established theories.

The legal environment (L)

Laws quickly age. Financial penalties stated in an Act on the Statute Book may quickly be eroded by inflation; new technological developments such as video cassette recorders and personal computers give rise to arguments over the question of copyright over software and film; social trends such as a rise in illegitimate births create problems over the inheritance of property on the death of a parent; social change motivates pressure for that which was previously taboo, e.g. Sunday opening of shops in Britain. In other respects, far from being anachronistic, the law may exhibit certain curious anomalies. For example, it is possible for video shops to be raided by police and to be served a summons for offering rental videos deemed to be pornographic and yet, the movie version has been approved for nationwide general release in cinemas throughout Britain.

Increasingly, the interpretation of national laws has a great bearing on the activities of the international marketer. Polaroid started proceedings against Kodak when the Kodak instant film camera was launched in Britain. Kodak withdrew the camera from sale in all markets as a precautionary measure. Although the High Court of England has no jurisdiction outside of England, a favourable judgement might then give rise to lawsuits in other countries. Returning to Polaroid vs Kodak, this action ended up costing almost one billion pounds. It is important therefore to check out the legal position before, and not after, any market activities are undertaken. In a slightly different way, a decision by the FDA in the USA that a certain drug is found under certain conditions to produce carcinogenic reactions will usually ensure a blanket ban in the UK as well, not because of jurisdiction, since the USA has no jurisdiction over the UK, but as a precaution for the public well-being. In the same way the British Committee on the Public Safety of Drugs and Medicines may produce a similar effect in the USA.

One of the great weaknesses of the age in which we live is that there is no international law for commercial disputes, only domestic law travelling imperfectly abroad. For example, in the creation of joint ventures with overseas partners, the terms of jurisdiction in the event of a breakdown have to be agreed at the outset of the agreement. Very often a neutral country such as Switzerland proves useful, although its legal code may later be found to be lacking and so industry-wide international agencies may then be asked to arbitrate in case of dispute. No nation state has yet enacted laws within its national legal code or constitution which will allow it to deal effectively with all international trade disputes. Consequently in 1965 the World Bank Convention established the International Centre for the Settlement of Investment Disputes (ICSID) which provides a conciliation service between a government and an investor. Where both parties are private persons or trading companies they can go to conciliation under the rules of the United Nations' Commission for International Trade Law (UNCITRAL) established by the General Assembly of the United Nations in 1966, which lays down a procedure. Under conciliation it is the responsibility of the parties themselves to reach an agreement. The decisions of industrial arbitration councils or international bodies such as the International Chamber of Commerce in Paris are always considered carefully in the event of a subsequent court hearing. As more countries sign and ratify the various UNCITRAL Conventions more national case law will arise and the position of arbitration will become clearer.

At present, because of advantages such as cost and privacy, arbitration has moved from a second-best alternative position to becoming the preferred choice of parties in dispute. Litigation brings with it unwanted public exposure to confidential areas of disagreement as well as the costs of professional legal representation to present argument, the costs of executive time measured over the duration of a court decision, and the uncertainty of enforcing any damages awarded. The situation overall is unsatisfactory. Joint ventures which fail are therefore severally allowed to lapse rather than be subject to divorce proceedings. Companies realize that once a venture fails it is probably too late for litigation, it being seen that litigation in the local courts may produce only an unfavourable outcome anyway. Litigation then is only really for rather conspicuous cases where large sums of money have been lost through a failure of one partner to comply with his contractual responsibilities.

Arbitration may be preferred to litigation on grounds of cost and privacy. Generally arbitration is regulated by the New York Convention of 1958 on the Recognition and Enforcement of Foreign Arbitral Awards, the UNCITRAL Arbitration Rules adopted in 1976, the UNCITRAL Conciliation Rules of 1980, the Model Law on International Commercial Arbitration of 1985 and the UNCITRAL Notes on Organizing Arbitral Proceedings of 1996. Normally there are three arbitrators who have been selected and approved by the two parties in dispute.

Government everywhere has generally failed to keep pace with the demands of the business world. A fine example of this is that multinational corporations are incorporated under articles of association in a particular sovereign country (most commonly Britain and Delaware in the case of the USA). There is no international body as yet equipped to standardize international articles of association for multinational corporations. There is no such thing either as a body of international law, only the application of domestic law to international disputes. For joint ventures, which are increasing worldwide, the question of legal jurisdiction and of arbitration in the event of a dispute is very important. Very often a neutral third country may be chosen but whereas neutrality reassures us on impartiality of judgement, there is as yet no national code or constitution sufficiently comprehensive to easily embrace all the problems of international trading, although UNCITRAL has gone some way to solving this particular problem.

Increasingly, the EU is projecting itself as a legislator on regulations for trading within its boundaries, but although the EU accounts for the home base of very many large multinationals (British, German, French, Swedish, and Italian), this does not solve a global problem of accountability and control. Meanwhile, the USA is increasingly acting in the eyes of its NATO allies as *ultra-vires*, or 'beyond its legal power', in its desire to control not only US multinational corporations at home but their subsidiaries and technology licensees abroad.

For example, at the time when the Soviet gas pipeline was being constructed to bring Soviet gas into Western Europe, diplomatic difficulties arose over the US ban on General Electric rotor blade technology in the British export of turbines for the pipeline. Attempts were made by the US Administration to influence the British firm of John Brown to stop the shipment or else face reprisals against its subsidiaries in the USA. At the same time, the British Government took the line of threatening reprisals directly at the British company if it did not proceed with the export order immediately. The company found itself placed between two governments in dispute and both of which refused to back down.

Extraterritorial reach is becoming an even more important issue as these trading blocs, such as the EU, take on the rights of a legal person, able to conduct negotiations and sign treaties in their own name as well as impose duties, quotas and tariffs. Extraterritorial reach goes beyond these organizations, though, to certain national legislatures, which take it on themselves to regu-late national enterprises wherever they may be located in the world, and so, in effect, world business. The US Administration has passed legislation, such as the Foreign Corrupt Practices Act, which affects not only US companies but companies from other countries as well which have a stock market listing in the USA.

In other respects, the law and practice relating to commerce and industry can lead to changes in the social fabric. Product distribution in developed markets provides an example of various channels of distribution existing alongside each other: direct selling, retailing, wholesaling, 'cash-and-carry', factory-direct, door-to-door selling and house party selling. Mail-order and the 'house party' is US in origin but the concept has travelled well to other countries, including Japan. Nevertheless, it is possible for a country to make a quantum leap from developmental to advanced forms of retailing as France did in the 1960s or Poland in the 1990s, with the introduction of hypermarkets (characterized by approximately 200,000 sq ft of sales floor space, usually like a very large warehouse conveniently sited close to a main highway with good parking and loss-leader petrol [gasoline] sales in the forecourt), without first experiencing a switch towards the US-style supermarket. Legal flexibility allowed this to happen in France but has constrained its development in the UK as local councils feared for the continuation of high-street shopping in the main city centres now being faced with this challenge to their continued existence by the out-of-town hypermarkets and their lower cost buildings and ground rents.

The economic environment (E)

A macro-environment is created when trade and transactions take place across, rather than within, national frontiers; but it is important to note that there may well be greater similarity in comparing market segments across countries than within the same country. Within any one country there are often large gaps between disposable incomes and prices in one area relative to another part of the country. This is a marketing problem and yet these differences pose both problems and opportunities for foreign firms. Selecting market segments and comparing size, measurability, access and substantiality of market segments across markets often reveals greater similarity across countries than within, lending support therefore to the concept of international market segmentation.

Uncompetitiveness leads to protectionism despite the best efforts of GATT and now the WTO to dismantle obstacles to trade; and so the constraints which are imposed on foreign firms are less in the form of tariff barriers than 'non-tariff' or 'invisible' barriers such as health and safety standards, or hygiene standards. The rationale behind these measures is simply to stem the flow of imports into the country, sometimes also to protect an infant indigenous industry from the pressures of overseas competition flooding better, cheaper products into the home market.

Defining the market

Having examined the functions of a market it is important now to assess this in terms of the firm. Kay (1990) defines the strategic market as 'the smallest area within which it is possible to be a viable competitor.' In terms of competition, Porter identifies five main forces (as shown in Figure 2.6).

Kay separates the dimensions of the market from those of the industry whether product or geographically based. Take the car market as an example (see Figure 2.7). Porter argues that the type and scope of advantage can be used to develop a typology of strategies clearly emphasizing that there is no one type of strategy appro-

priate for every industry but that different strategies can and do coexist successfully in many industries (see Figure 2.8).

Kay shows how it is possible to compete either by differentiating across product classes or focusing within a product segment as does BMW for example in luxury cars. This ties in with Porter (1990) who uses similar examples in talking of competitive scope and different paths to globalization. The drug Zantac is adapted for local markets and so is a multidomestic brand rather than a global brand. Yet in assessing markets it is sometimes difficult to arrive at the necessary level of disaggregation to obtain the information necessary for planning and control. Standard industrial classifications lack specificity. Kay cites the example of refrigerators and washing machines being grouped together because they are often made by the same firms and use some interchangeable technology and componentry.

As marketers know, it is not necessary to serve the whole of a single market but to identify those segments which the firm is best equipped to serve. It is important to identify the market correctly, neither too narrowly nor too widely (see Figure 2.9).

Source: Porter, M. E. (1990) *The Competitive Advantage of Nations*, Macmillan, The Free Press, New York

Figure 2.6   Porter: five competitive forces that determine industry competition

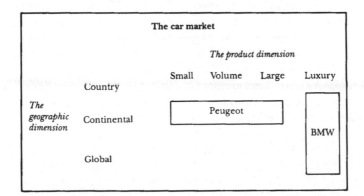

Source: Kay, J. A. (1990) Identifying the strategic market. *Business Strategy Review*, **Spring**, 2–24

Figure 2.7   The car market

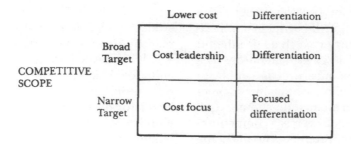

Source: Porter, M. E. (1990) *The Competitive Advantage of Nations*, Macmillan, The Free Press, New York

Figure 2.8   Porter's generic strategies

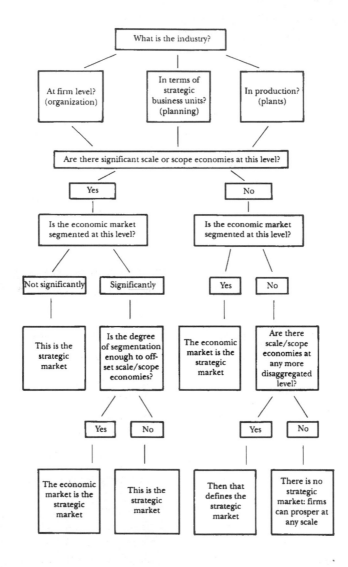

Source: Kay J. A. (1990) Identifying the strategic market. *Business Strategy Review*, **Spring**, 2–24

Figure 2.9   Deriving the strategic market

Over time, new possibilities for competing will arise typically either through discontinuity or a change in the industry structure. These, again, according to Porter (1990) will arise out of:

1.   new technologies,
2.   new or shifting buyer needs,
3.   emergence of a new industry segment,
4.   shifting input costs or availability,
5.   changes in government regulations.

Porter's generic strategies differentiate in terms of cost and differentiation. Focused differentiations have concentrated on specialized areas of production which command higher prices. The error that companies make according to Porter is to try to pursue simultaneously all of the strategies.

From General Agreement on Tariffs and Trade (GATT) to World Trade Organization (WTO)

The General Agreement on Tariffs and Trade (GATT), founded in 1948, is not just one treaty but a large cluster of around 180, involving 103 governments called the 'Contracting Parties' which have shaped the constitution and thus direction of GATT, its membership and mission. The basic principles of GATT are:

1. The 'most favoured notion clause' or non-discrimination in trade.
2. Domestic industry should be protected only through customs tariffs.
3. Measures such as dumping and subsidies should not interfere with fair competition.
4. Tariffs should be reduced through multilateral negotiations and 'bound' against subsequent increases.

Instituted to reduce tariff barriers, each of its seven negotiating 'rounds' has lasted an average of nine years which illustrates clearly the difficulties involved in freeing trade. The most recent, the Uruguay round (launched 1986, completed 1994) was the most difficult because negotiations were already taking place in a changed world trading situation moving further into recession and towards protectionism of areas in which the developed countries are strong and the developing countries weak, as is the case in services. Examples of protectionism abound in the practices of industrial countries *vis-à-vis* the less developed nations of the world.

The ninety-seven member countries of GATT accounted for more than four-fifths of world trade. The basis of GATT is that trade should not be discriminatory and that preference should be given to the developing countries which account for two-thirds of the membership. Under the terms of GATT membership, nations agree to apply their most favourable or lowest tariff rate to fellow GATT signatories, but within GATT it is possible still to have preferential tariff rates. There is a basic GATT signatory tariff rate but also a preferential rate which the UK, for example, may wish to use to encourage

Exhibit 2.2   Spoiling world trade

By the sorry standards of much of this century, world trade looks in rude health. In the 1930s, protectionism helped poison the world economy. After the Second World War, tariffs and other trade barriers fell too slowly. However, over the past decade, many of the restrictions that stifle international commerce have been relaxed – thanks in large part to the lengthy Uruguay round of GATT talks, completed in 1993. Since 1990 world trade has grown by 6% a year, compared with less than 4% a year in the 1980s. As if to confirm the importance that governments now attach to the subject, there is now a World Trade Organisation (WTO), with 126 members, to police the new regime and to take the cause of free trade further into areas where there are still far too many restrictions, such as agriculture, services and investment.

From this perspective, the WTO's first big ministerial meeting, which starts on December 9th in Singapore, is going to seem disappointing. Ministers are preparing to squabble publicly over all manner of things – from the pace of trade reform to the terms on which China should be admitted to the WTO. On the last day there will be a bland communiqué of some sort, which will do nothing to beat back the protectionists that lurk in America and Western Europe. However, the greatest damage in Singapore will not be done by what is said, but what is left almost unmentioned: the threat that 'regionalism' poses to global trade.

When the feasible is the enemy of the good

Thanks to the recent explosion of regional trade arrangements, whose members agree to liberalise trade among themselves, the WTO is just one cook among many stirring the free-trade broth. Only a handful of the WTO's members are not already part of some other local club. The European Union has 15 members and could soon have more. Some Americans are already looking for ways to meld together the North American Free-Trade Agreement (NAFTA), which was formed with Mexico and Canada, with Mercosur, a customs union formed by four South American countries. Free-trade areas are planned in both South-East Asia and South Asia. And the 19-strong Asia-Pacific Economic Co-operation (APEC) forum has a grand plan for 'free trade in the Pacific' by 2020.

→

→ **Exhibit 2.2** *continued*

Put this way, it sounds like something to applaud. *The Economist* has given qualified support to many of these agreements as and when they have appeared. What is it about their cumulative effect that should give pause for thought?

Most governments and many free traders believe that regional free-trade areas are a step in the right direction. Their defence is usually a mixture of economic principle, practical diplomacy and visionary politics. First, they ask, how can it be possible for countries to agree to scrap tariffs among themselves and not make trade freer? Then they argue that it is often easier to make a deal in a small group than in the unwieldy WTO. And, finally, trade agreements, they say, are politically valuable: if countries are tied by commerce, they are less likely to start shooting at each other.

The first of these arguments, plausible as it seems, is simply false. Regional 'free-trade areas' need not make trade freer. By liberalising trade only with their neighbours, countries are by definition discriminating against those not lucky enough to be in the local club. Some goods will be imported from other members of the free-trade area at the expense of producers elsewhere; and members will begin to specialise in industries in which they lack comparative advantage.

Thus, the EU has a bloated farming industry while many producers in poorer countries suffer from not being able to serve its markets; and NAFTA has complicated 'rules of origin' requirements, stipulating how much of a car needs to be made in Mexico to qualify as 'NAFTAn', and so enter America tariff-free. It is always better to liberalise without discrimination than to open up only to neighbours; sometimes, selective opening is worse than doing nothing at all.

The argument that, despite this danger, regional trade areas represent a speedier, more practical way to proceed than does the WTO, is also open to question. True, the Uruguay round lasted more than seven years, and even now governments are struggling to finish off some outstanding negotiations, but slow progress bedevils regional arrangements, too. Despite much talk about expansion, the membership of NAFTA is stuck at three. APEC is moving at a glacial pace. Similarly, although the local clubs sometimes broach subjects long before the WTO (for instance, NAFTA has a treaty on foreign direct investment), they can also introduce possible bugbears (NAFTA also contains worrying agreements on standards for labour and environmental protection).

Moreover, the standard against which each regional trade pact needs to be measured has, mercifully, been raised. Back in the 1950s, the idea of a customs union in Europe (even if it was linked to an idea as awful as the common agricultural policy) was attractive because the alternative (no customs union at all) was plainly worse. Now, the emergence of the WTO has raised the hurdle: the architects of regional agreements know they will have to defend their plans against the charge of setting back liberal trade, and adjust their plans accordingly. That is fine, but it raises a question: would it not be simpler, after all, to make these deals at the WTO?

That leaves the last 'political' argument – that bodies such as APEC and Mercosur have brought old enemies together. So they have. Again, however, would this be any less true of broader multilateral agreements? And there are limits to how far the goal of international amity, worthy as it is, should be used to justify economic lunacy. Invoking France's post-war friendship with Germany seems an odd way to defend the EU's limits on imports of Argentine chocolate.

If governments paid more attention to the threat of regionalism, that would be an excellent start. One excuse for their not doing so is that the WTO's own system for policing regional trade agreements is a mess. At present, each new free-trade area or customs union is appraised by a committee, open to all members and with extremely vague terms of reference. Unsurprisingly, only six of the 70-odd committees formed since GATT began have ever reached a firm conclusion. It would be much better if agreements were examined by a smaller team of independent scrutineers with a precise mandate to assess the effect on world trade – and, in particular, the way that the new agreement treats outsiders.

It can be hard to say whether any free-trade area is so restrictive that its costs outweigh its benefits – though Mercosur, by some calculations, fails the test, and the case for the new ASEAN agreement also looks weak. Most agreements are a mixture of good and bad. The long-term challenge for the ministers about to meet in Singapore is thus twofold: to change the worst details in their own regional deals; and, even more important, to press ahead with multilateral trade liberalisation in the WTO. Governments now have a chance to make this new institution the strong catalyst for liberal trade which they have long said they wanted. They should seize the opportunity.

Source: The Economist, 7 December 1996

trade with Commonwealth countries, particularly the less developed countries. Much Favoured Nation (MFN) status is the highest degree of preferential treatment that may be accorded to a fellow GATT signatory and is accorded on a bilateral basis. MFN status became a political means of rewarding or punishing countries.

With regard to farm subsidies, the EU, now accounting in itself for 38 per cent of world trade, is divided among its members. The EU has its own famous surpluses of agricultural produce and so is unable to make concessions in the way of trade for developing countries which are crop dependent. The situation for both industrial and less developed countries was exacerbated by the world trade recession of the early 1990s in which agriculture looked likely to tear down the structure of GATT itself. The GATT Council is impotent, lacking con-sensus among its members to take any firm action that cannot be easily circumvented. Exhibit 2.2 sets out the issues facing GATT which in the Uruguay round focused on trade in services, trade-related aspects of intellectual property rights and trade-related investment measures.

The previous Tokyo round 1973–9 had been successful in addressing a number of the increasing non-tariff barriers to international trade. Yet there was a price to be paid for GATT was unable to rewrite its own constitution and so as regards the results relating to the non-tariff measures of the Tokyo round, these have been incorporated into 'side' codes which bind only those nations

Exhibit 2.3   WTO needs to take wider view after narrow escape

The World Trade Organization (WTO) escaped disaster at its first ministerial meeting in Singapore in December. The question now is whether it can turn that escape into something more credible by the time ministers meet again in Geneva in 1998.

That meeting is designed to coincide with the 50th anniversary of the General Agreement on Tariffs and Trade (GATT), the WTO's predecessor. When it rolls around the WTO will be four years old and its members will presumably be able to assess whether it is succeeding in its stated aim of putting more teeth in the policing of world trade. So far it isn't, although most trade officials admit it is not totally failing either. But there is a general agreement that things are not working as well as they were supposed to when the Uruguay Round negotiations brought the WTO into being in 1994. And the presumed arrival of Russia and China on the scene this year will make a cohesive policy even more difficult to achieve.

Russia's application seems on track and Moscow has said it is confident of being in the WTO by the end of this year. But the continuing bilateral fight between the United States and China is delaying things on that front and there may even be signs that the Chinese are getting fed up with waiting. Newspaper articles in Beijing in December said that the WTO needs China more than vice-versa, and that if the endless delays continue, China will let matters rest. This may be another case of conflicting signals coming out of China, but if it is true it will mean that Taiwan will not get in either. The world's 16th-largest economy has been promised membership only when China joins. Hong Kong is already a member, but many officials question whether it will continue to have much influence after the Chinese takeover this July.

American toughness on the Chinese issue is one example of why the promise of 1994 has not turned into a new era. A major architect of the WTO agreement, Washington blew hot and cold on the organisation in the past two years. If this continues, the north-south divide will accentuate further this year, at the same time as the US and the EU do battle on Helms-Burton (US legislation passed last year designed to penalise foreign companies who deal with Cuba). Sir Leon Brittan, the WTO's trade commissioner, was rebuffed in Singapore when he tried to launch a new round of global trade talks, simply because most countries want to avoid the eight years of tortuous gestation of the Uruguay Round process. But Sir Leon promises he will return to the attack.

The outlook for this year therefore is more of the same, with individual trade disputes subordinated to the overall theme of how the China issue will be handled. Will the US be as co-operative as before, even though it is probably going to be defeated on Helms-Burton? And can Director General Renato Ruggiero head off a north-south fight on such issues as trade and the environment and textiles?

Ruggiero's term of office ends next year, which means that by the end of this year electioneering will have begun for his successor. Developing countries are already starting to say it is their turn. Ruggiero, who is from Naples, has been telling reporters that the pressure of work is such that he cannot afford the time to eat a plate of his beloved pasta. Another year of keeping the disputants apart should see him longing for retirement and a chance to do just that.

Source: The European, 2–8 January 1997

which separately accept them. Amending GATT rules requires a two-thirds acceptance of its members. Nevertheless, the Tokyo round produced nine special agreements, four 'understandings' on special issues describing procedures which were arguably already followed and protocols on tariff reduction.

GATT's major shortcomings:

1.   Disuse. Complaints totalled 38 for the twenty years between 1960 and 1980, then there were 115 complaints in the 1980s. Dispute settlements were not working.
2.   There were delays in the establishment of panels.
3.   There were delays in appointing panel members.
4.   There were delays in the completion of panel reports.
5.   The uncertain quality and neutrality of panelists and panel reports was always a factor.
6.   Blocked panel reports.
7.   The implementation of panel reports.

The World Trade Organization

The World Trade Organization was created in 1994 out of the GATT because GATT was no longer able to function effectively in the 1990s. Its constitution had been set in quite different times, almost fifty years before. What brought crisis to this organization was the increasing incidence of non-tariff barriers together with a proliferation of regional trade deals, the cumulative effect of which was to pose the biggest threat to free global trade since the inception of GATT. The dialogue continues now with the WTO. The World Trade Organization is therefore concerned with multilateral agreements on trade in goods and to bolster areas in which previously there was little control, including services and non-tariff barriers. The international agreement establishing the WTO states:

A member may apply a safeguard measure to a product only if that Member has determined, pursuant to the provisions set out below, that such product is being imported into its territory in such increased quantities, absolute or relative to domestic production, and under such conditions as to cause or threaten to cause serious injury to the domestic industry that produces like or directly competitive products.

It is required therefore that an investigation take place before any action is undertaken and that these investigations be made open to the public. Where there is due cause to protect confidentiality then non-confidential summaries will be provided. The Agreement defines 'serious injury' as meaning a significant overall impairment in the position of a domestic industry, and 'threat of serious injury' as being serious injury that is clearly imminent as based on facts not on allegation, conjecture or remote possibility. Where a quota is applied as a corrective action, then imports of the good in question cannot fall below the average of imports over the last three years unless clear justification is given that a different level is necessary to prevent or remedy serious injury.

Provisional safeguards are permissible where delays would cause damage which it would be difficult to repair. Provisional measures cannot extend beyond 200 days during which period a full investigation has to take place. If an investigation subsequently fails to find serious injury then higher tariffs applied as an interim measure have to be refunded. The total period for a safeguard measure cannot exceed eight years including provisional safeguards. Liberalization of existing safeguards of more than one year in duration is expected to take place. With measures of more than three years' duration a review should take place at mid-term. Protection can be reapplied but not more than twice in five years and there has to be at least one year between applications. Special consideration is made also for developing countries where action can only take place where that developing country has more than 3 per cent import share. Developing countries are also allowed longer periods of protection by two years more than the normally permitted maximum. Existing safeguards in force at the time of the WTO Agreement have five years or eight years after first application, whichever comes later. Members shall not take or maintain any voluntary export restraints, orderly marketing arrangements or any other similar measures on the export or import side. Member states have until December 1999 to terminate any existing arrangements, after which the limit is one exception per member state. The EU therefore has until 31 December 1999 to resolve its dispute with Japan over passenger cars, off road vehicles, light commercial vehicles, light trucks up to 5 tonnes, and the same vehicles in wholly knocked down form (CKD sets). The WTO Committee on Safeguards has to be kept notified of any possible measures that might be taken and provided with full documentary evidence. The Committee on Safeguards will provide a trade monitor role and an annual report on the implementation of the Agreement and make recommendations as to its improvement and also assist member states if they so request. Whether WTO will succeed where GATT failed has yet to be seen. WTO's powers in terms of dispute settlement have yet to be put to the test.

Exhibit 2.4   Red light on Korean car deals

The European Union is stepping up pressure on Poland and Romania to modify import agreements with South Korean car maker Daewoo, amid indications that Korea is preparing to use east Europe as a manufacturing base for a major export drive into the EU.

Trade commissioner Sir Leon Brittan flies to Warsaw this week for talks with the Polish government, and Korea's car making plans are expected to be high on his agenda. Talks between European Commission and Polish officials, which failed to reach agreement in Brussels last week, also continue in the Polish capital.

The chief EU negotiator in the talks with Poland, Pierre Mirel, said last month that the issue was the single biggest threat to Poland's chances of joining the EU.

In a separate initiative, Commission officials are considering action at the World Trade Organization (WTO) against an agreement Romania struck with Daewoo, which includes the production of 200,000 cars in the country by 2000.

When Sir Leon arrives in Warsaw on 7 February he will repeat Commission demands for Poland to impose duties on 110,000 Korean-built Daewoo cars which enter the Polish market via Slovenia under an agreement concluded last year. To avoid Polish duty, the cars are taken apart in Slovenia, shipped to Poland and reassembled. They are 25 per cent cheaper than similar models in Poland.

The EU can only export 35,000 tariff-free cars a year to Poland. EU car makers believe Korea's deal breaks world trade rules on non-discrimination and the EU's association accord with Poland. But Warsaw says Korea is only doing what other EU car makers such as VW and Fiat do when they import parts for assembly, and that the

issue should be resolved by the World Customs Organization.

A spokesman for the Brussels-based Association of Car Manufacturers of Europe said: 'You have to see the issue in the light of the EU accession of Poland. The Polish government is clearly violating existing agreements and they have to bring their legal system into line with the EU very soon.'

Jaroslaw Pietras, director of Poland's Committee for European Integration, said: 'This is the biggest problem we have with the EU, because it is the biggest in terms of economic importance. You can't turn down an investor willing to invest $1.25 billion.'

The Commission fears that Korea's ultimate aim is to export 'locally-built' cars from Poland to the EU.

The Korean export drive to Poland coincides with a clampdown by Seoul on luxury car imports from the EU and US by subjecting buyers to tax inquiries. EU car makers have just 0.4 per cent of the Korean market of 1.2 million cars a year. Korea has 1.5 per cent of the EU market and is the fastest growing supplier.

Talks between Romania and the Commission centre on a 1995 deal under which Daewoo imports 20,000 cars at preferential tariffs, using the proceeds to pay for its $156 million stake in a Romanian state car company. In exchange for tax and excise concessions, Daewoo agreed to manufacture at least 200,000 cars by the year 2000, buy 60 per cent of parts locally and export half the cars made.

Commission officials have already talked informally with the WTO about Daewoo's agreement with Romania, which they feel contravenes trade rules on subsidies and incentives.

Source: The European, 2–8 February 1997

Exhibit 2.5   Egypt confronts car tariff dilemma

Once, most cars in Egypt looked as if they were held together by a good sailor's knot; now the streets gleam with new Jeep Cherokees and Peugeots, thanks to the rapid emergence of a domestic car assembly industry.

The industry relies on extremely high tariffs for imported cars – from 40 per cent on vehicles under 1,000cc to 135 per cent on those over 2,000cc.

Now some are questioning the economic logic of this protectionist policy which makes Egypt one of the most expensive countries in the world in which to buy imported cars.

Egypt first started assembling cars in 1961 when the state-owned El Nasr Automotive Manufacturing Company (Nasco) started to produce Fiat cars. Nasco was the only producer and the authorities provided heavy protection to the infant industry.

The awakening of this stagnant industry came in late 1993 when the government removed restrictions on commercial car imports and better credit facilities became available for customers.

Car sales have jumped from a low of 20,000 units in 1992 to an expected 65,000 last year,

→ **Exhibit 2.5** *continued*

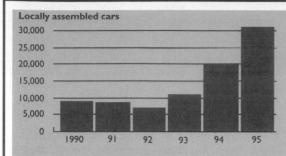

Source: Egyptian government

Egypt: Car output accelerates

about half of them assembled locally. Though the numbers are small, given Egypt's 60m inhabitants, car dealers are banking on doubling sales by the year 2000.

With the opening of the car market, the local industry has attracted E£5bn ($1.5bn) of investment and created 72,000 jobs in the past five years. A 40 per cent local-content law has helped to generate a strong component industry.

Since the first GM Opel Vectra rolled off the assembly line in November 1993, local private companies have begun assembling Suzuki Swifts, Hyundai Excels, Peugeot 405s, Citroen AXs and the Cherokee four-wheel drive, greatly extending consumers' choice from the 1970s Fiat models still produced by Nasco. Though the capacity of the seven assembly lines in operation in Egypt is 85,000 units a year, output is only one third of this.

Mr Shaker Abaza, assistant managing director of Peugeot Egypt, says: 'Thanks to the tariffs I sell my local Peugeot at E£85,000 whereas the imported Peugeot is around E£135,000'.

The luxury Mercedes-Benz E-series and the BMW 5-series will be assembled in Cairo from CKD (completely knocked down) kits this year – BMW's first Middle East venture. Talks are also under way for the assembly of Skoda, Daewoo, Kia, Nissan and Volkswagen.

Mr Luder Paysen, BMW sales director for the Middle East, said the new plant would enable BMW to offer high-quality cars at competitive prices. He said price advantage was the number one reason for setting up in Egypt, as BMW only sold 250 cars there in 1995. The new plant will be able to make 2,500 cars a year.

Despite the growth of Egypt's car-assembly industry, critics say its protectionist wall should be removed, since the Egyptian government is committed to an IMF programme which has trade liberalisation at its core.

Mr Shafic Gabr, chairman of Artoc Group for Investment and Development, which owns the Skoda dealership in Egypt, is sceptical of the long-term viability of the car assembly industry under present arrangements. 'You've got to be able to compete, or else you are creating a false economy,' he says. 'It's a short-term vision chasing a quick hit.'

Mr Gabr is critical of the licence agreements the nascent Egyptian car assemblers have with the parent manufacturers. 'Not one of them has rights to sell their assembled vehicles outside Egypt, which in an unprotected market would be vital for survival.'

Artoc is negotiating with Volkswagen to set up a 50/50 joint venture to assemble cars in Egypt for distribution throughout the Middle East.

Even though the Egyptian government cut tariffs by up to 50 per cent last year, the assembly industry has managed to sidestep competitive forces. The maximum tariff on imported cars was cut only from 160 per cent to 135 – and the retail price of cars has not dropped one piastre.

This is because the protectionist minister of industry and the strong car assembly lobby won a battle against the pro-liberalisation minister of finance. The industry minister, who is said to believe that production should take priority, regardless of the circumstances, persuaded his colleague to increase the sales tax on imported cars by an amount equal to the cut in import duties.

Many doubt the car assemblers could survive without protection. Dr Adel Gazarin, the former managing director of Nasco, says the assembly industry in Egypt is based not on economic reasoning but rather on protection.

Car factories are not automated, and though Egypt has cheap labour, it is not very productive. Imported kits arrive in special sep-arate packages, each sprayed with preservatives, increasing their cost by about 17 per cent. Egyptian assemblers have to keep two to three months' stock because of inefficient supply systems, both for local and imported parts.

Mr Karim Ghabbour, acting manager of Mercedes Commercial Vehicles Egypt, says the industry needs protection for 15 years before being exposed to international competition.

Source: *Financial Times*, 9 January 1997

Tariff barriers

Tariff barriers include:

- Taxes, duties comprise the following:
  1. *Ad valorem.* This is a percentage of the value of the goods, calculated on the landed CIF cost at port of entry.
  2. *Specific duty.* This is a specific amount of currency per weight, volume, length, or number of units of measurement. It is expressed in the currency of the importing country.
  3. *Alternative duty.* Applicable rate is that which yields the higher amount of duty.
  4. *Component or mixed duties.*
  5. *Temporary import surcharges.* Under WTO rules these must only be temporary. This device has been used in the past by Britain and the USA.
  6. *Compensatory import taxes.* Manufacturers in VAT countries do not pay VAT on exports to non-VAT countries but all US manufacturers still pay and have no tax relief from the tax equivalent in the USA.
  7. *Anti-dumping duties.*

- Customs union or common market such as EC which maintains an external tariff.
- 'Countervailing' duty is designed to raise the price of the cheapest import to the price of the nearest domestic competitor by adding the necessary additional tax to the import.
- 'Drawback' duty repaid if imported goods re-exported.
- Tariff schedule
  single column (same tariff regardless of origin)
  multi-column (discriminated with regard to origin).
- 'MFN' or 'much favoured nation' status, which has traditionally been accorded between trading nations, is permissible under previous GATT regulations, and allows for bilateral trade or preferential rates of tariff duty.

Non-tariff barriers (NTBs)

These are becoming increasingly more common. As WTO continues to fight for the reduction of tariffs worldwide, sovereign states apply their ingenuity to the creation of 'invisible tariffs'. These may take many forms but their ultimate aim is to exclude, or at least stem the flow of, foreign imports of any given good or politically sensitive item. NTBs may take the following forms:

1. Specific limitations including quotas and import restraints (VER = Voluntary Export Restraints). Once the quota is filled, the price mechanism is not allowed to operate. With VERs there is a 'voluntary' agreement which demands compliance.
2. Discriminatory governmental and private procurement policies, e.g. 'buying national'. One of the major barriers to fall within the EC after 1992 is public procurement previously closed to all but national suppliers. Also state trading and subsidies.
3. Restrictive customs procedures on validation, classification, documentation, health and safety and hygiene.
4. Selective monetary controls and discriminatory exchange rate, controls, e.g. the requirement for an advance deposit equal to the value of the imported goods.
5. Restrictive administrative and technical regulation including standards for products, packaging, labelling and marketing.

The political environment (P)

Government procurement and corporate 'buy-national' policies

It is a common enough phenomenon to find companies pursuing an implicit or explicit 'buy national' policy. Governments do likewise as they have to consider the employment effects of sourcing. They also have to consider the national interest in the placing of any orders for defence equipment or for products resulting from a research programme that has been heavily funded by government finance. Local government authorities often also choose to exercise their political right to choose suppliers of equipment on such bases as these. What has changed is that some of the largest international companies are moving towards single sourcing of components. This makes open-tender contracts more lucrative and the loss of such contracts can have a serious impact on the firms involved. EU regulations are now being used to challenge the status quo and open up competitive bidding to outsiders.

The Single European Market is discussed in more detail in Chapter 11, but this issue of public procurement is an important one as it has traditionally been a market closed to all but national suppliers and yet is estimated as being worth more than 15 per cent of GDP within the European Union. Good reason has now to be provided for any member state of the European Union going outside of what is now established EU policy. Defence is an area which is more integrated than before on a European-wide scale but in which national government discretion may be used in the choice of suppliers.

Increasing rationalization creates problems not just with supplier selection but also supplier

Exhibit 2.6   Japan to ease unfair tax on Scotch

Jubilant Scotch Whisky producers last night welcomed a Japanese tax climbdown that industry experts predict will boost their trade by £200m.

After almost two decades of campaigning against 'unfair' discrimination on Scotch, the Japanese Government announced it would slash export taxes that have favoured its national spirit, sochu.

The battle to win a fair trading field abroad for Scotch is now to be extended by the European Union to cover Chile and South Korea, which both operate similar tax rules to Japan favouring their home-produced spirits.

A spokesman for European Trade Commissioner Sir Leon Brittan said: 'This success with Japan sends out a very political signal to other countries that they can expect a similar campaign by the EU on behalf of Scotch whisky.'

Yesterday's agreement between Japan and the EU comes in the wake of a World Trade Organisation edict last year that the Japanese tax system was in contravention of international trade rules.

Annual whisky exports to Japan are currently more than £119 m. The market doubled to this figure after a GATT ruling in 1987 that Japan should scrap a previous tax system that had favoured home-made whiskies such as Suntory.

At present, tax accounts for about half the £12 retail cost of a bottle of Scotch in Japan. Sochu is taxed at different strengths but tax accounts for about £1 for a bottle retailing at £5 to £6.

Under the deal, Japan will double the tax on sochu and in a series of reductions over the next three years will cut the tax on Scotch by £2.

Last night, the director-general of the Scotch Whisky Association, Mr Hugh Morison, said: 'This is wonderful news for Scotch whisky   producers.

'The industry has been pressing its case for fair tax treatment in Japan for almost 30 years.

'We now have a definite timetable for the removal of the tax advantage faced by Scotch whisky, with major steps towards total reform in the next few months.'

Mr Morison added: 'There are many other markets throughout the world where we face tax discrimination but this move gives out a very strong signal that it is unacceptable and must be changed.'

The Japanese deal with the EU also includes a timetable for cutting taxes on Irish whiskeys, brandy, and cognac.

Mr Morison said: 'Although the tax cut for whisky amounts to £2, it will be for the individual brands to decide how much of this to pass on to the drinker.'

Japan is the fourth most valuable export market for Scotch. The industry is now looking for steady growth in Japan rather than a sudden bonanza.

One of its first tasks will be to make up the ground Scotch has lost to sochu – Scotch sales in 1990–91 were around £180m.

Source: Glasgow Herald, 5 February 1997, p. 3

---

exclusion. The new regions choose from suppliers within their own boundaries rather than seek competitive tenders from outside. National preference in large civil engineering projects is no longer possible within the EU. For example, in Britain, the Skye Road Bridge was built by a British–German consortium.

Whereas before national preference was the problem today it is regional trade bloc preferences. This was one of the hardest problems for GATT to handle. In the United States, a report is prepared for Congress identifying countries, whether signatories or not to the Government Procurement Code, and the nature of the violation of their code obligations. The three criteria used for identification are:

1. A significant and persistent pattern or practice of discrimination in procurement practices against US goods and services.
2. Identifiable harm to US businesses.
3. Significant purchases by the US government of products or services from that country.

The US has identified the European Union and Japan in this way. Where a country or bloc is a persistent offender it is placed under constant monitoring which is called Title VII of the 1988 US Omnibus Trade and Competitiveness Act. Countries which have been singled out for attention but not action have included: Australia for the Information Technology sector, Brazil for computer, software, telecommunications and digital electronics sectors, China for the non-transparent procurement practices and Japan for the supercomputer and computer sectors.

Japan will be discussed in detail in Chapter 12 but the Japanese government has established voluntary measures designed to increase market access beyond that established under the WTO agreement on government procurement. These measures cover procurement of goods and services by 30 government ministries and

Old economy	New economy
Table 2.7 The evolving economy	

Old economy	New economy
(a) Standardized output Assembly lines	(a) Customized goods and services Increased variety and bundling of goods and services
(b) In-house production services	(b) Externalization of services, networking, interlinkages
(c) Local, national markets	(c) Internationalization of production and competition
(d) Vertical integration Large corporations	(d) Vertical disintegration Small firms, large transnational conglomerates
(e) Rigid embodiment of technology	(e) Flexible production modes
(f) Material inputs, outputs	(f) Non-material investments, human resource and knowledge-based inputs
(g) Factory, blue-collar employment	(g) Office, white-collar employment
(h) Sectoral regulation	(h) New forms of regulation

Source: Nicolaides, P. (1989) *Liberalising Service Trade*, Routledge, London

agencies and 84 government related entities and include:

1. Clarification of government procurement procedures.
2. Expanded use of general tenders.
3. Improved qualifying procedures.
4. Improved distribution of government procurement information.

Dumping

Anti-dumping regulations are aimed at preventing the sale of products in one country at prices lower than those fixed in the country of origin. The EU follows the ruling of the USA in this matter, namely that for 'dumping' to be established two criteria need to be met: firstly that these are not cheap imports but goods sold for less than in their country of origin; and, secondly, that these imports are injurious to domestic industry. The difficulty is the time that it takes to substantiate allegations of dumping by which time permanent market disruption may have taken place with the closure through bankruptcy of domestic suppliers. Dumping may be of three types:

1. *Sporadic* – where it makes better commercial sense to unload surplus abroad at advantageous prices rather than on the home market where discounts once offered would create a precedent for future behaviour.
2. *Predatory* – when foreign producers use low prices to weaken indigenous competition abroad. Accusations of hidden governmental subsidies have been levelled against Italian producers of refrigerators and washing machines. These subsidies support a low price structure and allow the company to buy market share abroad. The EC outlaws such activity in restraint of trade but too often the damage is done and once done, cannot be corrected.
3. *Persistent* – the continued sales of products at prices lower than those of its country of origin. The case of Polish exports of electric golf-carts to the USA, which arose in early 1970s and lasted for many years, illustrates the difficulty in implementing these regulations. Firstly, Poland did not have any golf courses nor need for electric golf-carts so there was no comparable domestic price which in any event would be distorted, because in a communist country all prices are politically set and need not bear any relation to their material or labour costs. This situation was later corrected but only through political pressure from the USA. Since 1990, Poland has moved towards a free market economy.

While developing countries, particularly those without an indigenous industry of their own, are likely to welcome what will be seen as 'cheap imports'; it is generally the case that the most contentious imports for any nation to receive are steel, textiles and agricultural produce, together with basic industrial chemicals such as ethylene or soda ash, which would also come under similarly close political scrutiny.

With textiles, the problem has been that the industrial countries have been successful in selling textile machinery to less developed countries who then quickly start to produce textiles at lower cost and in higher volumes than indigenous Western textiles industry, and so in a very short space of time, direct competition ensues over the end product. When it became apparent that an industry response was required in Western Europe to meet this damaging threat, a body known as CIRFS emerged. This body, known by its French acronym, is a European man-made fibre producers' association, and has acted to reduce West European production capacity.

It is often alleged that dumping incorporates hidden subsidies from the home government, whether in manufacturing location, selective employment assistance, favourable taxation treatment, etc. As these subsidies reduce factor costs, they may also reduce final price, hence the accusation of dumping. Dumping only occurs, though, if goods are sold at one price in the home market, and at another in a foreign market, or at least that is one of the main criteria. While the EU will institute anti-dumping measures on behalf of its member states, it will nevertheless 'dump' butter and other surplus dairy products in the FSU because (a) agricultural prices have to be protected within the EU and (b) storage costs for butter and beef mountains and milk and wine lakes are high and the costs of selling off this produce cheaply is lower than the costs of keeping it in refrigerated storage. To the FSU, with its centralized inefficient agricultural system, these sales constitute a windfall. For the EU it is only a temporary respite as the agricultural system is designed to over produce. Only in the last few years have measures been implemented to halt the growth of EU agricultural produce yet rather than just be halted, it needs instead to be cut back.

The EU concluded new agreements in 1982 with 25 leading Third World textile exporters. It took two years of negotiation to conclude the new Multi-Fibre Agreement, to stay in force until mid-1986. The only country not to have initialled an agreement with the EU is Argentina, but there will now be unilateral controls on Argentinian exports. The British Textile Confederation was particularly concerned at exports from the Mediterranean countries in general and from Turkey and China in particular. In the case of three dominant suppliers – Hong Kong, South Korea, and Macao – the regulations provide for a 7–8 per cent cut from 1982 levels on the import of T-shirts, jeans, and certain other clothing products.

Agriculture is a contentious topic within the EU as overproduction means that surpluses have either to be stored, destroyed, or exported by means of subsidies. GATT has faced pressure over this question but it is argued that the disciplines of industrial trade cannot be applied to agriculture as the products and technology are different. While demands then are made for some new international committee or forum to examine the question, those countries enjoying surpluses in agricultural production are able to benefit from the market disarray and to exploit their particular commercial advantage. Organization may lead to unpalatable changes for the developed countries with regard to prices, competition and perhaps the ending of export subsidies on agricultural produce. In the EU the farming community is too powerful, and over-protected by a Common Agricultural Policy which ensures that farming is the only industry in the free world to be assured guaranteed prices for output. The USA and Canada have important grain interests but they may well find that their own self-interest is not best served by 'free trade' and so are likely to abstain from anything other than merely talking about it, preferably not too often, nor for too long.

Does anyone practise unregulated 'free trade'?

While professing belief in a free and open exchange of goods and services many nations in effect practise something quite different. Britain, throughout the 1980s, while professing 'free trade', has been actively trying to discourage French exports of milk and has been using hygiene standards to block importation at the docks. The French, too, pursued an effective 'invisible tariff' against Japanese exports of video cassette recorders (VCRs) into France by channelling all Japanese-sourced exports of VCRs through Poitiers, a small town known not to have the resources to deal with this traffic. Of course, being undermanned, this caused interminable delays which were the designed aim of this policy. Known as the Second Battle of Poitiers for its parallel with the French repulsing the Arab advance outside this town in 728 AD, this policy was effective in persuading the Japanese manufacturers that they had to come to some form of accommodation with the French.

In theory, neither France nor Britain, as members of the EU, have the unilateral right to impose tariffs as these are decided now by the EU in Brussels. The system works in the following way. Each member state has an anti-dumping unit which collects information and sends it to Brussels, which then decides on official action for the Community as a whole. In some rather sensitive areas, such as steel, agreement is easily reached; in others, where one member may be benefiting at the expense perhaps of another, agreement on action is delayed. In practice then unilateral action continues to exist. Britain has a voluntary restraint agreement with the Japanese car manufacturers restricting them to 11 per cent of the market; France has a similar understanding whereby they revealed that their market research showed that the Japanese could not hope for more than 3 per cent of the French market while Italy has continually blocked them almost entirely. The case indeed of 'an iron hand in a velvet glove', but these are illustrations only of a much greater and more general *malaise*.

Moving to finance, another important facet of trade (discussed more fully in Chapter 10), 26 countries including all the Western industrialized nations established in 1934 the regulatory framework of the Berne Union to try to prevent a disastrous 1930s-style price war taking place between rival government-backed export credit guarantee departments and their lines of credit. In theory, this meant that Hermes, the export-credit guarantee body in West Germany, could not offer lower terms than, say, the Export Credit Guarantee Department (ECGD) of Britain, but they could match ECGD terms where these may be lower. Here was the danger. Proof was not always required. Hearsay may be enough to panic a government export insurance department into lower terms and allowing a higher percentage of foreign sourcing in a contract than may otherwise be normal practice. ECGD insists on British content to qualify for the lines of credit which they insure, Hermes and others are much less strict. Where the companies involved are multinationals, the bidding situation develops where one country is set against another for the prize of winning perhaps a large export order. Precedents once established cannot be easily dismissed. Multinationals may exercise choice as regards to which subsidiary, in which country, should deal with which markets, and obviously will choose to base their business in the more accommodating countries.

To restore order to what was becoming a 'merry-go-round' with each Western partner bidding one against the other, the Western nations met in summit in 1977. As this was in breach of existing conventions, the meeting was therefore under the aegis of OECD, but due to the pressures of finding profitable trade in a recession, these meetings have been taking place rather regularly and as they have been successful in finding agreement between themselves over export finance, this grouping of the Western industrialized states has become known as the 'Consensus'. The Consensus sets minimum interest rates and maximum lengths of credit for a wide range of capital goods sold on officially supported credit terms of two years or more.

The framework of the 'Consensus' (dis-cussed at more length in Chapter 7) has since evolved to the point where it was asked by the US Administration to implement higher interest rate charges for the Soviet Union and its East European allies as a political retaliation over the invasion of Afghanistan. Politics can never be far removed when trade is taking place across two quite different social, political and economic blocs which throughout the postwar years have traditionally viewed the other as the 'enemy'.

Article 80 of the Treaty of Rome is supposed to prohibit any measures in defiance of free trade within the EU area. In the case of the USA, domestic legislation while national in character has always had international ramifications. The Foreign Corrupt Practices Act, for example, applies to companies with an American Stock Exchange listing; therefore many multinationals from different countries of origin will find themselves under the jurisdiction of this legislation, which relates to acts of bribery and corruption, in fact anywhere the company may operate. It can and does mean that a company will be pilloried for activities viewed as 'unseemly' from a US domestic economy viewpoint even where such an activity may otherwise be totally in keeping with the commercial practice of the country concerned. Bribery and corruption are emotive words; the question is whether local nationals will recognize this in their dealings. There may be questions of scale relating to the frequency of such events or the size of sums or other inducements offered, but it has also to be said that even in countries where it may be seen to be normal to have to agree to 'facilitating' payments, bribery and corruption are still something which will not be tolerated by the local populace.

Yet another development which has arisen in the economic environment of the past ten years has been increased government activity in enticing foreign investment into its boundaries by means of tax holidays, low-cost factory buildings, low-interest loans or grants, and employment subsidies. Governments are becoming more involved and, as they become more proactive in enticing foreign companies to invest, they are demanding a say in the running of operations which are based within their jurisdiction. This has meant a sharp increase in the number of countries now seeking joint ventures with local partners rather than 100 per cent direct foreign investment. Countertrade is another area of operations in which national governments are becoming involved. It is now a major worldwide phenomenon practised by developed and developing countries alike. More will be said of countertrade and the many variants of goods-related payment terms and conditions in Chapter 7. Whereas previously Japan was the only country actively pursuing the benefits of foreign equity and participation but with some degree of local control, there are now a number of developed countries eager for this form of investment.

The Triad of Europe, North America and Japan

While Ohmae sees the triad in the above terms, other observers including futurists such as Toffler point to the focus of future attention being Germany, USA and Japan which may well prove to be the case, as Germany before unification was the largest and economically most powerful member of the European Community. However, confining ourselves to the three regions previously stated we notice that the rationale for this triad is that the bulk of global trade and economic power rests within these three regions. The global economic size of these three: Europe, USA and Japan is disproportionate to their actual number or physical size. Ohmae cites Japan and the USA alone as accounting for 30 per cent of the Free World Total and that with the addition of UK, West Germany, France and Italy, this increases to 45 per cent. Aside from economic wealth, these countries share other similarities as well: mature stagnant economies, ageing populations, unemployment among skilled trades while dynamic technological

developments are taking place, costs of research and development are constantly escalating as are production facilities. This is all part of the new reality as Ohmae sees it.

This triad creates a market of 600 million with marked demographic similarities and levels of purchasing power as a result of:

*   growth of capital intensive manufacturing,
*   accelerated tempo of new technology,
*   concentrated pattern of consumption.

A reaction to any of those forces above is protectionism. Ohmae shows that industries critical to wealth generation in the 1980s were all concentrated in Japan, USA and Europe, constituting more than 80 per cent of global production and consumption. Ohmae argues that these 600 million share the same desires for the same goods: Gucci bags; Sony Walkmans; McDonald's hamburgers, etc. While there is an international youth market for denims, CDs and tapes, tastes are not the same nor is purchasing power equal either. Psychographic segmentation based on values and attitudes which may be shared also across national boundaries is what is important. However, Ohmae's triad does not stop there. Each high technology player is in the three triad regions plus one developing region making four: Japan in Asia; Europe in Africa and the Middle East; USA in Latin America.

Therefore the shape that emerges is that of a tetrahedron as shown in Figure 2.11. The answer

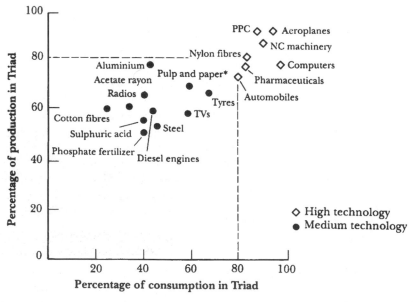

Source: Ohmae, K. (1985) *Triad Power, The Coming Shape of Global Competition*, Macmillan. The Free Press, New York

Figure 2.10

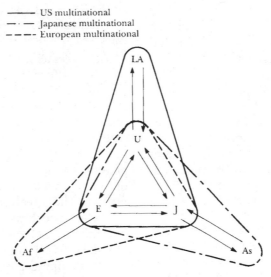

------- US multinational
—·— Japanese multinational
----- European multinational

Note: Af, Africa; As, Asia; E, European Community; J, Japan; LA, Latin Ameria; U, USA

Source: Ohmae, K. (1985) *Triad Power, The Coming Shape of Global Competition*, Macmillan, The Free Press, New York

Figure 2.11   Becoming a triad power

to market presence in each of the triad regions comes through consortia and joint ventures which pose a new challenge for the corporation as Ohmae points out, of learning how to communicate institutionally with the very different corporate cultures and languages of other companies. This ties in with the networking approach of the IMP research group.

Technological dimensions (T)

The company looks at international markets

This review of international market potential has to be undertaken by means first of an internal diagnosis of the firm: establishing strengths and weaknesses with regard to production; finance; human resources; and the current standing and client base of the firm. Against this, the opportunities and threats of the foreign market may be viewed with regard to legal; ethical; market; competition; and technology variables.

Information

Analysis ———▶Objectives ◀——— resources of the company?

Setting commercial targets

Each firm has its own needs and these influence its strategic thinking. A useful addition to this growing literature on business strategy has been Ansoff's 1987 revision of his previous matrix. Instead of the two dimensions of the original matrix (product and mission) Ansoff now uses a

three-dimensional cube to define the thrust and ultimate future scope of the business as in Figure 2.13. Market need is defined in broad rather than product terms, e.g. need for personal transportation or need for amplification of weak electrical signals; product/service technology whether it is present technology or new technology; and market geography which defines the regions or nation states in which the firm intends to do business. The extreme choices possible are to continue serving traditional needs and traditional markets with traditional technology or move to offer new product technology to serve new product needs in new markets. In between, there are also several possible permutations on the three dimensions.

We need to measure overall market size and competitive market conditions. Given that many of the 149 countries listed by the World Bank Atlas with a population in excess of one million have very limited market data, particularly among the less developed countries, to undertake this market study and fulfil these information requirements, an eight-point plan is proposed (see Table 2.8) which systematically evaluates prospects and therefore helps make recommendations for definite action.

International risk perception

The title may imply a short-term approach be taken to identify simply an opportunity for a 'quick kill', perhaps the off-loading on a once-only basis of overproduction of home goods or a windfall shortage of goods in a foreign market that are in over-supply at home or again, a low-labour cost production advantage abroad. This though, is not the intention. The difference between what may be called a 'sales' approach and an 'entry strategy' approach has been outlined by Root (1987). The approach is quite different in a number of important respects including objectives: time horizon; resource commitment; product adaptation and innovation; price; promotion and distribution.

The same point was made equally forcibly by Virgil Dewey Collins (1935) in *World Marketing* published by the JP Lippincott Company, London:

Throughout this practice, I propose to use the term 'world trade' rather than that of exporter in common usage at present, not because world trade is a catch phrase but because it more aptly implies the broader responsibilities of one who engages in the Science of World Trade as distinguished from the more common or garden variety of exporter making less than the sustained and intelligent effort required in this field of endeavour to insure the fullest measure of success. Exporting, in itself, is confined merely to that techni-

cal procedure and the mechanical processes by means of which an order from a foreign customer is embarked to its destination.

Market research of foreign countries is open to all able to afford it and the governmental assistance available will be discussed later in this chapter. Further practical help may also be found in Paliwoda (1994). Before proceeding further, though, it must be recognized that a marketer contemplating a foreign market cannot possibly be as knowledgeable about all aspects of that market as he is about his own domestic market. The greatest mistakes are made by marketers who think they know a foreign market 'like the back of their hand' often to find after an ill-fated product launch that they do not. Product usage, shopping patterns and the unfortunate meanings which some brand names can have in colloquial everyday slang are merely some of the pitfalls which will be discussed in Chapter 6. The areas in which a marketer cannot hope to be fully appraised prior to market entry without actually visiting the country itself include:

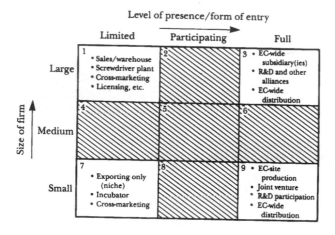

Figure 2.12

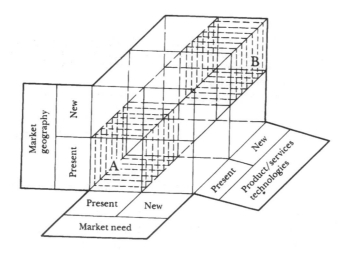

Source: Ansoff, I. (1987) *Corporate Strategy*, revised edn, Penguin Harmondsworth, Middlesex

Figure 2.13

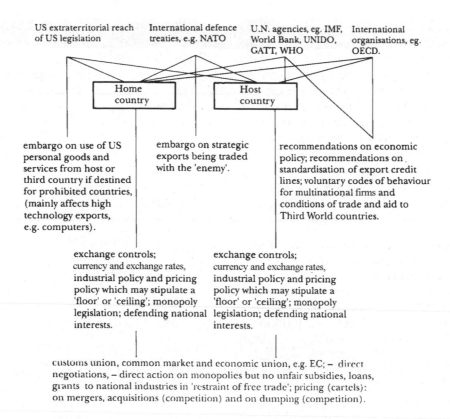

Figure 2.14   Political intervention in business

1.   political risk,
2.   economic risk,
3.   commercial risk,
4.   taxes and legislation relating to company incorporation.

These risks may be properly assessed through an acquaintanceship with the facts. This will involve both secondary data, i.e., published sources of information and primary data analysis, i.e. interviews, surveys and different types of field work conducted in the target market itself.

Political and economic risk appreciation

In a world which appears to be becoming a 'global village' with ever-increasing interdependencies between nations, going international has become a necessity for companies rather than a luxury. Speed has therefore become a critical element in an international strategy which dictates that all important markets must be approached simultaneously.

The opportunities for internationalization

Table 2.8 Operationalizing 'SLEPT' and 'C' Factors				
	Corporation	*Countries*	*Currency*	*Competitors*
Social, Cultural				
Legal				
Economic				
Political				
Technological				

Note: This is like a SWOT analysis but specific rather than random. The first column is devoted to the corporation which may exclude markets or different forms of trading or incorporation on policy grounds. Currency is another interesting variable in that it may be fully convertible, semi-convertible or inconvertible so it may be a legal trade but when viewing the economic factors, the dominant currency may well in fact be the US dollar, in which case there may be political requests for countertrade. Viewing how competitors respond to the same variables can be equally enlightening.

Table 2.9				
		Perceived investment quality climate		
		High	Medium	Low
	High	Wholly owned sales and production venture	Screwdriver assembly	Franchising
Actual cost of entry	Medium	Joint equity venture	Strategic alliances contractual joint venture	Licensing: know-how agreement
	Low	Sales subsidiary	Management contract	Agent; Distributor; exporting only

offered by the expansion in information technology (IT) are great but so too are the risks. Companies are controlled and managed by people and people may often prefer to operate within their region or within their political and economic bloc. This often clouds their thinking in that political risk is to be found only in certain geographic regions of the world. The uncertainty may be higher in the Middle East or Africa but political risks are to be found everywhere including otherwise stable regions such as Europe.

Another type of political risk arises with the extraterritorial reach of US legislation. In December 1981, martial law was imposed in Poland and so the USA imposed an embargo on the export of all equipment of US origin, which included gas transmission equipment, services and technology to the former Soviet Union, even if made overseas under licence. The political boycott of the Soviet oil pipeline by the USA created difficulties for Western countries determined to meet their obligations and yet thwarted by the US refusal to deliver any parts or supplies for this project. This posed a significant problem for the British company, John Brown Engineering, which had bought a licence to produce turbine blades from General Electric of the USA. As this licensed technology formed a major functioning part of their turbines ordered by the FSU, they then found themselves in the impossible predicament of being threatened with repercussions likely to affect their US operations by the US Administration, if they did go ahead with their delivery of turbines to the FSU, and being threatened with repercussions also by the British Government, if they did not deliver to the FSU.

Political risk may be

1. Obvious, where a new government comes into power with fixed and (to business) unfavourable ideas on the role of foreign companies in the economy.

2. Latent, where, like a slowly burning fuse, there is the danger of suddenly and unexpect-

edly losing one's assets in a possible action of expropriation or nationalization.

3. Partial, in that it may refer particularly to certain sectors of industry and commerce and not others with regard to investment, local national pricing, local content laws, and taxation.

Instead of conducting a proper evaluation of the facts, a 'Go-No-Go' study as to whether or not to enter a market will be accepted or rejected on the basis of a subjective, cursory examination of one or two characteristics, often made by a junior company employee visiting the foreign market for less than a week and not fully conversant with the local language or business practice customs.

It may be appropriate therefore to look first at a few more realistic methods for assessing the environment of a target market (see Table 2.9).

Another way of looking at this has been provided by Ishikawa (1990) looking particularly at the EU Single Market as in Figure 2.16.

Business Environment Risk Intelligence (BERI)

Launched in 1972, the Business Environment Risk Intelligence was developed by Frederich Haner, of the University of Delaware, USA. It has since expanded into country-specific forecasts and country risk forecasts for international lenders, but its basic service is the Global Subscription Service. BERI's Global Subscription Service assesses 48 countries, four times a year, on 15 economic, political, and financial factors on a scale from zero to four. Zero indicates unacceptable conditions for investment in a country; one equates with poor conditions; two with acceptable or average conditions; three with above average conditions; and four with superior conditions. The key factors are individually weighted according to their assessed importance as with ingredients. Thus, if the panellists score a country's political stability at an average of 1.7, this is multiplied by the top weighting of 2.5 and becomes 4.2. Since the total weighting adds up to 25 and the top of the rating scale is four, 100 are the maximum points any one country can score.

At present more than 500 companies use the BERI service, which also includes detailed in-depth reports on countries personally visited and assessed by its founder; each quarter 98 unpaid panellists sit down to assess up to 12 countries each.

There are two points worth mentioning here: firstly, BERI tries to get nationals of each country examined as panel members as they tend generally to be more objective; secondly, to elim-inate a bias within the panel, the original panel of 34 was increased to 98 by asking each panellist to find two other panellists. The panellists, how-ever, remain anonymous and unpaid. More recently, the panel has been increased to 170 busi-ness, banking and political specialists. The users of the service are seen to be varied. It may, for example, allow a company to determine more fairly how their managers around the world are performing other than on a profit and loss basis. For example, a manager may be able to hold sales even when the economy is on a downturn, or to evaluate expansion projects and new investment possibilities, to decide whether and where to conclude licensing and trade agreements.

It is also worth pointing out that not every country in the West has the same number of people reporting on it, so Haner has started a computer program which tests each statistic and sends out an alarm if there are inadequate statis-tics for any country. Since major investment decisions require three or four months delibera-tion, panellists try to predict nine months or a year ahead. Panellists receive their sheet back every quarter and if they wish to change their assessment of any country they simply mark over the old ratings with a red pencil. Total points are a possible 100 but a country that rates 80 or more has a very advanced economy plus an environment favourable to foreign investors. A score of over 70 would also imply an advanced economy, but not so favourable an investment climate. The range between 55 and 70 embraces developing countries with investment potential, but also includes '. . . a few mature economies having mentalities not fully compatible with modern business.' The next level, 40 to 55, includes high risk countries which sometimes offer profits in relation to the risks. But even when potential earnings are in proportion to the risk, the quality of management 'has to be supe-rior to realize potential.'

With a score below 40 it would take a very unusual situation to justify the commitment of

capital. Generally, ratings do not change very much nor very quickly, although Chile and Venezuela have proved to be exceptions. Polit-ical upheavals will always occur as have taken place following the Tiananmen Square massacre in Beijing, and its subsequent effects on Chinese trade and diplomatic links with the rest of the world. Equally, the dramatic quantum leaps made by the East European nations since the political convulsions of 1989 have been unparal-leled. The subsequent unification of Germany in October 1990 created a new global awareness of the speed with which events were taking place in Europe. The Single Market of 1993 is now being treated more seriously as a result. Prior to this, some observers had not anticipated 1993 to take place before 2005!

The country environmental temperature gradient

What follows is a review of literature which is dated only because it has not been added to. In total, they provide alternative ways of assessing country markets. In a study ostensibly of the marketing middleman – the agent – in interna-tional business, Litvak and Banting (1968) pre-pared a classification system of country environmental factors on a temperature gradi-ent whereby when the temperature was 'too hot' the agent would find himself pushed towards new institutional structures in order to survive. The variables which Litvak and Banting identified were: the nature of the product; con-centration of customers; intensity of competi-tion; resources of the middleman; market potential; degree of industrialization; cultural, linguistic, and geographical distance; legisla-tion; and degree of political stability.

It was found to be the case that agents will be used: the greater the degree of political volatility; the greater the degree of cultural, lin-guistic and geographic, distance; and the greater the degree of legislation relating to foreign investment.

Countries were defined as being 'hot' where the market was dynamic and the agent was forced to adapt to meet the needs of the market. A market was 'cold' where there was less com-petition, and the agent was allowed complete freedom of movement. The variables of classifi-cation as to whether a country is 'hot', 'moder-ate' or 'cold' are as follows: political stability; market opportunity; economic development and performance; cultural unity; legal barriers; physiographic barriers (obstacles created by the physical landscape); geo-cultural distance. (See Table 2.11)

Table 2.10 Business Environment Risk Index

Rate up to 12 countries Identify any 6 for weight	Political stability	Attitudes Foreign Investor & Profiles	National-ization	Monetary Inflation	Balance of pay-ments	Bureau-cratic delays	Economic growth	Currency convert-ibilities	Enforce-ability of contracts	Labour cost-produc-tivity	Profes-sional services & contracts	Communi-cations—tele, mail, air, telex	Local mgt.	Short-term credits	Long-term loans/venture capital	MAIL To: P. T. Hamer P. O. Box 4697 Newark. Del. 1971 USA. Negative Adjustment *Worker Co-determination Impact on Profits
	3	1?	1?	1?	1?	1	2?	2?	1?	2	?	1	1	2	2	
	1	2	3	4	5	6	7	8	9	10	11	12	13	14	15	

AMERICAS: 9   0 1 2 3 4

1 Canada
2 Mexico
3 United States
4 Argentina
5 Brazil
6 Chile
7 Colombia
8 Peru
9 Venezuela

ASIA/AUSTRALASIA: 14   0 1 2 3 4

10 Australia
11 China (Taiwan)
12 Indonesia
13 Japan
14 Korea
15 Malaysia
16 Philippines
17 Singapore
18 India
19 Iran
20 Israel
21 Lebanon
22 Pakistan

	0 1 2 3 4
23 Turkey	

EUROPE/AFRICA: 20

24 Belgium	
25 Denmark	
26 France	
27 Ireland	
28 Italy	
29 Germany (West)	
30 Greece	
31 Netherlands	
32 Norway	
33 Portugal	
34 Spain	
35 Sweden	
36 Switzerland	
37 United Kingdom	
38 Kenya	
39 Libya	
40 Morocco	
41 Nigeria	
42 South Africa	
43 Egypt	

	0 1 2 3 4
NEW COUNTRIES:	
44 Equador	
45 Saudi Arabia	

Ratings: 0 – Unacceptable conditions

1 – Poor conditions

2 – Acceptable or average conditions

3 – Above average conditions

4 – Superior conditions

*Give a number on the 1–4 scale for your impression of worker co-determinator's impact on profits from operations in the country being rated.

Taking an example of an agent in Canada, a score may emerge of five 'hot' and two 'moderate' variables which would place Canada as relatively 'hot'. An example of an agent in South Africa may reveal four 'cold' and three 'moderate' variables which would place South Africa as relatively 'cold'. It is emphasized, however, that all such ratings will of course change over time. The positioning on the gradient scale is approximate but finer calibration is possible with the introduction of further subjective weights. The gradient scale shows the susceptibility of agents to change, and also predicts how the institutional structure is most likely to evolve. A firm operating with heavily committed investments in a 'hot' country may be guided by this gradient to relinquish control if the environment becomes 'cooler'.

The gradient depends on continual auditing. However, it does suggest the favourability of new markets and the ease with which their opportunities may be realized; the degree of control other foreign principals can exercise; and the degree of local control in the planning and development of operations in the foreign country.

This threefold classification (hot–moderate–cold) of countries using seven environmental factors on a hot–cold scale has since been further developed. Firstly, as a guide to long-range planning, it presents a method of allocating scarce resources selectively. Secondly, it specifies both the magnitude and type of foreign investment involvement depending on the 'temperature' of a country. Thirdly, the conceptual framework suggests how a large body of secondary data or environmental factors can be effectively utilized to undertake long-range planning.

The following shortcomings of the Litvak–Banting model were identified by Sheth and

Lutz (1973) before proceeding to describe their own multivariate model within the Litvak–Banting framework.

•   No analytical framework is developed to transform values into the gradient of 'hotness'.
•   The operational indicators from secondary databanks are not described.
•   The threefold classification is judgmental and arbitrary rather than empirically derived.
•   There is no weighting attached to the individual environmental factors.
•   Market opportunity, being specific to an industry or product, is different from the other six variables. This factor requires primary data whereas the other six can use secondary sources of information.

The Sheth–Lutz model classifies countries on six factors and then investigates the market potential in those countries which appear to be most promising for foreign investment. To do this, Sheth and Lutz used three data sources related to 1961–2 which gave profiles of 82 countries including China and the USSR; this left 80 countries which were then examined from the point of view of US corporate foreign investment. Fifteen variables were finally selected which related to the six environmental factors. Political stability is indicated by governmental stability, freedom from group opposition and political incultivation. Cultural unity is represented by religious, racial, and linguistic homogeneity, each on a three-point scale. Economic development and performance are reflected by economic development on a four-point scale; and energy consumption in megawatt hours. Legal barriers are indicated by two indirect variables. The first is the level of imports and exports measured in millions of US dollars. It is argued

Table 2.11	Litvak and Banting: country environmental temperature gradient		
Degree of environmental characteristics	*Hot country*	*Moderate country*	*Cold country*
Political stability	High	Medium	Low
Market opportunity	High	Medium	Low
Economic development and performance	High	Medium	Low
Cultural unity	High	Medium	Low
Legal barriers	Low	Medium	High
Physiographic barriers	Low	Medium	High
Geo-cultural barriers	Low	Medium	High

Source: Litvak, I. A., and Banting, P. M. (1968) A conceptual framework for international business arrangements. In *Marketing and the New Science of Planning, American Marketing Association Conference Proceedings,* (ed. King, R. L.) (Chicago, Fall) pp. 460–67

Table 2.12 The 'hot-cold' gradient from a historical US viewpoint

Country	Value	Country	Value
USA	13.22	Venezuela	−0.40
UK	4.60	Panama	−0.41
W Germany	3.44	Costa Rica	−0.47
France	2.64	Turkey	−0.47
Netherlands	2.12	Bulgaria	−0.47
Canada	2.01	Ecuador	−0.52
Belgium	2.00	Libya	−0.60
Denmark	1.44	Bolivia	−0.61
Italy	1.32	Philippines	−0.64
Taiwan	1.16	Egypt	−0.72
Japan	1.13	Peru	−0.73
Sweden	1.13	Lebanon	−0.80
Poland	0.93	Haiti	−0.88
Switzerland	0.86	Guatemala	−0.93
Ireland	0.83	Liberia	−0.94
Argentina	0.81	Ceylon	−0.97
Australia	0.76	Albania	−0.99
Norway	0.73	Thailand	−1.00
Austria	0.73	Mongolia	−1.07
E Germany	0.72	Paraguay	−1.13
Mexico	0.58	N Korea	−1.16
Finland	0.47	Iran	−1.23
Brazil	0.46	Indonesia	−1.23
New Zealand	0.40	S Korea	−1.24
Czechoslovakia	0.33	Ethiopia	−1.25
Spain	0.23	Cambodia	−1.28
Colombia	0.22	Saudi Arabia	−1.31
Greece	0.16	Syria	−1.32
Hungary	0.05	S Africa	−1.33
Portugal	−0.00	S Vietnam	−1.37
Uruguay	−0.13	Jordan	−1.42
Yugoslavia	−0.16	Iraq	−1.44
Honduras	−0.16	Pakistan	−1.52
El Salvador	−0.17	Burma	−1.55
Chile	−0.18	Israel	−1.57
India	−0.19	N Vietnam	−1.62
Nicaragua	−0.23	Nepal	−1.68
Cuba	−0.26	Afghanistan	−1.86
Dominican Rep	−0.29	Laos	−1.89
Romania	−0.29	Yemen	−1.99

Source: Sheth, J. N., and Lutz, R. J. (1973) A multivariate model of multinational business expansion. In *Multinational Business Operations*, (eds Sethi, S. P., and Sheth, J. N.) 3, *Marketing Management*, Goodyear Publ., California

that a greater degree of international trade will be present in a country characterized by fewer legal barriers, and vice versa. Similarly, the second variable is the level of tariff on imports as a percentage of the total value of imports. Again, the greater the number of legal barriers, the more likely it is to find a higher levy of tariffs, and vice versa. Physiographic barriers are also included, although indirectly, by the three models of transportation. It is assumed that the greater the

physiographic barriers present in a country due to mountains, deserts, and rivers the less will be the density of air, road, and railroad transports. By simultaneously taking into account all the three major surface and aerial methods of transportation, we presume that substitution effects among them, if any, are included. Finally, geocultural distance is measured in two ways, both of which are related primarily to the distance of a country from the USA – the first measure is an index of Westernization on a six-point scale; the second is the air distance from the USA.

The multivariate method which follows, resembles factor analysis except that:

- In factor analysis, typically the interest is in the correlational structure among variables (R-type factor analysis) whereas here the interest is in the structure among countries (Q-type factor analysis).
- Typically factor analysis is performed as a correlation matrix. This model obtains the rank of the data matrix X through its cross-products matrix.
- The emphasis in factor analysis is on the overall parsimony of the data matrix. In this model, parsimony is directly related to the specific viewpoints the researcher is interested in. Accordingly the rotational procedures may vary between the two methods.

The relative positive values of countries reflect the degree of 'hotness' and the relative negative values of countries reflect the degree of 'coldness' from the viewpoint of US corporate foreign investment.

Generally, advanced countries were found to have the highest 'hot' values. Although Canada and Mexico are closer in geographical proximity, other countries were found to be better candidates for investment purposes. Relative to other countries, Portugal was found to have a zero value from an investment viewpoint. The East European and other Communist countries in Latin America, Africa, and Asia do not systematically cluster together in the cold spectrum

of the continuum. For example, Poland (rated 12), Czechoslovakia (rated 24), and Hungary (rated 28) have positive values. It is somewhat surprising to find that even the 'hottest' country, the UK, is considerably separated on the continuum from the USA. This implies that overseas investment in general is more problematic than domestic investment.

Goodnow and Hansz (1972) have further refined the Litvak-Banting model with stepwise multiple discriminant analysis. The 59 variables used in a cluster analysis of 100 'free-world' countries were gathered from published sources and expert opinion. The aim was to determine:

- how many unique groups of countries would best portray the 100 countries,
- in which group a country belonged,
- a statistical profile of the environmental characteristics of each group.

Variables were selected which best predicted group membership: seven economic and market-opportunity variables, six political and legal variables, three cultural variables, and one physiographic variable. The discriminant model was tested to determine its ability to reproduce the original country groupings. Ninety-eight out of 100 countries were classified correctly by the 17 variable discriminant factors. This was a result, firstly, of the country groupings being statistically determined by a 59-variable hierarchical cluster analysis, and, secondly, the model being tested on the same data that was used to construct it. Overall, the 17-variable discriminant model was found to fare far better than the traditional univariate method of GNP per capita.

Table 2.13 Goodnow, Hansz: correlations of corporate behaviour with environmental indicators

Strategy	GNP per capita Variation r^2 explained		Environmental index Variation r^2 explained		% increase in variance explained
Ranking of countries by % of US companies entering market	.63	40%.	.75	56%	40%
Ranking of countries by % of US companies going via direct channels given market entry*	.49	24%	.63	40%	67%

*Direct market entry channels include: wholly or partly-owned subsidiaries and branches, licensing agreements and direct export through overseas company owned channels or company sales forces overseas.
Source: Goodnow, H. D., and Hansz, J. E. (1972) Environmental determinants of overseas market entry strategies. *Journal of International Business Studies*, **3** (Spring), 45

Table 2.14   Undertaking a foreign market study: Information requirements

1. *Background information*
    This is derived from published secondary sources of information and would include:
    - rates of growth of the population, workforce, and GNP (but, as mentioned earlier, GNP per capita has its limitations as a credible measure of anything)
    - balance of payments (although this has not stopped anyone exporting to the USA!)
    - composition of exports and imports
    - consumer expenditures
    - formation of fixed capital in construction and equipment.

2. *Analysis of supply*
    - *External competition* can be ascertained by analysing import statistics, via
      UN World Trade Annual
      UN Commodity Indexes for the Standard Industrial Trade Classification, 2 vols.
      OECD Trade by Commodities (Foreign Trade Statistics, Series 'C', Paris, half-yearly).
    - *Import analyses* usually show:
      import flows over past five years, by major supplying countries, by quantity, and by value
      percentage growth of imports over the years studied.
    - *Apparent domestic consumption* may therefore be computed as
      Total supply = (local production − exports) + imports.

3. *Demand and end-use analysis*
    The aim is to study the various kinds of principal users of a product to discover where the growth points may be. The following need to be studied:
    - economic sectors that use the product
    - each sector's share of total consumption
    - growth pattern of each of these sectors
    - plans and forecasts of future growth for each major sector and the related sectors (future secondary demand).

4. *Demand forecasts*
    It is best to concentrate on five- to ten-year prospects. The following points should be noted:
    - Examine long-term trends, remembering cyclical pattern associated with industrial development
    - Examine substitutability of the goods in question
    - Ignore short-term economic forecasts as current events can bias thinking
    - Examine national plans.
    - Listen and interpret intelligently, e.g., ask a manufacturer about his competitors.

5. *Information of prices*
    - Extrapolation of unit prices over a five-year period may indicate the way in which prices are moving
    - Field enquiries at home can yield manufacturer and f.o.b. prices
    - Field enquiries in target country can yield cif prices and distribution costs.

6. *Access to the market*
    Conditions of access to the market may be influenced by the following:
    - customs tariffs
    - import charges
    - non-tariff barriers
    - import regulations.

7. *Trading practices*
    - sizes and grade of goods most often in demand
    - preferred types of packaging or product presentation
    - most popular qualities/assortments of goods
    - standardization at national/international level
    - usual channels of trade
    - condition of payment
    - problems of transport
    - insurance terms.

8. *Sales promotion*
    - evaluate target audience and coherent theme of message
    - when, where, how should this sales message be delivered?
    - media availability
    - publications readership profile
    - costs of advertising per prospective customer, by various media
    - strengths and weaknesses of present and prospective customers
    - what marketing approaches have been effective there in the past?
    - trade fairs—which groups attend them and what are the conditions for participating?

Note: An initial feasibility study may be conducted by means of secondary data, but before market entry much better, more timely information will be required which can only be gained from visiting the target market itself such as prices; potential new entrants to the market; potential substitute products for outside the industry; and the prevailing degree of buyer − supplier dependency in the target market itself.

Target market-selection decisions

It is a sad fact that the literature on foreign market selection points to it as often being only an informal decision on which little research has been conducted. It may be the result of a competitive move; or a chance sighting of a product from a particular market; the result of a business conversation, a chamber of commerce seminar; the result of a foreign inward trade mission; or else a market is chosen simply because it is a pleasant location, the people are nice and the managing director's spouse enjoys going there on holiday! Curiously, more attention appears to be paid to 'industry talk' which amounts to unsubstantiated rumour than to the reports and publications produced by different trade and governmental bodies. This behaviour has been reported in the UK and in the USA as well, although it must be remembered that since the USA does not have the same degree of dependence on trade as we have in the UK, this only serves to make the finding more incomprehensible.

Market selection means choosing the markets to which to devote your resources. Now, here without apologies, we wish to cite a reference that is 20 years old, the BOTB report on Key Market Concentration, because the findings still have relevance today. It found from taking a representative sample of a quarter of British companies that companies were spreading their resources too thinly over too many markets. Assuming a Pareto relationship, where approximately 20 per cent of a company's markets could be found to account for perhaps 80 per cent of its exports, BETRO exhorted exporters to concentrate their resources on their 'best' markets. Newcomers to exporting, the report suggested, could build a prosperous export trade by dealing with five or six countries only. Concentration would therefore bring:

- less administration,
- better market knowledge,
- more opportunity to compete on non-price factors,
- less distraction,
- higher market share.

The BETRO report concluded that British companies exported to too many markets. Piercy (1982) qualified this theory of 'market concentration' by viewing this, not in terms of limiting the company as to the market where it may sell, but to markets where it may market itself. By selling wherever demand arises but maintaining a certain selectivity over the use of marketing resources, Piercy then, and only then, confesses to a certain benefit in market concentration. Other commentators have pointed to the BETRO report and the advice on key market concentration as being responsible for the bankruptcy of many British exporters since the date of its publication, concentration being little different from 'placing all your eggs in one basket'. When disaster strikes, everything may be lost.

International market segmentation

Market segmentation follows the rationale of concentrating resources on the best prospects. In the pursuit of market segmentation, one is adopting a 'rifle' strategy at a given target segment as opposed to the general market at large, which would constitute a 'shotgun' approach. Sometimes firing far and wide, the latter will strike a target segment but at a cost and over time, and so the 'rifle' strategy is probably the more effective of the two as there are likely to be greater similarities across similar market segments than between two country markets. For example, BMW has effectively tapped into the international segment which is attracted by sporty family cars.

Three overall possibilities exist:

- market differentiation, whereby competitors make different offerings across the entire market and with the flexible manufacturing systems made possible by computerization this has become a feasible strategy much less costly than ever before;
- market segmentation, whereby specific target markets are identified and offerings are designed especially for these segments;
- market positioning whereby competitors position their offerings differently for each market segment.

There are degrees of segmentation, but certain criteria have to be fulfilled to make segmentation a feasible strategy:

1. Measurability. The target segment must be capable of some form of measurement, or at least, a 'best guess'.
2. Size. The target segment has to be large enough to make the marketing effort financially worthwhile.
3. Accessibility. Targeting is useless unless this group can be accessed by promotion and distribution.
4. Responsiveness. The target group should react to any change in the marketing mix elements. Failure to do so indicates that this is not a proper segment that has been drawn.

If a company chooses to ignore the differences between consumers, it will be practising undifferentiated marketing. If, on the other hand, it segments the market on the basis of consumer differences, it can choose to practise either differentiated marketing – in which a marketing mix is used for each segment – or concentrated marketing – in which all or most marketing efforts are focused on one or a few segments.

Wind and Douglas (1972) tie in market segmentation with their recommendations on international market research, as may be seen in Figure 2.15, which separates enduring characteristics such as the topography of the country, which will affect distribution networks and situation-specific characteristics, which are unique to an industry or perhaps sub-culture and should not be seen as either lasting or universal outside of that particular segment.

Mandell and Rosenberg (1981) mention also 'market integration' and 'market orchestration'. Market integration unites certain market segments, finds a basic characteristic that several otherwise different groups share in common, and designs a product that appeals to all of them. One example offered is in the area of snack foods. Market integration arose as a response to oversegmentation. Market orchestration arises where different market segments are to be included in the target range and lack compatibility. The price factor is therefore the most common means of orchestration; since high and low prices will encourage some segments and discourage others.

Selecting a strategy then, is by means of a review of five factors:

- *Company resources,* whether limited in terms of capital and/or marketing.
- *Product homogeneity,* degree of similarity within

a product class.
- *Product age* (PLC theory of product phase and corporate response).
- *Market homogeneity,* depending on where consensus needs are like/unlike.
- *Competition,* moving into several segments or a mass market will influence corporate response.

Primary sources of information

Excellent, but expensive is the problem. First determine what the company has to offer, undertake some research of secondary sources of information on that country and that industry. When the focus of the research has been narrowed down to perhaps one market, and the trail of secondary information has petered out, then this is the time for primary information gathering, provided enthusiasm for going into this market is still riding high.

There comes a time when only primary data collection can be conducted. Secondary sources are secondary because they are always collected for another and are presented for a specific purpose, e.g. governmental demographic data. Although cheap they lack specificity and timeliness. This is what primary data can offer. They can offer a custom-built survey of attitudes and perspectives on a new product to that market, but it takes money and time and needs to be handled by local nationals so as to eliminate much of the confusion and nonsense that often creeps in when questionnaires are transferred over from a head office at home and translated roughly into the foreign language of the country concerned.

Also under the heading of primary data comes the internal examination of the company; the suppliers; channels of distribution; and

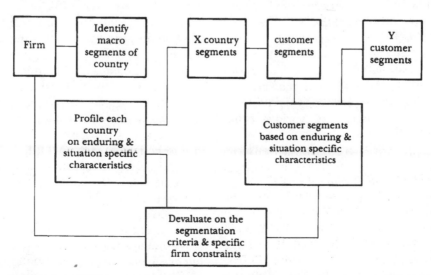

Source: Wind and Douglas (1972), International market segmentation. *European Journal of Marketing,* **6** (1)

Figure 2.15   Segmenting international markets

industry in the target foreign market. This then involves an examination of what Porter (1985) calls the 'value chain' for each of the companies; suppliers; climate and industries. The all-important linkages within these value chains and the determination of what is value itself as perceived within the target foreign market cannot be gauged from a review of secondary published sources of information.

The value chain is composed of nine generic categories of activities which are linked together. The activities in a firm's value chain are linked to each other and to the activities of its suppliers, channels and buyers. These linkages affect competitive advantage. The firm's value chain is determined by its history, strategy, its approach to implementing strategy and the underlying economies of the activities themselves. The firm is a series of functions and the value chain is a system of interdependent activities. Simply stated value is the amount buyers are willing to pay for what a firm provides them. Creating value for buyers that exceeds the cost of so doing, is a common strategic goal and so value, rather than cost is used to explain how companies, which offer value are able to charge a premium for this and differentiate themselves also from the competition at the same time. This means, though, that the value has to be clearly seen and appreciated by the buyer. Value activities are the physically and technologically distinct activities a firm performs. These value activities are the building blocks of competitive advantage by which a firm creates a product valuable to its buyers. The value chain displays total value and consists of value activities and margin which is the difference between total value and the collective cost of performing the value activities.

Value activities can be divided into primary and support activities. Primary activities are further divided into five categories but are the activities involved in the physical creation of the product and its sale and transfer to the buyer as well as after-sales service. Support activities provide backup for primary activities and for each other by providing purchased inputs, technology, human resources and various other functions within the firm.

The economies of each activity, as well as its performance, determine whether a firm is high or low cost relative to competition. How each value activity is performed will also determine its contribution to buyer needs and hence differentiation. Comparing the value chains of competitors exposes differences that determine competitive advantage.

The value chain, rather than value added, is the appropriate way to examine competitive advantage. Porter (1985) maintains that while value added (selling price minus cost of purchased raw materials) has been taken as the base for cost analysis in the belief that it is an area in which the firms can control costs, it is in fact a misconception. Value added simply isolates raw materials from the many purchased inputs used in a firm's activities. The value chain, on the other hand, is not an accounting classification but examines the costs of all the inputs and looks also at the linkages which a firm may have with its suppliers to reduce cost or enhance differentiation. Supplier and channel value chains also relate back to the firm as they form vertical linkages and part of the total cost that will be borne by the buyer. To explore these linkages fully requires information systems so as to achieve the necessary optimal coordination. There are also tradeoffs in the system which increase the complexity of managing and controlling the entire system, e.g. higher costs in one area may result in lower costs in another. Another factor to be considered is the degree of vertical integration and the extent to which the firm divides its activities with its suppliers, channels and buyers. Differentiation may come through offering a range of buyer activities either internally or through supplier co-operation or coalitions and strategic business alliances with independent firms.

Secondary sources of information

Secondary sources, i.e., published sources of information are a good inexpensive place to start. There are more than 146 countries with populations greater than one million but available market data particularly from the less developed countries will be very limited. For governments in unstable economies a census can have a destabilizing effect particularly if it shows demographic shifts that indicate electoral underrepresentation of any significant part of the community, and if that community displays no likelihood of supporting the government in power, the census will only have served to underline and give statistical credibility to a societal wrong. Not surprisingly, then, there are countries where only estimates are available as to how large the population may be. Examples are to be found in the Middle East and Africa. This, despite the fact that population censuses have been taking place all over the world since before the birth of Jesus Christ.

Secondary sources of information vary greatly. The greatest publisher of information is government and where international agreements on exchange of information are in place, it will be possible to consult foreign governments' statistical publications locally as is the case in Britain with US statistics and vice versa. Supranational bodies such as the EU and the various UN agencies publish their own statistics as do other international organizations such as EFTA, OECD and other customs unions. At a local level it will usually be possible to find reports published by export trade associations, trade unions, employers' confederations and consultancies such as Business International SA or Booz, Allen and Hamilton.

Data interpretation problems

Conducting market research in one's own country, one enjoys the benefit of a certain degree of familiarity with the nature of the society, its values and laws. Foreign market research is like a great leap into the dark where many variables are unknown unless it is conducted by local nationals in the country concerned. The scope of error is vast, particularly so where a foreign company may be enquiring about the local acceptability of a product, concept, service, or slogan currently in use in other parts of the world. The problem of the Self-Reference Criterion comes into play here. An individual looks at a foreign market and evaluates it against experience and understanding of his own market. False perceptions, misunderstandings and unfulfilled expectations lead to costly mistakes. Even where the common language may be English there are many possible instances where the same word will not be used in popular conversation or advertising in Britain and in Canada, Australia or New Zealand. It is possible to create a totally negative effect through this inability to communicate across two English-speaking communities, although the comic occasions usually arise with translations, e.g. 'Come alive with Pepsi' may be a familiar slogan in the English-speaking world but how would the English-speaking manager react on hearing that his product slogan has been translated in China (PRC): 'Pepsi reawakens your dead relatives'? On a more positive note, it is likely that the product would have high brand-name recall among consumers. Careful checking and preparation cannot be over-emphasized. Generally, the problems revolve around language because language is a living thing and while the world of commerce is constantly innovating products and language to communicate new product concepts, their understanding is neither total nor universal.

Time is required for good market research and familiarity with the market and the product concerned. However, this may be a stated ideal and the pressures on executive time and finances may force a decision to be made on data which is often incomplete in many respects. One of the most serious problems is the lack of a common statistical base in data collected worldwide. Keegan (1989) illustrates how a confusing array of units of measurement for Pepsi consumption nationally – whether in can, bottle or glass; and in terms of frequency: whether daily, weekly or number of times daily – led to the lack of a coherent standardization of data within the Pepsico organization as a whole. The lack of complementarity between statistical bases is one of the single greatest problems of foreign market research. It means statistics cannot be directly compared and contrasted and severely limits any statistical analysis on a time series, demographic, socio-economic or regional basis. It is interesting to note how the OECD and EU are making moves towards international standardization of statistical reporting. Elsewhere, a consortium of international publishers have produced 13 national research companies, including Research Services in the UK, a 13 country Pan-European survey of readership habits and profiles for 23 daily, weekly, fortnightly, monthly and bi-monthly publications.

Demographic, economic, and social statistics are thus not comparable since they are compiled by different agencies for different purposes. To pursue a few of these distortions along the lines laid down by Barnes (1980):

- *Degree of concentration of population.* Figures may be distorted because not all of the land mass is actually habitable, as for example with Japan or Switzerland. Urban concentration will therefore be greater than the average mean which is 'smoothed' and will inevitably include lakes and mountain ranges in the number per square kilometre of land. Urban concentration in Britain or Japan will therefore be much higher than may be inferred from statistics drawn on this basis. Even so, Macao has a population density of 20,482 per km^2 and Australia 2 or Canada 3.
- *The extent of car ownership.* This may be distorted, firstly, by leasing and, secondly, by the fact that in a country such as Britain, approximately 70 per cent of the car market is accounted for by company cars as this is in turn influenced by the taxation system. Attempts to assess car ownership as against cars per household will yield quite different results, particularly if it is a study of usage. Language and the correct choice of words is important. GIGO or 'garbage in, garbage out' is the perennial problem with questionnaires where semantic nuances affect understanding and respondent evaluations.
- *Level of individual prosperity.* Beware again of

per capita GNP and also of self-reference criteria that suggest that foreign market X will, with increasing personal incomes, display the same consumer wants and desires as your own domestic market. This is the self-reference criteria at work. Even if consumers are willing to divulge personal information about household incomes either in actual numbers or by agreeing to being within a predetermined income band, there are the added problems of fluctuating exchange rates and differences in direct income taxes and benefits which go to make it all the harder to approximate equivalent purchasing parities.

• *Infrastructural level to be considered* – for example, whether there is adequate electricity power supply or simply, maintenance and repair facilities. A fax machine will require a telephone line but the telephone system may still be in another age. Photocopies require abundant supplies of paper. Computers require paper and floppy disks, etc.

• *Level of female emancipation.* The role of women in society differs greatly between Europe and North America and, for example, the Middle East. The UK, Sri Lanka, Israel, Poland and India have had women as Prime Ministers, while in some Middle Eastern countries women have still to walk cloaked totally in black, behind their husbands. It may be argued that they do this of their volition but it is nevertheless true that this is a societal expectation. Countries do differ in this regard and even within countries there may be differences. Again educational opportunities, career opportunities and equality of treatment between the sexes vary greatly between and sometimes within countries. In the extreme, 'the role of a woman is in the kitchen and the birthing-bed'. Opportunities to target executive toys or magazines at these women are limited. Statistics on numbers in higher education and entry to professions give some indication as to sexual equality, as does the time and the range of publications generally available in that market. Are there any specifically targeted at women in any profession or of any age?

• *Labour supply.* The shortage of labour and/or the cost of labour may not always be apparent. West Germany in the early 1970s had to import labour mainly from Turkey but when industrial conditions changed and labour unions began to complain about the societal consequences of importing perhaps three million workers, this method was dropped in favour of contractual joint ventures in Eastern Europe whereby production was secured with none of the attendant problems of immigrant labour, although new problems would soon have their place.

• *Level of industrialization related to the infrastructure.* It is costly to transfer a general technology; it is simpler and less expensive to transfer industry-specific or company-specific technology, i.e., a product or process. Markets must also be recognized as being at different economic stages of industrialization, some undergoing de-industrialization, some actually industrializing, others remaining essentially raw-material supplying countries.

• *Level of retail integration.* This gives some indication as to available channels of distribution, discussed more fully later. Enormous variances exist – from the longest channels worldwide in Japan to short retail channels in France where the hypermarket concept was first developed. Note, too, that quantum leaps are possible in development and that France made a quantum leap in retailing, bypassing the supermarket stage and moving directly to hypermarkets. Again, this was aided and abetted by a commercially favourable legal system which did not seek to obstruct this change as has happened in Britain where planning controls have been used to limit out-of-town hypermarkets and 'protect' urban shopping centres.

• Countries tend to 'adjust' published figures and learn to live with and discount statistics known to be imperfect. Fig. 2.16 shows the discrepancies in the annual bilateral trade balance as reported separately by Canada and by the USA.

Also, on national statistical reporting, Kenichi Ohmae argues the case for Japan in saying that no common industrial classification system exists between the USA and Japan which would allow statistical and economic figures between the two countries to be compared. The USA for its part has argued that Japan treats it as a developing country in terms of the commodity structure of its foreign trade with Japan. The same has also to be said of UK–Japanese trade. Ohmae argues the contrary that these classifications do not allow valid comparisons to be made and maintains that Japan is the USA's number one foreign purchaser of commercial aircraft, organic and inorganic chemicals, pharmaceuticals and photographic supplies; and the second largest foreign purchaser of medical and scientific supplies, measuring and testing devices, pulp and wood products, and semiconductors. The USA then will be constrained in terms of possible actions in its trade war with Japan, if Japan owns it!

Certainly, trade studies have numerous

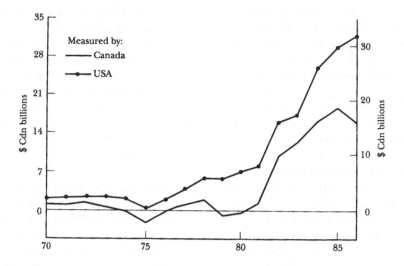

Source: United Nations Economic Commission for Europe, *Harmonisation of International Trade Statistics*.
TRADE/AC.25/R.2, 18 July 1990

Figure 2.16   Canada's merchandise trade surplus as measured by Canada and the US

built-in distortions. Another convention of trade figure reporting is that exports are always quoted FOB and imports CIF. Regardless of changes taking place in the INCOTERMS used for export trade quotations, this convention has been maintained. An export order FOB or 'free on board' will represent a lower value than an import quoted as CIF (cost, insurance, freight) as the FOB price may in its simplest form be the factory gate price with no overheads added for transportation, insurance, etc. as is a FOB quotation. This is the responsibility of the buyer or importer. This means then that exports FOB will have a lower price than imports CIF so comparing, say, British exports to France with French imports from Britain will not state the same values because of the FOB/CIF discrepancy as well as currency fluctuation. The added problem of different national statistical codes for products and services is a very difficult one. Technology soon renders obsolete any attempt at classifying industrial products but without a common industrial code we cannot really compare what one country imports under the heading of 'machine tools' with what another exports to it also understood to be 'machine tools'. The most

Table 2.15   What per cent of women are in the labour force?

	Census	OECD	International demographics	Statistical Abstract of Latin America	Statistics Canada	Annual Abstract of Statistics UK
USA	55 (1985)	63	54	—	—	—
Canada	52 (1981)	62	61	—	46	—
Japan	49 (1985)	57	57	—	—	—
Great Britain/	47					
UK	46 (1981)	59 (UK)	57 (UK)	—	—	49
Australia	46 (1981)	53	52	—	—	—
Fed. Rep. of						
Germany	39 (1980)	49	49	—	—	—
Italy	33 (1981)	41	41	—	—	—
Venezuela	31 (1984)	—	24	21	—	—
Mexico	28 (1980)	—	—	17	—	—
Brazil	27 (1980)	—	39	20	—	—

Source: Bartos, R. (1989), International demographic data? Incomparable! *Marketing and Research Today*, vol 17, no. 4, p. 207

recent industrial product classification has been TARIC introduced into the European Union in 1988. It is a genuine attempt to coordinate and standardize industrial classifications across the community. It has also been adopted by a number of countries outside the EU.

Yet the problem does not just lie with industrial products continually being updated and transformed with new technology into new products for new applications. The problem also lies in the human knowledge element embodied in software that makes technology function. This has traditionally been difficult to classify but, as may be seen from the table below other statistical definition problems arise as well. For example, not only do different statistical sources conflict on the issue of the number of women in the labour force but there is a fundamental split as to how to define a woman. In most countries, it will be age 15 but in the USA it is 16, in Italy 14, in Mexico, 12 and Brazil 10 (Bartos, 1989). (See Table 2.15).

Language creates difficulties particularly with regard to multicultural multilingual questionnaires. A researcher has to be quite certain that data gathered in English will be directly comparable with the same gathered in French. Aside from the problems of defining a similar sample frame across two countries and ensuring adequate representation of the sample among respondents, it also involves a great deal of cross-checking, testing and translation back into the original language once complete and so extends the time required for completion, the cost of final completion, and the credibility of the final effort to management.

Where contemporary data does not exist nor is specific to the problem in hand, then primary data collection – i.e., fieldwork – has to be undertaken. The costs and time involved cannot be exaggerated.

Where data exists to some degree but there is difficulty in establishing fieldwork, then certain approximation measures have to be turned to and this we shall deal with shortly. There are other sources – the political and economic press of the country concerned; possibly, too, discussions with importers and end-users; and reports of either government departments or trade associations. The dynamism of the marketplace means that competitors can often quickly find a lucrative market in an otherwise altogether undesirable market, politically, financially, and touristically. This then creates a pressure for competitors to follow into that market but without the prior knowledge and information of the leader. A 'bandwagon' effect is then created. Companies find themselves in markets, not entirely of their own choosing, simply by following the market leader or other close rivals, and assuming also that the leader has perfect knowledge of where he and the market in general is going, because they have not. Managing a business without a knowledge of the market that one is in has been compared to driving a car blindfolded in reverse. A lot of bruising will take place before some essential lessons are learned.

The section which follows exceeds the requirements of the Institute of Marketing Diploma syllabus. However, it may lead to a better understanding of identifying market opportunities if this section is read rather than omitted.

Commercial services such as BERI do not identify export opportunities at the firm level nor are they meant to provide criteria for foreign market selection. Instead, they are offered to help develop a decision-making framework in which the criteria important to the firm may be gauged against the opportunities offered. The pages which follow are designed to shrink the psychological distance between the marketer and his envisioned target market and lead hopefully to more objective and better decision-making based on better information.

Revision questions

1. Identify exactly the acronym 'SLEPT'.
2. What are the costs of involvement in international competition?
3. What are folkways or conventions, and how may a knowledge of the same be useful to an international marketer?
4. How would you define your own culture?
5. Illustrate with examples how language can get in the way of effective communication.
6. What is a 'Self-Reference Criterion'? How might this impact a country market feasibility study?
7. Rokeach states that man possesses far fewer terminal than instrumental values. What is the significance of that?
8. What is the meaning of semiotics, and what can they offer the international marketer?
9. Cite three possible dangers arising from the lack of an agreed body of international law.
10. What is ICSID and UNCITRAL and why are they important?
11. Identify three different forms of non-tariff barrier.
12. How do you define a 'strategic market'? What role does segmentation play in the identification of these markets?
13. Why was a World Trade Organization (WTO) created out of GATT?
14. What is Voluntary Export Restraint?

15. Explain the three different forms of 'dumping' and possible actions that may be taken to counteract it.
16. Why is it that politicians are afraid of unregulated free trade? Is it not a contradiction to want to regulate 'free trade'?
17. What is the significance of the Triad to a manufacturer of high tech electronic consumer goods?
18. Point out six ways in which political intervention occurs in international business.
19. What are the requirements of a foreign market study? How many stages are involved?
20. What are the key differences between primary and secondary data?

Key reading on foreign market research

Basic information

Advertiser's Annual, Reed Information Services, East Grinstead, Sussex RH19 1HE.
ASLIB Directory of Information Sources in the UK (ed. Codlin, E. M. and Reynard, K. W.), 3 Belgrave Square, London SW1X 8PL.
Benn's Media, Tunbridge Wells, Kent.
British Institute of Management, 'Where to find it: a guide for managers under pressure' ed. Richard Withey, Management House, Cottingham Road, Corby, Northants, NN17 1TT, 1986.
British Institute of Management, information sheets provided on a key-word basis.
BSI Buyers' Guide 1988/89 – listing of all British Standards Institute Kitemark and safety mark licences, registered forms and registered stockists, BSI Quarterly Assurance, PO Box 375, Milton Keynes, MK14 6LL.
Companies Registration Office, Crown Way, Maindy, Cardiff, CF4 3UZ and London Search Rooms, 55 City Road, London EC1Y 1RB. Company records on microfilm. Microfilm index of all live companies. Annual report published by HMSO.
Croner's Reference Book for Exporters, Croner Publications, Croner House, London Road, Kingston upon Thames, Surrey, KTZ 6SR, loose-leaf book with monthly supplements.
Croner's Reference Book for Importers.
Commonwealth Secretariat, *Commonwealth Organizations: a handbook of official and unofficial organizations active in the Commonwealth*, 2nd edn, 1979.
Department of Trade and Industry, *Register of Quality Assessed United Kingdom Companies*, 3rd edn, London 1986.
Directory of British Associations and Associations in Ireland, CBD Research, Beckenham, Kent.

Directory of Directors (Reed Information Services), Windsor Court, East Grinstead House, East Grinstead, West Sussex RH18 1XE.
Directory of Export Buyers in the UK, ed. M. Cummins, Trade Research Publications in association with the British Exporters Association, Berkhamsted 1993.
European Directory of Non-official Statistical Sources, 2nd edn. 1993, Euromonitor Publications Limited, 87–88 Turnmill Street, London EC1M 5QU.
Europa Yearbook, detailed information on every country in the world and international organizations, Europe Publications Ltd, 12 Bedford Square, London WC1B 3JN.
Hollis Press and Public Relations Annual, Hollis Directories, Lower Hampton Road, Sunbury-on-Thames, Middlesex TW16 5HG.
Key Business Enterprises, The Top 20,000 British Companies, Dun and Bradstreet, 26–32 Clifton Street, London EC2P 2LY.
Kompass Register of British Industry & Commerce, 4 volumes. Windsor Court, East Grinstead House, East Grinstead, West Sussex RH19 1XD.
OECD Economic Surveys, for all member countries, HMSO London.
Sell's Directory of Products & Services, Sell's Publications, Epsom, Surrey KT17 1BQ.
J. Padget *Chambers of Commerce Worldwide – a selected list: 1992* London Chamber of Commerce and Industry, 68 Cannon Street, London EC49 5AB.
Statesman's Yearbook, Macmillan Press, London.
Scottish Enterprise (1991) Register of Quality Assessed Scottish Companies, 4th Edn.
Company Handbook, two issues per year, Stock Exchange Press and Datastructure under licence from the International Stock Exchange.
Trade Associations and Professional Bodies of the UK, ed. P. Millard, Pergamon Press, Oxford.
UN Statistical Yearbook, New York. Also IMF, UNIDO, WTO, UNECE, FAO and other UN organizations publish their own statistics.
Whitaker's Almanac, published by J. Whitaker & Sons, 12 Dyott Street, London WC1A 1DF.
Who Owns Whom, separate volumes for Europe, Australia and North America, Dun and Bradstreet, London EC2A 4BU
Willings Press Guide, Reed Information Services, East Grinstead, Sussex RH19 1HE.
Europages, European Business Directory (annual) 7th edition, Thomson Directories, 296 Farnborough Road, Farnborough, Hampshire, GU14 7NU.
Europe's 15,000 largest companies: 1989, ELC International, Sinclair House, The Avenue, London, W13 8NT.
Major Companies of Europe, Graham and Trot-

man, Sterling House, 66 Wilton Road, London
SW1V 1DE.

Financial data

Annual Company Reports.
Euromoney
FT (Financial Times) Publications.
EIU (Economist Intelligence Unit) *Publications,*
various country, industry and product reports.
25 St James' Street, London SW1A 1HG.
Times 1000, Times Books, 16 Golden Square,
London W1R 4BV, annually.

Guides to British statistics

Central Statistical Office, *Guide to Official Statis-
tics*, HMSO, London.
Central Statistical Office, *Government Statistics,
a brief guide to sources*, Press and Information
Service, HMSO, London.
Mort D. and Siddall S., *Sources of Unofficial UK
Statistics*, Gower, 2nd Edition, 1990.

Indexes and abstracts

Anbar. Published in collaboration with the Char-
tered Institute of Marketing. Five abstracting
journals containing one paragraph abstract of
articles surveyed. Anbar is a division of MCB
University Press, 62 Toller Lane, Bradford,
West Yorks.
Business Periodicals Index. H. W. Wilson Ltd., 950
University Avenue, Bronx NY 10452, USA.
Chiefly US publications, somewhat difficult to
locate in the UK.
Contents Pages in Management. Monthly publica-
tion by Manchester Business School.
Predicasts Inc, *F & S Index*, monthly reports on
business, economics and industry. 11001
Cedar Avenue, Cleveland, Ohio, 44106 USA.
SCIMP European Index of Management Period-
icals. European Business School Librarians
Group, Helsinki School of Economics and
Business Administration, Runebarginkaty
22–24, 00100 Helsinki, Finland.
Marketing Surveys Index (pub. in association with
the Chartered Institute of Marketing), Marketing Strategies for Industry (UK) Ltd, Heath-
court House, Parsons Green, London SW6 4TJ.

International reports

Business International Corporation produces
several regional business newsletters, e.g.
Business Asia.
*Directory of US and Canadian Marketing Surveys
and Services*, pub. Kline, Fairfield, New Jersey,
USA.

European Companies: a guide to sources of
information, 4th edn. R. Rickson CBD
Research, Beckenham, Kent.
Euromonitor's Consumer Market Factfile,
Market Research Europe.
Industrial Marketing Research Association,
European Sources of Industrial Market Research.
Price Waterhouse – 2 series: *'Tax in . . .'* and
'Doing business in . . .'
Published Data on Middle and Far East, Industrial
Aids Ltd, 14 Buckingham Palace Road,
London SW1.
US Dept of Commerce, *Overseas Business Reports*
(thanks to an Exchange of Information Act
with the USA, American foreign market
research reports are to be found in the Dept. of
Trade and Industry's EMIC (Export Market
Information Centre), Victoria Street, London
SW1 (see Chapter 5).

Market research survey reports

British Library. *British Reports, Translations and
Theses*, monthly, Boston Spa, Wetherby, West
Yorkshire.
Mintel International Group, London, industry
sector reports.
Keynote Reports, a range of 220 industry sector
reports monthly, UK, some European, Keynote
Publications Ltd., Field House, 72 Oldfield
Road, Hampton, Middlesex TW12 1BR.
Marketsearch (formerly International Directory
of Published Market Research).
MEAL, Media Expenditure Analysis Ltd., 110 St
Martin's Lane, London WC2N 4BH.
Mintel: *Market Intelligence*, monthly reports of
consumer goods in Britain, Mintel Ltd, Brom-
ley, Kent.
National Economic Development Office, occasional
specific industry reports, Millbank, London.

Market sector reports

Business Monitor (aggregated sales, production,
exports, etc. for specific industrial sectors).
Business Statistics Office, Dept. of Trade and
Industry, London.
Predicasts *Overview of Markets and Technology
(PROMT)* quarterly abstracts, PREDICASTS
Inc., 11001 Cedar Avenue, Cleveland, Ohio,
USA. Available online on DIALOG.
Worldcasts, abstracts of published international
forecasts, for all countries, Predicast Inc., 200
University Circle Research Center, 11001
Cedar Avenue, Cleveland, Ohio, USA.

Newspaper indexes

Financial Times, Research Publishers Ltd, PO

Box 45, Reading RG1 8HF. Monthly Index. *Times Index*, Newspaper Archive Developments Ltd, Reading RG1 8HF

Wall Street Journal Index, Dow Jones & Company Inc., 200 Liberty Street, New York, NY 10281, USA.

Research Index. pub. Business Surveys Ltd, PO Box 21, Dorking, Surrey RH4 2YU. Fortnightly index of newspapers and products by keyword – also publish *Reports Index*.

McCarthy *Information Services*. Manor House, Ash Walk, Warminster, Wilts. BA12 8PY. Company as well as subject indexes.

References

Allport, G. W. (1961) *Pattern and Growth in Personality*, Holt Rinehart and Winston, New York.

Ansoff, I (1987) *Corporate Strategy*, revised ed, Penguin, London.

Barnes, W. N. (1980) International marketing indicators. *European Journal of Marketing*, **14** (2), 90–136.

Barnhill, J. A., and Lawson, W. M. (1980) Toward a theory of modern markets. *European Journal of Marketing*, **14**, (1) 50–60.

Bartos, R. (1989) International demographic data? Incomparable! *Marketing and Research Today*, **17** (4).

BETRO Trust Committee (1976) *Concentration on Key Markets*, British Overseas Trade Board (BOTB), London.

Brown, M. A. (1976) Values: A necessary but neglected ingredient of motivation on the job. *Academy of Management Review*, **1**, 22.

Bunn, J. H. (1981) *The Dimensionality of Signs, Tools and Models*, Indiana University Press, Bloomington, Indiana.

Business Environment Risk Intelligence (BERI), Long Beach, California, USA.

Clarke, Jr., D. S. (1987) *The Principles of Semiotics*, Routledge, London.

Collins, V. D. (1935) *World Marketing*, JP Lippincott Company, London reprinted 1978 by Arno Press Inc., New York.

Czinkota, M. R., Ronkainen, I. A., and Tarrant, J. J. *The Global Marketing Imperative*, NTC Business Books, Lincolnwood, Illinois.

Deely, J. (1982) *Introducing Semiotic: Its History and Doctrine*, Indiana University Press, Bloomington, Indiana.

The Economist, *Pooled World in Figures*, 1997 Edition, London.

Farmer, R. N., and Richman, B. M. (1971) *International Business – An Operational Theory*, Cedarwood Press, Bloomington, Indiana.

Freud, S. (1955) *Interpretation of Dreams*, translated by Strachey, A., Allen and Unwin, London.

Goodnow, J. D. and Hansz, J. E. (1972) Environmental determinants of overseas market entry strategies, *Journal of International Business Studies*, **3** (Spring), 45.

Griffin, T. (1993) *International Marketing Communications*, Butterworth-Heinemann, Oxford.

Hall, E. T. (1960) The silent language in overseas business. *Harvard Business Review*, May/June, 87–96.

Herzberg, F. (1966) *Work and the Nature of Man*, William Collins, Glasgow.

Hibbert, E. P. and Liu, J. (1996) *International Market Research: A financial perspective*, Blackwell, Oxford.

Kay, J. A. (1990) Identifying the Strategic Market. *Business Strategy Review*, Spring, 2–24

Keegan, W. (1989) *Global Marketing Management*, Prentice-Hall, Englewood Cliffs, N. J. Chapter 8.

Kosaka, H. (1992) A global marketing strategy responding to national cultures. *Marketing and Research Today*, November, 245–255.

Lange-Seidl, A. M. (1977) *Approaches to Theories for Nonverbal Signs*, Peter de Ridder Press, Lisse, Netherlands.

Litvak, Isaiah A. and Banting, Peter M. (1968), 'A conceptual framework for international business arrangements', in King, Robt. L. (ed), *Marketing and the New Science of Planning*, American Marketing Association Conference Proceedings, Chicago, Fall, 460–67.

Mandell, M. I. and Rosenberg, L. H. (1981), *Marketing*, 2nd ed, Prentice-Hall, Englewood Cliffs, N. J.

Martin, D. (1995) 'The Role of Research in International Marketing', in Michael J. Thomas (ed), *The Handbook of Marketing*, 4th edn, Gower, Aldershot, Hants.

Maslow, A. H. (1954) *Motivation and Personality*, Harper and Row, London, pp. 80–106.

McCall, J. B., and Warrington, M. B. (1989) *Marketing by Agreement: A Cross-Cultural Approach to Business Negotiations*, John Wiley and Sons, Chichester.

Montgomery, D. B. and Urban, G. L. (1969) *Management Science in Marketing*, Prentice-Hall, Englewood Cliffs, N. J., 4–6.

Murdock, G. P. (1945) The Common Denominator of Culture. In *The Science of Man in the World Crisis*, (ed. Linton, R.), Columbia University Press, New York.

Ohmae, K. (1985) *Triad Power: The Coming Shape of Global Competition*, Macmillan – The Free Press, New York.

Ohmae, K. (1995a) *The Evolving Global Economy: Making Sense of the New World Order*, Harvard Business Review Book, Boston, Mass.

Ohmae, K. (1995b) *The End of the Nation State*, The Free Press, New York.

Paliwoda, S. J. (1994a) International marketing –

getting started. In *The Marketing Book* (ed. M. J. Baker), 3rd ed, Butterworth-Heinemann, Oxford.

Paliwoda, S. J. (1994b) The International Marketing Environment. In *Marketing Handbook* (ed. M. J. Thomas), 4th edn, Gower.

Paliwoda, S. J., Ryans Jr, J. K., eds (1995) *International Marketing Reader*, Routledge, London.

Piercy, N. (1982) *Export Strategy: Markets and Competition*, George Allen and Unwin, London.

Ponzio, A. (1990) *Man as a sign: Essays on the Philosophy of Language*, Monton de Gruyter, Berlin.

Porter, M. E. (1985) *Competitive Advantage*, Macmillan Publishers, New York.

Porter, M. E. (1996) *The Competitive Advantage of Nations*, Macmillan, London.

Rokeach, M. (1973) *The Nature of Human Values*, Macmillan – The Free Press, New York.

Root, F. R. (1987) *Entry Strategies for International Markets*, Lexington Books, Lexington, MA.

Ruthstrom, C. R., and Matejka K. (1990) The Meanings of 'Yes' in the Far East. *Industrial Marketing Management*, **19,** 191–192.

Sheth, J. N., and Lutz, R. J. (1973) A multivariate model of multinational business expansion, In *Multinational Business Operations* (eds Seth, S. P., and Sheth, J. N.), **3,** *Marketing Management*, Goodyear Pub., California.

Terpstra, V. (1994) *International Marketing*, 6th edn, Dryden Press – Holt, Rinehart and Winston, Chicago and New York.

Whalen, B. (1983) Semiotics: An Art or Powerful Marketing Research Tool? *Marketing News*, 13 May, pp. 8–9.

Wind, J. and Douglas, S. (1972) International Market Segmentation. *European Journal of Marketing*, **6**(1).

Web Sites

Note that EMIC (Export Market Information Centre) London provides a list of World Wide Web Pages. For details please contact Ola Agboola on 0171 215 4352.

Other sites selected include:

Advertising and Marketing on the Internet
http://www.yahoo.com/
  Business_and_Economy/Marketing/

American Marketing Association
http://www.ama.org

Asia Internet Directory
http://www.asia-inc.com/aid/index.html

Asia Trade
http://www.asiatrade.com/index.html

Australia and New Zealand Comparative and International Education Society
http://www.macarthur.uws.edu.au/ssd/
  anzcies/

Australian Government Information Sources
http://www.nla.gov.au/oz/gov/
  ozgov.html

Bank of America: Global Capital Markets Group
http://www.bofa.com/capmkts4.html

Bank of England
http://www.bankofengland. co.uk

BBC
http://www.bbc.co.uk

Brazil general lists
http://www.embratel.net.br/
  dirweb.html

Brazil government information (communications)
http://www.telebras.gov.br/

Business Information Resources
http://sashimi.wwa.com/~notime/eotw/
  business_info.html

Business Information Server
http://www.dnb.com/

Business Statistics
gopher: University of Michigan:
  una.hh.lib.umich.edu
Choose: ebb Current Business Statistics

Businesses on the Internet
http://www.yahoo.com/
  Business_and_Economy/Corporations/

Business to Business Marketing Exchange
www.btob.wfu.edu/b2b.html

Cahners Manufacturing Marketplace: US manufacturers, distributors, products, news and hot links
http://www.cmm.net

Canada government information
http://info.ic.gc.ca/opengov/

Canadian WWW Central Index
http://www.csr.ists.ca/w3can/
  Welcome.html

Chartered Institute of Marketing
http://www.cim.co.uk

Chile general lists
http://sunsite.dcc.uchile.cl/chile/
  chile.html

Chile Government Information
http://200.0.148.2/homepage/catalogo/
    bases/dofi.html

China Garment Enterprise Association (200
    Member Companies across China)
http://www.sh.com/custom/cgea.htm

CNN Interactive
http://www.cnn.com/

Commerce Business Daily
    gopher:cscns.com
Choose: Internet Express Gopher by Subject
        Business–Commerce Business Daily-
        Softshare

Commercenet
www.commerce.net

Commercial Use of the Internet
http://pass.wayne.edu/business.html

Consumer Information Centre
http://www.gsa.gov/staff/pa/cic/cic.htm

CultureNet
http://www.culturenet.ucalgary.ca/

Currency Converter
http://bin.gnn.com/cgi-bin/gnn/currency

Czech Republic general lists
http://www.cesnet.cz/html/cesnet/
    wwwservers.html

Czech Republic Government Information
http://www.czech.cz/

Daily News – source of business and economic
    news
http://www.helsinki.fi/~Isaarine/
    news.html

Ernst & Young
http://www.ernsty.co.uk/ernsty

EWR (Early Warning Report) : Chokepoints for
    World Trade
http://www.subscriptions.com/beacon/
    mapchokepoints.html

ExportNet – Export Today Matchmaking Service
http://www.exporttoday.com

Foreign Exchange Rates
http://www.dna.Ith.se/cgi-bin/kurt/rates/

France general lists
http://www.urec.fr/cgi-bin/list

France government information
http://www.ensmp.fr/industrie

Friends of the Earth
http://www.foe.co.uk

GE Information Services – bringing together US
    buyers and suppliers
http://www.tpn.geis.com

Germany general lists
http://www.chemie.fu-berlin.de/
    outerspace/www-german..html

Germany – government information research
    and technology
http://www.dFin.de/bmbf/

Global Internet News Agency
www.gina.com

Global Trade Center
http://wwwtradezone.com/tz/

Hitchhiker's Guide to the Internet
ftp://nic.merit.edu/documents/rfc/
    rfc1118.txt

Homeworker
http://www.hmeworker.co.uk

Inc. Online
http://www.inc.com

Industry Net
http://www.industry.net/

Information Market Europe – European Com-
    mission
http://www.echo.lu/

Information Technology Laboratory
http://wwwubilab.ubs.ch/

Insight Information
http://avidinfo.com/

Institute of Management and Administration
    Information Services for Professionals
http://starbase.ingress.com/ioma/

International Chamber of Commerce,
    Paris
http://www1.usa1.com/~ibnet/
    icchp.html

Internet Address Finder
www.iaf.net

International Internet Marketing
www.clark.net/pub/granered/iim.html

ISO Online
http://www.iso.ch

Israel Web Servers
http://www.ac.il/

Israel Government Information
http://www.israel.org/

ITAR/TASS
http://www.itar-tass.com/

Japan Web Servers
http://www.ntt.jp/SQUARE/
www-in-JP.html

Japan: What's New in Japan
http://www.ntt.jp/WHATSNEW/

Japan Information Network
http://jin.jcic.or.jp/navi/category_1.html

JETRO (The Japanese External Trade
Organization)
http://www.jetro.go.jp/index.html

Metalforming Online Buyers' Guides
http://www.industry.net/metalforming

Mexico general lists
http://lanic.utexas.edu/la/Mexico/

Mexico government information
(communications)
http://ags.inegi.gob.mx/

Mexico: Internet growth
http://csgwww.uwaterloo.ca/~dmg/
mexico/internet/mexico.html

MexPlaza English language Internet page for
Mexico
http://mexplaza.udg.mx:80/ingles/

Moneyworld UK
http://www.moneyworld.co.uk

Moscow Libertarium
http://www.fe.msk.ru/libertarium/
ehomepage.html

NAFTANET – North American Free Trade
Agreement
http://www.nafta.net/

National Readership Surveys
http://www.nrs.co.uk

The New York Times
http://www.nytimes.com/

News from Russia
http://www.novosti.com/

Open University
http://www.open.ac.uk

Thomas Ho's Favourite Electronic Commerce
WWW Resources
http://www.engr.iupui.edu/~ho/
interests/commmenu.html

The Press Association
http://www.pa.press.net

Pointcast Network
http://www.pointcast.com

Politics & Economics WWW Virtual Library

http://www.w3org/hypertext/Data-
Sources/bySubject/politics/
Overview.html

Regional Information Guides by Price
Waterhouse
http://www.i-trade.com/infsrc/pw

Russia Alive!
http://wwwalincom.com/russ/politics.html

Russia Net Politics Page
http://www.russia.net/politic/pol_main.html

Russian Interfax
http://www.interfax-news.com/

Russian Media
http://www.hibo.no/stud/sh4/media.html

Singapore Web Servers
http://www.w3.org/hypertext/
DataSources/WWW/sg.html

SilverPlatter World: a worldwide library of
electronic information
http://www.silverplatter.com/

Singapore Info Web
http://www.technet.sg/InfoWEB/
welcome.html

South Africa Servers
http://www.is.co.za/www-za/

South African Government Information
http://www.polity.org.za/gnu.html

The Daily Telegraph
http://www.telegraph.co.uk

The Economist
http://www.economist.com

The European Business Directory
http://www.europages.com/g/
home.html

Time WarnerHome Page includes Time,
People, and Life plus news
http://www.pathfinder.com/

The Times
http://www.the-times.co.uk

Trade Compass
http://www.tradecompass.com

Trade Statistics
http://www.census.gov/ftp/pub/
foreign-trade/www/

UK Based Servers
http://src.doc.ic.ac.uk/all-uk.html

UNCTAD (UN Conference on Trade and
Development)
http://www.unicc.org/unctad/en/enhome.htm

United Nations
http:///wwww.undp.org

US Dept. of Commerce
http://www.doc.gov/
  CommerceHomePage.html

US Fedworld
www.fedworld.gov

US National Trade Data Bank
http://www.stat-
  usa.gov/BEN/Services/ntdbhome.html

USA–Economic Bulletin Board
gopher://una.hh.lib.umich.edu/11/ebb

UT-LANIC–University of Texas Latin
  American Network Information Center
http://lanic.utexas.edu/la/region.html

UT MENIC – University of Texas Middle East
  Studies
http://menic.utexas.edu/mes.html

Wall Street Net
http://www.netresource.com/wsn/

Web Page for Global Business
http://www.seattleu.edu/~parker/
  homepage.html

Web Sites for International Information:
http://www.ustr.gov/
http://www.i-trade.com/
http://www.stat-
  usa.gov/BEN/subject/trade.html
http://www.itaiep.doc.gov/

World Bank
http://www.worldbank.org/

World Wide Web Virtual Library
http://W3.org

WTO (World Trade Organization): Agreement
  Establishing the WTO:
http://www.soton.ac.uk/~nukop/data/
  fullrecs/1660.htm

WTO
http://www.unicc.org//wto/Welcome.html

WWW Yellow Pages
www.cba.uh.edu/ylowpges/
  ylowpges.html.

Yahoo Reuters
http://www.yahoo.co.uk/News

Yellow Pages UK
http://www.yell.co.uk

CHAPTER 3

Exporting – not just for the small business

Why export?

This is analogous to the question 'Why go abroad?' which was dealt with in the first chapter. An important factor relating to exporting is the low cost and low risk involved relative to any other form of market entry, the reason therefore why we have separated exporting from the other forms of market entry mode. Exporting, as we have seen, is different from international marketing in the resource employed as well as the time horizon for investment payback upon entry. Sales are the objective of exporting, while an international marketing approach involves the planned deployment of resources so as to build an effective market position within a three- to five-year period. The approaches are therefore quite different. Against a willingness to adapt product or service offering for long-term sales growth is an eagerness instead to maximize short-term sales with a standardized offering. International marketing differs considerably from export selling.

Exporting is an activity open to companies of all sizes. It is the least cost method and so is used often to test for a market response. Although the focus here is on the small business, the intention is not to exclude any other type of exporter.

Exporting by the risk averse

Perceptions of risk do influence market entry mode selection. The political, social, cultural and economic factors which influence risk have been discussed in the last chapter. However, we have also to be aware that in the long run, everything can change. This present generation has witnessed some momentous political change with the falling of the Berlin Wall, which symbolized the collapse of the Soviet Empire, and the ending of apartheid in South Africa. Both these political events have created new trading opportunities, because both have been in a political vacuum and subject to ostracization by the West.

New conditions have been created and nations and exporters respond accordingly, as we might expect. Exporting features prominently in such conditions because it is the least risky form of doing business overseas. Before long, however, competition will force successful exporters to consider new and more lasting long-term forms of market entry and representation. It is similar in many ways to the Wheel of Retailing, where low cost entrants soon find they have to offer more in terms of product and/or service, which adds to their value added but also adds to their cost structure and so makes them more vulnerable to competitive attack as time goes on. The low cost competitor is forever being seen to enter the market; it is the organizational response of existing competitors which determines survival. In the next chapter, we discuss other forms of market entry which do involve investment and longer projected payback periods than exporting.

First, though, we need to define what we mean by a small business.

Exhibit 3.1   US business data worst in world – and getting worse

Why is it our data on small business are so bad that we can't get a handle on straightforward questions like how many jobs small business produces?' laments Timothy Bates, a professor at Wayne State University, in Detroit. As it turns out, there is no easy answer.

Such numbers are simply hard to find. And the ones that are out there aren't particularly reliable. Bates tells the story of a fellow researcher who undertook a study using both Census Bureau data and Bureau of Labor Statistics (BLS) numbers. The researcher found that the two data sets

→

➤ Exhibit 3.1 *continued*

disagreed by 20 per cent on the number of self-employed people in the United States. 'We're talking about the two major statistics-gathering organizations,' grumbles Bates.

The situation is worsened, Bates continues, by dickering with classification criteria. Woman-owned businesses, for example, lose that designation when they grow big enough to register as C corporations, thus making the average woman-owned company look artificially small. The same is true for black-owned businesses.

Think that's absurd? It gets worse. A 1988 study showed that government data missed nearly all manufacturing companies with fewer than five employees. Meanwhile, the government required that all individuals who claimed a piddling $50 or more in self-employment revenues on Schedule C of their tax form be counted as 'small businesses.' The mind boggles.

What exactly is the problem? For one thing, there's little official support for a standardized national database that tracks such basics as company births, growth, and deaths. The Small Business Administration, which developed such a database in 1979, pulled the plug on it in 1991. 'Since it was discontinued,' says Bruce Kirchhoff of the New Jersey Institute of Technology, 'there hasn't been much information around.' 'What's worse,' reports Kirchhoff, 'is that apparently no one bothered to save the old database. A year expired, and the machine erased it. Just like that, the nation's primary source of small-business information vanished forever'.

The federal government has shown no eager-

ness to develop or promote alternative sources. Catherine Armington, formerly a consultant with the BLS, cites a prototype database built by the BLS that was based on annual reporting of unemployment-insurance tax payments for US businesses from 1989 to 1994. 'It's by far the best data on employment,' claims Armington. Yet when a government researcher prepared an article based on it last year, she says, the bureau – unwilling to defend the 'experimental' data publicly – 'squashed it' and has no plans to make any further use of the data.

All of that probably doesn't alarm many business owners, but it should. 'Research has effects,' says Bruce Phillips, data czar at the SBA's Office of Advocacy. 'It filters its way down into public policy.' He points out that many of the policy innovations that cleared the way for the recent entrepreneurial explosion – such as small-business-friendly clauses in the 1986 tax reform – came as the result of SBA-funded studies during the 1980s, when the agency's research budget was almost 10 times what it is now.

Unfortunately, data that might help further an innovative agenda may grow even scarcer. Congress withheld funding for SBA research for much of this year and toyed with the idea of wiping out the SBA's Office of Economic Research entirely. Ultimately, the research office may be killed for the same reason the SBA database was: because its custodians, according to Kirchhoff, 'couldn't find any small-business owners or politicians who thought there was any value in it.'

Source: Inc., October 1996, p. 26

Exhibit 3.2   Psychic distance too great!

Poland tried to export this very successful fudge to India hoping another developing country may prove sympathetic to her exports. Needless to say, the design was not checked out for India. It had been in use since the turn of the century and so was accepted as a given fact.

Defining the small business

Defining a small business is a difficult task and defining what is meant by a small business across various countries is even more difficult. In the manufacturing sector a small firm has been defined as one employing 200 or fewer people. To arrive at a more general definition, we will have to look elsewhere to pinpoint the essential characteristics which may have bearing on the firm's ability to export. For example, owner-management and the fact that 'the people who run it are those that bear the risks of the enterprise' is another characteristic; but it is not necessarily limited to small business either as this is to be found among Ford Motor Co., J. Sainsbury, Getty Oil, and others, which continue to be wholly-owned and controlled by the families who manage them. The importance of the small firm then has to be assessed in the light of other

Exhibit 3.3   Outline for an export plan

Table of contents

Executive summary (one or two pages maximum)

Introduction: Why a company should export

Part I – An export policy commitment statement

Part II – The situation/background analysis

- product
- operations
- personnel and export organization
- resources of the firm
- industry structure, competition and demand

Part III – The marketing component

- identification, evaluation and selection of target markets
- product selection and pricing
- distribution method
- terms and conditions
- internal organization and procedures
- sales goals: profit (loss) forecasts

Part IV – Tactics: action steps

- countries where firm has special advantages (e.g., family ties)
- primary target countries
- secondary target countries
- indirect marketing efforts

Part V – An export budget

- pro forma financial statements

Part VI – An implementation schedule

- followup
- periodic operational/management review (measuring results against plan)

Addenda – background data on target countries and market

- basic market statistics: historical and projected
- background facts
- competitive environment

Source: US Department of Commerce (1990)
A Basic Guide to Exporting, NTC Business Books, Lincoln-wood, Illinois, p. 4

criteria which assess its absolute and relative size in the marketplace. So, we offer the following identifying characteristics of the small firm:

- It has only a small share of its market.
- It is managed in a personalized way by its owners or part-owners and does not have an elaborate management structure.
- It is not sufficiently large to have access to the capital market for the public issue or placing of securities.

Once the firm has outgrown any of these three thresholds it ceases to be a small firm. Therefore to qualify as a small firm, the firm will have to simultaneously qualify under all three criteria. Naturally, it depends on the country; for New Zealand, the thresholds for small and medium sized would be lower than they are in the UK, as the concept of firm size is relative to the national market.

British exporting is now dominated by large firms. In the UK, 20 per cent of the visible exports derive from the activities of a mere ten

Exhibit 3.4   The firm founded on exports

The software allows major communication companies to compete more effectively with cable companies and Internet access providers by making better use of their networks through increasing the volume and speed of transmissions. In the USA, Bell Atlantic is using an Atlantech system to offer fast Internet access and video on demand to subscribers.

David Sibbald, chairman and managing director, says: 'In telecommunications, boundaries between domestic and foreign markets don't apply. We took a global perspective from Day One.

'All our initial customers were American and it was three years before we had our first British customer.'

In those three years the company's annual turnover has risen to £6.2 m, a factor which helped Atlantech win this year's Trailblazer of the Year award. Exports' share of business is 70 per cent and covers customers from South America to Australia.

The directors and senior staff have widespread experience of working abroad, and Sibbald himself has had long spells in America and south east Asia. 'It is only by living in the US that you have a sense of the size of the marketplace,' he says.

'In comparison, the European Union is a myriad of different standards and practices. The US market takes notice of what you have to offer, irrespective of the size of your company.

→ Exhibit 3.4 *continued*

'You've got to understand how to get into the market and align yourself closely with your strategic partners to reduce the risk of failure. Finding the right size of partner is the hardest part.

'We are now working with four partners on both project-related and product-related work and we can offer a combined package to the market.'

Even during the three years when the AccessVision software was being written and they were also acting as consultants, the directors made the time to learn more about the market to adapt and fine-tune their product.

As well as aiming to be the world's first producer of a software management system for the sophisticated demands of a telecommunications network, Atlantech also had to ensure it could satisfy the stringent service assurance standards. Typical orders vary in size from $250,000 to $1m and each project takes a year on average. Generically-produced systems account for 70 per cent of orders with the rest tailored to customers' requirements.

The scale of operations has led to the opening of a wholly-owned American subsidiary in Boston with a staff of four. The Cumbernauld office employs 50. 'It gives us a critical mass in the US market,' says Sibbald. 'It supports our partnership relationships and provides the 24-hour presence which we need. Building relationships in this market can take twice as long compared to the UK and likewise funding requirements might be double.'

Communications links are given top priority. 'As well as a very high investment in IT systems, we have high-speed Internet links and access to a shared database which covers product specifications,' Sibbald adds. 'I make regular monthly visits to the States.'

The Scottish contribution to operations is the professional skill of the development engineers and marketing team. 'They are the best in the world,' says Sibbald. 'If only there were more . . . as it would speed up our growth.'

Source: The Herald, 12 September 1996

Table 3.1   US top 100 high tech exporters

Rank	Company	Revenue $mn.	Top exec.	Product	Employees
1	The West Co. Inc. Lionville, PA 19341	410.9	William G. Little	Noningestible pharmaceuticals	5,210
2	Mine Safety Appliance Co, Pittsburgh. PA 15230	424	Tom Hotopp	Safety products	5,000
3	Therm-O-Disc Inc., Muskegon MI	300	James A. Knight	Temperature sensors	5,000
4	Bourns Inc, Riverside CA 92507	250	Gordon Bourns	Electronic components	4,500
4	Chloride Power Electronics, Caledonia NY 14423	260	Richard King	Uninterruptible power systems	4,500
6	The Cherry Corp., Waukegan IL 60087	339	Peter B. Cherry	Subassemblies & components	4,400
7	Imo Industries Inc., Lawrenceville NJ 08648	463.8	Donald Farrar	Subassemblies & components	4,000
8	Esco Electronics Corp., St.Louis MO 63124	441	Dennis J. Moore	Subassemblies & components	3,700
9	General Binding Corp., Northbrook IL 60062	420.4	Govi C. Reddy	Computer hardware	3,500
9	Qualcomm Inc., San Diego CA 92121	386.6	Dr Irwin M. Jacobs	Telecommunications (digital wireless)	3,500

Rank	Company	Revenue $mn.	Top exec.	Product	Employees
9	Rowan Companies Inc., Houston TX 77056	438.1	C. R. Palmer	Off-road heavy equipment	3,500
12	Woodward Governor Co., Rockford IL 61125	379.7	John A. Halbrook	Factory automation	3,439
13	Logica North America Inc., Lexington MA 02173	350	William Engel	Computer software	3,400
14	Cordis Corp., Hialeah FL 33014	443.1	Robert C. Strauss	Medical products	3,370
15	Aptor Group Inc., Crystal Lake IL 60014	474	Ervin J. Lecoque	Factory automation	3,300
15	General Instrument Corp., Melville NY 11747	315	Rick Friedland	Rectifiers and transient voltage suppressors	3,300
17	BW/IP International Inc., Long Beach CA 90802	448.7	Bernard G. Rethore	Seals and pumps	3,000
17	The Carborundum Co., Niagara Falls NY 14302.	250–500	Luiz F. Kahl	Advanced materials	3,000
17	Eaton Corp., Hydraulics Division Eden Prairie MN 55344	360	James Earnshaw	Hydraulic valves, pumps	3,000
17	Idex Corp., Northbrook IL 60062	399.5	Donald N. Boyce	Subassemblies and components	3,000
17	International Rectifier Corp., El Segundo CA 90245	320	Eric Lido	Subassemblies and components	3,000
17	Marquette Electronics Inc., Milwuakee WI 53223	342	Michael J. Cudahy	Medical products (diagnostic & monitoring)	3,000
23	Jackson Lea, Conover NC 28613	356.6	William H. Talbert	Advanced materials	2,953
24	Helmerich & Payne Inc., Tulsa OK 74114	329	Hans Helmerich	Energy (oil and natural gas drilling)	2,700
24	Measurex Corp., Cupertino CA 95014	335	David A. Bossen	Computer hardware (sensor based systems)	2,700
26	Dynatech Corp., Burlington MA 01803	488.7	John F. Reno	Telecommunications (support products & service)	2,630
27	Biomet Inc., Warsaw, IN 46581	454	Dane A. Miller	Medical products (trauma devices, electrical bone growth stimulators)	2,600
27	Harnischfeger Corp./P&H Mining Equipment Division, Milwaukee WI 53201	480	Bob Hale	Energy (shovels, excavators, mining equipment)	2,600
27	Hoechst Celanese Corp., Dallas TX 75234	250–500	Thomas F. Kennedy	Chemicals (acetic acids, formaldehyde, methanol and other petrochemicals)	2,600
27	Moog Inc., East Aurora NY 14052	374.2	Robert T. Brady	Transportation (propulsion, missile and motion controls)	2,600

Rank	Company	Revenue $mn.	Top exec.	Product	Employees
31	Advanced Technology Laboratories, Bothell, WA 98041	366	Dennis Fill	Medical products (diagnostic ultrasound medical systems)	2,500
31	J. Ray McDermott & Co. Inc., Morgan City LA 70381	250–500	Mike H. Lam	Energy (marine pipeline and platform installation services for oil industry)	2,500–4,999
33	Varlen Corp., Naperville IL 60566	342	Richard L. Wellek	Locomotive and laboratory equipment	2,500
34	DeKalb Genetics Corp., DeKalb IL 60115	320	Richard Ryan	Biotechnology (seed hybrids and hybrid swine breeding stock)	2,400
34	Fluke Corp., Everett WA 98206	382.6	William Parzybok	Electronic test equipment	2,400
34	Neles–Jamesbury Inc., Worcester MA 01615	290	Thomas Sturiale	Subassemblies and components (control valves)	2,400
34	Perot Systems Corp., Dallas TX 75251	470	Mort Meyerson	Computer hardware (systems integration & support)	2,400
38	Brown & Sharpe Manufacturing Co. Kingstown RI 02852	321	Frank T. Curtin	Factory automation	2,392
39	The Duriron Co. Inc., Dayton OH 45401	345.3	William M. Jordan	Subassemblies and components	2,350
40	Bio-Rad Laboratories Inc., Hercules CA 94547	355.2	David Schwartz	Biotech research products (analytical instruments)	2,300
41	St. Jude Medical Inc., St. Paul, MN 55117	359.6	Ronald A. Matricaria	Medical devices (cardiovascular)	2,250
42	Symbol Technologies Inc., Bohemia NY 11716	465.3	Jerome Swartz	Computer hardware	2,192
43	Aqualon, Wilmington DE 19899	250–500	Frazer Reid	Chemicals (advanced material additives, modifiers, water soluble polymers and cellulose ether)	2,186
44	J. D. Edwards & Co., Denver CO 80237	340.8	Ed McVaney	Computer software	2,150
45	VeriFone Inc., Redwood City CA 94065	309.1	Hatim Tyabji	Computer hardware	2,100
46	Graco Inc., Minneapolis MN 55440	360	George Aristides	Test and measurement (systems to move and measure fluid materials)	2,075
48	Mentor Graphics Corp., Wilsonville OR 97070	348	Walden C. Rhines	Computer software	2,050
49	Jarvis B. Webb Co., Farmington Hills MI 48331	330	George H. Webb	Factory automation (materials handling systems)	2,000
49	Watkins–Johnson Co. Palo Alto CA 94304	387	W. Keith Kennedy Jr.	Defence industry (advanced electronic products, semiconductor equipment)	2,000

Rank	Company	Revenue $mn.	Top exec.	Product	Employees
51	Adaptec Inc., Milpitas CA 95035	466	Grant Saviers	Computer hardware	1,900
52	AAR Corp., Elk Grove Village IL 60007	451	Ira A. Eichner	Transportation (aviation and aerospace)	1,940
53	Logitech Inc., Fremont CA 94555	370	Pierluigi Zappacosta	Computer hardware	1,900
54	Brush Wellman Inc., San Rafael CA 94903	369.6	Gordon D. Harnett	Engineered materials including ceramics and metals	1,856
55	Autodesk Inc., San Rafael CA 94903	454.6	Carol Bartz	Computer software	1,800
55	California Microwave Inc., Sunnyvale CA 94086	468	Philip Otto	Telecommunications (satellite systems)	1,800
55	Systems Software Associates Inc., Chicago IL 60661	334	Roger E. Covey	Computer software	1,800
55	Telrad Telecommunications Inc., Woodbury NY 11797	320	Amon Toussia-Cohen	Telecommunications (digital keybox equipment)	1,800
59	Linear Technology Corp., Milpitas CA 95035	328	Robert H. Swanson	Subassemblies and components (amplifiers, converters, filters)	1,700
60	Morse TEC Corp., Ithaca NY 14850	257.6	Ronald M. Ruzic	Subassemblies and components (timing chains for fourwheel transmissions)	1,691
61	Silicon Valley Group Inc., San Jose CA 95131	319	Papken Der-Torossian	Manufacturing equipment (automated water processing equipment)	1,663
62	Coherent Inc., Santa Clara CA 95054	285.4	Bernard Couillaud	Photonics (lasers)	1,594
63	Acuson Corp., Mountain View CA 94039	350.4	Samuel H. Maslak	Medical (ultrasound diagnostic systems)	1,500
63	Cincinnati Milacron Inc./ Plastics Machinery Group, Batavia OH 45103	250–500	Harold Faig	Factory automation (plastic blow moulding)	1,500
63	Genicom Corp., Chantilly VA 22021	294	Paul T. Winn	Computer hardware	1,500
63	Houghton International Inc., Valley Forge PA 19482	253	William F. Macdonald Jr.	Petroleum and organic chemicals	1,500
63	Norton-Performance Plastics Corp., Wayne NJ 07470	270	Louis F. Laucirica	Advanced materials (high performance plastics)	1,500
63	SpaceLabs Medical Inc., Redmond WA 98073	252	Carl A. Lombardi	Clinical information systems and patient monitoring equipment	1,500

Rank	Company	Revenue $mn.	Top exec.	Product	Employees
63	Synopsys Inc., Mountain View CA 94043	265	Aart J. de Geus	Computer software	1,500
63	Trans-Resources Inc., New York NY 10019	385	Arie Genger	Fertilizers, herbicides, pesticides	1,500
71	Commscope General Instrument, Hickory NC 28603	250–500	Frank M. Drendel	Subassemblies and components (fibre optic distribution equipment)	1,400
71	Gerber Scientific Inc., South Windsor CT 06074	322.7	H. Joseph Gerber	Manufacturing equipment (robotics)	1,400
73	Life Technologies Inc., Gaithersburg MD 20884	272.2	Stark Thompson	Biotechnology (products for biomedical manufacturing and the study of disease)	1,354
74	Amcol International Arlington Heights IL 60004	347.7	John Hughes	Advanced materials	1,328
75	BMC Software Inc., Houston TX 77042	400	Max P. Watson Jr	Computer software (software for automating applications)	1,300
75	SunSoft Inc., Mountain View CA 94043	25–500	Janpieter Scheerder	Computer software (utility systems software)	1,300
75	Tencor Instruments Mountain View CA 94043	330.2	Jan Tompkins	Factory automation (semiconductor wafer inspection systems and film thickness measurement instruments)	1,300
75	UB Networks, Santa Clara CA 95054	365	Roel Pieper	Baseband-based and broadband-based LANs	1,300
79	Calgon Carbon Corp., Pittsburgh, PA 15230	274	Colin Bailey	Environmental (chemical purification equipment)	1,267
80	Ametek Inc./Lamb Electric Division, Kent OH 44240	250–500	George Marsinek	Subassemblies and components (vacuum and fractional horsepower motors)	1,200
80	Cargill Fertilizers Inc., Riverview FL 33569	330	Ray Larson	Phosphorus compounds used in production of fertilizers	1,200
80	Comsat RSI Inc., Dulles VA 20166	250	Richard E. Thomas	Telecommunications (satellite; microwave; air traffic control and earth stations)	1,200
80	Forest Laboratories Inc., New York NY 10022	404.8	Howard Solomon	Pharmaceuticals (cardiac drugs and cerebral function stimulants)	1,200
80	Nooter Corp., St. Louis, MO 63166	330	G. Bouckaert	Subassemblies and components (pressure vessels for the chemical and petroleum industries)	1,200
85	QMS Inc., Mobile AL 36618	292.6	James L. Gusby	Computer hardware (laser printers)	1,194

Rank	Company	Revenue $mn.	Top exec.	Product	Employees
86	Network equipment Technologies Inc., Redwood City CA 94063	280	Joseph Francesconi	Telecommunications (integrated digital exchange transmission equipment, network design systems)	1,150
87	Haemonetics Corp., Braintree MA 02184	262.4	John F. White	Medical (automated plasma collection systems and blood component therapy)	1,109
88	Huck International Inc., San Jose, CA 95161	250–500	Bruce Zorrich	Transportation (speciality fastening systems)	1,100
89	KLA Instruments Corp., San Jose CA 95161	442.4	Kenneth Levy	Factory automation (process control systems for semiconductor industry)	1,000
89	Panduit Corp., Tinley Park IL 60477	250–500	J. E. Caveney	Factory automation (electrical wiring components, fibre cables for telecommunications industry)	1,000–2,499
89	Pettibone Corp., Lisle IL 60532400	400	Larry Giles	Factory automation (sewer cleaning machinery, automated materials, handling systems)	1,000
92	Stratacom Inc., San Jose CA 95126	331.7	Richard M. Moley	Telecommunications (fast packet ATM switching systems)	988
93	PictureTel Corp., Danvers MA 01923	255.1	Norman E. Gaut	Telecommunications (PC video-conferencing systems, software)	950
94	Standard Microsystems Corp., Happauge NY 11788	379	Paul Richman	Telecommunications (computer integrated circuits and network management software)	800
95	Applied Industrial Materials Corp.,	250–500	Wayne Kocourek	Advanced materials (metals, minerals and alloys)	500
96	Tranter Inc., Augusta GA 30907	250–500	Kenneth L. Kaltz	Energy (heat exchangers, transformer radiators)	500
97	CIC International Inc., Astoria NY 11105	393.2	Michael Kane	Defence (engineering and installation services)	254
98	Mack Technologies Inc., Westford MA 01886	300	Ronald Ziffer	Computer hardware (design engineering services)	220
99	Astec Custom Power Inc., Carlsbad CA 92009	250–500	Richard Dubois	Subassemblies and components (switching power supplies)	100
100	53 Inc., Santa Clara CA 95051	316.3	Terry N. Holdt	Computer peripherals	79

Note: This listing comprises companies with up to $500 million in annual revenue, of which 25 per cent is garnered from international sales, and ranked by number of employees. Operating units or divisions of larger corporations or holding companies were excluded from the list in a bid to better reflect the small and midsized segment of US business in general and high tech industries in particular.

Source: *World Trade* (1997), 'World Trade 100: Our Ranking of America's High Tech Export Leaders', September, pp. 22–30

firms. Although small firms account for 20 per cent of the GNP, an examination of six key industries showed that small firms accounted for 5 per cent of the exports of these industries.

Martin Rumbelow, Secretary of the British Overseas Trade Board (BOTB), captured the essential difficulty of persuading small companies to think big when he was quoted as saying: 'the encouragement of small businesses to export is always an uphill battle, one that you can never win, but one that you must always fight so as not to lose' (*Financial Times*, 24 October 1985).

In Japan, the small company sector provides about 60 per cent of direct exports. In the UK, the figure is 8 per cent. The presence of the Japanese trading house makes it possible for small and medium-sized Japanese companies to regard their export markets as being just as accessible as their home markets, whereas some of their UK counterparts are unable to penetrate international markets at all. Japan may now be on the threshold of a new era in its relations with Europe, based on on-the-spot manufacturing and assembly, rather than direct exports, and on large-scale involvement in the economy of Europe rather than arms-length trading relations. More importantly there is the direct investment in the manufacture of cars by Nissan and domestic electrical equipment by Sony, Hitachi, and Toshiba. The UK accounts for the majority of Japanese investment within the EU.

For small business in the UK, the main outlet appears to be Europe. The EU take 45 per cent while other European countries take a further 20 per cent.

The main characteristics of the exporting activities of small firms include:

1. Export market research used by minority – the norm is for overseas orders to arise by chance and to be met, but that market is not then pursued further. Unexpected export orders do not generally give rise to market research.
2. Fairly low expenditure commitment in terms of total market research budgets and specifically export market research.
3. Prime selling techniques are personal visits, use of fairs and exhibitions, and employment of agents.
4. General ignorance of government support – little use made of BOTB services, with even less use made of management consultants, chambers of commerce and embassies overseas.
5. Limited resources lead to use of export houses and selling via UK buying offices of overseas department stores.

Exhibit 3.5   Fyne tuning overseas markets

On his first Hong Kong trade mission a decade ago John Noble, chairman of Loch Fyne Oysters, was told by an embassy official that there was no chance of winning orders for his smoked salmon produce. Now Hong Kong is the company's largest export market.

Success has followed in other Far Eastern markets: Singapore, Japan, Taiwan, Thailand and now China and Russia. Other distant markets are Argentina, South Africa and the USA with, nearer to home, many European countries. This was recognised in 1994 with the Queens Award for Export Achievement.

'Scotland is a very popular country abroad,' Noble says. 'In a niche market like ours, customers want the best. We sell to quality outlets, which are intelligent enough not to be bamboozled by the fraudulent claims of some producers.

'It is important that authentic indigenous food gets proper protection. We encourage customers to visit Loch Fyne to see what they are buying.'

Noble's own preference is for an Appellation Controlee style of system to cut out fraudsters who sell on the back of Scottish producers' reputation for top quality. Offenders are not restricted to foreign firms: a Cumbrian company has just been convicted for the 11th time on this type of charge. Loch Fyne Oysters is a founder member of the Scottish Salmon Smokers Association.

Salmon products account for 90 per cent of Loch Fyne Oysters' export sales, which are worth half of its turnover. This year its total output of smoked salmon is expected to be around 300 tonnes, earning at least £4 m. The company exports to 14 countries from its base at Cairndow in Argyll.

Andrew Lane, its managing director, points to the advantages of exports over home sales. Because the company deals only with one distributor in each market, compared to 400 UK trade customers, the size of orders means greater economies.

'Although margins are competitive, overseas consumers will pay a better price for a product where the quality and service is guaranteed,' he says. 'In comparison, Britain has a small independent retail sector and quality restaurant base.'

→

➡ **Exhibit 3.5** *continued*

Regular communication with customers, efficient delivery, patience and judgement are qualities which Lane lists as essential to export success. 'We judge each market on its merits and assess new ones for future promise,' says Lane.

'You develop an export culture, so that it becomes as easy to deal with a customer abroad as at home. You have to be sensitive to market fluctuations, organise promotions at the right time and get your pricing right.'

The Taiwanese market for smoked salmon was built up by the Norwegians, but the growing affluence and international hotel development on the island has created a demand at the top end of the market. In other countries the rewards from years of groundwork are now arising: four years'

presence in South Africa, four in Argentina and also in the USA.

Developments in European countries also favour Loch Fyne Oysters. The trend, notably in Italy and France, for groups of wholesalers to act in partnership has led to reduced distribution costs and quicker payment.

Lane gives credit to the expertise of the sales department for handling the complex export documentation and Arbuckle Smith, its shipping company.

Loch Fyne Oysters has also benefited from the Scottish Export Assistance Scheme (SEAS), which reimburses half of the cost of implementing an export marketing plan. In return, Scottish Enterprise receives a 5 per cent royalty on future sales in the target market up to twice the level of grant.

Problems for small exporters

Specific problem areas for small exporters include:

- A relatively large domestic market and lack of exposure to other cultures, making the selection of markets and identification of customers abroad difficult.
- The lack of management time and general resources.
- Reaching the foreign markets; selecting and motivating 'arm's length' commission agents. Finding the good agents and distributors and being able to keep them motivated.
- Controlling the foreign operation, channel policy, and physical distribution. The interest of principal and agent may often differ and small businesses because of their size may be more exposed to the varying degrees of political, economic and financial risk made uncertain by the indifferent attitude of a foreign agent.
- Paperwork and management of export operations.
- Cost of flying supervisory salesmen is often very high when costed per man year of effort in the field, even more so when costed separately on a per visit basis.
- Which language is the sales staff to learn if visiting many territories?
- Cost of overseas offices may not be justified by the sales potential of particular territorial makets. Going it alone retains independence of action but may be financially ruinous having the same effect as 'placing all your eggs in one basket.'

- Different safety and quality standards overseas may involve a small company in expensive modifications to achieve compatibility. This adds to the 'up-front' costs before a single product may be sold.
- A long-term perspective has to be taken of many markets which may require a long company presence before achieving any payback. This is particularly true where the product concept is new, existing distribution channels are unreliable and the manufacturer wants to assure himself that the customer receives quality and service. In these cases, vertically integrated distribution networks are the answer.

The magnitude of these problems was investigated in the USA (Rabino, 1980) by asking respondents to rank order by relative importance, and this produced the following 'rank order' or 'league table' of difficulty:

1. *Paperwork.*
2. *Selecting a reliable distributor.* Lists available from embassies and trade councils do not offer a qualitative assessment, which is what may be required. Increasingly the British clearing banks are offering their services in this area previously dominated by the merchant banks.
3. Comparative disadvantages due to *non-tariff barriers*, e.g., health and safety standards used to exclude imports. Small companies do not always have the resources to modify products and fight back.
4. *Honouring letters of credit*, although not where this has been endorsed by the local

bank thus creating an irrevocable confirmed letter of credit (LC) where the funds are guaranteed by a bank in the seller's country. LCs are still the most common form of payment.

5. *Communication with foreign customers.* Not only language is involved here but distance which may be both psychological as well as geographical. It may be comforting to visit a country where you feel people think,

act and feel as you do, the reverse is also true.

As regards Europe, Kaleka and Katsikeas (1989) reported differences in perceptions dependent upon the stage of export development. The most important export problems were associated with the intensity of competition in export markets and the lack of effective national export policies. Their study was

Exhibit 3.6   Painting Red Square Grant tartan

First it was Robert Burns' poetry, now the Russians have taken another time-honoured Scottish institution to their hearts: shortbread. Amid the grey bleakness of a Moscow winter, Walkers, the world's most favoured purveyor of shortbread, is opening a shop in the heart of the capital later this month resplendent in red Grant tartan and with a piper to add that extra touch of authenticity.

It may be an image Scots blanche at back home, but the Speyside company, which accounts for 60 per cent of world shortbread output, knows what sells abroad.

The Walkers store, owned by its local distributor, will be displaying 80 of its best-selling products and is expecting a healthy response. Sales and export manager Iain Armour said Russians have taken to shortbread with enthusiasm, the buttery biscuits reminiscent of good Russian home baking.

In general it is seen as another tangible link with Scots, whom they admire for their love of spirits, Burns . . . and their sweet tooth.

However, Walkers' start in Russia happened by sheer chance when a husband and wife team of entrepreneurs sat munching shortbread in an airport lounge waiting to fly back to Moscow.

Instead of importing and exporting car parts, which was gruelling and offered little reward because of over-supply, they decided to start dealing in shortbread.

Now Walkers' produce can be found all over the city in top class supermarkets and in department stores. Muscovites do not seem to be price sensitive. Boxes of shortbread cost 20 per cent more than in Britain, but this appears only to enhance their appeal.

Russians do not celebrate Christmas for religious reasons, but Armour says people are finding present giving more acceptable as time goes on and Western culture catches on.

It is a welcome luxury for hard-pressed Muscovites who are denied their own renowned chocolate which is largely exported for hard currency.

Walkers is pleased with its new business, although it is taking things slowly. The company has been in the exporting game a long time and is currently represented in markets all over the world. Its next move after Russia is likely to be into the Ukraine.

Its efforts were recognised recently with a special award at the Export and Business Enterprise Awards sponsored by the Scottish Council Development and Industry, Scottish Trade International and British Airways.

However, even an experienced hand like Walkers acknowledges the need for eyes and ears on the ground before tackling a new market. Before it set foot in Moscow it contacted Scottish Trade International's Russian office to check out the distributors before they were taken on.

'Any foreign business should build up trust with Russian companies, but it is difficult for an outsider to assess whether it has a good partner or a bad partner at the outset.' said Yuri Andreev, Scottish Trade International's advisor in Moscow. 'Russia is not an easy market. There is great potential but you need a long-term presence.'

Walkers will build on its own presence by exhibiting at the upcoming Food Expo. However it has not yet visited Moscow, preferring to deal through its distributor, whose name is fiercely protected in case of competition.

But for those who go there to work, they should remember that Russia is undergoing enormous change and not for nothing does its crime rate figure more highly in the international press than its trade figures.

The Confederation of British Industry, although it is encouraging about exploiting a country of 150 million people, warns: 'Russia can be one

of the most profitable markets on earth but it is
often a chaotic even dangerous place to conduct
business.' Russia, it says, is still very much the wild
west and many international businessmen refuse
to go about their work without the security of
bodyguards and car escorts.

However, Andreev believes it is too easy to
get caught up in stereotypes. 'There is a perception in Scotland that Russia is full of mafiosi and

political problems but this perception is not always
right,' he said.

'Change is still going on – you would not
imagine otherwise after 70 years of central control
– but you can operate freely without major obstacles provided you take a pragmatic approach.'

Source: Scotland on Sunday, 1 December 1996,
p. 2

conducted in Cyprus, a small but export-
intensive economy.

Perceptions of non-exporting small firms

Very often perceptions are judgemental and
purely subjective and so not based on fact,
thus creating psychological barriers to exporting.
It is not necessary to have knowledge of a subject
to have opinions about it! There may be an expectation of profit maximization within a specific
period, and although this expectation may be
based on domestic market experience, international business does take longer to develop.

If a decision to sell or produce overseas is

based on 'hunch', rather than substantiated by
fact, e.g. independent market research, self-
imposed market limitation factors may come
into play.

Companies may consider an export effort to
be too much trouble, or they may believe that
they could not cope with the resources required
for overseas selling, assembly, manufacture,
construction, engineering, consulting or licensing, in which case, they are probably right for
without commitment, failure becomes ever
more certain.

The geographical scope of overseas operations may discourage some firms, yet freight
costs may not be the largest component in the
foreign export price, as can be seen in the degree

Exhibit 3.7   Nardini's sell ices to Russia

A Largs family business looks set to begin an 'ice-
cold war' offensive in Russia.

But espionage will give way to special ices
when Nardini's invade the country this month.

The famous local company expects that their
unique flavours will melt the hearts of even the
toughest Cossack customer.

The first Nardini's Russian ice cream parlour
will open in Rostov-on-Don in southern Russia in
August. Despite frequent chilly weather in the
area company boss Aldo Nardini is confident the
shop and business will prove to be a great success.

He said: 'When I visited Kiev in January there
were ice cream sellers on the street who had
turned off their fridges, but still couldn't scoop out
the ice cream because it was so cold!

'And yet despite the weather Russians were
queuing up to eat the stuff – which didn't taste anywhere near as good as our home-made flavours.'

Nardini's were invited to open their newest
parlour by Russian businessmen who visited Largs
in May.

Partnership
The visitors proposed a partnership after

sampling some of the family's 40 flavours of ice
cream.

Aldo, who had already been looking at the
possibility of setting up in the Ukraine, promptly
accepted.

The new parlour, to be named Nardini-Don,
will be run by a Russian family called the Litvinov's.
Nardini's Operational Manager, Alasdair Woods,
has flown out to Rostov to advise them on production of 14 of the renowned Nardini recipes.

Aldo himself will go over to train staff for the
parlour's opening, while one of the   Litvinov sons
will visit Largs for work experience.

'There's going to be a small production plant
and outdoor carts as well as the parlour itself,'
Aldo said.

'We'll also be shipping out some of our special Italian ingredients and decorations for the parlour.

'I have no doubt the venture will prove a success and I would expect that we'll be opening
other parlours in southern Russia soon.'

Source: Largs and Millport Weekly News, 6205,
Friday 9 August 1996

Table 3.2 Non-exporters' reasons for not exporting (n = 48); problems encountered by exporters (n = 108)

Reasons	Percentage	Problem	Percentage
Focus was on satisfying domestic demand	27	Matching competitors' prices	81
Product not marketable in foreign markets	25	Promoting product overseas	77
Lack of foreign market contacts	13	Establishing distribution network overseas	76
Lack of financing	10	Getting information about foreign markets	73
Perceived difficulty in gaining market entry (due to price disadvantage, quality problems, tariff and tax, quota restrictions and regulations	10	Necessity to grant credit facilities to foreign buyers	66
Operational problems (manpower, size of firm, production capacity and expertise)	10	Establishing contacts with foreign customers	65
Lack of knowledge and exposure of market opportunity and demand	8	Employing good export sales personnel	64
Exports handled by agents	8	Developing new products	57
		Getting repeat business from existing buyers	48
		Quality of product	37
		Design and packaging	37
		Understanding import/ export documentation	36

Source: Keng, K. A. and Jiuan, T. S. (1989), 'Differences between Small and Medium Sized Exporting and Non-Exporting Firms: Nature or Nurture', *International Marketing Review*, **6** (4), 27–40

to which the Pacific Basin countries have become a global workshop. Telephone, fax, e-mail, satellite television conferencing and air travel can further minimize distance as can the commonality of language.

Yet, there may be structural constraints emanating from company policy as devised by owner-managers or the board of directors. For example, there may be a policy limiting the company to certain types of trading relationships,

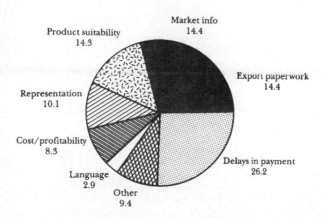

Figure 3.1 Greatest difficulties in exporting

	Low	**Commitment**	High
None	Non-exporter		Start-up exporter
Some	Passive-exporter		Active exporter

(Experience axis on left: None, Some)

Source: Cannon, T., and Willis, M. (1986) *How to Buy and Sell Overseas*, Business Books/Hutchinson, London

Figure 3.2   Export experience base

such as wholly owned subsidiaries. Or there may be financial self-imposed constraints, e.g., refusal to seek external debt or equity capital. Or there may be other corporate policies against trading with certain countries because of the political regime in power, or a system in force.

Identifying the exporter

Instead of simply using the terms 'passive' and 'active' as applied to exporting, Cannon and Willis (1986) see it in terms of a four-cell matrix, where the two axes are 'experience' and 'commitment'. The non-exporter is a fairly small group, too concerned with survival in the immediate local domestic market to get involved in exports, and too young to gain the interest of overseas buyers (see Figure 3.2).

The start-up exporter has no export experience but a commitment by top management to investigate export opportunities and invest some management time and effort.

The size of the cell containing passive exporters is by far the largest. For the UK, the Department of Trade report, *Into Active Exporting*, clearly described the economic significance of converting passive exporters into active exporters. If we take the upper limit scenario where the average ratio of all passive exporters could be raised to equal that of active exporters, then UK exports of manufacturers would increase by £5.2 billion at 1985 prices, an increase of 117 per cent equal to half of the total non-oil deficit on the 1985 current account.

In this particular study for the Department of Trade, active exporters were defined as exporting more than 15 per cent of their turnover in one of the past three years; non-exporters were the firms with export ratios of 1 per cent or less and passive exporters were the residual of these two categories.

Table 3.4   Management and exporting

1. Company size by itself is not an important factor unless linked to aspects such as financial strengths or variables related to economies of scale.
2. In companies where management is firmly committed to export, export performance tends to be higher.
3. Firms that have better management systems and plan export activities well are more successful than those that don't.
4. Export experience is important and firms that have experience are likely to do better than firms that are just starting.
5. Competencies are probably more important than firm characteristics. Unless management has an international vision, consistent export goals, favourable perceptions and attitudes towards export, is willing to take risks and is capable of engaging positively in export activities, a firm is not likely to become a successful exporter.
6. Technology may or may not be important for success. Export success through technology depends upon good management and what markets the firm decides to enter.
7. A substantial number of non-exporters perceive export to be risky, to require more resources, export assistance and tax incentives than may be required, which leads us to believe that pre-export programmes focusing on correcting management perceptions and erroneous beliefs may be worthwhile.

Source: Aaby, N. E. and Slater, S. F. (1989), 'Management Influences on Export Performance: A Review of the Empirical Literature 1978–88', *International Marketing Review*, **6** (4), 7–26

The significance of size is important. *Into Active Exporting* identified a situation in Britain where the hundred largest exporters in 1985 accounted for 85 per cent of UK exports of fuels, basic materials and manufacturers. The top fifty accounted for 47 per cent alone and the share of the hundred largest in total net output in manufacturing was 41 per cent. Against this difficult background, *Into Active Exporting* addressed three important questions:

Exhibit 3.8   Changing tastes of Scotland

Scotland cannot live by shortbread alone. But, judging by the Scottish presence at last week's international food show in Paris, it might well survive on naan bread.

Thirty Scottish companies clubbed together at the national pavilion at SIAL, Europe's largest food exhibition. Most were of the traditional salmon and spring water set, shamelessly pushing their tartan credentials and building on Scotland's international renown for premium-quality, natural produce.

But tucked among these established manufacturers was a small and equally confident group of companies launching products not so readily associated with hills and heather. From Asian fare to alcoholic spring water, the Scottish food and drink industry is stretching itself in new directions and taking the country's economy with it.

Shazia Gallam is managing director of Abel Eastern International, the UK's largest producer of naan bread and supplier to supermarkets such as Sainsbury and Marks & Spencer.

The company rose from the ashes after a fire last summer destroyed the old factory in Livingston. The blaze happened only hours after the property insurance ran out and a lengthy court battle ensued, with Abel Eastern going into receivership.

A £1m government package helped Gallam and her husband launch Abel Eastern International with a new factory, employing 160 people, in Cumbernauld. The company has since won an industry award for its products.

On the British food stand, at least three manufacturers of Indian and Asian foods are competing for attention. On the Scottish stand, Abel Eastern is unique and it is a position which Gallam shrewdly works to her advantage. 'I like the fact that we're known as a Scottish company,' she says. 'Producing something so different is not a disadvantage and it certainly helps people to remember us, and if it serves that purpose then it can only be a good thing.'

Abel Eastern was there to push its range of filled snack breads and ready spice kits. The week had already brought a large order from the US to provide bread for more than 200 stores by Christmas. Gallam is pleased that the company is finally strengthening its presence outside the UK. 'It's been absolutely superb. We couldn't have dreamed of a better week.'

As head of Scottish Enterprise's food team, Jonathan Tait likes hearing success stories such as Abel's. SE is midway through a five-year action plan for the food industry that aims to boost export sales by 60 per cent and create yet more jobs in an area that employs more than 70,000.

Tait takes heart from such stories and believes there is room for beef and balti in the national larder. 'It's a move which is going to continue and we have to look out towards the global market to improve. But we'll always have the traditional end of the Scottish products and what that gives us – the beef, the salmon, the whisky – is a strong traditional base which still forms the cornerstone of our exports.'

But even foodstuffs such as fish, the solid backbone of Scotland's culinary heritage, are being developed in increasingly novel ways.

At SIAL, the Orkney Herring Company was launching its latest lemon herring marinades, which join the whisky, sherry, juniper, dill and madeira ones sitting in the chill cabinet. The firm's managing director, Ken Sutherland, is in discussions with a major supermarket chain to create a brand marinade just for it.

Not every departure on the gourmet scene is necessarily a radical one. MacB Marketing, along with soft drink manufacturer Sangs (Banff), started by adding sugar-free fruit flavours to sparkling Scottish spring water.

Now its masterpiece the Wee Beestie, an alcoholic spring water drink, will be on the shelves in time for the festive season. Aimed at the 18–25-year-old bracket, the Beestie's slogan – 'Float like a butterfly . . .' – is bound to make it a winner with the youth market.

MacB's is the brainchild of John and Anne Hempstock, who embarked upon a populist approach away from the sophistication of rivals such as Highland Spring.

But Hempstock says his product still benefits from its Scottish pedigree. 'Wherever I've been there is a great benevolence to things Scottish and an acceptance that Scottish water is the best. 'So while we enjoy that, we're also trying to put a new spin on it.'

Source: Scotland on Sunday, 27 October 1996, p. 2

1. To establish the extent of untapped export potential among small and medium sized UK companies.
2. To ascertain the barriers and obstacles to exporting and their significance.
3. To establish what would encourage companies with export potential, but not exporting actively, to become active exporters.

The Institute of Export (1987) is in no doubt about this failing:

Too many companies, too many directors and managers still think that selling their products and services outside the United Kingdom is something for someone else. Undoubtedly, the reason for this attitude is the failure of our education and training system, which in many instances does not include automatically, the international dimension in the teaching of each management subject in business studies and management courses.

Peter Williamson (1990) in a comparative study of British, Japanese and West German exporters' strategies towards the US market commented on the very significant difference which affects both the types of products exported and degree of success in US market penetration.

The British strategy was seen to be ruled by domestic supply and demand consolidation. Pricing was volatile as it was tied to sterling, availability was affected by the attitude of British suppliers who regarded exports as a 'filler' for production capacity. Consequently, British involvement in distribution, sales and marketing was limited. Where competition was intense, British exporters did not fare well, with the exception of certain identifiable market niches, which were insulated from price fluctuation, erratic product availability and competition. The Japanese were at the other end of the spectrum working to build market penetration over an extended period. Whereas British exporters saw exports as an adjunct to their core business and as products sold from the UK, the Japanese positioned their products in the US marketplace with regard to local domestic competition in factors such as pricing and dedicated long-term support, distribution and sales as investment in a target market. The difference could hardly be more telling, whereas British companies were still thinking of actual exports abroad, the Japanese were treating these foreign sales as local market sales of Japanese products. Yet the British are not alone. Taking a measure such as per capita volume of foreign trade, the 1987 figures amounted to $5,343 in the EU, $4,314 in Japan and $2,599 in the USA, approximately half of the EU average. Two further points about US trade:

-   approximately 85 per cent of US exports can be traced to only 250 firms (Stoffel, 1985).
-   of the estimated 250,000 manufacturing exporters less than 19 per cent account for more than 80 per cent of the total export volume (Kaikati, 1984).

Dichtl, Koeglmayr and Mueller (1990), focusing on the foreign market orientation of managers, established that it was possible to empirically differentiate between export-experienced and inexperienced decision makers by using a measuring device based on managers who:

-   experience a greater than average psychic distance to foreign markets or countries,
-   are older, have a more limited education level, are less proficient in foreign languages and travel less to foreign countries than their colleagues,
-   are risk averse, rigid and unwilling to change, and expect lengthy, job-related stays abroad to have a negative effect on their careers and families,
-   display a principally negative attitude toward exporting as a possible company strategy,
-   are not foreign market oriented, and will, under comparable conditions be less likely to participate in export activities than foreign market oriented colleagues.

The resultant firm typology (see Figure 3.3) comprises five classes that are homogeneous and can be arranged into a matrix with the dimensions 'foreign market domestic market orientation' and objective conditions.

Factors in the exporting success of small firms

Conventional wisdom states that the following factors may be important for a firm to achieve success in exporting, by exploiting an advantage in foreign markets whether in:

-   high technology
-   substantial research and development (R&D)
-   sophisticated marketing
-   advanced form of organizational design

Monk (1989) points out that there is no across-the-board success or failure rate for any industry; that no country has exclusively the knowhow that puts all its industries one step ahead of the competition; and that success – and lesser success – occurs in all industries and across all markets. Nevertheless, Monk cites the following as criteria for success:

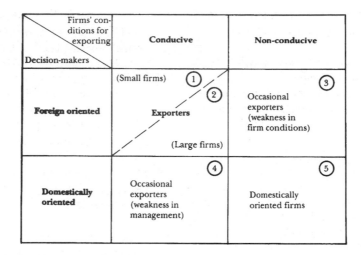

Source: Dichtl, E., Koeglmayr, H.-G., and Mueller, S. (1990) International orientation as a precondition for export success. *Journal of International Business Studies,* **21**, (1). 23–40

Figure 3.3   Classification of exporters and non-exporters based on personality factors and firm's conditions

1. geographic expansion of operations
2. degree of identification with the local market/country
3. sales growth per market
4. profit growth:
   - per market
   - intentional as a percentage of total profits
5. quality of corporate identity/reputation in local markets
6. corporate 'will' – staying power – long-term commitment.

Studies of successful small exporters in North America by Cavusgil, Bilkey and Tesar (Bilkey and Tesar, 1997; Cavusgil and Nevin, 1980) showed many of these points in the recipe for success. The successful firms were seen to:

1. hold patents and/or have a technological orientation
2. have a price advantage in the market
3. have already established fairly broad market coverage
4. have sales volume in excess of $1 million per year (a measure too quickly eroded by inflation, unfortunately)
5. hold high profit aspirations.

But another study by Kirpalani and Mackintosh (1980) took a different view, pointing out that the inputs which determine market effectiveness for the small firm could be different from those that apply to the large multinational corporation (MNC). Stating then, the factors which may contribute towards success, but including also a few rather general thoughts, we note that:

- Government assistance does not act as a motivator although its absence would be regretted.

- Top management effort and backing are required.
- Pricing and promotion are most important.
- Firms with one or two products are more successful.
- Mature products, if modified for export, can compete successfully.
- Sophistication of a firm's manufacturing process is not a prerequisite for exporting success.
- Information for control reporting is vital – quality of information, frequency of reporting, closeness of monitoring of foreign operations.

This has been conceptualized into a model of small firm export sales (Brasch, 1979) whereby export sales are a function of *Effort Opportunity Resistance,* i.e.

$$S = f(E \times O \times R)$$

where R is represented by ability to compete outside home market; cultural uniqueness; logistical barriers; and government regulations. It is imperative that an exporter obtain whatever information he can about these three sales variables before entering the export field. The exporter not only needs to evaluate the *opportunity* that presents itself in the marketplace: he also needs to identify the resistance factors which may make it more difficult to take advantage of this opportunity and could even prevent him from capitalizing on what might otherwise appear to be a lucrative market. Finally, the manufacturer must look at the *Effort* variable, objectively assessing the quantity and quality of inputs that he is capable of providing and willing to commit. After each variable has been analysed individually, some overall evaluation should be made.

Table 3.3 depicts 23 different activities which executives were asked by Howard and Herremans (1988) to evaluate in terms of overall importance to their exporting operations. Many of these relate to planning and if this is performed well, the likelihood of success is much greater.

Using networks

An 'intangible', it is often a very neglected resource stored out of sight and needing only to be unlocked. Cannon and Willis (1986) emphasize the importance of this unstructured in-house resource which includes:

- Previous business and business inquiries. This may involve searching memories as well as files for requests for product information as well as requests for tender. Comparison may be usefully made with what the competition is doing.
- Contacts, acquaintances formal and informal. Links with the parent group and the extended information resource of the grapevine. Can-

non and Willis point out though the common mistake of using a parent group's agency without examining whether it can handle all of the group's business or has the marketing expertise to succeed.

- External relationships. Many customers may be part of multinational firms whose annual reports will often highlight overseas activities, prospects, locations and details of senior personnel.
- Export organizations such as the Department of Trade and Industry's 'Export Initiative'; chambers of commerce; banks; buying houses; export clubs; export councils for specific trading areas, e.g. East European Trade Council and professional organizations such as the Institute of Export.

Small firms concentrate their activities on neighbouring countries to keep their problems within bounds (Verhoeven, 1988). Networking can work to the advantage of the company and its parent group exposing it to the opportunities of a global marketplace and possible partners if

Table 3.3 Importance of business activities ranked by successful small exporting firms

Activity	Importance (mean*)
	N = 101
1. Selecting agents/distributors	1.902
2. Maintaining agency/distributor relations	1.880
3. Completing exporting documentation	1.774
4. Pricing decisions	1.641
5. Providing technical advice	1.626
6. Understanding local business practices	1.587
7. Collecting foreign accounts	1.578
8. Developing export sales leads	1.570
9. Sales promotion activities	1.565
10. Providing parts availability	1.448
11. Sales force management	1.429
12. Researching foreign markets	1.418
13. Obtaining credit information	1.385
14. Providing repair service	1.376
15. Understanding cultural differences	1.348
16. Physical distribution activities	1.242
17. Adapting advertising messages	1.225
18. Advertising media selection	1.178
19. Physical product adaptation	1.146
20. Analysing political risks	1.022
21. Managing political risks	0.989
22. Packaging adaptations	0.967
23. Managing foreign exchange	0.956

Source: Howard, D. G., and Herremans, I. M. (1988). Sources of assistance for small business exporters: advice from successful firms. *Journal of Small Business Management*, July, 48–54

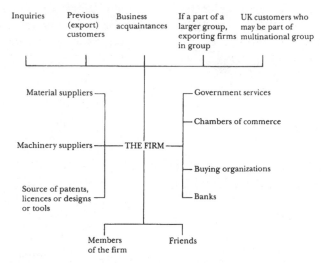

Source: Cannon, T. and Willis, M. (1986) How to Buy and Sell Overseas, Business Books/Hutchinson, London

Figure 3.4   A firm's network of possible points of contact with export markets

Exhibit 3.9 Woman of substance

Pat Grant, 52, the eldest girl of nine children, has collected accolades in the business world like most women accumulate lipsticks.

In the 25 years since she and her husband Alex established Norfrost at Castletown in Caithness, producing 12,000 freezers a week for export to 125 countries, she has been awarded an OBE, named Business Woman of the Year, become the first woman to receive the Captain of Industry Award and a European Women of Achievement Award.

Her own philosophy that an inner contentment is vital to an outward beauty says a great deal about her lifestyle.

Now she is using the business skills acquired over 25 years to establish a new company, Beauty Through Herbs, which produces a full range of beauty products and cosmetics and offers beauty treatments for the whole body.

So why the move from freezers to facials? 'I have always been interested in herbal medicine,' says Pat, in a break from a visit to her Aberdeen shop. 'For me, that is conventional medicine with everything else coming after it. I have always preferred to use natural remedies and cosmetics with natural ingredients which actually work.'

Pat was introduced to an Italian biochemist and cosmetologist Gabriel Segalla, working in a laboratory in Milan from a book of recipes, some dating back to the 14th century. She liked what she saw, and with his help established her own research and development laboratory in the city.

'Gabriel is a marvellous man with wonderful ideas,' says Pat. 'I know the ingredients he uses are natural – in some cases the products are 99.7 per cent natural and the remainder is preservative. As yet we haven't found a suitable natural preservative but as soon as we do, we will use it.'

The products are centred on herbs, fruits and natural essences in different ranges, including a skin therapy range to treat conditions like acne, rosacea and stretchmarks.

A second laboratory was set up in Thurso, close to her Norfrost HQ, and now beauty products are made in both Italy and Scotland and some in Yorkshire, under licence.

Next Pat researched beauty treatments including aromatherapy and reflexology, as well as facials, toning and slimming treatments using high-tech equipment.

But Pat, with lessons learned from Norfrost, wanted her new business to grow gradually. 'You have got to know exactly what you are doing and employ people with the best skills,' says Pat.' You must have products which people want to use more than once and you must tell your customers the truth about them.'

Research began eight years ago and all her treatments and products were refined and subjected to intensive testing and market research.

'I was lucky in that area because the 200 women at Norfrost are only too happy to try out the products,' says Pat. But there is nothing haphazard about the research as each woman is given a detailed questionnaire to record all her reactions to each product.

The all-natural range, which includes bath

➤ **Exhibit 3.9** *continued*

oils, soaps, shampoos, face and body creams, and fragrances for men and women was launched at Pat's first shop in Thurso almost five years ago. The second store in Aberdeen followed.

The range has now found great success in the Middle East, but the biggest launches – in Edinburgh and London – are planned in the next six months.

Pat has wasted no time in persuading women in the Middle East to sample her products. She already has shops in Cyprus, Bahrain and Saudi Arabia and plans to open in Kuwait in October. There are plans for Abu Dhabi, Dubai, Jordan and Cairo in 1997.

'I'm sure one of the reasons why we've been so successful in those countries is because women there have never moved away from natural products,' says Pat.

Debenhams liked Beauty Through Herbs' products, which are now on sale in the cosmetics department of their Middlesbrough store (just down the road from Pat's home town of Stockton) with an option to sell in six other towns.

Packaging is simple but smart, with a mid-price range.' I want people to have a good product and good advice at a price they can afford,' says Pat. 'I've used the products for eight years and I know that they work.'

Pat now divides her time between Norfrost and her new company. She is still responsible for all the buying and 50 per cent of the sales operation for Norfrost – she negotiated the export deal to supply Coca-Cola chillers for the USA.

Norfrost employs 400 staff and its philosophy of 'the best product at the best price' reflects a multi-skilled company in which nearly all components are produced in-house.

Pat admits one of her keys to success is her limitless energy. She admires other women with similar drive and energy and her one ambition concerns one of them. 'I'd love to get up on stage with Tina Turner for just one dance!' she says.

Source: *Topflight,* Gill Airways inflight magazine, February 1997

Table 3.5   Main reasons for failure

1.   Incorrect analysis of true market potential (often over-enthusiastic and underestimating the problems).
2.   Inappropriate company structure for the host country based on country-of-origin model. Keep financial controls and reporting systems constant or you will make the venture fail.
3.   Start-up cost control: including office location, quality of accommodation, level of manning, and hotel resource required.
4.   Job titles have an effect on employees and clients but it makes 'promoted' employees more expensive to discuss.
5.   Too rapid staff changes. Exporters may look for quick short-term results, whereas local nationals may take a longer view. The corporation is what is important and continuity of policy is as important as continuity of personnel.
6.   Too fast tie-ups with rural party distributors and representatives. The seduction of fast market entry may lead to market dependency and a constraint on further market development.
7.   Lack of an international career track within the organization. Successful companies have done this, creating executives that are broader in outlook, not parochial or xenophobic. Businesses will need executives like these to survive into the next century.

Source: Adapted from Monk, K. (1989) *Go International: Your guide to marketing and business development,* McGraw-Hill, Maidenhead

---

unwilling to go it alone either in terms of research, product development or market expansion.

The exporting consortium alternative

Assuming size is an important variable in the exporting success of small firms, we wish now to consider the possibilities for small exporters to form themselves into export clubs or industry-wide export trade associations.

This is known as 'consortium marketing', 'federated marketing' or 'grouping' depending on which country you are in. Basically, the concept is simply one of strength in unity. Good agents need a great deal of backup and supporting effort from home, which means frequent expensive visits are necessary, with management effort at a premium. Depending on the number of participants, and the degree of government financial support, costs for a company acting in consortium have been estimated at about one-tenth of those which the company would otherwise have had to meet for its own exclusive local presence, and about the same fraction for the equivalent cost of employing 'flying salesmen' to supervise agents.

Most importantly each member of the consortium keeps his own identity and sovereignty, while sharing in the combined strength; and small companies who constitute the growth sector of the economy and provide the new job opportunities, can in theory begin to sell into overseas markets as easily as they sell into the home market.

A union of three or four companies, offering complementary and non-competing products and services, collaborating through a joint organization in an overseas sales facility provides the advantages of cost-sharing and risk-sharing for the individual companies.

Other advantages may include:

- The group can deploy resources beyond the budget limits of the individual companies, and with a joint turnover which will justify the expenditure.
- On-the-spot professional top calibre sales staff arrange feedback, after-sales service, local distribution, and provide permanent sales presence.
- Concentrating on specific markets minimizes the language problem.

Forming an exporting consortium

Exporting consortiums usually develop along the following lines:

1. A target overseas geographical market is identified, in market and not product terms.
2. A group of two or three companies with complementary products/services agree to co-operate in their export efforts. A group of companies thus formed can between them supply and design a service or package system, and in addition provide financial credits and working capital.
3. A jointly owned overseas marketing consortium is created and registered as a public company with limited liability.
4. The consortium is managed by a board of directors with one director appointed by each company. The consortium appoints its own general manager and overseas marketing staff.
5. Communications are established between the overseas offices or marketing staff, and the member companies. The role of the overseas posts is very important in agreeing and implementing plans, collaborating, negotiating, and providing technical presence.
6. Local images may be all important. Equally a maintenance facility may be a prerequisite for sales, and the maintenance operation may in itself be very profitable.
7. The consortium will develop its own rules concerning managers and participants and third-party supplier's selling prices, stocks, publicity, and sales policies. All members are expected to quote fair prices to the

Table 3.6 Twelve most common mistakes of potential exporters

1. Failure to obtain qualified export counselling and to develop a master international marketing plan before starting an export business.
2. Insufficient commitment by top management to overcome the initial difficulties and financial requirements of exporting.
3. Insufficient care in selecting overseas distributors.
4. Chasing orders from around the world instead of establishing a basis for profitable operations and orderly growth.
5. Neglecting export business when the US market booms.
6. Failure to treat international distributors on an equal basis with domestic counterparts.
7. Assuming that a given market technique and product will automatically be successful in all countries.
8. Unwillingness to modify products to meet regulations or cultural preferences of other countries.
9. Failure to print service, sale and warranty messages in locally understood languages.
10. Failure to consider use of an export-management company.
11. Failure to consider licensing or joint-venture agreements.
12. Failure to provide readily available servicing for the product.

Source: US Department of Commerce (1990) *A Basic Guide to Exporting*, NTC Business Books, Lincolnwood, Illinois, USA

Table 3.7   The export decision – management issues

I Experience

 1. With what countries has business already been conducted (or from what countries have inquiries already been received)?
 2. Which product lines are mentioned most often?
 3. List the sale inquiry of each buyer by product, by country.
 4. Is the trend of sales/inquiries up or down?
 5. Who are the main domestic and foreign competitors?
 6. What general and specific lessons have been learned from past export experiences?

II Management and personnel

 1. Who will be responsible for the export department's organization and staff?
 2. How much senior management time:
     • should be allocated?
     • could be allocated?
 3. What are management's expectations for the effort?
 4. What organization structure is required to ensure that export sales are adequately serviced? (Note the political implications, if any.)
 5. Who will follow through after the planning is accomplished?

III Production capacity

 1. How is the present capacity being used?
 2. Will filling export orders hurt domestic sales?
 3. What will be the cost of additional production?
 4. Are there fluctuations in the annual workload? When? Why?
 5. What minimum order quantity is required?
 6. What would be required to design and package products specifically for export?

IV Financial capacity

 1. What amount of capital can be tied up in exports?
 2. What level of export department operating costs can be supported?
 3. How are the initial expenses of export efforts to be allocated?
 4. What other new development plans are in the works that may compete with export plans?
 5. By what date must an export effort pay for itself?

Source: US Department of Commerce (1990) *A Basic Guide to Exporting*, NTC Business Books, Lincolnwood, Illinois, p. 3

consortium and not take unfair advantage of individual key inputs, e.g., raw materials.

8. A countertrade member would supply financial credits for credit sales and provide working capital for contract operations.
9. The consortium appoints, if required, a consulting engineer as technical advisor so that it can take advantage of a strong consulting system.

Attracting more small firms into exporting

More small firms could be attracted into exporting by improving the trading environment and simplifying trading operations.

Christensen, de Rocha and Gertner (1987) examined 152 Brazilian companies exporting in 1978 and interviewed them again six years later to determine the factors that were correlated with continuation to export. Firm characteristics, export management practices and manager perceptions were each found to be correlated with exporting success thus supporting the basic contention that it is possible to predict export performance. Firms that discontinued exporting relied more on the Brazilian government export incentives, possibly to be competitive in international markets without making the necessary structural changes, thereby raising important questions about the long-run impact of the Brazilian export programmes and of government export subsidies generally.

Improving the trading environment

This could be achieved by:

• Eliminating the distrust among small businessmen of government departments by making the latter more responsive to the needs of small business.

- Correcting the mistaken perception of non-exporters who view the cost factors – executive time, packaging and insurance costs, clerical time, shipping costs – to be higher than do exporters.
- Encouraging exporters to be proactive rather than reactive in their approach to international marketing, focusing on the profit advantage of international marketing activities over domestic sales, and moving away from the idea of a market of last resort.
- Encouraging trade associations to participate in exporting on behalf of their members, also to develop export market research databanks.
- Encouraging the development of voluntary export consortia which can provide the financial strength and marketing resources so many small firms lack.

Simplifying trading operations

The key to this question is in simplifying and reducing paperwork. Arranging export credit and documentation may be a small task for the large company but for the small company taking perhaps its first large export order, the export preparations can be intimidating. In Britain, too, there is a polarization of all financial services towards the south. This means that, firstly, in the north of England the general level of awareness of services will be lower, and that secondly, the expertise is mainly to be found only by travelling to London and the south since most bank branches feel quite out of their depth in trying to handle export credit assistance and prefer to have such specialist questions answered by their head office based in London. The situation is changing, however, and the main clearing banks are beginning to move their financial services further north. Still, the banks impose a floor limit on the export credit facilities which they offer which they do not generally seek to go below. This may be of the order of £50,000. As this may well constitute a large order for the small company, it may feel, quite rightly, that its needs are not being served. Into this breach have stepped confirming houses such as the English Export Finance Association based in Rochdale. A licensed deposit taker by the Bank of England, it is not only physically present in its area but able and willing to handle a smaller scale of business.

With regard to paperwork particularly, much has been done by SITPRO (Simplification of International Trade Procedures), London to facilitate the processing of export documentation, also by providing task-specific pre-printed stationery, as well as occasional country reports.

The Confederation of British Industry (CBI) helps with world regional area trade specialists as does the Export Credit Guarantee Department (ECGD) although it often encounters the criticism that its lines of credit are designed for large companies and not the smaller size orders which would probably still constitute very large export orders for small businesses. With regard to the ECGD, too, a Matthews inquiry into its efficiency in March 1984 found a widely held feeling that the ECGD's service and premium charges to large exporters were adversely affected by the proportionately greater amount of time devoted by the department to servicing the small exporter. In the five years to 1983, all but the largest of the ECGD's comprehensive short-term guarantees failed to contribute enough to cover the cost of administration and claim payments. About 40 per cent of the smallest policies produced less than 3 per cent of premium income and accounted for nearly 20 per cent of administration costs. Matthews recommended that the ECGD should not have to meet the costs of services to small exporters beyond its obligation as an insurer.

The Department of Trade has centralized its services to exporters under the umbrella organization of the Export Initiative and these include:

- Export Marketing Research Scheme (EMRS) which provides free professional advice to help you decide whether specific market surveys are needed, advice on how to get them underway and offers financial support often in the form of grants for market research studies undertaken overseas. This can cover:
  - using professional consultants
  - using your own staff
  - purchasing published marketing research
  - research commissioned by your trade association
- Export Market Information Centre (EMIC) brings together the former Statistics and Market Intelligence Library (SMIL); the microfilm database of product information of the former Product Data Store (PDS) and so consult:
  - *statistics*: worldwide statistics are available
  - *market research reports*: a selection of overseas market reports supplements the statistics collection
- *Country profiles*: reports and forecasts
  directories: overseas trade and telephone directories
- *DTI Export publications*
  mail order catalogues: ideal for checking consumer goods preferences
- *CD-Rom databases*
  development plans: economic plans for selected countries are available on loan to exporters

- *Trade Fair catalogues*: export opportunities and sales leads
- *Business Travel Guides*
- *Other online databases*: a search service is available to selected commercial online databases.

EMIC is located at:
  Export Market Information Centre (EMIC)
  Department of Trade and Industry
  Kingsgate House
  66–74 Victoria Street
  London SWIE 6SW

  Tel: 0171–215 5444/5
  Fax: 0171 215 4231
  E. mail: EMIC@ ash001.0ts.dti.gov.UK

  Open 9:30–20.00, Monday to Friday and Saturday 09.00–17.30
  Export Market Information Research Service (EMIRS)
  EMIC's fee-based research service. Fax: 0171 233 6853
  World Aid Section, Kingsgate House
  66–74 Victoria Street,
  London SWIE 6SW

  World Bank Group: 0171–215 5369/4372
  Asian Development Bank, African Development Bank, Inter-American Development Bank, Caribbean Development Bank and United Nations Agencies:
  0171–215 4256/5053
  European Development Funds: 0171–215 4255/5616
  European Structural Funds: 0171–215 4279/5615

- Technical Help to Exporters. Removing technical barriers to trade is a vital element of the Community's Single Market Programme to ensure that member states recognize each other's terms and certification arrangements. As the Single Market is completed, the effect will be that any product which can be sold in the member state in which it is produced, will be freely marketable in all other member states of the community.

  Meanwhile, firms will still need to get to grips with differences in national rules and practice. Technical Help to Exporters (THE) is a service operated by the British Standards Institution (BSI) 389 Chiswick High Road, London W4 4AL. The BSI has been advising British manufacturers on foreign regulations and standards since 1966.

  THE is a service operated by the British Standards Institution and its staff of engineers and information specialists. It provides advice on foreign requirements including:

- National laws, particularly in relation to safety and environmental protection
- Technical standards
- Certification processes in relation to customer needs.

It also has a further range of services which include:

- A technical enquiry service to answer day-to-day problems
- A consultancy service
- Technical research
- Major updating services for particular industrial sectors
- A library of over 500,000 standards and regulations for over 160 countries, together with 10,000 English translations. The library also offers a related technical translation service for firms. A charge is made for this service.

The THE enquiry service can answer by telephone or telex questions on the day-to-day problems faced by exporters such as the identification of foreign standards, technical requirements and approval procedures in Community member states as well as those of non-EU countries. A more detailed study is sometimes needed of products affected by a wider range of requirements, and THE can research any combination of technical standards for a specific product in a foreign market. THE engineers can visit manufacturers' works to examine products intended for export and suggest technical modifications which may be needed. THE also arranges presentations and seminars for designers and production staff.

THE produces a wide range of publications and surveys covering mainly the electrical, mechanical and building industries, and a classified list of publications is available free of charge. A special updating service is available in some product fields where companies require a consolidated manual of up-to-date technical information. The full text in English of all current requirements overseas for the product is supplied, and regular updating sheets are produced.

Further information may be obtained direct from THE:

Tel: 0181 996 7111
Fax: 0181 996 7048

Revision questions

1. What is the difference between exporting and international marketing?
2. Why is exporting of interest to small companies?

3. How do you define 'exporting'?
4. How do you define a 'small' firm? What are the essential characteristics?
5. How does the UK compare with Japan in terms of the economic importance of small business to the economy? What political effects are likely to be seen as a result of this?
6. What are the resource implications of being a small firm? How do you counteract this?
7. What are the specific problems that small exporters face?
8. What are the essential characteristics of the profile of a small exporter?
9. In what significant ways do the perceptions of exporters and non-exporters differ?
10. How does adding 'experience' and 'commitment' to the mix aid in understanding the exporter or non exporter?
11. How does international orientation aid in understanding the exporter or non-exporter?
12. Which factors have been found to be present in the profile of unsuccessful exporters?
13. Do these success factors differ significantly from those general success factors identified by Monk (1989)? What success factors are necessary for the small firm to succeed?
14. Knowing that export sales are a function of effort, opportunity and resistance, how does this knowledge help a small firm assess a foreign market opportunity and plan for it?
15. How might networks be used most effectively for exporting?
16. What are the key features of an exporting consortium or alliance?
17. Why would a small firm be attracted to an exporting consortium?
18. What are the main reasons for export failure?
19. How might government improve the trading environment for exporters?
20. What assistance is offered to exporters by the Department of Trade and other agencies?

References

Aaby, N. -E., and Slater, S. F. (1989) 'Management Influences on Export Performance: A Review of the Empirical Literature 1978–88', *International Marketing Review*, 6 (4), 7–26.

Adams-Smith, K. (1996) 'The Trade Information Center takes export counseling services into Cyberspace via CompuServe', *Business America*, 117 (5), May, 18.

Beamish, P. W., Craig, R., and McLellan, K. (1993) 'The Performance Characteristics of Canadian versus UK Exporters in Small and Medium Sized Firms', *Management International Review*, 33 (2), 121–137.

Bilkey, W. J., and Tesar, G. (1997) The export behaviour of smaller sized Wisconsin manufacturing firms. *Journal of International Business Studies*, Spring, 93–98.

Bonaccorsi, A. (1992) 'On the Relationship between Firm Size and Export Intensity', *Journal of International Business Studies*, 23, Fourth Quarter, 605–635.

Branch, A. E. (1993) *Export Practice & Management*, Chapman & Hall, London.

Brown, R., and Cook, D. (1990) Strategy and performance in British exporters, *Quarterly Review of Marketing*, 15 (3), 42–61.

Browning, J. M., and Adams, R. J. (1988) Trade shows: an effective promotional tool for the small industrial business. *Journal of Small Business Management*, October, 30–37.

Burton, F. N., and Schlegelmilch, B. B. (1987) 'Profile Analysis of Non-exporters versus Exporters Grouped by Export Involvement', *Management International Review*, 27 (1), 38–49.

Cannon, T., and Willis, M. (1986) *How to Buy and Sell Overseas*, Business Books/Hutchinson, London.

Cavusgil, S. T., and Kirpalani, V. H. (1993) 'Introducing Products into Export Markets: Success Factors', *Journal of Business Research*, 27, 1–15.

Cavusgil, S. T. and Nevin, J. R. (1980) Conceptualization of the initial involvement in international marketing. In *Theoretical Developments in Marketing* (eds C. W. Lamb and P. M. Dunne), American Marketing Association Theory Conference, Phoenix, April.

Cavusgil, S. T., and Zou, S. (1994) 'Marketing Strategy–Performance Relationship: An Investigation of the Empirical Link in Export Market Ventures', *Journal of Marketing*, 58, January, 1–21.

Wong Kwei Cheong and Kwan Woi Chong (1988) Export behaviour of small firms in Singapore. *International Small Business Journal*, 6 (2), pp. 42–61.

Craig, R., and Beamish, P. W. (1989) 'A Comparison of the Characteristics of Canadian and UK Exporters by Firm Size', *Journal of Global Marketing*, 2 (4), 49–63.

Dichtl, E., Koeglmayr, H. G., and Mueller, S. (1990) International orientation as a precondition for export success. *Journal of International Business Studies*, 21 (1), 23–40.

Haar, J., and Ortiz-Buonafina, M. (1995) 'The Internationalization Process and Marketing Activities: The Case of Brazilian Export

Firms', *Journal of Business Research*, **32**, 175–181.

Howard, D. C., and Herremans, I. M. (1988) Sources of assistance for small business exporters: advice from successful firms, *Journal of Small Business Management*, July, 48–63.

Institute of Export (1987) *Export*, April, p. 1.

Kadar, A., and Whitehead, G. (1995), *Export Law*, Woodhead Faulkner, Hemel Hempstead.

Kaleka, A., and Katsikeas C. S. (1995) 'Exporting problems: The Relevance of Export Development', *Journal of Marketing Management*, **11**, 499–515.

Karakaya, F. (1993) 'Barriers to Entry in International Markets', *Journal of Global Marketing*, **7** (1), 7–24.

Katsikeas, C. S., and Piercy, N. F. (1993) 'Long Term Export Stimuli and Firm Characteristics in a European LDC', *Journal of International Marketing*, **1** (3), 23–47.

Keng, K. A., and Jiuan, T. S. (1989) 'Differences Between Small and Medium Sized Exporting and Non-Exporting Firms: Nature or Nurture', *International Marketing Review*, **6** (4), 27–40.

Leonidou, L. C. (1995) 'Export Stimulation Research: Review, Evaluation and Integration', *International Business Review*, **4** (2), 133–156.

Leonidou, L. C., and Katsikeas, C. S. (1996) 'The Export Development Process: An Integrative Review of Empirical Models', *Journal of International Business Studies*, **27** (3), Third Quarter, 517–552.

London Chamber of Commerce & Industry (1994) *The Export Handbook: A Complete Guide and Reference Source for International Traders*, Kogan Page, London.

Mahone, C. E. (1994) 'Penetrating Export Markets: The Role of Firm Size', *Journal of Global Marketing*, **7** (3), 133–148.

Monk, K. (1989) *Go International: Your guide to marketing and business development*, McGraw-Hill, Maidenhead.

Motoko Yesnde Lee, and Mulford, C. L. (1990) Reasons why Japanese small businesses form cooperatives: an exploratory study of three successful cases. *Journal of Small Business Management*, July, 62–71.

Naidu, G. M., and Rao, T. R. (1993) 'Public Sector Promotion of Exports: A Needs Based Approach', *Journal of Business Research*, **27**, 85–101.

Nobuaki Namiki (1988) Export strategy for small business. *Journal of Small Business Management*, April, 32–37.

Noonan, C. (1996) *The CIM Handbook of Export Marketing: A Practical Guide to Opening and*

Expanding Markets Overseas, Butterworth–Heinemann, Oxford.

Ortiz-Buonafina, M. (1991) 'Export Marketing Activities in the Internationalization Stages of the Export Firm', *Akron Business and Economic Review*, **22**, Spring, 45–55.

Rabino, S. (1980) Examination of barriers to exporting encountered by small manufacturing companies. *Management International Review*, **20** (1), 67–73.

Ramaseshan, B., and Patton, M. A. (1994) 'Factors influencing International Channel Choice of Small Business Exporters', *International Marketing Review*, **11** (4), 19–34.

Rao, T. R., and Naidu, G. M. (1992) 'Are the Stages of Internationalization Empirically Supportable?', *Journal of Global Marketing*, **6** (42), 147–170.

Root, F. R. (1994) *Entry Strategies for International Markets*, Revised and Expanded, Lexington Books, New York.

Samiee, S., and Walters, P. G. P. (1991) 'Segmenting Corporate Exporting Activities: Sporadic versus Regular Exporters', *Journal of the Academy of Marketing Science*, **19** (2), 93–1–4.

Styles, C., and Ambler, T. (1994) 'Successful Export Practice: The UK Experience', *International Marketing Review*, **11** (6), 23–47.

Verhoeven, W. (1988) The export performance of small and medium sized enterprises in the Netherlands. *International Small Business Journal*, **6** (2), 20–33.

Williamson, P. J. (1990) Winning the export war: British, Japanese and West German exporters' strategies compared. *British Journal of Management*, **1**, 215–230.

Wolfe, A. R. (1993) The Eurobuyer: how European businesses buy. *Marketing and Research Today*, February, 45–49.

Web sites

American City Business Journals: news from 28 weekly city business journals
http://www.amcity.com

AT & T Business Network-free site
http://www.bnet.att.com

Babson Internet Business Resource Links
gopher://gopher.babason.edu

Best of the Web
http://wings.buffalo.edu/contest

BEMs – Big Emerging Markets (US Classification)
http://www.stat-usa.gov/itabems.html

Business Information Resources

http://sashimi.wwa.com/~notime/eotw/
  business_info.html

Business Information Server
http://www.dnb.com/

Business Site of the Day
http://www.bizniz.com/eurocool/

Business Statistics
gopher: University of Michigan:
  una.hh.lib.umich.edu
Choose: ebb Current Business Statistics

Businesses on the Internet
http://www.yahoo.com/
  Business_and_Economy/Corporations/

Business to Business Marketing Exchange
http://www.btob.wfu.edu/b2b.html

Canadian Business Info World
http://csclub.uwaterloo.ca/u/nckwan/.html/
  directory

CIA Publications
http://www.odc.gov/cia/publications/
  pus.html

Clearinghouse for Networked Information
  Discovery
http://kudzu.cnidr.org/welcome.html

Clearinghouse for Subject Oriented Internet
  Resources
http://www.lib.umich.edu/chhome.html

Electronic Herald
http://www.cims.co.uk/herald/home.html

Entrepreneurs – Edward Lowe Foundation
http://www.lowe.org

Entrepreneurs – How to succeed in your Home
  Business
http://www.tdbank.ca/tdbank/succeed.index
  .html

Entrepreneurs – MCI Small Biz center
http://www.mci.com/SmallBiz

Entrepreneurs – Web Marketing Today
http://www.wilsonweb.com/rfwilson/
  wmt

Entrepreneurs on the Web
http://sashimi.wwa.com/~notime/
  EOTW.html

Ernst & Young
http://www.ernsty.co.uk/ernsty

Europages
http://www.europages.com

Europe – Business Monitor
http://www.businessmonitor.co.uk

ExportNet – Export Today Matchmaking
  service
http://www.exporttoday.com

Find it Fast
http://www.webcom.com/~tbrown/
  findpage.html

Homeworker
http://www.hmeworker.co.uk

Home Business Review
http://www.taab.com/Home.Business/

Internet Business Center
http://www.tig.com/IBC

International Small Business Consortium
http://www.isbc.com

Internet Sleuth
http://www.intbc.com/sleuth/

Importing and Exporting
Usenet: alt.business.import-export

Inc. Online
http://www.inc.com

Industry Net
http://www.industry.net/

Infomarket – gathers finance and business
  related links:
http://www.fe.msk.ru/infomarket/
  ewelcome.html

Information Technology Laboratory
http://wwwubilab.ubs.ch/

Insight Information
http://avidinfo.com/

International Business Resources on the WWW
http://ciber.bus.msu.edu/busres.htm

International Chamber of Commerce, Paris
http://www1.usa1.com/~ibnet/icchp.html

Internet Address Finder
http://www.iaf.net

International Internet Marketing
http://www.clark.net/pub/granered/
  iim.html

Japan Information Network
http://jin.jcic.or.jp/navi/category_1.html

JETRO (The Japanese External Trade
  Organization)
http://www.jetro.go.jp/index.html

Legal List Internet Desk Reference
http://wwwlcp.com

Legal Information Institute
http://www.law.cornell.edu

Moneyworld UK
http://www.moneyworld.co.uk

Thomas Ho's Favourite Electronic Commerce
    WWW Resources
http://www.engr.iupui.edu/~ho/interests/
    commmenu.html

Newsgroup for Importing and Exporting
news:alt.business.import-export

Regional Information Guides by Price
    Waterhouse
http://www.i-trade.com/infsrc/pw

Rice University, USA: Subject Information
http://riceinfo.rice.rice.edu/Riceinfo/
    Subject.html

Simpler Trade Procedures Board
http://www.sitpro.org.uk/index.html

Small Business Administration
http://www.sbaonline.sba.gov

Small Business Information
http://www.ro.com/small_business/
    homebased.html

Business Network International
http://www.bninet.com

Statistical Agencies on the Internet
http://www.science.gmu.edu/csi779/drope/
    govstats.html

Statistics UK
http://www.emap.com\cso

Statistics USA
http://www.stat-usa.gov

Statistics Canada – reputedly the best
    governmental statistical reporting
    service
http://www.statcan.ca

SunSITE Classic – Previous Best of the Web
    Award winner
http://sunsite.unc.edu/

The Economist
http://www.economist.com

The Scotsman
http://www.scotsman.com

Trade Compass
http://www.tradecompass.com

TradePort – extensive information on
    international business
http://www.tradeport.org

Trade Statistics
http://www.census.gov/ftp/pub/
    foreign-trade/www/

TradeWave Galaxy – Public and commercial
    information and services
http://www.einet.net/galaxy.html

UPS Online
http://www.ups.com

US West features 50,000 suppliers from USA,
    Mexico, Canada
http://export.uswest.com

US West Export Yellow Pages
http://yp.uswest.com

Web Page for Global Business
http://www.seattleu.edu/~parker/
    homepage.html

Web Sites for International Information:
http://www.ustr.gov/
http://www.i-trade.com/
http://www.stat-
    usa.gov/BEN/subject/trade.html
http://www.itaiep.doc.gov/

World Factbook
gopher: gopher.aecom.yu.edu

World Wide Web Virtual Library
http://W3.org

WorldClass Supersite
http://web.idirect.com/~tiger

WWW Yellow Pages
www.cba.uh.edu/ylowpges/ylowpges.html.

Yahoo Reuters
http://www.yahoo.co.uk/News

Yellow Pages UK
http://www.yell.co.uk

Yelloweb Europe
http://www.yweb.com/

CHAPTER 4

Market entry modes: strategic considerations of direct vs. indirect involvement

Company resources and objectives

Once again, it is worth repeating that there is no one, single universal 'best' foreign market entry strategy. The firm should consider all possible channel strategies when entering each market. The 'best' strategy will be the one which is situationally best, optimal in that it is often a satisficing strategy which takes into consideration market competition, perceived risk, and established corporate policy with regard to forms of market entry. Yet this will not last for ever. Once the decision is made, there should be continuous monitoring in place, a periodic review and evaluation and the possibility at least of a change of mode in the future.

It may be useful to think in terms of a company having to deploy a broad portfolio of international entry modes to deal with a diversity of market conditions worldwide. While the five basic characteristics of a market must still be found, namely: sizeable, accessible group of people, ability to buy, willingness to buy, a suitable product or service offering, and legality of consumption, conceptually, the forms of market entry, which we describe below, do not follow a sequential order or classification. It should not be assumed then that there is a linear progression or an incremental internationalization process moving from export sales being part of domestic sales through to wholly owned foreign subsidiaries. In fact, research undertaken within one major British multinational by one of the

Exhibit 4.1 Taking trade one step at a time

1.
Assess the needs of the potential market – identify potential customers.

2.
Assess your own capability to meet those needs.

3.
Identify the tools – technology, finances, regulatory expertise – required.

4.
Begin to match specific capabilities to specific needs.

5.
Lay the groundwork for an initial meeting with the client.

6.
Hold the first face-to-face meeting.

7.
Following the meeting, assess the results. Focus on the 'soft' side of the business relationship, the cultural and philosophical differences. Having done that, refine the needs and capabilities. Define follow-up and the products and services to be offered, the partnerships to be formed, the contracts to be suggested.

8.
Hold a second face-to-face meeting to discuss specific business relationships and to agree on follow-up.

9.
Implement the sales or partnership agreement.

10.
After an agreed-upon period, evaluate the arrangement, analyse the lessons learned. Review the experience for its applicability to other markets.

– *Arthur Jones*

Source: Jones, A. (1996), 'From the Ground: The 10 Steps of Global Trade', *World Trade*, September, 20.

authors established that board-level thinking was moving towards the need to justify the existence of a wholly owned foreign sales subsidiary in preference to a commission agent. Again, ownership of assets has traditionally been thought to be necessary to have local control, but this is debatable. Again, control has a price, too, and so the optimal market entry choice can only ever be situation-specific.

Corporate objectives vary but, aside from short-term opportunity, may include:

- growth
- profitability and economies of scale
- new products for existing markets
- new markets for existing products
- new products from new markets
- foreign earnings from existing products
- reducing vulnerability to domestic economic downturns
- access to foreign production inputs
- increased total potential market size over which to spread R&D costs.

Selection of market entry mode has an important bearing on strategy, and can later prove to be a severe constraint on future intended international expansion unless due care and attention has been exercised in terms of any contractual arrangement.

Selecting a market entry mode

The criteria to be considered include:

1. *Speed of market entry desired.* If speed is required, building up a wholly owned subsidiary is too slow and so acquisition and licensing or use of an agent/distributor will be the likely ways to ensure quick effective distribution in the foreign market.
2. *Costs to include direct and indirect costs.* Subjectivity which is ever present may force a wrong decision. Commitment to establishing a market presence does not mean blindness to facts. Possible savings may be outweighed by indirect costs such as freight, strikes, or disruptions to output, lack of continuity with the power supply, or irregularity in the supply of raw materials. Against this, the cost of doing nothing has to be considered; this may be higher than the attendant risks of moving into a relatively unknown market.
3. *Flexibility required.* The laws of a country exist to protect that country's nationals. There is as yet no such thing as international law (although it is important to recognize, UNCITRAL, the extraterritoriality of US law, and

also within the EU, Articles 36, 85, and 86, as they affect trade within the European Union). In disputes between two countries the domestic law of a neutral third country is often called on, so that domestic law then becomes used for a purpose for which it was never designed: international disputes. Agents are appointed or distributors given exclusive sales territory rights, usually only where it is deemed unlikely that there will be very much future expansion by the company directly into that market.

4. *Risk factors* – including political risk and economic as well as competitive risk. In a dynamic market, time is of the essence. No product remains 'new' forever. Getting the product to market is important but so, too, is avoiding the creation of a competitor, a common criticism of licensing. Risk may be diminished by minimizing the investment stake in the company by accepting a local joint- venture partner. Equally, investment activity in one market may lead to reprisals for the company elsewhere as has often been seen in the past with companies trading with Israel and then finding themselves subject to an Arab boycott.
5. *Investment payback period.* Shorter-term payback may be realized from licensing and franchising deals, whereas joint ventures or wholly owned subsidiaries will tie up capital for a number of years.
6. *Long-term profit objectives* – the growth envisaged in that market for the years ahead. Here, the question of distribution channel policy is very important. A wholly owned foreign subsidiary may build up its own technical service department alongside a small but growing sales team. Existing agents will then have to be given *ex gratia* payments to dispense with their services. Otherwise it will mean litigation which may well go against the company if heard in a local court, plus, of course, there are the costs of local legal representation.

The main features of the alternative modes of foreign market entry have been outlined (see Table 4.1). A company, perceived as being closely related to its country of origin, is termed 'ethnocentric'; if the company is based in a few countries with no conspicuous home country image, but instead a local market image in each market, it may be said to be 'polycentric': if its overall image is identifiable not with a country but a region of the world it may be termed 'regiocentric'; and, in the final category, of those very few companies, such as IBM, Coca-Cola, or Pepsi – viewed as being globally co-ordinated with their own complex global sourcing,

Table 4.1 Main features of market entry modes

Market entry method	Characteristics
Courier/Express Delivery Services	Generally courier companies such as DHL see themselves as express delivery not freight services. DHL have a weight limit of 30 kilos, UPS of 70 kilos, but the tendency now is for companies to send small shipments often rather than large shipments and break bulk.
Freight forwarder	Acting on behalf of producer. Documentation and delivery service to foreign destination. Goods are collected from the manufacturer and all paperwork and freight handling is done by the freight forwarder.
Export houses	Approx. 700–800 of these in the UK, accounting for 20 per cent of UK exports. Export house represents a buyer abroad. Trading company may be buying and selling on own account, or acting for a foreign principal.
Agents	Most common form of market entry worldwide. Paid on commission, usually handling products for more than one company and perhaps more than one product line. Low cost but very difficult to get rid of a bad agent other than with a 'golden handshake'. Agents vary in quality, and are sought for their market knowledge and ability to network.
Distributors	Differ from agents in that they 'take title to the goods' they sell, i.e. they have to buy the goods first, then sell them. For the producer, this lessens risk and improves cash flow, but weakens control as less is known about the final end-user and final sales price. Distributors will seek exclusivity of sales territory.
Piggybacking	An entry method much favoured by US multinationals and a feature of strategic business alliances. Uses the distribution channel of another company, and in this respect, overlaps with agents but complementarity sought of distribution outlets and products carried. Size is a factor. Returns are achieved by means of commission or outright sale of goods by one multinational to another.
Consortium exporting	Used by small companies and companies with narrow specific skills to combine their skills and resources, and bid for contracts and projects as a group, while still retaining their independent ownership.
Licensing	Often regarded as a second-best alternative to exporting. It confers a right to utilize a company-specific process in manufacturing a proprietary brand, and may also include a know-how agreement incorporating training and the licensor's learned experience of producing according to this process, plus continuing exports of components embodying the most advanced technology. This lessens the risk of copying and increases the value added for the licensor.
Know-how (knowledge) agreement	Usually incorporated into licensing sales, the know-how agreement is the sale of production experience using the particular process in question and training the licensee's operatives. A know-how agreement can halve the time required before a plant is fully operational.
Franchising	Experiencing high growth in Europe and North America. Introduces small independents with no prior business experience to a proven business concept. Transfers the right to use the company's name, logo and all that may be identifiable with the company. Examples abound in the services sector. May also include a management contract.
Management contracts	Transfer of management control and accounting systems, widely evidenced in the services sector, e.g. hotel industry, private hospital management where administration is contracted.
Joint ventures	Two distinct types: contractual, as in strategic business alliances (SBAs) and joint-equity. Contractual is of fixed duration; with responsibilities and duties well defined. Joint-equity involves investment, no fixed duration, and is continually evolving.

management reporting systems etc. – are labelled 'geocentric' and for these very few companies, planning on a world scale is a daily reality.

These terms, ethnocentric, polycentric, regiocentric and geocentric, are labels to describe outward manifestations of the company; they do relate to corporate structure, and have effects on corporate planning and policy as in Figure 4.1.

Knowledge is a valuable asset and, in an age of information technology, is constantly being repackaged. Knowledge is central to licensing, to franchising, to management contracts and to joint ventures, and particularly, strategic business alliances. Although licensing and franchising are

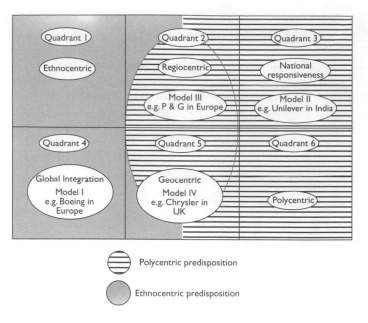

Source: Chakravarthy, B. S. and Perlmutter H. V. (1990) 'Strategic Planning for a Global Business'. In Thorelli,   H. B. and Cavusgil, S. T., *International Marketing Strategy*, 3rd Edition, Pergamon, Oxford

Figure 4.1   A framework for choosing strategic planning systems

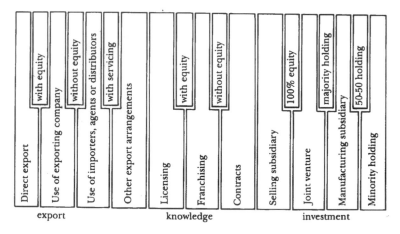

Source: Brooke, M. Z. (1996) *International Management*, 3rd Edition, Stanley Thornes publishers, Cheltenham, Glos.

Figure 4.2   Brooke's keyboard analogy of international strategies

sometimes used interchangeably, licensing confers a right to produce, using a patented manufacturing process, while franchising involves the right more often to sell a service under a brand name and within strict guidelines relating to all aspects of its merchandising. Licensing, franchising and management contracts (sometimes also called technical assistance agreements) are but three ways in which knowledge, rather than a product, is transferred from seller to buyer. Brooke (1996) classifies the different modes of foreign market entry into three categories: exporting, knowledge sales, and investment in that order, see his piano keyboard in Figure 4.2.

The keyboard analogy

Many of the notes have to be played at once, while the combinations and sequences are all important. This analogy is as exact as an analogy can be and, hopefully, illuminating. Unfortunately, as has been pointed out by more than one correspondent, it does not illuminate those who are unfamiliar with music. The author can only invite them to take on trust the statement about sequences and combinations. A glance at a keyboard instrument will usually demonstrate the truthfulness of the diagrams.

In this chapter, we will be dealing with

exporting and knowledge sales, and with those strategies related to investment. Regarding exporting, it must be said that the popular media is responsible for creating a distorted image of exporting as a pioneering activity which is fraught with danger, but somehow noble in itself, and also patriotic. Consequently, media focus undue attention on daily (spot) currency exchange rates as having an unequal weighting in winning export orders. A significant fall over the day in one currency will often be seen as heralding new export opportunities, ignoring the fact that exports often have a three, six or nine month time lag before a sales contract actually is fulfilled. Daily fluctuations in exchange rates are, therefore, no more than just simply fluctuations which can be dealt with by banks. The serious buyer will in any event buy forward, i.e., take out an option to purchase a fixed amount of foreign currency at a set date in the future and, so, guarantee himself a fixed exchange rate which will be unaffected by any subsequent currency revision. At the same time, it is difficult also to introduce some realism into popular conceptions that exporting is noble and

patriotic. Exporting is not a luxury nor is it an activity that requires bravado as much as research, skill and some luck. It often requires a great deal of patience and also resource before bearing fruit, but to an increasing number of companies of different sizes across the world, exporting has become the activity on which the very survival of the company often depends.

Companies do, however, find themselves being pushed into exporting and it is in this connection that we should first consider 'indirect' market entry strategies, remembering all the while that the rather grandiose term 'strategy' may commonly apply only to a strategy by default, where a company, faced with a certain market situation, chooses to do nothing. Over time, corporate attitude and strategy become more clearly visible. Those strategies termed 'indirect' are chiefly those whereby a domestic manufacturer is able to engage in the fortuitous sale of his products abroad with minimal outlay or use of his own company resources. Also in this category is the situation which is frequently encountered where a company may often be

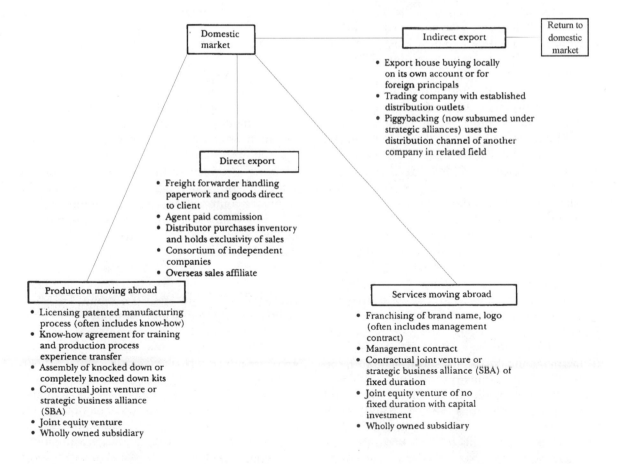

Source: Adapted from Terpestra, V. and Sarathy, R. (1994) *International Marketing*, 6th Edition, The Dryden Press

Figure 4.3 Charting the possibilities for direct and indirect exports, production and services

unaware that its products are even being exported. Foreign buying offices of department store chains are represented in the Export Buying Offices Association, London, which represents stores and fashion houses worldwide. This provides a prime example of an 'export-pull' effect, whereby goods are exported to a new market without the active participation of the producer himself. This may then create a demonstration effect within that foreign market which may lead to further export sales. Then, as envisaged by the product life cycle for international trade, foreign production increases imports, displacing domestic products chiefly on price. Foreign production strength leads to eventual foreign production penetration and saturation of the domestic market which first launched the product.

As indirect market entry methods involve the use of intermediaries who handle all documentation, physical movement of goods, and channels of distribution for sale, indirect exports may take place either with or without the knowledge of the manufacturer himself. Indirect market entry may occur in a number of ways.

An *export house*, of which there are many in the one mile square City of London, will buy directly from you on behalf of a foreign principal in which case the sale will be a purely domestic one with the export house arranging the export of the goods.

The *trading company* is in a quite different category. Britain owed its strength in international trading to these trading companies such as the East India Company, Hudson Bay Company and others firmly established in what were then British colonies. Today, the United Africa Company (UAC), which is part of Unilever, remains the largest trader in Africa, but Paterson Zochonis is another example of a very large trading company with well established roots. These trading companies have well connected distribution outlets in the countries in which they operate and are able to handle a diverse product range, in the case of UAC in Nigeria, from galvanized metal pails to motor car dealerships. The Japanese trading houses, the Soga Shosha (discussed in Chapter 11) offer an integrated range of financial and insurance services in addition, as they frequently incorporate their own bank into their organizational structure. The dominance of Japanese banks in world banking may be seen in Chapter 11. Offering then a range of integrated services, all the way through to the end-user, gives the Soga Shosha a competitive advantage.

Piggybacking is a quite different phenomenon and is increasingly being subsumed under strategic business alliances, of which more later.

Piggybacking remains primarily a US phenomenon occurring between consenting US multinationals! One-third of US companies were seen to be involved in piggybacking and so it is worth considering some of the reasons why this should be so:

1. Extending the product depth – the exporter may be seeking additional products in order to be able to offer a fuller product range, or else extend the associated benefits or services currently available.
2. Foreign customers may have asked the exporter for specific merchandise that is not currently available in the market. Here, the exporter is simply making available his distribution outlets to the manufacturer. Where the exporter is also a manufacturer or distributor of allied products, there may even be a synergistic effect in that where the goods are truly complementary to each other and non- competing, then they may lift total sales.
3. Some US exporters look for additional products to sell in foreign markets to increase their total sales. The exporters or piggybackers will ask a manufacturer to produce a product line under their own brand name.

Piggybacking seems to attract large companies rather than small, but it enables a non-exporter to exploit the distribution channels of an exporting company with a complementary, non-competing product. For the exporter, piggybacking offers the advantage of widening the product range carried, using the sales force to the full, and earning additional revenue from carrying products into distribution channels which would have to be served anyway. For the domestic company, there is the obvious advantage of a ready made overseas market with an experienced international exporting firm at the ready. There is less risk than going it alone and there is direct access to the market, as the channels of distribution already exist. With piggybacking there are two possible forms of payment: either outright full payment or an ongoing commission basis on volume sold.

This relationship may, therefore, vary from an order-to-order basis to one of established permanence. Finding a piggybacker may prove difficult and once established there is also the problem of the nature of the relationship, the product selling price, and the potential disadvantage that since the products are subordinated to the other company's lines they may not be promoted as aggressively. The exporting manufacturer may feel greater loyalty to his own wares and he may be under greater pressure from his management to sell his own wares. Profitable

Table 4.2 Market entry mode selection criteria profiles

	Agent	Distributor	Licensing	Franchising	Joint-equity venture	Strategic business alliance	Wholly-owned subsidiary
Speed of market entry	High	High	Slower	Slower	Slow	Slow	Slowest
Costs direct and indirect	Low	Low	Higher	Higher	High	High	Highest
Degrees of freedom	Low	Low	Contractual	Contractual	Limited	Limited	Total
Total exposure to risk	Low	Low	Moderate/high	Moderate	Moderate/high	Moderate	High
Investment payback period	Short	Short	Short/medium	Short/medium	Medium	Short/medium	Long-term
Perceived long-term profitability	Moderate/low	Moderate/low	Low	High/moderate	High/moderate	High	High
Foreign market competition							
low	Less likely	Less likely	Limited	Present	Less likely	Less likely	Present
high	Present	Present	Present	Present	Present	Present	Less likely
Ability to expand within mode	Present	Present	Limited	Present	Limited	Limited	Present
Stable mature product	Present	Limited	Limited	Present	Limited	Limited	Less frequent
Excess capacity utilization	Present	Limited	N/A	N/A	N/A	N/A	N/A
New product launch	Present	Present	With caution	Present	Limited	Limited	Present
Achieving market coverage	Present	Present	Present	Present	Present	Present	Present
Receiving feedback	Limited	Limited	Very limited	Moderate	Moderate	Moderate	High
Method of recovery income for sales	Commission	Outright sale	Royalty	Royalty + fees +ongoing sales of inputs	Shared	Shared according to agreed formula	Total profits
Control over market mode by principal	Limited	Limited	Contractual and limited	High	Moderate/high	Moderate/high	Total

* May also be other barriers as well.

Table 4.3   External and Internal Factors influencing the Entry Mode Decision

	Generally favours:				
	Indirect and agent/ distributor exporting	*Licensing*	*Branch subsidiary exporting*	*Equity investment/ production*	*Service contracts*
External factors (foreign country)					
Low sales potential	×	×			
High sales potential			×	×	
Atomistic competition	×		×		
Oligopolistic competition				×	
Poor marketing infrastructure			×		
Good marketing infrastructure	×				
Low production cost				×	
High production cost	×		×		
Restrictive import policies		×		×	×
Liberal import policies	×		×		
Restrictive investment policies	×	×	×		×
Liberal investment policies				×	
Small geographical distance	×		×		
Great geographical distance		×		×	×
Dynamic economy				×	
Stagnant economy	×	×			×
Restrictive exchange controls	×	×			×
Liberal exchange controls				×	
Exchange rate depreciation				×	
Exchange rate appreciation	×		×		
Small cultural difference			×	×	
Great cultural difference	×	×		×	
Low political risk			×	×	
High political risk	×	×			×
External factors (home country)					
Large market				×	
Small market	×		×		
Atomistic competition	×		×		
Oligopolistic competition				×	
Low production cost	×		×		
High production cost		×		×	×
Strong export promotion	×		×		
Restrictions on investment abroad	×	×			×
Internal factors					
Differentiated products	×		×		
Standard products				×	
Service-intensive products			×	×	
Service products		×		×	×
Technology intensive products		×			
Low product adaptation	×				
High product adaptation		×	×	×	
Limited resources	×	×			
Substantial resources			×	×	
Low commitment	×	×			×
High commitment			×	×	

Source: Root, F. R. (1994) *Entry Strategies for International Markets*, Revised and Expanded Edition, Lexington Books, Lexington, MA.

business can, however, emanate from this kind of relationship, although this relationship may mean either that A is purchasing from B to resell in foreign markets under his control, or else A is the agent of B and in return for providing suitable outlets for products complementary to his own, he receives a commission on sales. However, there is the added advantage also, though much less quantifiable, of increased sales resulting from augmented product range. The points to particularly note of a potential piggybacker are:

* the products the firm presently exports,
* how your product will be promoted – in particular, who will handle your product, how often he travels abroad, etc.,
* type of distribution used in major foreign markets,
* exporting pricing policies,

* identification of others being 'piggybacked' (check with these firms to find out if they are happy with the arrangement),
* estimated amount of export sales for your product; and
* countries covered by the exporting manufacturer.

The difficulty remains, however, of being stuck with an arrangement which could in the long term hinder your ability to expand your product range or establish your own export effort, or could not be changed if dissatisfied with the piggybacker's performance.

Direct exporting activities

These begin where the company may be actively involved in foreign sales, but perhaps due to

Table 4.4   McMillan and Paulden's classification of agents and distributors

Agent acting for exporter as principal
1. Agent on commission.
2. Commission/fee and commission/stockist agencies.
3. Salaried salesman (i.e. own company man).
4. Independent salesman (Jack-of-all-trades).
5. Agent/distributor.
6. Agent/warehousing.
7. Agent/servicing company.
8. Agent/design office (prefab buildings, central heating, etc.).
9. Agent/customer.
10. Agent/manager (e.g., French or British in Africa).
11. Factory representative/Agent controller (for agent supervision.)
12. Export management agency (acts as an export dept.).

Agent purchasing for himself as principal
13. Export merchant.
14. Distributor.
15. Stockist.
16. Wholesaler.
17. Trading company (esp. Japanese).
18. Agents who assemble (using percentage of local parts).
19. Sales agent who buys.

Agent acting for other buyers as principals
20. Buying offices, esp. American dept. stores, Australia (Myers).
21. Buying houses (serve a particular territory, cf 17).
22. Buying agents located abroad.

Agents understanding specialized aspect of export cycle other than selling
23. Confirming houses (guarantees payment on due date, intermediary).
24. Factors, operating for exporters, financial service – bills are discounted with or without recourse to money.
25. Shipping and forwarding agents.
26. Technical partnership.
27. Depot distribution agents.

Source: McMillan, C., and Paulden, S. (1974) *Export Agents: A Complete Guide to their Selection and Control*, 2nd edn, Gower. Aldershot, Hampshire

---

Table 4.5   Agents – how many to appoint?

Some variables to consider:

- market size and accessibility
- agent's own resource base – agent's network of contacts
- number of languages/dialects spoken in the target market
- important regional differences that require regional representation
- location of the agent

---

inexperience, arranges for all documentation and physical distribution to be handled on its behalf by a freight forwarder.

Beyond this stage, the most popular form of direct entry is the agent or distributor and here, the reader is recommended to turn to the 27 different types identified by McMillan and Paulden (1974) in Table 4.4. Note that these can, however, be grouped into four main categories.

Agents

Agents are the most common form of low-cost direct involvement in foreign markets. However, there are a number of disadvantages. Firstly, although foreign embassies and national trade associations are able to supply fairly complete lists of agents, it is often difficult for them to give any qualitative assessment or evaluation, or to recommend specific agents, perhaps out of a need for impartiality rather than a fear of libel. Service quality offered can prove extremely variable and, as an agent is paid commission only on sales, his loyalty may be further questioned if it is seen to rest purely on the company currently providing him with the greatest earnings. As agents may represent a number of separate companies and product lines, this may be a problem. Meanwhile, the company holds responsibility for whatever unsold inventory is held by the agent, while at the same time being virtually deprived of market information.

No agent will willingly expose himself to the risk of being supplanted by a branch of the company's own sales organization. In market situations where there is (in Boston Consulting Group terminology) a 'problem child' syndrome evident – i.e., slow growth for the company's product in an otherwise high growth market – it may be difficult to determine exactly why this has arisen. On the other hand, where there is high market growth, this creates pressures within the company to take over the foreign market from the agent. This may often require compensating the agent handsomely, especially where local legislation exists to protect his position. Elsewhere, the situation may arise where the company wishes to expand its product line or else diversify into a quite different product, and the local agent finds himself unable to meet this new expansion but still holds a company agreement to exclusivity of sales territory.

Distributors

Distributors usually seek exclusive rights to specific sales territories, but constitute yet another method of low-cost foreign market entry. The difference between the distributor and the agent is that the distributor will, like the foreign buying office, be placing an order similar to any other domestic purchase order in that the responsibility for the condition and sale of goods will end at some point to be agreed in the distribution channel between producer and distributor. The distributor actually takes title – i.e., owns the inventory which he carries – and represents the manufacturer in the sales and service of

---

Table 4.6   Assessing the potential agent

- date of incorporation and business experience of the principals
- resource base of the agent, including:
    human resource strength, e.g. technical skills
    financial strength
    goodwill associated to agency
- degree of motivation to accept your product line = high/low
- annual turnover of the agency
- number of foreign principals represented
- contact patterns established with the client base
- how does the agent perceive your product in terms of strengths and weaknesses?

Exhibit 4.2   Put it down to cultural difference

The north-south divide thrives in death as in life. The World Health Organization's latest statistics on suicide show southern Europe, as usual, lagging behind the north. Sunshine, perhaps, makes life more worth living. The cold and clouds depress.

League of gloom

Suicide rates per 100,000 1990–95	All	Men	Women
Hungary	38.6	58.0	20.7
Finland	29.8	48.9	11.7
Switzerland	22.7	34.3	11.6
Belgium	22.7	32.0	13.8
Austria	22.6	34.6	11.6
Denmark	22.4	30.0	15.1
France	20.1	29.6	11.1
Sweden	18.6	26.8	10.6
Germany	17.5	24.9	10.7
Japan	16.1	20.6	11.8
Norway	15.5	23.3	8.0
Poland	13.9	23.9	4.4
United States	12.2	19.9	4.8
Netherlands	9.7	12.3	7.2
Portugal	9.6	14.9	4.6
Ireland	9.5	14.4	4.7
Britain	7.9	12.4	3.6
Spain	7.7	11.6	3.9
Italy	7.5	11.2	4.1
Greece	3.5	5.5	1.5

Source: WHO

Compare Finland, the northernmost country in continental Europe, which has a suicide rate of almost 30 per 100,000, with Greece, at a mere 3.5. According to the WHO's global rankings (and remembering that countries have different national standards for establishing a death as suicide), northern European countries took up no fewer than eight of the top ten entries for men committing suicide. Spain, Italy, Greece and Malta, meanwhile, languished at the bottom of the list, alongside such island paradises as Barbados and the Bahamas.

France, by itself, illustrates suicide's latitudinal bent. The overall suicide rate is high, at 20 per 100,000, but almost all these deaths occur in the country's northern half. Stretches of the Breton coast have a suicide rate three times as high as the balmy beaches of Corsica. Similar trends appear in countries of the former Soviet Union. Lithuania reported over 70 suicides per 100,000 men, whereas Tajikistan mustered only 5.4. Russia counted 66 to Ukraine's 38.

Various statistical studies have tried to link the divergences to unemployment, urbanisation, religious beliefs and alcoholism — without much success. Even hours of sunshine do not, when one comes down to it, really provide the answer. Most suicidologists, as the professionals call themselves, attribute the highs and lows to the catch-all of 'cultural differences'.

Britain, it turns out, is very culturally different. Of all the countries in northern Europe, it has the lowest overall rate at 7.9 suicides per 100,000 people. Even Puerto Rico and Portugal score higher. Scholars put this poor performance down to the method of choice. Frenchmen prefer to hang themselves, and Germans to shoot themselves, but the average suicidal Briton tries to die by swallowing poison. And that, more often than not, does not do the trick. Once again, British perversity lands it outside the club of core European countries.

Source: The Economist (1996), 5 October, p. 50

the products which he carries. Thus, in return for his capital investment, he will usually seek exclusivity of supply and sales territory plus a reasonable turnover rate of the products handled.

Similarities between agents and distributors

McMillan and Paulden (1974) identified 27 different types of agents/distributors, as in Table 4.4 which shows many similarities beyond the essential differences described briefly above. Both agents and distributors are intermediaries in the distribution channel between the pro-

ducer and his final customer, and as intermediaries, share a number of similar characteristics. Many authors, therefore, use the term agent or distributor interchangeably, whereas, in fact, they are more correctly referring to the role of intermediaries. The distinction between agents and distributors has always to be maintained. So, assuming that we have discovered that the company has an exportable product and we have been able to identify a target market, we have then to decide on the best form of representation, finding an intermediary whose profile most clearly meets our needs, and then negotiate a working arrangement with that intermediary.

A great deal of risk and pure guesswork has

been removed from the selection procedure in that the clearing banks will now offer a financial appraisal of a foreign client, and that further help is also available from the London Chamber of Commerce and the Department of Trade and Industry in terms of qualitatively evaluating those intermediaries which appear on lists circulated by foreign embassies and consulates. The advantage of using a Chamber of Commerce is that the names put forward on either side can generally be assumed to be reliable firms.

In terms of selection, Beeth (1990) offers some very concrete advice:

1. Go personally to the country, allowing ample time. Talk to the ultimate users of the equipment to find out from which distributors they prefer to buy and why. Two or three names will keep popping up in the replies you receive.

2. Then go to those two or three distributors and see which one or ones you would be able to sign up.

3. But, before making the final choice, look for the distributor who has the key man for your line.

Beeth (1990) describes how in a company for which he worked, they had a scaling system of one to ten by which to evaluate intermediaries on 24 different activities and abilities. These ratings were then verified against their individual importance to the company and a final assessment produced. However, the final rating figure showed no correlation at all to their actual performance. Consequently they abandoned the

Table 4.7   Contracts with intermediaries

1. *General provisions*
    Identification of parties to the contract.
    Duration of the contract.
    Definition of covered goods.
    Definition of territory or territories.
    **Sole and exclusive rights.
    Arbitration of disputes.

2. *Rights and obligations of manufacturer*
    Conditions of termination.
    Protection of sole and exclusive rights.
    Sales and technical support.
    Tax liabilities.
    Conditions of sale.
    Delivery of goods.
    Prices.
    Order refusal.
    Inspection of distributor's books.
    Trademarks/patents.
    Information to be supplied to the distributor.
    Advertising/promotion.
    Responsibility for claims/warranties.
    Inventory requirements.
    **Termination and cancellation.

3. *Rights and obligations of distributor*
    Safeguarding manufacturer's interests.
    Payments arrangements.
    Contract assignment.
    **Competitive lines.
    Customs clearance.
    Observance of conditions of sale.
    After-sales service.
    Information to be supplied to the manufacturer.

** Most important and contentious issues.

Source: Root, F. R. (1994) *Entry Strategies for International Markets*, Revised and Expanded Edition, Lexington Books, Lexington, MA.

24 criteria and started to look more closely for any commonality that existed among the excellent intermediaries. This emerged as being able to identify one capable person within the intermediary who would be committed to the company and to the product and, in Beeth's own words, 'take the new line of equipment to his heart and make it his personal objective to make the sale of that product line a success in his country.' If unable to identify a suitable local intermediary, or else persuade an intermediary to switch from handling a competitor's product line to yours, it is better not to enter that market than to enter it with a mediocre intermediary.

Retaining and motivating good intermediaries are important. Usually this means financial rewards for volume sold, but it means also providing regular stimulus to the intermediary to maintain interest in your product line. Training may be paid for and warranty obligations must be met in full as these help create goodwill. The contract is the basis on which the relationship is to be defined, so it must define the setting of targets as well as penalties.

Similarly, there have to be awards for achievement. Mediocre intermediaries can only be improved at a cost and for most companies the price will be too high. There is a need, therefore, to be able to be ruthless and extricate yourself quickly from an arrangement that appears to be going nowhere. Cancellation clauses usually involve rights under local legislation, and it is best that a contract is scrutinized by a local lawyer before signature, rather than after a relationship has ended and a compensation case is being fought in the courts. Care should be exercised in contracts with intermediaries. (See Table 4.7.)

Management contracts

Management contracts are quite different again in that they often subsume some other form of relationship in addition, such as licensing,

---

Exhibit 4.3 PSA captures management deal in Aden

The Port of Singapore Authority (PSA) is set to operate the Ma'alla Terminal in Aden and is in talks to build a new container terminal in the Red Sea port.

PSA said it had a contract with Yemen Investment and Development International (YemInvest) to provide management and operations services at the existing terminal.

YemInvest, a consortium with government concessions to develop and manage Aden port and storage facilities, is backed by Saudi-based investors.

PSA also confirmed it was negotiating with the Yemeni authorities to build a new container terminal in Aden.

'PSA would be interested to participate in the development of the container terminal with YemInvest,' it said.

Sources close to the deal said negotiations between Yemeni authorities and PSA over the terminal were 'beyond the preliminary stages.'

The deal was expected to have been firmed up by the end of last month, they said.

The port project has attracted a number of operators, including Hong Kong and British groups. Philippine port operator International Container Terminal Services Inc (ICTSI) was a leading contender, together with Meneren Corporation of the United States.

ICTSI backed out because of disagreement over the deal. It is believed the local authorities would only offer it a short management term compared with the 25-year deal it wanted.

PSA is likely to accept an initial short term management of three years, one source said. The authority has tied this to clinching an equity stake in the deal, the source said.

Aden, located strategically on the main east-west and north-south shipping lanes, has been earmarked by Yemen for development into a commercial and industrial 'free zone'.

The government also aims to make it the major transshipment port for the Middle East region.

Aden's container traffic is low. Ma'alla Terminal is estimated to have handled only about 12,000 teus (20-ft equivalent unit) containers last year.

Government officials believe the terminal has potential to become a relay hub, saying that container ships using other ports in the area could cut two to three days off sailing time by transshipping containers through Aden.

Plans for the new container terminal, referred to as the North Shore Terminal by Yemeni port authorities, are well advanced and the authorities are pressing on with the first phase of development – dredging the port channel.

The channel is to be deepened to 16 metres to accommodate the latest generation of ships sailing between Europe through the Suez Canal and the Red Sea to Asia, East Africa and Australia.

Source: South China Morning Post, 4 April 1997

Table 4.8   Profile desired of intermediaries

- Trading areas covered.
- Lines handled.
- Size of firm.
- Experience with manufacturer's or similar product line.
- Sales organization and quality of sales force.
- Physical facilities.
- Willingness to carry inventories.
- After-sales servicing capability.
- Knowledge/use of promotion.
- Reputation with suppliers, customers and banks.
- Record of sales performance.
- Cost of operations.
- Financial strength/credit rating.
- Overall experience.
- Relations with local government.
- Knowledge of English or other relevant languages.
- Knowledge of business methods in manufacturer's country.
- Willingness to cooperate with manufacturer.

Source: Root, F. R. (1994) *Entry Strategies for International Markets*, Revised and Expanded Edition, Lexington Books, Lexington, MA.

Table 4.9   What intermediaries seek

- Differentiated, well-known, prestige product with good sales potential.
- Functional discounts that allow high markups.
- Exclusive distribution rights protected by the manufacturer.
- Contractual obligations assumed by the manufacturer for a lengthy period, with indemnities paid for any cancellation by the manufacturer.
- Right of the distributor to terminate the agreement without indemnities.
- Right to design and implement the marketing plan without interference or control by the manufacturer.
- Generous credit terms.
- Full support by the manufacturer – inventory backup, quick order servicing, technical and sales training, advertising allowances, special discounts, and so on.
- Product warranties.
- Freedom to handle other lines, whether competitive or complementary to the manufacturer's line.
- Paid visits to the manufacturer's headquarters or to regional meetings.
- Obligation to provide only minimum information to the manufacturer.

Source: Root, F. R. (1994) *Entry Strategies for International Markets*, Revised and Expanded Edition, Lexington Books, Lexington, MA.

franchising, strategic business alliance or joint-equity venture. Management contracts emphasize the increasing importance of services and know-how as a saleable asset in international trade. Based on a contractual form, it will concern the transferral of management control systems and know-how involving personnel training. The demand arises mainly from those countries where there exists a 'managerial gap'. Essentially, it is a 'software' package incorporating management and control systems, and frequently found in those industries where there is an expectation of quality, service, and attention.

Hotels and hospitals are just two areas in which management contracts have been usefully explored. Management contracts do constitute high value added, long-term business.

Franchising

Franchising is a marketing-oriented method of selling a business service, often to small independent investors with working capital but little or no prior business experience. Yet, it is almost like an umbrella term which is used to mean anything from the right to use a name to

Table 4.10	Franchising in Europe	
	# Franchises	% of total retail sales
Belgium	3,000	6%
UK	222,700	32%
France	25,750	6%
Germany	20,000	–
Hungary	5,500	2.5%
Italy	21,930	2.5%
Netherlands	11,975	12%
Sweden	9,500	6–7%

Source: Belgian Franchise Association cited in *Entrepreneur International* (1997) Feb/Mar, p. 5

the total business concept. Franchising's origins go back two centuries to when brewers in Britain created the tied-house system to guarantee outlets for their beer. In the US the concept was developed by the Singer Sewing Machine Company. Three growing markets account for two-thirds of all franchises in the UK – home improvements and home maintenance (31 per cent), food and drink (18 per cent), and business services (17 per cent).

Franchising transfers the legal right to a third party to use a company's registered trade name, trademarks and logo, products, packaging, and business system. For example, Kentucky Fried Chicken (part of Pepsico Foods International) have a standardized red and white corporate colour, a distinctive trademark, logo and carton packaging for food. Kentucky Fried stipulate the sources from which the raw materials must be obtained, the recipes for the preparation of the food, again to be strictly controlled, and the quantity to be served in each portion. The particular benefit which franchising confers is that it allows small independents with investment capital (average £26,000 in UK in 1985), but no industry or management experience, to enjoy the benefits of belonging to a large organization while remaining owner-managers. Sixty per cent of all franchisees are women. Usually the franchisee is under 40, married with a couple of children, but the franchise can cost between £5,000 and £250,000. Drain clearing is relatively low cost while fast food operations are considerably more expensive, perhaps because of training and support. The failure rate is low, about 2 per cent per annum in the UK, whereas 75 per cent of all small businesses fail in the first

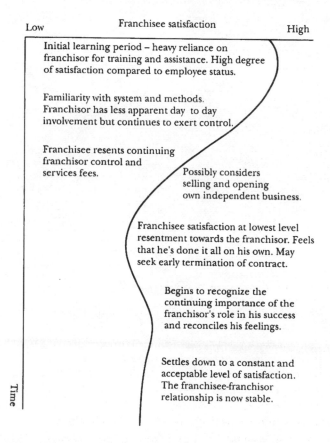

Source: Hall, P., and Dixon, R. (1989) *Franchising*, Natwest Small Business Bookshelf, Pitman Publishing, London

Figure 4.4   Franchisee satisfaction and the life cycle of the franchisee relationship

Exhibit 4.4   EUROPEAN FRANCHISE FEDERATION

EFF Member Franchise Associations

FRANCE
Chantal Zimmer
Féderation Française de la Franchise
60 Rue La Boétie
75008 Paris
Tel: +33 1 53 75 22 25
Fax: +33 1 53 75 22 20
E-mail: fff@club-internet.fr.Internet:
http://www.telecom.at/wklms/
   franchise

BELGIUM
Mr Pierre Jeanmart
Belgische Franchise Federatie
Bd. De L'Humanité 116/2
1070 Brussels
Tel: +32 2 523 97 07
Fax: +32 2 523 35 10

DENMARK
Dansk Franchisegiver – Forening
Amaliegade 37
1256 Copenhagen K
Tel: +45 45 88 77 18
Fax: +45 45 93 83 41

HUNGARY
Dr Istvan Kiss
Hungarian Franchise Association
POB 446
Budapest H-1536
Tel: +361 212 4124
Fax: +361 212 5712
E-mail:
100324.454@compuserve.com

POLAND
Mrs Jolanta Kramarz
Polskie Stowarzszenie
   Franchisingowe
Ul. Szpitalna 1, IIP., Room 5
00–020 Warsaw
Tel/Fax: +48 22 625 6956

SPAIN
Mr Jordi Ruiz de Villa Jubany
Associacion Espagnola de
Franquiciadores
Avda. de la Ferias S/N
PO Box 476
46080 Valencia
Tel: +34 6 386 11 23
Fax: +34 6 363 61 11

AUSTRIA
Mr Andreas Hacker
Osterreichischer Franchise-Verband
Nonntaler Haupstr. 48
5020 Salzburg
Tel: +43 662 82 56 70
Fax: +43 662 82 56 71

CZECH REPUBLIC
Mr Joseph Fidler
Ceska Asociace Franchisingu
Rytirska 18–20
110 00 Prag 1
Tel/Fax: +42 2 224 230 566

GERMANY
Peter-Alexander Sondermann
Deutscher Franchise Verband e. V.
Paul-Heyse Str. 33–35
80336 München
Tel: +49 89 53 50 27
Fax: +49 89 53 13 23

ITALY
Mr Michel Scardi
Associazione Italiana del
Franchisingso
Corso di Porta Nuova 3
20121 Milano
Tel: +39 2 2900 37 79
Fax: +39 2 655 59 19
E-mail: http://www.infodata-italy.com

NETHERLANDS
Mr Brouwer
Nederlandse Franchise Vereniging
Boomberglaan 12
1217 RR Hilversum
Tel: +31 35 6624 34 44
Fax: +31 35 6249 194
E-mail: franchise@nvf.nl

RUSSIA
Mr A Mailer
Russian Association for the Develop-
ment of Franchising
2nd proedz Perova polya,
9 Moscow
Tel: (095) 306 2526
Fax: (095) 305 5850

SWITZERLAND
Schweizerische Franchise
Lowenstrasse 11 Postfach
8039 Zurich
Tel: +41 1 225 47 57
Fax: +41 1 225 47 77

UNITED KINGDOM
Mr Brian Smart
British Franchise Association
Thames View, Newtown Road
PO Box 706
Henley-on-Thames
Oxon RG9 1HG
Tel: +44 (0) 1491 578049
Fax: +44 (0) 1491 573517

SWEDEN
Mr Stig Sohlberg
Svenska Franchise Fôreningen
Box 5512
S. 114 85 Stockholm
Tel: +46 8 660 86 10
Fax: +46 8 662 74 57

PORTUGAL
Mrs Pascale Lagneaux
Associaçáo Portugesa da Franchise
Rua Castilho, no 14
1250 Lisboa
Tel: +351 1 315 1845
Fax: +351 1 315 1845

YUGOSLAVIA
Dr Zdravko Glusica
Jugoslovenske Fransizing Asocijcije
Mokranjceva, 28
21000 Novi Sad
Tel/Fax: +381 21 614 2321

If you are involved, or interested in, international franchising,
THE EUROPEAN FRANCHISE FEDERATION and *THE EUROPEAN*,
the official publication of the EFF, are here to help you.

The EFF is dedicated to setting high standards within the franchise industry, and promoting franchising through Europe. If you want to reap the benefits of belonging to the Federation, contact your local association, listed above. If you want to promote your business across Europe and beyond in the Federation's only official international publication, contact Alan Cassidy on +44 171 418 7878 (tel) or +44 171 713 1835 (fax).

five years. This is partly due to the lack of capitalization and lack of personal motivation of the franchisee as well as lack of guidance and support from the franchisor. The British Franchising Association states that 98 per cent of franchisees are working with established franchises, but the emphasis should be on the word 'established'. Legislation varies from country to country and in some cases, franchises are sold for untested market ideas.

Nevertheless, the proven business idea behind a franchise appeals to banks, all of whom have established franchising departments. The *Good Franchise Guide* emphasizes that many franchises are little more than untested business ideas. Franchisees can get burned by paying high sums of money for a franchise, receiving little in return other than perhaps help with the preparation of company records, and having to pay highly also for supplies from a source to which they are contractually committed for the next ten years. Not all franchisors point out the need for planning permission to operate a business from home. Again, some franchises operate a chain of stocking-up that comes very close to pyramid selling, which is illegal. The *Good Franchise Guide* points to a disturbing number of franchises set up without first running pilot operations, also of poor prospectuses and poor PR. The *Good Franchise Guide* gives an honest portrayal of a form of business that contains a great many questionable operators. The return on initial capital invested may be recovered on average in just under two years, the return on the full cost in just over three years, but this depends on a number of variables, including the size of the franchised territory. A large fast-food restaurant may take four to five years for the investment to be recovered.

Franchising is rapidly increasing, as are the companies actively promoting it, e.g. Sheraton Intercontinental, Holiday Inns (hotels); Coca-Cola, Pepsi-Cola (soft drinks); Budget (car rental) and many of the fast-food companies; as well as others in drain clearing (Dyno-Rod), printing, and photocopying (Prontaprint).

Coca-Cola is held to provide the classic example of a franchise strategy, with its independent bottlers around the world preparing soft drinks from concentrate according to specifications supplied by Coca-Cola, which retains control over its trademark, recipe, and advertising. Franchising can often subsume a management contract and, thus, lead to profits from both royalties and management fees. It is still a relatively new concept in the international area and the tax treatment for this form of trading has yet to be standardized. Cadbury–Schweppes, who concluded a franchising deal with Asahi Breweries, part of the Sumitomo Group, to sell soft drinks in Japan, benefits also from the continuing export of essences and concentrates from the UK.

Mendelsohn (1992) points to the need for a contract stipulating the following:

1. There must be a contract containing all the terms agreed on.
2. The franchisor must initiate and train the franchisee in all aspects of the business prior to the opening of the business and assist in the opening.
3. After the business is opened, the franchisor must maintain a continuing interest in providing the franchisee with support in all aspects of the operation of the business.
4. The franchisee is permitted under the control of the franchisor to operate under a trade name, format and/or procedure, and with the benefit of goodwill owned by the franchisor.
5. The franchisee must make a substantial capital investment from his own resources.
6. The franchisee must own his business.
7. The franchisee will pay the franchisor in one way or other for the rights which he acquires and for the continuing services with which he will be provided.
8. The franchisee will be given some territory within which to operate.

An illustration of what can go wrong with a franchising deal is provided by the experience of McDonalds, the US fast-food chain, in France. McDonalds have 7,000 restaurants worldwide, but have been buying in franchises in the USA. (All of the first 126 British outlets were company owned.) McDonalds franchised a certain individual in the early 1970s to open a number of restaurants in Paris. The relationship soured when the US company charged him with not maintaining his restaurants to McDonalds' standards. There followed a long-winded lawsuit which was finally resolved in a Chicago court in 1982 in favour of the US company. McDonalds removed all names and references to the company from the franchised operation in Paris and set to work to catch up on the time lost to its rivals, including the Burger King chain, on the flourishing Parisian fast-food market. The franchisee renamed his restaurants O'Kitch. Meanwhile McDonalds selected for their re-entry to Paris an unusually stylish two-storey establishment which seeks to be very French, with granite bistro tables, art deco lights and lush plastic plants, plus the innovation of loose chairs for the first time in a McDonalds restaurant.

The maintenance of standards and the need also for standardization are two of the problems

Table 4.11   Advantages of franchising as a mode of market entry

A *To the franchisor:*
1. fast entry and withdrawal, so lower risk
2. moderate investment
3. limited overheads
4. avoid import duties and taxes as import/export content minimal
5. access to ready-made market
6. control.

B *To the franchisee:*
1. flexible business structure
2. shared financial responsibility
3. legal independence
4. tried and tested idea
5. economies of scale in distribution
6. motivation.

C *To the consumer:*
1. standardized product
2. fixed price
3. new technology fast
4. motivated/interested manager.

D *To the host country:*
1. technology transfer
2. creates employment and business opportunities
3. royalties often remain.

Table 4.12   A selection of international franchisors

France:

Quelle (photos)
Carrefour (hypermarkets)
Pronuptia (wedding dresses)
Phildar (wool)
Yoplait (yoghurt)
Yves Rocher (cosmetics)

USA:

McDonald's (hamburgers)
Subway (sandwiches and salads)
Yogen Fruz Worldwide (frozen yoghurt and ice cream)
KFC (chicken)
Jani-King (commercial cleaning)

UK:

Body Shop (premier environmentally-conscious cosmetics and grooming)
Burger King (hamburgers)
Clarks Shoes (family shoes)
Tie Rack (ties and scarves)
Dyno-Rod (drain cleaning)
Exchange Travel
Spud-U-Like (fast food restaurants)
Prontaprint (printshops)
Sketchley (dry cleaning)
Skirmish (paint-ball adventure games)

Table 4.13   Problems of franchising as a mode of market entry

A   *To the franchisor:*
  1. bureaucracy of host government regulations
  2. high import duties and taxes
  3. monetary uncertainties and royalty
  4. share royalties not profits
  5. logistical problems
  6. selection of franchisee
  7. control of a franchisee network
  8. quality of product and service must be standardized.

B   *To the consumer:*
  1. standardization of product with both good and negative aspects
  2. foreign technology directly exported
  3. high product price relative to domestic competitors.

C   *To the franchisee:*
  1. high cost of items supplied
  2. lack of independence in decision making
  3. franchisor lacks local knowledge
  4. doesn't keep or reap profits due to effort.

D   *To the host country:*
  1. direct import of foreign technology
  2. refusal often to use local substitutes
  3. negative culture effects.

Exhibit 4.5   Marketing to victory

If you thought French cooking was all about snails and frogs' legs, perhaps it's time you thought again. The runaway success of the franchised restaurant chain Pierre Victoire, with its simple decor and tasty but unpretentious fayre, suggests there is plenty of room in British hearts – and stomachs – for good French cuisine.

The first Pierre Victoire restaurant was established in Edinburgh in 1988 by French chef Pierre Levicky, four years after he followed a romance to Scotland.

Levicky, now 38, grew up in France with a part-Italian mother and Hungarian grandmother, and was introduced to good food from all over the world from an early age.

Pierre paid for his chef's education through a string of part time jobs before complementing it with the degree in business studies which would come to serve him well.

Arriving in Scotland in 1984 he landed a job as head chef at the Vintners Rooms in Leith, finally securing a lease for his own restaurant in Edinburgh's Victoria Street. His eccentric practices helped it to become one of the city's most popular restaurants.

He reportedly responded to complaints about the roof leaking by handing out umbrellas, and would reply to the question 'Are there any tables?' with 'No, but you could always bring your own'.

Word spread and Levicky quickly found himself opening more and more restaurants to satisfy demand. He decided to franchise the chain and, to ensure his exacting standards were maintained throughout, produced an operating manual and recipe book giving strict instructions about quality and service, as well as value for money.

All new franchisees and their chefs, as well as about 30 French chefs every week from the 18 restaurants still controlled directly by Pierre Victoire Ltd, have to go through a residential training programme at the new Pierre Victoire training school in Lochgelly. Levicky's book for franchisees has been updated and now contains some 500 recipes.

The restaurant chain includes Pierre Victoire, Chez Jules, Beppe Vittorio and Pierre Lapin restaurants, of which there are now more than 100 throughout the UK and Ireland, serving more than six million meals a year.

Group turnover has reached £44m, making Pierre Victoire one of the largest independent restaurant groups in the UK. Its target was to have 200 restaurants – 30 of them owned and controlled by Pierre Victoire Ltd – in operation by 1997, and it has already announced its intention to float on the stock market later this year.

Having first brought French cuisine to an appreciative audience in Scotland, Levicky is now taking Scottish cuisine to the continent. A pilot 'Scottish theme' restaurant opened in Brussels in last September.

The 300-seat restaurant has already proved enormously popular, attracting huge publicity and a considerable amount of business. It is entirely decorated on a Scottish theme, including stags' heads, claymores and wall-to-wall tartan.

Staff wear kilts and the bar boasts more than 50 malts, while cuisine ranges from Scotch pies and haggis to lobster and smoked salmon. The restaurant was even constructed by a team of Scottish

joiners, sent specially by Levicky to make absolutely sure his restaurant would have a genuinely Scottish feel.

The reception in Brussels to a Scottish theme restaurant has been overwhelming – it had to turn away more than 100 people on opening night – and Pierre Victoire Ltd is hopeful that its plans for expansion into Europe will be equally successful.

Levicky hopes to introduce 30 of his new theme restaurants across Europe, targeting major European cities such as Lille, Amsterdam, Antwerp, Cologne, Barcelona and Oslo. From there he will be expanding his empire into the United States. But that's another story . . .

Source: *Top Flight*, Gill Airways, Newcastle, January 1997

facing an international franchising operation. Meanwhile, it is interesting to note that the first 126 McDonalds' operations in the UK were wholly owned by McDonalds and not a franchise operation as found elsewhere among their 7,000 outlets worldwide. A legacy perhaps of their French experience, to ensure that they first got the quality right before expanding further, this has since changed and a few McDonalds franchises are now operational in the UK. Kentucky Fried Chicken called a temporary freeze on franchise recruiting and bought back 13 restaurants. Kentucky Fried Chicken own 60 stores out of 360 in the UK. Burger King, again in the UK, arc negotiating to buy in the last of their UK franchises.

Licensing

Licensing confers only a right to use a company-specific and patent-protected process in manufacturing. This right is conveyed in the transferral of original blueprints and designs. Operational experience in production of the licensed technology is usually a separately negotiable item, as will be any subsequent modifications to the product transferred, unless this has specifically been contracted and does not constitute 'new' technology. In its simplest form, then, it may involve the transmittal of original designs. Increasingly, though, use is being made of additional 'know-how' agreements which will include on-site training of supervisory staff plus an experience transferral in the operations of handling the licensed technology. Know-how, also referred to as technical cooperation or assistance, agreements are defined as: '. . . any

industrial information and techniques likely to assist in the manufacture or processing of goods and materials' (Mearn, 1987). 'Know-how' is estimated to save approximately two years on the tooling-up time for any major production plant. Where the licence does not include 'know-how', the buyer, while benefitting from a lower sales price, is hampered by the lack of available operational knowledge. The ability to cope with this situation depends on the technical levels of competence of the buyer and seller respectively.

When licensing agreements do turn out to be far from successful there may well be subsequent recriminations against the seller, perhaps even at a national level, for his refusal to update technology without further fee, particularly in the event of protracted delays in final production. Shortage of hard currency reserves leads to money having to be saved on licensing which usually means buying the blueprints only, ensuring, therefore, that the technological gaps will always be maintained.

The competitive 'advantage' incorporated in the licensing deal will in any event have a finite life. What licensors seek to do, therefore, is to protect the most secret part of their technology by continuing to export that particular component which embodies state-of-the-art technology. By so doing, they decrease the risk of creating a potential competitor – an accusation often levelled against licensing – while ensuring for themselves a steady revenue from export sales which can also be expected to increase as foreign production climbs. Licensing royalties, on the other hand, usually decrease over time and beyond a certain threshold of sales volume. Licensing may also create a future strategic

Table 4.14   Top 100 US Franchises

KEY: A: Africa **B:** Asia **C:** Australia/New Zealand **D:** Canada **E:** Eastern Europe **F:** Mexico/Central America **G:** Middle East **H:** South America **I:** Western Europe

FRANCHISE	ADDRESS	FAX NUMBER	DESCRIPTION	WHERE SEEKING
1. McDonald's	1 Kroc Dr., Oak Brook, IL 60521	(708)575–5645	Hamburgers, chicken, salads	Worldwide
2. Subway	325 Bic Dr., Milford, CT 06460	(203)876–6688	Submarine sandwiches & salads	Worldwide
3. Yogen Fruz Worldwide	8300 Woodbine Av., 5th Fl., Markham, ON, Can. L3R 9Y7	(905)479–5235	Frozen yogurt & ice cream	Worldwide
4. KFC	1441 Gardiner Ln., Louisville, KY 40213	(502)456–8255	Chicken	A,B,C,E,F,G,H,I
5. Burger King Corp.	P.O. Box 020783, Miami, FL 33157	(305)378–3502	Hamburgers	D,F,H
6. Jani-King	4950 Keller Springs, #190, Dallas, TX 75248	(972)991–5723	Commercial cleaning services	Worldwide
7. Dairy Queen	P.O. Box 39286, Minneapolis, MN 55439–0286	(612)830–0450	Soft-serve dairy products/sandwiches	B,C,D,H,I
8. Mail Boxes Etc.	6060 Cornerstone Ct. W., San Diego, CA 92121	(619)546–7488	Postal/business/ communications services	Worldwide
9. Pizza Hut Inc.	14841 N. Dallas Pkwy., Dallas, TX 75240–2100	(914)253–2070	Pizza	Worldwide
10. CleanNet USA Inc.	9861 Broken Land Pkwy., #208, Columbia, MD 21046	(410)720–5307	Commercial office cleaning	A,C,D,F,G,I
11. Coldwell Banker Residential Affil.	6 Sylvan Wy., Parsippany, NJ 07054	(201)560–1380	Residential real estate brokerage	Worldwide
12. Novus Windshield Repair	10425 Hampshire Ave. S., Minneapolis, MN 55438	(612)944–2542	Windshield repair	Worldwide
13. Coverall Cleaning Concepts	3111 Camino Del Rio N., #950, San Diego, CA 92108	(619) 584–4923	Commercial office cleaning	Worldwide
14. Midas Int'l. Corp.	225 N. Michigan Ave., Chicago, IL 60601	(312)565–7881	Brakes repair services	B,C,D,E,F,I
15. Holiday Inn Worldwide	3 Ravinia Dr., #2000, Atlanta, GA 30346	(770)604–2107	Hotels	Worldwide
16. TCBY Treats	425 W. Capitol Ave., Little Rock, AR 72201	(501)688–8246	Soft-serve frozen yogurt/ice cream	A,C,E,I
17. Blimpie Int'l. Inc.	1775 The Exchange, #600, Atlanta, GA 30339	(770)980–9176	Submarine sandwiches & salads	Worldwide
18. GNC Franchising Inc.	921 Penn Ave., Pittsburgh, PA 15222	(412)288–2033	Vitamin & nutrition stores	Worldwide
19. Chem-Dry	1530 N. 1000 West, Logan, UT 84321	(801)755–0021	Carpet, drapery & upholstery cleaning/ fabric care	Worldwide
20. Wendy's Int'l. Inc.	4288 Dublin Granville Rd., Dublin, OH 43017	(614)764–6894	Quick-service restaurant	D
21. Budget Rent A Car	4225 Naperville Rd., Lisle, IL 60532–3662	(708)955–7799	Auto & truck rentals	B,C,D,E,G,I
22. Century 21 Real Estate Corp.	339 Jefferson Rd., Parsippany, NJ 07054	(201)560–1362	Real estate services	B,C,D,F
23. Re/Max Int'l. Inc.	P.O. Box 3907, Englewood, CO 80155–3907	(303)796–3599	Real estate services	A,D,E,F,G,H,I
24 ServiceMaster	860 Ridge Lake Blvd., Memphis, TN 38120	(901)684–7580	Commercial/residential contract cleaning	Worldwide
25. Jazzercise Inc.	2808 Roosevelt, Carlsbad, CA 92008	(619)434–8958	Dance/exercise classes	Worldwide
26. Merle Norman Cosmetics	9130 Bellanca Ave., Los Angeles, CA 90045	(310)641–7144	Cosmetics studios	Worldwide
27. The Medicine Shoppe	1100 N. Lindbergh Blvd., St. Louis, MO 63132	(314)872–5500	Pharmacy	B,C,D,E,F,G,H,I

FRANCHISE	ADDRESS	FAX NUMBER	DESCRIPTION	WHERE SEEKING
28. Papa John's Pizza	P.O. Box 99900, Louisville, KY 40269–9990	(502)263–7352	Pizza	D
29. Choice Hotels Int'l.	10750 Columbia Pkwy., Silver Spring, MD 20901	(301)681–5687	Hotels, inns, suites & resorts	Worldwide
30. Great Clips Inc.	3800 W. 80th St., #400, Minneapolis, MN 55431	(612)844–3443	Family hair salons	D
31. Super 8 Motels Inc.	339 Jefferson Rd., Parsippany, NJ 07054	(201)428–0526	Economy motels	Worldwide
32. Applebee's Neighborhood Grill/Bar	4551 107th St., #100, Overland Park, KS 66207	(913)967–8910	Restaurant	D,E,F,G,I
33. Denny's Inc.	203 E. Main St., Spartanburg, SC 29301–0001	(864)597–7708	Full-service family restaurant	Worldwide
34. Matco Tools	4403 Allen Rd., Stow, OH 44224	(330)929–5008	Automotive tools	D
35. Cost Cutters Family Hair Care	300 Industrial Blvd. N.E., Minneapolis, MN 55413	(612)331–2821	Family hair salons	B,C,D,E,F,I
36. Merry Maids	860 Ridge Lake Blvd., Memphis, TN 38120	(901)537–8140	Residential cleaning	Worldwide
37. Terminix Termite & Pest Control	860 Ridge Lake Blvd., Memphis, TN 38120	(901)766–1208	Termite & pest control	Worldwide
38. Play It Again Sports	4200 Dahlberg Dr., Minneapolis, MN 55422	(612)520–8501	New & used sporting goods	C,D
39. Miracle Ear Hearing Systems	4101 Dahlberg Dr., Golden Valley, MN 55422	(612)520–9529	Hearing aids	A,B,E,F,G,H,I
40. Schlotzsky's Deli	200 W. 4th St., Austin, TX 78701	(512)477–2897	Sandwiches, soups, salads & pizza	B,C,D,F,G,H,I
41. Heel Quik! Inc.	6425 Powers Ferry Rd., #250, Atlanta, GA 30339	(770)933–8268	Shoe repair/alterations/monogramming	Worldwide
42. Churchs Chicken	6 Concourse Pkwy., #1700, Atlanta, GA 30328	(404)353–3312	Fried chicken & biscuits	Worldwide
43. Sylvan Learning Systems	9135 Guilford Rd., Columbia, MD 21046	(410)880–8717	Supplemental education	B,D,H,I
44. Manhattan Bagel Co. Inc.	246 Industrial Way, Eatontown, NJ 07724–2242	(908)544–1315	Bagel bakery & deli	D
45. Sir Speedy Printing Inc.	23131 Verdugo Dr., Laguna Hills, CA 92653	(714)348–5068	Printing, copying, digital network	Worldwide
46. Sbarro The Italian Eatery	763 Larkfield Rd., Commack, NY 11725	(516)462–9165	Quick-service Italian restaurant	A,B,C,D,E,F, G,H
47. Molly Maid	1340 Eisenhower Pl., Ann Arbor, MI 48108	(313)975–9000	Residential home services	D,E,I
48. Carlson Wagonlit Travel	P.O. Box 59159, Minneapolis, . MN 55459–8206	(612)449–2302	Travel agency	D
49. Floor Coverings Int'l.	5182 Old Dixie Hwy., Forest Park, GA 30050	(404)366–4606	Mobile floor coverings sales	D,I
50. Rent A Wreck	11460 Cronridge Dr., #118, Owings Mills, MD 21117	(410)581–1566	Auto rentals & leasing	A,B,C,E,F,G,H,I
51. Futurekids Inc.	5777 W. Century Blvd., #1555, Los Angeles, CA 90045	(310)337–9346	Computer learning centres for children	Worldwide
52. Orion Food Systems Inc.	2930 W. Maple, P.O. Box 780, Sioux Falls, SD 57101	(605)336–0141	Fast food systems	Worldwide
53. Fantastic Sams	5101 E. La Palma, #100, Anaheim, CA 92807	(714)779–3422	Hair salons	D,F
54. AAMCO Transmissions Inc.	One Presidential Blvd., Bala Cynnwyd, PA 19004	(610)617–9532	Transmission repair & services	D
55. Thrifty Rent-A-Car System Inc.	P.O. Box 35250, Tulsa, OK 74153–0250	(918)669–2861	Vehicle rentals, leasing & parking	Worldwide
56. Meineke Discount Mufflers	128 S. Tyron, #900, Charlotte, NC 28202	(704)358–4706	Exhaust systems/shocks/brakes/struts	D,F
57. Fastsigns	2550 Midway Rd., #150, Carrollton, TX 75006	(214)248–8201	Computer-generated vinyl signs & graphics	B,C,D,F,H,I

FRANCHISE	ADDRESS	FAX NUMBER	DESCRIPTION	WHERE SEEKING
58. Kwik-Kopy Corp.	P.O. Box 777, Cypress, TX 77410–0777	(713)373–4450	Printing, copying & related services	A,C,D,F,G,H,I
59. Precision Tune	748 Miller Dr. S.E., Leesburg, VA 20177	(703)779–0136	Auto tune-ups/repair services	Worldwide
60. A & W Restaurants Inc.	17197 N. Laurel Park Dr., #500, Livonia, MI 48152	(313)462–1017	Burgers, hot dogs, root beer	B,C,F,G,H
61. Popeyes Chicken & Biscuits	6 Concourse Pkwy., #1700, Atlanta, GA 30328	(404)353–3170	Fried chicken & biscuits	Worldwide
62. Golden Corral Fran. Systems	5151 Glenwood Ave., Raleigh, NC 27612	(919)881–5252	Family steakhouse/ buffet & bakery	C,D,F
63. Maaco Auto Painting & Bodyworks	381 Brooks Rd., King of Prussia, PA 19406	(610)337–6176	Automotive painting & body repair	D,F
64. Travel Network	560 Sylvan Ave., Englewood Cliffs, NJ 07632	(201)567–4405	Travel agency	Worldwide
65. Roto-Rooter Corp.	300 Ashworth Rd., West Des Moines, IA 50265	(515)223–4220	Sewer, drain-cleaning & plumbing svcs	Worldwide
66. Carl's Jr. Restaurants	1200 N. Harbor Blvd., Anaheim, CA 92803	(714)778–7160	Hamburgers & chicken sandwiches	B,C,F
67. Signs Now Corp.	4900 Manatee Ave. W., #201, Bradenton, FL 34209	(941)747–5074	Computerized 24-hr. sign-making services	Worldwide
68. Pizza Inn Inc.	5050 Quorum, #500, Dallas, TX 75240	(972)960–7208	Pizza, pasta, salads	Worldwide
69. Express Services Inc.	6300 Northwest Expwy., Oklahoma City, OK 73132	(405)720–0846	Staffing services/P.E.O.	Worldwide
70. Rainbow Int'l.	1010 N. University Parks Dr., Waco, TX 76707	(817)745–2592	Carpet/drapery dyeing/restoration	A,D,E,F,G,H
71. Furniture Medic	277 Southfield Pkwy., #130, Forest Park, GA 30050	(404)363–9797	Furniture restoration & repair service	Worldwide
72. General Business Services	1020 N. University Parks Dr., Waco, TX 76707	(817)745–2544	Business counselling/tax & accounting services	B,D
73. One Hour Martinizing Dry Cleaning	2005 Ross Ave., Cincinnati, OH 45212	(513)731–5513	Dry cleaning & laundry services	Worldwide
74. Realty Executives	4427 N. 36th St., #100, Phoenix, AZ 85018	(602)224–5542	Real estate w/ 100% commission	Worldwide
75. Uniglobe Travel	1199 W. Pender St., 9th Fl., Vancouver, BC, Can. V6E 2R1	(614)764–0112	Travel agency	Worldwide
76. Speedy Muffler King	8430 W. Bryn Mawr, #400, Chicago, IL 60631	(312)693–0309	Exhaust/brakes/suspen- sion/ride control	D
77. Minuteman Press Int'l. Inc.	1640 New Hwy., Farmingdale, NY 11735	(516)249–5618	Full-service printing centre	Worldwide
78. Hardee's	1233 N. Hardee's Blvd., Rocky Mount, NC 27804–2815	(919)450–4150	Fast-food limited- menu restaurants	A,B,C,E,F,G,H,I
79. The Athlete's Foot	1950 Vaughn Rd., Kennesaw, GA 30144	(770)514–4903	Athletic footwear & related sports accessories	A,B,D,E,F,G,H,I
80. Round Table Franchise Corp.	2175 N. California Blvd., #400, Walnut Creek, CA 94596	(510)974–3978	Pizza	A,F,H
81. The Chesapeake Bagel Bakery	6832 Old Dominion, #203, McLean, VA 22101	(703)893–0168	Bagel bakery & restaurant	D,F
82. Duraclean	2151 Waukegan Rd., Deerfield, IL 60015	(847)945–2023	Specialty cleaning/ restoration services	Worldwide
83. Comet 1 Hr. Cleaners	406 W. Division, Arlington, TX 76011	(817)861–4779	Dry cleaning & laundry services	F
84. Gateway Cigar Store/ Newsstands	30 E. Beaver Crk. Rd., #206, Rchmnd. Hill, ON, Can. L4B 1J2	(905)886–8904	Newsstand & sundry store	D
85. Gymboree	700 Airport Blvd., #200, Burlingame, CA 94010	(415)696–7452	Parent/child play programme	B,C,D,E,F,H,I
86. Steamatic Inc.	1320 S. University Dr., #400, Fort Worth, TX 76107	(817)332–5349	Cleaning services/ insurance restoration	D

FRANCHISE	ADDRESS	FAX NUMBER	DESCRIPTION	WHERE SEEKING
87. Jan-Pro Franchising Int'l. Inc.	300 Providence Hwy., #M-1, Dedham, MA 02026	(617)461–8471	Commercial cleaning services	D
88. The HomeTeam Inspection Service	6355 E. Kemper Rd., #250, Cincinnati, OH 45241	(513)469–2226	Home inspection service	D
89. Sign-A-Rama Inc.	1601 Belvedere Rd., #402 E, West Palm Bch., FL 33406	(407)640–7271	Full-service sign business	Worldwide
90. Jenny Craig Int'l.	11355 N. Torrey Pines Rd., La Jolla, CA 92037	(619)812–2711	Weigh-management services	B,E,F,G,H,I
91. Bruegger's Bagels	159 Bank St., P.O. Box 374, Burlington, VT 05401	(802)865–9739	Bagel bakery	A,B,C,E,F,G,H,I
92. ProForma	8800 E. Pleasant Valley Rd., Cleveland, OH 44131	(216)520–8474	Comm'l. printing/ promo. products & multimedia	D,F
93. American Leak Detection	888 Research Dr., #100, Palm Springs, CA 92262	(619)320–1288	Concealed water/ gas leak-detection services	Worldwide
94. Taco Time	3880 W. 11th Ave., Eugene, OR 97402	(541)343–5208	Mexican fast food	Worldwide
95. Gloria Jean's Gourmet Coffees	395 Del Monte Center, #152, Moneterey, CA 93940	(408)633–5920	Gourmet coffee, teas & accessories	B,C,F,G,I
96. Quizno's Corp.	7555 E. Hampden Ave., #601, Denver, CO 80231	(303)368–9454	Submarine sandwiches, soups, salads	D
97. Orange Julius of America	P.O. Box 39286, Minneapolis, MN 55439–0286	(612)830–0450	Fast food	B,C,D,F,G,H,I
98. Auntie Anne's Inc.	P.O. Box 529, Gap, PA 17527	(717)442–4139	Hand-rolled soft pretzels	Worldwide
99. Party City Corp.	400 Commons Wy., #C, Rockaway, NJ 07866	(201)983–1333	Discount party supplies	D,F,H,I
100. Once Upon A Child	4200 Dahlberg Dr., Minneapolis, MN 55422	(612)520–8501	Children's clothing & equipment	D

Source: Entrepreneur (1997) *Annual Franchise 500*, February/March, pp.19.27

limitation as Xerox Corporation in the USA found when they granted Rank-Xerox, a British–US company, rights to all markets outside the USA.

Licensing applies also to the increasing phenomenon of syndicating film personality and cartoon character rights to manufacturers of toys, clothing, stationery, etc. Disney cartoon characters perhaps started this trend many years ago with Mickey Mouse appearing on children's watches, but the growth in this area of characterization since then has been phenomenal. There have been the Smurfs displayed on petrol filling stations, the Flintstones on vitamin pills, plus Garfield (200 licensees) and Snoopy on a range of coffee mugs and stationery, including posters and greeting cards. The stars of the US television programme *Dynasty* promoted the merchandise of thirty-three different firms which paid to be associated with the series, with products ranging from 'Forever Krystle' perfume to Carrington House Carpets, plus jewellery and fashion wear bearing the Carrington family crest, including a $150 toiletry kit with a gold-plated toothbrush and razor, and a shaving brush made

of Chinese badger hair. The film industry, theatre and the arts, Olympic Games organizers, all seek to make additional revenue from the forward promotion of merchandise associated with either their current or forthcoming productions.

Where markets are fragmented and exporting the final goods is not possible, industrial process or product licensing remains a clear possibility. Where there is no direct investment permitted by law and no access to venture capital, etc., licensing remains a viable option. Curiously enough, there are no trade statistics on licences. The only organization which seeks to collect information in this area is the UN World Intellectual Property Organization (WIPO) based in Geneva.

Although criticized as being a 'second best' strategy to exporting, product or process licensing may prove to be the only way to enter a market. This was certainly true in previous years of Japan or Eastern Europe. Again, licensing may offer the best method of entry faced with a given level of risk. For smaller companies, licensing may hold many advantages such as lower level of capital required for market entry, lower risk, shorter term payback period. For the larger com-

Table 4.15

A. Conditions for adopting licensing policies

(1) The possession of patented devices and attractive trade marks, preferably in some novel or advanced technology, or special knowhow to which no one else has access.

(2) The ability to protect patents across different legal systems.

(3) That trading conditions in the licensee country inhibit other means of conducting business.

(4) That licensing is the most profitable option.

(5) That a general appraisal of the investment required by the licensee, both in plant and in promotional activities, has been undertaken. The length of time required for establishing the facilities has also to be estimated.

(6) That the results of market research are known, suggesting at least adequate sales in the first and subsequent years, and confirming the breakeven and other calculations. The licensee's profits can then be estimated.

(7) The type of licence has to be considered – whether it will confer exclusive or non-exclusive rights in the area, whether all or limited parts of the manufacture and sale of the product are included, and whether the right to sublet will be a part of the deal and if so on what terms.

B. Advantages of licensing

(1) To increase the income on products developed as a result of expensive research.

(2) To retain a market to which export is no longer possible or which is likely to become unprofitable due to: import prohibitions, quotas or duties, transport costs, lack of production facilities at home or other related factors.

(3) To protect patents, especially in countries which afford weak protection for products not produced locally.

(4) To make local manufacture possible where this is favoured, for other reasons than those listed above. Examples are the need to adapt the product, the opportunity to cash in on local nationalism, the lack of use for the particular patent in the domestic market. This last advantage may well apply to low-technology products for which there is still a market in developing countries.

(5) To make possible the rapid exploitation of new ideas on world markets before competitors get into the act.

(6) The penetration of new markets. Licensing agreements may open up parts of the world previously closed to a company, either in the licensee's own country or through exports from that country to others.

(7) There may be a valuable spin-off if the licensor can sell other products or components to the licensee. If these are parts for products being manufactured locally or machinery, there may also be some tariff concessions on their import.

(8) A means of entering a market where the nature of the competition – a few dominant and highly competitive firms for example – makes any form of entry apart from licensing too expensive to be contemplated.

(9) A means of entering markets that are less competitive than the domestic. This provides funds for extra Research and Development which then, in its turn, improves the chances of licensing where the competition is stronger.

(10) One considerable advantage for the small firm with an appropriate product is that licensing can be a much more plausible means of expanding abroad than exporting. It is easier to handle a number of markets this way.

(11) Licensing is a viable option where manufacture near to the customer's base is required.

C. Disadvantages of licensing

(1) The danger of fostering a competitor. This is strongly maintained when technical information is being provided; and there is no substitute for a satisfactory working arrangement to minimize the danger. The use of internationally promoted trademarks and brand names may also deter the licensee from setting up in opposition. To this end it is advisable that the parent company registers the trademarks in its own name.

(2) The danger of a reducing award.

(3) The fact that there is often a ceiling to licensing income per product, sometimes about 5% on the selling price. Innovating products, at least, could rate higher rewards if marketed in other ways.

(4) The danger of the licensee running short of funds, especially if considerable plant expansion is involved or an injection of capital is required to sustain the project. This danger can be turned to advantage if the licensor has funds available by a general expansion of the business through a partnership.

(5) The licensee may prove less competent than expected at marketing or other management activities; hence the licensor may find his commitment is greater than expected. He may even find costs grow faster than income.

(6) Opposition is encountered in some less developed countries to royalty payments on the grounds that too high a price is being charged for the knowledge provided.

(7) Negotiations with the licensee, and sometimes with the local government, are costly and often protracted.

Source: Brooke, M. Z. (1986) *International Management*, Century Hutchinson, London

pany, licensing payments may prove to be an effective means of siphoning funds out of a country, where exchange control regulations are in operation, by means of transfer pricing. A low transfer price rate from a high-tax country to a subsidiary in a low-tax country would have two effects. First, the manufacturer in the high-tax country is only marginally profitable, thus, minimizing his exposure to taxation. Secondly, the subsidiary overseas benefitting from a low transfer price will be able to record large profits in a low-tax country. For the company as a whole, the strategy may make sense. What this equation leaves out, though, is the role of customs officers in exporting and importing countries, and the effect of unprofitability on the morale of the workforce.

The disadvantages of licensing include then:

- creation of a potential competitor without the designation of specific sales territories,
- difficulties of maintaining control or 'leverage' over the licensee to avoid damage to trademarks or brand names as a result of the licensee's inferior quality control, after-sales service, etc.,
- increasing production by the licensee may result in lower royalties where there is a sliding scale in operation.
- the licensor is ceding certain sales territories to the licensee for the duration of the contract – should he fail to live up to expectations, renegotiation may be expensive,
- problems involved in the transfer of funds, e.g. exchange control restrictions, exchange parities, plus of course, the refusal to pay!

For some processes particularly – and one may think back to Pilkington's float glass technique – exporting is not a practicable affair. Market entry and market expansion for the product or process can only be effected by a presence within the market. Territorial sales boundaries can also be agreed so as to defuse the criticism of the potential threat in licensing a potential competitor. This is the greatest single accusation levelled against licensing, together with performance requirements and procedures for the settlement of disputes (Root, 1994) yet masks the simple fact that much profitable business can be obtained via licensing. For a company which is small but technologically efficient, licensing has much to commend it, particularly as the royalties received on overseas production may well go to finance further expansion or fuel the research and development effort which created this invention, thereby maintaining the technological lead.

Also, consider cross-licensing, where two companies will exchange rights to access patents or know-how. There will be no money exchanged, simply technology or know-how transfer. This adds a further layer of complexity, when it is found that one party has a patent which he cannot employ without the cooperation of another patentee so as to avoid infringing another's industrial property rights. Patents are discussed in Chapter 5.

'Screwdriver' assembly operations

Assembly as a form of market entry is usually found where there is insufficient market size and the host government is seeking some form of production base. As such, assembly is a compromise and, as it usually also involves small-scale operations, its assembled products are usually destined only for the home market. The label 'screwdriver', as applied to assembly operations, was introduced by the EU in July 1987 in scrutinizing Japanese assembly operations within the Community and elsewhere. The new rule, Council Regulation 1761/87, resulted from more than one year's lobbying by industrial organizations throughout the Community and was an amendment to the Community's anti-dumping rule.

Few products exist today which are manufactured from start to finish within one country. Instead, the components, sub-assembly, and finishing may well originate in several different countries, and yet the 'made in' label will be applied to the finished article on the last stage of its production cycle. The 'made in' label is important. Whereas few countries will ask for a label or plate to be affixed to the product in question indicating exactly where an individual product was made, the importation of final goods en masse to third markets is very often likely to arouse political action, particularly where it competes with local industry. Country of origin rules allow products preferential tariff treatment when sourced from one country as opposed to any other. The rules allow for the last 'substantial stage of manufacture' howsoever defined as to be sufficient to meet the criteria for a certificate of origin from the final producer. However, with Japanese investment in Europe being centred mainly in the UK, there is the accusation that Britain is inviting in a Trojan Horse which will then attack European industry from within the Community. The technical argument of what is a British car extends to British assembled Japanese Nissans now being exported to Community markets. If deemed to be Japanese, they would be excluded from the French and Italian markets, but if deemed to be British, would be allowed tariff-free entry to all Commu-

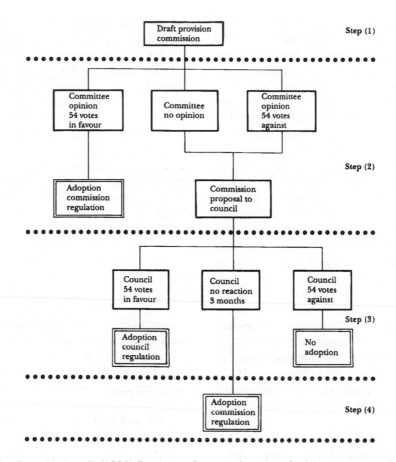

Source: Vermulst, E., and Waer, P. (1990) European Community rules of origin as commercial policy instruments? *Journal of World Trade,* **24**(3), 55–90

Figure 4.5   Determining rules of origin within the EU

nity markets. This then raises the question as to how to evaluate country of origin. The usual criteria is by means of measuring local content, but the French, for example, will not allow marketing costs to be included in this sum. Again, there are two means by which to gauge local content: by volume or by value.

If by volume, it would be possible to show that only a small percentage of the final car is still dependent on imports from abroad. However,

Table 4.16   Table of product-specific origin regulations

	Product	Step	Comments	Type of rule
1.	Eggs	2		Technical
2.	Spare parts	2		Technical
3.	Radio/television receivers	2		Value added
4.	Vermouth	2		Technical
5.	Tape recorders	2		Value added
6.	Meat/offal	4	No concurring opinion	Technical
7.	Woven textiles	2		Technical
8.	Ceramics	2		Technical
9.	Grape juice	2		Technical
10.	Knitwear	4	No opinion	Technical
11.	Textiles	4	No opinion	Technical
12.	Ball bearings	2		Technical
13.	Integrated circuits (ICs)	2		Technical
14.	Photocopiers	4	No concurring opinion	Technical

Source: Vermulst, E., and Waer, P. (1991) European Community rules of origin as commercial policy instruments? *Journal of World Trade,* June, 55–9

these continuing imports may contain the real added-value in that they encapsulate proprietary technology, and so, import costs may still be high. With cars, it may be possible to have an ongoing trade in engines which would fit our example of accounting for only a small import percentage of the total volume of the car, but a substantial part of the value. Politicians will choose whichever measure best suits their needs.

Within the Community, the rules are laid down in Regulation 802/68 and Article 13(7) of Regulation 2423/88 on protection against dumped or subsidized imports from third countries. The debate over the determination of rules of origin has moved to GATT and the Uruguay round of talks. The EU is a signatory to the Kyoto Convention of 1975 on the simplification and harmonization of customs procedures negotiated by the Customs Cooperation Council (CCC) in Brussels, which also says: 'When two or more countries have taken part in the production of the goods, the origin of the goods shall be determined according to the substantial transformation criterion.' While the CCC Secretariat is keen to devise a more substantive set of rules applicable to country of origin, its member countries are much less enthusiastic.

Present regulations 802/68 allow for a Committee on Origin within the EU which must record a majority role to continue an action. The Commission applies a technical test based on the change in tariff heading approach as opposed to a value-added test for the purposes of adopting product-specific origin rules. The EU for example, determined that Ricoh's photocopiers, made in the USA, actually had Japanese origins because the operations effected in California were not sufficient to confer origin. Examples of decisions made by the Origin Committee, and actions finally taken by the EU, are detailed in Table 4.16. Subsequent European Court rulings have taken issue with the substantiality of the last stage of manufacture, whether more than 10 per cent, and whether the objective was to change tariff heading and circumvent the existing regulations. As stated above, the technical test has been applied rather than an examination of value added. If the parts/sub-assemblies as assembled had acquired European origin, the whole parts/sub-assemblies would be treated as European even though they might have contained sub-parts from other countries. If, on the other hand, the parts/sub-assemblies had not acquired European origin in the production process, the Commission adopted a case by case approach, whereby it broke down the sub-assemblies into sub-parts.

As regards production from third countries, the EU may wait for a complaint from European industry of dumping, or they may dispute the origin of such products outright. Finding Ricoh's photocopiers to be of Japanese origin meant application of a tariff appropriate to Japanese imports into the Community. With regard to dumping, the adoption by the EU of 'selective normal value' (Didier, 1990) whereby only sales to unrelated domestic distributors are used as a basis of normal values and domestic prices to other categories of customers (dealers, end-users, etc.) are omitted from calculations.

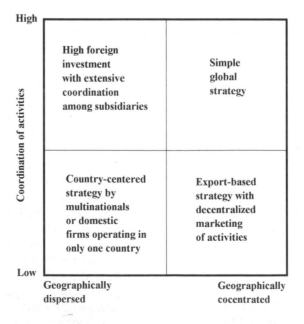

Source: Porter, M. E. (1990) *The Competitive Advantage of Nations*, Macmillan, New York

Figure 4.6   Types of international strategy

For a discussion of the issues, see also Matsumoto and Finlayson (1990), who identify:

1. arbitrary and unreasonable 'minimum' amounts, and unreasonably high imported rates for selling, general and administrative expenses and/or profit applied by certain countries,
2. use of fully allocated costs,
3. use of home market costs rather than export costs, and
4. administrative burden of preparing cost data in addition to price data.

It is useful to note, though, the Japanese reaction, as in Ishikawa (1990) who sees in EU legislation something quite sinister and in restraint of free trade: 'Its aim is to offer West European manufacturers protection in the new areas where the Japanese industry based in Europe has acquired a competitive advantage.'

Returning to Porter (1990), the types of international strategy are to be seen in Figure 4.6. A specific example for the car industry is shown then in Figure 4.7. The point that Porter is making is that coordination of dispersed production facilities, R&D laboratories and marketing is becoming increasingly important. Success will increasingly depend on seeking out competitive advantages from global configuration/coordination anywhere in the value chain, and overcoming the organizational barriers to exploiting them.

Exhibit 4.6   Where does your car come from?

A couple of generations ago most motorists here bought British cars, although a minority favoured French, German, Swedish or Italian makes. You could generally tell from the badge in which country a particular car was built, although there were some unusual arrangements like the production run of Citroens – from Light 15s and Big Sixes to the little plastic-bodied Bijous – manufactured in Slough.

Now the motor industry operates on a truly international scale. Cars with German badges may come from factories in Spain, Swedish ones from Holland, and 'Japanese' cars from the US, Hungary, Derbyshire, Wiltshire or Tyne and Wear.

This is just a fact of modern industrial life, and we have to accept it, although sometimes it causes a little embarrassment. A few years ago, for example, at the height of its anti-apartheid campaign, the former Glasgow District Council invested in some Ford P100 pick-ups, not realising (until after they had been delivered) that they were built in South Africa.

UK market Fiat Fiorino vans come from Brazil, the BMW Z3 to be introduced here next year is a product of Spartanburg, South Carolina, and the latest Mitsubishi pick-up, due to be launched in October at the Birmingham Show, is an import from Thailand.

Of the major British manufacturers, Rover's home-market cars are home-manufactured too. Ford brings in the Galaxy from Portugal, the Maverick from Spain, the Scorpio and the Escort cabriolet from Germany, the Probe from Michigan, and the Mondeo from Belgium.

Vauxhall, as part of General Motors, taps world-wide supplies. The Corsa and Tigra are built at Zaragoza in Spain. Astras come mostly from Ellesmere Port in Cheshire, but supplies are also fed in from Germany and Belgium, with convertibles coming via Italy, where Pininfarina carries out the open-top work. While the Frontera 4 × 4 is built in Luton, Montereys are produced by Isuzu in Japan.

The Omega is imported from Germany, and a remarkable thing about the Calibra is that 100 per cent of UK supplies come from Finland. The assembly plant there is at Uusikaupunki, whose name does not mean anything exotic like Where Elks Graze by Light of the Midnight Sun, but is simply the Finnish for New Town.

Finland is an example of a country whose motor industry is rarely thought of, but it also produces the Saab 900 convertible. All other Saabs are built at home in Sweden, and so are the bigger varieties of Volvo, although the 400 series as well as the new S40 and V40 come from Holland.

The Dutch connection is one of several examples of manufacturers from two countries establishing a joint production facility in a third. Volvo shares a factory near Maastricht with Mitsubishi, whose Carisma comes along the same production lines.

Fiat's Polish subsidiary pours out Cinquecentos. There is a Hungarian motor industry too, supplying UK dealers with Suzuki Swifts and the Subaru Justy, as well as building five-cylinder engines for Audi.

Next door, geographically speaking, Austria is the source of Mercedes G-Wagen supplies, and the Americans have moved in there too. While the Jeep Cherokee comes from the States, the Grand Cherokee is built for Europe in Graz.

The Renault 5 now comes from Ljubjlana in Slovenia. Italy concentrates on building cars for the

→ Exhibit 4.6 *continued*

Fiat empire, but there is a Japanese connection in Tuscany. A joint venture factory operated by Piaggio and Daihatsu produces the Daihatsu Hijet in all its many variants.

One Italian model in UK showrooms is built across the border in France. As part of the co-operative element in MPV production, the Fiat Ulysse is one of several types manufactured at Valenciennes.

The Iberian peninsula is the source of many cars, vans, MPVs and 4×4s sold here. Citroen imports AXs and ZXs from Vigo in Spain, and in the past brought in some RHD cars from Mangualde in Portugal.

Nissan's Serena and Terrano are built in Spain, and so are most UK-market Volkswagen Polos, while the Sharan is one of the products of the joint Volkswagen/Ford operation at Palmela in Portugal. When sales of the new Mercedes V-class MPV begin later this year, that will be from a factory at Vitoria in Spain. Honda brings in Civic coupes, Accord coupes and the Accord Aero Deck from Ohio. Mazda has a strong US connection too, but the MX-6 coupes marketed here come directly from Japan. Mercedes also operates across the Atlantic, and in 1998 when UK deliveries of the forthcoming M-class 4×4 begin, the vehicles will be shipped from Alabama.

While the home-financed and home-controlled British motor industry has been reduced to the likes of Rolls-Royce, Lotus, Bristol, Morgan, Marcos, Westfield and TVR, UK factories build large quantities of cars bearing 'foreign' badges.

Five-door Honda Civics and Accord saloons are manufactured in Swindon. The Mazda 121 rolls off Ford production lines at Dagenham. Nissan's Washington factory near Sunderland turns out Micras and Primeras. Peugeot builds all 306 variants (apart from the cabriolet and roadster) at Ryton on the outskirts of Coventry, and Toyota will soon be adding Corolla production to the range of Carina E models out of Burnaston in Derbyshire.

When you think of places like Slovenia, Hungary and Thailand all building vehicles which eventually find their way to Scottish dealerships, it goes against the grain to think that our own north-of-the-border motor manufacturing industry has just evaporated. Fortunately, there are still some substantial component and equipment suppliers in business here, but to consider anything else looks to be, on current form, just a mirage.

Source: The *Glasgow Herald*, August 16, 1996

Direct investment activities

The company may decide to do any or all of the following but the first issue to consider is the question of ownership and control. Although linked, the two words are not synonymous, and each of these three strategies, namely: wholly owned, merger/acquisition and joint venture, has to be examined in a situational context for optimal fit.

Wholly owned subsidiaries

Build up representation in the foreign country as a wholly owned subsidiary. This is slow to achieve, expensive to maintain and slow also to yield any tangible results. If a very favourable growth rate is envisaged for the market in question, it may be the only effective mode of entry because, although costly to maintain, it does allow for flexibility in future strategic shifts.

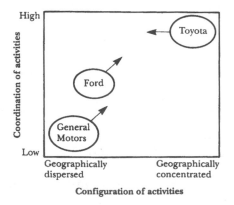

Source: Porter, M. E. (1990) *The Competitive Advantage of Nations*, Macmillan, New York

Figure 4.7   The dimensions of international strategy

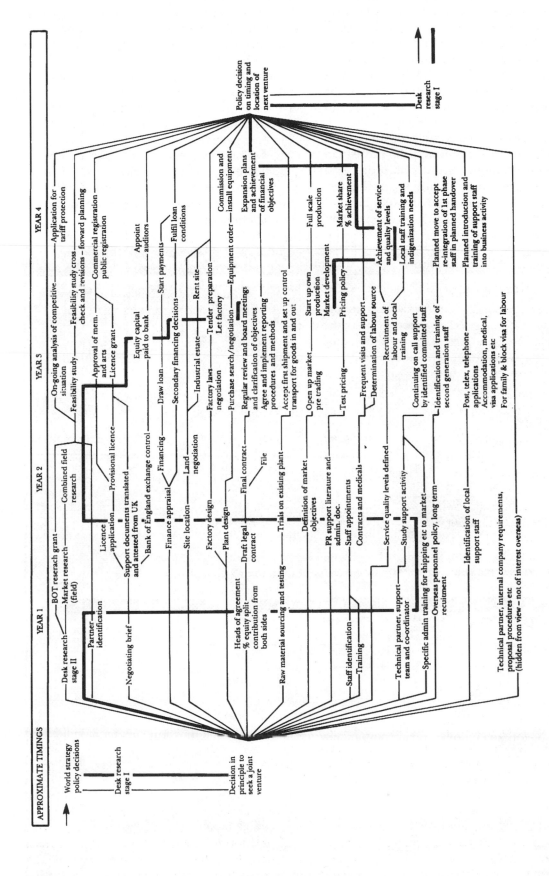

Source: Walmsley, J. (1982) *Handbook of International Joint Ventures*, Graham and Trotman, London

Figure 4.8

Issues of control and ownership continually surface in any discussion on joint ventures. Schaan (1988) concluded that there were two types of control; positive and negative. Positive control was an ongoing process of influence whereas negative control was seen more as an exercise of raw power designed to bring a recalcitrant child to heel. The joint-venture agreement, particularly from a negotiation skills perspective, is to be found in McCall and Warrington (1989).

Joint ventures (speaking generally) have been defined as 'the commitment, for more than a very short duration, of funds, facilities, and services by two or more legally separate interests, to an enterprise for their mutual benefit' (Tomlinson, 1970). This, then, goes deeper than mere trade relationships since it concentrates on the deliberate alliance of resources between two independent organizations in order to mutually improve their market growth potential (Walmsley, 1982). The anatomical structure of a joint-venture is fully delineated in Figure 4.8.

The reasons for a joint venture, leaving aside for the moment that there are essentially two types: the joint equity venture and the strategic business alliance, include:

1. Explicit pressures by the host government which may include a definite ruling.
2. Implicit pressure by the host government which may include suspicion or fear of discriminatory action.

Exhibit 4.7   BT pieces together a global jigsaw

The glare of publicity surrounding British Telecommunications' $20bn (£12.4bn) proposed acquisition of MCI of the US has obscured the quiet determination with which the UK operator is pursuing its international strategy.

It now has more than 25 equity joint ventures worldwide, together with 44 partnerships and distributorships for Concert, its existing international alliance with MCI.

'This is the result of a carefully orchestrated plan carried out over more than three years,' says Mr Alfred Mockett, head of BT's international division.

Nevertheless, BT and MCI between them have a mere 6 per cent share of the $670bn global telecoms market. More than 80 per cent of the market is still closed to competition, but a wave of liberalisation is opening up a host of opportunities.

If, as seems likely, Concert wins the battle for a 5 per cent stake in Portugal Telecom, BT will have done more than defeat rival alliances – including Global One combining Deutsche Telekom, France Télécom and Sprint of the US, and AT&T-Unisource.

It will essentially have completed its European jigsaw 20 months before EU markets, collectively valued at about $192bn a year, are opened to full competition.

It has already formed alliances in Germany, France, Italy, Spain and the Netherlands. 'We recognise there is a tremendous premium to be gained by

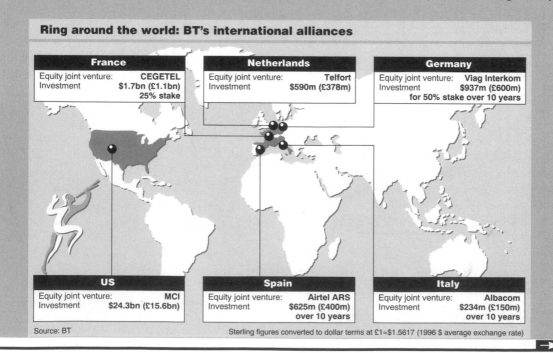

➤ Exhibit 4.7 *continued*

being the early mover. We need to be at the head of the queue for licences,' Mr Mockett says.

Opportunism is not enough, however. Mr Mockett says BT examined 200 French companies before agreeing to become part of Cegetel, a joint venture with Générale des Eaux.

The proposed MCI merger will give BT a significant position in North America. The US operator is planning to spend a further $700m this year attacking North America's local markets.

Through MCI's existing relationships it also will have a foothold in Mexico.

The Asia-Pacific region, where demand for telecoms services is rising fastest, remains BT's weak spot. It has failed to persuade NTT of Japan, the world's largest telecoms company, to join Concert, although the two are collaborating in a bid to secure the second national licence in Singapore. BT has had an office in Beijing for some years, but the Chinese market remains closed to foreign operators.

Analysts are impressed by BT's strategy. 'It has the most comprehensive global network of any operator,' according to Mr Andrew Harrington of Salomon Brothers.

This week the company released some of its financial criteria for overseas investment. It expects a 20 per cent annualised rate of return on investment, and to be both cash flow positive and profitable within three to five years. It aims to secure 10–15 per cent of the addressable market in the same timescale.

The proposed MCI investment apart, BT is spending comparatively little. It has an aversion to investing in infrastructure, preferring to provide technological leadership as its contribution to a partnership. This means that the partnership has the look and feel of a local operator, but uses the same technology as other partners in BT's global network.

Source: Financial Times, 18 March 1997

---

3. The desire to spread risk both:
   - normal business risks, and
   - the risk of unpredictability of the environment, e.g. national political and economic uncertainty.

4. The need for local facilities and resources best obtained through a local interest with local influence and local knowledge of the customs and legal systems.

5. The opportunity to participate in any local project undertaken by the local partner.

6. Local identity – the benefits accruing to a locally identified operation.

7. Internal company reasons, e.g. goodwill, or the desire to spread corporate capital over a wide range of interests and markets.

Killing (1983), writing on joint ventures, foresaw the coming of ever larger joint ventures more closely attuned to the mainstream business of the joint venture parents. He also foresaw that more favourable attitudes developing towards joint ventures would change as more experience was gained in managing them. Yet, making recommendations about choosing a partner was still a little like advising your daughter on the kind of man she should marry. Nevertheless, Killing did suggest:

1. The more similar the culture of firms forming a shared management joint venture, the easier the venture will be to manage. Culture is con-

sidered to have two components, one being the culture of the country in which a company is based, the other one corporate culture of the particular firm in question.

2. The more similar in size are the parents of a shared management venture, the easier the venture will be to manage. A significant size mismatch between a venture's parents can create a lot of problems for the venture.

In any event, the advantages must be strong enough to compensate for the initial lack of knowledge about economic, social, and legal conditions, and the market must be protected relatively well from entry by competitors. A US survey asking businesses to list the advantages of joint ventures revealed the following positive features:

1. the gaining of experience
2. risk reduction
3. capital saving
4. access to lower-cost skilled labour
5. improved government relations.

Harrigan (1987) went considerably further as may be seen from Table 4.18 which clearly outlines the internal, competitive and strategic motivations for joint venture formation.

In a study of the joint venture process in India and Pakistan, Tomlinson (1970) identified four clear stages in the investment environment:

1. *Unilateral antagonism.* The host nation fears the dangers of economic imperialism.

Exhibit 4.8

Analysis of prospective partners. Examples of criteria that may be used to judge a prospective partner's effectiveness by assessing existing business ventures and commercial attitudes.

1. *Finance*
    (i)   Financial history and overall financial standing (all the usual ratios).
    (ii) Possible reasons for successful business areas.
    (iii) Possible reasons for unsuccessful business areas.

2. *Organization*
    (i)   Structure of organization.
    (ii) Quality and turnover of senior managers.
    (iii) Workforce conditions/labour relations.
    (iv) Information and reporting systems, evdence of planning.
    (v)   Effective owner's working relationship with business.

3. *Market*
    (i)   Reputation in marketplace and with competitors.
    (ii) Evidence of research/interest in service and quality.
    (iii) Sales methods, quality of sales force.
    (iv) Evidence of handling weakening market conditions.
    (v)   Results of new business started.

4. *Production*
    (i)   Condition of existing premises/works.
    (ii) Production efficiencies/layouts.
    (iii) Capital investment and improvements.
    (iv) Quality control procedures.
    (v)   Evidence of research (internal/external), introduction of new technology.
    (vi) Relationship with main suppliers.

5. *Institutional*
    (i)   Government and business contacts (influence).
    (ii) Successful negotiations with banks, licensing authorities, etc.
    (iii) Main contacts with non-national organizations and companies.
    (iv) Geographical influence.

6. *Possible negotiating attitudes*
    (i)   Flexible/hardline.
    (ii) Reasonably open/close and secretive.
    (iii) Short-term or long-term orientated.
    (iv) 'Wheeler/dealer' or objective negotiator.
    (v)   Positive quick decision taking or tentative.
    (vi) Negotiating experience and strength of team support.

These suggestions only form an outline sketch of the type of information which can be used to grade partners and cover areas where there is a reasonable chance of forming a view by appraisal of published information and by sensible observation and questioning.

Source: Walmsley, J. (1982) *Handbook of International Joint Ventures*, Graham and Trotman Ltd., London

---

2. *Mutual suspicion.* Both foreign investors and capital-importing governments may have considerable doubt over the mutuality of their interests. There is concern over the stimulus of economic development with scarce resources, so both foreign capital and technology are required. Imports are paid for by earning from extractive industry exports. Entry conditions for foreign capital and labour are relaxed but still constrained.

3. *Joint acceptance.* The social benefits are perceived to exceed the social costs, and as the needs of development create their own self-generating momentum, their relaxation continues.

4. *Sophisticated integration* – the logical extension of the relaxation mentioned. Foreign investors may be permitted entry in any form of operation which they desire. In so far as local collaboration and participation are felt to be desirable or even necessary, they may well be promoted through discriminatory fiscal and financial incentives, rather than through legislative prohibitions.

These are universal truths. Grouping the possible reasons for partnership, Tomlinson (1970) produced six situations which still hold true today:

1. *Forced partnership.* The choice is effectively forced on the foreign investor either because of explicit host government direction, or indirectly because the partner preempts an exclusive licence.

2. *Convenience to the foreign partner of local facili-*

Table 4.18   Motivations for joint-venture formation

A. *Internal uses*
  1. Cost and risk sharing (uncertainty reduction).
  2. Obtain resources where there is no market.
  3. Obtain financing to supplement firm's debt capacity.
  4. Share outputs of large minimum efficient scale plants.
     a. Avoid wasteful duplication of facilities.
     b. Utilize by-products, processes.
     c. Shared brands, distribution channels, wide product lines, and so forth.
  5. Intelligence: obtain window on new technologies and customers.
     a. Superior information exchange.
     b. Technological personnel interactions.
  6. Innovative managerial practices.
     a. Superior management systems.
     b. Improved communications among SBUs.
  7. Retain entrepreneurial employees.

B. *Competitive uses* (strengthen current strategic positions)
  1. Influence industry structure's evolution.
     a. Pioneer development of new industries.
     b. Reduce competitive volatility.
     c. Rationalize mature industries.
  2. Preempt competitors ('first-mover' advantages)
     a. Gain rapid access to better customers.
     b. Capacity expansion or vertical integration.
     c. Acquisition of advantageous terms, resources.
     d. Coalition with best partners.
  3. Defensive response to blurring industry boundaries and globalization
     a. Ease political tensions (overcome trade barriers).
     b. Gain access to global networks.
  4. Creation of more effective competitors.
     a. Hybrids possessing parents' strengths.
     b. Fewer, more efficient firms.
     c. Buffer dissimilar partners.

C. *Strategic uses* (augment strategic position)
  1. Creation and exploitation of synergies.
  2. Technology (or other skills) transfer.
  3. Diversification.
     a. Toehold entry into new markets, products, or skills.
     b. Rationalization (or divestiture) of investment.
        Leverage-related parents' skills for new uses.

Source: Harrigan, K. R. (1987) *Strategies for Joint Ventures*, Lexington Books, Lexington, MA.

ties under *the control of the partner*. Among these would be a site or plant, marketing or distributive facilities, or a strong market position where the partner was already in the same line of business as that of the proposed joint venture.

3. *Resources*. Convenience of local sources of managerial and technical personnel, materials, components or local capital which can be contributed to the partner.

4. *Status and capability of the partner in dealing with local authorities and public relations*. This would also include status defined in terms of general financial and business soundness and standing.

5. *Favourable past association with the partner when the latter had been an agent, licensee, major customer or partner in a previous joint venture*. This category includes special cases in which there might have been strong personal contacts between individuals in the foreign and local parent companies, possibly individuals common to both.

6. *Identity*. A partner is chosen chiefly to obtain local identity, often through association with a potential sleeping partner.

	Product configurations cannot be standardized across markets	Product configurations can be standardized across markets
Customer sophistication and bargaining power is high	Multinational joint ventures: 'Spider's web' of co-operative strategies for cost reduction styling. Many short-term cross-licensing arrangements for new product features, cost reductions.	Few joint ventures, except as required to enter. High co-ordination control by global partner to keep costs lowest.
Customer sophistication and bargaining power is low	More longer term joint ventures (depends on competitors' activities), primarily for new product features.	Few joint ventures, except as required to enter (local partner allowed some co-ordination controls).

Source: Harrigan, K. R. (1987) *Strategies for Joint Ventures*, Lexington Books, Lexington, MA

Figure 4.9   Single firm analysis: hypothesized effect of customer bargaining power and market standardization on joint-venture formation and use (assuming firms will co-operate)

It is interesting, then, to compare this with Harrigan's (1987) four-cell matrix (see Figure 4.9). Nationality by itself was not enough justifi-cation in itself for entering a joint venture; a local partner would have to have something more to offer. Equally a shared management venture

---

Exhibit 4.9   Ford taps into Asia through Mazda

EVENT: Ford Motor Co. has acquired a controlling stake in Mazda Motor Corp. of Japan.

SIGNIFICANCE: Although Ford's move points to the increasing integration of the world's auto markets, other auto makers are unlikely to adopt this strategy for expanding in Asia.

ANALYSIS: On April 12, Ford raised its equity stake in Mazda, its Japanese affiliate, to 33.4 per cent, giving it effective control over Mazda's operations. This will allow it to make numerous changes to the ailing Japanese company. 'The Detroit car maker itself is also likely to benefit from the increased control.

1. Ford will be able to gain access to both the Japanese and fast-growing Asian car markets. Although in the short run, the former will be more important – particularly as demand picks up in response to the recovery – the regional market outside Japan will be increasingly significant over time. Sales in Asia (including Japan) are projected to reach 17 million units by the year 2000. Ford now has only 1 per cent of the Asian market share – compared with its market share elsewhere of 17 per cent – and lacks a significant manufacturing presence in the region. It will now be easier to build on this small base.

2. Ford gains greater access to Mazda's engineering capability, particularly important in the development of small- and medium-sized cars. Ford has experienced difficulties in this market segment in the past, and hopes links with Mazda will enable it to bring its products to market

sooner. It will also tap its Japanese partner's knowledge of the Asian market.

If successful, Mazda's Japanese competitors – which include Toyota Motor Corp., Nissan Motor Co. Ltd and Honda Motor Co. Ltd – stand to lose market share. These three combined now hold an estimated 50 per cent of the market throughout the region, and 85 per cent in the Asian newly industrialized countries.

3. Ford's relationship with Japan's Sumitomo Corp. group, Mazda's main backer, will be enhanced. Already one of Sumitomo Bank Ltd's largest foreign customers, Ford will benefit from;

- increased access to the conglomerate's vast financial resources
- links with its extensive insurance, logistical, electronics and machinery interests.

Sumitomo Bank approached Ford in December, 1993, asking it to raise its stake in Mazda and build a strategic relationship on a global scale. Had Ford not made the investment, it appears likely the bank would have sought another partner for Mazda, possibly reducing Ford's role in the company. Thus, Ford's decision to acquire a controlling stake was partly driven by a defensive motive.

Mazda's gains.
The move gives Mazda a badly needed infusion of cash. The company still carries a debt load of more than 773 billion yen ($9.9-billion). The inflow of new funds will enable it to:

- finish its restructuring program, which began about three years ago

→ Exhibit 4.9 *continued*

- invest in new products
- increase much-needed advertising and marketing activities in its domestic market.

Although Mazda's restructuring is largely complete, the company lacks products, particularly in the expanding 'recreational vehicle' segment. Mazda's cars are not well-known, even in their three major markets – Japan, Europe and the United States – and therefore tend to perform below their potential. Thus, the financial support for investment and advertising purposes will be particularly welcome.

In addition, Mazda will benefit from management support, particularly in marketing and sales. In fact, the company's new senior managing director, Henry Wallace, in charge of both global marketing and sales, comes from Ford.

Efficiency gains

Ford's increased stake also has the potential to bring benefits to both companies through platform sharing, joint-component development and sourcing, and will eliminate duplication in all aspects of their operations. Ford can expect to gain easier access to the Japanese market through Mazda's distribution system, and will now have the opportunity to build vehicles in one of Mazda's Japanese assembly plants.

With the U.S. dollar rising against the yen by almost 30 per cent since last April, Ford has benefited from a relatively favourable exchange rate. Furthermore, by selling at a substantial discount, Mazda has allowed its U.S. partner to invest at a minimum risk. The risk has also been reduced because Mazda has almost completed its restructuring and returned to operating profit in the second half of last year.

Asian market access

Last November, Ford and Mazda announced plans to produce pick-up trucks in Thailand. The project, to begin in mid-1998, involves investment of 11.8 billion baht ($837.3-million) in a new assembly plant.

A new joint-venture company, Auto Alliance, was established to run the operation. Ford and Mazda both hold 45 per cent direct equity in the operation, which is capitalized at five billion baht. The project enables Mazda to modernize its pick-up truck. Ford's pick-up range now lacks a one-tonne capability, along with double cabs and diesel engines. This development should help close that gap.

The deal also gives both companies much-needed access to the Southeast Asian market. Mazda depends heavily on the Japanese market, where sales have been static, and has been slower than its Japanese rivals to move production abroad. Similarly, Ford cannot rely on its declining sales in the U.S. market. The European market, where both companies have significant interests, appears set to remain weak, making an Asian presence more important.

Wider significance

In the context of overall U.S.-Japanese relations, the fact the announcement by Ford and Mazda was made immediately prior to U.S. President Bill Clinton's state visit to Japan was significant. Following last June's bilateral agreement on cars and car parts, both Japan and the United States were anxious to show that progress had been made by U.S. car makers in Japan. Ford's increased stake in Mazda enables Tokyo to claim its auto market is now open to the extent that a foreign company can take effective control of a Japanese firm.

But this is very much a unique deal, and further takeovers of this nature between U.S. and Japanese auto producers are unlikely.

In 1985, Chrysler Corp. sold the remainder of its equity stake in Japan's Mitsubishi Motors Corp., while General Motors Corp. lacks the financial resources to make a major investment. Moreover, GM already has a 38 per cent stake in Japan's Motors Ltd. Although this is bigger than Ford's 33.4 per cent stake in Mazda, Ford's influence over its Japanese partner is greater than GM's, because of the larger U.S. management presence at Mazda.

Over all, Japanese auto makers are now just emerging from a slump, linked to the recession. With the yen's recent depreciation as well as several years of cost-cutting now having an impact, the prognosis for the remainder of the decade is for moderate growth. It is unlikely any auto maker will now fold.

CONCLUSION: Japanese car makers are now emerging from the recession in relatively good shape. This will give them the opportunity to capitalize on the sharp growth in auto demand projected in the rest of the region.

Oxford Analytics is an international consulting firm providing timely analysis on world developments for business and government leaders. For information, contact Eric Noël by fax at 418-848-8853.

Source: Globe and Mail, (1996), May p. 310

had to be differentiated from a dominant parent venture. As Killing (1983) bluntly put it: 'A shared management volume should not be established unless it is abundantly clear that the extra benefit of having two parents managerially involved will more than offset the extra difficulty which will result.' This is a critical question which it seems all too few firms bother to ask. As one manager put it: 'You've got to have a very large carrot to keep both parents committed during the tough periods!' Killing (1983), however, emphasized that joint ventures are more successful if one company is willing to play a passive role. Having more than one parent led to dissension, confusion and inability to undertake clear concise and unambiguous decisions. Shared management ventures may work in theory but not in practice where uncertainty may predominate in various forms; political, economic and technical.

Joint ventures are of two types:

1. Joint-equity venture (JEV). There is the familiar form of a *joint-equity venture* which is well known, and documented, whereby each of the respective partners contributes a sum either in equity or technological know-how in return for a given stake in the operation of a joint venture. Unlike contractual ventures, these are open-ended and not of fixed duration.

2. Strategic business alliance (SBA). This is the increasingly popular form of *contractual joint venture* to be found in the aerospace industry and various other branches of engineering. It is to be found throughout the automobile industry as may be seen from the accompanying figures and diagrams which relate to Fiat. In the now defunct Comecon bloc, these contractual joint ventures are still referred to as industrial co-operation and such agreements known as 'industrial co-operation agreements' or ICAs, a term originally coined by the United Nations. Unlike equity ventures the investment stake may be in technology on one side only. The duration of the joint venture is laid down in the contract which designates the respective tasks and responsibilities of each party over the period of the joint venture. Any change or diversion has to be the subject of negotiation between the two partners. Lewis (1990) points to how companies can build operational strength through alliances, citing the example of how Boeing, pressed by capacity shortages, averted an operational crisis by turning to its rival, Lockheed, for a loan of 600 workers. For Boeing, in civil aircraft, flying these Lockheed workers to Washington

State made clear sense as these were experienced technicians. For Lockheed, where military aircraft were being built and jobs were dwindling, the deal retained a skilled workforce until new business could be developed.

Joint-equity ventures (JEVs) suffer in that the absorption of local equity capital from the foreign market will dilute the company equity base; whereas, an SBA, ICA or contractual joint venture, on the other hand, is quite different in that the respective duties of both parties are clearly designated over a fixed period of years within a legal contract and the issue of ownership does not exist while control is still maintained. Both forms of joint venture seek to answer claims for local national ownership and involvement in foreign-based firms, yet the means by which they do so vary quite widely.

Conditions which particularly favour the development of SBAs include:

*   low degree of centralization in marketing and/or production,
*   low research and development expenditures,
*   high diversification,
*   small size of firm or group, and
*   need for vertical linkages.

For Communist countries, Poliwoda (1981) pointed out reasons why the SBA may be particularly favoured:

1. The political and psychological attraction of an association with foreign investors which does not entail any degree of physical ownership of the host nation's resources. The latter remains in full legal control of its oil or copper deposits, while the foreign investor or consortium shares the capital expenditure, development costs, risks as well as profits, and contributes needed technical skill and equipment.

2. Lack of choice. The country in question may not allow wholly owned subsidiaries and there is a desire for more control than is found in simple licensing. Again, the question of payment in resultant goods produced under licence necessitates some form of partnership and market sharing agreement. Developments in terms of both market and product development are also jointly shared and this lessens the perceived risk of entry to that particular target market.

For the Western company, the responsibilities of a contractual joint venture are much easier to bear as it provides many of the advantages of a joint-equity venture without many of its attendant risks. The following advantages may be seen to include:

1. royalties from sales,
2. access to an increasing volume of low-cost output for marketing in the West,
3. no responsibility for management unless this has been specifically contracted for on a fee basis,
4. no company capital involved and so the return on investment – limited to personnel and technology – may be very high.

In cars, commercial vehicles, computers, robotics, video, telecommunications, office equipment, aerospace and all other key sectors, strategic business alliances are on the increase. This movement, forced by competitive pressures is linking archrivals such as Philips and Sony; Volvo and Clark Equipment; Fiat and Alfa Romeo; Rover and Honda; Rolls-Royce and Pratt & Whitney, to join forces to manufacture, sell, or conduct research development and yet still remain independent companies.

Research and development costs for the automobile industry together with the critical mass required to achieve economies of scale ensured that this industry would be one of the first to find ways to make savings through joint collaboration, where co-operation is close but clearly no one is particularly interested in ever owning any part of any other company. Instead, various links are forged between companies seeking to combine their engineering strengths in development.

Exhibit 4.10 The alliance from hell

From afar, it looks like the perfect transatlantic marriage, a soaringly successful union that's the envy of an entire industry. Acting in seamless harmony, Northwest and KLM Royal Dutch Airlines trade packed planeloads of high-paying customers between Northwest strongholds like Detroit and KLM's base in Amsterdam. The golden routes provide just a glint of the partnership's rewards. After nearly going bankrupt in 1992, Northwest staged a stunning revival that vastly enriched owners from both nations. U.S. investors Gary Wilson and Al Checchi, who own 20 per cent of the company, have made nearly $1 billion on an initial investment of $40 million. KLM, which controls 19.3 per cent of Northwest, saw its $400 million stake swell to $1.6 billion, half the Dutch airline's market value. To celebrate their oneness in the public eye, the two proud carriers have merged their logos into a single red-and-blue seal emblazoned on everything from cocktail napkins to 747s.

Don't let the facade fool you. Behind the scenes lurks a marriage from hell, a eye-gouging, rabbit-punching slugfest, with accusations flying like dinner plates, and one combatant, KLM, running to court hurling charges of spousal abuse. Though some signs of strife have popped up in public from time to time, the full story hasn't been told till now. *Fortune* assembled the first inside account by interviewing angry players on both sides and by mining a trove of internal memos, letters, and contracts. What emerges is the saga of a wealthy household that can't keep from tearing itself apart.

The conflict pits Checchi and Wilson, two highflying financial guys, against a bunch of stubborn airline burghers from KLM. The motives are basic: Both sides think they know best how to run an airline, and want to call the shots. Though they deny it, the Dutch have been trying to eject Checchi and Wilson for years and still haven't abandoned hope. KLM President Pieter Bouw has declared that he'd like to blend both companies into a single, binational organization along the lines of Unilever and Shell. That suggestion horrifies the Americans, who are certain KLM would end up running the show. Says Wilson: 'They can wrap themselves in tulips all they want. Their real agenda is controlling Northwest Airlines.'

So far, their amazing financial agility – the Dutch would say slipperiness – has enabled Wilson and Checchi to thwart KLM's bid for more power through the combination of a poison pill and creative money raising. Though it's currently illegal for a foreign carrier to own a U.S. airline, KLM has lobbied for changes in the rules, while pushing to acquire as much of Northwest as is legally allowed.

So bitter is the clash for control that the Dutch and the Americans threaten to wreck an alliance yielding $200 million a year in operating profits. 'This relationship is dysfunctional,' complains Wilson. The top brass from the two carriers don't even talk. In February the Dutch directors resigned from the three Northwest board seats KLM controls. Four months later, the seats remain vacant. In the latest twist, KLM is reportedly talking to American Airlines about replacing Northwest as its U.S. partner if the alliance falls apart.

In part, the fight is a classic clash in cultures, a collision of two diametrically opposed philosophies of doing business. 'It's the European way vs. the American way,' says Bouw, and the two agendas mix like wooden shoes at a Hollywood gala.

→ **Exhibit 4.10** *continued*

Each side takes pleasure in caricaturing the other. When they're not comparing Bouw's machinations with the antics of the hapless Inspector Clouseau, Checchi and Wilson paint the folks at KLM, which is 38 per cent owned by the Dutch government, as plodding bureaucrats envious of the millions Northwest's managers have earned on surging stock. 'That's laughable,' retorts Bouw. 'We're not jealous. We just appreciate our own values.' For his part, Bouw sees Checchi and Wilson as financial carpetbaggers.

Like most Europeans, the Dutch prize operating expertise over financial engineering, regarding LBO-types as speculators. They view themselves as experts in their chosen business. They are prudent, long-haul investors who shun high risk and leverage. They show a near-religious devotion to the concept of book value – they like to pile up cash and minimize debt. Picture their frustration flying with daring, on-the-edge dealmakers like Checchi and Wilson. 'We're airline people, they're not,' grouses Bouw. 'These guys are here for the short term. They're investing in hotels one day, airlines the other day, and who-knows-what tomorrow.' KLM argues Checchi and Wilson are betting on more good times ahead when they should be hoarding for stormy weather (see box). Says Bouw: 'You have to fix the roof when the sun shines to get ready for the thunderstorms.'

The cautious Dutch approach drives Checchi and Wilson just as crazy. Leverage and risk are in their blood. The Americans argue that sharp dealmaking – LBOs, spinoffs, or mortgaging assets – can dramatically boost stock prices and work well with a sound operating strategy. For the Yankees, cash flow is king. Why worry about Northwest's $3 billion debt, as long the company generates plenty of cash to cover its interest payments? Says Checchi: 'Pieter Bouw lacks financial focus and strategic expertise.'

While it's impossible to say for sure how all this rancor will play itself out, the two sides seem headed for more trouble. The Dutch would like to buy additional shares in Northwest, but Checchi and Wilson have stymied their adversaries by installing a poison pill that prevents KLM from raising its stake. If the Dutch exceed the 19.3 per cent of Northwest they already own, the pill would flood the market with millions of new shares, which would dramatically dilute KLM's position. Bouw retaliated in December by suing to undo the pill. In the end, the wrangling could lead to anything from a Dutch bid for Checchi's and Wilson's shares to a divorce that prompts KLM to sell its stake.

What their investments are worth now

1989
Checchi and Wilson buy 44 per cent of Northwest for $40 million. KLM gets 20 per cent for $400 million.

1992
NWA and KLM begin a transatlantic operating alliance linking hubs in Detroit and Amsterdam.

1993
Hemorrhaging money, Northwest plans for a Chapter 11 filing but averts bankruptcy with a last-minute deal to raise $870 million in labor savings over three years. KLM refuses to give final consent to the restructuring plan unless it receives new stock options and further board presence. Northwest agrees.

1994
Northwest stock goes public.

1995
Though KLM claims it has no intention of gaining control of the airline, the Northwest board directs management to negotiate a standstill agreement with KLM. KLM refuses. Board members vote for a poison-pill shareholder-rights plan to protect Northwest from hostile takeover. KLM files suit against Northwest to remove the pill.

1996
KLM's three directors resign. Checchi and Wilson's original $40 million stake is now worth $1 billion. KLM's initial $400 million investment has risen to $1.6 billion.

Bouw prized his investment in Northwest as an opportunity to bring global weight to his medium-size European airline. And he was right. In time the alliance proved visionary, lifting the two airlines' market share over the Atlantic from 7 per cent in 1991 to 12 per cent, and providing 30 per cent of KLM's profits.

Along the way, however, the deal hit lots of turbulence. In the early 1990s, Northwest, overburdened with debt, hit hard times. Just as the oil shock from the Gulf War swelled its fuel bill, a price war launched by American Airlines hammered revenues. Dealmaker Checchi had a challenge. He turned to the state of Minnesota (Northwest's home hub) and lobbied hard for a big

→ **Exhibit 4.10** *continued*

aid package, including a $270 million working-capital loan. To the chagrin of some local politicians, who felt the state was being taken, Checchi succeeded.

Despite the Minnesota bailout, the bankruptcy crisis continued. According to Checchi and Wilson, it was then that KLM bared its true intention: controlling Northwest Airlines. In 1992, with Northwest hurtling toward bankruptcy, KLM floated a plan to save the airline and dispatched a crew from Smith Barney to pore over Northwest's books. Under the plan, KLM and other investors would bail out the airline by injecting $500 million in fresh capital. But it was the draconian terms that shocked Northwest, terms that would open a way for KLM to wrest control away from the Americans.

The Dutch deny they ever wanted to control Northwest, citing the U.S. law barring foreign airlines from owning more than 25 per cent of a U.S. carrier. 'The idea is ridiculous,' thunders Bouw. But even today, the rules don't ban a foreign carrier from accumulating one-third of the board seats and exercising considerable power over big decisions like asset sales, restructurings, acquisitions, and partnerships. And in the push toward international deregulation, the guidelines on control could loosen.

Indeed, KLM's 1992 proposal gave it the right over time to buy a clear controlling interest of 51 per cent of Northwest's voting shares, providing that the U.S. government liberalized its rules on foreign ownership. It also seemed possible, since KLM was Northwest's sole savior, that the U.S. would make an exception to the 25 per cent rule to allow KLM a majority stake. In a 1994 letter to Northwest CEO John Dasburg, Bouw stated he did not intend to take control now, so long as Northwest continued to 'maximize shareholder value.'

Then, either as a result of a gross miscommunication or a strategic maneuver by the Dutch, the deal took a strange twist. To present the rescue package, Northwest, in November, invited its more than 100 worried bankers to a session at the Hilton Hotel in Minneapolis. 'We were ecstatic that KLM, in effect, was buying the airline,' says Jim Raff, then with Dutch bank ABN-Amro. 'We saw a big source of future cash.' But two days before the meeting, KLM abruptly withdrew the proposal, leaving a shell-shocked Northwest totally in the lurch. Bouw swears that the equity infusion was just an idea the two airlines kicked around. 'Our help was wishful thinking on Northwest's part,' he

says. But the banks contradict him. Declares Raff, who saw a list of the terms: 'We were all coming to hear about KLM's bailout.'

At the Hilton, the bankers reacted with horror. But by then Northwest had cobbled together a proposal for an emergency loan to tide the company over until it could produce a more durable restructuring. Bankers Trust, which was both a Northwest shareholder and its lead lender, agreed to arrange a $250 million temporary rescue loan, if other creditors also participated.

The lenders also demanded that KLM provide $50 million toward the short-term loan. KLM claims it embraced the second rescue package. Not so, recalls Bankers Trust vice chairman George Vojta: 'KLM had to be pulled kicking and screaming into the rescue package like a dog on a leash with its heels dug in.'

Bouw, seeing an opportunity to extract money and power from Checchi and Wilson, submitted a tough list of demands. He would lend Northwest the $50 million only if he were granted a series of options, including the right to buy some of Wilson and Checchi's stock at a steep discount. Overnight, and on the cheap, KLM could become the company's largest shareholder. However, there was a catch. To obtain the options, Bouw would have to secure, by the end of 1993, $500 million in permanent financing to save Northwest.

Bouw also tried unsuccessfully to force the pair to resign, or at least relinquish most of their power. Says the KLM chief, explaining his actions: 'If they had kept running things, it would have proved to the outside world that the short term had prevailed.'

Bouw says he targeted Wilson and Checchi for good reason. KLM deserved to buy their shares at a special discount because the Northwest co-chairmen, he says, refused to contribute to the bailout. 'I told them to put their money where their mouth is,' he asserts. 'I was annoyed and angry that they would not participate. It showed that they were not interested in saving Northwest.'

That's hogwash, say Checchi and Wilson, who claim that Bouw's reasons are really rationalizations created long after the fact. They swear that neither KLM nor the creditors demanded that they contribute to the rescue package. 'Bouw aimed at us because we were the biggest shareholders, and he wanted to dilute us,' says Checchi. 'It was a pure power play.' ABN-Amro's Raff recalls that at least a couple of banks asked Wilson and Checchi to participate – and didn't like their

■→

answer. Says Raff: 'The fact that they said no did not go over too well. A lot of people were upset.'

Checchi and Wilson believed KLM couldn't pull off the $500 million rescue package. And the bankruptcy clock was still ticking. So for the next six months they pursued their own restructuring. This time the key OPM contributor was labor. Checchi and Wilson proposed to the airline's unions $870 million in wage reductions over three years. At the end of that period, employees could recoup the deferred wages in cash or convert them into stock.

Against tall odds, Checchi and Wilson strove to orchestrate a giant package that encompassed not only separate deals with six unions but steep concessions from banks and suppliers as well. If one link snapped, the entire chain would fly apart. With its lawyers camped outside the bankruptcy court in Wilmington, Delaware, Northwest clinched the pivotal, final accord with the pilots' union in July 1993.

Now that they had regained the upper hand, Wilson and Checchi killed KLM's option to buy their shares at a low price. Bouw perceived that the co-chairmen were slipping away, but he had another move designed to once again give KLM the edge. The Dutch airline's board members had already agreed to Northwest's labor deal. But in its separate role as a stockholder, KLM – like the other owners – had to sign off on the accord a second time. Checchi and Wilson viewed shareholder approval as a mere formality. Then KLM uncorked a shocker. KLM announced to a stunned Northwest management that it would block the labor deal unless the airline met even more demands. The last-minute move caught everyone by surprise, and Checchi and Wilson had no choice but to agree. This time, KLM won still another option to buy shares at a discount from the two as well as from other shareholders. KLM also won a guarantee of at least three of 15 board seats until the year 2015. Says Bouw: 'The point was to get shares from Wilson and Checchi.'

By 1994 the airline industry's crisis had vanished. Buoyed by its new labor agreement and a resurgent economy, Northwest's profits came roaring back. Early that year Northwest successfully floated 20 per cent of its stock to the public. At that time the two sides tried to patch relations at a conclave in Amsterdam, featuring a dinner cruise on the canals and a banquet at the cavernous Rijksmuseum. With Rembrandt's *Night Watch* as his backdrop, Checchi tempered the festive ambience with a dramatic speech warning of the gaps in culture and trust that threatened to wreck the alliance. 'It's easy to understand why these alliances are so fragile,' warned Checchi. 'No one else has succeeded before.'

Around the same time, a KLM meeting with labor stretched the marriage to breaking point. Bouw invited Duane Woerth, head of Northwest's pilots' union, to lunch at the tony Sequoia Grill in Washington, D.C. An alliance between KLM and labor, which then controlled 30 per cent of Northwest's stock and held three board seats, would have spelled trouble for Checchi and Wilson. Together, KLM and the unions held about 50 per cent of the shares. In Bouw's version, he did little more than welcome Woerth to the board. Woerth remembers it differently: 'Bouw said that the long-term interests of KLM and labor were the same, and that Checchi and Wilson would get out as fast as they could.'

The encounter infuriated Checchi and Wilson, who voiced their outrage during an all-day meeting with Bouw at Checchi's townhouse in the Georgetown section of Washington. Wilson read an 18-page litany of complaints to an amazed Bouw, citing KLM's 'egregious behavior' and 'poor integrity.' 'It was hilarious,' says Wilson. 'I asked Bouw, "If I went behind your back to your pilots' union, wouldn't you be furious?" And he said, "No." I couldn't believe it.'

Checchi and Wilson demanded that Bouw sign a standstill agreement that would hold KLM's stake in Northwest to 25 per cent. If not, Wilson warned, the alliance would be in danger. KLM wanted to raise its stake to 25 per cent to exercise that valuable option it had won in 1993 to buy Northwest shares, including Checchi's and Wilson's. Because Northwest's shares have jumped, the option's a winner: Exercisable in 1998, it's now worth $129 million. But the standstill agreement would also include strict limitations on voting rights and board seats. Bouw left saying he'd think about it.

Soon after that rugged performance, 'the Armadillo' suffered a peccadillo. In August of 1994, Wilson was given a citation in the Boise airport for carrying a tiny amount of marijuana. The charges were dropped. He voluntarily stepped down as co-chairman at Northwest for 60 days. In private, KLM managers – who reside in the pot-smoking capital of the world – chuckled at the irony.

For the next 15 months the two sides sparred over the standstill agreement, with Bouw stubbornly refusing to sign. Finally, Checchi and Wilson turned the tables on their adversaries late

---

→ **Exhibit 4.10** *continued*

last year by springing a surprise haymaker of their own. They passed a poison pill limiting KLM to a nasty 19 per cent of the shares, meaning it can't add to its holdings. What about the option that was supposed to lift our stake to 25 per cent, howled Bouw. 'To us, a deal is a deal. This made us really see the kind of people we're dealing with.' In December, KLM filed suit to kill the pill.

Today, the alliance that has spawned both billions and bad blood could take a number of routes, most of them leading toward divorce. For now, KLM's power play has failed. Even if the Dutch win the lawsuit and raise their stake to 25 per cent, Checchi and Wilson will stay firmly in control, since the board – including the three labor directors – remains strongly in their camp. 'There is definitely a culture clash,' admits Bouw. 'It hurts in my heart to hear Northwest say the trust is gone.' Though Bouw swears he'd like to continue the union, he recognizes that the bruised feelings may make that impossible.

It's possible the Dutch will sell their Northwest shares but will stay in the alliance. If that's the case, Checchi and Wilson would be rid of a pesky shareholder while still hanging on to a venture that generates $200 million in operating profits a year. Bouw's dream of guiding Northwest would vaporize.

For the time being, Wilson and Checchi's luck seems to be holding. In April, their partnership could have ended in a famous, tragic plane crash. Checchi was scheduled to fly on the flight from Tuzla to Dubrovnik that killed Commerce Secretary Ron Brown and a group of businessmen, but he decided to take his own plane. Rush Limbaugh even announced Checchi's death on the radio. Wilson heard the report: 'For about 15 minutes, I was crazy.' His near-premature demise prompted Checchi to think deeply about all the great business colleagues he'd miss. Apparently, Pieter Bouw isn't one of them.

Source: Fortune, 24 June 1996

Exhibit 4.11   L'Oreal makes up strategies for the emerging markets

French cosmetics maker L'Oreal, trying to expand its share of developing markets, said that it will build another factory in China and restart production in Russia after a two-year absence. L'Oreal said that it has inaugurated its first plant in China and plans another at the start of 1997. It announced plans to build a 'significant' plant in Russia, where L'Oreal products haven't been manufactured since 1994.

The company, maker of Lancôme and Helena Rubenstein cosmetics and Biothem skin products, is expanding in emerging markets as its main Western European market is showing signs of maturing, analysts said. 'The company dominates the European market, which offers comparatively little growth compared to its competitors,' said Cedric Magnelia, a CS First Boston analyst.

The company's growth in developed markets has been helped by acquisitions Company-wide first-half sales rose by 11.7 per cent to FFr30.1 billion including the purchase earlier this year of US cosmetics maker Maybelline. Excluding Maybelline, sales would have risen by 7.7 per cent.

Meanwhile, L'Oreal has been investing in foreign markets. Last week, it bought Unisa, a Chilean seller of mass-market cosmetics, in an attempt to increase its market share in the country. The

financial terms of the transaction were not provided but Unisa, formerly owned by Gillette, had sales of $17m in 1995, and is Chile's top producer of mass-market cosmetics and suncare products, according to its new owner. The French firm had revenues in Chile of FFr260m ($51m) last year on sales of cosmetics, haircare products and perfume.

L'Oreal has also said that it will set up a joint venture in Japan to sell cosmetics by mail, and will buy a plant in Poland next year. 'What we want to do is get into markets that are developing rapidly,' said a spokesman, who refused to be quoted by name.

He added that the company posted a 111 per cent rise in sales in Russia in 1995 to FFr380m ($74.5m), but that it was too soon to disclose sales in China. L'Oreal stopped producing in Russia in 1994 after entering a venture known as Soreal with a local partner. The venture was privatised and taken over by a Russian firm that disputed L'Oreal taking a majority stake. L'Oreal subsequently bowed out and halted production in Russia. The L'Oreal spokesman said that the company will double the number of Maybelline outlets in China by the end of the year to 180 from 90 in January, and more than triple its L'Oreal Paris outlets in the country.

→

→ **Exhibit 4.11** *continued*

Magnelia, the CS First Boston analyst, said that the move into these countries remains largely symbolic in the short term, but represents a healthy investment down the road. 'The markets are minuscule compared to the overall growth of the company,' he said, 'but for every dollar they invest in tangible fixed assets, they generate about $3 in sales for the company.'

In Paris, L'Oreal stock closed down FFr37 last Tuesday, or 2.1 per cent, to FFr1,721 as shares of all exporters were hurt by the dollar's weakness, which cuts earnings when dollars are converted to francs. That closing price represented a retreat from L'Oreal's high of FFr1,844, a 51 per cent rise since the start of the year.

Source: Sunday Business, Trading Week Section, 3 November 1996

Table 4.19   Checklist for Joint-Venture Entry

A. *Purpose of joint venture*
   1. Objectives/strategy of foreign partner.
   2. Objectives/strategy of local partner.
   3. Reconciliation of objectives.

B. *Contributions of each partner*
   1. Knowledge of local environment.
   2. Personal contacts with local suppliers, customers, and so on.
   3. Influence with host government.
   4. Local prestige.
   5. Existing facilities.
   6. Capital.
   7. Management/production/marketing skills.
   8. Technical skills and industrial property.
   9. Other.

C. *Role of host government*
   1. Laws/regulations/policies.
   2. Administrative flexibility.
   3. Interest in this joint venture.
   4. Requirements for approval.

D. *Ownership shares*
   1. Majority (foreign partner).
   2. Minority (foreign partner).
   3. 50–50.
   4. Other arrangements.

E. *Capital structure*
   1. Legal character of venture.
   2. Equity capital.
   3. Loan capital (local and foreign).
   4. Future increase in equity capital.
   5. Limits on transfer of shares

F. *Management*
   1. Appointment/composition of board of directors.
   2. Supply/installation of machinery and equipment.
   3. Expatriate staff.
   4. Organization.

G. *Production*
   1. Planning/construction of facilities.
   2. Supply/installation of machinery and equipment.
   3. Operations.

4. Quality control.
5. R & D.
6. Training

H. *Finance*
   1. Accounting/control system.
   2. Working capital.
   3. Capital expenditures.
   4. Dividends.
   5. Pricing of products provided by partners.
   6. Borrowing and loan guarantees by partners.
   7. Taxation.

I. *Marketing*
   1. Product lines, trademarks, and trade names.
   2. Target market(s) and sales potentials.
   3. Distribution channels.
   4. Promotion.
   5. Pricing.
   6. Organization.

J. *Agreement*
   1. Company law in host country.
   2. Articles and bylaws of incorporation.
   3. Contractual arrangements (licensing, technical assistance, management, and so on).
   4. Settlement of disputes.

Source: Root, F. R. (1994) *Entry Strategies for International Markets*, Revised and Expanded Edition, Lexington Books, Lexington, MA.

There are, of course, some pitfalls associated with joint ventures generally. These include:

- Board level disagreement between the two parents on the priorities, direction and values of the joint venture.
- Difficulty of integrating into a global strategy with cross-border trading.
- Conflict when corporate headquarters endeavour to impose limits or even guidelines.
- Unacceptable positions can develop with a local market when the self-interest of one partner conflicts with the interest of the joint venture as a whole, as in the pricing of a single-source input or raw material.
- Objectives of the respective partners may be incompatible.
- Problems of management structures and dual parent staffing of joint ventures as well as nepotism perhaps being the established norm
- Conflict in tax interests between the partners particularly where one may represent the local government interest.

A joint venture requires sharing rewards as well as risks. Harrigan (1985) has identified the following as joint venture change forces:

1. Changes in the venture's industry (and success requirements therein).

2. Effectiveness of joint venture's competitive strategy.
3. Changes in partners' relative bargaining power *vis-à-vis* each other.
4. Changes in owners' strategic missions.
5. Changes in importance of the joint venture to owners.
6. Changes in venture's need for autonomous activities.
7. Changes in patterns of owner-venture coordination needed for competitive success.

The main disadvantage is the very significant costs of control and co-ordination associated with working with a partner. *Business Week* (21 July 1986) reported that seven in ten fall short of expectations and were disbanded. Franko (1971) revealed that more than one-third of the 1,100 joint ventures of 170 multinational corporations studied, were unstable, ending in 'divorce' or in a significant increase in the US firm's power over its parent. Killing (1983) also found this 30 per cent failure rate in his study of 37 joint ventures. Franko also found that joint ventures with a local government partner were more lasting. Research elsewhere has also shown that where business had the choice between joint-equity and SBA-type contractual joint ventures, they were increasingly moving towards contractual joint ventures. Note that

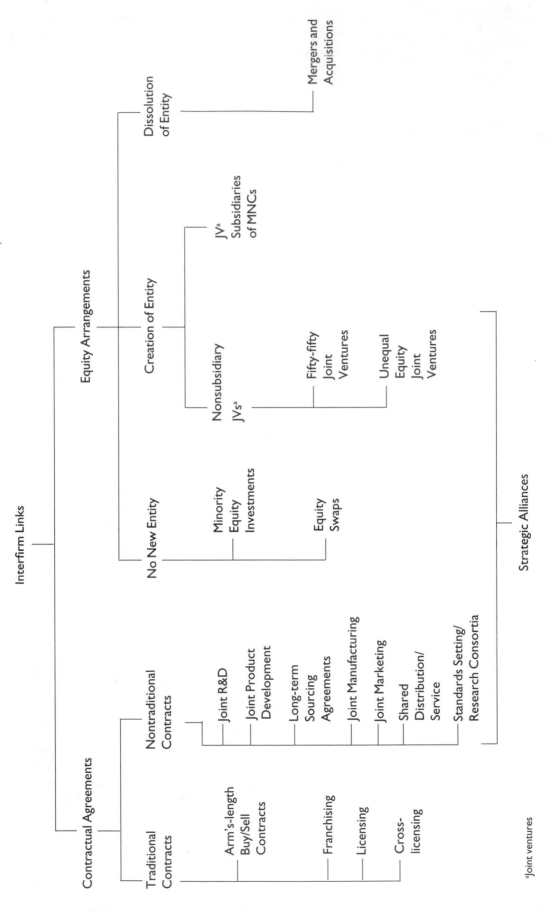

Source: Yoshino, M. Y. and Rangan U. S. (1995) *Strategic Alliances: An Entrepreneurial Approach to Globalization,* Harvard Business School Press, Boston, Mass.

Figure 4.10   The spectrum of alliances and joint venture

[a]Joint ventures

Table 4.20 Operational variable analysis contrasting strategic business alliances and joint equity ventures

Operation variables	Strategic business alliances		Joint equity	
	Possible advantages	Possible disadvantages	Possible advantages	Possible disadvantages
Ownership	None, no company finance involved	Lack of control	Equity stake	Weakening of company equity base
Venture control	Contractual limitations, plant, local partner responsibility	Limited control	De facto control greater than equity share	Inability to reconcile objectives
Venture capital	No capital investment by company	Entails acceptance of goods made under licence	Capital and managerial investment	Commitment of company resources
Return on investment (ROI)	Fast	Speed of project rests with local partner	Gradual ROI shows willingness to stay in market	Venture has to achieve profitability first
Risk sharing	Contractual liability only	Diminished risks diminish opportunity for spectacular profits	Half share only	Eastern partner may refuse to kill-off an unprofitable joint venture
Venture duration	Fixed duration	Renewal or extension requires separate contract	Unlimited	Termination a possible problem
Western company repayment	Hard cash and goods	Adjustment to Western business cycles	Goods made under licence and hard cash	Subject to local taxes
Manufacturing	Extra facility at cost	May flood market eventually	Extra plant at cost	Exposure to risk
Management skills	Limited, contractual obligations	Costs of this transfer may be greater than anticipated	Full access	Too great a dependence on the Western partner
Marketing	Lower cost goods made under licence	Co-ordination with Western business cycles	Lower cost goods made under licence	Investment in capital, machinery and management
Market expansion	Market access contractually limited	Ability to vary deliveries according to demand	Market access contractually limited	Sales priced only in 'hard' currency
Pricing	Lower costs	Western inability to forecast partner's expectation	Lower costs	All costs priced in 'hard' currency only
Quality control	Goods to Western quality standards	Free access but geographical distance and costs of quality control	Goods to Western quality standards	Free access but geographical distance and costs of quality control
Research and development	May be included or may develop	Dependent on mutual capabilities	Ability to capitalize on local partner	Difficulties of co-ordination
Updating of technology transferred	Contractual	Ambiguity of contract and defined limits	Close integration	Sharing of current company specific technology

Source: Paliwoda, S. J. (1981) *Joint East-West Marketing and Production Ventures*, Gower Press, Farnborough

in a later study (Franko, 1996) Franko assessed the degree of trade-off in MNC investment decreased among emerging economies.

As an innovative form, SBAs assume complex forms and do not readily correspond to the known established forms of commercial contracts and so the UN Economic Commission for Europe in its *Guide on Drawing up International Contracts on Industrial Co-operation*, in 1976, was forced to state:

the drafters of contracts relating to industrial co-operation are obliged to use their imagination and to resort to legal innovation while endeavouring to conform as closely as possible to the economic, financial and commercial realities of industrial co-operation transactions.

Tripartite ventures

Tripartite ventures are few in number. Originally they developed as a means of third country market exploitation by a joint company owned by two separate foreign principals, perhaps also from different politico-economic blocs.

East-West *détente* of the early 1970s facilitated the trade exchange. During this period a few joint stock companies were established such as Polibur based in Manchester, England, a joint venture in the chemical engineering consulting and services field, owned equally by Petrocarbon Developments as a subsidiary of Burmah Oil (which later sold out to the construction company, Costain) and Polimex-Cekop of Poland. The expectations for the joint venture were that the Poles would be able to access Socialist countries with Western technology; the British partners would have lower cost on Polish inputs to offer on Western markets. All profits would be shared equally. The identity and image of the company would change relative to the market which it was approaching. Unfortunately the downturn in the petrochemicals sector which has produced overcapacity has created problems for this joint venture. Its success overall has been limited.

Industrializing nations continue, however, to make demands of the developed industrial nations to form partnerships. Indian engineering companies took an unusual unprecedented step when they drew up a list of ten major contracts where they would like to be awarded subcontracts. Subcontracting is now a feature of consortium projects.

Foreign market servicing strategies

Buckley, Pass and Prescott (1990), in their empirical study on the impact of foreign market servicing strategies on the competitiveness of UK manufacturing firms in five industry sectors, point out:

1.   Choice of market servicing policy is highly constrained by the nature of the product, the firm's previous involvement with the market, the actions of competitors, demand conditions in the market, financial considerations and cost conditions.

2.   Firms have an approach to market servicing rather than a strategy. In many cases, the market servicing still is reactive rather than proactive.

3.   Choices made do not have a universally positive impact on the competitiveness of firms. In each of the categories: performance, potential, and management process, there are examples of changes in market servicing stance which had negative impacts. Two particularly problematical areas appear to be entry via exporting through a foreign distributor and the take-over of a foreign company, which form the opposite ends of the size and involvement spectrum.

4.   No definite causal relations were discerned between market servicing mode and competitive outcome.

In the *Future of the Multinational Enterprise*, Buckley and Casson (1985) acknowledge the role of the multinational corporation in the development and transferral of knowledge internationally, and, through foreign investment, the MNE's ability to bypass imperfect external markets for knowledge. While arguing for internalization as the explanation for multinational growth, Buckley and Casson foresee also a change to the multinational working environment in the lessening of competitive R & D, and through more effective marketing of knowledge. Such a change would affect competitive policy, rationalize R & D activities, and may substitute licensing for foreign direct investment. Through the advent of SBAs, this rationalization of R & D has come about but without any increase in licensing over foreign direct investment, so as an alternative to investment, licensing still appears to be commonly perceived by industry as having too many shortcomings.

Monitoring market entry modes

There is no one single mode of market entry that is optimal for all conditions. Market entry modes have to be assessed within their context. The expectations of head office management and the resources which they are willing to commit are important factors. Also a factor is the fact that at certain points in business history various forms of market entry have been fashionable. Over the years licensing gave way to franchising which is

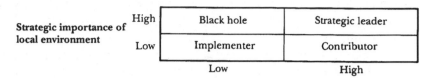

		Low	High
Strategic importance of local environment	High	Black hole	Strategic leader
	Low	Implementer	Contributor
		Low	High

Level of local resources and capabilities

Source: Bartlett, C. A. and Ghoshal, S., *Managing Across Borders: The Transnational Solution*, Hutchinson Business Books, London

Figure 4.11   Generic roles of national organizations

still buoyant in Europe but the greatest single trend has been towards strategic alliances. No one market entry mode is fault free or able to compensate for the deficiencies of alternative forms. For this reason, the mode must be assessed within the context within which it will be placed.

However, selection of a market entry mode is not the end of the process but the beginning. Evaluation starts as soon as the market entry mode is operational. Naturally, a reasonable period of time will usually be allowed against which to properly assess performance but a particularly poor or unimpressive performance may hasten withdrawal or replacement by another form of market entry. Seeing this process then as iterative it is useful now to consider the framework offered by Bartlett and Ghoshal (1989).

Bartlett and Ghoshal see the national environments as important to the firm's global strategy. A national subsidiary is placed in one of the four categories in Figure 4.11 depending on its strengths in technology, production, marketing or any other area that may lend competitive advantage. Strategic leaders develop organizational responses in certain areas. This is similar to the world product market advocated by Rugman and others. A certain area of competence may be developed to become the company's international specialist division or production or research base. Contributors are national subsidiaries who may have strong technological capability but a limited market. These subsidiaries feed into the worldwide network. Implementers are those who maintain operations in a non-strategic market but cannot contribute much to the strategic knowledge of the firm. They do not control resources or have access to critical information so they are limited in their operations but in pursuing what they do efficiently they can contribute greatly to the firm in pursuing their quest for ever greater efficiency in economies of scale perhaps and so competitive advantage. Most subsidiaries fall into the implementer category.

Finally, the 'black hole'. This exists where companies have only taken positions in the markets in which they are based. It has minimal

capability and is not held to be an acceptable strategic position. A strategy of a small monitoring unit to exploit the potential of the market does not work. 'One needs to be aware of developments as they emerge, and for that one must be a player, not a spectator' (Bartlett, Ghoshal, 1989). A strategic alliance is possible in these circumstances but it depends as much on the organizational capability of the parties as the motivating force of the potential to be tapped.

Relationship management and interaction theory

Unlike economists who still busy themselves with concepts such as pure competition which do not exist, businessmen take a different view of the marketplace. Academic theory is leagues behind practice in the area of international marketing. Various studies have been made on locational decision-making, on assumptions that companies move towards lower cost factor endowments. Less has been written on the organizational abilities of global corporations to exploit profitable sales rather than production or even to consider market entry as being a move that will later have strategic importance, as is evidenced in much investment being made in the EU prior to 1992.

When the importance of market concentration is considered and how with the ever increasing costs of research and development, the critical mass of production necessary to achieve economies of scale is forever being pushed upwards, it is not hard to imagine how hard the competition must be. Industries are not national but global and so, therefore, is the competition.

Interaction theory was developed by the Swedes but spread into France, Britain, Italy and Germany when a group of like-minded researchers formed what became known as the IMP Group, basing their research on the Interaction Model.

The interaction model recognizes the customer as important and puts at the very centre of its research the nature of this relationship between buyer and seller. Relationship

Table 4.21 Market Control and Modes of Entry

		Control over market strategy	Product policy	Pricing policy	Promotional policy	After-sales service
Exporting without presence	Agent	Weak to none	Standardization	Uncontrolled	Uncontrolled	Uncontrolled
	Exclusive agent	Weak to good	Standardization	Better control	Good control	Good control
	Concession	Contractual				
	Sale of patent or licence	None	Adaptation	No control	No control	No control
	Franchise	Rather good	Adaptation	Weak control	Weak control	Weak control
	Management contract	Good	Adaptation	Weak control	Weak control	Weak control
	Joint venture	Moderate	Standardization	Better control	Better control	Better control
	Wholly owned subsidiary	Excellent	Standardization	Well controlled	Well controlled	Well controlled
Small presence	Sub-contracting	Moderate	Adaptation / Problem of quality control	Badly controlled	—	—
	Joint venture	Moderate	Partial adaptation			
	assembly					
	production		Well controlled	Moderate control	Moderate control	Moderate control
	integration		Adapted / Badly controlled			
Heavy presence	Wholly owned subsidiary	Good	Partially adapted	Well controlled	Well controlled	Well controlled
	assembly					
	production					
	integration		Adapted			

Source: Translated and adapted from: de Leersnyder, J.-M. (1982), *Marketing International*, Dalloz, Paris, p. 106

management is crucial when one considers that for every customer complaint received, there are 27 who feel the same way but who would not otherwise complain. These, too, could be lost customers and when one considers that it takes five times as much to replace a customer than it does to retain one, the importance of relationship management becomes self-evident (*Marketing News*, 1991). This however requires market 'presence', see Table 4.21.

The differences which the interaction model brings to a study of market dynamics include:

- Recognition of an active dynamic market rather than a passive market, and its implications of simply manipulating marketing mix variables to achieve a response from a generalized, passive market.
- Questioning an atomistic structure to understand markets which assumes a large number of buyers and sellers with easy and costless change between suppliers and customers.
- Investigation of the characteristics of different organizations as they relate to other organizations.
- Analysis of the links between the units in terms of formalization, intensity and standardization.
- Relationships between buyers and sellers in the industrial context are frequently long-term, close, and involve a complex pattern

of interaction between and within each company.
- Tasks of marketers and buyers often have more to do with maintaining a relationship than with a straightforward sale or purchase.
- Links between buyer and seller often become institutionalized into a set of roles that each party expects the other to perform. This extends into product development, test procedures and the carrying of inventory.
- Importance of experiences of previous purchases, mutual evaluation and the relationship established during the course of that single transaction.

Figure 4.12 displays the interaction model with four groups of variables:

- parties involved both as organizations and individuals
- environment in which the interaction takes place
- elements of and the process of interaction
- unique atmosphere affecting and affected by the interaction.

Transactions are different from relationships which are frequently long term. To distinguish between them, the simple transaction is called an 'episode' which may or may not be repeated.

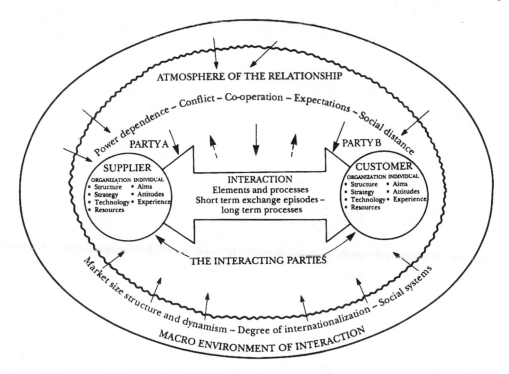

Source: Turnbull, P. W., and Paliwoda, S. J. (1986) *Research in International Marketing*, Croom Helm, London

Figure 4.12 The interaction mode

Table 4.22 Supplier/customer relationship: summary profiles of each country market

France	Germany	Italy	Sweden	United Kingdom
Highest average age	Highest average age among export markets	Lowest customer adaptations score	Highest customer adaptations among export markets	Lowest average age
Highest sourcing average	Lowest degree of reciprocal adaptations	Lowest supplier adaptations score	Highest combined volume of adaptations among export markets	Highest sourcing average among export markets
Highest customer adaptations score	Lowest human investment by customer	Lowest combined volume of adaptations	Highest degree of reciprocal adaptations	Highest supplier adaptations score
Highest combined volume of adaptations		Lowest human investment by supplier	Highest human investment by customers among export markets	Lowest degree of reciprocal adaptations
Highest human investment by suppliers		Highest stability of turnover		Highest human investment by supplier among export markets
Highest human investment by customers				
Lowest stability of turnover				

Source: Turnbull, P. W., and Valla, J.-P. (1986) *Strategies for International Industrial Marketing*, Croom-Helm, London

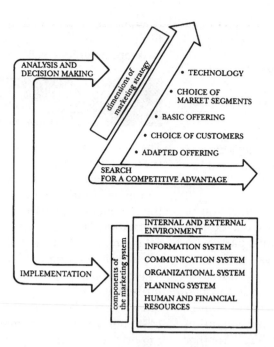

Source: Turnbull, P. W., and Valla, J.-P. (1986) *Strategies for International Industrial Marketing*, Croom-Helm, London

Figure 4.13   The multistrat model: a framework for industrial marketing strategies

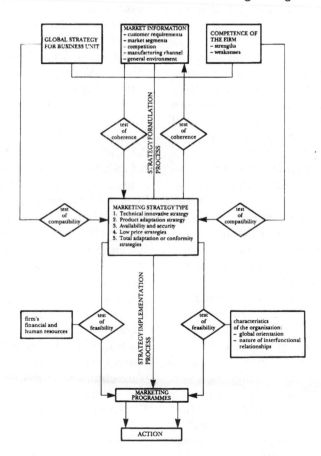

Source: Turnbull, P. W., and Valla, J.-P. (1986) *Strategies for International Industrial Marketing*, Croom-Helm, London

Figure 4.14   A framework for testing marketing strategies for coherence, compatibility and feasibility

It may evolve, if repeated over time, into a relationship. Episodes have four elements:

1. Product or service exchange which is at the very core of the exchange.
2. Information exchange which may be personal or impersonal.
3. Financial exchange.
4. Social exchange which helps also to further reduce uncertainty in a relationship based on market trust.

Relationships arise out of the routinization of these exchange episodes over time and so to a clear expectation on the part of either party with regard to roles and responsibilities. Again, over time, these expectations become institutionalized. Also, contact patterns become established between the two parties in terms of either individuals or groups seeking to transmit communications across the two organizations. Another important factor of relationships is the adaptations which one party may make either to the elements exchanged or the process of exchange. The structure of each organization and the extent of centralization, specialization and formalization will influence the interaction process. Individuals are also part of this process, usually several will be involved exchanging information, developing relationships, and perhaps building up the kinds of social bonds which may influence further future stages of their business relationship. Experience gained from individual 'episodes' becomes part of the total corporate memory of a relationship.

Market structure depends on the concentration of buyers and sellers and the degree of stability or change prevalent in that market. Markets are not just regional or national but may be international. This influences the interaction environment as the degree of dynamism is very central to interaction. Internationalism of the market as it affects buyers and sellers is another central issue shaping attitudes towards nationalism and so protection and perceptions about the ability of either parties to perform as is the position of either party in the distribution channel.

The unique atmosphere created between the companies is that of power and dependence; of conflict and cooperation; and of mutual expectations. The atmosphere affects, and is affected by, the other variables already mentioned. The parties can give each other valuable technical and commercial information but the ability to control the relationship is related to the perceived power of either party which may be low, or poorly understood, in the critical stages of the relationship but which will in any event,

change over time. A close relationship may be technologically advantageous but will in turn have opportunity costs.

International studies related to interaction theory

The first and major study of the IMP Group was the five country study of France, Germany, Sweden, UK and Italy whereby the perceptions of national suppliers were investigated by each of the national teams with the exception applying that national research teams were excluded from asking foreign buyers their perceptions of suppliers from their particular country. In this way, a certain bias that would otherwise have been introduced was completely eliminated at the outset. This study clearly showed supplier-customer relationship management to be an important issue. (See Table 4.22.)

A further IMP study was Hakansson, 1982 which was more industrial case study than international-marketing oriented. Then Turnbull and Valla, 1986 provided a country-by-country perspective of international industrial marketing strategies and the nature of relationships between national suppliers and their customers. Moving away from the industrial marketing mix concept, Valla proposed the multistrat model which introduces the five main marketing dimensions firms have to make: technology; choice of segments; basic offering; choice of customers; adapted offering. A sixth dimension is that the firm will normally look for one or more competitive advantage so as to be able to compete successfully. Against these six dimensions, there are five components of the marketing system: the information system; the communication system; the organizational system; the planning system and the human and financial resources. The IMP Group view industrial marketing as an investment process over time in which the interaction model provides a useful framework for understanding and presenting marketing strategy. Suppliers who have successfully entered into a relationship with a customer have an initial advantage over potential competitors, but this may be eroded if not maintained through continued investment activity. Figure 4.13 provides a framework for testing strategic alternatives although it should be emphasized that the nature of the business activity is an important factor in terms of value perceived or otherwise, i.e. commodity or stable or growing non-commodity may be simply one means of differentiation. The more the business activity resembles a commodity, the fewer are the strategic alternatives.

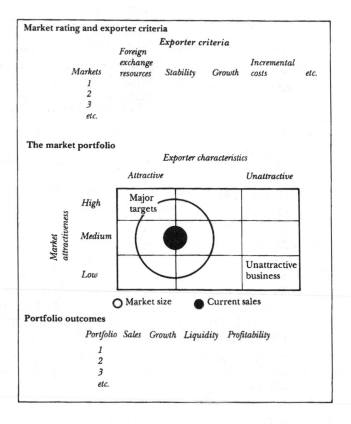

Source: Piercy, N. (1983) Export strategy – the market portfolio. *European Research*, 11, 168–176

Figure 4.15 Portfolio analysis for export market strategy

A strategic portfolio of market entry modes

Market concentration and spreading have been dealt with earlier. Piercy (1983) points to a portfolio approach which assesses market attractiveness against the company's competitive strengths by means of weighting a number of indicators representing several variables. This would allow a selection of the most appropriate markets which match the exporter's profile of needs. It blends hard data on export markets with a substantial examination of criteria appropriate for the individual exporter. A portfolio approach will also pinpoint change within market clusters and identify the appropriate strategy whether growth, hold, rebuild, harvest, or divestment. Designing an export market strategy requires information not just on growth and profitability but also risk and stability and to be meaningful, in a situational context (see Figure 4.15).

Conclusions

This chapter has sought to confront the measures against which relative degrees of success may be determined. Expectations are important as are resources, but what can be expected out of any investment is determined by what is actually put in, in way of investment. In order that the 'sharp-end' of the business, the actual contact with the foreign customer was not overlooked, a summary of interaction theory focusing on relationship management and the need to invest in customers to maintain relationships was provided.

Revision questions

1. What are the 10 steps in undertaking trade?
2. What criteria are employed in selecting a market entry mode?
3. Why is piggybacking so common amongst US multinationals?
4. What is an Export Buying Office? Is that direct or indirect exporting?
5. Identify the problems that may be encountered in using agents.
6. How do agents and distributors differ?
7. Explain how a management contract can be a form of foreign market entry.
8. Is it correct to say that licensing relates to products and franchising to services, or not?

9. Why would a franchisor want to buy back franchised outlets?
10. For a small independent investor, what are the attractions of franchising?
11. Licensing has often been called a second best alternative to exporting, why should that be the case?
12. What is a screwdriver assembly operation, and why does it exist?
13. Explain how rules of origin are determined within the EU.
14. Give few reasons as to why a joint venture may be justified.
15. Is a joint venture an organizational form that is inherently unstable from inception, a last resort?
16. Why are strategic alliances taking over from the traditional form of joint equity venture? Explain.
17. What is the Interaction Model and how does it lend further understanding to international marketing?
18. What is relationship management?
19. Explain how market control may be one means of classifying market entry modes. Is it realistic?
20. What is meant by having a strategic portfolio of market entry modes?

References

Attwood, T., and Hough, L. (1996) *The Good Franchise Guide*, Kogan Page, London.

Baer, J. R., Costello, K. R., Duvall, G. R., Mozero, J. G. and Wultt, E. B. (1995) 'Application of US franchise laws to international franchise sales', *Franchise Law Journal*, Fall, **15**(2), 41–52.

Bain, J. S. (1965) *Barriers to New Competition: Their Character and Consequences in Manufacturing Industries*, Harvard University Press, Cambridge, Ma.

Bartlett, C. A., and Ghoshal, S. (1989) *Managing Across Borders: The Transcontinental Solution*, Hutchinson Business Books, London.

Beamish, P. (1988) *Multinational Joint Ventures in Developing Countries*, Routledge, London.

Beeth, G. (1990) Distributors – finding and keeping the good ones. In *International Marketing Strategy* (H. Thorelli, and Cavusgil, S. T. 1990), 3rd edn, Pergamon Press, Oxford.

Blank, A. H. (1987) The growth of joint venture marketing. *The Banker's Magazine*, March–April, 60–63.

Brooke, M. Z. (1985) *Selling Management Services Contracts in International Business*, Holt, Reinhart and Winston, Eastbourne, East Sussex.

Brooke, M. Z. (1996) *International Management*, 3rd edn, Stanley Thornes Publishers, Cheltenham, Glos.

Buckley, P. J., and Casson, M. (1976) *The Future of the Multinational Enterprise*, Macmillan, London.

Buckley, P. J., and Casson, M. (1985) *The Economic Theory of the Multinational Enterprise*, Macmillan, London.

Casson, M. (1979) *Alternatives to the Multinational Enterprise*, Holmes and Merer Publishers Inc., New York.

Commission of the European Communities DG XXIII, and T.I.I. European Association for the Transfer of Technologies, Innovation and Industrial Information (1989) *Partnerships Between Small and Large Firms*, Graham and Trotman Ltd., London.

Didier, P. (1990) EEC anti-dumping: the level of trade issue after the definitive CD player regulation. *Journal of World Trade*, **24**(2), 103–110.

Doz, Y. (1986) *Strategic Management in Multinational Companies*, Pergamon Press, Oxford.

Dunning, J. H. (1985) *Multinational Enterprises, Economic Structure and International Competitiveness*, John Wiley and Sons, Chichester.

Entrepreneur (1997) Annual Franchise 500, January, 113–210.

Ford, D., and Leonidou, L. (1992) Research developments in international marketing: a European perspective. In *New Perspectives on International Marketing*, (S. J. Paliwoda), Routledge, London.

Forsgren, M. (1989) *Managing the International Process*, Routledge, London.

Franko, L. G. (1996) 'Strategic Rampages of Multinational Corporations to the Opening of Eastern Europe and the Former Soviet Union: And their impact on Competing Developing Countries, *Journal of East West Business*, **2**(1/2), 5–55.

Gemunden, H. G. (1991) Success factors of export marketing: a meta-analytic critique of the empirical studies. In *New Perspectives on International Marketing*, (S. J. Paliwoda), Routledge, London.

Gibson, M. (1996a) 'From Russia with years of expertise' (Russian franchise operating in the Western World), *The European*, 17 October, p. 27.

Gibson, M. (1996b) 'Getting the gumball rolling in Europe' (European franchising of American gumball machines), *The European*, 17 October, p. 27.

Goldenberg, S. (1988) *International Joint Ventures in Action: How to Establish, Manage and Profit from International Strategic Alliances*, Hutchinson Business Books, London.

Hakansson, H. (ed.) (1982) *International Marketing and Purchasing of Industrial Goods – An*

Interaction Approach, John Wiley and Sons, New York.

Hall, P., and Dixon, R. (1989) *Franchising*, Natwest Small Business Bookshelf, Pitman Publishing, London.

Harrigan, K. R. (1987) *Strategies for Joint Ventures*, Lexington Books, Lexington, MA.

Harrigan, K. R. (1985) Why joint ventures fail. *First Boston Working Paper Series*, Columbia University Graduate School of Business, FB–86–01, September.

Hooley, C., Shipley D., Fahy, J., Cox, T., Beracs, J., and Kolos, K. (1996) 'Foreign Direct Investment in Hungary: Resource Acquisition and Domestic Competitive Advantage', *Journal of International Business Studies*, no. 4, Fourth Quarter, 683–710.

Ishikawa, K. (1990) *Japan and the Challenge of Europe 1992*, Pinter Publishers, London, for the Royal Institute of International Affairs, London.

Katz, B. (1995) Agents. In *Marketing Handbook* M. J. Thomas, 4th edn, Gower, Aldershot, Hants.

Kedia, B. L., Ackeman, D. J., Bush, D. E., and Justis, R. T. (1994) 'Study Note: Determinants of internationalization of franchise operations by US franchisers', *International Marketing Review*, October, 11(4), 56–69.

Killing, J. P. (1983) *Strategies for Joint Venture Success*, Croom Helm, London.

Lewis, J. D. (1990) *Structuring and Managing Strategic Alliances*, Free Press, New York.

Marketing News (1991) American Marketing Association, Chicago, 4 February, p. 4.

Matsumoto, K., and Finlayson, G. (1990) Dumping and anti-dumping: growing problems in world trade. *Journal of World Trade*, 24(4), 5–20.

McCall, J. B., and Warrington, M. B. (1989) *Marketing by Agreement: A Cross-Cultural Approach to Business Negotiations*, 2nd edn, John Wiley and Sons, Chichester.

McMillan, C., and Paulden, S. (1974) *Export Agents: A Complete Guide to their Selection and Control*, 2nd edn, Gower, Aldershot, Hants.

Mendelsohn, M. (1992a) *The Guide to Franchising*, 5th edn, Cassell, London.

Mendelsohn, M. (1992b) Franchising in Europe, Cassell, London.

Mendelsohn, M. (1995) Franchising. In *Marketing Handbook*, (M. J. Thomas) 4th edn, Gower, Aldershot, Hampshire.

Paliwoda, S. J. (1981) *Joint East-West Marketing and Production Ventures*, Gower, Aldershot, Hampshire.

Perlemutter, H. V. (1969) Some management problems of spaceship Earth: the megafirm in the global industrial estate. *Academy of Management Proceedings*, New York, August.

Piercy, N. (1983) Export strategy – the market portfolio. *European Research*, 11(4), 168–176.

Porter, M. E. (1990) *The Competitive Advantage of Nations*, Macmillan, New York.

Preble, J. F., and Hoffman, R. C. (1995) 'Franchising systems around the globe : a status report' *Journal of Small Business Management*, April, 33(2), 80–9.

Roman, D. D., and Puett, E. F. Jr. (1983) *International Business and Technological Innovation*, North Holland.

Root, F. D. (1994) *Entry Strategies for International Markets*, Revised and Expanded Edition, Lexington Books, Lexington, MA.

Shane, S. A. (1996) 'Why franchise companies expand overseas', *Journal of Business Venturing* March, 11(2), 73–89.

Stopford, J., and Turner, L. (1985) *Britain and the Multinationals*, John Wiley and Sons, Chichester.

Tan, B., and Vertinsky, I. (1996) 'Foreign Direct Investment by Japanese Electronics Firms in the United States and Canada: Modelling the timing of entry', *Journal of International Business Studies*, no. 4, Fourth Quarter, 655–682.

Tomlinson, J. W. C. (1970) *Joint Ventures in India and Pakistan*, Praeger, New York.

Turnbull, P. W., and Cunningham, M. T. (1981) *International Marketing and Purchasing: A Survey Among Executives in Five European Countries*, Macmillan, London.

Turnbull, P. W. (1985) Image and reputation of British suppliers in Western Europe. *European Journal of Marketing*, 19(6), 39–52.

Turnbull, P. W., and Paliwoda, S. J. (1986) *Research in International Marketing*, Croom Helm, London.

Turnbull, P. W., and Valla, J.- P. (1986) *Strategies for International Industrial Marketing*, Croom Helm, London.

UN Economic Commission for Europe (1976) *Guide in Drawing up International Contracts on Industrial Co-operation*, Geneva, ECD/TRADE/124.

Vermulst, E., and Waer, P. (1991) European Community rules of origin as commercial policy instruments? *Journal of World Trade*, June, 55–59.

Walmsley, J. (1982) *Handbook of International Joint Ventures*, Graham and Trotman Ltd., London.

Wright, M. (1989) *Build Up Your Exports*, Tate Publishing Company, Milton Keynes, England.

Yoshino, M. Y., and Rangan, Y. S. (1995) *Strategic Alliances: An Entrepreneurial Approach to Globalization*, Harvard Business School Press, Boston, Mass.

Young, S. Hood, N., and Hamill, J. (1988) *Foreign Multinationals and the British Economy*, Croom Helm, London.

Contacts

British Franchise Association
Thames View
Newton Road
Henley on Thames RG9 1HG.
tel 01491 578 050   fax 01491 573 517

Franchise Consultants Association
57 Nottingham Road
London SU17 7EA.
tel 0181 767 1371   fax 0181 767 2211

Franchise Development Services
Castle House
Castle Meadow
Norwich
tel 01603 620 301   fax 01603 630 174

Web sites

AC Nielsen
http://www.nielsen.ca

Asia Trade
http://www.asiatrade.com/index.html

AT & T Business Network – free site
http://www.bnet.att.com

Australia general lists
http://www.csu.edu.au/links/ozweb.html

Southeast Asian Information:
http://www.channelA.com/
http://www.asia 1.com.sg/htmlBank of
    America:Global Capital Markets Group
http://www.bofa.com/capmkts4.html

Best of the Web
http://wings.buffalo.edu/contest

BEMs – Big Emerging Markets (US
    Classification)
http://www.stat-usa.gov/itabems.html

Brazil general lists
http://www.embratel.net.br/dirweb.html

British Exporters Web Site
http://www.export.co.uk

Business Europa – business throughout Central
    and Eastern Europe
http://www.business-europa.co.uk

Business Information Resources
http://sashimi.wwa.com/~notime/eotw/
    business_info.html

Business Information Server
http://www.dnb.com/

Business Site of the Day
http://www.bizniz.com/eurocool/

Businesses on the Internet

http://www.yahoo.com/
    Business_and_Economy/Corporations/

Business to Business Marketing Exchange
http://www.btob.wfu.edu/b2b.html

Business Week
http://www.businessweek.com/

Canadian Business InfoWorld
http://csclub.uwaterloo.ca/u/nckwan/.html/
    directory

Canada Newswire
http://www.newswire.ca

Canadian WWW Central Index
http://www.csr.ists.ca/w3can/Welcome.html

CBS Television
http://www.cbs.com/

Chile general lists
http://sunsite.dcc.uchile.cl/chile/chile.html

CIA Publications
http://www.odc.gov/cia/publications/
    pus.html

Clearinghouse for Networked Information
    Discovery
http://kudzu.cnidr.org/welcome.html

Clearinghouse for Subject Oriented Internet
    Resources
http://www.lib.umich.edu/chhome.html

CNN Interactive
http://www.cnn.com/

Commerce Business Daily
gopher:cscns.com
Choose: Internet Express Gopher by Subject
    Business-Commerce Business Daily-
    Softshare

Commercenet
www.commerce.net

Commercial Use of the Internet
http://pass.wayne.edu/business.html

Cool Site of the Day
http://cool.infi.net/

D & B Market Place
http://www.mktplace.com/home2012

Electronic Shopping – BarclaySquare, use your
    BarclayCard(VISA)
http://www.itl.net/barclaysquare.

E-Mail Directory Assistance
http://www.bigfoot.co.uk

Entrepreneur International
http://www.leadnet.com

Ericsson (Telefonaktiebolaget LM Ericsson)
http://www.ericsson.com

Export – Import Pathfinder
http://mickey.queens.lib.ny.us/guides/
    export_i..html

ExportNet – Export Today Matchmaking service
http://www.exporttoday.com

Fax – use the Internet as a fax machine
http://www.jfax.co.uk

Federal Express (FedEx)
http://www.fedex.ca

Financial Times
http://www.ft.com/

Find it Fast
http://www.webcom.com/~tbrown/
    findpage.html

France general lists
http://www.urec.fr/cgi-bin/list

Franchising – Access WWW Franchise
    Directory
http://www.entremkt.com/access/index.html

GE Information Services – bringing together US
    buyers and suppliers
http://www.tpn.geis.com

Geek Site of the Day
http://www.owlnet.rice.edu/~indigo.gstod/
    index.html

Germany general lists
http://www.chemie.fu-berlin.de/
    outerspace/www-german.html

Glaxo-Wellcome
http://www.glaxowellcome.co.uk

Global Economic Forum
http://www.ms.com/GEFdata/digests/
    960129-mon.html

Global Internet News Agency
www.gina.com

Global Trade Center
http://wwwtradezone.com/tz/

Guinness plc
http://www.guinness.ie

Home Run – magazine for those running a
    business from home
http://homerun.co.uk/

Hong Kong Business Directory
http://www.hkdir.com.hk

Internet Business Center
http://www.tig.com/IBC

Importing and Exporting
Usenet: alt.business.import-export

Inc. Online
http://www.inc.com

Industry Net
http://www.industry.net/

International Business Forum
http://www.ibf.com

International Business Practices Guide
University of Missouri St. Louis
Gopher: umslvma.umsl.edu
Choose: The Library
    Government Information
    International Business

International Business Resources on the WWW
http://ciber.bus.msu.edu/busres.htm

International Chamber of Commerce, Paris
http://www1.usa1.com/~ibnet/icchp.html

Internet Address Finder
www.iaf.net

International Internet Marketing
www.clark.net/pub/granered/iim.html

Israel Web Servers
http://www.ac.il/

Kodak
http://www.kodak.com

Land's End – the famous clothing catalogue
    company
http://www.landsend.com/

Malibu Island – Internet Magazine Site of the
    Month
http://www.maalibu-rum.bb/

MBE Mail Boxes Etc
http://www.mbe.com

Mexico general lists
http://lanic.utexas.edu/la/Mexico/

Mexico government information
    (communications)
http://ags.inegi.gob.mx/

MexPlaza English language Internet page for
    Mexico
http://mexplaza.udg.mx:80/ingles/

Midas International Franchise
http://www.midasfran.com

Mungo Park – travel and adventure in bizarre
    and dangerous locations
http://mungopark.msn.com

Netherlands Foreign Investment Agency
http://www.nfia.com

New Scientist
http://www.newscientist.com

New Zealand Government Web Pages
http://www.govt.nz/

New Zealand Information
http://manuka.lincoln.ac.nz/libr/nz

Newsgroup for Importing and Exporting
news:alt.business.import-export

On-Line: Tracking time spent on-line
http://tucows.cableint.net/softime.html

OOCL (USA) Inc. freight forwarding
http://www.oocl.com

PC Daily News
http://www.zdnet.co.uk

Pizza Hut
http://www.pizzahut.com/

The Press Association
http://www.pa.press.net

Pointcast Network
http://www.pointcast.com

Pointcast Network Canada
http://www.pointcast.ca

Regional Information Guides by Price
    Waterhouse
http://www.i-trade.com/infsrc/pw

Royal Bank of Scotland
http://www.rbos.co.uk

J. Sainsbury plc
http://www.j-sainsbury.co.uk/

Saturn – the idiosyncratic GM subsidiary, its
    cars and advance information
http://www.saturncars.com/

Schweppes
http://www.schhh.com

Scottish Tourist Board
http://www.holiday.scotland.net

Scottish Virtual Memorial Garden
http://www.hebrides.com

Simplification of International Trade
    Procedures Board
http://www.sitpro.org.uk/index.html

Singapore Web Servers
http://www.w3.org/hypertext/
    DataSources/WWW.sg.html

SilverPlatter World: a worldwide library of
    electronic information
http://www.silverplatter.com/

Singapore Info Web

http://www.technet.sg/InfoWEB/
    welcome.html

Sony
http://www.sony.com/

South Africa Servers
http://www.is.co.za/www-za/

South African Government Information
http://www.polity.org.za/gnu.html

Statistical Agencies on the Internet
http://www.science.gmu.edu/csi779/drope/
    govstats.html

The Times
http://www.the-times.co.uk

The White House Home Page
http://www.whitehouse.gov/

Thomas Ho's favourite Electronic Commerce
    WWW Resources
http://www.engr.iupui.edu/~ho/interests/
    commmenu.html

Trade Compass
http://www.tradecompass.com

TradePort – extensive information on
    international business
http://www.tradeport.org

TradeWave Galaxy – Public and commercial
    information and services
http://www.einet.net/galaxy.html

Virtual Shopping Mall
http://www.Itl.net/shopping/
    index.html

UT-LANIC – University of Texas Latin
    American Network Information
    Center
http://lanic.utexas.edu/la/region.html

UT-MENIC – University of Texas Middle East
    Studies
http://menic.utexas.edu/mes.html

Wall Street Journal
http://wsj.com

Wall Street Net
http://www.netresource.com/wsn/

Web Page for Global Business
http://www.seattleu.edu/~parker/
    homepage.html

Web Sites for International Information:
http://www.ustr.gov/
http://www.i-trade.com/
http://www.stat-
    usa.gov/BEN/subject/trade.html
http://www.itaiep.doc.gov/

Web TV Networks Inc.
http://webtv.net

What's new on the Internet
http://www.whatsnew.com

World Factbook
gopher: gopher.aecom.yu.edu

WWW Yellow Pages
www.cba.uh.edu/ylowpges/
    ylowpges.html

Yahoo: National Yahoos: Canada, France,
    Germany, Japan, UK, Ireland.

Metros: Chicago, Los Angeles, New York, San
    Francisco Bay Area, My Town

Yahoo Reuters
http://www.yahoo.co.uk/News

Yellow Pages UK
http://www.yell.co.uk

Yellow Pages for the Web
http://www.yell.co.uk

Yelloweb Europe
http://www.yweb.com/

CHAPTER 5

International product policy considerations

Considering products as well as services in our definition, we ought to remember that services differ in terms of how we may perceive them with our five senses. They are intangible – we cannot see, touch, smell, hear or feel services, the possible exception being prostitution, which is not usually regarded as being a service which is legally offered, and so we can discount it from our reckoning. Aside from intangibility, services also exhibit perishability in that they have a very finite life which is the present and cannot be saved or held over. Heterogeneity is another feature, because services differ in delivery and are often inseparable from the service provider, for example the hairdresser or taxi driver. Consumption of service therefore takes place at the same point as where the service is offered, the barber shop or taxi.

What may sell abroad

A useful starting point is to examine the definition of a 'product'. The definition used here is that offered by Philip Kotler (1994). It remains the most suitable for our purposes in that it is concise, measurable and comprehensive.

A product is anything that can be offered to a market for attention, acquisition, use or consumption, that might satisfy a want or need.

A product may, therefore, be seen to embrace more than a branded, packaged good offered for sale. The definition has been widened to include services which include tourism, as well as the benefits and services that products bring with them. Black and Decker is an example of one company which has for many years had a marketing orientation which is evident in the way in which they perceive their customers. Asked about what business they are in, the company's response is that it is to sell solutions to clients who purchase their products with a particular problem in mind. Black and Decker do not see their mission as being particularly to sell electrical drills, but to make and sell equipment to meet

client needs. So, if clients wish to bore holes in wood, steel or plaster, Black and Decker will seek to meet that need with the best product formulation, incorporating the most up-to-date technology available. Looking at the business in these broad terms, it becomes clear that with 'technology push', the tools used to drill holes will change substantially over the years. By taking a broad view, Black and Decker are, therefore, prepared to consider alternative technologies, perhaps thermal lances or laser technology, as they become available. The problem of drilling holes leaves itself open to a number of possible future solutions.

Competition is changing globally and important writers, such as Levitt, Kotler and Drucker, have signalled this change in writing of the 'new competition'. Kotler (1994) has stated for example, that:

The new competition is not between what companies produce in their factories but between what they add to their factory output in the form of packaging, services, advertising, customer service, financing, delivery arrangements, warehousing and other things that people value. (p. 433)

This change is being driven by societal change and as change takes root, society proceeds then to challenge its structure and institutions. As Lannon (1966) pointed out, marketing is inextricably embedded in the social fabric. Developed societies are experiencing deep and important structural dislocations and disconnects in the way they operate, and flowing from these fractured interdependencies come profound implications for how consumers behave and thus how to market to them. This new age is not the age of modernity but of postmodernism where most of the certainties that anyone now over the age of 40 grew up with are being questioned. This state of affairs touches both more significantly and differently on the process of branding than is usually recognized. There is the decline of manufacture and the preeminence of services and information technology over branded products and a new global culture

Table 5.1   Modern and postmodern societies compared

Modern (industrial) society	Postmodern (post-industrial) society
Economic	
Wealth creation: manufacturing	Wealth creation: information/service
Restricted capital and people movements	Unrestricted capital and people movements
Social/consumers	
Authority vested in stable institutions	Institutional authority questioned, transference to 'media power'
Hierarchical, deferential social order	Egalitarian social order 'tribes'
Handed down, inherited values	'Discovered' individual values
Status reflected by things/externals	Status reflected by experiences/internals
National lifestyles	Mixtures of global lifestyles/bazaars
'Controlled closed' media	'Open/free access' media
Passive consumers	Active/educated consumers
Marketing/business	
Business activities back stage (covert)	Business activities front stage and transparent (overt)
Mass media	Fragmented specialist media
National markets	Global markets
'Mass' marketing	'Mass customization'/relationship marketing

Source: Lannon, J. (1996) 'What is Postmodernism and What does it have to do with Brands?', *The Journal of Brand Management,* **4** (2), 83–94

whereby the many existing value systems and lifestyles that have always existed but are not necessarily widely known are now very clear and visible via global television as well as mass travel. Fundamentalism, or absolutism as Lannon prefers, is confronted with pluralism, i.e. the ability to hold more than one view and still function normally. Lannon argues that in this new age, branding is more important than ever, that brands are needed to act as signposts but the communication of brands requires to be different, getting closer to consumers through micro segmentation while still producing fairly standardized offerings.

This emphasis on the attendant benefits and services that people value is what essentially separates the companies who practise the marketing concept from those who do not. If this is not presently being provided by a local competitor, the chances are that it will be provided by a foreign one. The internationalization of competition is apparent everywhere with the established multinational companies chasing each other around the world in a never-ending search for global market share. The multinationals have had to adopt a suitable 'positioning' strategy with regard to their products alongside local competitors, but derive instant benefit from the fact that their name and product are often already known, ahead of their actual physical arrival in that target market, as a result of the spill-over effects of international media: newspapers, magazines, cinema, radio and television. For multinational companies, the aim then is to seek also to transfer that same high level of product satisfaction across national boundaries.

Exhibit 5.1   Gucci set for rapid expansion

Upmarket Italian fashion house Gucci says it is looking at opening more outlets in China after sales at its first two stores quickly outstripped expectations.

The shops were opened together at the beginning of February in Beijing and Shanghai.

'Both stores, especially the Shanghai one, have performed well beyond our best expectations,' Gucci president and chief executive, Domenico de Sole said.

Mr de Sole said the 1,500 square foot Shanghai shop took more than US$100,000 in the first 15 days of March. The store in Beijing occupies 900 sq ft in the Palace Hotel.

Both stores are run directly by Gucci selling a similar range of the company's hallmark Italian-designed and manufactured goods.

Mr de Sole said consumers in China appeared to have more knowledge about branded goods

→ **Exhibit 5.1** *continued*

than he had expected, and admitted he had under-estimated the potential offered by the mainland.

'The Chinese market is much more important than I thought a year ago,' he said.

In the next two years, the company would look to open a store in Guangzhou or another one in Shanghai.

The latest set of Gucci results show Asia has become the most important revenue-earning market for the company. The company's main market in the region is Japan, where it has 20 directly operated shops.

Mr de Sole described increasing returns from repositioning Gucci's stores in Japan as the engine of growth in the region at the moment.

Gucci has five shops in Hong Kong and is considering one more.

It wants to move its existing store in Pacific Place to a better location within the complex and expand floor space. It is also trying to move away from reliance on tourist sales to appealing directly to the local population.

'Fifty to 55 per cent of our sales are to local customers now,' Gucci (Hong Kong and China) managing director Kenny Kwok said.

The company also has franchised sales in Singapore, Thailand, South Korea and Taiwan. It is opening a new directly operated outlet in Thailand at the end of this week.

Under the helm of Mr de Sole, Gucci has undergone a radical transformation in fortunes. From a position of near bankruptcy in the late 1980s it has been transformed into a group with no debts and operating profits last year of $239 million.

The Gucci family, which started the business in Florence in 1923, is no longer involved with the firm.

By 1993 and in severe financial difficulty, Maurizio Gucci, nephew of founder Guccio Gucci, sold the remaining family interest to Investcorp, an investment bank. Investcorp floated all its interest in Gucci between October 1995 and March last year.

Source: *South China Morning Post*, 2 April 1997

Exhibit 5.2   Czech brewers seek solace abroad

The beer was flowing freely last week when the Czech brewing industry gathered for its annual fair – a summit-cum-booze-up at which producers and customers forge alliances and break old ones, and forget for a few days the breweries' often illogical economics. Figures look different when viewed through the bottom of a glass.

Although Czechs drink more beer than any other nation, their breweries are barely profitable. Consumption is high because prices are extremely low. There is no brand loyalty, so competition is intense and usually based on price.

In a recent report on the industry, stockbrokers Ballmaier & Schultz noted that local consumption was not rising and may even decline in future, and that sales would gradually shift from pubs to supermarkets as more people drink at home. About 20 per cent of the industry's capacity was idle, the report said.

But against this sober background, this year's fair coincided with signs of a change in the fortunes of Czech breweries, after a long period of upheaval during privatisation and the breakdown of old monopolies.

Gone is the obsession with its own greatness and the insular thinking that dominated the industry in the past few years. Breweries are focusing more on lifting profits and seeking a decent return on the huge sums spent in recent years on modernising production and securing distribution rights.

The upheaval affected different brewers in different ways.

At Plzensky Prazdroj, the country's largest, a clear ownership structure emerged for the first time only last year. With that distraction behind it, management is now free to develop the business.

'Last year was the first year of normal operations, when we could concentrate on developing plans for the future,' says Mr Vladimir Perina, Prazdroj chief executive.

The company is now seeking to double output at its Pilsen brewery to 8m–10m hectolitres by the turn of the century.

Though sales of Prazdroj brands exceeded 4m hectolitres for the first time last year, preliminary figures show profits fell from more than Kč 150m ($5.1m) in 1995 to Kč 90m–Kč 100m.

In an effort to reverse this trend, the brewery raised prices by an average 10 per cent in December, higher than inflation but still below the cost increases experienced in the past few years.

Prazdroj is also considering licensing production of some of its brands abroad, and hopes to

→

→ Exhibit 5.2 *continued*

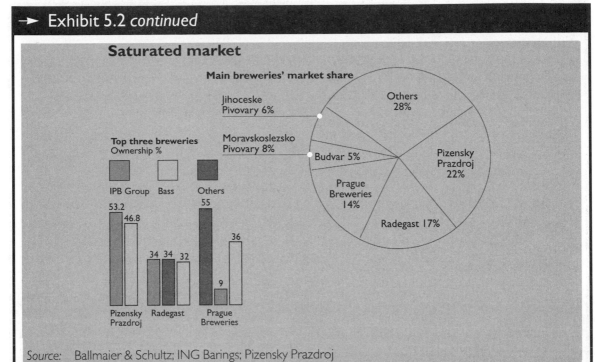

Saturated market

Source: Ballmaier & Schultz; ING Barings; Pizensky Prazdroj

boost exports after securing distribution deals in western markets.

The company would like to acquire another brewery in central Europe, after buying 51 per cent of Ragutis in Lithuania, where production of Prazdroj's Gambrinus brand – the biggest seller in the Czech Republic – will begin this spring.

At the same time, a battle looms for the top spot in the Czech market. Prazdroj has a 22 per cent share of national beer consumption. Radegast and Prague Breweries, the second and third biggest of the country's 49 brewing groups, have 17 per cent and 14 per cent, respectively.

Bass of the UK, which owns 51 per cent of Prague Breweries, has made no secret of its ambition to create a group with at least 25 per cent of the Czech market. It is in a tussle with the IPB banking group, which owns 53 per cent of Prazdroj, for control of Radegast, in which each has a 34 per cent stake.

Prazdroj, meanwhile, has approached the regional brewery Jihoceske Pivovary, which would add another 7 per cent to its market share.

Mr Perina says: 'We feel a strong group is being created around Bass, and we are trying to follow that. Concentration will continue if Czech brewers want to be able to compete.'

This concentration would make price rises more necessary and perhaps easier to implement.

This week Prague Breweries followed Prazdroj's lead by raising prices for some of its brands, though by only 4 to 5 per cent.

Cracking the export market should also be made easier by the shake-up under way.

Until 1990, only Pilsner Urquell, made by Prazdroj, and Budvar, perhaps the best-known of all Czech beers, were exported.

Budvar is still the most successful exporter, selling more than half its annual production of 1m hectolitres abroad.

Prague Breweries is rapidly expanding exports of its premium Staropramen beer, which is widely available in Bass pubs in the UK. Prazdroj increased exports last year by nearly 16 per cent to 442,000 hectolitres.

Exports of Pilsner Urquell, Budvar and Staropramen are likely to continue rising.

An executive at one of the top three breweries comments: 'In five years, domestic prices may not be much higher than they are now. So more and more beer will go for export. Exports are the key to making money from Czech beer.'

Source: *Financial Times,* 11 March 1997

Another important element of the 'new' competition is the arrival on world markets of the Japanese as a formidable trading nation. Using what has been termed as a 'cascading' strategy (Lorenz, 1981), they will initially seek penetration of well-defined segments, then move to volume stimulation and segment domination, before cascading into other areas and moving across.

This raises the question, why do products fail? Aside from the product or service itself and

Table 5.2   The number of people per telephone line, ranked by country

1	Bermuda	1.4		Belgium	2.2
2	Sweden	1.5		Malta	2.2
3	Denmark	1.7	25	Italy	2.3
	United States	1.7	26	Taiwan	2.5
	Switzerland	1.7		South Korea	2.5
	Canada	1.7		Israel	2.5
7	Iceland	1.8	29	Spain	2.7
	Norway	1.8		Macao	2.7
	Luxembourg	1.8	31	Puerto Rico	2.8
	Finland	1.8	32	Ireland	2.9
	France	1.8		Portugal	2.9
12	Hong Kong	1.9	34	Bulgaria	3.0
13	Netherlands	2.0		Barbados	3.0
	Australia	2.0		UAE	3.0
	United Kingdom	2.0	37	Slovenia	3.4
16	Germany	2.1	38	Bahamas	3.5
	Japan	2.1	39	Croatia	3.7
	Greece	2.1	40	Netherlands Antilles	3.9
	Singapore	2.1	41	Bahrain	4.0
	New Zealand	2.1	42	Estonia	4.1
21	Austria	2.2		Lithuania	4.1
	Cyprus	2.2	44	Kuwait	4.4

Source: Pocket Economist World in Figures, 1996

its particular marketing mix, there are the problems of tariff barriers, of non-tariff barriers or 'invisible' barriers which seek to exclude products or services from a given market. Where access is granted, tariffs or subsidies to a local competitor may mean inability to compete or even match on price. Related to this also is the question of 'dumping', which may upset a market sufficiently to persuade existing local suppliers that there is no long-term future for them.

Other reasons for failure would include cultural insensitivity; poor planning such that there is limited availability of the product in question; poor timing so that the regularity of supply or

even first appearance on the market is ill-timed; blind enthusiasm of top management concerned so as to ignore possible weaknesses; product deficiencies with regard to the target market; and, finally, lack of distinctiveness or what used to be called 'Unique Selling Proposition' (USP) generally, indicating that neither in the product, its accompanying benefits, nor its advertising, is there any criterion to differentiate this particular product from any of its competitors for the price at which it is sold.

With regard to product suitability for foreign markets, this depends on the product itself; its stage in the product life cycle – and the

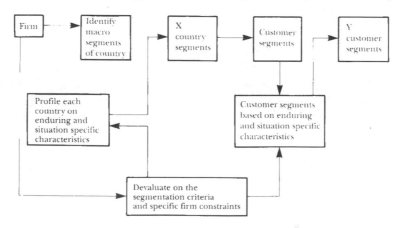

Source: Wind, J., and Douglas, S. (1972) International market segmentation. European Journal of Marketing, 6 (1)

Figure 5.1   International market segmentation

intended host country and its economic life cycle stage – whether mature industrial, or one of the types of less developed country; in addition to situation-specific characteristics, such as that market's current product offerings. Product life cycles have already been discussed, but it is important to remember also that this is only one part of the equation, and one must take cognizance of the state of development of transferor country and transferee. As Livingstone (1989) has pointed out, there are three important elements to consider in terms of production:

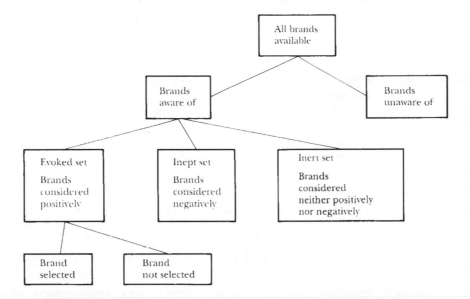

Figure 5.2

Table 5.3 Consumer goods: *Ownership*					
TV					
Number of people per receiver					
1	Bermuda	0.9		Malta	2.5
2	United States	1.3		Switzerland	2.5
3	Oman	1.4	28	Singapore	2.6
4	Canada	1.5		Russia	2.6
5	Japan	1.6		Czech Republic	2.6
6	France	1.7	31	Estonia	2.8
7	Germany	1.8		Hong Kong	2.8
8	Denmark	1.9	33	Lithuania	2.9
	Hungary	1.9		Luxembourg	2.9
	Uruguay	1.9	35	Netherlands Antilles	3.0
11	New Zealand	2.0	36	South Korea	3.1
	Finland	2.0		Argentina	3.1
	Netherlands	2.0		Ireland	3.1
14	Australia	2.1		Brunei	3.1
	Austria	2.1		Iceland	3.1
	Sweden	2.1	41	Trinidad & Tobago	3.2
	Latvia	2.1	42	Puerto Rico	3.3
18	Belgium	2.2		Poland	3.3
	United Kingdom	2.2	44	Slovenia	3.4
20	Italy	2.3		Jamaica	3.4
	Qatar	2.3		Israel	3.4
	Spain	2.3		UAE	3.4
23	Norway	2.4	48	Slovakia	3.6
	Bahrain	2.4		Macao	3.6
24	Kuwait	2.5		Moldova	3.6

Source: Pocket Economist World in Figures, 1997

1.   the size of the market.
2.   the level of local technology
3.   and the local distribution of the factors of production.

The example of McDonalds, the US hamburger chain, serves to illustrate this point with their entry to the UK. When this took place, the McDonalds mode of counter service and of production line hamburger preparation was new to Britain, so it meant that not only were McDonalds' US food recipes being introduced, but also the specifications for the fast-food catering equipment and McDonalds' distinctive style of packaging and merchandising. Once British suppliers were found, it made it easier for competitors to enter on the scene: profit-seeking suppliers now sought other potential clients for the fast-food equipment which they had imported or developed.

Suitability is not, however, the same as acceptability and it is worth noting at this point the work done on international market segmentation by Wind and Douglas (1972). They pointed out that segmentation could usefully be per-

formed after first conducting a study of the enduring characteristics, such as target market geography, topography and demography. Little could be expected to change among these variables except over time. The second set of variables were the situation-specific characteristics and here they included factors such as buying patterns and consumption. Figure 5.1 is a flowchart of their basis for segmentation.

At the same time, it should not be forgotten that prevailing local attitudes towards a particular product or product type should be monitored. Marketing can play an important role in influencing behaviour where stereotyped attitudes exist.

Where the source of origin is deemed to have a positive effect – which is only one of three possible outcomes – this may even allow a foreign product to remain competitive when not actually price competitive. The other two possible outcomes in relation to product recall are the 'inept set' and the 'inert set'. Only the 'evoked set', i.e. those products which consumers are bale to recall and react to favourably, is a really acceptable outcome. (See Figure 5.2).

Exhibit 5.3   Why Boeing scrapped super-jumbo plan

British Airways and United Airlines of the US both told Boeing that they wanted to buy new 550-seat jets, but were not prepared to place large enough orders to make production commercially feasible, according to Mr Bruce Dennis, Boeing's vice president for marketing.

Boeing recently scrapped its plans to build the super-jumbo, although its European rival Airbus is sticking to its own plan for a similar airliner.

Mr Dennis said designs of the planned Boeing 747–600 had been extensively tested in wind tunnels.

BA had played a substantial part in designing the proposed aircraft, he said.

In January, Boeing announced that the market for the 747–600 was not large enough to justify the $7bn development cost. Mr Dennis said Boeing had abandoned the project reluctantly as BA was one of its leading customers.

'You just hate to look at one of your best customers and say, 'We just can't do it at this time'.' He said Boeing would continue to re-evaluate the market for aircraft of more than 500 seats to see whether it was feasible to manufacture them.

BA last week told a UK public inquiry into the building of a fifth terminal at London's Heathrow

The shape of the world fleet

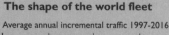

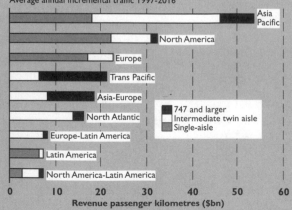

Source: Boeing Current Market Outlook 1997

→ Exhibit 5.3 *continued*

airport that it remained convinced that aircraft with more than 500 seats would be built.

Boeing has been arguing with Airbus Industrie, the European consortium, over the size of the market for aircraft of 500 seats or more. Airbus says the market is big enough for it to continue with plans to build the A3XX, family of aircraft with between 470 and 600 seats.

Mr Dennis said Boeing believed that if such an aircraft was built, only 480 would be sold over the next 20 years. Airbus is due to present its latest estimate of the market for large aircraft tomorrow.

Mr Dennis said Boeing, in its annual market forecast, predicted that airlines would buy a total of 16,160 new jets worth $1,100bn over the next 20 years. Almost 70 per cent of these would be smaller single-aisle aircraft. Aircraft of this size

would account for 43 per cent of aircraft spending between this year and 2016.

Intermediate-sized aircraft would account for 23 per cent of sales by unit and 39 per cent by value. The market for aircraft of 400 seats and above, including the Boeing 747, would account for 7.3 per cent by unit and 18 per cent of expenditure, Boeing said.

Mr Dennis said that by the end of this year, Boeing would be producing a record 40 aircraft a month. He said, however, that airlines were keeping orders in line with traffic growth, which is expected to rise by an annual average of 4.9 per cent over the next 20 years.

Mr Dennis said: 'There's no sign of the overheated airplane buying spree of the late 1980s.'

Source: *Financial Times*, 5 March 1997

Communication issues – language and media

The Plain English Campaign was founded in Britain in 1979. Politicians, including Margaret Thatcher who opened the first Plain English Exhibition, and more recently, John Major, have given strong endorsement to this campaign. British Government statistics indicate 16,000 forms have since been abolished and 21,000 forms clarified, including an indemnity payment form which until 1985 had a 55 per cent error rate.

The campaign cites a study in 1986 by pharmacists Reynor and Sillito which found that 40 per cent of patients questioned misunder-

stood 'complete the prescribed course', 31 per cent misunderstood 'to be instilled', and 33 per cent misunderstood 'use sparingly'. This failure to provide clear information has led to unnecessary deaths and injuries. Would patients readily understand this example?:

A non-greasy, water-miscible cream with a marked anti-pruritic and analgesic action. The special base achieves intimate contact with moist surfaces, thus having a drying effect on exudative skin conditions, and is particularly suitable for application to exposed surfaces.

Readers of plain English prescription labels made 15 per cent fewer incorrect statements than those reading the traditional labels. They also gave 5 per cent more correct statements.

Exhibit 5.4 Quebec falls to language police

Montreal's English-speaking shopkeepers are furious about new legislation in Quebec which will give the province's language 'police' far-reaching search-and-enter powers to check that French is being used.

The powers were described by opponents as 'more extreme than any police powers currently in place in the Western world' and 'worthy of Nazi Germany.'

Supporters of the controversial Bill 40 argued that it simply defended Quebec's partly French culture by setting up a commission for the protection of the French language.

Bill 40, which is expected to pass into law this month, will allow Quebec government inspectors

to enter businesses 'at any reasonable time' and 'examine any products or documents, make copies and take photographs'. No warrant will be required and the searches may be conducted at a suspect's home if it doubles as a business address.

If shopkeepers display signs which are in English only they are liable to fines. French-only signs are permitted. When signs are in both languages, the words in French must be bigger.

The Office de la Langue Francaise (OLF) is charged with enforcing the province's much-disputed language laws designed to protect the use of French in the bilingual province. Anglophones allege that the laws have led to 'bullying' of

→

→ Exhibit 5.4 *continued*

English-speaking and particularly ethnic minority-run businesses.

The office employs 217 people, with an annual budget estimated by opponents at C$30 million (HK$167 million).

David Black, of the Quebec Committee for Canada, a group which opposes francophone desires for Quebec independence, said: 'In its two decades of operation the OLF has managed to fine only 179 people, at about C$63 each. Why do they need so many employees?'

Under Bill 40, provincial funds and officials will be put at the use of anyone reporting abuses of the language laws.

'The commission shall provide assistance to complainants in drawing up their complaints,' the bill proposes.

In the past 30 years, during which time the French-speaking majority has exercised increasing muscle, more than 500,000 Quebeckers emigrated, the highest population loss for any Canadian province.

The mood among shopkeepers of Montreal's English-speaking areas suggests that more defections to federal Canada may be on the way.

Ruth Shine, who runs a bead shop in the city's Westmount – formerly a bastion of British values – said that she was repeatedly bothered by French language inspectors after being found to have a small sign in her shop which asked customers not to lean on the glass counter.

She accused the OLF of harassment and

'pettiness', but said that many of her fellow-business owners were seriously worried by enforcement of the language laws. Penalties for linguistic infringements were recently raised by as much as 400 per cent.

Robert Lecker, a McGill university professor who has been critical of the language laws, said: 'These are laws which can only be imposed with the use of a ruler. That shows how ridiculous they are.'

At Tabagie Rockland, an Asian-Canadian convenience store, court action beckons after language inspectors came across an elderly member of the proprietor's family who had difficulty expressing himself in French.

In the Laval quarter, a 30-year-old restaurant called Mr Melrucker's Diner has been ordered to alter its name because it is not French.

One English-speaking local, requesting anonymity, said this week: 'This is a subtle form of ethnic cleansing.'

Some businesses have used a loophole in the law to get round the difficulties. Under Quebec law, business signs must carry French but political organisations are granted exemption.

Accordingly, a political action group is now going around Montreal 'buying' English business hoardings for C$1, to save owners from being prosecuted. Apart from a very small sticker carrying the name of the political group, there is no visible difference.

Source: *South China Morning Post,* 5 April 1997

These modest improvements represent a reduction of approximately one error per twenty prescription items. With 400 million prescription items dispensed annually in Britain, the use of plain English labels could do much to improve the health of our nation. (See Table 5.4)

Examples of bad translation, such as the Zanussi cooker hood, are just incomprehensible: 'Please care that the superior border of the calibre is on the inferior border of the incorporated board.' I certainly could not answer questions on that, but too often professional people sound as though they are reading from an economics or legal textbook. Have you ever understood a statement on the economy from any political party or been led to believe that they understood it either? The same is true of courtrooms where, legal jargon aside, we hear of the former Head of the British Civil Service admitting in Court in Australia of being economical with the truth' or Lieutenant-Colonel Oliver North admitting that

he used 'additional input that was radically different from the truth.'

The campaign present awards for examples of English that are extremely good or hideously bad. In 1996, the Crystal Award winners were those shown in Figure 5.3.

Rather than just campaigning, the Campaign for Plain English operates a commercial service offering editing, design, testing, training and publications. This consultancy service offers specialist practical help on forms, leaflets, booklets, instructions, posters, standard letters and consumer contracts. Complex legal documents are often also revised into more everyday English without losing their precision. (Contact Plain English Campaign, Outram House, Whaley Bridge, Stockport SK12 7LS England, UK or Website: http://www. demon. co. uk/ plain english).

The Plain English Campaign have made many of the UK's largest commercial organizations more efficient by improving their commu-

Table 5.4	
Traditional style	*Plain English style*
The Eye Drops	The Eye Drops
One-two drops to be instilled into both eyes every six hours for four days.	Drop one or two drops into both eyes four times a day.
Not to be taken.	Do this at regular intervals for four days.
Discard 28 days after opening.	Don't swallow this.
	Throw this away one month after opening.
The Cream	The Cream
To be applied sparingly to the affected area twice a day.	Spread thinly on the affected skin twice a day.
For external use only.	Use on the skin only.
Discard 28 days after opening.	Throw this away one month after opening it.
The Tablets	The Tablets
One to be taken three times a day. Avoid exposure of the skin to direct sunlight or sunlamps. Do not stop taking this medicine except on your Doctor's advice.	One to be taken three times a day. Protect your skin from direct sunlight. Don't use sunlamps. Keep taking this medicine until your Doctor tells you to stop.
The Tablets	The Tablets
One to be taken every eight hours, with or after food.	One to be taken three times a day, with food.
Take at regular intervals.	Space the doses evenly through the day.
Complete the prescribed course unless otherwise directed.	Keep taking this medicine until it is finished.
Warning. Avoid alcoholic drink.	Don't drink any alcohol.

Source: S. Paliwoda (1988) 'Plain English Campaign', *MBA Review*, December

1. *Clearest public information*
   The British Red Cross for their leaflet 'Missing'
   North Derbyshire Health for their leaflet 'You and Your Doctor'
   The National Dairy Council for their booklet 'Healthy Eating for the One to Fives'
   The Association of Civil Enforcement Agencies for their complaints procedure leaflet.
   The Royal College of Psychiatrists for their leaflets 'Bereavement' and 'Sleep Problems'.

2. *Golden Bull Awards for the year's most baffling public information.*
   The Motor Insurers' Bureau for their form of assignment.
   British Telecom for their report into boundaries of local exchange areas.
   NBI Information Management Services for their letter about the FlowMan workflow system.
   Leeds City Council for one of their public notices.
   The Internal Revenue Service (USA) for one of their notices.

3. *The Global Pioneer Award for encouraging the use of plain English in all types of disclosure documents.*
   The Securities and Exchange Commission, Washington DC.

4. *The International Plain English Award.*
   NationsBank in the USA for their booklet 'Introducing your new Statement'.

Source: Plain English Campaign (1997)

Figure 5.3 Plain English Campaign's 1996 Crystal Award Winners for Clear Communication

nications. They are consulted now by just about every major organization in the UK and have worked for organizations in the USA, South Africa, Australia, Denmark, Ireland, Ghana, Hong Kong, Finland and Switzerland. They have been consulted by government departments in the UK, and in South Africa and by the United Nations in Geneva. As Tom McArthur,

Editor of the Oxford Companion to the English Language put it: 'In all the history of the language, there has never been such a powerful grass-roots movement to influence it as the Plain English Campaign.'

Modification versus standardization — the issues

The importance of the Triad of Japan, USA and Europe has been underlined by Ohmae (1985) in pointing to a market of over 600 million consumers with shared demand patterns because of a high standard of living. Indeed, the rich industrial countries, which make up the membership of the Organization for Economic Cooperation and Development (OECD), account for 15 per cent of the countries in the world, but 55 per cent of the global GNP. Jain (1989) points to a few reasons as to why this then should lead to standardization.

1. The purchasing power of OECD residents as expressed in discretionary per capita income is eight to fifteen times that of residents of the LDCs or NICs.
2. Television penetration within OECD countries exceeds 75 per cent, whereas in NICs it is 25 per cent and less than 10 per cent in LDCs.
3. More than one-third of OECD consumers graduate from high school or higher educational institutions.

Exhibit 5.5   Transvestites get special bank cards in Scotland

Edinburgh (Reuter) – A leading Scottish bank will allow transvestites to use two of its new cheque-cashing cards – one with a photo of them dressed as a man and the other as a woman.

'If any cross-dressing customers are confident enough to go shopping dressed as a woman it's possible for them to have a second card, so that they can avoid embarrassment or difficulties when paying by cheque,' a Royal Bank of Scotland spokesman said Wednesday.

'It's at their local bank manager's discretion and subject to the usual safeguards.'

The spokesman could not say how many cards were issued.

He pointed out it is easier when clients operate separate accounts in their male and female roles.

The Royal Bank said its introduction of cards carrying a photograph of the account-holder has cut fraud dramatically.

Source: Calgary Herald, 24 February 1994

Exhibit 5.6   Coke tries a curvy can

One of the few claims to fame of Terre Haut, Indiana, is that in 1916 it was the birthplace of Coca-Cola's contour bottle. Today, Coca-Cola plans to put Terre Haut back on the map as the birthplace of another revolution in packaging: the first-ever contour can.

Coca-Cola has chosen Terre Haut as one of five US test markets for a curvaceous can that it hopes will boost sales by mimicking the popular shape of its famous 'hobbleskirt' bottle, one of the world's best-recognised icons.

Cans for food and other products have come in various shapes and sizes over the years, but Coca-Cola claims this is the first time a soft drink has been marketed in anything other than a conventional straight-sided cylinder.

'We view cans as one of the last bastions of non-differentiation when it comes to the marketing of non-alcoholic beverages,' says Frank Bifulco, vice-president for marketing at Coca-Cola USA. 'We felt we needed to probe that opportunity as a

way for us to connect more strongly with the consumer and, at the end of the day, to sell more product.'

Oddly, for all its longevity, the contour bottle came about by accident. It was invented by a Coca-Cola bottle manufacturer in Terre Haut who was searching for a design that would distinguish Coca-Cola from its imitators. The bottler looked up 'coca' in the *Encyclopaedia Britannica* and mistakenly took his cue from the fluted contours of the totally unrelated cocoa bean pod.

The bottle caught on because of its pleasing feel and shape, which matched the contours of the human grasp. The bosomy lines of the original design caused it to be known as the Mae West bottle for many years, but a slimmed-down version was dubbed the hobbleskirt after a women's fashion of the time.

Today, the contour trademark ranks almost as high in recognition as the Coca-Cola logo. So, in

→

→ Exhibit 5.6 *continued*

the last few years, Coca-Cola has been looking for ways of exploiting its value by adopting it for other containers. In 1993 it scored a big success by starting to sell Coke in a contoured, 20oz plastic bottle, a move that has subsequently delivered strong sales growth in the otherwise mature US market and elsewhere.

But about 50 per cent of all Coke sold in the US is canned, and executives have long pondered how to apply the contour shape to this market segment. The main obstacle was technological: how to overcome the problems of filling, shipping and stacking an irregularly shaped, and therefore structurally weaker, container.

By 1994, Coca-Cola had developed an experimental can made of steel, and showed it to consumers in Germany. After getting an enthusiastic response, it moved ahead and developed today's aluminium version, with the help of the Chicago-based American National Can.

Coca-Cola's Frank Bifulco says the can is 'just another tactile as well as visual cue to consumers to tell them that Coca-Cola is different, better and special'. It starts, he says, with what you feel in your hands, before the product even reaches your throat.

This seems to confirm what many have always said: that the mystique of Coca-Cola has little to do with how the stuff tastes. But one question that will have to be established by test marketing is whether people are prepared to pay more for a funny-shaped can than for the regular article, since it costs more to produce.

Source: Financial Times, 3 March 1997

According to Jain (1989), this standardization among OECD countries is feasible because of their educational level (what they read and see), their television watching (their level of awareness), and their purchasing power, and makes OECD residents similar to each other in behaviour and distinguishes them from the rest of the world.

However, global branding does not automatically include global advertising. Ritchie (1986) emphasized how a global perspective must not override local market requirements. Thus, according to Ritchie (1986), whatever cost benefits there may be in standardizing production, and even if there are financial advantages in standardizing the advertising process (which may in practice prove to be less than anticipated), the local dimension has to be maintained to withstand local segmentation and local commodity brands.

The chairman of a US multinational corporation was once quoted as having said that, all things being equal, given that his company had completely standardized global products and given the potential economies of scale in production, he would ideally have only one worldwide production centre in the USA from which he would then source worldwide. However, this is an imperfect world and so there proved to be numerous obstacles in the way of what was for the company perhaps an ideal cost-efficient sourcing solution. Apart from a few companies fortunate enough to enjoy global products such as Coca-Cola and Pepsi, the question for the remainder is not single sourcing of a global standardized product, but, instead, the degree to which they will be able to standardize or have to bow to local modification. Economies come from standardization, but the local pressures, which may arise from consumers as well as governments, may be in favour of some degree of local modification. We shall now examine these factors under the separate headings of standardization and modification.

Before doing so, however, it is worthwhile to consider what Livingstone (1989) says on product orientation which he sees as taking three policy forms among the larger international companies:

1. A policy of designing a 'universal' product, universal in the sense only that the design takes account of conditions in economies similar to the major market.
2. A policy of introducing the product into markets for which it is not very obviously designed if this is going to be cheaper than giving the market what it would prefer.
3. A policy of phasing out the product as and when it becomes obsolescent in the major market, and only then manufacturing in the less important market, satisfying any remaining demand for that product by exporting.

A life cycle profile of the product in relation to the market offers some insights into the strategic alternatives available.

Exhibit 5.7   Polish marketing Grandma's choice

When arrogant Western companies first hit Poland's fledgling consumer market, they thought their names would be enough. Keep the advertising budget high, get the brand known, and Poles would flock to buy high quality Western products. But it wasn't that simple. Now some multinationals, beset by poor sales in key brands, are belatedly accepting the need for better market research.

The classic case is Hellman's real mayonnaise, launched three years ago in Poland. The company gathered research documenting the Poles' extensive use of mayonnaise and their receptiveness to quality foreign brands. It spent millions bolstering the brand. TV spots guaranteed widespread taste trials for shoppers, because Hellman's believed there would be little trouble getting repeat buyers.

There was. 'Hellman's didn't quite gel with the Polish taste,' says James Moser, managing director of advertising agency BBDO Warszawa. Many focus groups later, Hellman's realised it had got the recipe wrong. Tests revealed that Poles liked milder mayonnaise, with less salt and vinegar, like that made by Winiary, a former monopoly spice-and-sauce company.

In its attempt to salvage the launch, Hellman's rejected one option, that of re-issuing the original brand with a Polish recipe. Instead, in March they brought out a second brand – Hellman's Babuni or grandmother's mayonnaise. It was promoted as being made the old-fashioned way, with natural ingredients, and was priced 10 per cent lower. Sales have soared.

The new brand also had an unexpected side-effect. Instead of acting as competition to Hellman's Original, it acted as brand reinforcement, increasing sales of both brands. Nobody is quite sure why that happened.

Certainly, Hellman's had hit on a popular formula. At least four other food producers simultaneously came out with 'babuni' foods. 'The traditional Polish grandmother has become an icon for quality,' says Matt Bartels, senior account manager at advertising agency DMB&B Warszawa. The consumer focus groups used to try out names for a mini-croissant overwhelmingly chose a grandmother image, with its connotations of tradition and careful preparation, over alternative foreign names such as *tete a tete* or *la petite*.

The food sector was not the only one where multinationals were forced to undertake additional market research after getting it wrong the first time. In the toiletries market, Benckiser, Unilever and Cussons inadvertently set themselves up for a fall by focusing on the quality of their soap and shampoo products.

The problem was, says DMB&B's Central European manager Carol Schuster, that consumers came to equate quality with cost. Cost-conscious Poles bought the expensive Western brands but saved them for special occasions. For everyday use, they found cheaper options among new or improved Polish brands. The multi-nationals are now introducing economy ranges in Poland to increase the volume of sales and promote their brand name to a wider target group. Western arrogance is giving way to consumer preference.

Source: Business Central Europe, September 1996

Exhibit 5.8   Kiddi just fine in the UK, but in the USA it's Binky

When it comes to bringing up baby, or at least buying for baby, parents in the United Kingdom have much in common with their counterparts in the U.S.

But when Lewis Woolf Griptight decided to bring its new Kiddiwinks line of infant and toddler accessories over to the States, it took some research to ferret out those small, yet crucial, differences.

There was the whole 'help, my baby's having a bad hair day' thing, for example.

It appears that American parents are far more concerned than those in the U.K. that their little tykes look well-coiffed.

So the company dutifully added a grooming set to the U.S. line.

First introduced as Kiddiwinks in the U.K., the line was designed based on extensive research with parents in those countries, said Elizabeth Lee, marketing manager for the company.

But Lee, who was brought over for the U.S. launch, contends the work was 'very appropriate to the market here.'

'There are subtle differences, but many problems are the same. Whether a cup spills here or in Madagascar or in the U.K., moms aren't going to like it,' she said. 'We didn't need to redo all the research to find out that people didn't want cups that spill, but we still had to do research on things like color and packaging.'

To transform Kiddiwinks into Binkykids for the American market, the U.S. based

→ Exhibit 5.8 *continued*

*600 million consumers in the Triad.

Source: Ishikawa, K. (1990) *Japan and the Challenge of Europe 1992*, Pinter Publishers

Figure 5.4   Strategies should be developed to capitalize on similarities and potential for shared resources

Binky-Griptight division made some important changes.

When it talked to parents in the U.K. about the Griptight brand name being used before the new line was launched, the company discovered that it was 'the most un-user-friendly name,' she said. 'People thought it was a carpet glue, a denture fixative, a kind of tire.'

The brand name became Kiddiwinks, a British word for children.

In the U.S., however, recognition of the Binky name was high, with some consumers using it as a generic term for pacifiers.

'We didn't want to lose the Binky's name because it was so associated with pacifiers,' Lee said. 'Yet we wanted to make a strong distinction between Binky's and the new brand.'

One of the most dramatic changes was in the packaging graphics. The Kiddiwinks package relies primarily on white because research revealed that Brit mums were 'a little bit more conservative,' viewing items for the tykes 'almost as medical products,' said Lee. In the U.K., for example, parents typically sterilize bottles and pacifiers after every use. In the U.S., however, the products are usually sterilized the first time and then just washed.

'For baby goods, one has to be taken very seriously,' Lee said.

The Binkykids packages have a quite stylish look and prominently feature the line's signature green and lilac colors.

'In the U.S., the safety aspect is paramount,

but it can be cute and cuddly, too,' Lee said. 'You can get away with a much more flamboyant look in the U.S.'

American parents also were 'a lot more into things that are new and different,' she said. The company's flagship product here is a pacifier that plays one of three lullabies when the baby sucks on it. That product isn't available in the U.K., however, because of safety regulations that would require a redesign.

The research showed 'a lot of similarities between the U.S. and the U.K. market, perhaps not even shared by the European market,' Lee said.

Glass bottles, in modern shapes and patterned with boffo designs, were all the rage in Germany. And the product did have its advantage: It was environmentally friendly, was more scratch resistant so it was more hygienic, and it kept milk warm longer.

But when the company asked consumers in both the U.S. and the U.K. about it, it found that the risk of the bottle breaking caused parents to say they wouldn't buy it.

The company also looked into using more environmentally friendly packaging for its bottles, replacing the outside box with a sticker connecting the two parts of the bottle.

'They thought having no packaging was a fabulous idea, but they said they wouldn't buy it. It's a psychological thing,' Lee said. 'People think that baby products should be wrapped.'

Source: Marketing News, 28 August 1995

Product modification

Mandatory product modifications arise as a result of the following:

1. *Legal requirements.*
2. *Tariffs; 'invisible' tariffs.*
3. *Nationalism* as a response to lack of company presence on the market other than just in sales; unfortunate brand name; high perceived degree of 'foreignness' in the product offered.
4. *Technical requirements* are another means of excluding a product from a market until the technical specifications have been met. Regulations for such things as foodstuffs, drugs, electrical equipment are a few examples.
5. *Taxation* has to be considered. For example, with regard to cars, Britain has a system whereby the 'road tax' is levied as a flat rate on all users. Whereas in France it is dependent on engine size and the age of the car. Indeed, it is a much more equitable system, but it is likely to add significantly to the running costs of luxury cars in France.
6. *Climate* plays a part, too, in that special modi-

fications need to be made often with regard to higher and lower working temperatures for machinery, and with special packaging for consumer goods to ensure freshness in actual use. North America contains all these possible climatic extremes, from the snowy wastes of Northern Canada to the sunshine of Florida.

Other factors influencing modification include:

1. *Consumer tastes.* Traditionally, food has been held to be society's most culture-bound product, but perhaps it is time to rethink this, in view of the fact that Kentucky Fried Chicken is now sold in Japan and that McDonalds and others are now to be found in France, the gastronomic capital of the world. Consumer tastes will have an important bearing on the name used; product features, labelling, packaging and materials; pricing and sales and advertising promotion.
2. *Low personal disposable income* in the target market will affect frequency of purchase as well as product sizes offered.

Table 5.5 Product profile and strategic implications

Product profile	Yesterday's products	Today's products	Tomorrow's products
Strategy			
Critical function	Marketing	Product development	New product assessment
Nature of turnover with time	Sharp decline	Limited life	Growth potential maximum
Penalties for mistakes	Very high	High	Can be compensated
Advertising and sales promotion	To push the demand to the maximum	To maintain the demand at an increasing rate	To pull the potential demand to the highest possible value
Customer education and training	Limited efforts	Increased efforts	Vigorous efforts
Service function and spares policy	Very important	Important	Increased importance
Competition monitoring	Not very critical	Keep a watch	An alert lookout
Scope for exporting	Minimum	To other developing countries	Joint ventures with developed countries
Integration of marketing with other functions	Active interaction with production,	Interaction with production finance, and sales	Active interaction with R & D

Source: Pal, S. K., and Bowander, B. (1979) Marketing challenges of technical industries in developing countries. *Industrial Marketing Management,* **8,** 69–74

3. *Illiteracy and low levels of education* will necessitate product simplification with the use of symbols instead of words. Within the EU it has been the case for many years that all the instrumentation in the dashboard of the car is now labelled with symbols rather than words. It is presumably no reflection on the prevailing standards of education and general literacy levels within the EU but a means devised by the multinational automobile companies of standardizing their cars for all West European markets. Symbols travel more easily than does the written word.

4. *Poor maintenance standards* will necessitate product change, perhaps prolonging periods between overhauls and regular servicing.

5. *Local labour costs.* Where these are low, they encourage a greater labour content in work carried out. Where labour costs are high, production switches to being capital intensive. As Livingstone (1989) has pointed out, labour intensive production is most easily achieved where the obsolescent techniques are being used in the manufacture of obsolescent products, even if obsolescent in this sense means different from the most up-to-date methods used in the home plants.

Another factor to consider is environmentalism which has been something which has swept through the rich industrial countries, perhaps a little guilt-ridden about the way in which they had been spoiling the environment for generations in their search for economic gain. Environmentalism is now a major factor to be considered in the marketing of consumer products, not only in Western countries but worldwide. Additives are now frowned on, and biodegradability of materials is expected of both products and their packaging. This has created a new competitive environment in some industries where traditional suppliers now find themselves under threat as suppliers of environmentally unfriendly products.

Product reformulation, and often relaunch, has been required, even of soaps and detergents, whereas in other products where brand names carry less weight, such as refrigerators, furniture and polystyrene drinking cups, materials used have been strongly questioned. CFCs used in refrigerants and air conditioning units have been reduced at least in Western manufacturing plant operations. In furniture, the restricted use of materials includes that of foam and vinyl, and the use of flame retardants, which may kill the occupants of a house from inhalation of fumes long before the flames ever reach them.

Similarly, with materials used in disposable nappies (diapers). Worldwide sales in nappies amounted to $5 billion in 1989, and so environmentalism is striking hard at a very important market, forcing the manufacturers to rethink their product formulation or help local authorities, responsible for handling waste management, to break these products down by means of systems known as 'accelerated composting', which supposedly breaks down organic matter in ten weeks. Up to 98 per cent of the disposable nappy should, therefore, break down in these compost systems. The alternative of just leaving them cannot be entertained as the plastic would otherwise take 400–500 years before deterioration.

Product standardization – influencing factors

Factors which encourage product standardization include:

1. *Production economies of scale.*
2. *Development costs* as reflected in the increase in contractual joint ventures to counteract the escalating costs of new product development in the automobile industry or the aircraft industry.
3. *Stock costs* as a result of the maintenance of a wide range of products and high level of service.
4. *Components that are interchangeable* across product models.
5. *Technological content* is standard internationally for the industry.
6. *Consumer mobility* as a result of increasing travel opportunities which leads to familiarity with international products, such as perhaps Gillette or Bic razors; Coca-Cola; Pepsi; and a wide range of clothing, toiletries and other articles. The brand name, rather than the country of origin, is what sells the product.
7. *Market homogeneity* is increasing with the market concentration effects of the EU for example. Concentration has taken place in many areas, leading to European industries rather than national industries. As the costs of research and development increase, and as the needs of critical mass become apparent, then companies begin to treat neighbouring country markets as an extended regional market rather than as a number of separate foreign markets.

The benefits of standardization are:

1. Cost savings through experience-curve effects and economies of scale.
2. Consistency, with customers acknowledging consumer mobility and cross-border flows of

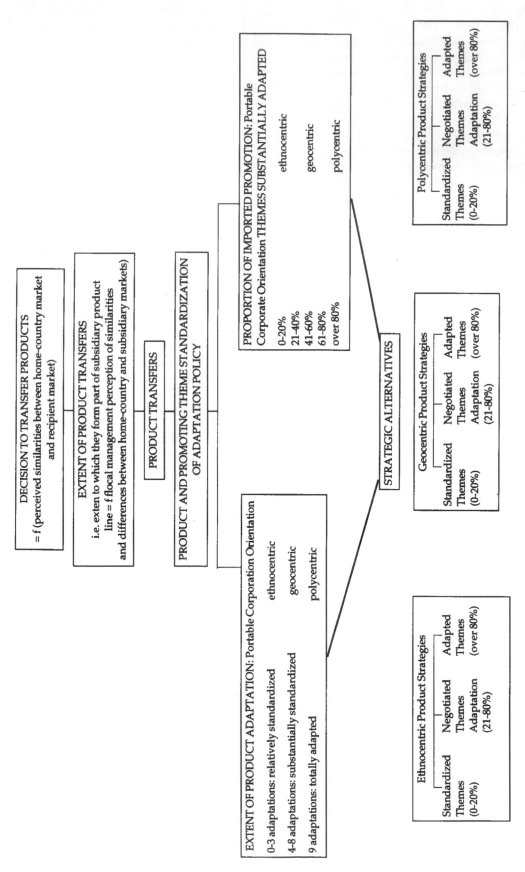

DECISION TO TRANSFER PRODUCTS
= f (perceived similarities between home-country market and recipient market)

EXTENT OF PRODUCT TRANSFERS
i.e. exten to which they form part of subsidiary product line = f flocal management perception of similarities and differences between home-country and subsidiary markets)

PRODUCT TRANSFERS

PRODUCT AND PROMOTING THEME STANDARDIZATION OF ADAPTATION POLICY

PROPORTION OF IMPORTED PROMOTION: Portable Corporate Orientation THEMES SUBSTANTIALLY ADAPTED

0-20%	ethnocentric
21-40%	
41-60%	geocentric
61-80%	
over 80%	polycentric

EXTENT OF PRODUCT ADAPTATION: Portable Corporation Orientation

0-3 adaptations: relatively standardized	ethnocentric
4-8 adaptations: substantially standardized	geocentric
9 adaptations: totally adapted	polycentric

STRATEGIC ALTERNATIVES

Ethnocentric Product Strategies

Standardized Themes (0-20%)	Negotiated Themes Adaptation (21-80%)	Adapted Themes (over 80%)

Geocentric Product Strategies

Standardized Themes (0-20%)	Negotiated Themes Adaptation (21-80%)	Adapted Themes (over 80%)

Polycentric Product Strategies

Standardized Themes (0-20%)	Negotiated Themes Adaptation (21-80%)	Adapted Themes (over 80%)

Source: Keegan, W. J., Still, R. R. and Hill, J. S. (1987) Transferability and adaptability of products and promotion themes in multinational marketing in MNCs and LDCs. *Journal of Global Marketing,* **1** (1/2), 85–103

Figure 5.5 Transfer and adaptation process of consumer non-durable products – a conceptual framework

Table 5.6   Extent of adaptation of US/UK products in LDC markets

Number of adaptations	Number of products	Per cent total	Corporate orientation
0	15	8.6	
1	17	15.5	Ethnocentric
2	15	8.6	
3	9	5.2	
4	18	10.3	
5	21	12.1	Geocentric
6	39	22.4	
7	22	12.6	
8	3	1.7	
9	5	2.9	Polycentric
Totals	174	100.0	

Source: Keegan, W. J., Still, R. R. and Hill, J. S. (1987) Transferability and adaptability of products and promotion themes in multinational marketing in MNCs and LDCs. *Journal of Global Marketing*, 1(1/2), 85–103

television, radio, newspaper and periodical advertising.

3. The remaining barriers are common to all markets, such barriers as social conventions regarding product use and purchasing patterns.

Keegan, Still and Hill (1987) undertook a study of the transferability and adaptability of products and promotion themes in marketing by multinationals in the LDCs. They set out with three questions:

1. To what extent are products transplanted from one market into another? Products have to be transferred between nations before any standardizing or adapting occurs.
2. What is an adapted product? Products have multiple components, e.g., packaging and labelling. A change in any component is an adaptation, and 'degree of adaptation'

better describes product change than does the dichotomous 'adaptation-standardization'.

3. When products are transferred, what proportion of their promotion themes undergo substantial change?

A conceptualization of the process of product and promotion transfer and adaptation by Keegan, Still and Hill (1987) is to be found in Figure 5.5. Overall, 19 MNCs responded to their survey (18 US; one UK) from both international headquarters and from the LDCs. Finally, 61 responses were computer analysed. In all, the 174 products sold in LDCs had 718 adaptations, an average of 4.13 changes out of a possible nine. (See Table 5.6.)

Firms changing three or fewer components believe they reap many of the advantages of standardization for one of three reasons:

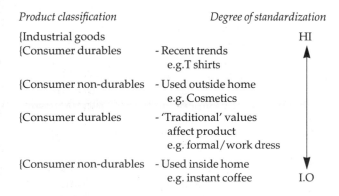

Product classification		Degree of standardization
{Industrial goods		HI
{Consumer durables	- Recent trends e.g. T shirts	
{Consumer non-durables	- Used outside home e.g. Cosmetics	
{Consumer durables	- 'Traditional' values affect product e.g. formal/work dress	
{Consumer non-durables	- Used inside home e.g. instant coffee	I.O

Source: Whitelock, J. M. (1987) Global marketing and the case for international product standardisation *European Journal of Marketing*, **21** (9), 32–44

Figure 5.6   A standardization/modification decision framework

Table 5.7 Obstacles to standardization in international marketing strategies

Factors limiting standardization	Product design	Pricing	Distribution	Sales force	Advertising and promotion, branding and packaging
Market characteristics					
Physical environment	Climate Product use conditions Income levels		Customer mobility Consumer shopping patterns	Dispersion of customers Wage levels, availability of manpower	Access to media Climate Needs for convenience rather than economy
Stage of economic and industrial development	Labour costs in relation to capital costs	Income levels			Purchase quantities
Cultural factors	Custom and tradition Attitudes toward foreign goods	Attitudes toward bargaining	Consumer shopping patterns	Attitudes toward selling	Language, literacy Symbolism
Industry conditions					
Stage of product life cycle in each market	Extent of product differentiation	Elasticity of demand	Availability of outlets Desirability of private brands	Need for missionary sales efforts	Awareness, experience with products
Competition	Quality levels	Local costs Prices of substitutes	Competitors' control outlets	Competitors' sales force	Competitive expenditure messages
Marketing institutions					
Distributive system	Availability of outlets	Prevailing margins	Number and variety outlets available Ability to 'force' distribution	Number, size, dispersion of outlets	Extent of self-service Media availability, costs, overlaps
Advertising media and agencies				Effectiveness of advertising, need for substitutes	
Legal restrictions	Product standards Patent laws Tariffs and taxes	Tariffs and taxes Antitrust laws Resale price maintenance	Restrictions on lines Resale price maintenance	General employment restrictions Specific restrictions on selling	Specific restrictions on messages, costs Trademark laws

Source: Buzzell, R. D. Can you standardise multinational marketing? *Harvard Business Review*, November–December, 1968, 98–104

1. Their products have universal appeal, e.g., Coca-Cola or Pepsi.
2. They are moving toward greater standardization, e.g., Kodak or Gillette.
3. Consumers prefer some products with strong modern images, e.g., Max Factor cosmetics.

Three important findings emerged from this study:

1. Economic and cultural gaps between modern markets, e.g., US or UK, and LDCs do not deter MNCs from transferring modern consumer products between them.
2. The MNCs sampled substantially adapt most modern products before marketing them in LDCs, suggesting that universal products, e.g., Coca-Cola and Colgate toothpaste, are the exceptions rather than the rule. However, this finding may not hold for less culturally sensitive products, such as consumer durable and industrial products.
3. Although many modern themes are transferred into LDCs without substantial change, the extent of theme adaptations parallels the degree of product adaptation, suggesting interdependence between marketing adaptations and standardization decisions.

Whitelock (1987), in her study, *Global Marketing and the Case for International Product Standardisation*, acknowledged this gap of consumer durables and incorporated it into her framework (see Figure 5.6).

Exhibit 5.9   Made in Korea, driven by ambition

Koreans may have studiously copied every western manufacturing trick to produce cars which at least do the basics efficiently. But they still have some way to go on the creative side.

Advertising certainly does not appear to be a strong point for Samsung, the latest of the giant chaebols, or South Korean conglomerates, to express global car assembly ambitions. With two years to go till its first car runs off the assembly line, it is trying to drum up anticipation among potential customers with the less than catchy slogan: 'Samsung Will Roll Out Its First Car in 1998'.

But if the billboards are dull, the response to the news is not. On the day the ads began running, 3,000 people signed up for Samsung credit cards, which let them accumulate up to one million won, or £800, over five years towards a new Samsung car.

'I have no idea what Samsung's car will be like, but I think it's a hell of a bargain,' said banker Sohn Hee Shik, flashing his card. Since May 7, an average 3,500 people a day have signed up.

All this excitement over a car Samsung Motors has not even described yet, except to say it will probably be a family model and cheaper than its competitors.

Samsung has deep pockets to make the launch successful. The Samsung Business Group, South Korea's biggest conglomerate, took in £53.3bn last year by selling stocks and insurance, construction equipment, newspapers, petrochemicals and by building ships. Just for good measure, it is also the world's largest producer of computer-memory microchips.

Samsung tried to enter the car business three years ago when it started buying shares in Kia Motors, South Korea's second-largest automotive assembler. But the public does not like the big chaebols and raised a stink that forced Samsung to back away.

But Samsung persisted in bending the government's car about the economic sense in allowing it to make cars, and finally won approval – perhaps in return for leaving Kia alone. Now Samsung has the car industry fretting again.

In response to its initiative, rivals Hyundai and Daewoo have been forced to issue their own loyalty cards, and Kia has made it known that it plans to launch a version soon.

Hyundai, South Korea's biggest player in the motor industry, gives its card holders 0.8 per cent of what they charge toward buying one of its models while Daewoo, the third-largest manufacturer, offers those who sign up this year 4 per cent of what they charge. But both of these deals pale comparison with the 3 per cent–8 per cent Samsung allows.

Established in March 1995, Samsung Motors has a lot of ground to catch up on its Korean rivals, which means there is a chasm separating it from American and European manufacturers. But it intends to close this gulf with money. By 1998 it plans to spend as much as £800m on design, marketing, engineering and on a factory complex capable of turning out half a million cars a year.

This is not exactly the best time to get into the car business in South Korea. The market had been expanding by one fifth every year until last year, when it slowed to only half that (see table).

Hyundai, Kia and Daewoo can already make 3.3 million cars and trucks between them, and are shooting for double that by the turn of the century. That is much more than the £18bn South Korean market can absorb.

➤ **Exhibit 5.9** *continued*

'If all these carmakers go ahead with their ambitious plans, I expect a serious glut,' said Lee Sang Bae, an analyst with Dongsuh Economic Research Institute. 'Samsung may be better off doing what it's best at, such as microchips, and let others do the cars.'

investment in India for example, should produce stronger growth beyond 2000.

By 2010, South Korea is predicted to have a minimum of two firms among the world's top 10 motor companies. These will probably be Hyundai and Daewoo, unless Kia is acquired by Samsung,

South Korea: Forecast car production

Manufacturer	1996	1997 (all figures in thousands)	2000
All makes	2,196	2,332	2,669
Hyundai	1,060	1,100	1,225
Daewoo	550	575	625
Kia	533	545	580
Samsung	0	53	151
Ssangyong	47	53	81
Asia Motor	6	6	7
Annual change	+10.8%	+9.7%	+3.5%

Source: Economist Intelligence Unit

The only way to sell all those cars is to export. Samsung has not said which foreign markets it will concentrate on, though it will do test marketing in the US and Europe by 1998.

In general the South Koreans sold about 40 per cent of their output abroad last year. The export-led strategy means South Korea's motor industry is set to become the new global pacemaker, according to the Economist Intelligence Unit.

Annual increases in production of passenger cars are forecast to slow in the remainder of the decade, but the expansionist strategy overseas, which has seen Hyundai commit to a large

making that the largest company. By 2010, Samsung itself hopes to produce 1.5 million cars every year.

Daewoo is aggressively attacking the European market and Hyundai, which has traditionally focused on own-brand sales in developed markets such as North America, also sees the EU as a vital export market.

The EIU predicts that, despite problems at home of overcapacity, financial losses, weak component supply chains and rising labour costs, Korea could nevertheless move from fifth to third in the world production league for cars, trucks and vans by 2005.

Source: *Scotland on Sunday*, 28 July 1996, p. 5

Product standardization and World Product Mandates

The World Product Mandate is to be found chiefly in the Canadian literature deriving from the internalization aspect of Dunning's Eclectic Theory. A world product mandate (WPM) is defined as the full development and production of a new product line in a subsidiary of a multinational company, thereby changing the nature of the subsidiary–parent multinational relationship to that of a strategic business unit or division. It is rapidly becoming a major topic of public policy discussion, although there still remain many unresolved technical and conceptual issues.

A World Product Mandate permits the subsidiary to be responsible for the development and worldwide marketing of a specific innovation. The subsidiary needs to bargain with its parent to secure a potentially profitable mandate, but once it has it, the subsidiary can use the internal market of the multinational organization to distribute and control the new process. It is necessary, therefore, to examine the cost benefits from the viewpoint of the three parties involved: host country, subsidiary company, and parent multinational.

Host countries seek employment, growth, and development technology and expertise from companies located within their boundaries. As was pointed out earlier, host countries

Table 5.8 World product mandates from the points of view of the respective parties

Host country	Subsidiary	Multinational corporation
1. Economies of scale and expertise	1. Reduced dependence on local market	1. Decentralization of power in R&D
2. More efficient, higher value-added production lower unit costs	2. Increased stability with market diversification	2. Loss of some control
3. Relative independence from local market	3. Market research information now required	3. Restricted to source of supply
4. Local content ratio up to 100 per cent	4. Staff product support to sister subsidiaries	4. Need to protect the mandate and avoid duplication
5. Creation of local suppliers	5. International marketing skills required even if using parent network	5. Mandate must ensure continued competitiveness
6. Local purchasing eliminates transfer pricing disputes	6. Interact with host government	6. Safeguards to ensure product compatibility worldwide
7. High exports with low imports	7. Illustrate benefits clearly to host government	7. Subsidiary needs now to be kept informed of product changes/ legislation and research
8. Ongoing R&D at subsidiary diary level	8. Stronger management team required	8. MNC has to ask all sub-sidiaries to cooperate with the mandated subsidiary
9. Possible future exporter of technology	9. Subsidiary becomes a centre for that product's R&D	9. Mandated subsidiary must be fully integrated and accepted within the MNC organization
10. Access to world markets	10. Convince parent MNC that benefits outweigh costs	10. Smooth communications between sister subsidiaries
11. Pressure to remain competitive supplier for a world market		11. More intense planning and coordination necessary as options now reduced and dependence increased
12. Improved relations with subsidiary		12. MNC has to act as an adjudicator in the event of dispute
13. Improved relations with MNC		

Source: Adapted from Etemad, H. (1983) World product mandates in perspective. In *Multinationals and Technology Transfer: The Canadian Experience* (ed. Rugman, A.). Praeger, New York

do complain about the perceived quality of investment made by multinationals within their boundaries. Such complaints may include:

- absence of, or insufficient, R & D at the sub-sidiary level, especially when the market size is small,
- insufficient transfer or diffusion of tech-nology,
- employment of obsolete technology,
- inefficient subsidiary operation/no economies of scale,
- high transfer pricing for goods imported from other sister subsidiaries,

- downward pressure on the host's currency and drain on foreign exchange,
- low local content ratio,
- low or no exports,
- negative or neutral effect on economic growth and development,
- low, or no, adherence to host country's national goals.

For the most part, host countries have refused to bear a proportionate share of the cost or risk of developing technology, a product, or a market. Furthermore, they have been the primary source of environmental, sovereign, and political risk.

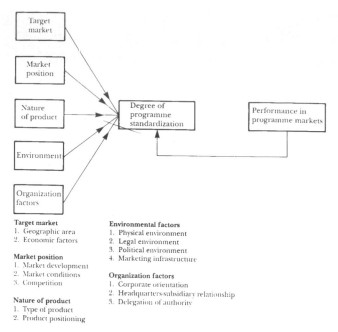

Source: Jain, S. C. (1989) Standardization of international marketing strategy: Some research hypotheses, *Journal of Marketing,* **53** (1), 70–79

Figure 5.7 A framework for determining marketing programme standardization

The WPM is an arrangement whereby the MNC allows the subsidiary to transcend the restrictions of miniature or truncated operations by enlarging the subsidiary's mandate, and hence its associated responsibilities, above and beyond the geographical or political boundaries of the host country. The sphere of the new mandate's activity and coverage depends on the interactions between the costs and benefits of the mandate in terms of economies of scale and learning, transportation charges, added cost of logistics, cost of tariffs, non-tariff barriers, etc. For example, when economies of scale are reached at relatively low volumes or economies of learning are realized in comparatively short periods of time, the mandate is expected to be more united in geographical scope than the global coverage implied in WPM.

It is possible to have regional product mandates (RPMs), especially when the demand of the contiguous region is larger than, or as large as, the optimal plant size. In that case, instead of a real WPM, a more limited mandate in terms of authority and responsibility with respect to at least one product is given to the subsidiary, but this is awarded on a competitive basis and a mandate must be earned.

From the host country viewpoint, there are the advantages of having relatively autonomous and internally directed institutions which are operating on a worldwide basis without much of the actual costs associated with developing such institutions. Young, Hood and Hamill (1988) state that whereas multinationals such as NEC

and Philips have been quoted as examples of firms which have made considerable strides in these directions, it is doubtful whether many others exist.

The parent MNC has very little incentive to grant a WPM to any subsidiary. Doing so defeats the very basic feature of MNCs – flexibility and freedom of choice with regard to source and location of supplies. In so far as worldwide procurement of the mandated product is concerned, a fully developed or natural WPM implies that the parent enterprise gives up this privilege and commits itself to the mandated subsidiary as the sole source in control of supplies for its worldwide markets.

In order to receive a mandate, a subsidiary must become highly competitive or find other sources of support. As a result of a mandate, the host country receives substantial benefits. Indeed, there is such a great deal at sake for the host country that it cannot remain indifferent. It finds itself obliged to lend active support to the subsidiary to bid for and finally secure a mandate. Given the profound future benefits to the subsidiary (due to the mandate), a subsidiary finds it difficult not to accept the help and support from an old adversary in fighting for the mandate. In this process, a new coalition (i.e., subsidiary–host country) is formed and the old coalition (i.e., subsidiary–parent) is weakened. As a result, in order to receive, operate, and continue with the mandate successfully, the subsidiary will need the host government's continued active and substantial support.

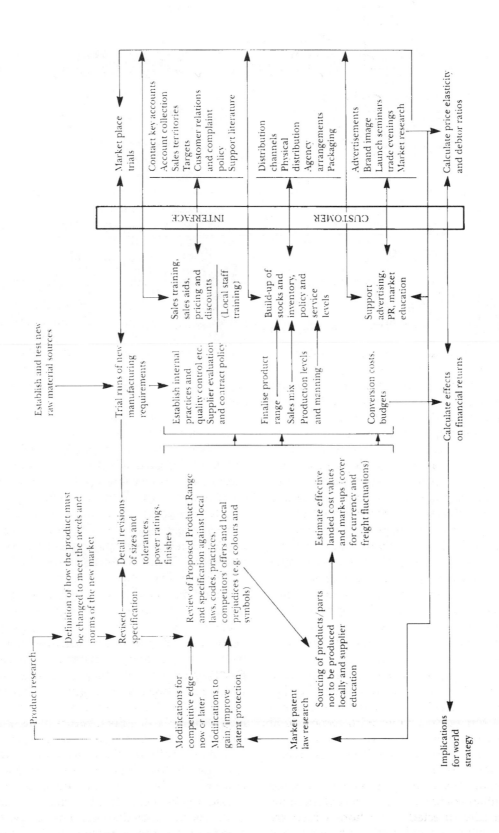

Source: Walmsley, J. (1989) *The Development of International Markets*, Graham and Trotman, London

Figure 5.8 An overall view for 'translating' a product for a new market and introducing and maintaining that product

A WPM restores a sense of power and accomplishment to the newly formed subsidiary; it can produce a new coalition between the subsidiary and the host country; while it increases their interdependence with the rest of the MNC's system simultaneously.

In summary, WPM cultivates an environment which is highly conducive to efficient, complete, and co-operative operation for all the participants the host country, the subsidiary, and its parent company.

Exhibit 5.10   Ford 'Super Car' project passes rivals

Dearborn, Michigan – An ambitious 'super car' project initiated by the White House 3½ years ago to build a new generation of highly efficient vehicles is moving closer to putting some wheels on the ground.

Ford Motor Co. unveiled its 'P2000' plan to build prototypes of a lightweight, high-mileage, low-emissions family car of the future later this year. In doing so, Ford jumped significantly ahead of the previous timetable for the joint government-auto industry program. It also seemed to move closer to realizing the project's goals than General Motors Corp. or Chrysler Corp., though both those companies have made significant announcements this year, too.

'We're moving into a new stage of development, and the research is starting to bear fruit,' said Virginia Miller, the government's communication director for the Partnership for a New Generation of Vehicles.

The 10-year research program, launched in September 1993, set out to develop new technologies intended to enable U.S. auto makers to put low-emission family cars that consume just a gallon of gas for every 80 miles (128 kilometers) on the road by the middle of the next decade.

Ford's P2000 prototype cars will be made of aluminum and other lightweight materials and will weigh just 900 kilograms, about 40 per cent less than today's midsize Ford Taurus, but it will be capable of carrying as many passengers and as much cargo. Ford said a new type of powerful, small, 1.4-liter four-cylinder engine will be able to meet the government's most-stringent so-called ultra-low emissions standards and will be capable of running 60 to more than 70 miles on a gallon of fuel, depending on how it is paired with an electric motor.

Separately, Ford confirmed that it plans to indefinitely idle the car production line at its Lorain, Ohio, assembly plant at the end of the 1997 model year in the third quarter, at least temporarily discontinuing its famous Thunderbird luxury sport coupe and the sister Mercury Cougar. Ford said the shutdown, which won't affect the Lorain plant's production of Econoline vans, will idle about 2,500 Ford employees, 1,800 of them at the Lorain unit and 700 at related parts plants.

In addition, Ford said that at the end of this model year it will drop production of the Aerostar minivan and the Probe sports coupe. Neither move is a surprise. The rear-drive Aerostar was scheduled to be phased out earlier, and the Probe is due to be replaced next year by a Mercury sports coupe – which may be called the Cougar. Neither of those product decisions will result in any layoffs because the plants that make them will increase output of other vehicles.

Jacques Nasser, president of Ford's automotive operations, said the discontinuations will result in a write-off of about $150 million, probably during the second quarter. He said the moves are part of an annual review of product plans and vehicle-making capacity, but he added that he doesn't expect any more major moves in North America in the next two years and that he believes Ford's 55 per cent truck-45 per cent car capacity mix is about right.

He did say that more capacity adjustments are likely in Europe.

Ford's unveiling of its 'super car' program follows significant announcements by its U.S. rivals. GM recently started building and offering for lease in California and Arizona its EV1 electric car, which the company says amounts to a large-scale commercial test of a research vehicle. Besides the electric-power technology, the EV1 uses advanced, light-weight vehicle construction methods.

For its part, Chrysler earlier this year described advances in fuel-cell technology, in which hydrogen is extracted from gasoline or the air and is used to generate electricity to power a vehicle. Also, Chrysler says it expects to have test vehicles running later this year that will be powered by prototype hybrid equipment that combines diesel and electric motors. And Chrysler's aluminum-body Plymouth Prowler sports car uses lightweight technology developed in the 'super car' program.

Ford's plan to have 12 to 16 prototypes of its P2000 car running by late this year seems to put it significantly ahead of the 'super car' program's goal that each Big Three company would have 'concept' cars ready by the year 2000 and pre-production prototypes ready by 2003. The No. 2 U.S. auto maker seems to have taken a lead in combining

→

→ Exhibit 5.10 *continued*

various technological developments into a vehicle package that approximates something that might eventually be sold in volumes similar to today's best-selling Taurus.

However, Bob Mull, Ford's manager of the P2000 project, acknowledged that the test car would be 'many thousands of dollars' more expensive to build than today's Taurus, even at high volumes. He said part of the high cost involves materials and processing expenses related to the aluminum body, but other high costs are related to the vehicle's sophisticated electronics. Ford engineers acknowledged that the hybrid electric-diesel technologies they are exploring are 'many

times more complex than any car on the road today.'

By pushing ahead with test vehicles, Ford hopes to learn how to cut the costs to commercially viable levels and how to further advance the new technologies. Ford said that by the end of 1998, it hopes to have three fully refined versions of the P2000 in operation – one operating only on the new aluminum diesel engine; one a hybrid using that engine and a relatively simple, low-energy-storage electrical system; and one a hybrid using the diesel engine and a more sophisticated electrical system with more capabilities.

Source: Asian Wall Street Journal, 19 March 1997

Branding

Branding is important as a means of distinguishing a company offering, and differentiating one particular product from its competitors. To the company with a product with any commercial life left in it, branding is able to offer an advantage. Given all the other factors already mentioned – pricing, distribution, and promotion – branding is a means whereby the consumer can identify a particular product, and, if satisfied with it, ask for it by name. For the company concerned, there are clear advantages to branding in that branding enables the company to differentiate its product

more clearly, but also to fetch a higher return than could be expected from generic products. Shalofsky (1987) points to 'producer quality' and 'consumer quality'; the former determined in the manufacturer's laboratories, R&D department, and takes into account product characteristics.

'Consumer quality' is what in the store may move it off the shelf. The 'consumer quality' of an international brand entering a new market may well be poor. Something then will have to be found to increase consumer acceptance and this may be in the area of brand image. When Interbrand arranged for Rank Hovis McDougall's brand names to be listed as assets, the balance sheet rose by £678 million (Birkin, 1989).

Exhibit 5.11   More than you wanted to know about Spam

Spam: Spiced ham. Arguably the planet's most recognizable portmanteau word (closely followed by 'Gidget' and 'infomercial') and certainly among its most popular foodstuffs. More than five billion cans have been produced – and, more tellingly, consumed – since Hormel Foods Corp. introduced it in 1937. This year, about 70 million North Americans will eat Spam, mostly because they like it.

As recent D-day commemorations showed, Spam sticks in the public consciousness perhaps most enduringly as war fare, but those who believe the luncheon meat to be long past the best years of its life are mistaken. In fact, several recent developments hint at a large and passionate Spam subculture. While there is no national fan club, Spam lovers regularly exchange, often electronically, news about recipes for, and panegyrics to, the cameo-pink canned meat. To the astonishment of Hormel, its mail-order business in Spam giftware, introduced just before Christmas, has exceeded all

expectations and may soon expand to department stores. Spam sales have risen consistently over the past three years, and while Hormel officials won't reveal Spam's exact contribution to annual profits, they will admit the company's total annual sales exceed $2.8-billion.

Spam is huge. Ask the Smithsonian. Ask Margaret Thatcher. Ask David Letterman. Spam is on line. Need we say more?

If so, here are your Spam questions answered.

Q: What is a common misconception about Spam?

A: That it contains meat byproducts ranging from the unsavoury to the unspeakable. (Those lips, those eyes.) A base canard. Spam is pork shoulder, ham, salt, water, sugar and sodium nitrite.

Q: Did the person who named Spam earn millions?

A: No. Kenneth Daigneau, an actor and the brother of a Hormel executive, received only $100 as winner of a meat-naming contest in 1936. According to corporate lore, Jay C. Hormel, son of the company's founder, wanted to find a good use for several thousand pounds of surplus pork shoulder. He cooked up a canned blend known as spiced ham. When competing meat-packers began marketing similar products, creating a catchy brand name became imperative. Hence a name contest. Had Mr. Daigneau chosen to emphasize the pork shoulder rather than the ham aspect of the product, we might all be eating Sporsh.

Q: Why was Spam drafted for the Second World War?

A: Because it was nutritious, filling and shelf-stable, says Hormel. The British government wanted to honour the tinned soldier by holding a Spam fritter-cooking contest during D-day celebrations last month. Veterans' groups criticized the event as 'trivial.' But was that really fair to the food that fuelled the Normandy invasion?

Q: What did Nikita Khrushchev say about Spam?

A: In *Khrushchev Remembers*, the Soviet leader remembered: 'We had lost our most fertile, food-bearing lands. Without Spam, we wouldn't have been able to feed our army.'

Q: What about Margaret Thatcher?

A: She recalls it as a 'wartime delicacy,' shared on Boxing Day, 1943, with friends and family. 'I quite vividly remember we opened a tin of Spam luncheon meat. We had lettuce and tomatoes and peaches, so it was Spam and salad.'

Q: Where do folks buy the most Spam?

A: In the U.S., in Hawaii, Alaska, Arkansas, Texas and Alabama. Hawaiians put away 4.3 million cans a year. Among the 50 foreign countries where Spam is sold, Britain and South Korea are the largest markets.

Q: Why is Spam so popular in Hawaii?

A: The military brought Spam to the islands, its novelty imparted cachet and Second World War food rationing firmly entrenched the Spam habit, says Suzan Harada, who heads a program in Hawaiian culture at Kapiolani Community College in Honolulu. 'This was a period when having Western things was really important. Even if you had access to fresh pork and chicken, being able to afford canned food showed status.' Now it's tradition.

Q: What about Alaska?

A: 'Spam is cheap, convenient and delicious and it doesn't freeze,' says Mr. Whitekeys, pianist for Whitekeys and the Fabulous Spamtones and owner of Whitekeys's Fly by Night Club in Spenard, Alaska, where the menu prominently features Spam. 'It gets pretty stiff, but it doesn't freeze.' (A spokeswoman at Hormel insists she has managed to freeze a slab of Spam.)

Q: If you wire a can of Spam to the exhaust manifold of your snowmobile when the temperature is –45 degrees, how many kilometres must you travel before the meat is perfectly browned?

A: About 60 kilometres, according to the team of snowmobilers that breaks trail for the annual Iditarod Dogsled Race.

Q: How does the selection of Spam-based dishes at a typical restaurant in Hawaii or Alaska compare with the selection at the Green Midget Café made famous by Monty Python?

A: The Ala Moana Poi Bowl in Honolulu serves Spam *musubi* (a sort of oversize sushi) and Spam, eggs and rice. Mr. Whitekeys' Fly by Night Club just outside Anchorage offers Cajun Spam, Spam nachos and specials like pasta with Spam and sun-dried tomatoes in cream sauce. The Green Midget Café's bill of fare included egg and Spam; egg, bacon and Spam; egg, bacon, sausage and Spam; Spam, bacon, sausage and Spam; Spam, egg, Spam, Spam, bacon and Spam; Spam, Spam, Spam, Spam, egg and Spam; Spam, Spam, Spam, Spam, Spam, Spam, baked beans, Spam, Spam, Spam and Spam; or lobster thermidor aux crevettes with a mornay sauce garnished with truffle pâté, brandy and a fried egg on top and Spam.

Q: Did an overzealous Hormel lawyer ever go after the Monty Python comedy troupe?

A: No, but an overzealous Hormel lawyer did once send a cease-and-desist order to the fabulous Spamtones. Mr. Whitekeys subsequently learned that the lawyer wasn't with the company long. Hormel executives remain haunted, however, by fears of generification. They think the two scariest words in the English language are Xerox and Kleenex.

Q: How can you get a free plate of Spam cuisine at the Fly by Night Club?

A: Purchase a bottle of Dom Perignon and your Spam is on the house.

Q: Are there many Spam-related festivals and gatherings throughout the U.S.?

A: You bet. Sixty-eight state and regional fairs hold Hormel-sanctioned Spam recipe contests. Spam Jamboree, held every Fourth of July weekend, in Austin, Minn., is the only Spam shindig Hormel officially sponsors.

The company looks benignly, however, on the annual Spamorama in Austin, Tex., a Spam cook-off on Maui and Spam carving contests held annually in Seattle. Spam has also been suggested as the subject for the fourth annual Smithsonian Conference on Stuff, to be held next spring. (The 1994 conference dealt with marshmallow.)

Q: Are beloved cult novelists ever judges in the Seattle Spam carving contest?

A: Yes. This year the panel included Tom Robbins. The winning sculpture was called *Nude Descending a Staircase*. Among previous winners were works representing Spamhenge and Spammy Wynette. 'The idea came to me in a dream,' says Ruby Montana, a founder of the contest. 'Spam is a humorous and carvable medium and serves a useful purpose in that form.'

Q: What interesting use for Spam was suggested by David Letterman?

A: Spam on a rope, for snacking in the shower.

Q: What interesting use for Spam was suggested by Hormel employees and used as a T-shirt slogan after a bitter year-long strike that ended in 1986?

A: 'Cram Your Spam!' Members of Meatpackers' Local P-9 walked out of Hormel's Austin plant when the company cut wages and benefits despite high profits. The strike was the subject of the Oscar-winning 1990 documentary *American Dream*, directed by Barbara Kopple.

Q: Is it true that in South Korea, Spam is a gift as prized as jewelry or premium whisky?

A: Yes.

Q: Where can a person buy gifts with a Spam motif closer to home?

A: From the Hormel Foods Gift Center catalogue, which features Spam-logo T-shirts, watches, sweatsuits, bars, boxer shorts, fanny packs, mugs, golfballs, magnets, sunshades, windsocks and more.

Q: Can brides register for Spamware at the Hormel Gift Center?

A: Sorry, no. Hormel just doesn't have the staff. But according to Mary Harris, who took the order, this spring a Florida woman bought Spam underwear for all the groomsmen in her wedding party.

Q: What's the best-selling item in the catalogue?

A: The classic T-shirt, with the word Spam in yellow on a field of blue.

Q: Any other gift items Hormel should consider?

A: Well, at Long's Drugstore chain in Honolulu, you can buy a *musubi* press that will mold a mound of rice into the shape of a Spam can.

Q: Which is stronger. Spam or supernatural forces?

A: Spam. In Hawaii, it's considered bad luck to carry pork in any form over the Pali Highway, the mountainous main route from Honolulu to the other side of Oahu. But this doesn't deter the suppliers of Spam. 'I know for a fact that the drivers don't alter their course because Spam's on the truck; to do that it would triple their travel time,' says Hoagy Gamble, president of L. H. Gamble, one of the state's largest food brokers and Hormel's representative since 1950. 'But there hasn't been any trouble. I think it has something to do with the integrity of the container. The can keeps all that wonderful pork sealed up nice and tight and deflects bad luck.'

Q: Does anyone have a Spam licence plate?

A: Chuck Hudson, a retired graphic designer in Virginia Beach, Va., whose Isuzu Trooper plate reads MMSPAM.

Q: Has anyone ever Spaminized a car?

A: Yes, Lew Cady, a Denver copywriter, at the Spamposium, a 1983 national gathering of 33 Spamophiles who delivered scholarly papers and gave demonstrations, including making explosives from Spam. 'It rained,' recalls Mr. Hudson, a participant, 'and that sucker really beaded up.'

Q: Does Chuck Hudson put his money where his mouth is?

A: Indeed. He bought Hormel stock and 'it suddenly took off. My stockbroker said, 'What do you know that I don't?' The broker's theory is that after Eastern Europe shrugged off the yoke of communism, the best Polish hams were no longer exported. 'And as soon as Polish ham stayed home,' says Mr. Hudson, 'stock in Hormel, which has the second-best ham in the world, went up.'

Q: Does Spam make good bait?

A: Ann Kondo Corum, author of *Hawaii's Spam Cookbook*, recommends it highly.

Q: What are some really cool Spam recipes, besides bait?

A: Ms. Corum's book covers everything from Spam Chowder to Spam Fu Young. The Hormel folks suggest Spam Salad Cones, made with tortillas. Hearts of Spam is Lew Cady's specialty.

Q: What kind of wine goes best with Spam?

A: A riesling or a gewürztraminer. 'Both tend to be fruity and slightly sweet, qualities that go well with ham,' explains John Osborne, the buyer for Astor Wines and Spirits in New York.

Q: How many times a week does Senator Robert Byrd of West Virginia enjoy a Spam sandwich with mayo on white bread?

A: Three, by his own accounting.

Q: What's the buzz on the Spamnet?

A: A recent peek at Prodigy's Spam Exchange

> ➡ Exhibit 5.11 *continued*

yielded a recipe for S'pam S'mores and some household hints. (Confidential to Heloise: Spam purportedly makes good furniture polish, and can also be used to keep condensation off the bathroom mirror when showering.) Someone calling himself Spamurai just got back from Maui and suspects that Hawaiian Spam is a tad darker than the mainland variety.

Q: How do mental-health professionals explain the enduring appeal of Spam?

A: 'Spam is a happy thing to organize around,' says David Levitsky, professor of nutrition and psychology at Cornell University, N.Y. 'It doesn't cause harm, gives a sense of identity and, as with any other shared interest, binds people together. Like other foods that origin-ated in a culture of poverty – for example, chicken soup and chopped

liver brought from Europe – Spam helped people survive difficult times.'

Q: Is Spam a cruel muse?

A: Jack Collom, a poet from Boulder, Colo., and the winner of two National Endowments for the Arts, doesn't think so. Here are a couple of his Spam-inspired acrostic poems.

Suddenly, masked hombres seized
Petunia Pig
And
Made her into a sort of dense Jell-O.

Somehow the texture, out of nowhere,
Produces a species of
Atavistic anomie, a
Melancholy memory of 'food.'

Source: The Globe and Mail, 23 July 1994

Table 5.9   Products for markets

	Market stage	Government attitudes and business policy	Corporate control	Brand product protection	Target product market
Corporate perspective of the market					
Short term	Mature/declining	Weak	Expensive bureaucratic control if pursuing a 'build-up or acquire' strategy	Weak	Standardized brand or generic
Medium term	Mature	Indeterminate	Build-up	Strong	Standardized brand or generic
Long term	Innovative	Strong	Standardization potential of a homogeneous market with similar requirements	Strong	Non-standardized brand/niche market servicing

Branding is perceived as a means of guarantee of quality offered by the manufacturer to the consumer. There is the expectation of standardization, that each and every product will meet these same specifications. Where there is a high degree of standardization accompanied by a high degree of customer satisfaction, the brand is likely to become, if it has not already done so, the market leader. Brand names, according to Interbrand (Fisher, 1989), can be seen to fall into three categories:

Table 5.10   Eight product quality variables

Performance:	Effectiveness of product primary operating characteristics.
Features:	Make-up, shape, proportions and attributes.
Reliability:	Measured over a specific period of time under stated conditions of use.
Conformance:	Degree to which physical and performance characteristics of a product match pre-established standards.
Durability:	Period of time a product is in use before suffering deterioration.
Serviceability:	Speed, courtesy and competence of repair.
Aesthetics:	How a product looks, feels, sounds, tastes or smells.
Perceived quality:	Subjective assessment resulting from image, advertising, or brand name.

Source: Garvin, David A. (1987) Competing on the Eight Dimensions of Quality, *Harvard Business Review*, Nov–Dec, p. 101

Table 5.11	Branding perspective (from manufacturer's viewpoint)

Advantages	Disadvantages
No Brand	
Lower production cost	Severe price competition
Lower marketing cost	Lack of market identity
Lower legal cost	
Flexible quality control	
Branding	
Better identification and awareness	Higher production cost
Better chance for production differentiation	Higher marketing cost
Possible brand loyalty	Higher legal cost
Possible premium pricing	
Private brand	
Better margins for dealers	Severe price competition
Possibility of larger market share	Lack of market identity
No promotional problems	
Manufacturer's brand	
Better price due to more price inelasticity	Difficult for small manufacturer with
Retention of brand loyalty	unknown brand of identity
Better bargaining power	Requiring brand promotion
Better control of distribution	
Multiple brands (in one market)	
Market segmented for varying needs	Higher marketing cost
Creating competitive spirits	Higher inventory cost
Avoiding negative connotation of existing brand	Loss of economies of scale
Gaining more retail shelf space	
Not hurting existing brand's image	
Single brand (in one market)	
Marketing efficiency	Assuming market homogeneity
Permitting more focused marketing	Existing brand's image hurt when trading up/down
Elimination of brand confusion	Limited shelf space
Good for product with good reputation (halo effect)	
Local brands	
Meaningful names	Higher marketing cost
Local identification	Higher inventory cost
Avoidance of taxation on international brand	Loss of economies of scale
Allowing variations of quantity and quality across markets	Diffused image
Worldwide brand	
Maximum marketing efficiency	Assuming market homogeneity
Reduction of advertising costs	Problems with black and grey markets
Elimination of brand confusion	Possibility of negative connotation
Good for culture-free product	Requiring quality and quantity consistency
Good for prestigious product	LDC's opposition and resentment
Easy identification/recognition for international travellers	Legal complications
Uniform worldwide image	

Source: Onkvisit, S. and Shaw, J. J. (1989) The international dimension of branding: Strategic Considerations and decisions. *International Marketing Review*, **6** (3)

Table 5.12 Top ten European brands				
Brand	*Manufacturer*	*Country*	*Value ($bn)*	*World Ranking*
1. Nescafé	Nestlé	Switzerland	10.3	10
2. Louis Vuitton	LVMH	France	4.5	25
3. Philips	Philips	Netherlands	4.1	28
4. Hennessey	LVMH	France	3.4	39
5. Nestle	Nestle	Switzerland	3.3	40
6. Johnnie Walker Black Label	Guinness	UK	2.8	47
7. Michelin	Michelin	France	2.7	49
8. L'Oreal	L'Oreal	France	2.6	51
9. Guinness	Guinness	UK	2.3	55
10. Danone	Danone	France	2.3	56

Note: Worldwide, the top three were Coca-Cola, Marlboro and IBM.
Source: *Financial World* cited in David Short (1995) 'Europe lags in the Battle of the Brands', *The European*, 28 July, p.19.

1.   *descriptive*, like Corn Flakes and British Rail
2.   *associative*, like Fruit Bursts and InterCity
3.   *stand-alone*, like Hob-Nobs or Casey Jones.

Occasionally, though, brands suffer the fate of being too successful in that they pass into the language and lose the distinctiveness which they once had. Sometimes, this is due to market dominance because of patent protection, sometimes implying just market leadership. Where a brand becomes the name for all products of that type, it has become a generic. The German firm Bayer once had the rights to Aspirin, which was a protected brand name until after the war. Bayer has since gone out and bought back the rights to the name Aspirin in several countries, including Canada.

Pharmaceutical products are likely to be standardized, but as reflected in Keegan's *Five Strategies for Multinational Marketing*, brand names often meant that although the name is the same, the ingredients may be quite different from the product sold in the home country. *The Economist* in 1982 carried a report on how Bangladesh imposed a ban on 2,000 drugs. The aim was to both save foreign exchange and save also on drugs that did not work. For nearly three-quarters of these prohibited drugs had been listed by the World Health Organization or by US or British drug authorities as useless, harmless, or both. Madawar and Freese (1981) raised this issue of branded pharmaceuticals as well as adequate instructions and directions for use. Their reservations include:

1.   Drugs which are simply dangerous. Clioquinol and Aminopyrine, both banned in some countries, yet actively being promoted in others, are two particularly horrifying examples.

Exhibit 5.12

Polish Mineral Water

2. Products which are more or less undesirable as 'bad medicine'. An example of these would be a mad combination of antibiotics and other drugs. Combination drugs are bad because if a patient suffers from more than one complaint, each complaint should be treated with the appropriate dose of the appropriate medicine. The reason combinations are commercially preferred is, of course, that they allow the manufacturer to promote something 'unique'.

3. Products which do no harm, but which are not needed and which account at best for serious economic waste. Tonics and vitamin pills are obvious cases in point.

4. In addition to this, the instructions and precautions for use supplied with such products may be wholly inadequate, if not dangerously wrong. Two recent examples include: a migraine treatment where the maximum dose recommended in developing countries was twice the maximum recommended elsewhere; and an anti-nauseant, contra-indicated for use in pregnant women in the USA but specifically recommended for the control of 'morning sickness' elsewhere.

Ethical questions arise equally over products sold in the Western hemisphere. Citing one example which arose in the USA, a Dallas federal district judge denied an injunction to end a ban on a cereal which was promoted as a drug to reduce cholesterol levels (*Marketing News*, 1991, 13 May).

A quite separate example entirely is that of cigarettes where high tar level cigarettes are freely available in some of the less-developed countries, although now withdrawn from sale in the West. Branding may be international but the assurance of branding varies with national frontiers.

Yet branding lies behind the success of franchising. Franchising conveys the right to use a name, logo, plus access to company-specific know-how, including management systems. The key to this form of market representation is the importance attached to an established brand name, many of which are quite international: McDonalds hamburger chain, Budget Rent-a-Car; Kentucky Fried Chicken. All derive their income from the use of their names.

Marks & Spencer, the British firm with a quality image chain of department stores, has no manufacturing capacity of its own, but, nevertheless, controls 600 stores worldwide. Marks & Spencer have three strategies. The first is to grant the St Michael brand name franchise to free-standing sales outlets. The second is to establish shops within shops that sell the St Michael marque exclusively, as in Finland. The last is to sell directly to selected retailers or to market through a wholesaler. The company policy is not to export to countries where they already have stores, i.e., France, Ireland, Canada and Holland. Marks & Spencer have 282 company stores in the UK, 3 in Eire, 23 in the rest of Europe, 6 in Hong Kong; 40 in Canada. There are also 133 operated by Brooks Brothers in the USA and Japan, 19 run by Kings Super Markets in the USA, 106 operated by D'Aillairds in Canada plus 76 franchised stores worldwide.

Exhibit 5.13 Prescription drug sales advance

Sales of prescription drugs in the world's top 10 markets rose 7 per cent to $143.8bn (£88.2bn) last year, according to data published today.

The increase conceals wide variations between countries and medical areas, according to IMS International, the specialist pharmaceuticals industry market researchers. Sales advanced 8 per cent in 1995 and 1994.

The star performers last year were anti-depressants such as Eli Lilly's Prozac and cholesterol-lowering agents such as Zocor and Mevacor from US company Merck.

Anti-depressants are included in nervous system drugs, which recorded a 14 per cent year-on-year increase in sales to $20.3bn.

Sales of blood agents, which include cholesterol-lowering drugs, rose 16 per cent to $7.9bn.

From this year, IMS will be switching choles-terol-lowering drugs to the heart disease category. Heart disease drugs remain the biggest single category, but sales have grown slowly in recent years because of tough competition between drugs aimed at lowering blood pressure.

Heart drug sales last year rose 3 per cent to $25.5bn, keeping them just ahead of digestive system drugs, where sales climbed 9 per cent to $24.6bn. Digestive system drugs include the world's two biggest sellers, Zantac, made by Glaxo Wellcome of the UK, and Losec/Prilosec from Swedish company Astra.

Anti-infectives, which include fast-growing Aids drugs but also antibiotics, where buyers are more price-conscious, saw sales rise 6 per cent to $14.6bn.

The world's biggest market, the US, was also one of the fastest growing. Drug sales climbed 10 per cent to $60.2bn. Only Italy grew faster, rising

→ Exhibit 5.13 *continued*

11 per cent to $9bn, at constant exchange rates. The Italian expansion followed two years of slow or negative growth due to government measures to control the drugs budget.

biggest market, with sales up 5 per cent to $16.5bn.

The world's second biggest market, Japan, recorded relatively slow growth of 3 per cent to

World pharmacy drug purchases January–December 1996 ($m)

	US	Japan	Germany	France	Italy	UK	Spain	Canada	Belgium	Neths
Cardiovascular	8,645	3,550	3,741	4,057	1,908	1,124	1,001	717	387	334
Alimentary/Metabolism	9,810	4,783	2,730	2,315	1,463	1,348	838	579	292	436
Central Nervous System	11,294	1,188	1,912	1,984	969	1,052	682	630	334	250
Anti-infectives	5,952	2,670	1,248	1,828	1,165	443	602	262	243	121
Respiratory	6,348	2,006	1,723	1,394	678	1,008	542	362	212	288
Blood Agents	3,135	2,230	778	342	507	188	300	279	101	125
Genito-urinary	3,815	475	967	829	431	380	186	210	94	115
Others	11,211	6,445	3,430	2,326	1,847	1,279	967	698	333	322
Total	60,210	23,347	16,529	15,075	8,968	6,822	5,118	3,737	1,996	1,991
% Change**	10	3	5	2	11	10	9	4	6	1

Source: IMS International   *Non-hospital market only   **Increase excluding currencies

The UK grew at the same rate as the US, to £6.8bn ($11.1bn), but its market is smaller than those in Italy and France, which have similar populations. French drugs sales rose 2 per cent to $15.1bn. Germany remained Europe's

$23.3bn. Tokyo introduced mandatory price cuts in April – and will do so again this year – and winter's influenza season was mild, hitting sales of antibiotics and respiratory drugs.
Source: *Financial Times*, 11 March 1996, p. 3

Coca-Cola and Pepsi-Cola have licensed bottlers around the world who pay for the right to use the name. Pepsi is now based in 145 countries but they never patented their recipe as they feared they might lose it after the traditional 15–16 year period of first registration. Coca-Cola dates back to 1893 as originally a cure for peptic ulcers. Although both Coke and Pepsi are seen as virtually interchangeable today to the majority of the buying public, 40 years ago the situation was quite different. Pepsi then was identified with the working classes and perceived as being better

value than Coke. Pepsi first began to receive television advertising in the USA from 1939, but the development of the two giants is fascinating.

Coca-Cola benefited from the Second World War when the US army took it with them overseas, but Coke was still being sold in war-time Germany. There was a Coca-Cola manager, Max Keith, who was head of soft drinks for all occupied Europe. Fanta was developed at this time because sugar was short in Hitler's Germany. Elsewhere, the US Defence Department was paying for bottling plants to be sent to the front line.

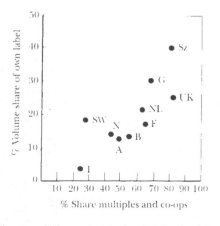

Source: Davies, G.(1990) Marketing to retailers: a battle for distribution? *Long Range Planning*, **23**(6), 101–108

Figure 5.9   Own-label penetration and multiple-co-operative market share in European grocery retailing

Exhibit 5.14   Elastic brands

Jeremy Bullmore, a director of WPP, the world's top marketing-services group, has for many years played a game called Brandicide. The rules are simple. Players choose a well-known brand and think of extending its name into a new area that would kill the brand stone dead.

It is not that easy. Bullmore and his friends thought After Eight chewing gum a good opening shot, but on reflection concluded that an upmarket, premium-priced chewing gum might sell well. It was not until someone suggested After Eight bubble gum that Brandicide had been committed.

Some might argue that to suggest Persil produce a chocolate bar, or Listerine make a whisky would not be playing the game properly – such Brandicide would be too crude. But who could have imagined that Cadbury would apply its name to a cream liqueur, Del Monte launch a range of cook-in sauces or that Sainsbury would sprout a bank?

The announcement from Sainsbury highlights a new culture of brands. Companies are increasingly attempting to stretch their proven expertise into new areas. In particular, the weakness of most financial-services brands is under attack.

Sainsbury is not alone in targeting the financial-services sector. Marks & Spencer has already made inroads and Richard Branson's ubiquitous Virgin has made the leap from retailing and air travel into personal equity plans and pensions without missing a step.

The boundaries are breaking down, not just between one sector and another but also between manufacturers and retailers. To the consumer, a company such as Tesco or Virgin is as much a brand as Kit-Kat or Pampers. And few of them seem to know their place any more.

Many of the most powerful brands are being stretched beyond any limits their inventors could have imagined. Instead of 57 varieties, Heinz now has 360 in the UK and more than 4,000 worldwide. There are 15 varieties of Heinz Baked Beans alone.

Even Unilever, the consumer-goods giant that has championed free-standing brands, is stretching those it is hanging on to while culling its weak ones. To new generations of shoppers, Persil is a washing-up liquid and Vaseline is a deodorant.

Much of this is not new. But a combination of factors has made companies more eager to stretch their brands further and more boldly than before. Advances in technology have reduced the barriers to entry in new sectors. Companies have developed stronger and more knowledgeable relationships with customers. And the cost and difficulty of developing new brands is encouraging people to exploit what they already have.

Peter Wallis, founding partner at SRU, the management consultancy, and better known by his *nom de plume*, Peter York, has a Brand-stretch Programme and has identified three levels of stretchability. The first is licensing, where a strong brand, such as Harley Davidson, allows its name to be used on smaller items, often including scents or after-shave. The second is when a brand is stretched gently, usually within its sector. Mars, for example, has put its name on an ice cream.

The third is when a brand appears to leap into unknown territory, relying on its relationship with its customers to bring it success in a new area of activity.

'The third phenomenon, where the brand almost seems to leap a species barrier, is the thing that has got everyone agog,' says Wallis.

Experts are divided on the wisdom of the Sainsbury Bank launch. Some believe it is an innovative use of the company's relationship with its 12m customers and will create a useful income stream. Others say the company, already a profitable petrol retailer, is taking a big risk. Instead of offering a fresh alternative to the financial-services giants, the Sainsbury name may lose its lustre. Paul Edwards, deputy chairman of the Henley Centre, says: 'Sainsbury is trying to make a big jump in one go. Maybe it thinks it will overtake Tesco. I would worry it was a step too far.'

Most of the world's biggest brands go back a long way. Kodak, Coca-Cola and Gillette have all been market leaders since the 1920s or before. And Heinz surfaced even further back, in 1869.

Since then some of the biggest and wealthiest companies have spent hundreds of millions of pounds dreaming up names and packages for their products. They have picked up ideas from their product-development departments, hired design companies to create appropriate packaging, and invested heavily in advertising. Yet 99 per cent have sunk without trace.

The difficulty in establishing a new brand is illustrated by the familiarity of Britain's 50 top-selling grocery brands. Four were launched while Queen Victoria was on the throne; 16 between 1900 and 1950; 21 between 1950 and 1975, coinciding with the emergence of commercial television; and only nine since 1975.

In the 1980s, many predators justified the price paid in takeover bids by citing the value of the brands they acquired, and finance directors struggled to find ways of valuing these assets. Grand Metropolitan, which bought Heublein, owner of Smirnoff in 1988, later included acquired brands on its balance sheet at £588m.

Yet all this attention shed remarkably little light on the true personality of different brands, their strengths and weaknesses and their relationship with customers.

For all the philosophising and debate, some of the world's most sophisticated brands hurtled down what turned out to be cul-de-sacs. Kellogg, the king of cereal, decided it would become king of breakfast and introduced an orange juice drink in a sachet. Cadbury allowed its name to be plastered on salted snacks, tea bags and instant mashed potato, before retreating back to chocolate and confectionery. 'Today the Cadbury name appears only where it relates to a chocolate product,' says a spokeswoman.

Such examples have not deterred marketers. The proliferation of brand-stretching is greater than ever. Companies are relentlessly extending their brands, apparently without stopping to count the cost.

Bullmore likens brands to night-storage heaters, in need of regular replenishment. The launch of a sub-brand, he says, invariably takes heat from the parent. 'Some people call it leveraging brand equity,' says Bullmore, 'which makes it sound penalty-free. But there is a cost.'

If a brand loses credibility in one sector, that virus can contaminate everything that bears its name. The potential downside is almost always greater than the possible benefits.

The new battleground is over trust and credibility. Fame should not be confused with potency. Almost everyone has heard of Barclays Bank, Domestos and Ratners. That does not mean they would make very stretchy brands. In the new environment, many of the traditional consumer-goods companies are at a big disadvantage compared with retailers. Shops have expertise in selecting things, whereas a manufacturer is expected to

have credibility in making them, leaving less room for manoeuvre.

'Manufacturers have been slow to recognise that in the eyes of the consumer, retailers can have as much authority as they do,' says Bullmore.

So-called own-label products from Boots the Chemist are market leaders in their sectors. That does not mean Boots could credibly move into selling cars or mortgages.

The most common mistake made by chief executives in their quest to maximise profits is a failure to understand fully the personality of their brands, according to Wallis. 'The set of meanings attached to a brand has more to do with attitude and culture than attributes,' he says.

In an analysis of a dozen of the world's best-known brands, Wallis has singled out only two as being superstretchy, brands capable of leaping categories.

Marks & Spencer, the retailer, has come to be trusted absolutely and can be relied on to deliver 'democratic luxury' in whatever field it chooses. Virgin, has proved that its David versus Goliath approach has also earned it credibility almost everywhere. Behind them comes Nike, the hugely successful sportswear company. It has pulled away from its rivals by establishing a reputation for attitude and youth, and shows enormous potential. They all make Coca-Cola, the world's most famous brand, look a trifle stiff.

Few brands are capable of leaping their categories, though more and more are eager to try. Wallis says: 'People are constantly coming to me with unrealistic expectations of their brand and I have to let them down tactfully.'

Robin Wight, chairman of WCRS, the advertising agency responsible for BMW, warns against the fashion. 'There seems to be an irresistible pressure to extend the equity of brands, but it is a very dangerous activity,' he says, 'Brands aren't like tins of paint that can be slapped on any wall you like, they have to have parameters.'

Source: Sunday Times, 3 November 1996

Banking provides other quite different illustrations of the importance of branding, as with travellers' cheques and plastic bank cards which are now universal. In travellers' cheques, Thomas Cook was in at the very beginning, followed by American Express, and the travel and entertainment cards of Diners Club and American Express which were the first truly global cards, followed belatedly by the various banking consortia such as Visa International – who now

issue travellers' cheques as well as credit cards – and Master Card. These last two are consortia which allow local member banks to append their name to an internationally recognized and standardized card format. Obviously, a local bank will gain more respect from its clients when its travellers' cheques are readily accepted abroad at a wide variety of outlets instead of just correspondent banks. Here the power lying behind the name of the consortium constitutes the differential advantage. Interestingly, British television advertisements for travel and entertainment cards emphasize the freedom of international movement and purchasing power, while for the bank credit cards, the high number of outlets which will accept their cards. The approach in either case is quite different, but here is an example of banks now being able to offer a highly standardized globally branded product.

Selecting a brand name

Textbooks and management checklists often state that a good brand name should be able to meet a number of criteria, such as being short, unique, memorable and able to connote an important quality or image. Above all, it has to be available to use, registrable and protectable. The name should describe the product, be distinctive, be pronounceable, lend itself to graphic display, be acceptable, be legal (i.e., not an already registered name), be suggestive of the product that it represents, and be easy to remember.

In the international marketing arena, many products fail to meet these criteria once transferred to the foreign market. An unfortunate branding example is GEC-Osram, a long and well-established lighting division of the British General Electric Corporation (GEC). Now, although both GEC and Osram are well respected quality brand names, the name Osram in Polish is very close to the word for excrement!

Products sometimes travel better than do brand names, although brand names are often well-known before even the product arrives. 'Coke' and 'Pepsi' are known worldwide, even in markets where there is general scarcity. General Motors sell a small hatchback car throughout Europe known as the Opel Corsa, using the German subsidiary name although the car is actually manufactured in Spain. In Britain, again with the same car, General Motors decided to use instead the name Vauxhall Nova as Vauxhall is the GM British subsidiary. Curious to relate then that 'Nova', in Spain, where this car is after all made, means 'doesn't work'!

Types of branding

1. *Individual brand names.* This was a policy pursued by Rowntree-Mackintosh who, only in the last few years (before being bought over by Nestlé), introduced a corporate logo onto their packs. Products were stand-alone brands, such as 'Smarties', or 'Kit-Kat', or 'After-Eight', with little mention of who the

manufacturer was. It mattered little as they are all quality products, but there was no association with the parent manufacturer. This has always been the case, too, with the promotion and sale of soaps and detergent washing powders with Unilever and Proctor & Gamble fighting an international battle for market share with competing brands in each sector, few identifiable with their parent company.

2. *Blanket family name for all products* is what is practised by Heinz who used to emphasize 'Heinz 57 Varieties', although the total product range must extend now into hundreds. The phrase '57 Varieties' is attributed to the French philosopher Voltaire who on a visit to England, commented favourably on the freedom of speech and the 57 varieties of religion.

3. *Separate family names for all products.* This is practised by department stores who may have different in-house brand names for different types of merchandise. Woolworth's and Littlewoods practise this.

4. *Company name and individual product name* is the strategy adopted by Kellogg's who emphasize their name strongly alongside all of their brands. Similarly, Ford Motors do likewise with each of their cars.

5. *'No-name', unbranded merchandise.* In grocery stores, this has been adopted by Carrefour hypermarkets in France and Britain, and by International Stores in Britain. Woolworths have introduced a range of generic 'no-name' products at discontinued prices. Germany has experienced this effect quite markedly with cigarettes, particularly where the 'no-name' cigarette packs made abroad now account for 40 per cent of the supermarket trade, and has led to the market leader Reemstra having to slash its prices. The market had been rocked also by a rise of 39 per cent in the German tax on tobacco which influenced smokers to trade down. The problem then for the established brands, such as Peter Stuyvesant, Ernte, Marlboro, HB, etc., was to re-establish themselves as being value for money brands offering premium quality at a premium price.

Brand names take account of good commercial sense – making use wherever possible of a local subsidiary name, culture, and language. There is no good reason to explain why a Fiat Ritmo which sold well in Europe could not sell well in Britain, or why it should sell better as a Fiat Strada in Britain when Strada means only 'Street'? The Japanese did have a car called the Cedric and a small truck in Japan which was not exported but known locally as the 'Little

Table 5.13 Brand names from the totally abstract to the completely descriptive		
Completely freestanding arbitrary or coined	Associative or suggestive	Completely descriptive
Kodak	Slalom	Sweet 'N' Low
Exxon	Visa	Supa-Save
Schweppes	Coca-Cola	Bitter Lemon
Formica	Sunsilk	
Replay		

Source: Blackett, T. (1989) Brand-name research – getting it right? *Marketing and Research Today*, May, pp. 89–93

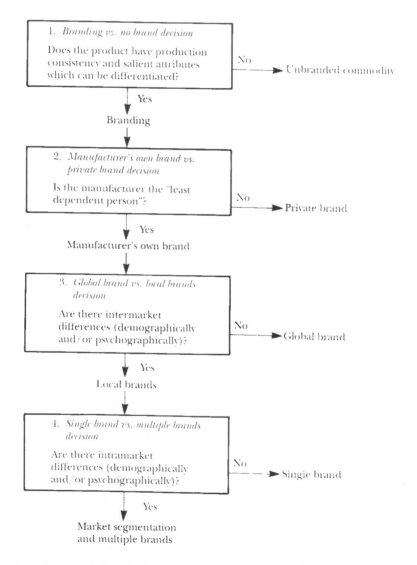

Source: Onkvisit, S., and Shaw, J. J. (1989) The international dimension of branding; strategic considerations and decisions. *International Marketing Review*, **6** (3)

Figure 5.10   The international dimension of branding

Bugger'. Sales of Tide in Denmark were low until it was deduced that it was the Danish word for menstrual flow. However, the Danes do sell successfully a hair product called Blackhead which obviously must have a different meaning over there but that is the translation of the German founding brand of hair care products: Schwarzkopf. (See Table 5.14)

Table 5.14   Conceptualizing the next new product
1. Be aware of trends, use them and respect them.
2. Do not discount demographic trends.
3. North America and Europe show the same trends of the bulk of the population moving into middle-age.
4. Acknowledge the post-war baby boomers as now a greying set.
5. Appreciate the home as a comfort zone.
6. Acknowledge the increased value society puts on time.
7. Do not adulterate the environment.
8. Participate in the electronic revolution.
9. Acknowledge that the marketing environment of the 1990s is different from that of years before.
10. Do not steal market share.

Source: Adapted from Clark, A., and Femina, D. (1989) Ten most important trends that will impact your next new product, paper to the American Marketing Association New Product Conference, February 16th. Reproduced in the AMA 'Worth Repeating' Series.

The folklore of brand names is very rich – some companies use agencies to help them. Some will make a computer search, but the difficulty always with a brand name is that unfavourable associations are usually because it is connected with a slang or colloquial usage, and dictionaries do not usually provide any help whatsoever in this regard.

Taking an established legend in international advertising folklore, Esso's 'Tiger in your tank' was undoubtedly a successful standardized campaign, but it did undergo modification. To the French, the concept of putting a tiger in the tank was bizarre and so it had to be translated as putting a tiger in your engine. Shell used to have a slogan 'I love Shell' and they benefited greatly from French colloquial usage when they used their slogan in France 'C'est celle que j'aime', a phrase used to point out an attractive lady more often than a motor oil, but the closeness of 'celle' and 'Shell' made it effective. The point is that it is not just translation that is necessary, but the transposition of a concept into another culture. Without checking back on the original, disasters do arise.

The problem with names is that more and more are being registered, making the search for a suitable name more difficult and creating a market for professional name search companies, such as the US company, Namestormers, or the British company, Interbrand. Namestormers follow a six-step approach:

1. *Information gathering* using one or more in-depth telephone interviews with key members of the organization. During these conversations, a fairly lengthy series of questions are asked about what it is you are naming, what you want the name to communicate, your target market, your competitors' names, how your name will be used, the positioning and brand strategy for the product or company, and other related issues.

2. *Old-fashioned brainstorming.* After reviewing notes with the entire naming project team (typically five people) and calling back with a few more questions, Namestormers conduct a series of informal brainstorming sessions. Often held over breakfast or lunch, these sessions are designed to encourage a very creative, non-defensive interplay between team members. At this point, there is no such thing as a stupid name or bad idea (having discovered that some of the worst initial ideas often ultimately yield some of the best name candidates).

These sessions focus on identifying naming 'dimensions' or avenues of thought to pursue for developing the names themselves, rather than immediately trying to develop specific name alternatives. For example, 'textures' and 'shapes' may be identified as two dimensions to pursue when naming a new kind of doughnut, and specific name candidates (like *RingLeaders* or *Softballs*) will be arrived at after reviewing a long list of existing texture and shape words, roots and names. Or, if the object is a company name, the question may be, 'If this new company were an automobile, what kind fits the company's objectives and desired image the best – would it be a Mercedes, a Honda, or ...?' Once the type of car is identified, related naming dimensions can then be pursued.

3. *Individual name development.* Independent of the brainstorming sessions, individual team members start exploring different naming dimensions and building their own list of favourite name candidates. Some members will make extensive use of computer naming programs, name-part dictionaries, synonym finders, and databases of words and roots

categorized by connotation and industry group. Others will go on 'field trips' to look at competitive products on the grocery store shelf, take a long drive out in the country, or hibernate in a restaurant for a few hours scribbling ideas. The individual approaches vary as greatly as the resulting names do.

4. *Feedback and evaluation.* As the individual name development proceeds, team members submit their name candidates for inclusion on the master list. This list is then sorted and distributed back to the entire team. A group session is held to discuss, critique and rank everyone's name ideas. This step involves team members identifying the worst and best names, defending their favourites and lambasting many others. After what often becomes a fairly heated and lengthy debate, each member's scores and comments are combined together and turned over to the team leader.

5. *Limited trademark search and profanity check.* The team leader takes the top name candidates and has preliminary trademark and profanity checks performed on each name. The preliminary trademark check compares each of the top name candidates to a directory of US registered trademarks. The comparison is based on exact spelling matches from the relevant International Classes. If a match is found, the name is flagged as potentially unavailable. While this preliminary check often catches many of the obvious problems and, saves considerable time and money (from having to perform the more exhaustive

search on a lengthy list of name candidates), it is not a substitute for the comprehensive computer search. Since the trademark database Namestormers use is typically six to twelve months out-of-date, and includes no state or common-law information, a patent and trademark counsel is still needed to conduct a comprehensive trademark search (for similar as well as exact spellings) using the most current data available.

The preliminary profanity check uses a database of obvious vulgarities and obscenities in five languages: English, Spanish, German, Italian and French. Other languages are not checked and Namestormers do not reference an exhaustive listing of all the contemporary negative or obscene words in a language (e.g., in English, you might not want to name a product *Valdez* given the tie with the Exxon oil spill, even though it wouldn't be flagged during the profanity check). This check does give you an early warning of many possible vulgar or obscene meanings connected with a name.

6. *Report preparation.* Namestormers then print an eight section report which includes the three lists of name candidates, sample results from some of the computer runs, and results of the limited trademark search and preliminary profanity check. The top 40 name candidates are ranked on the criteria jointly established during the initial interview and displayed in a format shown in Table 5.15 (these categories and rankings are fictitious).

Table 5.15   Avoiding the ten great blunders in brand name selection

1. *The newly minted mystery.* People respond most positively to names they can immediately understand, and are least enthusiastic about abstract and meaningless names.
2. *The rational dud.* Names that simply explain products lack imagination, memorability and emotional appeal.
3. *Alphabet stew.* Replacing corporate names with a string of letters works only for highly visible and established companies with large advertising budgets.
4. *The nearsighted name.* Too specific a name may threaten future expansion if tied too closely to a single market, product or service.
5. *The equity exterminator.* Names build up equity and imagery which can easily be lost with a name change. Retaining the old name with a fresh visual image may be equally effective.
6. *The dirty word.* Names need to be checked for vulgar meanings in popular slang.
7. *The ugly duckling.* The look of its name, its graphic potential and sound are important to be able to pronounce and memorize.
8. *Names without a market.* Names communicate to an already defined market, they do not create markets.
9. *The absentee veto.* Market testing may suggest popular associations with names that may have escaped management's attention.
10. *The legal quick kill.* Avoid lawyers for names as they will offer legally safe names without marketing value.

Source: O'Neill, T. (1986) Avoid the 10 great naming blunders. *Marketing News*, **12** September, p. 72

Packaging

The example above of the movement on Western markets into plain, unbranded generic products is providing satisfaction for the consumerist lobby, long anxious about the size of advertising budgets and questionable promotional costs being added to overheads and, hence, final selling price. However, in Britain already, the packaging industry and the printing trades federation have made representation to trade and industry bodies about the effects that this is having on their industries.

Branded products fetch a premium over generic products. Aside from actual product qualities, there is the expectation of a 'no-nonsense' package which is purely functional rather than aesthetically or intrinsically appealing. Branded products offer the highest value-added to the packaging industry. Quality is implicit in the presentation of the product and that presentation is usually the package itself. Materials used are often laminated rather than single thickness. Lacquering of the printing inks gives an impressive sheen and means there is no smell or tainting from the inks. On generic products, this does not matter, it may even be expected as a result of lower price. Packaging, then, is no longer a promotional tool, but simply a barrier medium with generic products to protect the product as best it can and as cheaply as possible until final sale. Generic products display high-volume, low-value unit sale characteristics, so specifications change quite dramatically over the branded products. There is need only for an identification label of the contents only, and as the lower priced product has a higher turnover rate, the degree of protection may be reduced for a projected shorter shelf life. This will lower packaging costs further.

Packaging is often seen merely as a barrier property, but for many products it is the product that you see on the shelf. Dehydrated soups, for example, are sold in sachets, or pouches as the

Americans call them, but this container represents the product visibly to the buying public, whereas actual sight of the dried powder itself may not appear quite so appetizing.

Packaging sizes change with personal disposable income, but also with the available channels of distribution. There may be a clear split also in the infrastructure available to urban and rural dwellers. There may be special characteristics of the distribution channels, such as a proliferation of wholesalers, or alternatively the large supermarket chains may effectively control distribution. These factors, in addition to the nation's topography, influence shelf life, and that in turn is affected by climate: again, a packaging problem. Packaging, therefore, has not only to act as a barrier, but to come in what the end-user perceives as being the 'right' sizes; and to be easily identifiable in terms of contents and labelling. It is possible, therefore, to pursue a dual-brand strategy whereby the same product, or a very similar product, is sold through two quite different channels of distribution as they are intended to be targeted at two or more quite different market segments. This is quite separate from the argument over 'own-label' manufacturing where the large supermarket chains in Britain now have manufacturers producing under their own label. Tesco and Safeway now both offer an 'own-label' whisky so their range is quite extensive. It is sometimes assumed that the contents are identical with the brand leader. This is often a false assumption. Indeed, it may be quite wrong to assume so, for both Nestlé, with their Nescafé, and Kelloggs, with their Corn Flakes brand, have been advertising that they do not manufacture for anyone other than themselves, nor under any other name than their own registered brand names. British supermarket chains, such as Tesco, Sainsbury, etc., have become both irritating to manufacturers over this issue, but at the same time, attractive because of the size of their market dominance. For manufacturers it may not be their first choice entering into 'own-label', but

Table 5.16

Name	Memorable	Clarity	Descriptive	Value	Total
Pandora's Secrets	5	4	3	5	17
Orbitoes	5	3	4	3	16
Double Think	3	4	5	4	14
BioStar	4	4	3	5	16
Yieldflex	4	4	4	3	15
Vision Quest	4	4	4	2	14
Accucheck	3	4	4	3	14
Power House	5	4	3	2	14

Source: The Namestormers, Tel: (214) 692–9091

Table 5.17 Samples of a few of the names the Namestormers have helped develop over the years

Names	Description	Client
Aegis	A family-oriented health care organization	Bowman Gray Hospital
All Systems Go	Automotive repair centres	Goodyear
Alliant Select Alliant Plus	Two health plans: an HMO and a Point-of Service plan	Group Health Cooperative
AutoSource	An automotive parts and repair service centre	Auto Source
CareStream	A company name spanning a variety of medical systems	FoxMeyer
Cool Peppers	Mexican Restaurant	Concordia
GENEX	A corporate name that doesn't sound so focused on rehabilitation	General rehabilitation
Halo	Water sprinkler nozzle	L. R. Nelson
Imagineer	A variety of engineering-oriented software products	Intergraph
InterGo	Internet-based software	TeacherSoft
Jet Solutions	Jet leasing company	AMR Combs
Laforza	Italian-designed automobile	Fissori
Member One	A federal credit union	North & West Federal CU
Minuet	Bar code scanner engine	PSC, Inc.
MobileWare	Mobile networking systems	21 Cennet
Pizza Cravers	A Doritos snack flavour	Frito-Lay
Positive ID	A computer/telecom security system	Southwestern Bell
PowerShot	A digital camera	Canon
Pyramis	An ECG management system	Burdick
SatisFAXtion	A fax board for PCs	A Technology Company
Sensible Chef	A line of frozen meals	ConAgra
Traxxis	Power seat system	Johnson Ctrls

The Namestormers, 2811 Declaration Circle, Lago Vista, TX 78645–7523
Phone: 512-267-1814 Fax: 512-267-9723
Web Site: www.namestormers.com

the volume considerations must surely make this a proposition worthy of consideration.

Two other categories of names are the arbitrary name, such as Guess ? Jeans, and the suggestive name. The arbitrary name has no real meaning relative to the product, service or company. It describes whatever meaning becomes attached to the name as the result of a company's marketing efforts and thus enjoys excellent protection under the law. As Unikel (1987) points out, arbitrary names are a lawyer's first choice, but frequently undesirable from a marketing point of view. Unless a company is able to invest sizeable marketing dollars to give meaning to an arbitrary name, it has little intrinsic value.

Suggestive names are a compromise between legal and marketing requirements, e.g., 'Suave' shampoo and 'Accent' flavourings. However, where a manufacturer chooses a descriptive name, e.g., 'chocolate fudge drink', then this cannot be protected, whereas had this come to be expected of a brand name drink, then it would be protectable (Unikel, 1987).

Intellectual property

There are perhaps six main kinds of intellectual property:

- Patents, which are for inventions, i.e. new kinds of technology.
- Copyright for literary, artistic, dramatic and musical works.

- Trademarks which are words, symbols or pictures – or combinations of these – used to distinguish the goods or services of one person from those of another.
- Industrial designs which are for the shape, pattern or ornamentation of an industrially produced object.
- Integrated circuit topographies refer to the three-dimensional configuration of the electronic circuits embodied in integrated circuit products or layout designs.
- Plant breeders' rights apply to certain new varieties.

All sorts of people have a stake in intellectual property – people in business, inventors, artists, designers, electronic microchip manufacturers, plant breeders and others. Intellectual property is a saleable asset. Licensing and franchising both revolve around the sale of company specific know-how. Like any other form of asset, know-how requires protection and that will be our focus. Protection of the know-how behind a branded good or service and protection of the brand as well. Note that brand names, trademarks and trade names have an important market value, hence the propensity to copy, and are often referred to as industrial property rights.

Industrial property rights

Licensing confers the right to produce under a company-specific technology in return for a fee or royalty. It allows access to an outsider to technology that has been protected by patents. In the past, industrial property rights which concerned technology have been the easiest to protect, but in today's world markets there is a great deal to be gained from product imitation or closely related brand names, sometimes even instituting a brand name that looks quite different but is phonetically identical in the local market abroad. Another large loophole at the moment is the question of computer software, for the regulations have to be rewritten in order to encompass rights to authorship over computer software programs where development costs are high and duplication may be carried out with ease.

At the moment, there are three international agreements on patent protection in addition to the Paris Union and Madrid Arrangement which cover trademarks as well. The European Patent Convention encompasses 16 countries; the European Community Patent Convention, its member countries; and the Patent Co-operation Treaty has 20 signatures including all the major Western trading nations. Registration in one member country is effective for all nations signatory to the agreement.

A patent is granted only for the physical embodiment of an idea or description of a plausible working product or a process which produces something saleable or tangible. It is not possible to patent a scientific principle, an abstract theorem, an idea, a method of doing business, a computer program or a medical treatment. Nor it is possible to patent inventions having illicit or immoral purposes.

CIPO (1993) *A Guide to Patents*, Ottawa.

A successful patent application in Canada has to establish within the application:

- novelty,
- utility,
- inventive ingenuity.

Note that the novelty criterion is jeopardized if the invention was made public before the patent application was filed. The Internet and the freedom of information legislation could therefore jeopardize the chances of registering a patent. Patent law in both Canada and the US has the same provision – publication of information about an invention can prevent a patent from being issued. The issue now arises as to whether discussion on the Internet constitutes public domain publishing. The Internet can be easily 'browsed' and many powerful search engines are now widely available to access data held in countries all over the world and bring it within seconds to a personal computer or notebook located perhaps in another country. Data access can be achieved without knowing anything of the identity of the inquirer; the 'who' or 'why' this is taking place is never known but every second of every hour of every day more and more people are looking to the Internet to access timely information for whatever purpose. Search engines retrieve information by identifying keywords and can quickly scan massive databases, so the issue of what constitutes publication is very real. The principle of electronic publishing has as yet to be tried in any court. However, there are two prongs to this possible attack on confidentiality. First, e-mail systems, Usenet newsgroups, and specialist forums are not secure. Next, the freedom of information legislation often makes government the culprit. By revealing information on applications as perhaps required by law, government agencies can then be held responsible for disclosing sufficient information as to jeopardize a patent application.

The Paris Convention for the Protection of Industrial Property allows for 'convention priority' which means that filing in one member

Exhibit 5.15   Harrods Internet win

Harrods has won a ground-breaking victory against 'pirates' who hijacked the top store's name on the Internet.

A High Court judge has ruled that Internet firm UK Network Services infringed Harrods' trade mark when it registered the store's name on the hi-tech computer network.

Other company names registered by UK Network Services include Cadbury's, Iceland, Ladbroke, RAC, Vodafone, Waitrose and even Olympic 2000.

By registering the name, UK Network Services effectively blocked Harrods and others from using the system to advertise their wares around the globe. Had the verdict gone against Harrods, it would have been forced to buy the Internet address from UK Network Services, or been unable to use it.

The number of Internet users doubles every eight months and the network is seen as the key to many companies' future success.

Harrods spokesman Michael Coles said: 'The verdict is very important for thousands of companies who may find pirates trying to steal their reputations. There was a very important point about ownership that needed to be made.'

Ladbroke says it will look closely at the judgment.

Source: Daily Express, 11 December 1996

country will provide a one year period of grace in which to file in all others. The exception to this rule is the US where prompt filing is required.

Application for a foreign patent is made possible through the Patent Cooperation Treat (PCT) administered by the World Intellectual Property Organization (WIPO) in Geneva, providing for a standardized industrial filing procedure for up to 43 member countries through a single application. Filing under PCT provides a 'prior art' search which checks the application against other applications and patents and a preliminary examination with an opinion on the patentability of the invention.

This report provides a good indication as to the value in seeking multiple patents in foreign countries.

Compulsory licences and the abuse of patent rights: the Canadian case

Under certain circumstances, compulsory licences may be granted by the Canadian government to Canadian firms for manufacturing new foods or pharmaceutical products.

Exhibit 5.16   Abuse of patent rights

Compulsory licences may also be granted to remedy what is called 'abuse of patent rights.' Such abuse occurs if you, the inventor, fail, within a period of three years after grant, to take steps to make your invention available on a commercial scale in Canada without good reason. (You may be allowed additional time if you need it.) It's considered an abuse because you are hindering trade and industry. Abuse situations include:

- hindering manufacture of the invention in Canada by importing the product from elsewhere;
- not meeting demand in Canada;
- hindering trade or industry in Canada by refusing to grant a licence (if such a licence is in the public interest), or by attaching unreasonable conditions to such a licence;

- using a process patent to unfairly prejudice production of a non-patented product, or allowing the patent on such a product to unfairly prejudice its manufacture, use or sale.

If someone applies for a compulsory licence because they believe that an abuse situation exists, you may be required to prove that you are not abusing your patent. In making a decision about such a situation, the Commissioner tries to ensure the widest possible use of inventions in Canada, maximum advantage to the patentee, and equality among licensees.

You may appeal compulsory licence decisions to the Federal Court of Canada.

Source: CIPO (1993), Ottawa

Table 5.18 The terminology of industrial property rights	
Intellectual Property	A form of creative endeavour that can be protected through a patent, copyright, industrial design, trademark or integrated circuit topography.
Patents	Patents are for new technologies (process, structure and function). Through a patent the government gives the inventor the right to exclude others from making, using or selling the technology in question from the day the patent is granted to a maximum of 20 years (in Canada) after the day on which the patent application was filed. The inventor can profit from a patent by selling it, licensing it or using it as an asset to negotiate funding.
Copyright	Legal protection for literary, artistic, dramatic or musical works or computer software.
Industrial Designs	Legal protection against imitation of the shape, pattern or ornamentation of an industrially produced object.
Trademark	A word, symbol, or picture – or combination of these – used to distinguish goods or services of one person or organization from those of competitors.
Trade Name	The name under which business is conducted whether it be the name of the owner or the name of a corporation or a partnership or a name adopted for a segment of that business i.e. a division of a company. The trade name can be registered as a trademark only if it is used to identify wares or services.
Integrated Circuit	The three dimensional configuration of the electronic circuits embodied in integrated circuit products or layout designs.

Source: CIPO – Canadian Intellectual Property Office, (1993), Ottawa

Brand names and trademark protection

Brand names operate under two separate conventions internationally – either prior use elsewhere of the brand name or first registration, which would allow a private citizen to record all rights for one country to what may well be protected brand names of another elsewhere. A certain South American individual was reputed to have registered over 300 brand names in the early 1960s and to have bartered furiously with multinationals subsequently seeking entry to that particular market. The same behaviour is now being witnessed with the registration of e-mail and Web site addresses. It would appear at first incomprehensible for such an action to take place but a Dutch individual has been able to register the name 'euro' as a trademark for coins and securities. History just keeps repeating itself.

Brand name protection, therefore, means registration in each country likely to be a market for the product concerned. It all depends on the market potential of the product concerned and the resources of the company. Nevertheless, these costs of brand name protection are expensive, amounting often to 10–20 per cent of the development costs of certain new products.

Registration and protection, add to total costs, while protecting the commercial advantage embodied in the product concerned from external competitions. This means, though, that either the product or the process itself has to be offered to a wider market in order to recover the costs of development. Ironically, this emphasizes both the need to go abroad as well as the need for international protection.

Trademarks is a separate area from brand names, yet although the name is what you would probably ask for or look for in a shop, the trademark is what would probably help you recognize the product even though a pack may be redesigned. A trademark can be any word, symbol, or device, or any combination of these which identifies goods or services. Registration at the Patent Office confers on the proprietor a statutory right to exclusive use of the mark. For example, the style of a typeface can be registered. Consider the distinctiveness of the typefaces used in the Kellogg's logo or the IBM logo or the Wrangler logo on shirts and denim jeans. Trademarks are the manufacturer's way of assuring the consumer that he is purchasing an authentic product at a time when brand piracy is certainly on the computers from the Far East. A standard pack of Kellogg's Corn Flakes, therefore, has protected rights to the Kellogg's logo: the Cockerel graphic; the slogan in 'the Sunshine breakfast'; and the slogan underneath the brand name, 'the best to you'. Loss of control over any or all of these could invite product imitation, which Kelloggs have been able to avoid completely in the UK until the advent of generic products.

It is interesting, therefore, to note how the Coca-Cola bottle was found not to be registrable as a trademark in a reapplication by the Coca-Cola company to the Court of Appeal, January 23, 1985. From the early 1920s, the company had been selling Coca-Cola in unusually shaped bottles in the UK, and there was ample evidence to show that the public in the USA, and in the UK, associated the shape with Coca-Cola. The verdict was that a line drawing of a bottle may be registrable as the trademark of a beverage if the bottle depicted is unusual and distinctive; but the bottle itself or its shape are not registrable in that they are not 'marks' capable of being applied to or incorporated in the beverage. However the legal situation has since changed with the new Community Trade Mark regime.

Goods are classified under different sections at the Patent Office, so a name in use under one category would not prevent registration of the same name by a different company in a different product category. Examples of names used by different companies for different products include Colt, which can be a gun, a car, a lager, or ventilating equipment; Titan and Jaguar, both of which can be aircraft or motor vehicles; and Lloyds Bank and Lloyds, the insurance market.

Trademarks are protected by the Paris Union, known formally as the International Convention for the Protection of Industrial Property, established in 1882, which allows a company registering in one country six months grace to register in any other it chooses. Russia is a member. The Paris Union allows for:

1. Mutual recognition and reciprocity in that each signatory nation has to provide the same degree of protection to nationals of other members states as to its own nationals.
2. Filing a claim in any other member state within twelve months of first registration and have the original date of application recognized.
3. Common rules and regulations applicable to all member states.

Note though that this is a convention and does not form part of English law. The UK Copyright Act stems from the Berne Convention and the current Patents Act from the European Patents Treaty.

The second agreement is the Madrid Arrangement, known formally as the Madrid Arrangement for International Registration of Trademarks of 1891. This is mostly European, has only 25 members, and does not include the USA or Britain, but allows for registration in one country to be effective for all member countries.

Trademarks licensed to the sole distributors of pharmaceuticals, and protected under national trademark laws, were in the past often used as a barrier against imports of identically branded goods sold by the manufacturer on another national market at a lower price. The EU has been waging a long and successful war against such trademark-assisted compartmentalization, and has received powerful support from the European Court. The European Court ruled, in the *American Home Products Case*, that two different trademarks must not be used for the same or similar product with the sole purpose of separating the national markets, or at least they must not be used to stop the parallel importer. The EU Commission's proposals would go much further. It would lead to an automatic invalidation of trademarks if the protected goods were marketed in another member state under another trademark. The EU has decided to follow the principle of first registration.

Exhibit 5.17 Rules of the patenting game

Q: My son has an interesting idea for a board game and is in the process of developing it. How can he safeguard his idea at this early stage against copying and what is the best way to proceed once he has a working model? – Reader in Montrose

A: You can get patent protection for board games provided they meet the normal criteria for novelty and innovation, says chartered patent agent Campbell Newell of agents Cruikshank and Fairweather. A patent would probably not be appropriate 'if it was just a case of a board game with some pieces on it and you move the pieces around' but it would be if the game had novel physical characteristics.

Agents will normally give a free initial consultation as to whether an idea is suitable. But patent agents tend to be a little wary of board games, simply because there are so many.

Consultancy Games Talk, which tests games for leading manufacturers, receives around 100 game ideas a week from the companies. Only around 40 a year will be seriously considered and a dozen may reach the shops. It says most ideas fail because they duplicate existing games based on

➤ **Exhibit 5.17** *continued*

sports, business or strategy and advises budding inventors to keep the rules simple and choose a broad theme with maximum consumer appeal.

Once you decide to go for patent protection you have to file a comprehensive description together with a set of patent claims which define the scope of what you want to protect. When the Patent Office assesses the application, it carries out a search of 'prior publications' which even under a new fast-track service still takes three months.

You can also file a 'provisional' or 'informal' application to start with, which has to be formalised within 12 months. This allows the inventor to disclose the invention or offer it for sale without prejudicing his rights or committing more patent money.

Costs start at £700 to £1,200 for an informal application and the same again later, or £900 to £1,700 for a complete application. Further costs will be incurred later, such as the present £285

for a full examination of the application within two years.

Copyright arises automatically in original works, whereas applying for registered design protection costs around £200 plus the cost of preparing drawings and photographs, and protection must be applied for to the Designs Registry before any non-confidential disclosure of the design.

There is also Design Right. If the board embodies original artistic, literary or design features, these could be copyrighted. 'The way to establish that is to send it to yourself by recorded delivery and don't open it,' says Newell. 'The alternative is to file it with your solicitor or bank and establish a date of creation.'

Source: Francis Shennan, 1996 'Rules of the Patenting Game', *Scotland on Sunday*, 3 November 1996, p. 7

Exhibit 5.18   Unravelling

Trouble looms for weavers of Harris Tweed

On this remote island in the Outer Hebrides, off Scotland's northwest coast, Donald Roddy Macleod pedals a noisy loom, weaving the fabric of his life.

Mr MacLeod is making Harris Tweed, the famous material woven here for more than 150 years. 'When it's a howling day and pouring rain, there's nothing like being in here weaving,' the 61-year-old Mr MacLeod shouts over the *clack, clack, clack* resonating through his tiny loom shed. 'But how's it going to last?'

This island is the only place in the world where the exclusive hand-woven fabric is made, but lately trouble looms large.

In fact, large looms are the trouble.

Hoping to reverse years of declining sales, the biggest mill operator, Derick Murray, wants weavers to replace their cast-iron looms with faster, larger – and more expensive – modern looms. His mill, Kenneth Macleod Ltd., which controls 90 per cent of the world's Harris Tweed trade, takes orders from apparel manufacturers, spins raw wool into yarn and then supplies the yarn to the weavers who make the material. Many weavers fear his plans to change the industry will unravel it and their way of life. So a small band of rebels has started a tweed mill and called on

anti-trust regulators in faraway London to investigate Mr Murray.

And thus have modern times intruded on this placid island's 21,000 residents. The feud has created an unprecedented caste system in the weaving world and left many weavers worried that the future of Harris Tweed is hanging by a thread.

These days, it isn't easy being in Harris Tweed. Although the fabric was fashionable 20 years ago among well-heeled Britons and Ivy League professors, sales have tumbled from a high of seven million yards in 1966 to just one million last year. In the past 10 years, the total sales of the tweed have dropped to about £12 million from £28 million.

Why? The weavers' looms, many 50 years of age or older, produce swaths of tweed too narrow – 75 centimetres – for modern clothing designers. As sales have dropped, a half dozen mills here have closed down or been bought up by Mr Murray. And the weavers' ranks are down to just 400 from 2,000 around 1970.

But change doesn't go over well here. Villagers still hike out to the moors to cut through the turf for peat to heat their homes. Road signs are in Gaelic.

So talk of changing Harris Tweed, which, along with fishing and sheep ranching, is the island's economic lifeblood, seems nothing short of sacrilegious. To qualify for the Harris Tweed

➡

→ **Exhibit 5.18** *continued*

trademark, the tweed must be woven from 100-per-cent virgin wool dyed, spun and finished by mills in the Outer Hebrides. It also must be woven by weavers in their own homes, on their own looms, with their own energy (no motor-powered looms allowed). And if more than two people weave in the same place at the same time, it's no longer Harris Tweed. 'That would be mass production,' says Angus Morrison, a teacher at the island's Lews Castle College weaving school.

Despite their proud traditions, most weavers earn less than £6,000 a year. Many are on the dole, and others raise sheep or vegetables – or pose for camera-toting tourists in hopes of selling some tweed.

Local tweed promoters believe that sales could be revived by the new looms, which weave tweed twice as wide – 150 centimetres – and enable weavers to make a wider variety of patterns using softer, lighter-weight yarns. But the big looms are expensive. A £10-million grant from local and European Union funds helps defray the £13,000 cost of each one, but weavers put in

£3,900. So far, fewer than a fifth of them have acquired the new equipment.

Indeed, many say the new looms threaten the very traditions of Harris Tweed. Over the years, they have essentially practised socialized weaving, handing out all tweed orders equally. Now an order for wide tweed goes only to weavers with the new looms.

Concerns about the looms and the fact that one company controls most of the business prompted a group of rebel weavers to start a co-operative, Harris Tweed Weavers Co. To Mr Murray, that is war. He told weavers that if they join it, they lose his business. And he decided to offer contracts to his own group of 'premier weavers,' most of whom have large looms, rather than distribute orders equally.

But that decision prompted the co-operative to complain to antitrust regulators that Mr Murray is trying to monopolize the industry. The Office of Fair Trading says it is investigating the matter.

Source: Globe and Mail, 5 October 1996

Exhibit 5.19   Caught up in the copyright web

The advent of the Internet has created new problems for the law, especially in relation to copyright, the main way in which information and computer software are protected from copying on the Internet.

Copyright gives the originator or subsequent owner of the product or information exclusive rights to do certain things, including exclusive rights to copy and distribute it.

It is difficult to reconcile the maintenance of these exclusive rights with the nature of the Internet, which allows the user to send e-mail or post a message on a bulletin board or include information on a web-page. This information is then available on a vast network spanning the entire planet.

The ease with which exact digital copies can be made of the information and then subsequently used, makes this reconciliation even more difficult.

The copyright owner will continue to retain the exclusive rights where information is posted in any manner on the Internet. Therefore the downloading, copying and printing of such information may be a breach of copyright. It is not clear what users of the Internet are entitled to do with information posted on the Internet.

A recent case in Scotland may well have far reaching implications for every company with web

sites in Scotland. It centred on the common practice of linking information from one web page to another using hypertext links. By clicking on a portion of text, the user can move to another page developed by a separate company with related information.

The Shetland Times, a well-known local newspaper which recently established a web site, alleged that its copyright was being breached by the use of such links by an Internet news reporting service calling itself The Shetland News.

The Shetland Times home page shows news items and photographs from the paper. It hoped to sell advertising space on its home page once it had a regular readership.

The Shetland News has a home page consisting of headlines and a number of advertisements. It also included headlines which were verbatim copies of headlines in The Shetland Times.

These news headlines were linked to the text of the stories contained on the Shetland Times web pages. The link allowed direct access to the text of the stories and did not take the user via the Shetland Times home page, thus by-passing the Shetland Times advertising.

Shetland Times took Shetland News to court, asserting that the existence of the link was a

→ Exhibit 5.19 *continued*

breach of copyright which would result in a loss of advertising revenue.

The Shetland Times raised an interim interdict to stop the Shetland News using the link until the full case on copyright infringement at some later date. Interim actions are common in copyright cases, and normally the alleged infringement will be stopped.

The Shetland Times argued that its web headlines were 'cable programmes' within the meaning of the copyright legislation. For this to be the case, information must be sent by the system.

It was argued for the Shetland News that Internet communication did not involve 'sending' information, and even if it did, it was an 'interactive' service which was an exception provided by the legislation.

The judge decided that the Shetland Times had shown that Internet communication did amount to the sending of information, and did not fall within the interactive exception. He also accepted The Shetland Times' argument that its headlines might be regarded as literary works and capable of protection by copyright.

He concluded that on an interim basis the link on Shetland News' home page should be removed.

The judgment clearly has important implications for all those involved with web pages.

To date, information on the Internet has been primarily regarded as literary works stored in electronic form, as opposed to cable programmes.

I would argue that the Internet should not be regarded as broadly equivalent to receiving cable television, as it does involve an element of interactivity in that information and data are sent to the server where the pages are stored.

If information on web pages was held to constitute a cable programme this would prevent companies from creating links to another company's web site using the titles or headlines of the other company as this would amount to infringement of copyright. This is the most common way of making links and the one which makes the most sense to the user, but may require a rethink in light of the court decision.

A change in referencing may have an effect to the use of search engines, as exact titles or headlines could not be used.

In the wider context, some of the arguments of the Shetland Times and the comments of the judge may have more significant implications. In his conclusion he refers to the fact that it was crucial to the setting up of the Shetland Times site that access to its material should be only through its home page.

It is technically possible to prevent direct access to your web pages other than through a home page, but much of the benefit of linking pages would thus be lost.

It is to be hoped that in the final judgment the judge examines the technical operation of the Internet and excludes it from the definition of cable programmes.

Source: Glasgow Herald, 23 January 1997

The Trademark Registration Treaty (TRT) of August 1980 opened up the possibility of having simply one application for registration, channelled through the UN World Intellectual Property Organization (WIPO), and valid for all countries. However, to date this has attracted only five signatories, including the USSR and four developing countries: Burkina Faso, Congo, Gabon, and Togo. The main obstacle is that Britain and the USA presently enjoy strong trademark registration and, while aware of the advantages which a common international system would bring, they view this as meaningless if the degree of protection conferred is to be in any way reduced. WIPO continues to act as the prime mover, but is seen to have a bias towards the less developed countries seeking easier access to Western technology. In 1985, talks were held on what is called a Third Variant, i.e., a third variant of the Madrid Arrangement, the TRT being the second, the intention being to super-sede the Madrid Arrangement, and yet incorporate more flexibility to try to entice US and British participation.

Brand piracy (product counterfeiting)

In an interview, Robert Littas of Interpol (Bresler, 1987) stated that there were 30 main categories of fraud, of which brand piracy then forms only part, although a prominent part.

Kaikati (1981) identified five different basic ways of forging famous trademarks which have been developed:

1. *Outright piracy* – false product in the same form and same trademark as the original. Records and tapes are common examples.
2. *Reverse engineering* – stripping down the original product and then copying it, underselling

the original manufacturer. This is happening currently in the electronics industry.

3. *Counterfeiting* – altering the product's quality without altering the trademark. Clothing companies, such as Levi Strauss, Lacoste and others, suffer heavily from this. The addition of an identifiable logo or trademark, such as the Lacoste crocodile, increases the perceived value of the product to the customer. Fake Cartier watches can be bought for $5 to $10 and then sold for $40 to $50, as against more than $700 for the original. In this case, the consumer believes that he is getting a good deal and that no-one is being hurt by this practice.

4. *Passing off* – modifying both the product and trademark, adapting a trademark that is similar in appearance, phonetic quality, or meaning, to the original product. All that is normally associated with the product is copied, e.g., Del Mundo for Del Monte; Coalgate for Colgate toothpaste, or Pineapple for Apple Computers. Yet, it may not be illegal to produce imitations. It raises a legal question as to whether all 'me-too' products are not imitations and whether any market follower would not then become a counterfeiter. Sony introduced the Walkman but many companies have since introduced very similar competing products.

5. *Wholesale infringement* – this involves the questionable registration of famous brand names overseas rather than the introduction of faked products. Although Kaikati (1981) cites this as a form of brand piracy, it is entirely within the law, and applies chiefly to those markets adhering to the Madrid Convention and the concept of 'first registration'.

Brand piracy or product counterfeiting is becoming much more prevalent than ever before, and entering into more and higher value-added areas such as microcomputers. A British response to this has been to establish the Anti-Counterfeiting Group (ACG) which is financed by 38 major companies seriously concerned with the growth of this activity. This works in conjunction with the American IACC (International Anti-Counterfeiting Coalition), International Chamber of Commerce based in Paris, Interpol, also based in Paris, and the Comité Colbert, a French organization formed in 1954 to combat counterfeiting. There are also international organizations such as the Software Publishers Association (SPA) and the Business Software Alliance (BSA).

Some of the activities of product counterfeiters are comic, such as the Asian manufacturer who promised Scotch Whisky made from real Scottish grapes and matured in the cellars of Buckingham Palace! There was also the Singapore manufacturer who tried to imitate the steering wheel covers of a West German company called Arus by even having a similar name, but his choice of 'Anus' in bold in the middle of a steering wheel met with some consumer resistance!

Elsewhere, the activities of these counterfeiters are not so funny. While Levi's and Wrangler clothing have long suffered from product imitations, and few have grieved over this except when challenging the manufacturers over the poor quality of their goods to find that they were in fact counterfeit, this is now spreading to higher value-added products as well, such as heart pacemakers and to birth control pills which are look-alikes but contain only chalk. G. D. Searle now mark their pills using more than one method. The House of Courrèges says that it only has 40 per cent of its 'own' market, worth $15 million a year; its image so devalued by copies that most retailers have given up hope of restoring it. Other designer houses, such as Gucci and Celine, also suffer from this trade as do Cartier watches, Apple computers and Raleigh bicycles. Much of this sourcing is based on the freeports of the Far East, but whereas before it was being sourced from the export hungry 'Four Dragons of Asia': Singapore, Hong Kong, Taiwan and South Korea, today it is coming from the Philippines, Thailand, Indonesia, Argentina and to a very great extent China where the value of such products is estimated at $2 billion. The US has repeatedly threatened trade sanctions against China. So far, a trade war has not developed. The ACG estimates that there are 30 different countries involved in product counterfeiting and that their output reaches most parts of the world. There is the obvious loss of revenue to the genuine company whose brand has been stolen but there is often a serious danger associated with the use of certain of these products. While heart pacemakers and pharmaceutical prescription drugs are newer, counterfeits, imported brake linings and tyres of poor quality have long been a problem. The involvement of organized crime becomes apparent with the realization that an estimated two-thirds of the video business in Britain is illicit, costing the industry £130 million in Britain alone or £700 million internationally. However, these estimates always assume that the market in question is equally willing to buy the same products at the full price which is a risky assumption to make. Software is now the number one target for piracy followed by music but generally all forms of added value attract product piracy. Extensive computerized dossiers are now being exchanged and legal action is being taken where the parties are identified, while dossiers are being sent also to WTO headquarters in the hope that some internationally co-ordinated action might be taken to remove this menace. Converted to job losses, it means 6,000 jobs lost in Europe alone just in one industrial sector.

The difficulty for individual customs authorities, such as the UK Customs and Excise Department, is that they are mainly concerned with ensuring that consignments entering the country are properly labelled and that duty is paid. Action needs to be taken by the company whose product is being counterfeited. For example, British Customs and Excise are willing to hold goods pending civil action, but they are not empowered to seize. The losses, therefore, on tax revenue and lost company sales are almost impossible to estimate.

The EU has joined with the USA in pressing for firm action against counterfeiting under WTO but has revealed a plan which will block and possibly ultimately prevent counterfeit goods crossing community frontiers. Suspected counterfeit goods would be impounded for ten days during which time the trademark holder would be allowed to prove his case. If the goods were found to be counterfeit they would then be confiscated and 'disposed of outside the normal channels of commerce.'

Exhibit 5.20   Cyberspace alien to US court dealing with Internet case

Washington – The US Supreme Court, which must rule on the constitutionality of a law forbidding indecency on the Internet, has shown that it has little acquaintance with cyberspace.

Free-speech activists and those seeking to protect children against smut in cyberspace clashed on Wednesday in a court that has no Internet site. Only two out of the nine judges – whose average age is 62 – use a computer.

Mr David Souter, 57, one of the youngest judges, has banned personal computers in his office and writes his rulings in longhand.

Television cameras and tape recorders have never entered the neo-classical courthouse and members of the public are not allowed to take written notes.

The lawyers' desks are equipped with a quill pen, a tradition dating back to the court's first session in 1790.

The court's anti-electronic code means that advocates and opponents of the Communications Decency Act of 1996 are not allowed to argue their cases by presenting the Internet's numerous pornographic websites.

The case, one of the most closely watched disputes this term, immerses the court in a complex and unexplored area of free speech with potential implications for lawmakers and parents, librarians and educators, and a multitude of online businesses.

At issue is a law passed last year that makes it illegal to transmit sexually explicit material to anyone under age 18. The law excludes from prosecution those who make a 'reasonable, effective and appropriate' attempt to keep indecent material out of the hands of minors.

While some judges suggested on Wednesday that Congress was stifling constitutionally-protected conversations between adults, it seems unlikely the court will rule with the unanimity of the special three-judge panel that resoundingly struck down the law last summer.

Justice Sandra Day O'Connor described the Internet as 'a public place . . . much like a street corner or a park'. But reflecting some of her ambivalence as well, as that of others on the bench, she later suggested that Congress may have authority to restrict a narrow category of 'patently offensive' materials.

Arguing in defence of the federal law, Deputy Solicitor General Seth P. Waxman said that an unregulated Internet 'threatens to give every child with access to a computer a free pass to the equivalent of every adult bookstore and theatre in the country'.

He also asserted that 'it is technically feasible to screen for age'. Although the lower court that first reviewed the law said it would be prohibitively expensive for non-commercial Internet users to verify the ages of potential recipients, Mr Waxman insisted that young teenagers could be stopped from accessing indecent material through the use of identification numbers that would be distributed only to adults.

Justice Stephen G. Breyer questioned whether the law was so broadly written that high school students, using their home computers to talk about their sexual exploits, would be open to prosecution and potentially imprisoned, as the law allows. Mr Waxman conceded the students might violate the law.

Justice Breyer also likened an Internet exchange to a telephone conversation and suggested that if Congress can monitor what goes on in cyberspace it also can monitor telephone conversations. – AFP, WP.

Source: The Straits Times, 21 March 1997

Interpol devised a piece of model legislation in 1985 which they then sent around the 142 member states of the organization. They also publish the *Counterfeits and Forgeries Review*.

Five corporate strategies to handle counterfeiting

Kaikati (1981), who has been one of the most important researchers in this area, has advanced the following counter-strategies from his research of counterfeiters and their victims:

1. *Compete and attempt to overcome the opposition.* A feasible strategy when the firm's stakes and power are relatively high. The objective is domination and forcing the counterfeiters out of the market. Many large companies, as well as the International Anti-Counterfeiting Associations themselves, now have a security force tracking down counterfeiters and pursuing them with legal actions wherever and whenever they are found.
2. *Avoid conflict and withdraw from the fray.* This is feasible where the firms' stakes and power are relatively low. The strategy objective is to throw in the towel on move or to 'greener pastures' at the lowest possible cost.
3. *Accommodate the opposition, where the objective is appeasement.* Customers may switch to their brand if they knew their products were being faked. The company which is the victim of such action is hoping that the problem will disappear. There is a further consideration in that pursuit of the offenders requires conclusive evidence which is a difficult and expensive proposition as it entails hiring private detectives for lengthy periods of time. Again, criminal action is speedier and more effective than civil action, but loopholes in the law are being fully exploited by very professional criminals.
4. *Collaborate.* This is likely to be best when the firm's relations with the opposition are relatively positive. Fiorucci, an Italian jeans maker with outlets in the USA, has been charged with ordering cheap Korean copies of its own luxury jeans and marketing them as though made in Italy. There have even been occasions when the quality of the counterfeit exceeds that of the original!
5. *Compromise.* In this situation, the firm's stakes are moderate and power is slight. The trademark Persil is owned by Unilever in Britain and France, and by Henkel in Germany, Belgium, Luxembourg, Holland, Italy and Denmark. Agreement had to be reached when Britain entered the EC and there were price differentials between the manufacturers, Unilever being cheaper than Henkel. Also, price differentials between countries, which gave rise to parallel exporting opportunities. The two manufacturers agreed to respect each other's trademark, and agreed that Henkel would use the name Persil on pockets in red inside a red oval whereas Unilever would use a green Persil trademark.

Distribution of counterfeit goods

Where goods are offered for sale by street traders, the public are right to be suspicious when massive discounts are being offered, although even at this level more professionalism has crept in. In the past few years there has been a problem with street traders in Britain offering supposedly French perfumes for sale at very low prices. To support their sales talk, they flaunt glossy colour advertisements allegedly from quality magazines, which refer to these perfumes. In fact, these advertisements are also fake. The appeal of some of the 'knock-off' perfumes is also hard to understand. Since 1981, a Connecticut based firm, Perfums de Coeur, has been advertising: 'If you like Opium, you'll love Ninja.' They also offer Confess (similar to Obsession), Primo (similar to Giorgio), and Turmoil (similar to Poison). They use comparative advertising copy, comparing their product with the brand leader (Sloan, 1987), but give it a different name so not actually promising the original.

However, counterfeit goods are well beyond the level of just street traders, but have entered many high street retailers and department stores in Britain and the USA. In the USA alone, it is a trade which has penetrated the major retailers but proposals to deal with the counterfeiters, including seizure of any goods suspected of being counterfeit, has run into opposition from US cut-price retailers. Jordache refuses to sell to K-Mart directly because it looks for outlets which reflect the image which it wishes to portray. K-Mart, therefore, obtain their supplies from middlemen known in the trade as 'diverters', and it is these people whom Jordache are keen to pursue, although there is nothing illegal in the practice of 'diverting' or selling to outlets that the manufacturer may not approve of.

While opinions are divided as to what role government should have in this situation, eighty-five US corporations have meanwhile formed the International Anti-Counterfeiting Coalition. An international code to let trademark owners intercept and seize shipments of suspect merchandise is the next step for the Coalition.

The code being considered by the (WTO) is opposed by Brazil, India, Hong Kong and Singapore because it is alleged that they fear that their trade in low-cost imitations will suffer. A few developed countries, including Austria and Switzerland, are opposing the code as well. Meanwhile, the Reagan Administration passed a law in 1984 which allows for goods to be confiscated, and distributors to be fined or even sent to jail. The US software industry estimates losses due to piracy in 1989 as $1.5 billion, and for Canada at $190 million. For software, the ratio of pirated to legitimate copies is around 5:1. An industry action group, the Software Publishers' Association, based in Washington, DC, now has 645 members.

Technology provides another part of the answer in that companies, now more security conscious than ever before, spent $50 million in 1985 on a variety of high technology gadgetry which provides a means of unobtrusively authenticating products with hidden magnetic or microchip tags, disappearing–reappearing inks, holographic images, and digitized 'fingerprints' of labels which read the unique pattern of fibres in each label. The verifiable label was developed by Light Signatures Inc. in 1981, and has been used by Nike Inc. (running shoes), MCA Inc. (records) and Levi Strauss, whose attorney, Peter M. Phillipes, was able to boast: 'We have virtually eliminated our counterfeiting problem in the US'. Clearly, other developments are not so encouraging, for in 1986 Sue Goldstein, author of *The Underground Shopper*, along with the Irving Texas-based mail order house, IMOCO, started 'Facsimile', a catalogue offering designer look-alikes of clothes from Ralph Lauren, Calvin Klein, Adrienne Vittadini, and others. The cover caption reads: 'If you like the Ralph Lauren look, you'll love Facsimile' (Sloan, 1987).

Britain has recently changed its position quite substantially in this area. The Copyright, Designs and Patents Act 1989 extended copyright to computers and satellite broadcasts, and changed the provisions relating to industrial designs allowing ten years' protection. Copying necessary to make spare parts, as with cars, is allowable. Yet, designs with 'eye appeal' are to be given 25 years' protection. 'Moral rights' are accorded authors, artists, and film directors, giving them the right to be identified with their work. Penalties have been introduced for making, importing or infringing copies of any kind of copyright material, allowing for an unlimited fine and up to ten years' imprisonment. Copyright ownership in relation to literary, dramatic, musical and artistic works produced by an employee is now automatically granted to the employer. The question of copyright, and of its ownership, and of obtaining payment for the use of copyright material has, therefore, been resolved to some degree.

Parallel or 'grey' exporting

With increasing regionalization and the harmonization of tariffs and duties worldwide, but perhaps especially in the EU, opportunities now abound to source branded products from low cost, low tax countries and sell them in high cost, high tax markets with no tariff applied to the export transfer. This practice is not illegal but it obviously undermines the channel of distribution which a producer will already have in place. As such, this is viewed as a distribution channel issue so this will be dealt with in detail in Chapter 7. This is a highly complex issue which involves everyone in the distribution channel at home and abroad, risks weakening the value of the brand and often brings company, nation state and a supranational body such as the EU into open conflict. Is it about cheap imports or safeguarding jobs at home, or protecting the integrity of the brand name or simply a matter of company control versus free trade?

After-sales expectations and service

There are obvious advantages where it is possible to standardize, if not globally, at least regionally, the level of service accorded to customers. From cars to electronic hi-fi stereo systems, product guarantees and warranties are common in all parts of the world. Where previously they were national, the clear trend is now international. In the past there may indeed have been valid reasons for separate warranties, country by country. With cars, for example, servicing periods were at 3,000-mile intervals, whereas in more recent years this has been extended to six months or 9,000-mile intervals. Products have improved but alongside this, there needs to be a uniformity on the dealer network internationally. Standardized servicing facilities, availability of parts, even standards of training of mechanics and maintenance personnel, are all factors to be considered before internationalizing a product warranty. It does add to company prestige and the consumer perception of product quality and reassurance in the event of breakdown. There may well, however, be instances of local market requirements, as in the case of the USA or the EU but these needs can still be met. Production costs on the warranty booklets can be reduced by producing them in large numbers, and comprehension can be aided by having it contain warranty guidelines in several languages.

Appendix
Dilmah and the history of Ceylon tea

Many remarkable stories are told about the origin of tea, the boldest of which suggests that it was known as a beverage in China at the time of Chi Nung, 2737 BC. A clear reference to tea appears in 'She King' a classical work compiled by Confucius about 500 BC, yet it is likely that it was only in the sixth century AD that tea became a beverage of any important scale in China. In 780 AD Lo-yu, a learned Chinese author who lived in the Dynasty of Tang, in an enchanting little dissertation on tea, said: 'Tea tempers the spirits, harmonizes the mind, dispels lassitude and relieves fatigue; awakens thoughts and prevents drowsiness, lightens and refreshes the body and clears the perceptive facilities.'

The first samples of tea reached Europe in 1610, arriving in Holland via the Dutch East India Company. Within a few years, tea had become a popular drink among the Dutch aristocracy, who drank it as much for its supposed medicinal properties as for its pleasant taste.

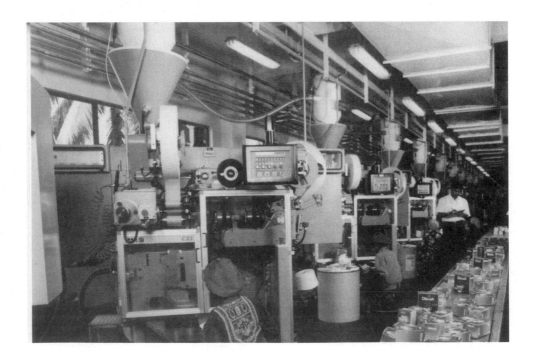

Tea reached Britain around 1650, where it immediately became so popular that the limited quantities available fetched astronomical prices. By the end of the seventeenth century, when a high duty had been placed on all grades of tea, smuggling became rife. In the early eighteenth century, two-thirds of all imported tea was in the form of contraband. It was during this period that tea became the favourite beverage of all classes.

In America, tea became the symbol of British oppression when George III used it as a test case to exert his right to tax the colonies. In 1773, the entire cargo of the East India ship 'Dartmouth' was emptied into Boston Harbour and the event became immortalized as the 'Boston Tea Party'.

Early in the nineteenth century Britain's East India Company began to investigate other possible sources of tea to China which, until then, had been the world's sole producer. It was feared that China might return to a completely insular way of life and that the world's tea supply would thus completely cut off. Tea trees were discovered in the Upper Assam region of North East India and the very first chests of

Indian tea reached London in 1839. In the same year, Assam tea seeds were successfully test planted in Ceylon.

The rise of Ceylon Tea – James Taylor and the Loolecondera Estate

Tea plants did not figure among the local flora on the island of Sri Lanka, a British crown colony, until the early nineteenth century when several entrepreneurs used their estates as test plots. In 1839, Dr Wallich, head of the botanical garden in Calcutta, sent several Assam tea plant seeds to the Peradeniya estates near Kandy. This initial consignment was followed by 250 plants, some of which went to Nuwara Eliya, a health resort to the south of Kandy, situated at an altitude of 6,500 feet. The Nuwara Eliya experiment produced excellent results. Seeds of Chinese tea plants, brought to Sri Lanka by travellers such as Maurice de Worms, were also planted in the Peradeniya nurseries.

But this time the results were disappointing, and Chinese plants were gradually abandoned in favour of the Assam variety that is now grown on every estate in Sri Lanka.

Tea cultivation nevertheless remained a minor activity for 20 years. Coffee remained the island's main export crop. However, in the 1870s the dreaded blight *Hemileia vastatrix* systematically destroyed coffee plants. The entire coffee industry was destroyed. Tea then appeared as a godsend, and the entire local economy shifted to the new crop within a few years. This rapid substitution owed a great deal to the fruitful initiative of a man names James Taylor.

Back in 1851, near Mincing Lane, which was later renowned as the tea centre of the world, Taylor had signed on for three years as an assistant supervisor on a coffee plantation in Ceylon. This 16-year-old Scot, son of a modest wheelwright, would never see his native land again. But throughout his life he sent letters to his father back home, providing a unique description of the daily life of a planter in that epoch. Five years after he took up his post, his employers, Harrison and Leake, impressed by the quality of his work, put Taylor in charge of the Loolecondera estate and instructed him to experiment with tea plants. The Peradeniya nursery supplied him with his first seeds around 1860.

Taylor then set up the first tea 'factory' on the island. It was in fact a rather rudimentary setup. Historian D.M. Forrest quotes a description provided by Taylor's neighbour, planter E.G. Harding: 'The factory was in the bungalow. The leaf was rolled on tables on the verandah by hand, i.e. from wrists to elbow, while the firing was done in chulas or clay stoves over charcoal fires, with wire trays to hold the leaf. The result was a delicious tea which we bought up locally at Rs 1.50 per lb.' The factory soon became famous throughout the island. In 1872, Taylor invented a machine for rolling leaves, and one year later sent 23 pounds of tea to Mincing Lane. Taylor trained a number of assistants, and from that point on Ceylon tea arrived regularly in London and Melbourne. Its success led to the opening of an auction market in Colombo in 1883, and to the founding of a Colombo tea dealers' association in 1894.

Taylor continued to test new methods and techniques at the Loolecondera estate (which he would never own) until the end of his life. He was well-liked by both European planters and native workers, yet remained somewhat solitary. He never left the estate, except for a single short vacation in 1874 – spent at Darjeeling, needless to say, in order to study the new tea plantations. His talent and determination were officially recognized when Sir William Gregory, governor of Sri Lanka, paid Taylor a visit in 1890 to congratulate him on the quality of his tea. The Sri Lanka Tea Growers Association, founded in 1886, gave him a silver tea service engraved with an inscription citing his pioneering work.

But the rise of the tea industry nurtured by James Taylor was also the cause of his downfall. Rapid growth was accompanied by a concentration of capital in the hands of large corporations based in Britain, and a wave of property consolidation forced out smaller planters. Taylor, like other planters, was dismissed. Terribly disappointed, he decided to remain on his estate despite an order to quit; not long afterwards, in 1892, he died suddenly of dysentery at the age of 57, on his beloved soil at Loolecondera.

The 1884 and 1886 International Expositions held in London introduced the English and foreigners to teas produced in the British Empire. But it was at the 1893 World's Fair in Chicago that Ceylon tea made a tremendous hit – no fewer than one million packets were sold. Finally, at the Paris Exposition of 1900, visitors to the Sri Lanka Pavilion discovered replica tea factories and the 'five o-clock tea' that became so fashionable. As a contemporary chronicler put it, 'The charming colonial house with bright shutters, the deliciousness of the beverage, the beauty of the Singhalese people – living statues of bronze wrapped in shimmering white loincloth – everything contributes to the success of this delightful stand at Trocadero . . .'

The planters' association supported this propaganda campaign by organizing various publicity events. In 1891, Kaiser Wilhelm II, Czar

Alexander III, Grand-Duke Nicolas, the queen of Italy and Emperor Franz-Josef all received 60 coffers of tea accompanied by an illustrated album on Ceylon.

The promotional policy was so effective that by the end of the nineteenth century, the word 'tea' was no longer associated with China, but with Ceylon. The island's prosperity sparked covetousness on the part of British companies and London brokers, who wanted to acquire their own plantations and cut out the middlemen. This marked a turning point in the saga when tea-pioneers gave way to merchants whose name or label would soon become more important than the country in which the tea was grown.

The rise of the big brands

As brand names became more important than the origin of the tea, the decline of Ceylon tea began. Multinational brands which built up consumer loyalty over the years by using only Ceylon tea in their packs started moving to cheaper, more recent origins for tea. Most consumers did not notice the gradual reduction in the quality of their favourite brand. Most consumers know of Ceylon Tea as the finest in the world, and still think that their favourite Brand X contains Ceylon Tea. In fact, Ceylon Tea has all but disappeared from retail shelves in traditional markets.

The secret of Ceylon tea

Mild breezes, light, clear air and a rolling landscape lend the gardens of Ceylon a very pleasant aspect. The brightly coloured saris scattered among the greenery provide an appropriate touch of beauty. Most tea gardens are located on the island's central hills. The best gardens are, as always, found at the higher altitudes, from 3,000 to 7,000 feet on the eastern and western slopes of the high plateaus. Depending on the direction in which they face, the gardens are influenced by one of two monsoons; on the eastern slopes, the finest tea is plucked from late June to the end of August, whereas on the western slopes the best harvesting takes place from 1 February to 15 March.

It is now midday at Dimbula or Uva Highlands, Devonia or perhaps Pettiagalla. Women in saris wear a long white cloth on their head to protect their shoulders from the sun. Their graceful and fragile silhouettes, slightly stooped, blend well with the tall tea plants left to grow like trees every 30 feet or so to provide a little shade and mark out the plots. Here and there, men dressed all in white – turban, jacket and long skirt down to their ankles – supervise the plucking. And when the baskets are full, they follow the pluckers to the door of the factory, where the tea is weighed. This tea factory in Ceylon, a long white building occupying the end of a small valley, looks somewhat like an Alpine sanitarium mistakenly set in the tropics. Although the soul of a garden resides in the hands of the pluckers, the factory represents both its heart and brain.

The freshly picked leaves undergo a long process of transformation, for black tea must be fermented. And the fermentation of tea requires as much care and close, scientifically controlled attention as does the fermentation of wine. This industrial art constitutes the modern, technological face of these exotic and apparently unchanging tea gardens, and merits the same detailed description as the colourful swirl of saris. But whereas it is pleasant to linger under a shade tree to watch the plucking, ears lightly humming with the music of wind in leaves or the voices and murmured songs of the pickers, once at the door of the factory it becomes impossible to tarry for long – much less day-dream – in the thundering din of machines.

Here, men do most of the work. Barefoot labourers and technicians in British-style shorts bustle among an indescribable clutter of machines, amid dim shade, heat and incessant noise.

Everywhere it is produced, black tea undergoes five successive stages. The leaves are first softened by a withering process that reduces their moisture content by half and enables them to be rolled without breaking. They are spread in thin layers on wide screens stacked eight inches apart to allow a current of warm air to circulate for roughly 24 hours. The most modern factories now accomplish the task in tunnels or vats, reducing withering time to six hours. Withering is followed by rolling (or maceration). The leaves are rolled to break down cell walls and release their essential oils. This was once done in the palm of the hand, but has long since been performed by rolling machines composed of heavy metal disks rotating in opposite directions.

The rolled leaves are then placed on long mats to be sorted according to size and condition – whole or broken. This sorting is still done entirely by hand in some gardens, enabling the leaves to be 'graded' into various classes of black tea. In the finest gardens, whole leaves are classified according to size and the way in which they are rolled, yielding Orange Pekoe (O.P., leaves rolled lengthwise and measuring from eight to fifteen millimetres), Flowery Orange Pekoe (F.O.P., leaves rolled in the same way yet smaller, from five to eight millimetres),

Golden Flowery Orange Pekoe (G.F.O.P. and F.O.P. in which certain leaves have a golden tip), or Tippy Golden Flowery Orange Pekoe (T.G.F.O.P., all tips are golden). Leaves that have been broken, deliberately or not, yield high-quality grades of Broken Orange Pekoe (B.O.P.), Golden Broken Orange Pekoe (G.B.O.P.) or Tippy Golden Broken Orange Pekoe (T.G.B.O.P.). Finally the so-called 'crushed' leaves, which are in fact small pieces, are called Dust (less than one millimetre) and Fannings (one and a half millimetres).

Next comes fermentation, the crucial operation that endows black tea with its colour and, above all, the subtlety of its flavour. Experts agree that the process remains something of a mystery. No one knows exactly what alchemy produces the flavours, for certain cellular reactions during fermentation have never been fully understood or even identified. We do know that fermentation is produced by exposing leaves to a highly moist atmosphere (at least 90 per cent humidity) after having been spread on broad slabs of cement, glass or aluminum. The air temperature must be carefully monitored and controlled (between 72° and 82°F), because a slight rise in temperature will give the tea a burned taste, whereas a slight drop will halt fermentation. When maintained at constant temperature and humidity, the leaf first heats up from the effect of several chemical reactions, then begins to cool off. A tea-maker's skill includes an adept sense of timing – for best results, fermentation should be halted just when the leaf stops heating, which may take from one to three hours.

The leaves are then dried in an enormous machine comprising a dryer and conveyor belt, exposing them to a temperature of at least 175°F for roughly 20 minutes. Drying, the last stage of transformation, also requires well-honed skills. If it is too brief, the tea may become mouldy in time; too long, and the tea will lose much of its flavour. All this expertise goes into the black tea that emerges from the greatest tea gardens in the world.

Tea and health

The nutritional value of tea could be attributed to its chemical components beneficial to the human body. Of these, caffeine, polyphenol fractions and anti-oxidants are considered to be the most important, since many of the beneficial effects claimed by the tea have been traced to these constituents.

Caffeine is known to stimulate the central nervous system and respiration. Other desirable effects of caffeine include relief of fatigue,

increase of alertness and aiding digestion. Excessive caffeine is said to have adverse effects on the human system; however, tea has only half the caffeine levels of coffee and research proves that the presence of caffeine in tea does not produce unhealthy results due to its combination with tea polyphenols.

The polyphenols present in tea act in many ways beneficial to human health. A cup of tea contains about 1,000 ppm (parts per million) polyphenols. The catechins available in tea polyphenols has the capacity to suppress an excessive rise in cholesterol, inhibit hypertension, reduce glucose levels in the blood, prevent cardio-vascular diseases, lower high blood pressure and keep the intestines in good order.

In density, a level of 1 ppm of fluoride in potable water is identified as having a prophylactic effect against dental decay. A tea infusion contains about 1 ppm fluoride which is of benefit in the prevention of dental caries.

Many beverages are high in calories yet it is essential to replace body fluids, especially in hot weather. Tea is the natural choice – it is a low calorie drink and a great thirst quencher. A glass of iced tea contains only 3 calories against a glass of cola with 70. 100 calories a day more than the body needs will cause a 4.5 kg weight gain in one year, while 100 calories fewer per day can bring about a 4.5 kg weight loss.

The nutritional value of tea, apart from its being a low calorie drink, is attributed to its mineral content. Tea contains the elements of manganese, zinc, potassium and magnesium which the human body needs daily.

Tea can reduce the risk of death from coronary heart disease and the chances of having a first heart attack. Tea has a high content of a natural group of chemical antioxidants known as flavonoids. According to research published in the British medical journal, *The Lancet*, tea drinkers who consumed four cups of tea per day or more saw their risk of dying reduced to 45 per cent compared to people who consumed little or no tea. The role of tea in reducing cancer risk has also been tested and is being researched further. No wonder tea is widely regarded as an additive-free health drink!

Dilmah Tea: an introduction

The MJF Group's origins date back to the 1950s, just after Ceylon (now called Sri Lanka) became an independent nation, after several hundred years of colonial rule, first by the Portugese, then the Dutch and finally the British. The founder of the Group, Merrill J. Fernando, was one of the first Sri Lankans to break into the field of tea blending and export, which was still a bastion of the British who remained in Sri Lanka after independence. He started in the tea trade with a reputable British firm, and was trained at the Mecca of tea, Mincing Lane, in London. Within a few years he bought a large stake in the firm and became its managing director, at a young age. Over the next few years, he became one of the largest exporters of Ceylon tea, well known in tea circles.

Ceylon Tea Services Ltd, a public company in the MJF Group, pioneered the value-added tea bagging industry in Sri Lanka. Tea has long been Sri Lanka's biggest and most important export, employing well over a million people. However, until recently Sri Lanka was merely a supplier of raw material in the form of bulk tea to blenders and packers overseas. This company was incorporated with the express purpose of developing an export market for pre-packaged Pure Ceylon Tea, thus ensuring all value-added benefits remain in the country where they are most needed. The company, acknowledged as a role model for successful marketing of a Third World commodity under an own brand name, is now the largest manufacturer and exporter of teabags in the tea growing world. It operates a purpose built factory equipped with the most modern machinery.

The company introduced a proprietary brand of tea, Dilmah, in an effort to reintroduce to consumers 100 per cent Pure Ceylon Tea at reasonable prices. Ceylon tea is widely acknowledged as the finest in the world but rising prices had resulted in multinational tea packers sourcing from other, cheaper origins.

Since it is freshly packed at source and unblended, Dilmah is far superior to most other brands which contain a blend of teas from several origins. Packaging is in a class of its own and the range of products is unmatched. The Dilmah range of teas has been commented upon in major markets as 'the finest available under a single brand'.

Dilmah's success is no secret

The success of Dilmah is due to insistence on quality to provide tea drinkers with a refreshing cup of fine tea every time. Dilmah therefore guarantees:

- 100 per cent pure Ceylon tea.
- Traditional methods of hand picking and preparation.
- Freshness, picking, flavour sealing and delivering direct from the high Tea Gardens of Ceylon.
- Real leaf tea taste and flavour also in teabags.

100% Pure Ceylon Tea

Until the 1960s, most consumers drank only Ceylon tea. However, the sudden growth in wealth of the Arab world in the mid-1970s created unprecedented demand for Ceylon tea. (Arabs drink tea black – and therefore appreciate the finer flavour of Ceylon tea. As they consider Ceylon tea to be an aphrodisiac, many Arabs drink up to 40 cups per day!)

The demand drove up the cost of Ceylon tea, and the international food companies turned to cheaper sources of tea. As a result only a fraction of previous volumes are shipped to traditional markets. However, the taste of fine Ceylon tea need not be a pleasure of the past any longer. Dilmah Teas are 100 per cent pure Ceylon tea of the finest quality – grown at an altitude of between 5,000 and 6,000 feet – where the crisp, cool air brings out the fine taste and flavour in the tea-leaf.

Traditional methods

Dilmah uses only the traditional methods of growing, picking and processing tea. Many tea growing countries now use mechanical harvesting, and cut, tear and curl (CTC) manufacture which brews faster, but at the expense of quality and flavour – which are the hallmarks of fine Ceylon tea. No CTC therefore guarantees real leaf tea flavour.

Dilmah teas are picked only by hand with just two tender leaves and bud being harvested. It is here that Dilmah's refreshing and distinctive flavour is concentrated. As a result, no other tea can taste like Dilmah.

Freshness

Good wine improves with age – not so with tea! Tea is a hygroscopic product, and therefore absorbs moisture from the moment it leaves the plantation. Tea imported in bulk from various origins for blending and packing in consuming countries can be several months old by the time it is available to consumers. This long period from plantation to teacup means the tea is stale, with a significant moisture content. Dilmah tea instead is picked, perfected and flavour sealed within days, right where it is grown, to preserve its distinctive fresh flavour. Like Chateaubottled wine, Dilmah is garden fresh and unblended – but not aged!

Real leaf taste in a tea bag

Using traditional methods of tea picking and preparation, Dilmah guarantees real leaf tea taste even in a tea bag. Dilmah therefore offers the convenience of a tea bag, without compromising quality.

Caring for the environment

Dilmah uses unbleached and oxygen bleached tea-bag paper and thread plus recycled boxes.

Revision questions

1. How do you define a product, and how does it differ then from a service?
2. Why do products fail?
3. Is international marketing segmentation possible?
4. If the use of plain English is a good idea why do so few companies practise it?
5. What is the importance of the Triad . . . and to product standardization?
6. What are the drawbacks of product standardization and of some local adaptation?
7. Under what circumstances might product modification be mandatory?
8. What are the obstacles to standardization in international marketing strategies?
9. What is a World Product Mandate?
10. How is a World Product Mandate viewed by its three constituent parties: host country, subsidiary and multinational parent corporation?
11. What is branding?
12. What are the eight product quality variables?
13. What are the advantages of branding from a manufacturer's viewpoint?
14. How are brand names screened and selected?
15. What different forms does branding take?
16. What are the ten great blunders to avoid in brand name selection?
17. How important a marketing tool is packaging in the overall marketing mix? What problems might be incurred with taking standardized packaging overseas?
18. How are brand names and trademarks protected? What about the Internet?
19. What are industrial property rights?
20. What is brand piracy and how can it be counteracted?

References

Banks, B. (1988) Double trouble. *Canadian Business*, **61** (5), 40–44, 97–103.

Baumwell, J. (1986) Life cycle for brands? Forget it!. *Advertising Age*, **57** (21), 18, 22.

Blackett, T. (1989) Brand-name research – getting it right? *Marketing and Research Today*, May, 89–93.

Bresler, F. (1987) The man from Interpol. *Business Life*, February/March, 30–34.

Buzzell, R. D. (1968) Can you standardize multinational marketing? *Harvard Business Review*, November-December, 102–13.

Chan, A. K. K. (1990) Localisation in international branding: A preliminary investigation on Chinese names of foreign brands in Hong Kong. *International Journal of Advertising*, **9**, (1), 81–91.

Chui, S. (1996) 'Creating Brands that Sell: an Interview with Unilever's Steve Chui', *Direction*, Hong Kong Institute of Marketing, **5** (4), July/August, 4–5.

Clark, T. (1990) International marketing and national character: A review and proposal for an integrative theory. *Journal of Marketing*, October, 66–79.

Collar, L. (1990) Effective management of international research and planning in brand and advertising developments. *European Research*, June, 109–114.

Dalby, J. (1996) 'A Mark of Protection in the Single Market', *The European*, February 15, no. 301, pp. 24–25.

Davies, R. (1985) Coke bottle not registrable as trade mark. *Financial Times*, 30 January.

Etemad, H. (1983) World product mandates in perspective. In *Multinationals and Technology Transfer: The Canadian Experience*, (ed. Rugman, A.) Praeger, New York.

Evans, R. (1996) 'A Giant battles its Drug Dependency – Glaxo Wellcome, the world's biggest seller of pharmaceuticals, gets 40 per cent of revenues from two medicines whose patents are about to run out', *Fortune*, August 5, pp. 88–92.

Feucht, F. N. (1989) It's symbolic. *American Demographics*, **11**, (11), 30–33.

Fisher, P. (1989) The name is the game. *Intercity*, July/August, 16–18.

Glemet, F. and Mira, R. 'The Dilemma of the Brand Leaders', *International Journal of Retail & Distribution Management*, Summer, **23** (6), 9–10.

Globerman, S. (1988) Addressing international product piracy. *Journal of International Business Studies*, Fall, 497–504.

Hankinson, G. and Cowling, P. (1996) *The Reality of Global Brands*, McGraw-Hill, Maidenhead, Berkshire, in association with the Marketing Society, London.

Harrell, G. D. and Kiefer, R. O. (1995) 'Multinational Market Portfolios in Global Strategy Development', in Paliwoda, S. J. and Ryans Jr, J. K. (1995), *International Marketing Reader*, Routledge, London.

Howard, D. G., and Mayo, M. A. (1988) Developing a defensive product management philosophy for third world markets. *International Marketing Review*, Spring, 31–40.

Jain, S. C. (1989) Standardisation of international marketing strategy: Some research hypotheses. *Journal of Marketing*, **53**, (1), 70–79.

Kaikati J. C. (1981) How multinational corporations cope with international trademark forgery. *Journal of International Marketing*, **1** (2), 69–80.

Keegan, W. (1970) Five strategies for multinational marketing. *European Business*, January, 35–40.

Keegan, W. J., Still, R. R., and Hill, J. S., (1987) Transferability and adaptability of products and promotion themes in multinational marketing in MNCs and LDCs. *Journal of Global Marketing*, **1** (1/2), 85–103.

Kern, H. Wagner, H. C., and Hassis, R. (1990) European aspects of a global brand: The BMW case. *Marketing and Research Today*, February, 47–57.

Kotler, P. (1994) Marketing Management: Analysis, Planning and Control (8th Edition), Prentice-Hall, Englewood Cliffs, NJ, p. 432.

Lannon, J. (1996) 'What is postmodernism and what does it have to do with brands?', *The Journal of Brand Management*, **4** (2), 83–94.

Leonidou, L. C. (1996) 'Product Standardization or Adaptation: the Japanese Approach', *Journal of Marketing Practice and Applied Marketing Science*, **2** (4), 53–71.

Livingstone, J. M. (1989) *The Internationalisation of Business*, Macmillan, London.

Lorenz, C. (1981) How Japan cascades through Western markets. *Financial Times*, 9 November.

Macrae, C. (1991) *World Class Brands*, Addison-Wesley, Wokingham, Berkshire.

Macrae, C. (1996) The Brand Chartering Handbook Addison Wesley Publishing and Economist Intelligence Unit.

Mallet, V. (1990) Seeking a wider market for a perfume of Arabia. *Financial Times*, 3 May.

Marketing News (1991) Judge rules Kellogg wrongly promoted cereal as drug. 29 April 12.

McLoughlin (1983) Japan acts to avoid car clangers. *Guardian*, 6 December.

Miller, C. (1995) 'Kiddi stuff just fine in the UK but here it's Binky', *Marketing News*, August 28, p. 8.

Mitchell, A. (1995) 'Trade Mark travails', *Management Today*, December, 86–88.

Morris, B. (1996) 'The Brand's the Thing, not so long ago, just about everyone had given up brands for dead', *Fortune*, March 4, **133** (4), 72–80.

Murray, J. Y. (1996) 'Research Note: Product Strategies of European and Japanese Multinational Firms in the US Market – an Empirical Investigation', *International Marketing Review*, **13** (6), 58–69

Nakhai, B., and Neves, J. S. (1995) 'The Demong,

Baldrige and European Quality Awards', in Paliwoda, S. J. and Ryans Jr, J. K. (1995), *International Marketing Reader*, Routledge, London.

Noble, K. (1990) Alleviating guilt of disposable diapers. *Globe and Mail*, Toronto, 10 October.

Olins, R. (1996) 'Elastic Brands', *Sunday Times*, November 3.

Olins, W. (1995) *The New Guide to Identity: how to create and sustain change through managing identity*, Gower, Aldershot Hants for The Design Council, London.

O'Neill, T. (1986) Avoid the 10 great naming blunders. *Marketing News*, 12 September, 72.

Onkvisit, S., and Shaw, J. J. (1989) The international dimension of branding: Strategic considerations and decisions. *International Marketing Review*, **6** (3).

Pal, S. K., and Bowander, B. (1979) Marketing challenges of technical industries in developing countries. *Industrial Marketing Management*, **8**, 69–74.

Paliwoda, S. (1988) Plain English Campaign. *MBA Review*, December, 9–11.

Paliwoda, S. J, and Ryans Jr, J. K. (1995) *International Marketing Reader*, Routledge, London.

Redwood, D. (1995) 'Terrible twins' (copycat products), *Marketing*, August 24, p. 23–24.

Ritchie, R. (1986) Global branding need not mean global advertising. *Admap*, January, 39–42.

Roth, M. S. (1995) 'The Effects of Culture and Socioeconomics on the Performance of Global Brand Image Strategies', *Journal of Marketing Research*, **32** (2), 163–176.

Samiee, S., and Roth, K. (1992) 'The Influence of Global Marketing Standardization on Performance', *Journal of Marketing*, **56** (2), 1–17.

Schmidt, K. (1995) *The Quest for Identity: Corporate Identity Strategies, Methods and Examples*, Cassell, London.

Shalofsky, I. (1987) Research for global brands. *European Research*, May, 88–93.

Smit, B. (1996) 'Euro trademark may engineer a fortune' (Robert Apon, Dutch engineer who registered euro as a trademark), *The European*, June 13, no. 3 18, pp. 26–27.

Sloan, P. (1987) Knock off deliver blows to fragrance market. *Advertising Age*, **58** (9), 3/4.

Srikantham, S. Ward, K., and Neal, R. (1989) Brand accounting: myth or reality? *Management Accounting*, **67** (4), 20–22.

Strauss, M. (1991) Cashing in on the clear Canadian image. *Globe and Mail*, Toronto, 13 March.

Szymanski, D. M., Bharadwaj, S. G., and Varadartajan, P. R. (1993) 'Standardization versus adaptation of International Marketing Strategy: an Empirical Investigation', *Journal of Marketing*, **57** (4), 1–17

The Namestormers, 2811 Declaration Circle, Logo Vista, TX 78645 – 7523, USA

Thomas, M. J. (1994) Product development and management. Ch. 17 in Baker, M. J., ed. The Marketing Book, 3rd edition Oxford: Butterworth-Heinemann Ltd. pps 422–446

Thomas, M. J. (1995) 'The Relevance of Global Branding', *Journal of Brand Management*, Vol. 2, No. 5. pp. 299–307.

Ughanwa, D. O., and Baker, M. J. (1989) *The Role of Design in International Business*, Routledge, London.

Unikel, A. I. (1987) Imitation might be flattering but beware of trademark infringement. *Marketing News*, 11 September, 20–21.

Whitelock, J. M. (1987) Global marketing and the case for international product standardisation. *European Journal of Marketing*, **21**, (9), 32–44.

Wind, J., and Douglas, S. (1972) International Market Segmentation. *European Journal of Marketing*, **6**, (1).

Young, S., Hamill, J., Wheeler, C. and Davies, J. R. (1989) *International Market Entry and Development*, Harvester Wheatsheaf, Hemel Hempstead.

Web sites

AC Nielsen
http://www.nielsen.ca

American City Business Journals: news from 28 weekly city business journals
http://www.amcity.com

American Marketing Association
http://www.ama.org/

AT & T Business Network – free site
http://www.bnet.att.com

Babson Internet Business Resource Links
gopher://gopher.babason.edu

BEMs – Big Emerging Markets (US Classification)
http://www.stat-usa.gov/itabems.html

Brainstorm Business Forum – home of CBI, Chambers of Commerce, Best Practice
http://www.brainstorm.co.uk

Business Europa – business throughout Central and Eastern Europe
http://www.business-europa.co.uk

Business Information
www.businessmonitor.co.uk

Business Information Resources
http://sashimi.wwa.com/~notime/eotw/business_info.html

Business Information Server
http://www.dnb.com/

Business Network International
http://www.bninet.com

Business Site of the Day
http://www.bizniz.com/eurocool/

Business Statistics
gopher: University of Michigan:
una.hh.lib.umich.edu
Choose: ebb Current Business Statistics

Businesses on the Internet
http://www.yahoo.com/Business_and_Economy/Corporations/

Business to Business Marketing Exchange
http://www.btob.wfu.edu/b2b.html

Canadian Business InfoWorld
http://csclub.uwaterloo.ca/u/nckwan/.html/directory

Canadian Egg Marketing Agency: Unique for Eggological Information
http://www.canadaegg.ca

Canada Newswire
http://www.newswire.ca

Canadian WWW Central Index
http://www.csr.ists.ca/w3can/Welcome.html

Chartered Institute of Marketing
http://www.cim.co.uk

CIA Publications
http://www.odc.gov/cia/publications/pus.html

Clearinghouse for Networked Information Discovery
http://kudzu.cnidr.org/welcome.html

Clearinghouse for Subject Oriented Internet Resources
http://www.lib.umich.edu/chhome.html

Commerce Business Daily
gopher: cscns.com
Choose: Internet Express Gopher by Subject Business-Commerce Business Daily-Softshare

Commercenet
www.commerce.net

Commercial Use of the Internet
http://pass.wayne.edu/business.html

Cool Site of the Day
http://cool.infi.net/
Copyright on the Internet
http://www.fplc.edu/tfield/copynet.htm

Copyright for training materials and products – Training Media Association
http://www.trainingmedia.org

Copyright – 10 Big Myths about Copyright
Explained
http://www.clari.net/brad/copymyths.html

Copyright Law for Electronic Media
http://rpi.edu/dept/IIc/intelprop/
index.html

Currency Conversion Information – Olsen and
Associates, 164 Currency Converter, Zurich,
Switzerland
http://www.olsen.ch/cgi-bin/exmenu/

Currency Converter
http://bin.gnn.com/cgi-bin/gnn/currency

Disney Channel – fun and games with a hidden
educational agenda
http://www.disneychannel.co.uk

Disneyworld
http://www.disney.com/Disney World/

Environics
http://www.environics.ca

Europages
http://www.europages.com

Export-Import Pathfinder
http://mickey.queens.lib.ny.us/guides/
export_i..html

ExportNet – Export Today Matchmaking service
http://www.exporttoday.com

Federal Express (FedEx)
http://www.fedex.ca

Find it Fast
http://www.webcom.com/~tbrown/
findpage.html

Foreign Exchange Rates
http://www.dna.Ith.se/cgi-bin/kurt/rates/

Glaxo-Wellcome
http://www.glaxowellcome.co.uk

Holiday Inn
http://www.holiday-inn.com

Hotel & Travel Index On-Line
http://www.traveler.net/htio

Internet Sleuth
http://www.intbc.com/sleuth/

ILT Guide to Copyright
http://www.ilt.columbia.edu/projects/
copyright/index.html

ILT Web – Copyright Resources to Education
Online
http://ilt.columbia.edu/projects/copyright/
ILTcopyO.html

Importing and Exporting
Usenet: alt.business.import-export

Inc. Online
http://www.inc.com

Industry Net
http://www.industry.net/

Infomarket – gathers finance and
business-related links:
http://www.fe.msk.ru/infomarket/
ewelcome.html

Information Market Europe – European
Commission
http://www.echo.lu/

International Business Forum
http://www.ibf.com

International Business Practices Guide
University of Missouri St.Louis
Gopher: umslvma.umsl.edu
Choose: The Library
    Government Information
    International Business

International Business Resources on the
WWW
http://ciber.bus.msu.edu/busres.htm

International Chamber of Commerce, Paris
http://wwwl.usal.com/~ibnet/icchp.html

International Trademark Classes
http://www.naming.com/naming/
icclasses.html

Internet Address Finder
www.iaf.net

International Internet Marketing
www.clark.net/pub/granered/iim.html

Irn-Bru (famous Scottish soft drink)
http://www.irn-bru.co.uk

Japan: what's new in Japan
http://www.ntt.jp/WHATSNEW/

JETRO (The Japanese External Trade
Organisation)
http://www.jetro.go.jp/index.html

Land's End – the famous clothing catalogue
company
http://www.landsend.com/

Legal List Internet Desk Reference
http://wwwlcp.com

Legal Information Institute
http://www.law.cornell.edu

Levi's – includes an online game called
'Riveted'

http://www.eu.levi.com/inner-
  seam/eu/vol2/iss3/game/intro.nhtml

Levi's 501 jeans
http://www.levi.com/menu

Magazine Publishers of America
http://www.ima.org/members/
  mmm02.html

Malls of Canada: The world's largest shopping
  malls
http:///www.canadamalls.com/provider/

MBE Mail Boxes Etc
http://www.mbe.com

Microsoft/NBC
http://www.msnbc.com

New Scientist
http://www.newscientist.com

Newsgroup for Importing and Exporting
news:alt.business.import-export

OOCL (USA) Inc. freight forwarding
http://www.oocl.com

Packaging Waste Legislation – the Sequoia
  Group
http://ourworld.compuserve.com/
  homepages/SeQuoia

Plain English Campaign
www.demon.co.uk/plainenglish

Political Risk Services
http://www.polrisk.com

Royal Family
http://www.neosoft.com/~dlgates/
  uk/ukspecific.html? pix_windsors.

Royalty – an entertainment
http://www.royalnetwork.com

Sainsbury plc
http://www.j-sainsbury.co.uk/

The New York Times
http://www.nytimes.com/

Thomas Ho's favourite Electronic Commerce
  WWW Resources
http://www.engr.iupui.edu/~ho/interests/
  commmenu.html

Pizza Hut
http://www.pizzahut.com/

The Press Association
http://www.pa.press.net

Pointcast Network
http://www.pointcast.com

Pointcast Network Canada
http://www.pointcast.ca

Ragu pasta sauces
http://www.eat.com

Regional Information Guides by Price
  Waterhouse
http://www.i-trade.com/infsrc/pw

Rice University, USA: Subject Information
http://riceinfo.rice.rice.edu/Riceinfo/
  Subject.html

Saturn – the idiosyncratic GM subsidiary, its
  cars and advance information
http://www.saturncars.com/

Schweppes
http://www.schhh.com

Scotch Malt Whisky – Laphroaig
http://www.laphroaig.com

Scotch Malt Whisky – Glenmorangie
http://www.glenmorangie.com

Scottish Tourist Board
http://www.holiday.scotland.net

Scottish Enterprise, help for small companies
  going international
http://www.scotent.co.uk

Scotweb
http://www.scotweb.co.uk

Sellafield
http://www.bnfl.com

Simpler Trade Procedures Board
http://www.sitpro.org.uk/index.html

SilverPlatter World: a worldwide library of
  electronic information
http://www.silverplatter.com/

Sony
http://www.sony.com/

Statistical Agencies on the Internet
http://www.science.gmu.edu/csi779/drope/
  govstats.html

Statistics UK
http://www.emap.com\cso

Statistics USA
http://www.stat-usa.gov

Statistics Canada – reputedly the best
  governmental statistical reporting service
http://www.statcan.ca

SunSITE Classic – Previous Best of the Web
  Award winner
http://sunsite.unc.edu/

Trade Compass
http://www.tradecompass.com

TradePort – extensive information on
  international business
http://www.tradeport.org

Trade Statistics
http://www.census.gov/ftp/pub/
  foreign-trade/www/

Trade Wave Galaxy – Public and commercial
  information and services
http://www.einet.net/galaxy.html

UNCTAD (UN Conference on Trade and
  Development)
http://www.unicc.org/unctad/en/
  enhome.htm

United Nations
http:///wwww.undp.org

UPS Online
http://www.ups.com

US Dept.of Commerce
http://www.doc.gov/
  CommerceHomePage.html

U.S. Fedworld
http://www.fedworld.gov

US National Trade Data Bank
http://www.stat-
  usa.gov/BEN/Services/ntdbhome.html

US West features 50,000 suppliers from USA,
  Mexico, Canada
http://export.uswest.com

US West Export Yellow Pages
http://yp.uswest.com

USA – Economic Bulletin Board
gopher://una.hh.lib.umich.edu/11/ebb

Web Page for Global Business
http://www.seattleu.edu/~parker/
  homepage.html

Web Sites for International Information:
http://www.ustr.gov/
http://www.i-trade.com/
http://www.stat-
  usa.gov/BEN/subject/trade.html
http://www.itaiep.doc.gov/

Virtual Shopping Malls
http://www.itl.net/shopping/index.html

Virtual Vineyards
http://www.virtualvin.com/

Winter Web Wonderland
http://banzai.neosoft.com/citylink/xmas

World Bank
http://www.worldbank.org/

World Factbook
gopher: gopher.aecom.yu.edu

World Health Organization
gopher: gopher.gsfc.nasa.gov

World Wide Web Virtual Library
http://W3.org

WorldClass Supersite
http://web.idirect.com/~tiger

WWW Yellow Pages
http://www.cba.uh.edu/ylowpges/
  ylowpges.html.

CHAPTER 6

Pricing, credit and terms of doing business

Domestic and international price setting

Pricing is a highly conspicuous element of the marketing mix and therefore has many publics to satisfy. As well as the buying public, there are many other interested parties such as competitors, society, government – particularly if there is a domestic prices and incomes board, other governments if the item is exported, and possibly even supranational bodies, such as the EU, if there is any hint of the exported product being 'dumped' within the European Union, or enjoying any subsidy, or artificial advantage which may be in contravention of free trade as laid down in the Treaty of Rome.

For management, there is no such thing as 'perfect knowledge' of any market situation nor is there ever any such thing as 'perfect competition' where all companies active in a market are equal. The major problem with price-setting is that there are few goal posts. Pricing within the domestic market, there are strategic implications as to whether one chooses to price high, low, or merely be a price-follower, and these same strategies can be pursued internationally, provided one is sure that there is a market segment to be found abroad, and that it is of a size and ability to buy and consume. For example, pricing high and producing in low volume, and so skimming only the cream of the market, is the strategy employed by Rolls-Royce, which enjoys a global niche market position in luxury cars. Following the product life cycle theory, when companies first introduce a new product and it embodies a new product concept, or where there is no clear competition in supply, there is the temptation to charge what the market will bear. In the initial stage at least, there is for a time a certain exclusivity and this helps build a product image and maintain a high product price. It helps ensure exclusivity but also pays for the sunk costs of research and development.

At the other end of the pricing spectrum is market-penetration pricing which means a low price but requires a high volume market. This strategy was encapsulated by Sir Jack Cohen, founder of Tesco food supermarkets: 'Pile it high and sell it cheap!'. This is a valid strategy for a product that is either mature or reaching saturation, and so lowering the price may draw in further sales, exactly as economists predict with elasticity of demand. For the manufacturer, penetration pricing may also help keep out competition because of the low final price and through the perception that low final prices are the result of economies of scale. With mature products, the cost savings are due to the experience curve effect (which produces cost savings of approximately one-third whenever production doubles). There are many examples that may be drawn of products adopting penetration-pricing once they had moved along the product life cycle, including calculators, digital watches and personal computers.

Exhibit 6.1 Watch your language

Contracts with consumers must be clear and fair. Rebecca Attree explains the new regulations

'I'm from the government and I'm here to help you.' This often-used saying is rarely believed. However, it is quite genuine in the case of the Office of Fair Trading's approach to the recently implemented law governing the small print in consumer contracts.

In a recent bulletin on the Unfair Terms in Consumer Contracts Regulations 1994, implemented on 1 July 1995, the OFT says it is seeking to work constructively with companies to improve their contract terms and, while it does not provide a drafting service, it will point companies in the right direction.

➡ **Exhibit 6.1** *continued*

Where did it all begin?

In common with so much UK legislation of the '90s, the latest consumer-driven initiative derives from an EC Council Directive – 93/13/EEC of 5 April 1993, on unfair terms in consumer contracts. This was aimed at harmonising what manufacturers and suppliers could and could not say in their contracts with consumers.

It required member states to implement its terms into national law by 31 December 1994. Very few did so and even now only a few have complied. These are the UK, Ireland, Finland, France, Greece, Italy and Denmark.

The tardiness with which the directive is being implemented nationally in the EU should not be seen by sellers of consumer goods as a good excuse to rest on their laurels and put off until another day the painful process of revisiting their terms and conditions.

This is because, first, as a result of various doctrines that have been developed by the European Court of Justice, a consumer may be able to obtain the protection of a directive notwithstanding its non-implementation into domestic law. The directive could therefore potentially be applied to sales made to consumers anywhere in the EU. Second, for those selling in the UK, the OFT is taking the regulations seriously and has examined no less than 550 cases in nine months.

What does it say?

The directive applies to almost all oral or written contracts for the supply of goods or services concluded between a seller or supplier and a consumer. It says that any unfair term which has not been individually negotiated shall be voidable.

It therefore principally applies to preformulated standard form contracts. The law does not give chapter and verse on what constitutes an 'unfair' term. It merely states, rather vaguely, that a term will be 'unfair' if it causes a significant imbalance in the parties' contractual rights and obligations, to the detriment of the consumer.

Of more help is the list of terms (albeit indicative only and non-exhaustive) annexed to the directive which may be regarded as unfair. Even the OFT in its bulletin admits that the test of unfairness is 'complex' and applying it is 'challenging.'

A term found to be unfair will be unenforceable. The remainder of the contract will still stand, provided the deletion of the unfair terms still leaves a binding contract.

The law also required standard consumer contracts to be written in plain, intelligible language. The OFT comments that although many suppliers have rewritten their standard contract, many still lack clarity and need improvement in content, style and presentation.

Many people apparently still think they can bury particularly onerous terms in small print but this is pointless and counter-productive. Illegible print and obscure wording can, by themselves, make terms unenforceable because consumers must be able to see what they are agreeing to.

What should you do?

If you are in the business of making and/or selling consumer goods in Europe you should dust off your terms and conditions and ask a lawyer to check that they comply with the law and are enforceable. If there is any doubt, it may be worth being pro-active and consulting the OFT, which will give its view. It may even suggest alternative wording to render otherwise unenforceable clauses binding.

If you do not review your standard terms and conditions, you may find that certain of them are unenforceable. At worst, you may also be on the receiving end of an injunction brought by the OFT to stop you using the terms.

At the end of the day, no matter what the law says, consumer businesses can only gain by presenting a better public face and writing contracts more clearly and fairly. Sending a simple and straightforward message about fair dealing can only help companies to gain the edge over their competitors.

Common unfair terms

In the UK the most common unfair terms are:

- Entire agreement clauses, which exclude from the contract anything said or promised by a salesman or agent of the company.
- Hidden clauses – e.g., those which consumers do not see until after they have signed the contract.
- Penalty clauses – e.g., those which enable a company to keep deposits with no counter-balancing penalties on the company if it does not comply with its obligations.
- Exclusion clauses – which exclude liability for every possible eventuality, including death and personal injury.
- Variation clauses – which typically give the supplier the right to put up prices with no realistic right for the consumer to get out of the contract without penalty.

This article provides an outline of the law; in specific cases legal advice should be sought.

Source: Export Today

As the product becomes more established, the buying public becomes more aware and knowledgeable, and the need for a branded product can now often be satisfied with a generic equivalent. The product life cycle affects all four Ps of the marketing mix simultaneously and not just price alone. With digital watches, the price lowered, the volume increased and changes took place in the promotion and distribution as well. The channel of distribution moved from specialist jeweller to 'blister packs' on supermarket shelves. The jeweller is not redundant, however, since he now chooses to specialize in higher value added goods, which means lower volume growth, but provides a higher unit return. Calculators are another interesting product which have made themselves virtually indispensable to a public who did not know them one generation before. As a mass-market product, calculators fulfil a basic function and are difficult to differentiate, thus pricing plays a major role. The PLC also provides an explanation for what has been happening with the sale of personal computers. As these have moved along the PLC to become mature products, a knowledgeable buying public is less concerned with brand name, knowing the componentry to be virtually identical across different brands. This has shifted the focus away from brands and specialist retailers to pricing, and so lower cost distribution outlets. While specialist computer retailers have been trying to expand, an ever-increasing volume of sales has shifted to the traditional retailers now selling their own in-house label personal computers. This in turn has created a massive shakeout among the specialist retailers unable to differentiate their product offering in any way, as for example, offering added service warranty or after-sales care that would help justify their higher levels of pricing. Training, for example, would be a useful value added service for the consumer purchasing a new computer but it is not being offered.

Appropriate pricing over the cycle depends on the development of three different aspects of industry, which usually move in parallel paths:

1. *Technical maturity*, indicated by declining rate of product development, increasing standardization among brands, and increasing stability

    of manufacturing processes and knowledge about them.
2. *Market maturity*, indicated by consumer acceptance of the basic service idea, by widespread belief that the products of most manufacturers will perform satisfactorily, and by enough familiarity and sophistication to permit consumers to compare brands competently.
3. *Competitive maturity*, indicated by increasing stability of market shares and price structures.

Somewhere in between the two strategies of skimming and of penetration, there is the flock of sheep, the companies who diligently follow the market leader, fearful of lowering prices and meeting retaliation or raising prices and losing sales. The danger which often passes unrecognized is that the company following the price of the market leader may not have a true knowledge of his own costs, particularly in industries where there is a critical mass that has to be produced, or of economies of scale, or of experience curve effects that may be reached beyond a certain level of production, and so there are inherent dangers always in basing sales/prices on someone else's costs. Skimming, penetration, and price-following (or me-too prices) are features to be found in all markets. What often happens though, is that when a product travels abroad it will, in seeking to position itself in the foreign market, allow itself to be influenced by domestic experience, and so perhaps just extend whatever pricing strategy is used in the domestic market to this new foreign market, thus failing to optimize on pricing. At either end of the pricing continuum there are international products which may be identified with a standardized pricing strategy, e.g., disposable razors, pens, and ladies' tights, where the price is cognizant of the fact that these are disposable products and so are sold cheaply in high volume. At the other end of this continuum would be those products which ignore a mass market and essentially appeal to an international market segment (if not niche), such as Rolls-Royce in cars or Mont Blanc in pens. Essentially, a premium price is being paid for a quality product and all the prestige that ownership of that quality marque may confer on the consumer.

Exhibit 6.2   Meeting for change on a more positive footing

The powerful men behind the world's leading sports brands meet in Atlanta today in one of the biggest tests yet of whether global business can have a conscience.

When we pay £50 for a pair of Reebok or Nike trainers, £1.50 is shared by the 40 workers who make them in the Philippines. Chinese sports shoe workers earn 22p an hour, and work in conditions where they are exposed to dangerous chemicals and fire risks. Most soccer balls are made by children on a production line in Pakistan. Do we care?

➤ Exhibit 6.2 *continued*

Yes we do, says Tom Hunter, the Scots entrepreneur behind Britain's biggest sportswear chain, Sports Division/Olympus. He told *The Herald*: 'I think our customers these days are more concerned about where things are made, and if you explain that environment, even if it costs a bit extra, that is a price all of us are willing to pay.'

But are we going to be asked?

On the agenda today, at the Atlanta meeting of the World Federation of Sporting Goods Industries, is the adoption of a 'model code for ethical conduct for the production of all sporting goods'. It would set new standards on child labour, low wages, and dangerous conditions in the unglamorous factories around the world which supply the glamorous star-endorsed sportswear.

Reports three months ago, before the WFSGI's last meeting, suggesting that a code would be quickly agreed, proved optimistic. The signs are that the collective conscience of an industry which generates sales of $100bn a year is stirring very slowly.

Reebok, Nike, and other multinationals have been on the defensive since the publication of a Christian Aid report on the 'globetrotting sports shoe' just over a year ago.

The charity complained that the companies 'market themselves as progressive, wholly short-changing the Asian workers who make the shoes'.

Then last September, in a surprise move, Reebok called on its arch rival Nike to collaborate in improving factory conditions and stamping out child labour. Reebok itself had launched a Human Rights Production Standard in 1992 after earlier criticism. Nike, meanwhile, is still considering Reebok's invitation.

Who gets what from a £50 pair of trainers

Retailer £23

Brand owner £16.40

Manufacturers £9.40

Factory worker £1.20

Source: Christian Aid

In November the WFGSI suddenly announced a programme to eliminate child labour from the soccer ball industry, and said an ethical code was now being discussed.

Stephen Rubin, chairman of WFSGI and of Pentland Group (which has Mitre, Speedo, and other top brands) said: 'These announcements reflect the commitment of the worldwide industry to develop a comprehensive, sustainable, and responsible framework to ensure that sporting goods are made in accordance with the highest ethical standards.'

But while welcoming the progress, Christian Aid warned yesterday: 'Companies such as Nike and Reebok already have codes of conduct, which they monitor themselves. If a code is going to be anything more than a PR stunt, it has to be independently monitored from outside the industry.'

Opinion polls suggest that ethical shopping will be the next big wave of consumer power. UK supermarkets, who deal with a far greater range of suppliers in more countries than the sports multinationals, are beginning to take it seriously.

The Fair Trade Foundation said: 'Sainsbury's is developing a code of conduct with its suppliers, beginning with four countries, and they are opening their procedures to independent scrutiny, working with us to set up a monitoring programme.'

Reebok said this week: 'We have people whose job it is to monitor the facilities.'

Phil Wells, director of the Fair Trade Foundation, said: 'We need to be addressing employment standards generally. It is only through that route that eventually child labour is going to disappear.

'The big companies need to work in partnership with groups who have credibility with consumers and can represent the interests of communities. You can't just wander in with a clipboard. It all needs to be independently verified, but the industry seems to have set its face against that.'

Aid and trade agencies have warned that focusing on the emotive issue of child labour in a vacuum will be counter-productive. Wells warned that the likely response from today's meeting, because of the need to 'move at the pace of the slowest', was a kneejerk policy on centralising labour in the Pakistani soccer ball industry. 'People working at home who are dependent on the production will be denied access to a job. What is needed is a long-term and proactive response which goes much deeper.'

Lesley Roberts, who was recruited by Pentland Group three years ago from Anti-Slavery International as its group business standards adviser, said the model code would cover not only child labour but working conditions, discrimination,

---

➤ Exhibit 6.2 *continued*

right of association, health and safety, and community involvement 'in recognition that members have a wider role within the community'.

But standards were difficult to agree on, she claimed. 'Is it ILO standards, UN standards, the Beijing agreement, or the minimum laws of the country'? If the intention was a dramatic improvement in working conditions, 'you have to be reassured that it is going to be worthwhile in terms of developing the product – people may be prepared to pay extra, but how much?' And again, 'with high levels of unemployment we are not talking about workers bidding up the wages because that is not going to work. There is a lot of waffle about a fair wage but what does that mean in a local context?'

How the WFSGI would deal with monitoring companies' own codes was 'an issue for the future', Roberts said. It was also far harder for smaller companies to improve standards. 'They would like to do these things, but they do not know what they are supposed to be doing and they are not experts in human rights or health and safety.'

But on the other hand she admitted: 'This is a

new science – every company will hope the whole thing will just go away, because it is just added on top of other worries.'

According to Pentland, one of the main problems is 'most companies don't own these factories, they just buy from them. You can't just walk in.'

But Wells said: 'The sports firms are in a much stronger position than most industries to do something about it, they are so dominant in relation to their suppliers. Buyers like Reebok in effect control these factories in Indonesia, Thailand, and elsewhere. We are advancing ILO standards which have been ratified by most developing countries.'

Pentland agreed: 'Certain companies do a lot, others don't do anything.'

And Tom Hunter, who has 240 shops across the UK, said: 'I would rather see a code which everybody adhered to, and then information could be available to say "these goods are made in this type of environment" – I would support that positive message.'

Source: *Glasgow Herald*, 2 February, 1997, p. 13

Consumer sensitivity to pricing

Sampson (1964) has argued that many desensitizing factors operate to diminish the impact of price changes. Insensitivity will, therefore, be greater where the following conditions prevail:

* personal selling, and therefore, variation in point-of-sale effectiveness
* promotion is local rather than standardized nationally
* service after sale is important
* consumer loyalties are significant
* products are highly differentiated and difficult to compare
* there are multiple dimensions of product quality
* unit price is low
* the product is sophisticated.

Shapiro and Jackson (1978) cite five principles of a customer approach to pricing, which are:

1. The customer chooses products by measuring benefits against costs.
2. Benefits include more than physical attributes, and additional components such as services are important in differentiating products.
3. Cost involves more negative aspects of the purchase than price alone.
4. Benefits and costs must be understood in

terms of a complete usage system, not as an isolated part of the system.
5. Different customers view benefits and costs in different ways, meaning that careful market segmentation is necessary.

A multi-stage approach to pricing

There are six major elements which have been identified by Oxenfeldt (1960) in a domestic pricing decision, which in sequential order are:

1. Selecting market targets.
2. Choosing a brand image.
3. Composing a marketing mix.
4. Selecting a pricing policy.
5. Determining a pricing strategy.
6. Arriving at a specific price.

However, international pricing has to take many more variables into consideration, and this is, of course, assuming that payment will be made almost immediately and in the seller's currency. Credit, payment in other currencies, barter and the new and important forms of countertrade, introduce new and urgent problems, given the levels of competition prevailing in world markets.

International price standardization

In an ideal world the same price for one's product would prevail everywhere, but this does not happen. When it does happen within a domestic market, it happens as a result of resale price maintenance (abolished in Britain in the early 1970s, but still practised in Japan). However, price standardization cannot happen within international marketing because of currency fluctuations, different factor costs, different product requirements, national standards, tariffs, duties and specific product category taxation plus official governmental controls on pricing and discounting. It is impossible to find the exact same product available for sale across different markets at exactly the same price. The next best thing that happens is that this price differential may be contained within a band of a few percentage points across markets, thus preventing the movement of this particular product across markets because of price differential alone. Nevertheless, price deviation will always occur for the same product across different markets.

The Economist (1996), together with McDonalds of fast food fame, publishes an annual 'Big Mac' index. The index is based around McDonalds' 'Big Mac' hamburger made locally to strict standards in more than 50 countries, and so free from the distortions that international transportation and distribution costs might otherwise introduce. *The Economist* sees this index as one of purchasing power parity and so revealing to some degree whether a currency is under- or overvalued. This index is based on purchasing power parity which has its own weaknesses, but it also has some strengths. For example, PPP is able to indicate the purchasing power of a local currency better than a straight conversion into US

dollars. For one thing, the domestic currency will often have a higher purchasing power locally than is indicated by a spot rate for US dollar conversion. In this way, prices such as for accommodation and just the general cost of living can easily become quite distorted. In the case of the Big Mac Index, the components making up the Big Mac are all locally sourced, hence there should be an opportunity to compare what one unit of the domestic currency will buy in the foreign market when converted at some equilibrium rate of exchange. PPP is also used to predict currency movements, either devaluations or revaluations, as it constantly tracks inflation. While interesting, the Big Mac Index is a laboratory experiment and no more. The Big Mac is not after all traded and there is no allowance made here for impediments to trade including transportation costs, tariffs, duties and taxes. For meaningful comparisons in terms of exchange rate mechanics, the exchange rate has to be in equilibrium. Short-term movements in exchange rates are beyond the capacity of this mechanism. However, another equally awful statistic for marketers to consider is GNP or GDP per capita where the national wealth is simply divided by the total population as if that were ever to be achieved. The arithmetic mean of national wealth so derived is not the monetary amount that citizens have in terms of disposable income and so, as with any smoothing device that is employed, it is impossible to predict the high and low points of the spectrum and so enable market segmentation strategies to be implemented. This is just another entertainment devised by idle economists.

Exhibit 6.3   McCurrencies: where's the beef?

How seriously should you take the Big Mac index?

Ten years on, *The Economist*'s Big Mac index is still going strong. Mad-cow disease notwithstanding, it is time to dish up our annual feast of burgernomics. The Big Mac index was devised as a light-hearted guide to whether currencies are at their 'correct' level. It is not intended to be a predictor of exchange-rates, but a tool to make economic theory more digestible.

Burgernomics is based upon the theory of purchasing-power parity (PPP). This argues that, in the long run, the exchange rate between two currencies should move towards the rate that would equalise the prices of an identical basket of goods and services in the two countries. Our basket is a McDonald's Big Mac, which is made to roughly the same recipe in more than 80 countries. The Big

Mac PPP is the exchange rate that would make a burger cost the same in America as it does abroad. Comparing this with the actual rate is one test of whether a currency is under-valued or overvalued.

The first column of the table shows the local-currency prices of a Big Mac; the second converts them into dollars. The average price in America (including sales tax) is $2.36. However, bargain hunters should head for China, where a burger costs only $1.15. At the other extreme, the Swiss price of $4.80 is enough to make Big Mac fans choke on their all-beef patties. This implies that the yuan is once again the most undervalued currency, and the Swiss franc the most overvalued.

The third column shows Big Mac PPPs. For example, if you divide the Japanese price of a *Biggu Makku* by the American one, you get a dollar PPP of ¥122. The actual rate on April 22nd was ¥107, implying that the yen was 14 per cent overvalued

→ Exhibit 6.3 *continued*

against the dollar. Similar sums show that the D-mark is overvalued by 37 per cent. In general, the dollar is undervalued against the currencies of most big industrial economies, but overvalued against developing countries' ones.

Thanks partly to the dollar's recovery, the example of this is Japan, where the price of a Big Mac was slashed by more than a quarter late last year. This reduced the yen's over-valuation from 100 per cent to 14 per cent.

The Big Mac index was originally introduced as a bit of fun. Yet it has inspired several serious

The hamburger standard

| | Big Mac prices | | Implied PPP* of the dollar | Actual $ exchange rate 22/4/96 | Local currency under(−)/over(+) valuation, † % |
	In local currency	In dollars			
United States‡	$2.36	2.36	−	−	−
Argentina	Peso3.00	3.00	1.27	1.00	+27
Australia	A$2.50	1.97	1.06	1.27	−17
Austria	Sch36.00	3.40	15.3	10.7	+43
Belgium	BFr109	3.50	46.2	31.2	+48
Brazil	Real2.95	2.98	1.25	0.99	+26
Britain	£1.79	2.70	1.32††	1.5††	+14
Canada	C$2.86	2.10	1.21	1.36	−11
Chile	Peso950	2.33	403	408	−1
China	Yuan9.60	1.15	4.07	8.35	−51
Czech Republic	Ckr51.0	1.85	21.6	27.6	−22
Denmark	DKr25.75	4.40	10.9	5.85	+87
France	FFr17.5	3.41	7.42	5.13	+46
Germany	DM4.90	3.22	2.08	1.52	+37
Hong Kong	HK$9.90	1.28	4.19	7.74	−46
Hungary	Forint214	1.43	90.7	150	−39
Israel	Shekel9.50	3.00	4.03	3.17	+27
Italy	Lira4,500	2.90	1,907	1,551	+23
Japan	¥288	2.70	122	107	+14
Malaysia	M$3.76	1.51	1.59	2.49	−36
Mexico	Peso14.9	2.02	6.31	7.37	−14
Netherlands	Fl5.45	3.21	2.31	1.70	+36
New Zealand	NZ$2.95	2.01	1.25	1.47	−15
Poland	Zloty3.80	1.44	1.61	2.64	−36
Russia	Rouble9,500	1.93	4,025	4,918	−18
Singapore	S$3.05	2.16	1.29	1.41	−8
South Africa	Rand7.00	1.64	2.97	4.26	−30
South Korea	Won2,300	2.95	975	779	+25
Spain	Pta365	2.89	155	126	+23
Sweden	Skr26.0	3.87	11.0	6.71	+64
Switzerland	SFr5.90	4.80	2.50	1.23	+103
Taiwan	NT$65.0	2.39	27.5	27.2	+1
Thailand	Baht48.0	1.90	20.3	25.3	−20

* Purchasing-power parity: local price divided by price in the United States † Against dollar
‡ Average of New York, Chicago, San Francisco and Atlanta †† Dollars per pound

Source: McDonald's

other rich-country currencies look less over-valued than a year ago. Adjustment to PPP can also come from changes in relative prices rather than exchange-rate movements. The most dramatic studies over the past year. Li Lian Ong, an economist at the University of Western Australia, wrote her PhD thesis on the index.* She concludes that 'the Big Mac index is surprisingly accurate in

→ Exhibit 6.3 *continued*

tracking exchange rates over the longer term.' Another study, by Robert Cumby of Georgetown University in Washington, DC, also found that deviations from 'McParity' are usually temporary.**

But a third study, by Michael Pakko and Patricia Pollard of the Federal Reserve Bank of St Louis, is more sceptical.† It concludes that 'the Big Mac does as well – or as poorly – at demonstrating the principles and pitfalls of PPP as more sophisticated measures.'

Their study concludes that although Big Mac PPP may hold in the very long run, currencies can deviate from it for lengthy periods. There are several reasons why the Big Mac index may be flawed:

- The theory of PPP falsely assumes that there are no barriers to trade. High prices in Europe, Japan and South Korea partly reflect high tariffs on beef. Differences in transport costs also act as a trade barrier: shipping perishable ingredients such as lettuce and beef is dear.
- Prices are distorted by taxes. High rates of value-added tax in countries such as Denmark and Sweden exaggerate the degree to which their currencies are overvalued.

- The Big Mac is not just a basket of commodities: its price must cover rents and the cost of other non-traded inputs. Deviations of PPP may simply reflect differences in such costs.
- Profit margins vary among countries according to the strength of competition. In the United States, the Big Mac has many close substitutes, but in other countries McDonald's is able to charge a premium.

Despite these weaknesses, which *The Economist* has long acknowledged, the Big Mac index still comes up with PPP estimates that are similar to those based on more sophisticated methods. Burgernomics has its methodological flaws, but our money is where our mouths are.

* 'Burgernomics: The Economics of the Big Mac Standard'. University of Western Australia, November 1995.
** 'Forecasting Exchange Rates and Relative Prices With the Hamburger Standard: Is What You Want What You Get With McParity?'. Georgetown University, July 1995.
† 'For Here or To Go? Purchasing Power Parity and the Big Mac'. Federal Reserve Bank of St Louis, January 1996.

Source: The Big Mac Index, *The Economist*, 27 April 1996, p. 110

Parallel or grey exporting

This topic is discussed also in Chapter 7, as this phenomenon owes its existence to distribution channels and imperfections in the market mechanism which therefore present opportunities for low-cost distribution. While simply an irritation to manufacturers and to their legitimate distribution channel members overseas, it is not an illegal activity and is often supported by government and the like as an expression of the free market and of free trade in action. It is becoming increasingly common, perhaps as a result of this tacit support.

Parallel exporting is an activity undertaken by intermediaries in the distribution channel who often find unofficial export sales more lucrative than selling on the domestic market. By taking advantage of retail price maintenance and currency differentials, these exporters – often wholesalers or retailers – are able to earn returns many times what could be gained by simply

Exhibit 6.4   Coke imports flunk test in Hong Kong

Hong Kong. Along with untaxed cigarettes and illegal immigrants, shadowy importers are bringing into Hong Kong unauthorized cans of 'the real thing' – Coca-Cola.

The wholesale price of locally canned Coke is pegged at $77 Hong Kong ($13.50) for a 24-can carton in this British colony where salaries and the cost of property and many other goods are high, the South China Morning Post said yesterday.

Imports from Canada, Singapore and even Jordan costing as little as $10.50 a carton are showing up at noodle bars and small retailers, eating into the profits of the local agent, the newspaper said.

The imports are just as much 'the real thing' as the local product and all come in Coke's distinctive red and white cans, although some are different sizes and the Arabic writing on the Jordanian cans stand out.

But the Post said its taste test showed the local brew was more 'real' than the others, with 60 per cent saying it was fresher, sharper and had a stronger taste.

A Coca-Cola Co. spokeswoman said the problem of outside importation occurs from time to time but the amounts involved are very small.

Source: Globe and Mail, 11 August 1995

selling in the domestic market. What they are doing is not illegal but unofficial and without the prior consent of the manufacturer or producer concerned, they undercut the manufacturer's official prices in the entry market concerned, thus affecting his profitability and his established channel of distribution, and perhaps also consequently bringing his brand into disrepute.

Electrical equipment, for example, has to be constructed to different standards across Western Europe; pharmaceutical preparations may also be slightly different for different national markets, but such differences are often glossed over in the search for large price differentials and quick profit. This is not marketing that is being practised, it is scanning for short-term market opportunity. Pharmaceutical price differences have already been signalled out by Cecchini in his report on the costs to the European Community of not having the standardization measures being adopted as 'Europe 1992'. While Portugal, Spain, France and Greece are relatively cheap, Benelux, Scandinavia, the UK and Germany are more expensive. The UK is the major consumer

of re-imports of pharmaceuticals in Europe, estimates going as high as 10 per cent of UK drug sales being re-imports or in this sense 'grey'. No European country has a free market in pharmaceuticals nor is there as yet a single European approvals board. Companies still prefer to pursue multiple applications in several countries than wait to see whether in fact the concept of reciprocity works in practice. Delays can cost many months of lost sales to a rival that will never be made up. Equally, the politics of the situation, where one European Community country is expected to recognize the standards of another has not been fully put to the test as yet. Meanwhile, this practice of grey imports continues. An example of this is Zantac, produced by Glaxo of the UK and held to be the world's best selling drug. It is exported to Greece, then bought by the UK wholesalers in Greece and re-imported to the UK, where wholesalers, licensed by the UK Government, are alleged to relabel the packaging (*Financial Times*, 1989). Even more ludicrous is to consider that the sole buyer in the UK for prescription drugs is the UK Government itself.

Exhibit 6.5   Raids on Mercedes and Opel

European competition authorities have raided offices of Mercedes-Benz and General Motors' Opel subsidiary in an investigation into complaints that some of their dealers refused to sell cars to cross-border bargain hunters.

The European Commission has received complaints from European Union consumers trying to exploit the often large differences in car prices across the union. They said dealers told them they could not buy cars outside their home countries.

Last year Commission officials raided German carmaker Volkswagen and its subsidiary Audi in a similar investigation into allegations that dealers were under pressure not to sell cars to nonnationals. The news came as the Brussels executive published its latest six-monthly report on EU car prices, showing that price differences are widening, rather than closing.

For 40 out of 75 models monitored, the difference between the highest and lowest prices of the same car within the EU exceeded 20 per cent. The biggest price differences were on Fiat, Ford, Opel, Citroën, VW, Nissan and Mitsubishi models.

For some models, such as the Opel Astra/Kadett, the difference was almost 33 per cent.

Although value added tax rates and currency fluctuations contribute to the price gaps, the Commission said the gaps suggested manufacturers were continuing to follow different pricing policies according to the country. Price differ-

ences had been predicted to narrow progressively after the creation of the European single market.

Of the 75 models, 23 were cheapest in the Netherlands and 21 in Portugal. Germany had the highest prices for 17 models, the UK for 15 and France for 13.

'Customers still encounter obstacles in certain member states,' the Commission said, citing Germany, Belgium, Spain and the Netherlands.

The raids on Mercedes are understood to relate to sales in all four countries, but those on Opel only to the Netherlands.

If a manufacturer is found to have violated EU competition rules – which say consumers must be free to buy similar products anywhere within the single market – it could be stripped of its anti-trust exemptions. That would stop a carmaker signing exclusive or restricted distribution arrangements with dealers.

The Mercedes and Opel inquiries are at an early stage, but the Commission wrote to VW and Audi in November giving them two months to provide detailed information on their dealership arrangements, particularly in Italy.

Austrian car buyers had complained they were unable to buy VW or Audi cars in Italy, where they are cheaper.

VW and Audi are expected to have a hearing with the Commission in April.

Source: Financial Times, 15 February 1997, p. 18

Table 6.1 Reactive strategies to combat grey market activity

Type of strategy	Implemented by	Cost of implementation	Difficulty of implementation	Does it curtail grey market activity at source?	Does it provide immediate relief to authorized dealers?	Long-term effectiveness	Legal risks to manufacturer or dealers	Company examples
Strategic confrontation	Dealer with manufacturer support	Moderate	Requires planning	No	Relief in the medium term	Effective	Low risk	Creative merchandising by Caterpillar and auto dealers
Participation	Dealer	Low	Not difficult	No	Immediate relief	Potentially damaging reputation of manufacturer	Low risk	Dealers wishing to remain anonymous
Price cutting	Jointly by manufacturer and dealer	Costly	Not difficult	No, if price cutting is temporary	Immediate relief	Effective	Moderate to high risk	Dealers and manufacturers remain anonymous
Supply interference	Either party can engage	Moderate at the wholesale level; high at the retail level	Moderately difficult	No	Immediate relief or slightly delayed	Somewhat effective if at wholesale level; not effective at retail level	Moderate risk at wholesale level; low risk at retail	IBM, Hewlett-Packard, Lotus Corp, Swatch Watch USA, Charles of the Ritz Group Ltd, Leitz, Inc., NEC Electronics
Promotion of grey market product limitations	Jointly, with manufacturer leadership	Moderate	Not difficult	No	Slightly delayed relief	Somewhat effective	Low risk	Komatsu, Seiko, Rolex, Mercedes-Benz, IBM
Collaboration	Dealer	Low	Requires careful negotiations	No	Immediate relief	Somewhat effective	Very high risk	Dealers wishing to remain anonymous
Acquisition	Dealer	Very costly	Difficult	No	Immediate relief	Effective if other grey brokers don't creep up	Moderate to high risk	No publicized cases

Note: Company strategies include, but are not limited to, those mentioned here.

Source: Cavusgil, S. T., and Sikora, E. (1988) How multinationals can counter gray market imports, *Columbia Journal of World Business*, Winter, 75,85.

Table 6.2 Proactive strategies to combat grey market activity

Type of strategy	Implemented by	Cost of implementation	Difficulty of implementation	Does it curtail grey market activity at source?	Does it provide immediate relief to authorized dealers?	Long-term effectiveness	Legal risks to manufacturer or dealers	Company examples
Product/service differentiation and availability	Jointly, with manufacturer leadership	Moderate to high	Not difficult	Yes	No; impact felt in medium to long term	Very effective	Very low risk	General Motors, Ford, Porsche, Kodak
Strategic pricing	Manufacturer	Moderate to high	Complex; impact on overall profitability needs monitoring	Yes	Slightly delayed	Very effective	Low risk	Porsche
Dealer development	Jointly, with manufacturer leadership	Moderate to high	Not difficult; requires close dealer participation	No	No; impact felt in the long term	Very effective	No risk	Caterpillar, Canon
Marketing information systems	Jointly, with manufacturer leadership	Moderate to high	Not difficult; requires dealer participation	No	No; impact felt after implementation	Effective	No risk	IBM, Caterpillar, Yamaha, Hitachi, Komatsu, Lotus Development, insurance companies
Long-term image reinforcement	Jointly	Moderate	Not difficult	No	No; impact felt in the long term	Effective	No risk	Most manufacturers with strong dealer networks
Establishing legal precedence	Manufacturer	High	Difficult	Yes, if fruitful	No	Uncertain	Low risk	COPIAT, Coleco, Charles of the Ritz Group, Ltd.
Lobbying	Jointly	Moderate	Difficult	Yes, if fruitful	No	Uncertain	Low risk	COPIAT, Duracell, Porsche

Note: Company strategies include, but are not limited to, those mentioned here.

Source: Cavusgil, S. T., and Sikora, E. (1988) How multinationals can counter gray market imports. *Columbia Journal of World Business,* Winter, 75.85.

As a strategy, parallel exporting is similar to encyclopaedia selling in that it forever requires a large pool of customers to be replenished as there are all kinds of barriers to repeat business. Those who sell in this way lack the resources of the original producer which they undermine. Product guarantees may, therefore, be suspect, and reliability of subsequent deliveries doubtful being dependent on the continuation of a price differential which in turn is subject to continued product availability on the domestic market at the same terms as before, plus the good fortune that currency devaluations do not take place to a degree that eliminates this differential.

Cavusgil and Sikora (1988) in Tables 6.1 and 6.2 chart out the proactive and reactive strategies that a company can adopt to counteract grey market channels. This is now becoming a critical management issue, since both the European Commission and the US Supreme Court (in 1988) have ruled on the legality of grey market imports.

Exhibit 6.6   EU fines P&O £315,000 for price fixing

The P&O shipping group was yesterday fined around £315,000 (400,000 Ecus) by the European Commission, which also imposed fines on four other ferry companies for operating a price cartel on cross-channel freight shipments in 1992.

The other companies named are Stena-Sealink, Brittany Ferries, Sea France and North Sea Ferries. P&O received the largest penalty followed by Stena-Sealink (£79,000). Total fines imposed amounted to around £500,000.

P&O, which also announced third-quarter progress yesterday, and Stena-Sealink were described as 'the main instigators of the practice', initiating and organising the joint action, said the Commission.

The fines imposed on Brittany Ferries and Sea France (around £47,000 each) and the £20,000 on North Sea Ferries reflected their 'minor role' in the affair.

P&O, which yesterday revealed that its third quarter showed that European ferry rates were still under pressure despite a smaller percentage drop in volumes than seen earlier this year, said that the Commission's decision to fine it more than any other ferry company reflected the size of its freight business.

The group's statistics showed that the company's container traffic division also faced 'a tough competitive environment with strong downward pressure on rates, particularly in the Far East to Europe trade'. This has led to a fall back in revenues.

The European ferries business saw third-quarter passenger, tourist vehicle and freight carryings down 6.8 per cent, 9.6 per cent and 3.6 per cent respectively on a year ago.

Tough competition from the Channel Tunnel led to P&O and Stena Line announcing a merger of their businesses on the cross channel ferry market on October 3 under a new joint venture.

The group's cruises operations were more upbeat, with higher yields than last year and a good outlook for the remainder of the year and the start of 1997. In Princes cruises, third-quarter capacity rose 17 per cent on 1995 helped by the introduction of a new liner in December last year.

Source: Glasgow Herald, 31 October 1996

Exhibit 6.7   You can seal that contract with a handshake, but the pen is better

There is a popular misconception that a legally binding contract only comes into existence once it has been confirmed in writing. Although most commercial agreements tend to be confirmed in writing, primarily in the interests of commercial certainty, other forms of contracting, such as oral contracts sealed by a handshake, may also be enforceable in certain situations.

In general, oral contracts are enforceable unless Polish law requires that the particular type of contract be confirmed in writing. The principal (but not the only) reason for requiring that certain commercial arrangements be in writing is to pro-vide greater certainty as to the terms on which the parties agreed.

For example, contracts for the purchase of real estate must be concluded in the form of a notarial deed in order for legally binding rights to be created. An oral agreement for the sale of real estate will be invalid and will not impose any enforceable obligations or duties upon the parties, nor will it operate to transfer ownership. Not surprisingly, there are analogous provisions in most countries.

In some cases it is necessary for evidentiary purposes to have written confirmation of the

→ **Exhibit 6.7** *continued*

parties' agreement. Where Polish law prescribes that a contract must be evidenced in writing, without stipulating that the contract will otherwise be void, the contract will only be enforceable to the extent that the parties concur on what was actually agreed. It may therefore be difficult to enforce the contract where there is disagreement as to its terms, since the evidence of witnesses and the parties to the effect that it was executed, will not always be admissible. For such purposes, where the value of the contract exceeds zł. 2,000 ($740), the terms of the parties' agreement should be confirmed in writing.

For purposes of zł. 2,000 test, if a contract confers a right to periodic performance (for example, a lease), the value for the contract during each year (or where the contract is for less than one year, the entire period) will be taken into account.

By way of example, we take the case of an oral agreement for the lease of an apartment for an indefinite period where the annual rent is more than zł. 2,000. The agreement will be valid, but the evidentiary problems mentioned above could arise in the event of a dispute.

In other cases, the law may insist on contracts being in writing in order to give effect to particular provisions of the contract. As an example, a contract for the lease of premises should be concluded in writing if it is intended to be for a fixed period exceeding one year.

If the contract is not in writing, the lease will be valid and enforceable, but it will be deemed that the lease was concluded for an indefinite period of time.

Despite these legal and evidentiary requirements for written contracts, there are many situations in which oral contracts can be binding. Generally, however, these are contracts whose value does not exceed zł. 2,000 and where there are no additional formal requirements.

Typical everyday examples of enforceable oral contracts include contracts for the sale of food and household goods at the grocery store (situations where we do not necessarily stop to consider whether a contract has been created).

In addition to the general requirements, which arise from Polish civil law, on the form of a contract, other legal criteria may have an effect on the manner of contracting, for example, consumer protection requirements or tax regimes. In the case of sales of consumer goods, for example, the seller must (upon the customer's request) confirm each sale in writing in order to safeguard the customer's statutory consumer rights, such as to sue the seller if the product is defective.

It is now a requirement of the tax regime that certain transactions are confirmed in writing for the purposes of making VAT returns, through invoices or receipts. Similarly, where a transaction is subject to stamp duty, it must be reduced to writing even if it was executed orally.

In cases where there is no strict requirement of a written contract, there may, in any event, be compelling administrative reasons to confirm contracts in writing. If, for example, you purchase a car from your uncle, you will want to have at least some written evidence of the transfer in ownership for the purposes of registering the vehicle in your name.

Thus, Polish law recognizes as binding, many oral contacts that are concluded every day. But in an age, where information technology makes more rigorous organizational demands on the way in which we conduct our everyday business, however mundane, it is likely that all but the most basic transactions will now be recorded in a physical form to a greater or lesser extent. In the commercial world at least, the days of the gentlemen's agreement concluded by a handshake (whether enforceable or not) has almost certainly been superseded by the demands of the information age, if not the law itself.

Source: Warsaw Business Journal, 2–8 September 1996, p. 11

Export market overheads

Overheads arise with the sale of goods to their final destination, the consumer. In international marketing, there are the costs of freight and of distribution if the goods are simply to be exported but remain competitive on the foreign markets; and, the problems of critical mass and economies of scale if the products are to be produced locally in that foreign market. The decision between exporting abroad and producing locally is often made more difficult by the frequent imposition by local governments of tariff and non-tariff barriers including 'countervailing duties', which seek to ensure that foreign goods will not undercut local manufacturers in price, this price differential now being replaced with the imposition of additional taxation to make its price similar to the nearest domestic competitor.

The cost of market entry and representation is an overhead, as is any required product modification or any modification to advertising and promotion, where modification is primarily for one market and cannot easily be replicated in whole or in part elsewhere. More will be said of

Table 6.3   Short guide to export credit terms

Berne Union (International Union of Credit and Investment Insurers.)

This is an association of thirty-six export credit insurance agencies founded in 1934.

It works for sound principles of credit insurance and maintenance of credit insurance discipline in international trade.

Buyer credit

A financial arrangement under which a bank or export credit agency in the exporting country extends a loan directly to a foreign buyer or to a bank in the importing country.

Consensus Arrangement (The Arrangement on Guidelines for Officially Supported Export Credits)

The arrangement, which first came into force in 1978, is adhered to by twenty-two member countries on the Paris-based Organization for Economic Co-operation and Development (OECD).

It aims at limiting competitive subsidization of export financing. The arrangement sets minimum allowable interest rates and maximum repayment terms for officially financed or subsidized export credits of at least two years duration.

Mixed credits

Arrangements which cunningly bundle export credits with aid funds. The French are past masters at this art; the Americans are not amused. The Consensus Arrangement discourages their use.

Paris Club

The forum in which creditor countries meet with the debtor country to consider a request for rescheduling of payments on official debts. Terms hammered out in such meetings are embodied in an Agreed Minute, and then recommended to the governments concerned.

The club has no fixed membership and no institutional structure. It is open to all official creditors who accept its practices and procedures.

Short-term commitments

Export credit undertakings on which the credit terms do not normally exceed six months. In some cases the term may be as long as two years.

Supplier credit

A financing arrangement under which the supplier (exporter) extends credit to the buyer in the importing country.

Source: Export credit agencies seek new strategies, *Euromoney* (1989), February, 5–8

this in later chapters. Bear in mind, though, that the exchange that is being effected between buyer and seller may often also require the use of an intermediary – whether an agent, distributor or even countertrade specialist – who has been engaged to realize cash from the manufacturer's or buyer's goods. Also, the terms agreed between buyer and seller may subsequently change the entire profitability of a contract if there is a dramatic rise or fall in currency exchange rates, world commodity prices, or imposition of any governmental action leading to 'force majeure' and the inability to complete a contract.

For the moment, then, we assume that the product being exported is one which is known to the domestic market. The company may then reduce the product price to the actual costs of production plus an overhead contribution, i.e., it is assumed that research and development originally invested in the product is now a sunk cost, which has already been recovered from domestic market sales. Theoretically, the seller may price lower for this product. If he does, however, he is guilty of dumping as he is no

longer selling in foreign markets at a price comparable to that in his own domestic market. If existing domestic demand is sluggish, this strategy of dumping may prove beneficial. Firstly, it does not damage his share of the domestic market. Secondly, the lower prices abroad are usually acceptable on a short-term basis and are preferable to the much longer term damage which would result from offering similar product discounts on the domestic market. Once the precedent of offering domestic price discounts has been established, it is difficult to break. As a strategy, dumping may, therefore, protect the domestic price structure. Elsewhere, dumping may be predatory, as when an exporting manufacturer working with factor costs much lower than his local foreign market competitors, offers a low price in the foreign market with the intention of buying market share. Persistent dumping of this kind will lead to a restructuring of market supply as it will force many companies out of business, at which point the dumping company may then revert back to price levels closer to pre-existing market levels.

Dumping and anti-dumping measures have become issues of increasing concern to the world trading system, and the complexity of dumping within a global economy is seen from the six topics of an international symposium in Tokyo in 1989 concerning the need for reform in the GATT Anti-dumping Code (Matsumoto, Finlayson, 1990):

1. Symmetry in the comparison of normal value and export price.
2. Calculation of constructed value.
3. Sale prices below the cost of production.
4. Like products.
5. The definition and treatment of related parties.
6. Anti-circumvention measures.

The EU have outlined a new calculation formula which attempts to bring more fairness into dumping calculations. When export sales are made to distributors (whether related or not), only sales to unrelated domestic distributors should be used as a basis of normal values. Domestic prices to other categories of customers (dealers, end-users, etc.) should be omitted from calculations. In EU terminology, this new method is called 'selective normal value'. It means that export prices to distributors are now compared against domestic prices to distributors. Exclusion from the average normal value of usually high sales prices to other domestic clients, e.g., dealers, retailers, end-users, yields a lower normal value, thus, a lower dumping margin. However, where there are no, or not enough, domestic sales to unrelated distributors (e.g., when goods are sold by the manufacturer/exporter to a related distributor), the normal value is still calculated, as in the past by averaging all domestic sales prices on the open market, including those charged by a related distributor to unrelated customers. The EU imposes certain conditions for accepting to calculate normal values in a selective way. Respondents have to prove that their domestic unrelated distributors have functions clearly distinct from those of other categories of un-

related customers, such as dealers. Only if these conditions are met will selective normal values be admitted by the EU.

Export quotation terms

Trade results from the negotiations between a potential exporter and an importer. Either side will wish to maximize its return. Given an otherwise acceptable product, the first problem is currency. The exporting firm way wish to quote in its own domestic currency, particularly if it is inexperienced or it is a small firm uninterested in currency speculation and buying on forward currency markets. In any event, exporters will studiously seek to avoid inconvertible currencies and those experiencing now, or in the past, rapid depreciation and/or high inflation rates. The problem is lessened to some degree in that anticipated foreign currency earnings can often be sold on the forward market at a premium (depending on the currency).

The exporter will seek an export quotation which will lessen his responsibility or terminate it at the earliest opportunity. This can be one through a form of contract known as FCA, which means free carrier i.e main carriage on the shipment is unpaid or 'EXW' which means 'ex works'. On this contractual basis, it is the foreign client's duty to collect the goods from the manufacturer and arrange shipment himself. The exporter's responsibility is probably less here than that of a domestic sale. Importers prefer a delivered price such as DDP (delivered duty paid) or CIP (carriage and insurance paid). These mean that the responsibilities of the importer begin only when the goods are in his own country. Importers prefer these means because they provide an instant price comparison between competing foreign exporters and local suppliers. (See Chapter 7 for a discussion on the new Incoterms.) Note, too, that this issue of when ownership is transferred is still unclear. With the transfer of ownership there is also the transfer of responsibility for the shipment in question.

Exhibit 6.8   A widespread confusion

Candidates in a recent Institute examination were asked if there is any way in which a company trading internationally can minimise the effect of the spread in foreign exchange transactions. Their answers, surprisingly, showed a marked ignorance of what is meant by the term, the circumstances in which it is likely to be an important factor for consideration by credit controllers or finance directors and the effects it may have on profitability.

The spread is the difference between the rate of exchange applied when a customer is selling currency to the bank and that applied when he is buying the same currency from them. Thus in foreign exchange quotations appearing in our morning newspapers we may read that, on the previous day, US dollars were quoted on the London Foreign Exchange Market at 1.5710–1.5718 spot.

This indicates the banks were requiring exporters to deliver \$1.5718 in order to receive £1 but would only provide \$1.5710 to importers

---

→ Exhibit 6.8 *continued*

for each £1 paid by them. The spread on that day was therefore 0.08 of a cent, a seemingly small amount but sufficient to yield the bank a satisfactory profit on its total deals. The spread represents the bank's remuneration for dealing.

If a company is solely an exporter, it has only academic interest in spread. It is always a seller of currency to the bank when invoices are in currency other than sterling.

Many candidates confused exchange risk with spread when answering the question. Exchange risk, of course, represents the danger to an exporter, selling in say US dollars, that the dollar-sterling exchange rate will be less favourable when proceeds of an export are received than it was at the date the contract for the sale of goods was entered into.

The result is a loss unless, as so many candidates pointed out, a forward exchange contract is taken out protecting the exporter. Prudent though this course may be, it has no relevance to spread.

If we look at the forward rate for one month US dollars in the same newspaper we shall see it quoted as, say, 0.085–0.065 centre premium, reflecting a spread in exactly the same way as in spot rates.

When then, if many exporters are not concerned with spread, is the question of minimising its effect worthy of consideration?

The answer lies in its significance for two categories of exporter. The first comprises companies which seek to satisfy their customers' demands for a complete range of products from which to make their choice by importing goods complementary to their own and, in turn, export their manufactures to companies in other countries who are wrestling with a similar problem in their home markets. Secondly, many exporters will import raw materials or components which are incorporated into their own product.

In both instances this can create receipts and payments in the same non-sterling currency. Add to this situation a sustained business with frequent transactions, both buying and selling the currency against sterling, and it is not difficult to

appreciate that the spread between the rates can be a major factor in reducing profitability.

What can be done to ease the problem?

Many companies in this position endeavour to keep to an absolute minimum the number of foreign exchange deals against sterling. It may be possible, through maintaining an account in the currency in question either with the exporter's UK bank or one in the country whose currency is involved, to credit export receipts and debit payments to suppliers, merely selling the surplus periodically for sterling.

Should circumstances justify running such an account in deficit, then periodic purchases against sterling may be made as necessary. In either event, the occasional exchange transaction involved will replace the series of deals, both sales and purchases, each one of which incurs spread.

In some cases where deficits are envisaged on a temporary basis only, due to time mismatches between imports and exports, it is normally practicable to seek overdraft or loan facilities on the currency account. Naturally, in making its decision on the cost effectiveness of maintaining a currency account, a company will weigh the costs of the account, including any interest differential in comparison with a sterling account, against the saving on spread.

There may also be other benefits in holding a currency account. For example, bank charges on frequent and, particularly, low value remittances can be disproportionately high due to 'minimum' charges. Each case must be judged on its merits.

It may be wise for an exporting company invoicing its customers in a non-sterling currency to ascertain if raw materials, components and complementary products imported can be invoiced in the same currency. This may significantly influence the decision as to whether or not a currency account is desirable and it will also make the calculation of profit margins easier and more exact.

Source: Export Today

When the supplier company is faced with a cash-flow crisis, money owing to them constitutes collateral and may be sold, i.e., factoring or else discounted or forfaited – not for the full value, but at a discounted value, of which more will be said later. Risk may be covered by national export credit insurance schemes which cover governmental lines of credit, plus commercial

and industrial projects and exports worldwide for a fee based either on the company's global insurance business as in the case of the ECGD or on the risks inherent in the market concerned. The insurance terms for a market will be influenced by perceived exposure to risk in that market; or changed economic market conditions which affect the local market's ability to repay;

Exhibit 6.9   WTO forecasts Internet trade to hit $300 billion by 2000

Big changes likely for financial services

The Internet will open new vistas for trade in goods and services – particularly financial services – possibly revolutionising it within a short span of time, says the Geneva based World Trade Organisation (WTO).

It estimates that the value of goods and services traded via the Internet would grow 20 times to US$200 billion (S$300 billion) between last year and the year 2000.

Similarly, the Internet will also have a profound effect on the financial services industry, though it has no estimates, the global trade watchdog says in a new study.

An advance copy of the study, 'Open Markets in Financial Services and the Role of the GATS', was obtained by The Straits Times.

It is the first of a WTO series of studies on topical issues. GATS stands for the General Agreement on Trade in Services.

The Internet was likely to transform dramatically the way business was conducted in many areas, including financial services, said WTO.

'The Internet cuts transaction costs, provides new channels for commercial transactions and lowers barriers to entry for smaller, geographically remote competitors. Businesses have a direct link to consumers worldwide, who can order practically anything, from airline tickets to cars, without leaving their homes,' the study noted.

For the financial services industry, the Internet's global reach means that banking, insurance and brokerage services can be bought from anywhere in the world.

'In fact, the Internet is likely to boost strongly international trade in financial services at the retail level – an area which has so far been little affected by globalisation,' says the WTO.

The cost of an average payment transaction on the Internet, for example, is as low as one US cent, compared with 27 US cents for an automatic teller machine (ATM), 54 US cents for a telephone banking service and US$1.07 for a transaction conducted via a traditional bank branch, the study points out.

A growing number of banks have, therefore, started offering banking services via the Internet, such as online payments and checking account statements.

WTO said recent studies suggested that more than 1,200 banks were already maintaining a 'Web' presence, and 60 per cent of the banks in the OECD countries will offer Internet transactions by the year 1999.

The 29-member Paris-based OECD, which stands for the Organisation for Economic Cooperation and Development, groups the world's economically most advanced nations.

Brokerage firms are offering online securities trading as well as access to real-time market data and sophisticated investment management tools, the study noted.

In the United States alone, there were some 1.5 million online stockbroker accounts, and this figure is growing by 50 to 150 per cent every year, said the WTO.

'Despite its great potential, the future of financial services trade on the Internet will depend largely on the ability to ensure the security of online transactions and information.

'Sophisticated encryption systems, plus the use of digital certificates that verify the parties to a transaction, will play an important role in establishing the security of online transactions,' it added.

WTO noted that there had been calls for multilateral rules towards establishing a free trade zone on the Internet. Discussions on a framework for governing Internet transactions feature customs and taxation issues, electronic payments methods, commercial code-related issues, intellectual property protection, privacy and security, it added.

Source: The Straits Times, 22 September 1997

Table 6.4   OECD consensus credit guidelines

Countries of destination		Maximum repayment terms
Category I:	Relatively rich	Five years; but after prior notification in accordance with paragraph 14 b) 1), eight and a half years
Category II:	Intermediate	Eight and a half years
Category III:	Relatively poor	Ten years

Source: OECD (1990) The Export Credit Financing Systems, 4th edn, Paris

Table 6.5 Volume of business supported by official export credits[1] (SDR Millions, credit value)				
Country	1982	1984	1987	1988
Volume of export credit repayment term over five years				
USA	2,008	1,542	772	548
Canada	1,489	903	455	478
France	4,465	4,321	1,544	4,131
Germany	2,035	745	789	868
Italy	630	513	233	1,359
Japan	3,112	728	669	382
UK	2,539	645	744	560
Seven Major Countries	16,278	9,397	5,206	8,326
All OECD Countries	18,792	10,783	6,304	9,414
All OECD (US $)	20,747	11,455	8,152	13,652

[1] Data reported to the OECD. SDRs were used for this table to minimize the effect of US dollar exchange-rate fluctuations.

Source: Letovsky, R. (1990) The export finance wars. *Columbia Journal of World Business*, Spring/Summer, 25–34

as well as by the export credit agency's total portfolio and exposure.

Foreign currency invoicing and financing

When a UK supplier sells abroad he can either price in sterling, in which case he will be sure of receiving the exact price requested, or else price in a foreign currency and bear an exchange risk. The exchange risk arises since national currencies continually fluctuate one against another and even when one country will devalue, this will not be uniform against all other countries. So currencies may weaken and find themselves devaluing against stronger currencies, or, they may appreciate relative to other currencies, or remain stable irrespective of currency movements elsewhere. Except in extreme cases, the more usual is for a few percentage points of difference although such differences may be crucially important in high-value industrial contracts. The solution for the foreign buyer is, therefore, to consider buying forward foreign exchange markets.

Foreign currency is sold either at the spot rate, which is the daily rate prevailing on the day of the requested exchange transaction, or 'forward' for any number of months ahead, usually three, six or nine. An exporter may wait until he receives payment for his goods and then convert it at the spot rate. However, production and delivery lags often mean a few months have

elapsed since the initial order was taken and, while it is possible for an exporter to speculate on future movement of foreign currencies, he is as liable to lose as to win. Much better to stipulate a fixed sum in an agreed currency and transfer the exchange problem to the buyer. Forward rates of exchange remove further uncertainty because the bank agrees to buy the exporter's foreign currency payment and change it into sterling when it falls due in six months' time. The important point to note here is that the rate of exchange is specified and known to the exporter when the forward contract is made. Accordingly, he can assure himself of his return plus perhaps benefit from a possible upturn in the value of the foreign currency relative to his own in the intervening six-month period. The forward rate will, therefore, specify a premium or discount over the spot rate, meaning that the financial markets expect that particular currency to appreciate or devalue over that given period.

The advantages of foreign currency invoicing include the following:

- The ability to invoice in international currencies such as the US dollar which may be more attractive to buyers in the country concerned.
- The buyer is relieved of exchange risk where the price quotation is given in his own currency.
- When sterling is at a discount on the forward exchange markets, an exporter can sell his expected foreign currency receipts forward

Table 6.6 Export credit agencies, relationship of government, and services offered

Country	Organization		Insurance	Loans
Australia	Export Finance and Insurance Corporation (EFIC) – a Division of the Australian Trade Commission	Division of a statutory authority	×	×
Austria	Oesterreichische Kontrollbank AG (OKB)	Statutory body reporting to the Ministry of Finance	×	×
Belgium	Office National du Ducroire (OND)	State guaranteed public agency	×	
	L'Association pour la Coordination du Financement a Moyen Terme des Exportations Belges (Creditexport)	Non-profit joint venture involving public and private sector institutions		×
Canada	Export Development Corporation (EDC)	Crown corporation wholly owned by the Government of Canada	×	×
Denmark	Eksportkreditradet (EKR)	Governmental council responsible to the Ministry of Industry	×	
	Dansk Eksportfinsieringsfond (DEFC)	Corporation owned jointly by the Central Bank of Denmark and various private sector banking associations		×
Finland	Export Guarantee Board (VTL)	Government agency reporting to the Ministry of Trade and Industry	×	
	Finnish Export Credit Ltd.	Joint stock company majority owned by the Republic of Finland, with minority holdings by private sector banks and firms		×
France	Compagnie Francaise d'Assurance pour le Commerce Exterieur (COFACE)	Semi-public joint stock company	×	
	Banque Francaise du Commerce Exterieur (BFCE)	Public institution		×
Germany	Hermes Kreditversicherungs AG/Treuarbiet AG	Private sector consortium operating for the account of the federal government	×	
	Kreitanstalt fur Wideraufbau (KfW)	Corporation majority owned by the federal government with minority ownership by various governments		×
Italy	Sezione Speciale per l'Assicurazione del Credito	Section of the National Insurance Institute, a statutory authority	×	

Country	Organization		Insurance	Loans
	all'Esportazione (SACE)			
	Mediocredito Centrale	Public financial institution supervised and financed by the Ministry of the Treasury		×
Japan	Export Insurance Division (EID) Ministry of International Trade & Industry	Division of a government ministry		
	Export-Import Bank of Japan	Government financial institution		×
Netherlands	Nederlandsche Credietverzekering Maatschappij N.V. (NCM)	Privately owned consortium, reinsuring political as well as medium- and long-term risks with the Dutch government	×	1
Sweden	Exportkreditnamden (EKN)	Official agency of the Swedish Government		
	AB Svensk Exportkredit (SEK)	Joint stock company majority owned by the Swedish government (50 per cent) and the private sector (50 per cent)	×	
UK	Export Credit Guarantee Dept. (ECGD)	Government department responsible to the Secretary of State for Trade and Industry	×	2
USA	Export-Import Bank of the United States (Eximbank)	Independent agency of the US government	3	×

Notes:
1. The Netherlands does not have a designated official institution for granting medium- or long-term export credits. However, the Central Bank of the Netherlands does have an arrangement with Dutch banks which permits the banks to offer such financing at below market rates.
2. The UK does not have a designated official institution for granting medium- or long-term export credits. However, ECGD does provide guarantees to commercial banks for buyer and supplier loans with terms of two or more years.
3. The Foreign Credit Insurance Association, a consortium of private insurance companies, acts as the exclusive agent of Eximbank for short- and medium-term coverage.

Source: Letovsky R., (1990) The export finance wars. *Columbia Journal of World Business*, Spring/Summer, 25–34

for more sterling than he would receive at currently prevailing spot rates. This may enable him to quote a more competitive price in foreign currency or may provide him with a higher profit than would otherwise be the case.

Another point is that it is increasingly common for finance to be provided in foreign currency. One way of minimizing exchange risk is to borrow the currency in which the contract is invoiced. Provided there is no default, this means that the debt outstanding will be covered. Financing in foreign currency may also allow the exporter to obtain cheaper supplies of finance credit, depending on relative interest rates. The UK Government has actively promoted the use of foreign currency financing to ease pressure on the international role of sterling, and the ECGD has had a ceiling on prospect finance, beyond which underwriting will only take place in a foreign currency. However, interest rates may lead the unwary into thinking that foreign loans are attractive, but if, for example, sterling swings sharply against the Deutschmark or French franc, repayment of loans in these currencies could prove to be particularly expensive when the buyer does not have any earnings in that currency.

Methods of payment

Many exporters still rely on overdrafts un-connected to the company's export business, but overdrafts are for short-term needs and must be repaid on demand. In the following pages we shall be discussing the use of credit and export finance with and without recourse to the exporter.

Payment in advance

Payment may be either cash with order (CWO) or cash on delivery (COD), but this has very limited application and is quite rare. It would kill a relationship before it started to ask for cash upfront so this may be requested only where the buyer is unknown or known to be unstable and there is little likelihood of further orders being requested and being paid for.

Open account

As this is based purely on trust, it offers the least security to the exporter, so should be limited to the most creditworthy customers, as well as sub-sidiaries and affiliates. Seventy per cent of UK exports are said to be paid for in this form, but this may be explained by the high degree of internationalization among UK firms who may, therefore, simply be transporting goods still within the company by exporting to subsidiaries and affiliates overseas on open account. It saves money and procedural difficulties, but increases risk. It is popular within the EU. Goods are sent to an overseas buyer who has agreed to pay within a certain period after the invoice date, usually not more than 180 days. Consignment Account is a variation of Open Account where the exporter retains ownership of the goods until they are sold.

Bills of exchange

A bill of exchange is defined as 'an unconditional order in writing, addressed by one person to another, signed by the person giving it, requiring the person to whom it is addressed to pay on demand or at a fixed or determinable future time, a certain sum in money to, or to the order of, a specified person, or the bearer'. The exporter draws a bill of exchange on an overseas buyer or third party as designated in the export contract for the sum agreed. When the customer signs it, it becomes 'accepted', and this means that the customer has accepted the terms and agreed to pay by the date designated in the document.

If the amount payable falls due on delivery of the goods, this is a sight bill, i.e., payable on receipt; otherwise the variation is a time bill which allows perhaps 30, 60 or 90 days before payment falls due. For exporters, a 'sight' bill would be preferred to a 'time' bill as it would delay payment once the goods had already been delivered.

Letter of credit

Worldwide, letters of credit are very important and very common, although less so in Britain and the rest of Europe. According to a rather dated SITPRO estimate, 20 per cent of British exports are undertaken by letters of credit. How-ever, letters of credit do not predominate in the countries of destination of the majority of British exports. Western Europe accounts for 56 per cent of British foreign trade; North America 15 per cent, and Australia 2 per cent. Thus, 78 per cent of British exports fall outside of this means of facilitating payment. A letter of credit (or docu-mentary credit) is a conditional undertaking by a bank regarding payment. It is a written under-standing by a bank (issuing bank) given to the seller (beneficiary) at the request and in accord-ance with the instructions of the buyer (appli-cant) to effect payment (that is, by making a payment, or by accepting or negotiating bills of exchange) up to a stated sum of money, within a prescribed time limit and against stipulated docu-ments. A letter of credit offers both parties to a transaction a degree of security combined with a possibility, for a creditworthy partner, of secur-ing financial assistance more easily.

The letter of credit is an undertaking by a bank and so the seller can look to the bank for payment instead of relying on the ability or will-ingness of the buyer to pay. It has three forms: revocable, irrevocable, and confirmed irrevoc-able. In its simple form, it is a conditional under-taking and so the seller must meet all his obligations. Only if all his obligations are met can he then demand payment. In its simple form, this is a *revocable credit* (now rare) which gives the buyer maximum flexibility as it can be amended or cancelled without prior notice to the seller up to moment of payment by the bank at which the issuing bank has made the credit available. An *irrevocable credit* is much less flex-ible and can only be amended or cancelled if all parties agree. A *confirmed irrevocable credit* means that a bank in the seller's country has added its own undertaking to that of the issuing bank, confirming that the necessary sum of money is available for payment awaiting only the present-ation of shipping documents. While it guaran-tees the seller his money, it is much more costly to the buyer. Generally, the buyer pays a fixed fee plus percentage of the value, but where the letter of credit is confirmed, the confirming bank will also charge a fee.

The different forms of a letter of credit, therefore, have the following characteristics:

- They are an arrangement by banks for settling international commercial transactions.
- They provide a form of security for the parties involved.
- They ensure payment, provided that the terms and conditions of the credit have been fulfilled.
- Payment by such means is based on documents only and not on merchandise or services involved.

However, it is worth pointing out that a Midland Bank International Division survey of 1,200 letters of credit showed that because of mistakes in documents and delays, in one in every two transactions the documents are rejected by the bank on first presentation. This means that payment is denied and that in turn may produce a cashflow crisis for the seller, having then to resort to borrowing at high interest rates to cover perhaps a short-term cash crisis. The Midland Bank report found a quarter of all transport and insurance documents to be flawed and one in seven invoices to be incorrect. Given the high levels of computerization and the standardization of exporting paperwork with the introduction of UN overlays, such statistics are really unforgivable.

Leasing

Exporters of capital equipment may use leasing in one of two ways:

1. To arrange cross-border leases directly from a bank or leasing company to the foreign buyer.
2. To obtain local leasing facilities either through overseas branches or subdivisions of UK banks or through international leasing associations.

The second is a more common arrangement. In both cases, it may also be possible to take advantage of ECGD facilities.

With leasing, the exporter receives prompt payment for goods directly from the leasing company and at the same time avoids any recourse. A leasing facility is best set up at the earliest opportunity, preferably when the exporter receives the order.

Bonding

This was very fashionable in the Middle East particularly in the 1980s. In the Middle East, contracts may be cash or short-term. Whereas this is an ideal situation for suppliers, it means that the buyer loses some of his leverage over his supplier as he cannot withhold payment as elsewhere where contracts are of a longer duration. In this situation, a bond or guarantee is a written instrument issued to an overseas buyer by an acceptable third party, either a bank or insurance company. It guarantees compliance by an exporter or contractor with his obligations, or the overseas buyer will be indemnified for a stated amount against the failure of the exporter/contractor to fulfil his obligations under the contract.

Bonds are of three types which may be either conditional or unconditional (known as 'on demand'). With a conditional bond, the onus is on the buyer to prove default by the exporter. 'On demand' bonds can be called for any reason at the sole discretion of the buyer, whether or not the exporter has fulfilled his contractual obligations. ECGD has a scheme designed to provide cover for the issue of all types of bonds for overseas contracts which are worth a quarter of a million pounds or more, and are on cash or near-cash terms. At the same time a recourse agreement is concluded with the contractor so that if he is held to be failing in his duties, ECGD may have recourse to him. The three types of bond, then, are:

1. *Tender or bid bond* which provides the buyer with an assurance that the party submitting the tender is making a responsible bid. If the contract is awarded to the bidder, the latter will comply with the conditions of the tender and enter into the contract. If he does not, the surety is liable to pay the costs incurred by the buyer in re-awarding the contract, subject to a limit of liability set by the amount of the bond. The amount may vary but generally represents between 2 and 5 per cent of the tender value.
2. *Performance bond* guarantees that the exporter will carry out the contract in accordance with its specifications and terms. The liability of the surety is limited to the total amount of the bond, which is generally 10 per cent of the contract price but can be as low as 5 per cent or as high as 100 per cent.
3. *Advance payment or repayment bond* – A buyer often requires a bond guaranteeing that if the contract is not complete, the surety will make good any loss suffered by the buyer as a result of making the advance payment.

Discounting and factoring

The factors are mainly owned by the large banks. They offer two services – invoice discounting and factoring. Invoice discounting is a means of financing whereby the exporter sells his invoices to the factor at a discount in return for up to 80 per cent of purchase price in advance. This service is most suited to exporters selling on open account with charges normally at a margin above usual bank borrowing rates. Payments are made by the customers to the exporter and customers are usually not aware of the invoice discounting facility with the factor. Bad debt losses are taken by the exporter.

The second service is that of factoring. The types of business likely to be acceptable for invoice discounters will be the same as for export factoring. The factor investigates the creditworthiness of customers and establishes credit limits. The exporter sells within the credit limits, and delivers to and invoices customers in the usual way, but sends a copy invoice to the factor. The factor maintains the sales ledger and also produces statements and reminders. If the exporter sells above the credit limit, this may be allowable, but the factor then has recourse to the exporter in the event of non-payment by the customer. Customers are asked to pay direct to the factor.

With factoring, the exporter is able to sell his export debts and relieve himself of the task of credit checking, ledgering, some documentation, and collection as well as usually eliminating any risk of bad debt or currency loss. Factoring companies do not usually purchase trade debts on terms exceeding 120 days, but some companies will exceptionally accept debts arising from contracts which provide for terms of up to 180 days. Thus, factoring is clearly most appropriate for exports on open account terms. It is used by exporters of all sizes and is particularly appropriate for those who are expanding rapidly. The factor charges a service fee of between 0.75 and 2.5 per cent of the sales value, depending on the workload and risk carried by the factor. The factor agrees to purchase without recourse the exporter's debts as they are invoiced, on terms up to 180 days, and to pay a proportion of the invoice value to the exporter immediately.

The advantages to the exporter of factoring include:

1. Only one debtor – the factor.
2. No sales ledgering necessary.
3. No need to credit check or credit insurance.
4. Non-recourse finance available.
5. Regular cash flow.
6. No foreign currency risk.
7. Substantial savings in staff and collection systems.

The disadvantages are:

1. Factoring companies are inevitably selective in their choice of client and of the debts they will factor. The country of distribution will be a major consideration.
2. The service charge may be greater than the cost of employing own staff and systems.
3. Contact with customers is reduced or eliminated.
4. As the business grows and the factor's charge becomes unacceptable, the exporter will not not have developed in-house experience.

Factoring is simply a method of exchanging book debts for cash on an agreed and regular basis. Apart from smoothing cash flow, it increases working capital. Factoring is not lending. It does not increase a company's debt so banks have found it an ideal source of new business while small businesses see in it a means of easing cashflow difficulties.

Forfaiting

This was developed in the 1950s by the Swiss bank group, Credit Suisse. The word is derived from the French term 'à forfait'. It is a form of medium-term non-recourse financing which is always denominated in leading Western currencies. In Switzerland, 75 per cent of special trade financing is in the form of forfaiting while leasing accounts for 20 per cent and factoring for 5 per cent. Worldwide exports of between two and three billion US dollars are forfaited each year. It is estimated also that two-thirds are claims on the socialist countries of Eastern Europe and developing countries in Latin America, Asia, and Africa.

Forfaiting is an arrangement whereby exporters of capital goods can obtain medium-term finance, usually for periods of between one and seven years. Under this arrangement, the forfaiting bank buys at a discount bills of exchange, promissory notes or other obligations arising from international trade transactions. Promissory notes are the preferred instruments of payment because it is then possible for the exporter to free himself from all recourse obligations. The purchasing bank (forfaiter) may commit itself to buying promissory notes even before the supply contract is signed. A commitment fee is then payable.

For a transaction to be eligible for forfaiting, it has to carry an internationally known banking name as guarantor.

Unless the importer is of first-class undoubted financial standing, any forfaited debt must carry a security in the form of an 'aval', or unconditional bank guarantee acceptable to the forfaiter. This condition is of the utmost importance because of the non-recourse aspect of the business: the forfaiter relies on such a bank guarantee as his only security for lending. The bill or promissory note must also be unconditional and not dependent on the exporter's performance, since the forfaiter has no right of recourse against the exporter. The forfait agreement then carries 80–90 per cent of the value of an export, as 10–20 per cent is usually paid in cash at the time an order for capital goods is placed. The forfaiter must consider risk, liquidity, and the fixing of the rate of return. To spread risk in terms of size and also geographical region, larger forfaiting transactions in excess of US$2 million are often syndicated.

When the forfaiter accepts the business, he often gives a declaration waiving right of recourse to the drawer as by law the drawer always remains responsible for the payment of the bills. For the exporter, the most important advantage is that he can sell his capital goods on credit and receive cash payment immediately from the forfaiter, who then assumes the rights and responsibility for collection of the debt. The only disadvantage is the high forfaiting rate, but this is due to the fact that the forfaiter combines the service of a bank in financing with that of an insurance company in the assumption of risk, so the forfaiting role must include not only a margin for financing but also a risk margin. Forfaiting is being seen as particularly appropriate for the export of capital goods. It is medium-term business, unlike factoring, and could range from one to seven years, although in practice a forfaiting financier will impose his own limits determined largely by market conditions and assessment of the risks involved for particular transactions.

Forfaiting is carried out by discounting in advance the interest for the whole life of the credit, and is done at a previously agreed fixed discount rate: thus, the exporter receives immediate cash and is liable only for the satisfactory delivery of the goods, all other risks being borne by the forfaiter. It is primarily this latter fact, coupled with the fixed-rate nature of the business, which makes forfaiting generally a very attractive service to the exporter, although occasionally relatively expensive on a short-term view.

Countertrade (CT)

The term, now commonly used as a generic umbrella term for all the increasing variants of goods-related payment, was previously (and wrongly) known as 'barter'. Countertrade is a genuine response to a difficult world trading environment, although much disliked by banks and international institutions such as the IMF and World Bank since it suggests a return to bilateralism. It is a means of payment for countries with limited reserves of convertible currency to purchase goods from the West, and pay partially in cash and partially in goods. There have been numerous conflicting estimates of the value of countertrade (CT). GATT estimates countertrade to account for 8 per cent of total world trade, which would value it at $2 trillion (i.e., million million), but this is held by bankers to be grossly underestimating the situation. The Organization for Economic Cooperation and Development (OECD) estimates countertrade to have accounted for 20 per cent of world trade at its peak in the late 1980s while Japan's External Trade Organization (JETRO) believes the figure may have been as high as 30 per cent. Certainly, whereas 20 years ago there were perhaps only ten nations involved in countertrade, the figure now includes practically all of the 209 nations listed by the World Bank. For Britain alone, it is

	MNC seller strong (near capacity)	MNC seller weak (has excess capacity)
Buying country's currency strong	Sale made / No CT needed	Sale made / CT sometimes not requested
Buying country's currency weak	No deal / Cash on barrelhead or seller goes elsewhere	Perhaps a sale / CT needed

Source: Elderkin, K. W., and Norquist, W. E. (1987) *Creative Countertrade: A Guide to Doing Business Worldwide*, Ballinger Publishing Company, Cambridge, MA, p. 11

Figure 6.1 Do we need countertrade?

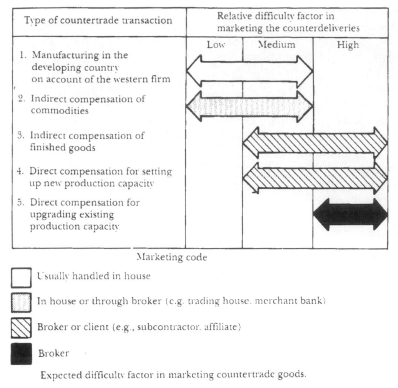

Figure 6.2   Expected difficulty factor in marketing countertrade goods

estimated to be equivalent to around 5 per cent of British exports, but this alone will represent £3 billion. It is a highly secretive world in which countertrade operates, so estimates of its value are usually always on the low side.

Countertrade (CT) has arisen because of:

1.   Acute shortages of both foreign exchange and international lines of credit. Many developing countries are now no longer eligible for traditional medium and long-term export finance because of indebtedness to Western banks.
2.   World markets for raw materials and low technology manufacturers are weak.
3.   CT can be used to fight protectionism in developed countries.
4.   Fierce competition exists between Western exporters of manufactured goods and capital equipment.
5.   Philanthropic and political attraction of bilateralism.

Countertrade is a generic term for a number of variants previously all collectively known as barter. Before discussing the variants, it is as well to remember that countertrade produces its own problems. Payment in goods is always a poor substitute for cash and even where the countertrade goods may be used within the exporting firm,

there is a potential threat created to existing suppliers as well as the continual danger implicit in using a new supplier with unknown reliability in quality, reliability, and continuity of supply. The value of countertrade is increasing in both the developed and developing world, where in some instances, it has become mandatory. Indonesia, for example, has used a mandatory countertrade policy to increase her non-oil exports. However, the US at an annual Inter-Governmental Group Meeting on Indonesia, which is composed of 14 countries and four international aid organizations, attacked the countertrade policy for the following reasons (Maynard, 1983):

1.   Countertrade degrades the contract process by focusing on countertrade requirements rather than price, quality and financing.
2.   Countertrade raises prices for goods the Indonesian Government buys.
3.   Countertraded goods will cause prices to fall on international markets which are based on supply and demand.
4.   Countertrade is not tied to world demand; the marketplace is more efficient.
5.   Barter is an antiquated system – a very rigid way to operate.
6.   Competition for contracts is reduced because source companies choose not to participate in countertrade.

Countertrade involves the participation of specialists who may be found in major clearing banks as well as merchant banks, trading houses and many multinational corporations, including Ford, which have specialist trading departments which will act on behalf of third parties for a commission (disagio). Countertrade does introduce its own problems, including increasing the cost of deals by 20 to 40 per cent (Michaels, 1989), and long-term traditional supplier displacement effects, particularly with regard to offsets. Nigeria's economy might have been different if it had actively pioneered the use of countertrade on a 'maxima' strategy basis rather than being an indecisive market follower, waking up to see more of its customers committed to other countertrade suppliers and fighting back only when a crisis arises with an oil price fall (Asiwaju, Paliwoda, 1986). Long-term compensation agreements of high value may give rise to complaints of injury to the domestic industry and so, charges of 'dumping'. As countertraded goods are most often sold at a discount, this leaves them particularly vulnerable also to a countervailing duty.

Antitrust legislation is another potential obstacle as the countertrade acceptance has introduced a distortion to the practice of free trade, so excluding other competitors. Taxation treatment in the home economy is yet another issue, whether to use the nominal sales price or the actual resale value of the goods in determining whether the exporter had a gain or a loss. Use of a foreign sales corporation may be one solution to allow deferral of income on the export sale, while any losses from the discounted resale of the countertraded goods could be used immediately by the parent to offset other income and reduce its taxes (Downey, Aldonas, 1985). Having said this, the US Government is also concerned with the growth in tax evasion, bribery, dumping and unfair competition as a result of increased countertrade activities (Michaels, 1989). Countertrade deals could be used to disguise bribes.

In the different variants of countertrade described below, it is important to remember that the type of countertrade goods offered will depend on the nature, and the economic priority to the importing nation, of the product to be acquired. High technology and high priority items will be accompanied by more favourable countertrade offers than, for example, consumer goods where the capacity to trade has only been made possible through the offer of a countertrade. A proactive attitude towards countertrade can yield success because more than just acceptance of CT, it means being able to integrate CT into the customer offer, and planning ahead as to how to accommodate a given value and volume of CT products, and how and where to dispose of it, if it is not being used directly by the company or in the company's production processes.

1. Bilateral trading clearing account

This occurs where an exchange of goods is effected under a mutual payments agreement between two sovereign states. It also involves the central bank or centralized foreign trade organization which runs a clearing bank account in the name of the importing partner, and a designated bank that in turn pays the exporting partner in local currency. This currency is inconvertible, and so termed 'soft', as opposed to 'hard' currency which is convertible. This gives rise to barter, where no surpluses and no deficits are allowable. When these deficits and surpluses exist because of an imbalance created by the economic structure of the two trading partners, an intermediary is often required to restore equilibrium, and this will then introduce 'switch trading'. It is politically expedient to have bilateral trading agreements, but they do not work in practice as developing countries are unable to find within themselves the goods and services in which they are most lacking. Bilateral trading agreements between nations are on the increase and GATT had voiced concern that this trend threatened its very structure. Note that GATT has since been replaced by the WTO.

2. Bartering

Barter stems directly from bilateral trading agreements. It is a means whereby one partner trades with another and all resultant balances are cleared by an exchange of goods and/or services. Bilateral trade agreements among the developing nations have traditionally been hailed as examples, but in case it should be thought that this is a phenomenon solely of trading with African and Asian countries, it exists also in trade within Europe – with Greece and Finland to take but two examples. Many years ago when the Swedish pop group Abba performed on a tour of Poland they received payment for their services in potatoes. Abba undertook so much business with the then communist bloc that they organized their own deals in Russian heavy machinery, Polish potatoes and Czech glass among other things. Where the goods offered cannot be readily used for the supplier's own consumption, the next best alternative may be to employ the services of a specialist trader who will off-load these unwanted goods on a third market and realize cash for them. However, his services will cost about 10 per cent, and the goods handled may require to be heavily discounted by up to 50 per cent in the case of machine tools, for example.

3. Switch trading or triangular trade

This arises where one of the two parties to a bilateral trading agreement introduces a third party who then accepts the obligation to take any outstanding surplus or unwanted goods offered under the bilateral agreement and thus convert them into cash or else effect a further series of international exchanges before converting them into goods which are actually wanted. Here, an imbalance in a bilateral trading clearing agreement is simply being bought by a third party who purchases the goods at a discount of 20–50 per cent and then sells them, perhaps through a number of exchange deals, for hard currency which may then settle the trading account and restore equilibrium to the bilateral account.

4. Escrow account trading

This is simply a 'blocked' account and useful where the buyer is unknown. This form of trading involves a third party, usually a specialist countertrader. Exports are made only when sufficient funds have been raised from the sale of goods on behalf of the buyer. Payment is then made against the usual shipping documents from a blocked or trust account in convertible currency as normal. There are time lags involved in the sale of countertraded goods to release of the funds. Escrow accounts are generally used only where there is some doubt about the ability of the buyer to complete a transaction.

5. Evidence accounts

Where the government of the country concerned has a mandatory countertrade policy for all foreign suppliers, companies will find it in their best interests to have all transactions duly noted by the appropriate customs authorities. The evidence account ensures compliance with this legislation and gives a parent group the flexibility of using one subsidiary's CT purchases to another subsidiary's possible advantage in that same country. Where subsidiaries often trade under different names from the parent holding group, the evidence account eliminates all possible confusion and may well work to the group's advantage. The evidence account operates like a revolving line of credit, where a debit is recorded for any exports to the country and a credit recorded for purchases made by the Western exporting company. An evidence account may prove to be useful for any company considering being in the market for the long term but not for a single deal.

6. Compensation trading

Compensation trading is another variant whereby the form of contract will usually allow part payment in convertible currency with the remainder being paid from a restricted selection of goods. The goods available are limited, and are usually restricted to those which could not readily be sold for convertible currency on Western markets. Again, the specialist services of a trading house may be necessary to realize cash from these goods. Russia commonly requests compensation trading but where the Western goods which they seek are earmarked for a national priority project and/or are of a high technology nature, then they will pay cash.

7. Buyback

'Buyback' is now a specialist term to denote the relationship whereby payment for a licensed product or process will partly be made by means of the resultant product. The duration of these contracts is usually in excess of three years and can extend to 16 on occasion. Buyback has been found in the past in Eastern Europe where Polish factories producing Fiat cars and International Harvesters crawler tractors discharge their obligations by sending back a certain volume of production to the original licensor. There are some advantages on either side. For the licensor, it ensures a new production plant coming on stream with no investment and with product price and quality control assurances. For the host country, it means the acquisition of new or state-of-the-art technology; access to 'know-how', which is often only contained in the minds of company personnel as in production, for example; plus softer terms on which to buy technology with guarantees of exports of a fixed percentage. In order not to conflict with corporate suppliers elsewhere, the contract would have to ensure either that new markets were capable of being accessed or that transfer prices to the licensor were on a par or lower than those of corporate subsidiaries elsewhere, a margin being allowed for freight costs. Buyback is still being practised but as it is usually still a state enterprise, there are now conditions for this in Central and Eastern Europe where instead, a foreign multinational can now engage in direct foreign investment.

8. Parallel trading (or counterpurchase)

'Parallel trading' (or counterpurchase) is quite separate and totally different from 'parallel' or 'grey' exports. Parallel trading occurs, for example, when a country agrees to purchase a certain, usually much sought-after, item such as a computer for hard currency, but wishes to tie the seller down to spending some of the purchase price in his country. For desperately sought-after items, convertible currency is always available. What changes the situation slightly is that the convertible-currency contract will be dependent on the signing of a second contract, whereby the seller must agree to repurchase a certain amount of goods available from anywhere within the importing country – the goods thus purchased to be of an agreed value, say 30 per cent of the initial contract price. There is no limit on the goods that may be selected, so goods which are easily exchangeable on Western markets, including commodities, may be included. This form of contract perhaps incurs the least penalties, identifies new raw material sources of supply for the seller, but is reserved only for the most sought-after imports. This is a characteristic particularly of selling computer mainframes to developing countries.

9. Industrial offset trading

This is found in the aviation industry. There are two facets to this. Either the exporter has undertaken a direct commitment to incorporate locally produced certain materials or components into his final products, sourced from within the importing country, or, in the second case, a sale may be tied to making 'best efforts' to assist the importing developing nation to earn hard currency and ease the cost of the sale. Through offsets, the importing nation can ensure that its domestic industries earn a percentage sale of the contract value. Important in the civil aircraft industry, offsets has, for example, ensured a place for domestic avionics companies in high technology aircraft contracts. As the value of these offsets can often exceed 100 per cent, there is a significant supplier displacement effect to be noted. This was the case with the Boeing AWACS deal concluded with the British Government, but then again, it is worth noting that perhaps 60 per cent of the final aircraft will be contracted out by the airframe manufacturer.

10. Swap trading

This is not technically countertrade. It does not affect the buyer, but is an arrangement purely between suppliers, most commonly in the oil industry. For bulk products, such as oil, where the freight cost is heavy, it may be advantageous for one supplier to exchange an obligation to supply with another supplier closer to the market of the buyer in question. The producers save on transportation costs while the buyer has only to assure himself of the quality of goods delivered are similar to those for which he has contracted to pay. For commodities, such as oil, there are clearly defined standards, usually relating to sulphur content, e.g., North Sea Brent, Texas crude etc., which must be incorporated into the sales contract and must be complied with.

Transfer pricing

Transfer pricing essentially refers to the prices at which goods and services are transferred within the corporate family but across national frontiers, as they move globally – division to division or to a foreign subsidiary or minority joint equity venture. Generally, the clarity of the reference price for transfer becomes higher as the product concerned moves through the product life cycle (Cats-Baril *et al.*, 1988), but what constitutes acceptable international accounting practice has never been properly defined. Transfer pricing becomes a problem at two quite different levels – within the company and with trade with the outside world. Transfer pricing may be used to remove funds from a particular country by charging more for intra-corporate inputs. By means of low transfer prices, it could also be seen as a means to finance a foreign affiliate or to evade tax. The influences driving transfer pricing and its features are described in Tables 6.7 and 6.8. Note that when demand for a product is high, the intermediate buying unit may be glad to have assured supplies on a full-cost basis, but then also wants the opportunity to sell on to find customers at still higher prices.

Where a profitable international division is an intermediary, there will be an inevitable conflict over price when goods move from the manufacturing division to the international division, and from there to the foreign subsidiary. For the manufacturing division, the price should be

Table 6.7 Transfer pricing features
• Higher transfer prices permit funds to be accumulated within the selling country.
• Tax haven affiliates have been used to drain off income from transactions between related affiliates.
• Not subject to withholding taxes.
• Creates surplus cash to pay off debt, finance new investment, or acquire securities.
• Permits purchase of foreign securities to diversify risk.
But:
• Can create difficulties in performance evaluation and with governments.

Table 6.8   Influences driving transfer pricing
• Market conditions in the foreign country. • Competition in the foreign country. • Reasonable profit for the foreign affiliate. • Home country income taxes. • Economic conditions in the foreign country. • Import restrictions. • Customs duties. • Price controls. • Taxation in the host country, e.g., withholding taxes. • Exchange controls, e.g., repatriation of profits.

high enough to encourage a flow of products for export and build up export trade. Where service or follow-up is needed, the prices fetched should make the manufacturing division willing to provide it. Low prices have the effect of showing poor returns for the manufacturing division, and losses can have a very bad effect on morale. However, from the viewpoint of the international division, the transfer price should be low enough to enable it to be both competitive and profitable in the foreign market. The international division also likes to be able to register profits and successes. Given these conflicting objectives the only outcome can often be that of mutual antipathy and only stalemate as the company is no longer working together to a common objective. There is an important power imbalance which has to be resolved with the very creation of a joint venture.

Possible solutions for this impasse include eliminating one of these divisions as a profit centre. The manufacturing division could be judged on the basis of costs and other performance criteria instead of profit. Secondly, the international division may operate as a service centre rather than as a sales centre, but this downgrading may also have a bad effect on morale. Finally, it may be possible to use the international division as a commission agent, functioning purely on sales handled.

A second and more recent problem is that of transfer pricing to joint equity ventures. Should these ventures enjoy the same price levels as wholly-owned subsidiaries or pay a higher level of prices, but perhaps invite some political retaliation? This problem arises with the price paid for inputs from the corporation to the joint equity venture, as well as supplies from the joint venture to the corporation. For the joint venture, which may well even be a minority joint venture holding for the corporation, price setting of components must be competitive with the corporation's subsidiaries elsewhere. In terms of performance, the joint venture wishes to be profitable and to be successful in exporting. How-

ever, for the corporation this may occasionally present a dilemma over supplier choice. It may involve choosing among old, trusted suppliers; wholly owned suppliers, and untried, untested joint-venture partners – the corporate objective being not to upset anyone and yet act in the best way for the group overall. Interpersonal as well as intra-organizational disputes will arise.

To the outside world, an important feature of interest to politicians, consumerists, and trade unions alike, is the ability of multinational corporations to source globally for their components and sub-assemblies. To cite but a few examples, IBM does it in the computer industry, and so too, do multinationals in the automobile industry such as General Motors and Ford, but there are few sectors in which global products are not found, and these global products are, in turn, the final products of a very complex network of sourcing and multi-stage production.

Where this freedom exists, the possibility at least of abuse also exists. It is this that attracts the politicians. Host countries all over the world dislike losing tax revenue, yet there is the prospect here, that since the component engineering and pricing structure remains company-specific knowledge, with multinational sourcing it may be possible to move funds in the transfer of goods to a foreign country. Transferring at a low price from a high-tax country would allow a subsidiary in a low-tax country to make a larger than normal profit, and would best serve the interests of the firm (see Table 6.9). Some African countries, such as Nigeria, introduced import inspection procedures as a result of repeated allegations of over-invoicing on imports which has the effect of withdrawing money from the country.

Equally, restrictions may exist with regard to repatriation of capital or the payment of fees for consultancy, licences, etc., or there may just be the fear of losses through devaluation, high inflation, or impending tax legislation. In such circumstances, the prospect of being able to pay lower taxes in another country must seem

Table 6.9 Tax effect of low versus high transfer price on net income

	Manufacturing affiliate	Distribution affiliate	Consolidated company
Low-markup policy			
Sales	$1400	(Sales) $2000	$2000
Less cost of goods sold	1000	1400	1000
Gross profit	$ 400	$ 600	$1000
Less operating expenses	100	100	200
Taxable income	$ 300	$ 500	$ 800
Less income taxes			
(25 per cent/50 per cent)	75	250	325
Net income	$ 225	$ 250	$ 475
High-markup policy			
Sales	$1700	(Sales) $2000	$2000
Less cost of goods sold	1000	1700	1000
Gross profit	$ 700	$ 300	$1000
Less operating expenses	100	100	200
Taxable income	$ 600	$ 200	$ 800
Less income taxes			
(25 per cent/50 per cent)	150	100	250
Net income	$ 450	$ 100	$ 550

Assumptions: Manufacturing affiliate pays income taxes at 25 per cent. Distribution affiliate pays income taxes at 50 per cent.

Source: Eitemann, D. K. and Stonehill, A. I. (1986) *Multinational Business Finance*, 4th edn, Addison-Wesley Publishing Co., Reading, MA.

enticing. In effect, it is difficult to establish whether these transfers are in fact taking place. For these reasons, customs authorities check values on imports more closely than exports, but it is not always possible to have a reference point on the value of exports of either parts or components. Because there is an important political issue here, many multinationals, including Exxon, IBM and Caterpillar, actually publish a code of business ethics.

The strategic choices in transfer pricing are either then to transfer at direct manufacturing cost, which may seem suspect to the local country's customs authorities; at cost plus, at a percentage to be agreed – usually of the order of 10 per cent; and finally, at arm's length.

'Arm's length' pricing means in fact that one is charging company divisions the same amount as one would an outside client. 'Arm's length' is, therefore, the term that is most often quoted by bodies such as the International Chamber of Commerce, but it is also very difficult to narrowly define and to enforce, which probably also helps explain its popularity.

Conspiracy to fix prices

This is outlawed under anti-trust legislation in the USA and by the EC under Section 80 of the Treaty of Rome. Even so, tacit collusion is much more difficult to establish than is an actual price cartel. A US lawyer writing in the *Harvard Business Review* pointed out that even price fixers who do not get caught may not benefit by conspiring. His 22 rules on how to conspire to fix prices were:

1. Do not overlook the fact that the purpose of a price-fixing conspiracy is to make more money than you would have made had you not conspired in the first place.

2. Don't wink at a conspiracy unless it is a moneymaking proposition.

   • Get your economists and analysts busy. Do not continue a profitless conspiracy. And, if you are not now conspiring, do not overlook this potentially profitable marketing technique.
   • Price-fixing works best where no one conspirator has a substantial cost advantage over his co-conspirators.

3. Threaten a reluctant conspirator with antitrust action in order to bring him into the fold.

4. Before conspiring, be sure that follow-the-leaderism and conscious parallelism are not in the cards. They are much less dangerous and work every bit as well.

	Manufacturing affiliate	Distribution affiliate	Consolidated company
Table 6.10 Tax-neutral impact of low versus high transfer price on flow of funds			
Low-markup policy			
Sales	$1400	(Sales) $2000	$2000
Less cost of goods sold	1000	1400	1000
Gross profit	$ 400	$ 600	$1000
Less operating expenses	100	100	200
Taxable income	$ 300	$ 500	$ 800
Less income taxes			
(50 per cent)	150	250	400
Net income	$ 150	$ 250	$ 400
High-markup policy			
Sales	$1700	(Sales) $2000	$2000
Less cost of goods sold	1000	1700	1000
Gross profit	$ 700	$ 300	$1000
Less operating expenses	100	100	200
Taxable income	$ 600	$ 200	$ 800
Less income taxes			
(50 per cent)	300	100	400
Net income	$ 300	$ 100	$ 400

Assumptions: Both manufacturing affiliate and distribution affiliate pay income taxes of 50 per cent.
Source: Eitemann, D. K. and Stonehill, A. I. (1986) *Multinational Business Finance*, 4th edn, Addison-Wesley Publishing Co., Reading, MA.

- A successful leader-follower constantly repeats the incantation: 'A like price is a competitive price, a like price is a competitive price . . .'
- Conscious parallelism may be illegal but is certainly not as illegal as conspiring. Moreover, it is hard to prove.
  - Get to know your competitors.
  - Develop effective lines of inter-firm communication.
  - Get in the habit of announcing policy and price changes in the press.

5. Do not have more active conspirators than necessary; do not have working-level meetings if not absolutely necessary; and do not include personnel any further down the hierarchical ladder than is 100 per cent necessary.

6. Do not take notes; do not leave papers, work sheets, scratch pads, and the like lying around in hotel rooms and other meeting places; do not register under your real name; do not travel with your co-conspirators in public transportation to or from meetings; do not make conspiratorial telephone calls from your office (particularly if your efficient secretary keeps a log); in other words, do not keep records of any kind.

7. Do not meet in hotel rooms if you can avoid doing so.
8. Avoid complicated schemes.
9. Have some reason for meeting besides fixing prices.
10. Gripe a lot, especially about prices.
11. Develop a jargon.
12. Send up 'trial balloons'.
13. Remember that the line between overt price collusion and mere discussion of a common problem is fine indeed.
14. It is advisable to have at least one member in the conspiracy who has monopoly experience.
15. Do not be greedy.

   - The share of each individual conspirator relative to the shares of any or all of his co-conspirators must be, by mutual consent, treated as irrelevant.
   - If you are getting more than you would have expected, stay in; if you are not, get out.

16. Do not overlook the possibility of dividing up sales revenues at the end of a prearranged conspiracy accounting period, irrespective of who actually made the sales.
17. Have an adequate contingency fund for educating (or eliminating) mavericks.

- Avoid giving the appearance of selling below cost. It antagonizes the Federal Trade Commission.

18. Conspiracies work best on shelf items, but are least necessary. They work worst on special-order items, but are most needed in these areas.

- If you sell special-order items, do not allow your enthusiasm to conspire to get out of hand.

19. When the heat is on, get out.
20. Do not worry about being a good citizen and a respected member of the community. It will not help you.
21. Do not worry about avoiding identity of price. This will not solve your problem.
22. Get the advice of an experienced conspirator.

Cartels

In a domestic situation these are illegal but for exporting, they are permissible, just as questionable payments may be illegal in the home market but, if for international trade promotion, suddenly become allowable for tax allowances. This is similar to the consortium or federated approach to exporting, where several independent companies may choose to collaborate to make a concerted pitch to a target foreign market.

Exhibit 6.10 US court challenge to price of CDs

The world's six largest record companies are facing a new court challenge over the price of compact discs.

A class action has been launched in the United States against the companies – including British giants Polygram and EMI – claiming that prices are being kept artificially high even though CD production costs have fallen.

If the action succeeds, prices are expected to fall in both the US and Europe where the same CDs already cost up to a third more.

Last Friday, a federal judge ruled, despite fierce opposition from the companies, that the case must be heard in a state court. Campaigners for lower prices were jubilant, saying that tougher consumer laws at state level increased their chances of winning.

Since their launch in 1983, CDs have taken over from vinyl and cassette tapes as the preferred form of musical recording. In Britain, CDs account for the bulk of sales within the £800m-a-year record market.

When Britain's Monopolies and Mergers Commission investigated allegations of unjustified pricing in the UK two years ago, it ruled that price differences between the US and the UK were acceptable.

Since then CD prices in the UK have risen by 10 per cent on average, almost three times the rate of inflation and far faster than in the US. Any cut in US prices would bring renewed pressure from consumer groups for a corresponding downwards revision in British charges. At present, the average price of a CD in Britain is £12.61 compared to around £9 in the US.

In the first lawsuit brought by consumers, the industry is accused of conspiring to fix and keep CD prices artificially high at a time when the cost of production has plummeted from £1.87 to around 62p.

Cited in the case apart from EMI and Polygram are Sony Music, WEA, Uni Distribution, and Bertelsmann Music which between them control an estimated 85 per cent of America's £6bn CD market. An inquiry into possible price-fixing by the US Federal Trade Commission is also thought to be under way.

The US lawsuit, being heard in Nashville, alleges that the companies have used illegal tactics such as colluding on what to charge retailers. The companies are also not passing on to consumers the savings as manufacturing costs fall. The suit also alleges that the defendants use 'minimum advertised price' policies to punish retailers that sell CDs below a specific price.

Such illegal practices mean consumers are paying about £2 too much per disc, says Joseph Barton, one of the attorneys representing the plaintiffs.

Music industry analysts agree that CDs are over-priced. Bruce Haring, an entertainment editor at USA Today newspaper, said prices were pegged to what the companies believed the market would bear. 'The music companies are making an obscene amount of money,' he said.

The companies argue that the music business is unusually expensive because of production and the costs of developing artists, and that higher profits on high-selling releases are necessary to cover losses on the many that are less successful.

They are unlikely to give up without a hard fight. Industry insiders say the £10m spent in legal costs during the MMC investigation was money well spent.

Source: Scotland on Sunday, 2 February 1997, p. 4

Revision questions

1. Why is there no such thing as a company possessing 'perfect knowledge' or participating in 'perfect competition'?
2. Explain the difference between technical maturity, market maturity and competitive maturity.
3. Why should it be dangerous to be a 'price follower'?
4. What are the six elements in the multi-stage approach to pricing?
5. Suggest a few reasons why international price standardization proves so elusive.
6. Cite five principles of a customer approach to pricing as outlined by Shapiro and Jackson.
7. What is the significance of purchasing power parity? What does the Big Mac Index really tell us?
8. Is 'parallel' or 'grey' exporting just an extension of free trade?
9. List typical market overheads that would have to be factored into any final price projections for an export.
10. What proactive and reactive strategies exist to combat grey market activity?
11. What is the significance of the Berne Union?
12. Explain what is meant by 'dumping'. Why should it be so sensitive an issue?
13. Cite the advantages of foreign currency invoicing and financing. What are the drawbacks?
14. What is the difference between a bill of exchange and a letter of credit?
15. How might leasing be used in international marketing?
16. Explain the difference between discounting, factoring and forfaiting.
17. What is an escrow account?
18. What is the difference between compensation trading and buyback?
19. How might countertrade be seen to lead to supplier displacement? Should that be of strategic concern?
20. What is understood by the term 'transfer pricing'?

References

ACECO (1985) *Practical Guide to Countertrade*, Metal Bulletin Inc., Park House, Park Terrace, Worcester Park, Surrey.

Asiwaju, G. O. A., and Paliwoda, S. J. (1986) Nigeria rethinks the countertrade basics. *Countertrade and Barter Quarterly*, **10** (3), 51–56.

Capoglu, G. (1990) The internationalisation of financial markets and competitiveness in the world economy. *Journal of World Trade*, **24** (2), 111–118.

Cats-Baril, W., Gatti, J. F., and Grinnell, D. J. (1988) Transfer pricing in a dynamic market. *Management Accounting*, **69** (8), 30–33.

Cavusgil, S. T., and Sikora, E. (1988) How multinationals can counter gray market imports. *Columbia Journal of World Business*, Winter, 75–85.

Cremer, H., and Pestieau, P. 'Distributive Implications of European Integration', *European Economic Review*, April, **40** (3–5), 747–758.

Didier, P. (1990) EEC anti-dumping: the level of trade issue. *Journal of World Trade*, **24** (2), 103–110.

Diller, H., and Bukhari, J. (1994) 'Pricing Conditions in the European Common Market', *European Management Journal*, June, **12** (2), 163–171.

Dow, F. (1990) *Understanding Documentary Bills and Credits: A Practical Guide for Exporters, Importers, Forwarders and Bankers*, Croner Publications Ltd., Kingston Upon Thames, Surrey.

Downey, A. T., and Aldonas, G. D. (1985) US legal implications of countertrade deals, *International Financial Law Review*, September.

Duhan, D. F., and Sheffet, M. J. (1988) Gray markets and the legal status of parallel importation. *Journal of Marketing*, **52**, (July), 75–83.

Elderkin, K. W., and Norquist, W. E. (1987) *Creative Countertrade: A Guide to Doing Business Worldwide*, Ballinger Publishing Co., Cambridge, MA.

Gardner, D. C. (1996) *Introduction to Documentary Credits*, Financial Times/Pitman Publishing, London.

Gardner, D. C. (1996) *Introduction to Finance of Foreign Trade*, Financial Times/Pitman Publishing, London.

Gaul, W., and Lutz, U. (1994) 'Pricing in International Marketing and Western European Economic Integration', *Management International Review*, April, **34** (2), 102–126.

Krarup, T. (1995) 'Banking Challenges in the European Union', *The World of Banking*, October–December, **14** (5), 25–30.

Leeflang, P. S. H., and van Raaij, W. F. (1995) 'The Changing Consumer in the European Union: A "Meta-Analysis"', *International Journal of Research in Marketing*, December, **12** (5), 373–388.

Lawyer, J. Q. (1963) How to conspire to fix prices. *Harvard Business Review*, March–April.

Matsumoto, K., and Finlayson, G. (1990) Dumping and anti-dumping: growing problems in world trade. *Journal of World Trade*, **24** (4), 5–20.

Maynard, C. E. (1983) *Indonesia's Countertrade Experience*, American Indonesian Chamber of Commerce, New York City.

Michaels, P. (1989) Countertrade: a powerful global competitive strategy for US international traders. *SAM Advanced Management Journal*, Summer, 8–14.

OECD (1990) *Export Credit Financing Systems in OECD Member Countries*, Paris.

Okoroafo, S. C. (1988) Determinants of LDC-mandated countertrade, *International Marketing Review*, Winter, 16–24.

Oxenfeldt, A. A. (1960) Multi-stage approach to pricing. *Harvard Business Review*, July–August.

Paliwoda, S. J. (1989) Countertrading. In *Marketing Handbook*, Thomas, M. J., 3rd edn, Gower, Aldershot.

Paliwoda, S. J. (1996) 'The International Environment', in M. J. Thomas, *The Marketing Handbook*, 4th edn, Gower Press, Aldershot, Hants.

Paliwoda, S. J., and Ryans Jr, J. K. (1995) *International Marketing Reader*, Routledge, London.

Publications of the International Chamber of Commerce (ICC):
Uniform Rules for Collections, ICC Publications #522, ICC Publishing, Paris
Guide to Documentary Credit Operations, ICC Publication #415
Guide to Incoterms, ICC Publication #461/90

Rice, M. R. (1988) Four ways to finance your exports. *Journal of Business Strategy*, July–August, 30–33.

Rockwell, K. M. (1993) 'British Executives defend Exporter Pricing Policies', *Journal of Commerce and Commercial*, January 22, **395** (27899), 2A–3A.

Roth, D. (1996) 'Rationalizable Predatory Pricing', *Journal of Economic Theory*, February, **68** (2), 380–397.

Sampson, R. T., (1964) Sense and sensitivity in pricing. *Harvard Business Review*, November–December.

Serwer, A. E. (1994) 'How to escape a Price War', *Fortune*, June 13, **129** (12), 82–88.

Shapiro, B. P. and Jackson, B. B. (1978) 'Industrial Pricing to meet Customer Needs', *Harvard Business Review*, November–December, 119–127.

Sinclair, S. (1993) 'A Guide to Global Pricing', *Journal of Business Strategy*, May–June, **14** (3), 16–20.

Strodes, J. (1989) Banana bonds: the movie. *Financial World*, 13 June, 24–26.

UN Economic Commission for Europe (1991) *International Buyback Contracts*, Geneva.

Thomas, M. J. (1996) 'Pricing Issues in Marketing',
in M. Warner (ed.) *International Encyclopedia of Business & Management*, International Thomson Business Press, London.

Watson, A. J. W. (1994) *Finance of International Trade*, Bankers Books Ltd, London.

Web sites

American Metal Market
http://www.amm.com

AT & T Business Network – free site
http://www.bnet.att.com

Bank of England
http://www.bankofengland.co.uk

Bank of Montreal
http://www.bmo.com/

BradyNet Inc
http://www. Bradynet.com/m-local.html

Cahners Manufacturing Marketplace: US manufacturers, distributors, products, news and hot links
http://www.manufacturing.net

CIA Publications
http://www.odc.gov/cia/publications/pus.html

Commerce Business Daily
gopher:cscns.com
Choose: Internet Express Gopher by Subject Business-Commerce Business Daily-Softshare

Currency Conversion Information – Olsen and Associates 164 Currency Converter, Zurich, Switzerland
http://www.olsen.ch/cgi-bin/exmenu/

Currency Converter
http://bin.gnn.com/cgi-bin/gnn/currency

Diners Club – Global weather, currency conversions, language translations, dealing with stress
http://www.dinersclub.com

Ernst & Young
http://www.ernsty.co.uk/ernsty

Europages
http://www.europages.com

Federal Express (FedEx)
http://www.fedex.ca

Find it Fast
http://www.webcom.com/~tbrown/findpage.html

Foreign Exchange Rates
http://www.dna.Ith.se/cgi-bin/kurt/
rates/

GE Information Services – bringing together US
buyers and suppliers
http://www.tpn.geis.com

Legal List Internet Desk Reference
http://wwwlcp.com

Legal Information Institute
http://www.law.cornell.edu

Manufacturing Marketplace from Cahners
http://www.cmm.net

Political Risk Services
http://www.polrisk.com

Purchasing On-Line
http://www.purchasing.net

Packaging Waste Legislation – the Sequoia
Group
http://ourworld.compuserve.com/
homepages/SeQuoia

Save Your Marriage: find the closest flowers,
champagne, restaurant and directions
http://www.zip2.com

Trade Compass
http://www.tradecompass.com

TradePort – extensive information on
international business
http://www.tradeport.org

TradeWave Galaxy – Public and commercial
information and services
http://www.einet.net/
galaxy.html

US Dept. of Commerce
http://www.doc.gov/CommerceHome
Page.html

U.S. Fedworld
www.fedworld.gov

World Bank
http://www.worldbank.org/

World Factbook
gopher: gopher.aecom.yu.edu

CHAPTER 7

Strategic international logistical and distribution decisions

Natural channels of distribution

The definition which follows is taken from Griffith and Ryans (1995):

Distribution channels evolved through the utilization of natural resources contained within an area of trade; Thus the term 'natural channel'. Through the utilization of the natural resources available within each market, an efficient distribution channel was formed. In the international arena, this is illustrated by the highly labour intensive channels, often complete with market bazaars, found in many developing countries and the continued presence of the popular neighbourhood bakers' shops, meat shops etc. in Western Europe.

Distribution channels in the Information Age

The advent of information technology (IT) has brought with it another popular acronym found in all spheres of commercial activity: EDI. This is electronic data interchange. EDI has been defined in the British International Freight Association (BIFA) Yearbook 1990 as, 'The transfer, by electronic means, of structured data from machine to machine, using agreed standards.'

Computer terminals in this sense are being used, not just to receive and read a message, but to interpret it, notify the user of significant items, and update the user's database with the new information. BIFA estimates cost savings for EDI of anything up to 10 per cent of turnover. Consider that distribution channels account for 15 per cent to 40 per cent of the retail price of goods and services in an industry and it becomes clear the potential which exists for productivity gains. (Bucklin et al., 1996) It affects everything now, including the movement of goods, the documentation which accompanies the goods and so, payment as well. Later, we shall discuss INCOTERMS but it is worth noting that they were introduced because of a need to accommodate EDI. Through an internationally agreed

set of rules, buyer and seller can be assured of equality of treatment for EDI messages as for formal documents. For the movement of goods, within the EU where the Single Administrative Document (SAD) is used most, there is an EDI version and electronic signatures are permissible.

EDI has had an important effect on buyer–seller relations within the international as well as national context. Payment delays resulting from a variety of different sources, are still common although the means of payment have increased, such as the use of plastic credit cards. For consumers, the ability to pay with credit cards while away from home has meant not having to exchange foreign currency. Some card companies offer their clients the more favourable commercial rate of exchange on their purchases abroad, making spending easier while allowing banks to retain their monopoly over the exchange of foreign currency. In other areas even including defence, travel and entertainment cards such as American Express have been issued to air force pilots whereas once they would have had to carry an emergency cash 'float' in case of a sudden need to purchase fuel. Similarly for businesses, some credit card companies will offer a specialized detailed monthly statement of expenses. Overall, service is generally improving, and much is due to information technology, but the ramifications of the IT revolution have yet to be experienced in their entirety.

EDI creates a databank of clients and their spending patterns which has effectively transferred some of the traditional market power and knowledge possessed by the manufacturers to those retailers offering the store cards. Manufacturers, even with large market research expenditures, are often lacking the specificity of detail to be found in credit card databanks as controlled by major retailers. Instant processing and debiting by means of computers being able to communicate with each other across nations have made life more comfortable than before for the retailers. Direct connections with the credit card issuing company eliminate much of the fraudulent use that was prevalent before, although major differences between world time zones still mean that British credit cards stolen in Hong Kong, for example, will not be logged onto the central computer for some hours. Counterfeiting of credit cards has been especially prevalent in France, but as the companies seek continually to make their cards more secure, the costs of doing so escalate while the pressure for lowering charges to both card carrying clients and retailers continues unabated. While the card companies experiment with photographs and laser-etched facsimile signatures on the card, France, meanwhile, is at the forefront of what is now called the 'smart card', a plastic card which incorporates a microchip rather than just a magnetic stripe. This allows the card itself to be updated if, for example, it carries a memory bank of transactions. It is more secure but more costly.

To the consumer, these electronic networks control money. Information is exchanged but, provided no one is blacklisted as a very poor credit risk, there is no finite number as to the quantity of credit cards which one may apply for and receive. In the industrialized countries, 'plastic money', as it has come to be called, has changed shopping patterns. Instead of saving to buy a certain item as our parents used to do, one can buy it immediately on credit. A materialistic society is therefore being built on a foundation of credit. For the developing countries, the situation is the opposite: the more unstable the economy, the more likely the request by the supplier for immediate payment in convertible currency. The disadvantaged are thus further disadvantaged because of an inequitable system where credit is most readily given to those who need it least.

EDI has also had two other important effects which relate to purchasing and procurement. Firstly, electronic cash register tills, and modern laser reading check-outs require a computerized bar-coding system on all products. Would-be suppliers are of necessity required to have a bar-code system in place before being considered. This creates a further, and quite new, barrier to entry.

In a similar vein, many industrialized Western nations have developed a national system of quality awards, to recognize quality in manufacturing or service within an industry. The need to compete for a quality award, or to retain an existing one, presents further additional barriers to entry for would-be suppliers. A company that presently has such an award will want to deal only with suppliers who either have one or are willing to submit themselves for inspection for

such an award. This, in turn, creates a further effect, whereby Western developed nations are forced to trade with each other and cannot afford to go outside of a concentrated network of suppliers for fear of endangering their quality status.

In sum, EDI has created many parallel interfaces with distribution networks, giving a new and prominent identity to certain key players internationally who were only peripheral before, such as in banks, finance and insurance, who are now heavily involved to a degree quite unprecedented in lubricating new wheels of finance which they have created to help turn the machinery of industry.

Virtual value chain vs. physical value chain

The value chain is a set of value adding activities. Rayport and Sviolka (1996) pointed out how by studying available information, new forms of value added could be found for the customer, many of which could be found on the Internet or through the use of IT. Music, for example, could be promoted and distributed through the Internet whereas new events such as recording and interviews could be made more interactive through the Internet. Federal Express (FedEx) allow customers to track their packages through the company's Web site. With the use of these new tools, managers have the ability now to plan beyond the constraints of what is just available today. Raport and Svioka point out how the China Internet Company, backed by the Xinhua News Agency, has produced a network of Internet sites for 40 industrial cities in China with multimedia presentations.

Logistics

Logistics is frequently used as a term to describe the movement of goods and services between supplier and end-user. So, let us begin by tracing its origins. According to the *Oxford English Dictionary*, the term 'logistic' could be defined up to 1644 as 'pertaining to reason', then after 1706, 'pertaining to reckoning or calculations'. Its root meaning embraced the elementary processes of arithmetic. In its plural form, 'logistics' has become synonymous with distribution, but in this context it has strong military associations, it is 'the art of moving and quartering troops' (i.e., quartermaster's work), now especially of organizing supplies. However, it is to be hoped that it has not lost its connection with rationality. As Dr Ian Canadine of the Institute of Logistics pointed out: 'You don't outsource logistics. You might outsource distribution or even sourcing but logistics is strategic thinking and part of the whole way the company operates. If you outsource it, you have lost half the company thinking.'

Military objectives, such as speed and continuity of supply, may be shared with marketers also, but the essential difference between marketing and the military is that military strategists have never considered the satisfaction of the final consumer of their product as being their main focus! Marketers deal with competition, in the shape of a much less visible target, and use weapons of persuasion which may be forceful in their own way, but are much less direct than armaments, take longer, are wasteful and so relatively more expensive.

moving goods from supplier to end-user when this involves crossing international frontiers; also, to compare channels of distribution within local markets for similar goods. It must be noted that worldwide the length of marketing channels, as a result of increasingly necessary cost reductions, is becoming shorter between supplier and end-user, and so this entails a reduction in the number of intermediaries who require price maintenance or recommended prices, discounts and rebates. Distribution costs are not uniform across markets, the peculiarly long and rather anachronistic distribution channels of Japan will be dealt with separately in Chapter 11. However, do note that the Japanese are world leaders in the handling and management of inventory.

Exhibit 7.1   What is a logistics alliance?

Van Laarhoven and Sharman (1994) defined a logistics alliance as an agreement that met three conditions:

* It must involve at least one full year of cooperation.
* It must offer both transportation and warehousing services.
* It must employ a single provider for the services.

The network economy

Corporate restructuring was taking place because of disappearing borders, greater distances to

market, and improving transport networks which have prompted the creation of European or regional distribution centres. Van Laarhoven and Sharman see these logistics alliances becoming what they call 'building blocks', the very foundations of the 'network economy'. They define the network economy as a system in which companies will increasingly focus on their core competencies and outsource other activities to service providers that can execute them more cheaply, more efficiently, and/or more effectively.

As Davies (1987) pointed out, there are a number of differences between national and international distribution as the documentation for an international sale:

1. costs more,
2. involves more parties,
3. involves higher financial penalties for errors,
4. requires more data and knowledge.

The average export order size is much larger than the domestic order, requiring more rigorous credit checks and, often, the services of an intermediary. A way to deal with this is to develop a style of thinking of international logistics as a concept emphasizing the movement of the export order rather than just the movement of goods. It does, however, require close integration of export shipping and sales.

Market entry decisions have already been discussed in Chapters 3 and 4 so here, the intention is to examine the decision areas involved in

International conventions have meant that companies operating within Europe are finding that border controls between member states have eased; regulations on packaging and labelling have been standardized throughout the European Union; and the ever-increasing volume of traffic between member states has become a permanent feature.

Cabotage remains a problem, however. Cabotage is the freedom for truckers registered in one EU country to collect and deliver loads between two points inside a second EU country. Cabotage remains a problem also for the airline industry to the same degree.

Movement of goods across frontiers

The speed employed in the transit of goods is an important consideration, but is cost relative to the total value-added of the item in question.

Exhibit 7.2   The more they see, the less they like

Purchasing professionals are fast gaining access to the Internet and are rapidly expanding their cyber-skills, according to a recent *Purchasing* poll. It seems, however, that greater access and expertise is causing buyers to narrow rather than expand their notion of how the Internet can be used on the job.

Getting connected

Eight in ten purchasing pros now have – at work – both the hardware and software they need to go online, according to the survey. Seven in ten say they have work-based access to the World Wide Web and other Internet services. Just one year ago, the corresponding numbers were roughly seven in ten for equipment and just 2.5 in ten for access.

Purchasing's poll also finds that buyers are advancing rapidly up the Net's learning curve. More than half (56 per cent) rate themselves as familiar or very familiar with the medium, up from just 18 per cent a year ago. And 43 per cent rate themselves as skilled to very skilled at finding what they want, up from 11 per cent a year ago.

Beyond equipment, access, and know-how, nearly six in ten buyers polled say they have found ways to use the Internet on the job. And of the 40 per cent who do not yet use the Internet for work, 65 per cent say they will in the near future. Eighty-seven per cent of the pros polled are interested or very interested in using the Internet as a business tool, up from 51 per cent last year. And 45 per cent say they are either comfortable or very comfortable with the prospect of conducting business via the Internet versus 26 per cent a year ago.

Stop the revolution – we want to get off!

These data are guaranteed to excite marketing execs, but the study gives no indication that the Internet will inspire real revolution in business-to-business relationships. Indeed, as buyers have gained experience with the Internet, their expectations for using it in research, transactions, and communications seem to be declining. Examples:

- Twenty per cent of buyers surveyed either use or plan to use the Internet frequently to obtain technical data about parts or materials – a ten-point drop from last year.
- Twenty-two per cent think the Internet will be a frequent source of information about what parts a supplier makes, compared to 31 per cent one year ago.
- Eleven per cent will use the Internet frequently to conduct legally binding purchase transactions, down five points from a year ago.
- Five per cent see the Internet as a good way to check a supplier's financial performance, down from 19 per cent a year ago.

The numbers did rise in five (out of twenty) applications categories. However, the nature of these uses suggests that purchasing pros view the Internet more as a replacement for the telephone or postal service than as a catalyst for competitive supply chain management. To wit:

- Thirty-three per cent will use the Internet frequently for supplier e-mail communications, up one point from last year.
- Seventy-one per cent will frequently dispatch RFQs via the Internet, up from 61 per cent last year.
- Sixty-five per cent will use the Internet to obtain pricing information, up from 57 per cent in 1995.
- Sixty-two per cent see the medium as a good way to perform order-status inquiries up from 58 per cent last year.
- Percentage of buyers planning to use the Internet frequently to research new suppliers rose from 36 per cent a year ago to 38 per cent now.

Asked to offer other potential work-related uses for the Internet, responses are few and far between. One buyer sees the Internet as a good way to 'share information on suppliers.' Another will use it frequently for 'tracking shipments,' via UPS and Federal Express sites. Conspicuously absent in this category is any suggestion that the Internet will be used to gain market intelligence or to otherwise inform sourcing decisions.

Better questions

The results of *Purchasing*'s poll raise, in fact, more questions than they answer:

- Do purchasing professionals view the Internet as a competitive or strategic business tool?
- Can the Internet be used efficiently and cost-effectively to inform purchasing decisions?
- How does the rise of (secure) Intranet technology affect expectations for the (insecure) Internet?

To weigh in on these topics, e-mail Anne Millen Porter at amp.purchasing@cahners.com or fax comments to (617) 630 – 4577.

Source: Purchasing

Table 7.1   Moving goods across frontiers: international transportation conventions

Sea transport:
  Hague-Visby Rules, 1968, which amended the Hague Rules, applies to all UK exports, but only to UK imports where the source country is party to Hague-Visby.

Road transport:
  CMR Convention, or the Convention on the Contract for the International Carriage of Goods by Road, devised by the UN Economic Commission for Europe, 1956.

Rail transport:
  COTIF/CIM Convention, 1985, mainly European in force. The railway authorities have quasi-common carrier status, the exporter designates the route to be followed.

Air transport:
  Warsaw Convention, 1929, and amended at the Hague in 1955, and in Guadalajara in 1961, but with fewer signatories.

Notes:
1. There is no convention relating to multi-modal transportation using a combination of the above.
2. These conventions have been incorporated into the laws of the UK.
3. The USA and Japan are not parties to the Hague-Visby Rules, and so goods from these countries imported into the UK will be subject not to the Hague-Visby rules, but the unamended Hague Rules.
4. There is no uniformity in the basis of the carrier's liability. Where multi-modal transportation has been used, there may be a contractual clause to the effect that any claims must be addressed to the carrier who had actual custody of the goods at the time of the loss (i.e., if that can be worked out!).

Another factor is the packaging cost of the product for the export market, which will be affected by availability of materials and by local legislation relating, for example, to the recycling of containers for re-use and, therefore, perhaps requiring a system for deposits and returns into the distribution channels. Additional protective export packing is another factor, although in recent years, this has become greatly simplified by the use of low-cost polystyrene moulded to fit the shape of the product in question, and so adding very little extra weight. Packaging has also been simplified by palletization, which has moved into computer systems software which now designs individual product packaging to maximize the number of units per pallet, and thus per container load. Palletization with shrink wrap protection and containerization has served both to protect goods against damage and to diminish losses through theft, otherwise referred to within the haulage industry as 'shrinkage'.

Logistics is primarily an operations research tool to contain costs and optimize efficiency in the flow of goods or services. However, within the channel between supplier and end-user, there will usually be a number of intermediaries, such as in the auto industry, where there may be an importer who is an agent or distributor, a national stockholding centre; then regional wholesalers; perhaps smaller wholesalers, then the retailers. The channel depends on the good or service itself, as much as local prevailing market conditions, but the exporter will be seeking the provision of accompanying services, as well as a return on his product and his general investment. The uncontrollable elements with regard to distribution are the political and legal systems of the foreign market; economic conditions; degree of competition prevailing in the given market; level of distribution technology available or accessible; the topography related to the infrastructure i.e., the geographical relief of the country's market (i.e, whether mountainous or flat, well endowed with good highways, main rail routes and navigable rivers); and the social and cultural norms of the various target markets.

Changes in approach and practice brought about by multi-modal transportation apply equally to ordinary through-container transportation. Much of our deep sea shipping trade operates on a port-to-port basis with optional pick-up and on-carriage. There is separate liability for each stage of handling. The operations of booking and delivering goods are the same as for combined or multi-modal transportation, but when damage or loss occurs, the different system of separate liabilities creates some special problems. Export staff need to be aware of whether they are dealing with goods under a full combined transport bill of lading/waybill, or through a container bill of lading/waybill. Yet, as noted earlier, EDI is changing this documentation quite dramatically, creating internationally accepted changes towards simplification of procedures for electronic processing.

Air freight must now be seen as a form of through or combined transport, involving other modes. Goods are trucked, for example, from Manchester to Heathrow under a flight number and air waybill, for onward carriage by air to their ultimate destination. Some airfreight to Western Europe is transported by surface, often by airlines themselves, under flight and air waybill routines. Some long-distance air-sea services are quicker than all-surface and cheaper than air alone. Any airfreight movement has by definition to be multi-modal as, unless both the exporter and importer are airport-based, a pick-up and delivery leg cannot be avoided. For all these reasons, export departments should see airfreight movement as door-to-door transport and organize their routines accordingly. For example, exporters should make sure that their air forwarders consolidate, fly, and break down consignments at destination as promptly as possible.

In selecting the means of transportation, rail freight, air or other through/combined transport movements, the export department must concern itself with the optimal means of delivering goods to the customer rather than the characteristics of individual conveyancing modes.

Marketing logistics

Recent studies by the Council of Logistics Management indicate that if a firm has an internal department handling foreign shipments, the knowledge and experience of the personnel is often country-specific. Successful global companies face international markets as a team rather than as a group of disparate functions (Trunick, 1989). General Motors, who implemented an

International Logistics Operation in 1977, differentiates between logistics and materials management (Krapfel *et al.*, 1981). The generic term at GM is materials management while international logistics focuses on transportation, packaging, and handling of both inbound and outbound freight. GM has 48 major overseas operations with plants in 60 cities. Nearly 200,000 GM employees live outside the USA, and overseas activities are responsible for the employment of an additional 60,000 within the USA. Outside of the USA, the largest market is Europe where GM own Adam Opel AG of West Germany; Vauxhall Motors of the UK; assembly and component plants in Belgium, France, Ireland, Netherlands and Portugal; and major factories in Austria, France and Spain. At present, virtually every European car manufacturer uses some GM components.

GM are found to practise the total-cost approach, i.e., material availability is accorded first priority followed closely by cost accordance or reduction. Alterations in transportation and packaging, and the qualification of costs with possible alternatives, lead to reasoned tradeoffs being made, prejudgments being made on total corporate benefit rather than divisional benefit alone.

International logistics have been introduced within GM to a divisional structure and must be held to be a good idea at local level rather than be seen as a measure of centralization, but they have not been able to accommodate and analyse the data necessary to its operations other than manually. GM is also constrained by what may be termed 'local infrastructure deficiencies', namely the state of port and local transportation and warehousing facilities – limited or no container handling at dockside, lack of weather-protected warehousing, different national groups in different regions or across political boundaries, and largely impaired highway systems. Taken together, the effect of these factors is cost multiplication due to delay, multiple handling, and damage in transit or storage.

Table 7.2   Some signs of latent opportunity and their solution

Opportunity	Solution
Unhappy end-users	Clarify and emphasize key drivers of customer satisfaction
Unexplored new channels	Quantify the value of each channel
Gaps in market coverage	If new channels required, transition by carefully defining roles
Deteriorating economics	Restructure networks to improve economics
Complacent intermediaries	Realign incentives
Dated systems at interfaces	Redesign systems

Source: Bucklin *et al.* (1996)

On the one hand, customer service levels must always be attained or improved; on the other, the cost of GM logistical activities to support worldwide operations must constantly be reviewed. This leads then to the consideration of new institutional arrangements and modes of operation.

Magrath (1996) points to the dilemmas which arise for the distribution manager with:

1. *Shifting channel coverage concerns.* Markets have splintered many times with the speed of competition and the constant rush of products to market and so channels that formerly met a supplier's objectives may no longer do so.
2. *Cost.* Channels usually involve transferring cost to improve margins. The largest single cost is holding inventory but most disagreements are over selling.
3. *Control.* There is channel crossover with companies giving products to multiple channels. Next, there is the growth of the private label brand and the sheer market size of certain retailers such as Wal-Mart.
4. *Capabilities.* This involves increasing the capabilities of the distributor to higher levels.

Trade procedures and documentation

With regard to documentation, the work of SIT-PRO, the Committee for the Simplification of International Trade Procedures, has achieved international agreement on certain items of trade documentation, including pre-printed computer paperwork for trade procedures, which they design, print and sell, and offer systems software to complete multiple documentation tasks from one typing. The increasing availability of relatively inexpensive small business computer systems facilitates this, and avoids the need for stocks of preprinted stationery and forms which may become obsolete. SITPRO systems are designed to international standards, incorporating the UN Layout Key.

Information handling by traditional means has come under review because of questions over cost and efficiency. As to these costs, SIT-PRO in their 1979 report, *Costing Guidelines for Export Administration*, commented:

In analysing the cost aspect of trade procedures and documentation, SITPRO has been able to draw on a number of assessments of the overall cost of present systems. We have, for example, the US figures following a detailed examination of procedures in that country which showed that the costs of compliance with essential documentation and procedures in typical export and import transactions were of the order of 7½ per cent of the average consignment value – that is 15 per cent for a full two-way transaction assuming that costs in other countries are not greatly different. As a very general indication of the possible orders of cost in the UK in export transaction, we would be quite ready to accept this ratio – viz. one seventh of the value of the goods exported.

Since then, of course, there had been the introduction of SAD, the Single Administrative Document, within Western Europe, as a direct result of European Union harmonization.

INCOTERMS 1990

In 1936, the International Chamber of Commerce, based in Paris, established the first set of international rules for the interpretation of the most commonly used terms in foreign trade. These became known as 'INCOTERMS 1936', and later, additions and subsequent amendments followed, to bring the rules in line with current international trade practices.

'INCOTERMS 1990' is the latest version, based on suggestions from governments, major importers, exporters and trade organizations, to adapt to the use of containerization, door-to-door intermodal transportation, roll-on/off and electronic data interchange (EDI). This revision incorporates some new terms as well as revising and dropping altogether some existing ones. The 13 INCOTERMS can be grouped into four categories (see Table 7.3):

1. E-terms, where goods are made available to the buyer at the seller's premises.
2. F-terms, where the seller is required to deliver goods to a carrier.
3. C-terms, where the seller contracts for carriage, but does not assume the risk of loss or damage after shipment.
4. D-terms, where the seller has to bear all costs and risks needed to bring the goods to the destination point.

INCOTERMS relate only to trade terms used in the contract of the sale, and are used to delegate responsibility to each party for customs clearance, packaging, inspection and destination.

The ICC continues to operate an international arbitration service, and further recommends that resort to ICC arbitration be clearly and specifically stated in the contract; the incorporation of INCOTERMS alone in a sales contract does not constitute in itself an agreement to have resort to ICC arbitration.

Long-established terms, such as 'FOB', are now restricted to port-to-port maritime movement, and 'FOB airport' is among the terms now

Table 7.3   INCOTERMS 1990

Group	Abbreviation	Explanation	Mode of transport usage
Group E:			
Departure	EXW	Ex works	Any
Group F:			
Main carriage	FCA	Free carrier	Air/rail
unpaid	FAS	Free alongside ship	Sea/waterway
	FOB	Free on board	Sea/waterway
Group C:			
Main carriage paid	CFR	Cost and freight	Sea/waterway
	CIF	Cost, insurance, freight	Sea/waterway
	CPT	Carriage paid to	Any
	CIP	Carriage and insurance paid to	Any
Group D:			
Arrival	DAF	Delivered at frontier	Any
	DES	Delivered ex ship	Sea/waterway
	DEQ	Delivered ex quay	Sea/waterway
	DDU	Delivered duty unpaid	Any
	DDP	Delivered duty paid	Any

Source: Adapted from: *INCOTERMS 1990*, ICC Publiication No. 460 (published in its official English version by the International Chamber of Commerce, Paris)

dropped. Multi-modal transportation should now use the term 'free carrier' or FCA. Similarly, CIF is also being restricted to maritime transportation. The more common term replacing CIF is 'Carriage and insurance paid' (CIP). The USA, with its own American Foreign Trade Definitions (AFTD), developed in 1919, and revised only once in 1941, has, according to BIFA (1990), agreed to accept INCOTERMS for international transactions.

Distribution efficiency and the national environment

We have the ability to market to the consumer in the store, and we are at a point where we have to focus on the consumer at an individual store level. There's something like 19 square feet of retailing space for every man, woman and child in the US. In 1967, there was something like 6 square feet. That's a very, very competitive business, we have to be efficient in what we do.

(William Fields, former CEO Wal-Mart, the world's largest retailer, Chicago, 1996)

Distribution is an integral part of the marketing programme and so should always be considered in relation to product positioning strategy, price, and communications. On a comparative country market basis, little has been done since Bartels produced his work in 1963 on wholesaling and retailing in 15 countries.

Direct comparisons are difficult between a

Table 7.4   Ten distribution myths

1. A channel of distribution is the movement of a product from the manufacturer to the ultimate consumer.
2. A channel's structure is determined by the characteristics of its products.
3. A distribution channel is managed by the manufacturer.
4. A firm should strive to maximize co-operation within its distribution channel.
5. The primary function of a warehouse is storage.
6. A firm sells to, or buys from, another firm.
7. Eliminating the middlemen will reduce distribution costs.
8. Administered channels are more efficient than non-administered channels.
9. A profitable channel is an efficient channel.
10. Planning distribution strategy is the responsibility of the distribution manager.

Source: Pearson, M. M. (1981) Ten distribution myths. *Business Horizons*, May-June, 17–23

home market and foreign target market because size alone is not an indicator of efficiency; competitive pressures surrounding the two markets will differ; and there may well exist a very sophisticated 'black' market or 'dual economy', where goods officially banned from entering the country may be found to be easily and openly available for either high prices or convertible currency or both. The same 'black market' phenomenon occurs, too, where goods may be in short supply and not generally available at what may be officially determined governmentally controlled prices, but available nevertheless to those willing to pay a little extra.

Technology also imposes change on channels of distribution as with containerization, in the use of freeports based near existing airports for the assembly and manufacture of duty-free goods for export only; and in electronic payments transfer, which allows for instantaneous transfer of funds between countries. Technology also affects the distribution channel ranging

Exhibit 7.3   Europe turns on to TV shopping

Electronic home shopping is already a massive phenomenon in the US, and Europeans seem likely to follow suit. By far the largest electronic home shopping business owned by Europeans is TV Shop, based in the small Swedish city of Malmö. After a 1989 start-up, annual growth has averaged an astonishing 40 per cent, and its 1996 sales totalled Skr490 million ($71.5m). TV Shop is active in 19 European countries, of which Germany is the biggest market, and it now aims to expand into Asia, particularly China.

TV Shop is 94 per cent owned by the MTG group, itself part of the Kinnevik organisation. Kinnevik has its roots in the steel and paper industries and last year had a turnover of $1.3 billion. It also operates radio stations in Scandinavia as well as TV3, TV1000, TV6, and ZTV. It is the largest shareholder in TV4. One of its subsidiaries is Scandinavia's largest private producer of television programmes. Kinnevik also operates digital cellular systems in Scandinavia and has cellular telephone networks in South America, east Europe, Asia and Africa.

The mail order catalogue is still today's predominant home marketing medium. But while those who advocate electronic marketing do not think that TV and Internet selling will be the end of mail order, TV Shop chief executive Jan Sjöwall says that electronic selling, particularly through the Internet, gives vendors more capacity to be 'super-responsive' compared with mail order houses. Furthermore, catalogues are expensive to produce, require long lead times and have a high transaction cost.

Sjöwall says: 'We can hit the public with single products through infomercials, mostly using dead time on terrestrial TV, and sell until we think saturation point has been reached. This year, our big seller is fitness machines, exercise devices of various kinds. For a while, it was household products, and before that, car body polishers.'

For the uninitiated, an infomercial is a 30-minute TV programme during which the virtues of, say, a multipurpose kitchen device are enthusiastically discussed by 'experts' before an admiring audience. Sjövall says 80 per cent of the infomercials his firm airs are imported from the United States, 'although we make about a dozen a year'. He says the selling programmes are 'presentations which are entertaining enough to attract their own audience'.

Sitting in his 26th floor office, the 39-year-old chief executive says: 'Although there are European firms in electronic home shopping, our only real competitors are in the US. The principal reason for continuing American strength in this sector is their big, relatively homogeneous, mainly unilingual market. So we are establishing an electronic shopping mall in Europe, a comparable if multilingual area.'

TV Shop's activity range is startling. Besides infomercial sales, which account for 60 per cent of turnover, it is Scandinavia's largest producer of commercial videos and short form commercials. It puts together programmes, operates TVG, its own Swedish shopping channel, runs sales operations through the Internet (in 14 countries), has its own computerised order processing system and runs a growing chain of retail outlets.

Although now the focus is on infomercials, Sjöwall finds them limiting in terms of the number of products you can present. He sees Internet sales as the way of the future: 'Then this business will no longer be entertainment-driven. The drive will come from customer conviction and price.'

He adds: 'If you think Internet marketing is a far-away dream, glance at this Philips Web TV Box that has just appeared in the United States. It should be on sale in Europe by June. For $300, if you have an electric plug and access to a phone line, you can surf the Internet on your TV screen without buying a computer. What that means is that very soon we shall be able to make Internet sales to a public that only needs to own a TV set and one of these boxes.'

Source: The European, 2–8 January 1997, p.19

from vending machines to goods material handling, as in laser scanning of purchases at checkouts in large supermarkets or even larger hypermarkets. One example is the development of home shopping in Britain via a home computer keyboard link through the public telephone system to a specially adapted television set, whereby it is possible to view data on anything from bank statements to household items, book holidays, transfer money in and out of bank accounts, and make purchases. This works through the British Telecom service, Prestel, which through a computer mainframe system gives a guide to goods on offer from the main retailing chains, and all companies including airlines, subscribing to the service.

Yet, it is still far removed from the sophistication of the French Minitel system, which opting for a penetration pricing strategy, succeeded in getting the necessary communications hardware into the majority of French households. Similar to a computer keyboard with a modem, it offers many advantages over the British system in terms of speed and the total number of subscribers to it, whereas previously they would never have considered a telephone number. Most French advertisers now include a Minitel number for further information. Technology is changing also in the home, and marketers must take cognizance of this as growth in the percentage of the population with personal computers, microwaves, compact disc players, fax machines, and other consumer durables affects not only what they buy, but how they buy, in what quantities, and how frequently. Both Prestel and Minitel have been relegated to the back of the pack internationally with the advent of the Internet. Without their own markets Prestel and Minitel have a presence but Prestel in Britain is fading fast.

Distribution is also affected by environmental change whereby changes arise within the society itself in terms of consumer mobility; consumer attitudes; available means of distribution; and the role that distribution is expected to fulfil. In many of the developed countries, the trend has been towards inner city decline in both industry and population, and towards the growth of suburbia. However, with near zero growth in population, this trend has been arrested, and is being reversed in some countries, Britain included.

Alternatively, environmental change may affect the profile of the channel, and the respective role to be adopted by the intermediaries who will be used, from importation or assembly, down to final sale to the consumer or end-user, and the relationships between these intermediaries and the manufacturer. The state may even decide that all importing has to be undertaken via a state trading enterprise.

Rising levels of personal disposable income in France created the postwar phenomenon of the hypermarket: an enormously large commercial shopping complex usually comprising a very large supermarket and general household departments, all located under the same roof on one ground level store located outside of town, and strategically positioned for major highway intersections. As an incentive, hypermarkets, such as the French chain Carrefour (which incidentally translates as 'crossroads'), operate petrol filling stations at their out-of-town locations which offer low-priced petrol for their customers as a draw to get them to visit their locations.

This quantum leap which France made in retailing with hypermarkets illustrates the fact that in distribution there can never be any guarantee against obsolescence. The hypermarkets in France have changed not only the buying situation for consumers, but also the selling situation for manufacturers, as the hypermarkets have become important customers for all the large manufacturing companies, not just in food but for all items which they stock, such as domestic electrical equipment and clothing.

Retailers are now increasingly going international. Barth *et al.* (1996) outline three new models of retailing abroad:

- *Superior operator.* Where a company expands internationally on the strength of its operating capability.
- *Concept exporter.* Export a distinctive concept but let someone else run it as Benetton does via franchising.
- *Skills exporter.* Companies export entire systems of doing business as Price/Costco has done.

For the foreign company, the question of location will be important. There is the question of ownership and control, whether it be a matter of finished goods, inventory or assembly. Manufacturers may choose to extend into retailing, as some multinational companies, such as Singer and Philips, have done, or take part-ownership of channel intermediaries, whether wholesalers or retailers. It is also possible for a foreign company to engage in some other means of distribution, such as direct mail order involving lower costs against the fixed costs of shopfronts and retail staff. However, against this are the heavy costs of postage in some countries, together with pilferage, high illiteracy rates and the fact that there may be a significant gap between dispatch of goods and receipt of payment. This lead time may create a cash flow problem for the company which is to maintain high levels of stock, and herein lies another problem. Interest rates are not equal between nations. If borrowings are expensive and inflation is high, then, there may be no advantages whatsoever in direct mail order unless there are also important differences in local taxation. Other possibilities include exclusivity of sales for a retailer whether he is continuing with the manufacturer's name or having his 'own label' added, an area of operations that has been increasing significantly over the past ten years in Western Europe.

In terms of transit of goods there is a wide variation in the possibilities on offer, not only of the mode of transportation, as already discussed, but also in terms of whether the company should decide to lease plant, equipment, vehicles, etc. – as is common in France or the USA – or buy, which would involve tying up capital. Aside from the relative advantages and disadvantages inherent in each respective method, there is always the guiding influence of competitive pressure to help shape the corporate decision as to the overall cost structure. (See Figure 7.1).

It is accepted that to create sales it is necessary to have a communications package, but aside from the problem of devising a successful communications package that will make sense in a foreign country, there is the perennial problem of acquiring meaningful foreign market intelligence and feedback, other than in waiting for sales figures. Choice of distribution channel may inhibit or eliminate the flow of market information from the country concerned. One may expect to receive less information from an agent than from a sales subsidiary, and virtually no information to emanate from a distributor who has exclusive sales territory rights.

Questions as to packaging and the necessary barrier and promotional properties of products for export are dealt with separately in Chapter 5. For the moment, let us just bear in mind that for small retailers, the product packaging is also the promotional material he is most likely to use within his shop-wide displays. For the manufacturer, there are certain cost advantages in having a standardized product package design which is acceptable to several markets: it eliminates the need for separate designs for each market, allowing the firm to capitalize on its presentation which at the same time benefits the production area, facilitates transit and enhances corporate image and brand awareness internationally, as well as helping small retailers with regard to product recognition, storage and display.

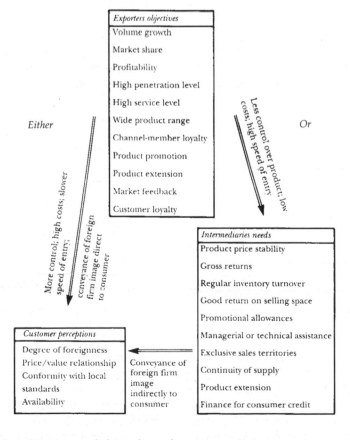

Figure 7.1   Comparative objectives and channel member expectations

Changing customer perceptions

The combined effect of market dynamics and the ability of computerization to detect patterns has produced some very useful thoughts on the subject. Perry (1989) interprets the market dynamic as leading to fierce competition, which will in turn force companies towards new and innovative distribution channels tailored to individual market niches. This will result from a fine-tuning of the segmentation process that has been in force since the late 1970s, and is seen as being the only way for US companies to compete with foreign competitors who are all-too-often satisfied with occupying the lower end of any market. Figure 7.2 depicts on the right a matrix which pinpoints customer needs with greater accuracy, and will be serviced by a portfolio of a multiplicity of distribution channels, including non-traditional channels.

Marketing intermediaries

The exporter's overall objective is to achieve some target rate of return on investment. The first point to consider is that irrespective of whether or not we use intermediaries in the channel, the functions of a conventional or vertical marketing system do not change. In a vertical marketing system, the company is simply bringing 'in-house' certain activities which would be performed by others. It is still necessary to fulfil these functions, however. As we go down the channel, these functions change from design,

production, branding, pricing, promoting, and selling, to a new set with a greater emphasis on functions, such as inventory, promotion, display, selling, delivery, and finance. Whenever a manufacturer looks grudgingly, therefore, at discounts offered to intermediaries, it is worthwhile remembering the importance and the cost of the functions that these intermediaries perform before deciding to bring these activities within the company. The cost savings, once the discount structure has been abolished and the activities have been brought in-house, may then only be marginal.

The benefits of using intermediaries have to be set against the disadvantages of loss of control. Primarily, where speed of market entry is important there may be instant access to a number of outlets, low selling costs, and the advantage of an experienced distribution outlet; but intermediaries, whether agents or distributors, may not give a product the attention which the manufacturer would like. Given that some of these intermediaries may be handling products for a number of companies, their motivation may lie more with the product earning them the highest returns in commission. This loss of control for the manufacturer is difficult to quantify. The manufacturer may not have any reasonable marketing objectives or sales projection figures established for the market in question, and so the intermediary may simply be a low-cost presence for an anticipated low level of sales. Control, though, is lacking. Information, too, is likely to be limited or biased in view of the fact that if the market is booming then the intermediary will only commit economic suicide by admitting it to

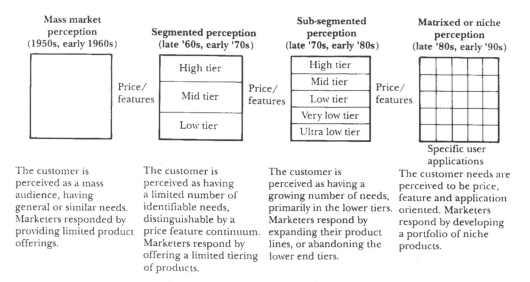

Source: Perry, D. (1989) How you'll manage your 1990s distribution portfolio. *Business Marketing,* **74** (6)

Figure 7.2   Changing marketing perceptions of the customer

the manufacturer, thereby inviting him to bring in his own sales organization and gear up for a future anticipated higher level of sales without intermediaries. Similarly, customer service may also be seen to be at risk. International warranties and brand awareness break down in markets where there is inadequate provision for service maintenance personnel and spare parts. Direct distribution avoids these problems but means a higher degree of investment is required, and perhaps also a greater length of time before a local sales team is recruited and trained for the task.

Exhibit 7.4 Compaq's compact solution

Fewer can be better when it comes to the strategic location of distribution centres. That is the finding of Compaq, which lays claim to being the world's biggest supplier of personal computers.

Four years ago the company had 13 service centres in 12 European countries, fed from its manufacturing and repair base in Erskine, Scotland. A review, led by Pearse Flynn, service manager for Europe, Middle East and Africa, highlighted the fact that there was inconsistency in the operating and stock control systems of the various national service centres. All held a full inventory of parts, yet the level of customer service varied dramatically from centre to centre.

A more cohesive European logistics strategy was needed which would bring about improvements in customer service while simultaneously cutting costs through reduced stockholding and more efficient distribution.

It was decided to bring in a logistics partner for this purpose. A qualifying questionnaire was sent out to some 100 companies across Europe, of which 13 were short-listed and invited to tender. These included freight forwarders, parcel companies, groupage operators and contract distribution specialists.

The objective was to find an alternative to having a network of national warehouses across Europe. The solution arrived at was to have a main parts store close to the Dutch-German border, supported by zonal warehouses in the UK and France. The result would be reduced inventory levels – but it was essential to ensure that country service levels were not compromised.

Not one but two logistics partners were appointed. Hays Distribution was given the task of managing all stockholding and co-ordinating trunking between the three parts centres and the Erskine plant, while parcels specialist UPS handles deliveries from the centres to Compaq's customers.

The contract was awarded at the end of September 1994. 'While we had earmarked two existing Hays warehouses for the zonal distribution centres, we had to find a totally new site in Holland,' recalls Hays Distribution's project manager, Jeremy Shepherd. 'Compaq wanted the new centre up and running by the year end, giving us three months to finalise the property, design and install the warehouse, and recruit and train staff.'

The site selected was at Helmond, near Eindhoven, close to the German border and well-placed for the motorway network and airport hubs. The warehouse was ready and staffed by mid-December, allowing Compaq to start closing its 13 local operations and transferring inventory.

The Paris centre, operated by the Hays French sister company Hays Fril, opened in February 1995. The UK zonal centre in Aldridge, Birmingham, was up and running in April.

By May 1995 all the old distribution centres had been closed. Throughout the transition period, customer service had been fully maintained.

The central distribution centre at Helmond holds 190,000 items of stock at any one time, across 4000 different parts. These range from docking stations and monitors to memory chips, badges and technical literature in several languages. Paris and Birmingham hold critical stocks of the thousand fastest-moving parts.

Trunking operations are scheduled to ensure that deliveries to each centre are completed by 10am daily. By 4pm, every item has been checked, logged and is available on the stock inventory system. The warehouse order entry system developed by Compaq allows the three warehousing operations to be viewed as a single entity, with complete stock visibility across all sites. This information can be accessed by all Compaq locations in Europe.

Orders received at Helmond by 5pm are collected by UPS that night, with the majority delivered across Europe the next morning. It is calculated that over the next 12 months more than two million parts will be shipped.

Compaq measures the effectiveness of the service in terms of the availability of parts against customers' orders. By this measurement, customer service has been improved from its former level of around 70 per cent to over 95 per cent.

At the same time, inventory levels have been cut by 40 per cent. The combined Hays/UPS operational costs are 15 per cent lower per part shipped than under the old network.

'We are now taking on new responsibilities,' says Jeremy Shepherd. 'For example, for deliveries to many African and East European countries, the distribution centres have to produce pro forma invoices.'

Source: Export Today (1996)

Avon Cosmetics maintain an approach of selling door-to-door wherever possible through a workforce of freelance agents who are also technically self-employed. Tupperware is another example of a US company that has been successful in transferring its house-party style of selling to other markets, including Japan. Elsewhere, the pattern seems to be that wherever direct control is not possible or desirable, settle for the next best alternative. In this regard, it is worth bearing in mind how Avon Cosmetics have traditionally sold their cosmetics into the Central and East European countries, and how Marks & Spencer successfully export their name and branded product range into countries where they are not officially represented other than as a brand name administered by a distributor. Retailing has become an international activity for many because of franchising, including Marks & Spencer, House of Fraser, Tie Rack, Benetton and Body Shop.

Identifying marketing intermediaries

Intermediaries may take various forms, but must also be acknowledged to be specialists of considerable experience, often with an important network of trade contacts. They include importers who are wholesalers, importers who are cash-and-carry wholesalers; brokers; commission agents; exclusive distributors; sales offices; and international co-operative food and grocery distribution groups, such as the Dutch based VG and Spar purchasing associations, which have themselves undergone profound organizational change in recent years. Spar is a member of the Schuitema group, which is majority-owned by the Dutch supermarket chain, Ahold, but rival Unigro also maintains an equity stake, buying out through Sagara of Spain the Spanish wholesaler Penagrande, a supplier to independent Spanish Spar stores. In Belgium, the food distributor to Spar, Alimo, has been acquired by Unidis, a Belgian subsidiary of Unigro, which now control two of the three Spar dealers in Belgium. In conjunction with Axel Johnson (Sweden), Spar is opening a chain of stores in Sweden. In Germany, Axel Johnson is an established supplier to Spar, having a joint equity stake in each other's organizations. Axel Johnson subsidiaries handle Spar's overseas import activities, including exotic and tropical fruits. A joint purchasing organization has now been created by the two companies, further integrating their activities.

VG, meanwhile, is actively developing its activities in Spain, but has operations also in Britain, Italy, Austria, the Netherlands and Ireland. The cash-and-carry concept proved to be short-lived and is now in decline within Western Europe but enjoying high sales growth in Central and Eastern Europe which have cash-based economies. Three leading European retailers: Argyll from the UK; Ahold from the Netherlands; and the French Group Casino have carried out a cross-shareholding deal to cement their European Retailing Alliance (ERA), and are looking at the possibilities for a European own-label family of brands. ERA is now looking at the potential for packaging, labelling and distribution across Europe.

Relating to channel strategy, consideration should be given to the number, quality and type of outlets to be used, whether it would be possible for some of the distributive tasks to be absorbed at an acceptable cost, or, if not, which form of channel intermediary has to be engaged. Retailing operators at the lower level include door-to-door salespeople and street traders. Service levels, too, are important, but these may be influenced also by the margins made available to the intermediary by the manufacturer. Where labour is cheap and plentiful, labour may be hired. Elsewhere, the move is to automate. Allied to service level is the question of inventory, and who exactly takes title to inventory and so responsibility for it, as this is a cost to be borne in the foreign market. Finance and credit is another area for joint participation by both manufacturer and intermediary, as is promotional activity at the local level. Complete standardization of distribution strategy across markets is difficult to achieve because of customer expectations as to service levels, and the competitive pressures existing to ensure that one either responds to these local demands or else leaves the market. Expectations with regard to customer service levels vary as do local distribution costs. The problem for the company is one of demand management – developing a distribution mix which best serves each market in which the company is represented.

Total customer satisfaction is a good route to pursue. Figure 7.3, Perry (1989) depicts exactly how a matrix distribution may work towards the salvation of US companies threatened by foreign distributors. Short product cycles, low profit margins, changing management emphases, have led to a neglect of the customer. In aiming for value-added niche marketing, companies will not take customers for granted, but instead, seek to provide full service and need satisfaction through traditional and non-traditional channels, exploiting all opportunities for synergy along the way through perhaps even a strategic business alliance.

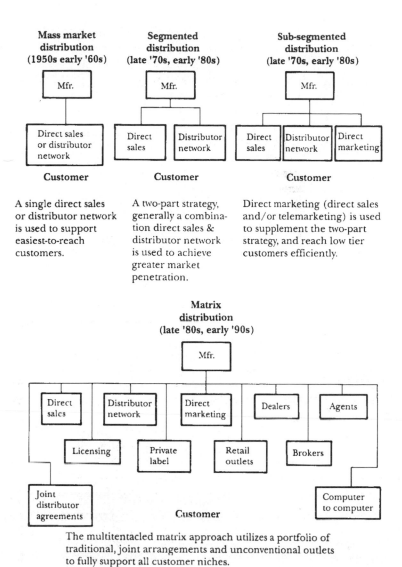

A single direct sales or distributor network is used to support easiest-to-reach customers.

A two-part strategy, generally a combination direct sales & distributor network is used to achieve greater market penetration.

Direct marketing (direct sales and/or telemarketing) is used to supplement the two-part strategy, and reach low tier customers efficiently.

The multitentacled matrix approach utilizes a portfolio of traditional, joint arrangements and unconventional outlets to fully support all customer niches.

Source: Perry, D. (1989) How you'll manage your 1990s distribution portfolio. *Business Marketing,* **74** (6)

Figure 7.3   Changing distribution strategies

Parallel or 'grey' exporting

This arises where domestic wholesalers begin to perceive greater returns available from the illicit exports of goods intended only for the domestic market. (See Figure 7.4). It undercuts the manufacturer's official recommended price abroad, upsets his foreign distribution channel members, and does damage to its corporate image at home, even where product specification between the two countries is different and is partly reflected in the price differential. The dilemma for the manufacturer is whether or not to withdraw the product from sale in the domestic market when this foreign leakage appears excessive. Alternatively, increasing the domestic product price may have a similar effect, making these illicit exports much less profitable, but will also develop hostility among domestic customers, consumer groups and even government in the home market.

The market may be upset by illicit exporting by wholesalers or retailers, as is seen in Figure 7.4, but sometimes also by third party clients who then resell to the manufacturer's distribution outlets in another country. L'Oreal has suffered the embarrassment of cut-price outlets in France obtaining supplies from third countries and supplying French customers at levels lower than L'Oreal's officially recommended prices. In the UK, there have been many similar examples. In the 1960s, Mallory Batteries tried to raise prices in the UK to discourage parallel exports taking place from the UK and ruining its official market price and distribution structure in France and Germany, but this ran foul of a UK Government Prices Board. Johnny Walker Red Label, a product of the Distillers Company, a subsidiary of Guinness plc, was taken off the UK market while it was still brand leader, and remained off the shelves for six years

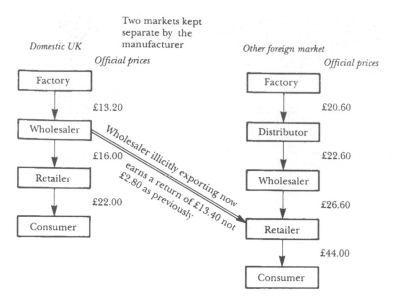

Note: To understand parallel exporting, one has to remember that countries have different tax regimes and that many have recommended resale price maintenance structures – making it virtually impossible for multinational corporations to standardize price structure – and that, combined with rises and falls in foreign exchange rates, can create market opportunities for channel members

Figure 7.4   Parallel or 'grey' exports

between 1977–1983, before a change of policy restored it. Red Label had had 12 per cent of the market when it was withdrawn. It was later reintroduced to a stagnant home market at the expense of Distiller's other brands (White Horse and Haig) and with no assurance that parallel exporting would not begin again.

Exhibit 7.5   Distributor takes on parallel importers

If you can't beat 'em, join 'em.

That is the strategy that Borneo Motors, one of the biggest players in the local car market, is adopting to face the challenge of parallel imports.

It distributes Toyota and Lexus cars here and will start with the seven-seater Ipsum which has so far been brought in only by parallel import.

Borneo Motors' general manager for marketing, Mr William Choo, said that from now on, his company would bring in new models, if enough customers asked for them, and that this was part of the strategy to be more sensitive to their needs.

He said: 'For example, we received more than 50 requests from people who were interested in the Toyota Ipsum but did not want to buy from parallel importers.

'We don't want to push them into the arms of parallel importers.'

He added that the vehicle, which major parallel importer Cheng Yong Credit Enterprises, started selling last October, would be available in the next few months.

There are more than 90,000 Toyotas on Singapore roads today and it has been a top seller for more than a decade.

Competition in the car market became keener after October 1995, when the Land Transport Authority relaxed its registration rules, allowing more parallel importers.

The first major parallel imports here were of Mercedes-Benz cars, distributed by Cycle & Carriage, and such imports have eaten into the distributor's virtual market monopoly.

Parallel importers then started bringing in Japanese cars, such as Toyotas and Nissans in significant numbers.

Mr Choo, who was speaking to The Sunday Times on Friday after announcing plans for the company's 30th anniversary this year, said that it would face the competition head-on and beef up on customer service.

For a start, it will soon bring in a new model, the 1.5 litre Soluna, which will cost at least $5,000 less than the 1.3 litre Corolla, a popular model now selling at $101,000 with a Certificate of Entitlement.

In a telephone interview on Friday, the managing director of Cheng Yong Credit Enterprises, Mr Neo Nam Heng, said that he was not worried about moves by distributors to counter parallel importers.

He said: 'I am prepared for it and welcome it.

➡

> → **Exhibit 7.5** *continued*
>
> It shows that we have succeeded in making the market more competitive, which is the way it should be.'
>
> 'For more than 30 years, they have enjoyed their monopoly now it's the customers turn to enjoy.'
>
> Tan Chong Motors, another major player, which distributes Nissan vehicles, said it was also working on its strategy against parallel importers, who have been bringing in the March, a small car.
>
> A spokesman declined to comment further, saying that all would be revealed soon at the launch of the company 40th's anniversary.
>
> As part of its celebrations, Borneo Motors is offering a $10,000 discount on 400 units of the Corona, with leather seats, sports rims and other extras.
>
> Other highlights include a charity drive to raise $300,000 for the Salvation Army.
>
> In a press statement on Friday, Cycle & Carriage announced the debut of a new three-litre model, the Mitsubishi Sigma saloon, going for $175,000 including COE.
>
> *Source:* *Sunday Times Singapore*, 23 March 1997, p. 30

The EU response to parallel exporting is clear from the *Hasselblad (GB) Ltd. versus Commission supported by Camera Care Ltd case*. Significantly, Hasselblad was prosecuted by the EU in 1981 for infringing Article 35(1) of the Treaty of Rome, which relates to free trade. The Commission contended that Hasselblad acted in concert with six sole distributors to prevent, limit, or discourage exports of Hasselblad equipment between the members states, and that the sole distributorships and selective distribution system operated, constituted infringements. Hasselblad (GB) Ltd. was fined £93,642. On appeal, this was reduced to £45,218. The aim of the concerted practice had been to prevent imports into the UK of Hasselblad cameras intended for Camera Care, and as such, constituted a flagrant breach of the EU competition rules. Although corporate responses to combat parallel exporting may include withdrawing the product or raising the price in the domestic market, the probability of EU intervention has also to be considered.

Waddington, the famous British games manufacturer, won an interim injunction in the Singapore High Court, in 1984, against a local importer, which involved the seizure of 559 sets of Monopoly and 531 sets of Cluedo purchased from a British export house and intended for sale and at a discount on sets made by Waddington in Singapore. However, in January 1985, when the case for the injunction was heard before the Singapore High Court, it was ruled that the injunction could not be continued as there had been no misrepresentation. The overall situation, therefore, is far from satisfactory. Although some consumers will temporarily enjoy the parallel importers' lower prices, there are important ramifications for foreign investment generally; for the licensed distributors who have invested in goodwill; and the employment effects if a

company like Waddington chooses to leave the foreign market as a response, particularly as this action will likely then be taken by other companies as well.

To turn to a more complex case of parallel exporting, that of the pharmaceutical products, here we have a case where opinions are divided about the morality of behaviour on either side. Firstly, to take the industry case, the British pharmaceutical industry believes that it is losing sales worth about £100 million a year to companies which buy British-made drugs cheaply in Europe and bring them back to the UK for resale. One large chemists' wholesaler, UniChem, which claims about 22 per cent of the wholesale market, said that they are losing about 10 per cent of their sales to parallel importers, costing them about £3 million per month.

Not all wholesalers have the same view, for in 1984, the Association of Pharmaceutical Wholesalers was formed by 32 wholesalers with the aim of establishing a code of conduct, lobbying MPs and mounting a public relations drive. Benefits obviously flow to the wholesalers and retailers making better margins on these parallel imports. The pharmaceutical companies themselves have been active in trying to curb the practice by conducting a campaign emphasizing the dangers to the public of being supplied with foreign language packaging or possibly slightly differently formulated products.

One such wholesaler, Malcolm Town, and his company, Maltown, were fined £6,360 in 1982 for illegally importing drugs which were then sold to health authorities and chemists for as little as half the manufacturer's list price. The defence counsel argued the case that the interests of his client were very much allied to the public interest. Nine summonses related to the import and sale of three drugs: Septrin, used for treating bronchitis, manufactured by the

Wellcome Foundation in Kent; Zyloric, prescribed for gout, made by the Wellcome Foundation in Spain and imported via Malaga and Gibraltar; and, Daonil, given to sufferers of diabetes mellitus, which was a Swiss drug that arrived in Britain via Hong Kong. The drugs were all being imported on a commercial basis and sold on a commercial basis. All drugs were sent for laboratory analysis before being sold on the British market.

The pharmaceutical price structure in Britain is a national agreement between the National Health Service and the industry, and allows for a 21 per cent profit margin to include advertising, promotion, research and development. However, this margin and this style of structure is sufficient to create disparities with other neighbouring European markets. Maltown has a list of about 300 imported drugs sold at prices substantially lower than the Health Service pays chemists for prescriptions. The trade price for 500 Septrin was £52.58, while Maltown obtained the same amount for £20.53. Zyloric was £14.34 for 100 milligrams, while Maltown paid £6.34, and Daonil listed at £9.64 for 5 milligrams was only £4.37. Ventolin, an asthmatic inhaler, made in Britain by Glaxo Pharmaceuticals costs the Health Service £2.91 per prescription, but Maltown reimports the drug at £1.45 from France, Belgium and Italy.

Although corporate responses to combat parallel exporting may include withdrawing the product or raising its price in the domestic market, the UK Government refused to act in the case of these pharmaceutical products, and was actually bringing the case against Maltown. The position of the EU with regard to this phenomenon has, therefore, to be considered. Any action viewed as being in restraint of free trade will invite EU intervention, and so the EU has maintained the right for individuals to shop around for cars and bring them back into their home market as a personal import. This right extends also to companies engaged in parallel or 'grey' exporting, which is not illegal and which the EU views as being an extension of free trade within the community.

Freeports

Freeports are based on the concept of manufacturing or processing in bond free of all taxes, but whereas this has always been the case with the manufacture of whisky, which by law required a minimum of three years to mature before being ready for sale at home or abroad, freeports usually exist only for the export market.

The term 'freeport' may be potentially misleading as the facility does not have to be based around a seaport, but may be a transit zone, a free perimeter or free trade zone. The terminology changes from country to country and includes free trade zone (FTZ), export processing zone (EPZ), free trade area (FTA), investment promotion zone (IPZ), export promotion processing zone (EPPZ), or just freeport. The term freeport will be used here as being synonymous with all the other terms presently in use.

Although freeports have attracted a good deal of attention in recent years, the concept started with the Phoenicians 3,000 years ago, although the first in Europe was Hamburg in 1189, when Frederick I, then Holy Roman Emperor, granted a charter to the City of Hamburg, releasing it from the payment of customs duties. Others then followed. The freeport concept in the Middle Ages included Bruges, Antwerp, Amsterdam, Marseilles, London and Genoa, which were important transhipment centres, as direct routes did not generally become available until a few centuries later with the steamships and the creation of established conference lines.

In 1982, there were reputed to have been more than 350 of these freeports around the world, of which more than two-thirds were in the developing world. They are estimated to have accounted for 9 per cent of world trade in that year and to have generated six million jobs. In a global economy experiencing little growth, this particular area of operations appeared to offer some promise, and, for this reason, the British Government in 1984 announced that six freeports were to be established, each based alongside an existing port or provincial airport, as with Belfast Airport, Prestwick Airport, Liverpool Port, Southampton Port, Cardiff Port, and Birmingham Airport, none of which is an important throughput centre in its own right, there being no equivalent of a Rotterdam among them. With the sole exception of Liverpool Port whose business is now 75 per cent import, all of these UK freeports have failed. Elsewhere, other examples of thriving foreign freeports in existence include: Hong Kong, Singapore, Hamburg, Amsterdam, Stockholm, Bombay, Sri Lanka, South Korea, plus an estimated forty-plus in the USA.

The Adam Smith Institute in London estimated, in 1985, the total number of freeports at over 500, and estimated that they accounted for 10 per cent of world trade in 1981 and would account for more than 20 per cent of world trade by 1985, but it should also be noted that the Institute's publication was the proceedings of a one-day seminar aimed at the promotion of freeports in the UK (Pirie, 1983).

Manufacturers operating within a freeport are not liable to the import duties or the local or governmental taxes which manufacturers would pay immediately outside of the freeport area, but items which are assembled or produced within this area are not allowed to enter the domestic economy without payment of appropriate taxes and duties. It is on this understanding, that the goods are produced solely for export, that these tax concessions are made. Freeports outside the UK also have certain important competitive advantages, such as relief from controls on planning, health and safety regulations, and legislative controls related to the workplace. Wages are generally 10–30 per cent of those in industrial nations.

The freeport advantage

1. Better cash flow for firms located on freeports. Goods may be imported from overseas for transhipment to other markets without the bureaucratic 'red-tape' of customs entries and subsequent withdrawals. Firms located on the zones do not pay customs duties or valued added taxes (VAT) on goods brought into the zone until they are released on to the domestic market. An exception to this arrangement is that VAT is payable on transactions between firms operating on the freeport, but this can be recovered if the goods are subsequently sold to customers outside the domestic market.
2. Freeports provide firms with a degree of flexibility in adjusting to market conditions. Goods can be stored on the zone without payment of duty until market prospects improve. For commodities which experience volatile shifts in pricing, this can be important for the nation state where it is economically dependent on a single commodity crop.
3. Freeports provide firms with freedom from paperwork and bureaucratic legislation.
4. Firms located on a zone can benefit from the concentration of export facilities therein, including customs, insurance, packing and certification.
5. Firms located on a zone could benefit from savings in insurance and policing costs. Freeports are fenced-in areas policed and monitored by customs authorities and provide a safe and secure environment for firms.
6. Freeports could make a substantial contribution to employment. They could be a source of both direct and indirect employment opportunities. Increased investment from both home and foreign sources would make a direct contribution to employment. Raw materials can be processed into finished or intermediate goods which may then be re-exported. In addition, there would be indirect job creation in the form of jobs attached to storage, warehousing and servicing the zones.

The test for success of a freeport is whether it is able to create investment additional to that which already exists, and avoid merely a dispersal and relocation of firms within the domestic economy. Another point is that trade within the EU is already exempt from duties and so, for the concept to work within the EU it would have to involve a manufacturing or assembly activity which relied on imports outside of the EU for re-export outside of the community. Because of this, and because of the geographical location of Britain which is not close to any non-EU country, British freeports would, obviously, hold little attraction for Continental European firms. As regards the VAT position, this has changed recently in the UK, whereby importers now have to pay VAT immediately on receipt of goods rather than when they are sold. As to the freeport, no tax would be paid on entry to the freeport zone, which has its own customs entry and departure points. Only if freeport goods were to enter the domestic market would payment of taxes and duties be required. Thus, should the expected strong export orientation

Table 7.5 Freeport advantages compared	
UK	*Rest of the world*
Concentration of exporting facilities, e.g., customs, certification, packing, forwarding	Concentration of exporting facilities, e.g., customs, certification, packing, forwarding.
Freedom from customs duty	Exemption from all forms of taxation
Politically located around declining centres of high unemployment	Located alongside thriving ports and airports
No locational advantage of freeport as entire EU is a free trade area	Exemption for wage and welfare legislation Generous depreciation allowances No trade unions (as in South Korea)

Table 7.6	The enabling environment for freeports
Duties	There should be no duties or tariffs on goods entering the freeport.
Taxation	Taxation must be lower in the freeport than outside. Examples of Belgium offering remission on seven different taxes affecting business, and of Spain offering no VAT and other concessions within the freeport at Cadiz.
Regulation	A lower level of regulation within the freeport to attract foreign traders unable or unwilling to cope with domestic regulations. Different standards, including product quality and packaging standards, can apply within the freeport. In some countries, this extends to there being less or even no legislation in respect of health and safety at work, and less or even no wage and price controls.
Independence	Freeports should be free of government and be independently managed by an authority largely outside the scope of political manipulation).

Source: Pirie, M. (1983) *Freeports*, Adam Smith Institute, London

fail to materialize, the future for the freeport is one of only becoming a bonded warehouse for imported goods awaiting entry to the domestic market.

The Malaysian port of Pasir Gudang is now operating in a freeport. Malaysian shippers are now able to store their goods at Pasir Gudang while waiting for prices of any particular commodity to pick up before exporting. It is hoped, too, that this freeport undergoing a $70 million expansion plan will take some traffic from neighbouring Singapore. It handled 3 million tonnes with a capacity of 3.5 million tonnes but has a projected capacity of 7.6 million tonnes. Taking another example, Bausch and Lomb base their European distribution at Schipol airport in the Netherlands, which allows them day-to-day delivery throughout Europe. Similarly, periodicals such as, *Time, Newsweek, Business Week*, are also distributed from this same base; getting information to the consumer on time necessitates air freight, but here, using a major hub and spoke airline distribution network, based on Schipol airport, there are the potential savings of bulk distribution.

The concept has spread so widely that there was even a suggestion in *The Times* of 5 January 1987 that the granting of freeport status to Port Stanley in the Falkland Islands might be one way to attract investment to those islands. Yet, like the UK freeports, it is difficult to see any clear locational or communications advantage for a Port Stanley freeport.

Distribution in the PLC stages

Companies each have their own corporate culture and corporate ethic – a belief as to which product and geographic markets they should be in, and which channels of distribution are most suited to their needs. However, the competitive environment does not always respect this, and in a multi-modal channel situation a product may have to forge a new channel of its own or die. Some companies have remained in business through the maintenance of a highly individual channel of distribution such as Tupperware or Avon, as mentioned earlier. The product life cycle works in two ways: first, with regard to the product itself and its stage in the cycle, and secondly, with regard to its distribution. Falling unit manufacturing costs leading to lower unit selling costs are signals of a mature product reaching into the saturation and decline phases of the cycle. Distribution, therefore, has to be adjusted accordingly, to minimize costs but still ensure product availability, and this may lead to a change in the choice of channel used; perhaps, following the example of Perrier bottled water in the USA, from low-volume specialist health foods or delicatessen retailer to high-volume general trader such as a supermarket chain. A differential advantage that may be identified when moving into a new channel or distribution away from the mainstream competition may not only provide a breathing-space, but a clear gain in profitability if it means leadership of a small but lucrative market segment now being accessed by means of this new distribution channel. Mature goods which are now being distributed in this way through new distribution channels include spectacles. Distribution channels, therefore, need to be reviewed periodically, and not just with regard to cost of the product, but with regard to customers as well (Combs, 1987). Even mature products, such as fruit and vegetables, can benefit as Del Monte found in Florida when they met with a five-fold increase in the sale of pineapples after providing retailers with a pineapple cutting machine. Research had shown that consumers would buy more pine-

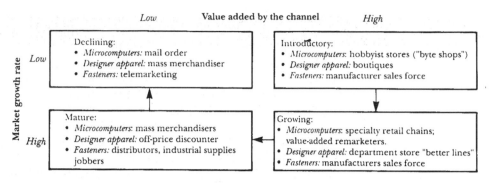

Source: Lele, M. (1986) Matching your channels to your product's life cycle. *Business Marketing,* **71** (2), 60–69

Figure 7.5   Value-added versus market growth matrix

apples if only they knew how to peel them. Del Monte showed them the way (Fortune, 1985).

Channel changes, according to Lele (1986), follow the product life cycle pattern, and the two factors responsible for this are value-added by the channel and the growth rate of the overall market. Firms then lose market share if they do not switch channels as the technology matures. In Figure 7.5, Lele (1986) shows how the two variables, 'value-added by the channel', in terms of services provided to the customer before, during and after the sale, and 'market growth rate', which measures the speed with which demand for that type of product is growing, interrelate. Each of the four cells corresponds to a stage of the PLC. The microcomputer is an example of a product that has moved very quickly from introduction to maturity, so while the dedicated vertical distributors were trying to expand, distribution was already moving to the mass marketers, the major retailing chains and mail order catalogues. Keeping pace with the PLC, marketers must shift to less costly channels that do not add as much value, or provide as much service, in order to achieve the strategic objectives of expanding the market and maintaining market share.

Lele emphasizes that no one channel will be sufficient to manage a product through all the stages of its development; that marketers ought to be responsive to market changes, and change their channels accordingly and not assume ever that channels can be controlled, even with attempts to motivate channels through volume-oriented financial incentives to intermediaries doomed to failure before they start.

Performance measures have to differ with each stage of the PLC and this, too, has to be considered in planning overall channel strategy. It should certainly lead to some further consideration before the implementation of an incentive campaign.

Returning to an Ansoff Mark I matrix of new and existing markets and new and existing products, Band (1987) offers a few recommendations:

1.   Market modifications:
     - convert non-users
     - enter new market segments
     - win competitor's customers
     - encourage more frequent product use
     - develop more usage per occasion
     - develop new and more varied uses

2.   Product modifications:
     - quality improvement
     - features improvement
     - style improvement

3.   Marketing-mix modifications:
     - prices
     - distribution – more or different channels?
     - advertising
     - sales promotion
     - personal filling
     - services

The selection and design of the distribution channel should be based (Mallen, 1996) on a decision matrix with six stages in selecting and structuring a company's channels of distribution, with the sixth being added for review and evaluation:

1.   Decision areas with five questions involving: how direct should the channels be? How selective should the distribution channel be? What types of middlemen are to be selected? How many channels for a given product? How shall the middlemen be chosen to fill the slots created?

2.   Guidelines. Four basic objectives: maximize sales; minimize cost; maximize channel goodwill; and maximize channel control.

3.   Determinants: the market; the marketing mix; the resources and the environment.

4.   Quantifying the options.

5.   Decision.

6.   Channel review and evaluation.

Interestingly, Wilkinson (1996) states that the choice of channel distribution that a firm opts for is a manifestation of its power/social influence. Managing these power plays can act to further a firm's business. Positive and negative influences which the firm can exert on the channel can dictate its working efficiency. Channels of distribution can therefore be viewed as social systems with firms as interdependent organizations. Power, according to Wilkinson, is the means by which co-operation between individual channel members' activities are co-ordinated and the means by which any conflict between firms is controlled. Co-operation and co-ordination require some form of power structure which sets up rewards (or positive sanctions) and punishments (or negative sanctions). Perceptions of anticipated gains and costs will shape corporate behaviour. At the same time, within any channel there will be a need for specialization which in turn creates dependence among participants but yet another important aspect is the separation of the physical movement of goods from the exchange of title contained in the accompanying paperwork. In all these respective tasks, channel members should be seeking to work together and explore respective areas of expertise.

Revision questions

1. What are the forces behind the creation of European or other regional distribution centres?
2. It is said that logistics alliances are posed to become a building block of the 'network economy'. What is a logistics alliance, and what is the 'network economy'?
3. What is the virtual value chain and how does it differ from the value chain as described by Michael Porter?
4. As international retailing expands, researchers are introducing new terminology such as the Superior Operator; the Concept Operator and the Skills Operator. Explain the characteristics of each of these three terms.
5. What are the six symptoms identified by Bucklin *et al.* which point to a developing channel opportunity?
6. What are the difficulties likely to be experienced by retailers who seek to export the standard retail formula which has been successful on the domestic market?
7. Retailers are turning to international sourcing to achieve a better price/value ratio at home. What are the likely longer term implications of this policy for policy-makers, suppliers and retailers?
8. What are natural channels of distribution?
9. What is the relationship between IT and Distribution channels?
10. What is SITPRO and what is its function?
11. What are Incoterms and why are they important? Identify the four main categories.
12. How does the environment affect the efficiency of the distribution channel?
13. Home shopping by television or on the Internet – which is likely to have the bigger client base in ten years' time, and why?
14. What is micro segmentation?
15. What is meant by 'parallel' or 'grey' exporting? Is it legal?
16. Explain what is meant by the term 'freeport'. Is there a universal definition?
17. How do PLC stages impact distribution channel effectiveness?
18. How does Ansoff's four cell matrix of markets and products stand up to present-day scrutiny? Does it still have relevance? Explain.
19. What are the conventions regulating international transportation by air, sea, road and rail? What about multi-modal transportation?
20. From the survey undertaken of purchasing professionals and their attitudes to the Internet, how do you foresee the future? Is Internet usage likely to be different, comparing companies and individual consumers?

References

Andel, T. (1996) 'CEO's share visions of supply chains (Intelligent Business Strategies Conference, Chicago, IL)', *Transportation and Distribution*, May, **37** (5), 109–112.

Band, W. (1987) Achieving success in mature markets requires careful approach. *Sales and Marketing Management in Canada*, **28** (2), 16–17.

Barks, J. V. (1989) Logistics broadens its horizons: international survey results. *Distribution*, **88** (10), 58–63.

Barth, K., Karch, N. J., McLaughlin, K. and Shi, C. S. (1996) 'Global Retailing: Tempting Trouble?', *McKinsey Quarterly*, No. 1, 117–125.

Basile, A., and Germidis, D. *Investing in Free Export Processing Zones*, OECD.

Bello, D. C. and Gilliland, D. I. (1997) 'The Effect of Output Controls, Process Controls and Flexibility on Export Channel Performance', *Journal of Marketing*, **61** (1), 22–38.

British International Freight Association, *Exporter and Forwarder: The Professional Guide 1990*, Feltham, Middlesex.

Brown, J. R., Lusch, R. F. and Nicholson, C. Y. (1995) 'Power and Relationship Commitment: their impact on marketing channel member performance', *Journal of Retailing, Winter*, **71** (4), 363–393.

Bucklin, C., DeFalco, S., De Vincentis, J. and Levis, T. (1996) 'Are you Tough Enough to Manage your Channels?', *McKinsey Quarterly*, No. 1, 104–114.

Clinton, S. R. and Calantone, R. J. (1996) 'Logistics Strategy: Does it Travel Well?', *International Marketing Review*, **13** (5) 98–112.

Combs, L. S. (1987) Fine-tuning the channels. *Journal of Business and Industrial Marketing*, **2** (1), 61–65.

Davies, G. J. (1987) The international logistics concept. *International Journal of Physical Distribution and Materials Management*, **17** (2), 20–27.

Davies, W., and Butler, E. (1986) *The Freeport Experiment*, Adam Smith Institute, London.

Eastman Kodak streamlines its product distribution (1990), *Industrial Engineering*, **22** (9), 42–44.

El-Ansary, A. I. (1986) How better systems could feed the world. *International Marketing Review*, **3** (1), 39–49.

Foster, T. A. (1990) The language of foreign trade. *Distribution*, **89** (10), 89–90.

Gassenhheimer, J. B., Calantone, R. J. and Scully, J. I. (1995) 'Supplier Involvement and Dealer Satisfaction: Implications for Enhancing Channel Relation ships', *Journal of Business & Industrial Marketing*, Spring, **10** (2), 7–13.

Gill, L. E. and Allerheiligen, R. P. (1996) 'Cooperation in Channels of Distribution: Physical Distribution Leads the Way', *International Journal of Physical Distribution & Logistics Management*, May, **26** (5), 49–64.

Griffith, D. A. and Ryans Jr, J. K. (1996) 'Strategically Employing Natural Channels in an Era of Global Marketing', *Journal of Marketing Practice & Applied Marketing Science*, **1** (4), 52–69.

INCOTERMS 1990, ICC Publishing S. A., Paris.

Industry Week (1996) 'On Your Mark', August 19, **245** (15), 102–103.

Laarhoven, P. van and Sharman, G. (1994) 'Logistics Alliances: The European Experience', *McKinsey Quarterly*, No. 1, 39–49.

Lele, M. (1986) Matching your channels to your product's life cycle. *Business Marketing*, **71** (12), 60–69.

Liu, H. and McGoldrick, P. J. (1996) 'International Retail Sourcing: Trend, Nature and Process', *Journal of International Marketing*, **4** (4), 9–33.

Magrath, A. (1996) 'Managing Distribution Channels', *Business Quarterly*, Spring, **60** (3), 56–64.

Mallen, B. (1996) 'Selecting Channels of Distrib-

ution: a Multi-Stage Process', *International Journal of Physical Distribution & Logistics Management*, May, **26** (5), 5–22.

Manning, K. H. (1995) 'Distribution Channel Profitability', *Management Accounting*, January, **76** (7), 44–49.

Moukheiber, Z. (1995) 'Scents Off', *Forbes*, August 14, **156** (4), 44–46.

Myers, H. and Alexander, N. (1996) 'European Food Retailers' Evaluation of Global Markets', *International Journal of Retail & Distribution Management*, **24** (6), 34–43.

Osborne, K. (1996) 'The Channel Integration Decision for Small to Medium Sized Manufacturing Exporters', *International Small Business Journal*, April–June, **14** (3), 40–57.

Pellow, M. (1990) Physical distribution in international retailing. *International Journal of Retail and Distribution Management*, **18** (2), 12–15.

Perry, D. (1989) How you'll manage your 1990s distribution portfolio. *Business Marketing*, **74** (6), 52–56.

Pirie, M. (1983) *Freeports*, Adam Smith Institute, London (based on a seminar).

Rayport, J. F. and Svioka, J. G. (1996) 'Exploiting the Virtual Value Chain', *McKinsey Quarterly*, No. 1, 21–36.

Rowe, M. (1986) What's in a word? A lot when it comes to trade terms. *ICC Business World*, **4** (3), 17–19.

Shiotani, T. (1988) Outline of Japanese distribution system. *Business Japan*, August, 89–97.

SITPRO, *Costing Guidelines for Export Administration*, 1979.

Trunick, P. A. (1989) International distribution is in your future. *Transportation and Distribution*, **30** (2), 12–15.

Value-added marketing (1989) *Global Trade*, **109** (5), 26, 28.

Wilkinson, I. F. (1996) 'Distribution Channel Management: Power considerations', *International Journal of Physical Distribution & Logistics Management*, May, **26** (5), 31–42.

Web sites

America Online Mailing List Directory
http://ifrit.web.aol.com/mld/production

BEMs – Big Emerging Markets
(US Classification)
http://www.stat-usa.gov/itabems.html

Brainstorm Business Forum – home of CBI,
Chambers of Commerce, Best Practice
http://www.brainstorm.co.uk

Business Europa – business throughout Central
and Eastern Europe
http://www.business-europa.co.uk

Business Information
www.businessmonitor.co.uk

Business Information Resources
http://sashimi.wwa.com/~notime/eotw/
business_info.html

Business Information Server
http://www.dnb.com/

Business Site of the Day
http://www.bizniz.com/eurocool/

Business Statistics
gopher: University of
Michigan:una.hh.lib.umich.edu
Choose: ebb Current Business Statistics

Businesses on the Internet
http://www.yahoo.com/Business_and_
Economy/Corporations/

Business to Business Marketing Exchange
http://www.btob.wfu.edu/b2b.html

CataList, the Catalogue of Listserv Lists
http://www.lsoft.com/lists/listref.html

CIA Publications
http://www.odc.gov/cia/publications/
pus.html

City.net – covers 4,300 destinations
http://www.city.net

Clearinghouse for Networked Information
Discovery
http://kudzu.cnidr.org/welcome.html

Clearinghouse for Subject Oriented Internet
Resources
http://www.lib.umich.edu/chhome.html

Commercial Use of the Internet
http://pass.wayne.edu/business.html

Disneyworld
http://www.disney.com/DisneyWorld/

Europages
http://www.europages.com

Europe – Business Monitor
http://www.businessmonitor.co.uk

Europe – see Yellowweb Europe and Europages

European Electronic Information Market
http://www2.echo.lu

European Union – Citizen's First
http://www.eu.com

EWR (Early Warning Report): Chokepoints for
World Trade
http://www.subscriptions.com/beacon/
mapchokepoints.html

Export – Import Pathfinder

http://mickey.queens.lib.ny.us/guides/
export_i..html

ExportNet – Export Today Matchmaking service
http://www.exporttoday.com

Federal Express (FedEx)
http://www.fedex.ca

Find it Fast
http://www.webcom.com/~tbrown/
findpage.html

Foreign Exchange Rates
http://www.dna.lth.se/cgi-bin/kurt/rates/

Inter-Links, searches the Usenet newsgroups
and mailing lists
Internet Business Center
http://www.tig.com/IBC

Internet Marketing List Archives
http://www.popco.com/hyper/
inet-marketing/

Internet Public Library
http://ipl.sils.umich.edu/

Internet Society
http://info.isoc.org/home.html

International Small Business Consortium
http://www.isbc.com

Internet Sleuth
http://www.intbc.com/sleuth/

Information Market Europe – European
Commission
http://www.echo.lu/

International Chamber of Commerce, Paris
http://wwwl.usal.com/~ibnet/icchp.html

JETRO (The Japanese External Trade
Organisation)
http://www.jetro.go.jp/index.html

Land's End – the famous clothing catalogue
company
http://www.landsend.com/

Legal List Internet Desk Reference
http://wwwlcp.com

Legal Information Institute
http://www.law.cornell.edu

Levi's – includes an online game called
'Riveted'
http://www.eu.levi.com/
inner-seam/eu/vol2/iss3/game/intro.nhtml

Levi's 501 jeans
http://www.levi.com/menu

Magazine Publishers of America
http://www.ima.org/members/mmm02.html

Malls of Canada: The world's largest shopping malls
http:///www.canadamalls.com/provider/

Manufacturing Marketplace from Cahners
http://www.cmm.net

MBE Mail Boxes Etc
http://www.mbe.com

MexPlaza English language Internet page for Mexico
http://mexplaza.udg.mx:80/ingles/

Microsoft/NBC
http://www.msnbc.com

Midas International Franchise
http://www.midasfran.com

Netscape In-Box Direct: E-mail based newsletters and newspapers
http://form.netscape.com

Political Risk Services
http://www.polrisk.com

Publicly Accessible Mailing Lists
http://www.neosoft.com/internet/paml

Purchasing On-Line
http://www.purchasing.net

Packaging Waste Legislation – the Sequoia Group
http://ourworld.compuserve.com/homepages/SeQuoia

Pizza Hut
http://www.pizzahut.com/

Regional Information Guides by Price Waterhouse
http://www.i-trade.com/infsrc/pw

Santa's Home Page
http://www.north-pole.org

Saturn – the idiosyncratic GM subsidiary, its cars and advance information
http://www.saturncars.com/

Schweppes
http://www.schhh.com

Singapore – Straits Times Interactive
http://www.asial.com.sg/straitstimes

Scottish Virtual Memorial Garden
http://www.hebrides.com

Simpler Trade Procedures Board
http://www.sitpro.org.uk/index.html

Sony
http://www.sony.com/

South China Morning Post
http://www.scmp.om/cdcom

Trade Compass
http://www.tradecompass.com

TradePort – extensive information on international business
http://www.tradeport.org

Trade Statistics
http://www.census.gov/ftp/pub/foreign-trade/www/

Trade Wave Galaxy – Public and commercial information and services
http://www.einet.net/galaxy.html

Transportation, logistics & shipping
http://www.transportnews.com/

Travel-Lonely Planet Travel Information – maps, facts and figures
http://www.lonelyplanet.com.au/lp.htm

Internet Guide to Transportation
http://www.iac.co.jp/~bobj/guide.htm

UNCTAD (UN Conference on Trade and Development)
http://www.unicc.org/unctad/en/enhome.htm

UPS Online
http://www.ups.com

US Dept. of Commerce
http://www.doc.gov/CommerceHomePage.html

U.S.Fedworld
www.fedworld.gov

US National Trade Data Bank
http://www.stat-usa.gov/BEN/Services/ntdbhome.html

US West features 50,000 suppliers from USA, Mexico, Canada
http://export.uswest.com

US West Export Yellow Pages
http://yp.uswest.com

US – Economic Bulletin Board
gopher://una.hh.lib.umich.edu/11/ebb

Scotch Malt Whisky – Laphroaig
http://www.laphroaig.com

Scotch Malt Whisky – Glenmorangie
http://www.glenmorangie.com

Virtual Shopping Malls
http://www.itl.net/shopping/index.html

Virtual Vineyards
http://www.virtualvin.com/

Winter Web Wonderland
http://banzai.neosoft.com/citylink/xmas

World Factbook
gopher:gopher.aecom.yu.edu

World Health Organization
gopher:gopher.gsfc.nasa.gov

World Wide Web Virtual Library
http://W3.org

WTO (World Trade Organization): Agreement Establishing the WTO:
http://www.soton.ac.uk/~nukop/data/fullrecs/1660.htm

WTO
http://www.unicc.org//wto/Welcome.html

WWW Yellow Pages
www.cba.uh.edu/ylowpges/ylowpges.html.

Yahoo: National: Canada, France, Germany, Japan, UK, Ireland.
Metros: Chicago, Los Angeles, New York, San Francisco Bay Area, My Town

Yahoo Reuters
http://www.yahoo.co.uk/News

Yahoo's List of Mailing Lists – updated links to mailing list resources
http://www.yahoo.com/computers_and_internet/internet/mailing_lists/

Yellow Pages UK
http://www.yell.co.uk

Yelloweb Europe
http://www.yweb.com/

CHAPTER 8

Promotion within the foreign market

In this chapter we deal with all the means by which marketers may communicate with their target markets and beyond. The communication task facing any company goes beyond its target market, it extends to its public image; employee morale; and shareholder perceptions of corporate efficiency often based on analysts' readings of annual company reports. Marketing's publics change with the ownership of the company, the nature of the product or service offered, the degree of acceptance found in the target market for the product or service in question and its parent company.

Communication has been made easier through the advent of telecommunications, fax and e-mail which has effectively eliminated geographical distance. The challenge which still remains is that of psychological or 'psychic' distance which may be felt to be greater between two neighbouring countries than two from different hemispheres. There has, for example, been a multiplicity of ties between Britain and the countries of the Commonwealth such as Australia, New Zealand and Canada, much less so between Britain and its neighbouring EU member states with 40 years of history as a European Union. Political positions have changed radically. Communication helps each of us as individuals to cope with these changes.

While cultural convergence remains a distant and purely theoretical concept, communications have brought about what Marshall McLuhan called the 'global village', where everyone buys similar products that are sold with similar messages. This demand for a particular product or product class and the homogeneity of the market offering has been brought about by communications which have helped shape aspirations of ownership and expectations of usage.

The great divide still exists, however, with the global brand. There are very few global brands beyond Coca-Cola, Pepsi-Cola, IBM and a few of the fast food franchises such as McDonalds or Kentucky Fried Chicken although there are many important regional brands such as Tiger Balm in the Far East or Stella Artois in Europe. The communication of a unified image of quality and service to the customer is paramount. Occasionally this may go awry because of either bad public relations; a 'whisper campaign' by competitors; the need to engage in 'corrective advertising' as a result of either advertising industry pressure or governmental pressure so as to rectify previous advertising deemed to be misleading or even practising deception; or finally just plain ill-founded rumour quite divorced from fact.

An example of how wild rumour is soon able to gather its own momentum is provided in the case of Proctor & Gamble:

The problem started in the Southern states of the USA where the word began to spread that Proctor & Gamble through the use of their trademark encourage satanism. The only supporting evidence was the Proctor & Gamble crescent moon and 13 stars, a registered trademark which no-one had probably examined too closely before, including most probably senior management of Proctor & Gamble themselves. In this particular case, Proctor & Gamble were being attacked from what is sometimes referred to as the 'bible belt' of the Southern states. The news of this scare took a while to reach Proctor & Gamble and to be taken seriously by its management but given the time lags of reporting market response even to sales, delay is inevitable, by which time considerable damage has already been done to market share. What would be their competitive response? Ignore it and continue to promote individual brands or take it seriously, and take on the Devil?

This example serves to show the difficult challenge sometimes presented to those in charge of promotion. The scare started in 1980 and did not die down and by 1982, had reached a peak where Proctor & Gamble were receiving 15,000 calls per month routed through to their consumer services department. Moving to the offensive, Proctor & Gamble then enlisted the support of one of the deans of the 'moral majority', Jerry Falwell; hired two detectives agencies to trace the culprits; filed six suits against people for spreading rumours and then set up a toll-free telephone number to handle anxious customer enquiries. The rumours, however, continued and calls were still pouring in at a rate of 5,600 a month when the company decided it had spent enough and suffered enough and was therefore discontinuing the use of its corporate logo on products over the next few years though they would continue with it on letterheads and at corporate headquarters.

The many facets of promotion

Promotion has many facets including:

* Personal selling
* Exhibitions
* Public relations
* Sales promotion
* Advertising

Too often, advertising is viewed to be simply promotion and vice versa. However, we shall see as we come to examine each of these in turn, that the differences which exist are not only between regions but within countries. There may well be a traditional way of doing things which has little bearing on how rich a particular economy may be, as is the case with the rather anachronistic distribution channels in Japan, for example.

Personal selling

The use of the salesperson particularly in selling high value-added industrial goods is unquestioned. Sound product knowledge and the ability to relate to consumers' needs is paramount. However, while it may be difficult to identify the members of a DMU or informal 'decision making unit' within one's own domestic market, the problem becomes greatly exacerbated when one starts to consider the different forms of ownership including outright state control which a monopoly over foreign trade may take. In that situation, the aim of identifying buyers, deciders, users, influencers and gatekeepers may well mean trying to identify individuals within different institutions all having some bearing or influence on the awarding of a contract to purchase. In such situations, the human element and being able to relate well to the customer are what often constitute the decisive element.

In international marketing, the use of a flying salesperson is without doubt expensive and many times that of a domestic field sales operative. Ironically, if this salesperson does move around a great deal then he or she is open to the

accusation of spreading himself or herself too thinly over too many markets, leading ultimately to personal exhaustion and poor company representation. The use of a consortium whereby small companies together may be able to afford the services of an expert salesperson is one way in which to defray the high costs involved. Yet there are many industries in which this is practised, without which you could not expect to compete. Speciality markets, highly specialized industries and high-risk countries make high demands on the use of personal selling. The costs may be high but so are the potential rewards without which no company would enter.

Exhibitions and trade fairs

Perhaps not surprisingly North America predominates in this sector. It is difficult to imagine a section of industry or interest so esoteric that is not represented in an annual meeting somewhere in North America. There is even an national association of suicidology although whether this is an academic association or group of practitioners is not certain. If it is an association of practitioners there may be problems in maintaining memberships! A selection of exhibitions and trade fairs across the rest of the world includes among others the 'International Brotherhood' Old Bastards Annual Conclave in Hong Kong.

As may be seen from Table 8.2, exhibitions and fairs may be general or specialist. Details of these fairs may be obtained from the Department of Trade's Fairs and Promotions Branch. Where specialist, the global competition will be seen to gather together in that exhibition hall for the duration of the show, to display their wares, but also check on what everyone else is doing within the industry. Trade enquiries are more likely to be converted into sales at such exhibitions because buyers worldwide will usually congregate there. The expense of exhibiting therefore has to be set against the cost or rather opportunity cost of being able to afford not to attend. For British companies, the Department of Trade usually offers some financial assistance to encourage participation in the national pavilion. Industrially and internationally, these exhibitions provide some degree of image building for the participants, the long-term goodwill value of which may greatly exceed the actual orders taken during the exhibition itself. In countries where one is dealing with a state buyer, this factor has to be taken into account. In Eastern Europe prior to the events of 1989, the importance of the national trade fair was inflated by having the signature of contracts postponed until the opening of the fair. This artificial mechanism inflated both the numbers attending and the volume of total business concluded during the national fair and because of this almost compulsory attendance, perhaps also the costs of individual contracts concluded.

The problem with trade fairs is that the costs are high and the rewards uncertain. Rosson and Seringhaus (1989) did a very good job of reviewing the existing literature in conducting their own survey. Lilien (1982) had found the most important variables to be: product complexity; sales level; purchase frequency and customer concentration. Furthermore that levels of spending were influenced by the magnitude of product sales and the stage in the life cycle.

detail important personnel changes; foreign contracts won; technological breakthroughs that have been made which give the company a 'leading edge'; or mergers, acquisitions or strategic alliances that have been entered into to ensure that the company remains competitive in the dynamic global market that exists for high technology products today. Certain high technology and some not so high technology companies have benefited from exposure of this kind which enhances their public image at large, informs the general public, including consumers of their products, and reassures shareholders and other interested bodies, all at the same time.

Word-of-mouth advertising is not only cheap, it is very effective. Public relations seeks

Categories and criteria	Rank
Audience quality	
Proportion of decision makers among visitors	1
Proportion of visitors in your target market	2
Show limited to specific types of exhibitors	8
Number of per cent of new contacts last year	9
Screening of visitors	15
Audience quantity	
Number visiting exhibit	3
Extent of promotion by show organizers	5
The show's audience size in past years	6
Display location	
Booth position/location on floor	4
Ability to specify/negotiate size, location, etc.	7
Aisle traffic density	13
Logistical aspects	
Easy registration or pre-registration	10
Security	11
Easily available move-in/out assistance	12
Move-in/out facilities	16

Table 8.1   Trade show criteria

Source: Dickinson, J. R., and Faris, A. J. (1985) Firms with large market shares, product lines, rate shows highly. *Marketing News*, 10 May, p. 14

Public relations/publicity

Public relations, also known as 'publicity', is of special significance. It is a form of free advertising whose value cannot be underestimated.

Any company can benefit from a favourable unsolicited media report. Television, radio and the press often look for free news stories of this kind. To meet this demand, many large companies employ a public relations agency to handle all external relations. Press releases are then distributed to the various media and these may

to enhance corporate image building and influence favourable media treatment. Not all companies are naturally gifted in putting the best possible face on their technological achievements or enlightened employee and customer care programmes. Public relations seeks to redress this balance as well as dealing often with fire-fighting situations which may emerge when, for example, an oil tanker has an accident and starts to lose some of its cargo of crude oil and creates problems of ecological and environmental concern not just locally or regionally but globally.

Table 8.2

Location	Date	Fair
Paris (France)	09.12–11.12/1998	*EXPO CONGRES Exhibition, Congress, Seminar and Business Travel Organization Trade Fair*
Moscow (Russian Federation)	07.09–11.09/1998	*LESDREVMASH International Exhibition Machinery, Equipment and Instruments for Woodworking Timber, Pulp and Paper Industries*
Moscow (Russian Federation)	07.09–11.09/1998	*EXPOGOROD International Exhibition on Infrastructure and Modern Town Development*
Moscow (Russian Federation)	07.09–11.09/1998	*Moscow Wholesale Fair of Merchandise and Machinery*
Gothenburg (Sweden)	08.09–11.09/1998	*INTERFOOD International Hot and Catering Exhibition*
Gothenburg (Sweden)	08.09–11.09/1998	*Scandinavian Fast Food Fair*
Gothenburg (Sweden)	08.09–11.09/1998	*Dagligvaruhandeln Grocery Exhibition*
Gothenburg (Sweden)	08.09–11.09/1998	*Wine & Spirits Expo*
Moscow (Russian Federation)	08.09–12.09/1998	*MIR DETSTVA International Exhibition World of Childhood*
Vienna (Austria)	09.09–13.09/1998	*HIT Consumer Electronics and Appliance Show*
Vienna (Austria)	09.09–13.09/1998	*HOME The Home, Interiors and DIY Show*
Vienna (Austria)	09.09–13.09/1998	*EUROMUSIC VIENNA Music, Show and Stage Fair*
Poznan (Poland)	15.09–18.09/1998	*Household Goods and Domestic Electronic Appliances Trade Fair*
Poznan (Poland)	15.09–18.09/1998	*International Packaging Technology and Logistics Exhibition*
Poznan (Poland)	15.09–18.09/1998	*International Advertising Fair*
Poznan (Poland)	0.10–06.10/1998	*International Agro-Industrial Fair*
Poznan (Poland)	01.10–06.10/1998	*National Horticultural Exhibition*
Nuremberg (Germany)	02.10–05.10/1998	*ÖKOWELT+ÖKO BAU Ecological Fair*
Moscow (Russian Federation)	05.10–09.10/1998	*AGROPRODMASH International Exhibition of Agricultural Equipment, Farming, Food Processing Industries, Trade Equipment, Packaging and Flower-growing*
Tel Aviv (Israel)	09.11–12.11/1998	*Telcom Israel Communication Systems Exhibition*
Stockholm (Sweden)	23.09–25.09/1998	*Scandinavian Travel Market and Bus Travel Market*
Wiesbaden (Germany)	23.09–25.09/1998	*Intergeo German Geodesists Congress and Trade Exhibition*
Stuttgart (Germany)	26.09–04.10/1998	*LWH Agricultural Trade Show – International Trade Exhibition for Farming and Agriculture*
Stuttgart (Germany)	29.09–01.10/1998	*VISION International Trade Fair for Industrial Image Processing and Identification Technologies*
Munich (Germany)	18.03–24.03/1999	*International Light Industries and Handicrafts Fair*
Stockholm (Sweden)	18.03–21.03/1999	*Nordic Trade Fair for Paint*
Zaragoza (Spain)	00.04–00.04/1999	*Shop Buyers* *FIMA Agricultural Machinery Fair*
Milan (Italy)	00.05–00.05/2002	*GEC International Exhibition of the Printing Publishing, Paper and Converting Industries*

Source: http://www.expobase.com

Exhibit 8.1   Beware, it grows on you

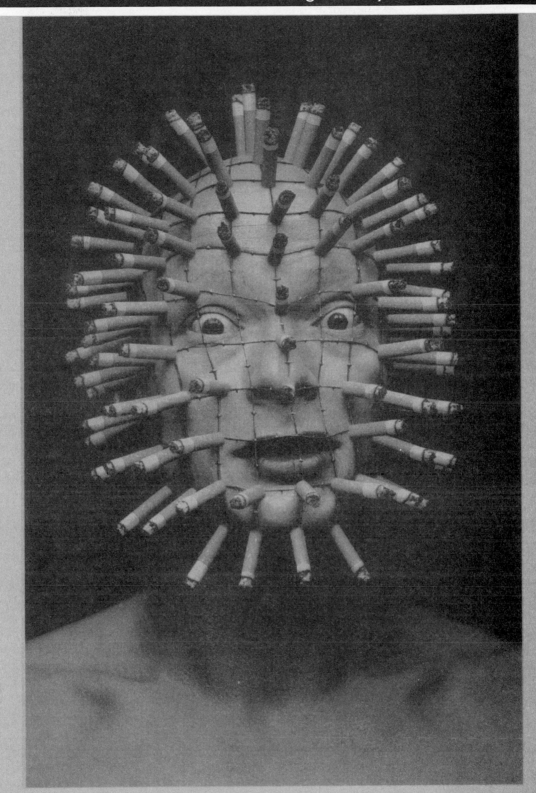

This is one of five dramatic posters seen in Rotterdam in the latest anti-smoking campaign in the Netherlands. The campaign is aimed at shocking Dutch youth into giving up smoking. The number of Dutch teenagers who smoke has risen to 25.5 per cent from 19.5 per cent in the past five years, according to the Dutch Foundation for Smoking and Health. – Reuters.

Source: Sunday Times, Singapore, 23 March, 1997

Photograph: Popperfoto

Sales promotion

The tools most frequently used singly, or in combination, would include:

- point of purchase advertising including displays
- premiums: self-liquidating; direct 'on-pack' or 'in-pack'; continuity premiums; tie-in premiums; and fulfilment premiums.
- speciality advertising; gifts to consumers to build goodwill that will generate future purchases
- coupons (goes back to 1885 in the USA)
- sampling
- deals
- sweepstakes and contests
- cooperative advertising between retailer, manufacturer or trade association
- booklets and brochures
- trade shows and exhibits
- directories and yellow pages
- trade incentives, price reductions, in the form of promotional allowances.

Above and below the line

These are all so-called 'below the line' activities including point of sale displays and demonstrations as well as leaflets, free trials, contests and premiums such as 'two for the price of one'. Unlike media advertising which is 'above the line' and earns a commission, 'below the line' sales promotion does not. To an advertising agency, 'above the line' means traditional media for which they are recognized by the media owners, entitling them to commission. When agencies are fee-based the situation no longer exists, so when the commission system operates – as it does in most countries – all those services which interfere with the earning of commission (usually 70 per cent of total income) go down below the line, that is, at the bottom of the list (Jefkins, 1976, 21).

Targeting directly at the potential buyer, the sales promotion material seeks to encourage a response to action and to actual trial of the product or service concerned. In some countries, this area of operations may be quite constrained because the market is small or sluggish because of political impediments, low personal disposable incomes and poor distribution and low product availability.

Advertising

Advertising was defined by the British Code of Advertising Practice, published in 1979 as: 'paid-for communication, addressed to the public (or some of it) with the purpose of influencing the opinion or behaviour of those to whom it is addressed'. Advertising exists to inform, persuade, and remind a buying public of a particular product or service and it does so at a lower cost per head to the company than personal selling or exhibitions. Advertising as defined by Kotler (1988) is: 'Any paid form of nonpersonal presentation and promotion of ideas, goods or services by an individual sponsor'.

Not all advertising is seeking a profitable transaction in the exchange of a good or service. Instead there are organizations such as the World Health Organization which have sought to nurture ideas of personal well-being through attention to diet and shaping attitudes towards tobacco and alcohol through promotion. There is now more to advertising than the creation of a brand image for a product, or corporate image for the company.

Taking brand advertising first, attention is paid first to the segments at which to target lifestyle advertising, so selective demand stimulation through advertising is what is sought. Primary demand stimulation would be a 'shotgun' approach to total demand for the product class whereas selective demand stimulation is a 'rifling' strategy narrowing in closely on the target.

In practice, where there is an oligopoly situation, advertising can create some confusion as to the identity of the advertiser as in the Vermouth sector. There is both Cinzano and Martini. However, when one advertises, even if confusion results as to the advertiser, it will lift total sales in this sector and so this confusion is not viewed as a problem. Increasingly though, own-label Vermouth is eroding the market share of these two very large companies.

Brand names wear out over time and so what were once branded products become generic, almost as a result of their own success. The effect of the brand name may then be seen to be greatly diminished if not lost totally. An example to quote is Aspirin which was once a branded protected name and Bayer is seeking now to restore that brand by acquiring rights to the brand name which were lost after the Second World War. Through popularity and common usage, certain products have become entrenched in the common everyday language of the country and in so doing have lost their significance as brand names, e.g. in Britain adhesive tape is always popularly referred to as 'Sellotape' whereas in France, Germany and elsewhere in Europe and North America it is known as 'Scotch' because of the 3M brand name. In Britain, people refer to a vacuum cleaner as a 'hoover' and will talk of 'hoovering' carpets or a staircase. Similarly, a Thermos flask is really a vacuum flask but is not popularly called that either.

'Pull' and 'push' strategies

Advertising seeks to stimulate demand for branded products and may do this in one of two ways either by means of a 'pull' strategy whereby a manufacturer might succeed in moving goods into retail shops by advertising to the end-users and ensuring that they ask for this particular product from their usual retailer. A 'push' strategy is where the manufacturer works down the channel of distribution 'pushing' the goods by means of financial discounts or incentives. The car industry which has its own tied distribution network has used the push strategy to get its cars into showrooms. Companies manufacturing convenience goods, for example, use 'pull' strategies in their fight against competitors for space on retailers' shelves.

With regard to advertising, choice has to be exercised as to the medium to be used whether press, television, radio, cinema or outdoor advertising. Points to note here are:

- *the reach*, i.e., the total number of members of the target audience who are expected to receive this message at least once,

- *frequency*, i.e., the number of times the target audience will be exposed to the message,

- *impact* dependent on the medium used and the message, this depends on compatibility between the two. EQ magazine continues to attract advertisers for high value-added consumer durables, e.g., cars, hi-fi equipment and clothes that are geared primarily to a high-income male segment.

- *continuity* which relates to the length of time a campaign will run and the pattern of timing of the advertising within a campaign.

Inevitably, therefore, there has to be a trade-off between high-frequency low-reach or low-frequency high-reach. Certain products identify with one or other strategy, e.g., soap powders will appear on television during the day, occasionally during the evening. Advertisements for cars will be shown primarily in the evening. This is partly a question of value of purchase, partly a question of appealing to all the decision-makers as well as to their users. Husbands may wish to be involved in the purchase of washing machines or dishwashers even if they do not wish to be around to physically operate these machines once purchased.

Exhibit 8.2   Britain's brewers get a head start in Canada and the US

If North Americans can be persuaded to drink their beer a little warmer and not freeze their glasses, Ms Jaclyn Bateman is confident of a growing market in the US and Canada for the ales that her family has been brewing in Lincolnshire since 1874.

Ms Bateman's company is one of 24 small and mid-sized UK brewers taking part in a drive to put more imported beers on the shelves of Canadian liquor stores. The US and Canada are 'opening up for our type of product', she says. 'North American taste buds are becoming more sophisticated.'

Beers like Titanic Stout, Freeminer Bitter and Summer Lightning are not exactly household names, even in the UK. Exports at present make up only a fraction of most micro-brewers' output.

But a combination of new opportunities abroad and obstacles at home, notably the difficulty of gaining a foothold in pubs owned by larger brewers, have persuaded many to venture outside the UK.

Peebleshire-based Traquair House Brewery, the smallest of the group visiting Canada, is banking on exports to justify a planned increase in capacity from 500 to 700 barrels a year.

The US already makes up almost a third of Traquair House's sales. Ms Catherine Maxwell Stuart, daughter of the brewery's founder, expects to sell another 50–75 barrels a year in Canada.

The UK brewers were attracted to Canada partly by the spectacular growth of domestic micro-breweries. Ontario-based Upper Canada Brewing, whose sales have doubled to C$24.4m ($17.8m) over the past five years, is in the midst of a public share offering.

Furthermore, changes in liquor distribution, which falls under provincial jurisdiction, have opened the door to imported beers. Alberta privatised its liquor outlets two years ago.

In Ontario, the two largest domestic brewers – John Labatt and Molson – have long enjoyed a stranglehold, thanks to their control of Brewers Retail, which handles 93 per cent of beer sold in the province. Brewers Retail agreed to provide access to imported brands a few years ago.

Foreign breweries must still pay hefty 'listing fees', as well as handling charges both to Brewers Retail and to the Liquor Control Board of Ontario, a government agency that oversees all liquor sales.

But the LCBO, which is the world's biggest liquor retailer, has become increasingly keen to sell imported beers through its own 600 outlets.

One concern, however, is that some micro-breweries do not have the resources to mount a sustained export campaign. Moves are afoot to launch a co-operative effort, in which four or five breweries may combine their products in a 'Taste of England' package.

Source: Financial Times, 21 February 1996

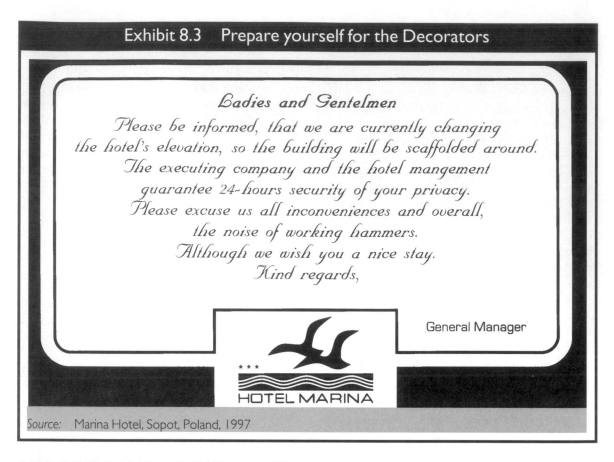

Exhibit 8.3   Prepare yourself for the Decorators

Ladies and Gentelmen

*Please be informed, that we are currently changing
the hotel's elevation, so the building will be scaffolded around.
The executing company and the hotel mangement
guarantee 24-hours security of your privacy.
Please excuse us all inconveniences and overall,
the noise of working hammers.
Although we wish you a nice stay.
Kind regards,*

General Manager

HOTEL MARINA

Source: Marina Hotel, Sopot, Poland, 1997

The communications process

The transmission of a chosen 'message' by a manufacturer through a suitable medium to an identifiable target segment audience is what we mean by the communications process. In this process, it is seldom that one manufacturer will be alone in proclaiming the benefits of its products, there will usually be many. This introduces the concept of 'noise'. We cannot hear clearly what this manufacturer is trying to tell us about his product because of this 'noise' from rival manufacturers making similar and often contradictory claims about their products. Thorelli and Thorelli undertook a study in the US a number of years ago to attempt to count the number of 'messages' that each individual received in the course of a day. From early morning, waking to radio or breakfast television, reading the morning paper that has been delivered to chatting over breakfast about perhaps a planned new acquisition or a neighbour's recent acquisition. As one walks along any street – or drives as is the practice in the USA – there are billboards, shop front displays and different advertising signs with product messages. This continues on public transport where there is also advertising; even the traditional British black taxis in Manchester now have small television advertising screens in the passenger compartments. To the office or place of work, the continual imperceptible bombardment of advertising messages continues even in conversations with colleagues who may share value judgements on good or bad experiences of products or services. This continues until returning in the evening and exchanging with one's spouse the events of the day and opening oneself up yet again perhaps to an evening newspaper, an evening of television or even if going out, to advertising in the cinema or theatre.

That we remember few of them is another important characteristic. As consumers, we screen out claims which conflict with our own attitudes and beliefs but make ourselves more open to advertising if we are about to buy a product in that product-class and want to know more or have a favourable leaning towards that particular brand because it is one which we have perhaps bought before. Reassurance is an important element in communicating with the consumer. Equally, the effectiveness of communications may be seen in terms of sales and of the consumers' ability to recall that particular brand. Moving from unawareness to the point where the buying public are able to recall unaided the particular brand and report strongly positive perceptions of it, is indeed the ultimate objective. The 'hypodermic model' is depicted in Figure 8.1.

We have spoken of 'noise' but the other important point to consider is the degree of 'fit'

Exhibit 8.4 Lager lout campaign passes sell-by date

After 12 years, it appears the British lager-buying public no longer gives a XXXX for the beer-swilling, cork-hatted Australian male.

In British television's most expensive television advertising blitz, the familiar Castlemaine XXXX bushman, who would rather lose his Sheila than his lager, is being replaced by a clean-shaven smoothie who lives in the suburbs, sees his girlfriend after work and, strewth, drinks his beer from a glass.

Research by Carlsberg-Tetley and Saatchi and Saatchi Advertising showed that in 1984, when the lager was launched in the UK, Australia had seemed 'remote and exotic'. But due to the proliferation of Australian soaps and increased opportunities for travel, the country had become more familiar and the appeal of Crocodile Dundee-type characters had worn off.

The results concluded: 'The XXXX personalities and values associated with outback life and extreme macho attitudes have become tired. People will view them as unsociable and un-successful and not as heroes . . . The advertising and its imagery increasingly sit uncomfortably with current attitudes.'

Dr David Lewis, a psychologist consulted by the companies as part of the research, said: 'Young people will no longer accept stereo-typical images of Australians as being hard and rugged outback types. Aussie soaps play a big part in shaping our view of the country and we see more macho behaviour in *Coronation Street* than *Neighbours* or *Home and Away*.'

The campaign opens on 17 August on ITV, during the screening of the movie *Demolition Man*. Nine different versions of the advertisement will be shown during the commercial breaks at a cost of £1m – the most money spent by one advertiser in one evening on British television and the most commercials for one product shown during a single programme. Eight different versions will be shown at later dates.

Source: *The Independent*, 7 August 1996

---

between medium and message. A wordy message would be better for the press than a visual medium such as television or cinema. Alternatively, radio simulates sounds to give vent to the imagination. On television, you have to see sandy beaches or the ski slopes; on radio, you can concentrate on the noises of travel, or of being on a beach or of skiis on snow. It is a different appeal to the senses as is the press for those who may prefer a totally dispassionate unemotional and purely factual statement. Newspapers and consumer reports carry detail with comment which would be omitted from advertisements on radio or television. The weakness of the hypodermic model is that it is injecting a message into the buying public but the leads and lags of advertising together with the presence of 'noise' make its direct effectiveness in achieving sales very difficult to assess.

Another factor to consider is the degree of newness of the product to the market in question. It has been said that success is more likely if the advertiser's goal is consistent with the goals of the target audience. Word-of-mouth advertising has been found to be important where one has been able first to influence those who, in innovation studies, are called 'opinion leaders' the 'early adopters' who make rational

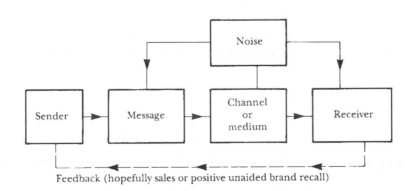

Feedback (hopefully sales or positive unaided brand recall)

Figure 8.1 Hypodermic communications model

purchasing decisions. These people are more open to the mass media than the people they influence. They are usually better educated and knowledgeable, they are the ones to turn to when seeking advice on a purchase about which you have no present knowledge either in terms of the meaning of product specifications or even in the recognition of reliable brand names.

Actually changing attitudes is beyond the scope of most advertising, as was pointed out in the discussion on cultural variables. Nevertheless it is possible to influence behaviour where opinions are not strongly held and do not have the strength of convictions. It is possible to persuade people to switch brands of toothpaste, or to accept trial of a new product which embodies a new concept and brings new benefits such as word processing, for example. In all of this, reference groups play an important role.

Figure 8.2 shows only a general model and it must be remembered then that the divisions may be somewhat arbitrary and may not apply to the same degree to all products. Yet Everett Rogers (1962) sees important differences in these five adopter groups as to their value orientations. The early adopters make a reasoned judgement and the early majority who follow may be seen to be adopting new ideas before the average person but they are rarely leaders like the early adopters. The late majority are composed of sceptics who will only accept an innovation once it is proven. Finally, the laggards. There may be many reasons here as to why they are so slow. Primarily this group consists of those without a fixed income so unable to fulfil all their wants. Students are grouped together here with all those without a fixed income, e.g. retired or unemployed. As a segment they may

be sufficiently numerous and advertising reduces 'psychic' distance that much further. Yet beyond this, there is little gain to be had from advertising to them.

Those who desire to acquire all new products just introduced onto the market, sometimes referred to as the 'lunatic fringe', account for only 2.5 per cent of those who will finally adopt the product. They do not therefore constitute a viable market segment of their own for any product. It is important then to emphasize that it is the early adopters, the opinion leaders, whom it is crucial to have on your side. Their behaviour influences others. People are not sheep but are influenced by others particularly when nervous about the purchase of a totally new product concept or high-value item. This is where word-of-mouth communication is so important.

Perhaps one may meet a friend or colleague and discuss his new car which was a personal import from Belgium and think 'strange, I didn't think it was so easy to import cars straight into the UK from Belgium and save 25 per cent on the British list price!' Again, at the office or place of work, the same is continuing even in a lunchtime visit to the bank (if you do not now use an ATM) since banks are now all active in a wide variety of secondary activities, and literature on their range of services may be everywhere apparent. The process is then repeated on the way home from work when an evening paper will be on sale, and one goes back home to listen to the family, listen about their day, what happened to their friends and perhaps watch television, read a newspaper or weekly television guide, or listen to radio.

As a means of self-protection each individual exercises **selective exposure** which means

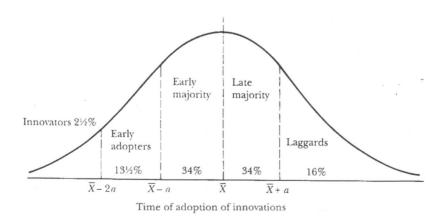

Figure 8.2 Innovation adoption cycle

exposure to messages that fit his/her existing attitudes and the avoidance of messages that are incompatible with his existing beliefs or attitudes. Second, individuals are guilty of **selective perception** that is they may distort or misinterpret the intended meaning of a message when it differs with their deeply-set values. The greater the gap between values held and messages presented, the greater the likelihood of message distortion. Third, being exposed to such a vast number of messages in the course of a day, we could never be expected to remember them all. Each individual has a capacity only for **selective retention**, remembering better those messages which reinforce his/her own values than those at variance. If it is of particular interest now or in the near future, it is more likely to be remembered.

Another point to note is that of **cognitive dissonance** whereby the individual having made a high-value purchase will experience a period of doubt immediately afterwards. During this period, he will be seeking reassurance in his purchase and may for a time read the manufacturer's advertisements more avidly for false or misleading claims. To this end, car manufacturers, to take one example, seek in their advertising both to persuade people to buy and reassure those who have just made a purchase. Flattering the client by telling him how wise he is in purchasing this particular model at this seasonal price is quite a common appeal in advertising which is also seeking to bring in new customers.

Advertising seeks to promote change by moving the individual through the following successive downward stages:

Unawareness	
Awareness	(that this brand exists)
Comprehension	(what this brand can do)
Conviction	(that this brand is supreme)
Action	(i.e., purchase)

Creating awareness is always the first step but beyond that, one has to remind customers of the availability of existing products and their relative competitive strengths. Within the distribution channel, this may have to be relayed perhaps in a different way to each channel member using a selection of trade press; direct mail; product demonstrations and salesforce visits.

Advertising induces mental readiness often pre-selling products. The USA has failed often to realize the global importance of Hollywood in its cinema and television dominance to pre-sell products or product concepts in virgin markets. Through cinema and television, the USA has been able to soften up a global market for its

brands. When those brands or concepts did finally arrive, they were approached by consumers who were inquisitive but already aware. Awareness then of brand names, product concepts and favourable perceptions towards these brands with accompanying expectations of their quality was a worldwide advantage which Hollywood gave to US companies through its marketing of US lifestyles.

Yet, not all advertising is designed to produce sales, as a certain percentage will be devoted to non-profit communication, as in the case of governmental health warnings on AIDS, alcohol abuse, tobacco, or road safety, which are to be found all over the world. Increasingly, companies now advertise their good corporate behaviour rather than their products. In situations where markets are already well saturated with commodity products such as petrol (gasoline) and the commodity market prices for the raw material are turbulent, there is perhaps more to be gained, in terms of consumer loyalty and non-government intervention, from an institutional advertising campaign showing the company to be an honest broker investing in the future of the market concerned. (This campaign may be repeated over several markets.)

Advertising – the global situation

First, irrespective of how low their per capita GNP may be, all countries engage to some extent in advertising. However, it is also important to note that countries report this expenditure data in different ways with expenditures in local currency, for example, and so there is not always consistency in reporting or comparability of the statistics provided. Moreover, the effectiveness of advertising reaches a point of diminishing returns in the more affluent countries as a result of competitive advertising, and hence a high degree of 'noise'. Keegan (1989) expressed it thus:

$$A = f[(B)(C)(D)]$$

where:

A = sales/awareness impact of any particular advertising message
B = effectiveness of advertising/media combination
C = potential market size
D = receptiveness of audience to additional advertising messages

So, as personal disposable income increases, the effectiveness of advertising decreases, thus C and D move in opposite directions to each other.

Advertising expenditure in national currencies gives only a distorted view since it may both conceal inflation in an outwardly growth trend, or else, give a false impression of importance or of total expenditure, so we shall examine advertising expenditure as a percentage of Gross Domestic Product, and market prices (see Table 8.3). Worldwide, advertising is increasing in terms of volume and in terms of media availability. The Former Soviet Union concluded an agreement in May 1989 with Saatchi and Saatchi for them to handle commercial television advertising in the Soviet Union.

Table 8.3 expresses what Figure 8.3 shows graphically. Having listed GNP, we have had to resort to other sources of information for advertising as a percentage of GDP because this was not available for GNP. There should only be perhaps a few percentage points, however, in the differences between GNP and GDP.

Japan is now a major player because as Japanese companies move abroad, Japanese advertising agencies follow, not in the 'camp-

Table 8.3 Population and per capita GNP (in US dollars) of selected countries, 1997

Country	Population mn.	GNP per capita	Country	Population mn.	GNP per capita
Switzerland	7.0	40630			
Japan	125.2	39640			
Norway	4.3	31250			
Denmark	5.2	29890			
Germany	81.8	27510			
USA	263.1	26980			
Austria	8.0	26890			
Singapore	2.9	26730			
France	58.0	24990			
Belgium	10.1	24710			
Netherlands	15.4	24000			
Sweden	8.8	23750	Venezuela	21.6	3020
Hong Kong	6.1	22990			
Finland	5.1	20580	Bulgaria	8.4	1330
Canada	29.6	19380			
Italy	57.2	19020			
Australia	18.0	18720			
UK	58.5	18700			
United Arab Emirates	2.4	17400			
Kuwait	1.6	17390	Mexico	91.8	3320
Israel	5.5	15920			
Ireland	3.5	14710	Poland	38.6	2790
New Zealand	3.6	14340	Jordan	4.2	1510
Spain	39.2	13580	Turkey	61.0	2780
Portugal	9.9	9740	Colombia	36.8	1910
Korea, Republic	44.8	9700	Thailand	58.2	2740
Greece	10.4	8210	Philippines	68.5	1050
Argentina	34.6	8030	Egypt. Arab Republic	57.8	790
Saudi Arabia	18.9	7040	Indonesia	193.2	980
Chile	14.2	4160	Kenya	26.6	280
Hungary	10.2	4120	Pakistan	129.9	460
Malaysia	20.1	3890	China	1200.2	620
Brazil	159.2	3640	India	929.3	340
			Nigeria	111.2	260
			Bangladesh	119.7	240
			Ethiopia	56.4	100
			Mozambique	16.1	80

Source: World Bank Atlas 1997, Washington DC

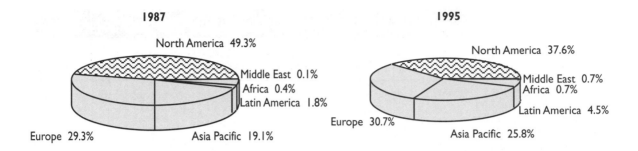

1987

North America 49.3%

Middle East 0.1%
Africa 0.4%
Latin America 1.8%

Europe 29.3%   Asia Pacific 19.1%

1995

North America 37.6%

Middle East 0.7%
Africa 0.7%
Latin America 4.5%

Europe 30.7%   Asia Pacific 25.8%

Figure 8.3   Distribution of total world advertising expenditure by continent

Table 8.4 Advertising as a percentage of gross domestic product						
	1995		1994		1987	
(Local currency units)	% of GDP	Rank	% of GDP	Rank	% of GDP	Rank
Costa Rica	1.57	1	1.68	2	1.17	4
Hong Kong	1.44	2	1.48	5	1.06	7
New Zealand	1.44	3	1.39	6	1.15	5
Panama	1.42	4	1.49	4	0.74	23
South Korea	1.33	5	1.26	7	0.72	24
Australia	1.25	8	1.22	8	1.36	2
Taiwan	1.23	10	1.06	14	0.90	12
United States of America	1.23	11	1.21	9	1.41	1
Brazil	1.18	12	0.83	31	n/a	–
United Kingdom	1.16	13	1.12	13	1.21	3
Portugal	1.16	14	0.99	17	0.45	35
Argentina	1.15	15	1.15	11	0.23	42
Malaysia	1.14	16	1.03	15	0.51	33
Switzerland	0.96	18	0.91	22	1.07	6
Israel	0.94	19	0.95	20	n/a	–
South Africa	0.94	20	0.92	21	0.62	28
Germany	0.91	23	0.89	24	0.88	14
Netherlands	0.90	24	0.89	26	0.79	18
Finland	0.89	25	0.86	30	1.04	8
Ireland	0.87	26	0.89	25	0.90	13
Singapore	0.87	27	0.90	23	0.77	22
Denmark	0.86	28	0.81	33	0.77	20
Spain	0.84	29	0.88	27	0.67	27
Sweden	0.81	32	0.80	34	0.77	21
Japan	0.77	33	0.75	36	0.79	17
Indonesia	0.74	34	0.60	44	0.22	44
Canada	0.73	35	0.73	38	0.81	15
Norway	0.73	36	0.69	39	0.93	11
Austria	0.72	37	0.73	37	0.59	29
Philippines	0.70	38	0.62	43	0.34	39
France	0.66	41	0.66	41	0.67	26
Poland	0.47	50	0.42	55	n/a	–
Kuwait	0.44	52	0.43	54	n/a	–
Saudi Arabia	0.22	65	0.22	66	0.12	46
Bangladesh	0.10	71	n/a	–	n/a	–
Côte d'Ivoire	0.01	75	0.01	75	n/a	–

Note: Figures are based on current price data.

Source: *World Advertising Trends*, 1997, NTC Publications Ltd., Henley on Thames, Oxon

Table 8.5   Total world advertising expenditure by continent

	World	North America	Europe	Asia/ Pacific	Latin America	Africa	Middle East
Advertising expenditure current US$m							
1987	136,423	67,193	40,012	26,117	2,465	508	127
1988	157,198	72,264	46,607	33,444	4,104	574	205
1989	167,341	76,133	48,720	36,729	4,903	593	264
1990	183,303	78,226	59,681	38,222	6,099	714	362
1991	185,607	74,957	60,730	42,214	6,433	903	371
1992	200,162	77,654	67,695	44,732	8,346	1,129	605
1993	200,567	80,795	59,013	47,957	10,951	1,150	700
1994	222,967	87,668	64,265	54,546	13,407	1,525	1,555
1995	247,498	93,140	75,860	63,849	11,133	1,758	1,758
Advertising expenditure, constant US$m							
1987	156,808	77,234	45,991	30,020	2,834	584	146
1988	173,700	79,850	51,499	36,955	4,535	635	227
1989	176,334	80,225	51,338	38,703	5,167	624	278
1990	183,303	78,226	59,681	38,222	6,099	714	362
1991	178,126	71,935	58,282	40,512	6,174	866	356
1992	186,370	72,303	63,031	41,650	7,771	1,051	564
1993	181,344	73,051	53,357	43,361	9,902	1,040	633
1994	196,620	77,308	56,671	48,101	11,823	1,345	1,372
1995	212,257	79,880	65,060	54,759	9,548	1,508	1,508
Annual % change in total advertising expenditure, constant prices							
1988	10.8	3.4	12.0	23.1	60.0	8.7	54.8
1989	1.5	0.5	−0.3	4.7	13.9	−1.6	22.6
1990	4.0	−2.5	16.3	−1.2	18.0	14.3	30.2
1991	−2.8	−8.0	−2.3	6.0	1.2	21.4	−1.5
1992	4.6	0.5	8.1	2.8	25.9	21.3	58.2
1993	−2.7	1.0	−15.3	4.1	27.4	−1.0	12.2
1994	8.4	5.8	6.2	10.9	19.4	29.3	116.8
1995	8.0	3.3	14.8	13.8	−19.2	12.1	9.9

Care should be taken when comparing year-on-year growth due to the addition of new countries.

Source: NTC Publications Ltd

Table 8.6   Media share, per cent of total world advertising expenditure

	World	North America	Europe	Asia/ Pacific	Latin America	Africa	Middle East
1987	100.0	49.3	29.3	19.1	1.8	0.4	0.1
1988	100.0	46.0	29.6	21.3	2.6	0.4	0.1
1989	100.0	45.5	29.1	21.9	2.9	0.4	0.2
1990	100.0	42.7	32.6	20.9	3.3	0.4	0.2
1991	100.0	40.4	32.7	22.7	3.5	0.5	0.2
1992	100.0	38.8	33.8	22.3	4.2	0.6	0.3
1993	100.0	40.3	29.4	23.8	5.5	0.6	0.3
1994	100.0	39.3	28.8	24.5	6.0	0.7	0.7
1995	100.0	37.6	30.7	25.8	4.5	0.7	0.7

Source: NTC Publications Ltd

© NTC Publications Ltd

follower' mode which has been found to explain the rise of certain service-industry multinationals in the West, but for a quite different reason. Japanese companies have financial ties with each other and long histories of supplying one another. It is like when one member of the family goes abroad, the rest of the family go abroad too. These family ties help explain also the lack of movement in the Japanese agency ratings for what is multibillion dollar business. Japan is clearly preeminent as may be seen now in the table of the top 50 advertising groups worldwide in 1989 (see Table 8.9).

problems are resolved (Killough, 1978). The famous Esso 'Put a tiger in your tank' campaign did create an image for an unromantic non-standardized product (petrol/gasoline). Yet what is forgotten is that this particular campaign happened a few generations ago. There are junior members of staff in advertising today who were too young to remember that campaign that is much spoken of in the advertising literature. That is not to say that standardization does not work or does not exist because it does. The degree, however, to which campaigns may be transferable is, however, limited. Perhaps 30 per

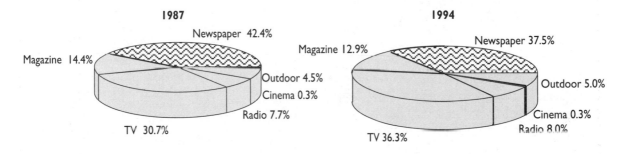

Source: NTC Publications Ltd.

Figure 8.4   Distribution of total world advertising expenditure by main media

If, however, we look at the top ten holding companies, the names change (see Figure 8.4).

Campaign transferability

Few brands are marketed on a worldwide basis for various reasons: because of language or lack of general transferability resulting from the product being climactically or culturally unsuitable, being too expensive, too large or too small. Smaller product sizes may be required for poorer nations. One is left then to standardize only on what is left in terms of the common component parts once all cultural, communicative, legislative, competitive and executional

cent of good campaigns may give rise to some international extension which may include modifications as well as language dubbing (Killough, 1978). See also how this campaign transposition is handled by Gruber (Paliwoda and Ryans, 1995).

In this search for product image, advertisers perceive the similarities more than the dissimilarities among global consumers (vindicating the Maslow Hierarchy of Needs) so potentially the same offering may be made to Malaysians or Nigerians as Americans or Europeans. This has held true for Hertz, Avis, Pepsi, Coke and McDonalds, but who are not representative of all multinational companies.

Exhibit 8.5   A harmonious Eurovision

The Green Paper on Commercial Communications, approved in May, could widely affect the £90 billion industry of pan-European advertising, direct marketing, sponsorship, public relations and sales promotions.

In essence, the Paper suggests that clauses in the Treaty of Rome, ensuring free movement of services, should also apply to commercial communications. Because of the fundamental importance

of the Green Paper for the industry as a whole, a closer look at the 13 restrictive measures the paper is trying to ameliorate is essential.

1. Misleading advertising

The definition of 'misleading' is itself misleading: advertising that is banned in one country might be viewed as informative in another. Comparative advertising is the classic example forcing

➤ Exhibit 8.5 *continued*

advertisers to adjust campaigns for France, Germany and The Netherlands where such advertising is banned.

2. Price, discounts and offers

Negotiating these restrictions can be a minefield. For example, in Germany cash discounts are limited to three per cent and advertising special offers is also restricted. Southern European countries have extremely detailed regulations on trading stamps and discounts. Some measures vary so widely that they effectively prevent any form of European campaign.

3. Telemarketing and direct mail

The EU is currently working on a distance selling directive to allow for the development of cross-border sales techniques. But stricter national rules may prevail which means complying with restrictive measures in The Netherlands, Italy, Germany and Denmark.

4. Promotions and competitions

Running a pan-European sales promotion, particularly one which involves a competition, is near impossible, as measures relating to promotional offers, competitions and lottery-style prizes are significantly different across Europe. The UK is one of the most liberal countries, while Germany claims the prize for being the most restrictive.

5. Media

Cross-border TV advertising can be tricky as restrictions range from no advertising at one extreme (for example, the BBC) to liberal systems at the other (such as Portugal).

6. Sponsorship

This is one of the most restrictive areas, with The Netherlands singled out as having the most restrictive measures. In terms of broadcasting the UK and Denmark came top of the restrictive list.

7. Tobacco

All EU countries have a ban on advertising tobacco products on TV. Only Spain and the UK allow radio advertising and in France advertising is only permitted at point of sale. An EU proposal which would harmonise national approaches by imposing a ban for all advertising is currently under discussion.

8. Alcohol

Cross-border differences create significant barriers for alcohol advertisers; Sweden and Finland,

for example, prohibit all advertising, while the UK and The Netherlands are much less restrictive.

9. Children

Strict rules exist in some countries. For example, in Greece, TV advertising of toys is banned until 10 o'clock in the evening. In Germany and Denmark advertising specific types of toys is banned. The concern is that such restrictions reduce sponsorship and advertising revenues for children's programmes.

10. Food

Creating and implementing a pan-European campaign for food products can be very expensive and problematic as the wide differences in the complexity of regulations regarding the content means producing separate TV ads is frequently the only solution.

11. Pharmaceuticals

National restrictive measures in this area are complex. Some countries ban non-prescribed pharmaceuticals advertising and others prohibit sales promotion. In addition, specific problems relate to warning messages about the product. The length of time for copy clearance is a major problem.

12. Financial services

Disparity between member states is particularly significant in the insurance and investment sector.

13. Societal values

This is a tricky area because it covers such diverse subjects as political advertising – party political advertising in the UK is banned from audio-visual media for example – to issues of 'taste and decency' relating to the use of the female body in advertising, the advertising of sanitary products, contraceptives and the kind of language allowed.

The Commission gave interested parties until the end of October to react to the proposals laid out in the Green Paper, so that the views of those who will be affected by any legislation can be taken on board before the European Parliament and the Council finalise a White Paper. The European Marketing Confederation, of which the CIM is an active member, is following these developments closely. If the consensus shows that current restrictions do present obstacles to marketing in the internal market, then European legislation will have a major impact for the industry.

Source: Marketing Business, December–January 1996/97, p. 50

Table 8.7 Total world advertising expenditure by main media

	Total	Print	TV	Radio	Cinema	Outdoor
Advertising expenditure, current US$m						
1987	136,306	78,000	41,364	10,521	358	6,063
1988	157,063	89,020	48,467	11,905	428	7,241
1989	167,179	94,482	51,771	12,775	446	7,705
1990	183,388	102,412	57,833	14,024	544	8,574
1991	185,921	101,371	60,103	14,115	538	9,800
1992	201,018	106,526	68,508	14,999	597	10,397
1993	202,895	103,153	72,750	16,191	670	10,131
1994	224,131	111,951	82,339	18,049	724	11,070
Advertising expenditure, constant 1990 US$m						
1987	159,753	90,741	49,082	12,371	443	7,116
1988	175,458	99,010	54,621	13,274	499	8,054
1989	176,980	99,872	54,957	13,532	478	8,142
1990	183,515	102,458	57,897	14,040	544	8,575
1991	177,788	97,083	57,323	13,489	510	9,387
1992	185,323	98,627	62,696	13,820	542	9,643
1993	180,893	92,568	64,177	14,408	589	9,095
1994	194,352	97,898	70,565	15,531	620	9,676
Annual % change in total advertising expenditure						
1988	9.8	9.1	11.3	7.3	12.5	13.2
1989	0.9	0.9	0.6	1.9	−4.3	1.1
1990	3.7	2.6	5.3	3.8	13.9	5.3
1991	−3.1	−5.2	1.0	−3.9	−6.2	9.5
1992	4.2	1.6	9.4	2.5	6.2	2.7
1993	−2.4	−6.1	2.4	4.3	8.8	−5.7
1994	7.4	5.8	10.0	7.8	5.2	6.4

Source: NTC Publications Ltd

Table 8.8 Media share, per cent of total world advertising expenditure

	Total	Print	TV	Radio	Cinema	Outdoor
1987	100.0	56.8	30.7	7.7	0.3	4.5
1988	100.0	56.4	31.1	7.6	0.3	4.6
1989	100.0	56.4	31.1	7.6	0.3	4.6
1990	100.0	55.8	31.5	7.7	0.3	4.7
1991	100.0	54.6	32.2	7.6	0.3	5.3
1992	100.0	53.2	33.8	7.5	0.3	5.2
1993	100.0	51.2	35.5	8.0	0.3	5.0
1994	100.0	50.4	36.3	8.0	0.3	5.0

Source: NTC Publications Ltd

This is the strategy employed by Coca-Cola and Pepsi. Food may generally be held to be culture-bound but both these products are global with a centrally produced advertising that incorporates local differences in language, etc. It coincides well with the production orientation because no differentiation is to be seen. This was true until Pepsico started to take market share from Coca-Cola who then changed their formulation to suit this new market change. It suited some but not others so Coca-Cola effectively split their market between the new and classic Coke. Since then, both Coca-Cola and Pepsi-Cola offer a range of carbonated drinks with different flavourings, sweeteners and caffeine levels.

In Keegan's second strategy, the same product can be communicated in different ways for different markets. Bicycles may either be for recreation or basic transportation; a small tractor may be a garden tractor in an affluent society or a small agricultural tractor in a less-developed country. However, that assumes that there is such a thing as a basic bicycle or a basic garden tractor and in this world of materialism, that is a difficult assumption to make. Next, there is the third strategy where the communications remain the same but the product formulation changes. The prime example here is the legend of Esso with its 'Put a tiger in your tank' campaign which remained constant despite the fact that in some markets only 91 octane petrol was available, yet the advertising image employed throughout was the same as for 100 octane and the promise of performance was the same. In the fourth situation, the product and the communications both change; here the examples offered

are greetings cards which vary with local and national holidays and feast days, but also in their nature, too, because of different attitudes to colour and the aesthetics of design. Clothing too, Keegan held, is culture bound. (See Table 8.9.)

However, in the past 20 years there has been the upsurge of multinational clothing led by the denim manufacturers behind Levi's and Wranglers, diversifying now into a full range of casual wear to a global market segment which is the youth market. Similarly, the syndicated franchises behind 'Snoopy' and 'Garfield' and the Simpsons cartoon characters have produced blank greetings cards for all occasions. One may well question whether the fourth case still remains applicable, as well as the actual examples offered. It includes no allowance either for the 'own label'/generic brand/acquisition or

Table 8.9 Keegan's five strategies for multinational marketing

	Product strategy	Communications strategy	Product examples	Product function or need satisfied	Conditions of product use	Ability to buy product
1.	Uniform	Uniform	Coca-Cola, Pepsi	Same	Same	Yes
2.	Same	Different	Bicycles	Different: recreation or transportation	Same	Yes
3.	Different	Same	Camay soap, Nescafé coffee, Petrol (gasoline)	Same	Different	Yes
4.	Different	Different	Clothing, greeting cards	Different	Different	Yes
5.	Invention	Develop new communications	Hand-powered washing machine	Same		No

Source: Keegan, W. (1970) Five strategies for multinational marketing, *European Business*, January, 35–40

Table 8.10 International product/communications standardization

	Generic/own label	Regional brand	International brand
Communication	No responsibility	Responsive and specific	Unresponsive and generalized
Distribution	No responsibility	Standardized	Varied
Pricing	No responsibility	Flexibility	No flexibility, fluctuations give rise to parallel importing/exporting
Profitability	Only on volume	Premium	Premium
Product	No change ensures long production runs	Quality/value	Constant reviewed safeguards the marque
Development	No responsibility	Under constant review	Constant monitoring locally and by headquarters

Table 8.11   The world's top 50 advertising organizations

Rank 1996	1995	Ad organization	Headquarters	Worldwide gross income 1996	Worldwide gross income 1995	1996–1995 % chg	Capitalized volume 1996
1	1	WPP Group	London	$3,419.9	$3,125.5	9.4	$24,740.5
2	2	Omnicom Group	New York	3,035.5	2,708.5	12.1	23,385.1
3	3	Interpublic Group of Cos.	New York	2,751.2	2,465.8	11.5	20,045.1
4	4	Dentsu	Tokyo	1,929.9	1,999.1	–3.5	14,047.9
5	6	Young & Rubicam	New York	1,356.4	1,197.5	13.3	11,981.0
6	5	Cordiant	London	1,169.3	1,203.1	–2.8	9,739.9
7	9	Grey Advertising	New York	987.8	896.6	10.2	6,629.4
8	8	Havas Advertising	Levallois-Perret, France	974.3	924.4	5.4	7,295.1
9	7	Hakuhodo	Tokyo	897.7	958.6	–6.3	6,677.0
10	10	True North Communications	Chicago	889.5	805.9	10.4	7,040.9
11	11	Leo Burnett Co.	Chicago	866.3	805.9	7.5	5,821.1
12	12	MacManus Group	New York	754.2	713.9	5.6	6,830.3
13	13	Publicis Communication	Paris	676.8	624.8	8.3	4,617.7
14	14	Bozell, Jacobs, Kenyon & Eckhardt	New York	473.1	404.5	17.0	3,675.0
15	15	GGT/BDDP Group	London	398.1	380.6	4.6	3,149.1
16	16	Daiko Advertising	Osaka, Japan	256.7	263.6	–2.6	1,853.4
17	17	Asatsu Inc.	Tokyo	242.0	254.2	–4.8	1,904.8
18	19	Carlson Marketing Group	Minneapolis	222.0	189.0	17.5	1,880.8
19	18	Tokyu Agency	Tokyo	214.0	231.1	–7.4	1,844.6
20	20	TMP Worldwide	New York	194.6	177.4	9.7	1,297.0
21	21	Dai-Ichi Kikaku	Tokyo	164.5	168.4	–2.3	1,249.0
22	22	Dentsu, Young & Rubicam Partnerships	Tokyo/Singapore	164.2	161.6	1.6	1,245.5
23	24	Cheil Communications	Seoul	152.0	124.9	21.7	1,005.1
24	28	Abbott Mead Vickers	London	137.1	106.5	28.7	1,079.0
25	23	Yomiko Advertising	Tokyo	125.9	133.0	–5.3	1,106.3
26	25	I&S Corp.	Tokyo	124.7	124.9	–0.2	969.1
27	27	Gage Marketing Group	Minneapolis	122.5	108.5	12.9	816.8
28	26	Asahi Advertising	Tokyo	106.7	114.7	–7.0	692.8
29	36	Campbell Mithun Esty	Minneapolis	94.2	79.2	19.0	785.2
30	31	Wilkens International	London	94.1	89.1	5.6	631.1
31	29	Man Nen Sha	Osaka, Japan	94.1	97.4	–3.4	608.8
32	35	DIMAC Direct	Bridgeton, Mo.	88.8	80.7	9.9	452.0
33	53	CKS Group	Cupertino, Calif.	86.4	49.1	76.0	548.1
34	33	Daehong Communications	Seoul	86.0	84.0	2.4	330.0
35	38	Oricom Inc.	Seoul	85.0	76.6	11.0	280.0
36	34	Clemenger/BBDO Group	Melbourne	84.3	81.6	3.3	503.0
37	40	Bronner Slosberg Humphrey	Boston	83.2	67.5	23.3	554.9
38	30	Oricom Co.	Tokyo	81.7	89.2	–8.4	547.9
39	51	Nelson Communications	New York	77.2	51.8	48.9	635.5
40	44	Wieden & Kennedy	Portland, Ore.	75.0	59.4	26.3	625.0
41	37	Nikkeisha	Tokyo	74.9	77.3	–3.2	454.5
42	39	Hal Riney & Partners	San Francisco	74.6	68.8	8.6	622.0
43	47	Arnold Communications	Boston	73.1	57.7	26.7	551.2
44	32	Sogei	Tokyo	70.4	85.3	17.5	458.1
45	43	LG Ad	Seoul	67.6	60.4	11.9	619.0
46	50	Hill, Holliday, Connors, Cosmopulos	Boston	66.5	52.6	26.4	443.6
47	52	Barry Blau Partners	Wilton, Conn.	63.7	49.9	27.8	425.0
48	46	Duailibi, Petit, Zaragoza Propaganda	Sao Paulo, Brazil	63.0	58.1	8.4	269.9
49	55	Frankel & Co.	Chicago	62.9	47.5	32.3	459.6
50	42	W. B. Doner & Co.	Southfield, Mich.	62.6	60.5	3.4	569.1

Notes: Figures are in millions of US dollars. Companies hold minority equity in each other as follows: True North owns 49% of Publicis Communication; Omnicom owns 46.67% of Clemenger/BBDO; Young & Rubicam and Dentsu each own nearly 50% of Dentsu, Young & Rubicam Partnerships.

Source: Ad Age's Agency Report

introduction of local brands. The final Keegan strategy is the market gap where no product exists but the needs exist. Here, the example offered is of Colgate who developed a hand-powered washing machine and then subsequently developed a communications package to accompany it. The realization that 600 million women still washed clothes by hand provided a feasible market for a multinational who saw possibilities of increasing sales of detergent powders at the same time. However, an alternative perspective could be as shown in Table 8.10.

It does not pay, however, only to listen to the company's advertising people or to the advertising agency. For one thing they all talk in jargon and for another in their search for creativity they are often quite divorced from how the customer perceives the product as Exhibit 8.1 shows.

Britt (1969) had long ago raised the question still to be answered: are so-called successful advertising companies really successful? Obviously, this was a question of setting clear objectives and if there were deficiencies in the statement of objectives, there would be problems devising criteria for assessment. Most advertising agencies he maintained then do not know whether their campaigns are successful or not and are unable to prove or demonstrate the success of the campaigns which they themselves had publicly stated were successes.

Multinational advertising agencies

Multinational advertising agencies have been in a state of flux over the past few years. What was seen always to be a US industry has now changed ownership but not without turmoil. When agencies are acquired or merge there is always a movement in account business, and a possible conflict of interest situation is seen to arise. Similarly when a multinational advertising agency is offered the worldwide business of a multinational company, it can often only make room by letting some accounts go.

Exhibit 8.6   Coke's kudos

A global brand is what every company dreams of spawning, but how many are there? The biggest survey yet of brand awareness, covering some 6,000 brands and 10,000 consumers around the world, indicates that only one, Coca-Cola, has definitely made it. Another 18 brands are close, all of them finishing among the top 50 in each of Europe, Japan and America.

The survey, carried out by Landor, a design consultancy, measures a brand's power in two ways: 'share of mind', or familiarity, and 'esteem', or how good consumers reckon the products are. Reliable and posh goods tend to do best: Rolls-Royce finished 23rd in share of mind and third in esteem, leaving it in 11th place overall.

Given that stress on esteem, polluters and drug-pushers do worst. Exxon finished 75th in share of mind and 157th in esteem, leaving it 94th overall. Marlboro, many marketers' favourite after Coca-Cola, finished 123rd, dragged down by its 328th rating in esteem; it finished 49th in familiarity.

Coca-Cola won by a landslide. The gap between Coke and its nearest rival, Sony, was enormous, but the distance between Sony and the rest was also considerable. Mr Alan Brew of Landor cites Sony as the marketing phenomenon of the past two decades. It finished top in esteem, elbowing aside brands like Mercedes-Benz and IBM. It also had a higher overall score than Coca-Cola among the under-40s.

Mr Brew says all the top ten brands, plus nine others (Rolls-Royce, Honda, Panasonic, Levi's, Kleenex, Ford, Volkswagen, Kellogg's and

Global brands

	Share of mind	
Esteem		
Coca-Cola	1	6
Sony	4	1
Mercedes-Benz	12	2
Kodak	5	9
Disney	8	5
Nestlé	7	14
Toyota	6	23
McDonald's	2	85
IBM	20	4
Pepsi-Cola	3	92

Porsche), can now be called 'global'. Some define their product categories so well that their names are used instead (e.g., a Kleenex instead of a tissue). Xenophobia, however, remains a problem. All the top 20 brands in America were home-grown – as were most in Japan. Global brands still have a long way to go.

Source: *Economist*, 15 September 1990, reproduced with permission

Advertising agency usage criteria

1. Multinationals may select an international agency group with strong central control capable of imposing decisions on regional offices. Kodak and the Ford Motor Company both use J. Walter Thompson in all markets. Colgate use Young and Rubicam in all their markets. Proctor and Gamble, Unilever, Mars all follow this pattern as well.
2. Foreign marketing may require the services of an international agency federation with more decentralized control giving greater local autonomy. (This would include minority interest and associate partner relationships.)
3. For local selling an agency in each territory is considered best for that territory. It may lead to fragmentation but it is the strategy adopted by ITT.
4. A home market agency devises the campaign strategy and places advertising directly into the chosen foreign target market media.
5. A company can go it alone without an advertising agency and place advertisements direct or via local correspondents.

The final choice of agency would be very much influenced by the relative strengths of agencies measured against the following criteria:

A. market coverage
B. quality of coverage
C. market research, public relations, and other marketing services available in-house
D. definition of the respective roles of company advertising department and agency
E. communication and control
F. international co-ordination
G. size of company's international business
H. image
I. company organization
J. level of involvement.

Multinational client/agency relationships

Historically, most of the big US advertising agencies owe their international expansion to their clients. In 1954, it was Coca-Cola which did it for McCann-Erickson. Next, it will be the French agencies in the European Union such as Publicis and strategic business alliances with the Japanese which will ensure that the US hold on global advertising is forever broken.

The 'mirroring' effect is a feature to note. Documented by Vardar (1989) this is an extension of point (J) above. Vardar and Paliwoda (1988) identified certain preconditions for successfully transferable global campaigns by examining the relationship between the local agency, the local client, the Agency Head Office (AHO) and Client Headquarters (CHQ). The findings revealed that apart from the actual head office, there was another body called the 'lead agency' which acted as the actual head office for each specific account.

The extent of involvement agencies experienced from their Head Offices was very much determined by their clients' corporate cultures, which was best displayed by the clients' organizational structure. The way clients organized themselves and their affiliates affected the extent of HQ involvement which would be exercised both in their own affiliates and indirectly in their agencies. Figure 8.5 provides a simplistic depiction of agency-client organizations.

Agency–client relationships never remain static, clients and agencies separately undergo organizational metamorphoses at certain periods of their corporate life, remodelling and reorganizing themselves accordingly. The relationship formed simply evolves and in the long term transforms into a new bond.

The findings show that clients were the initiators of any change which would take place within their own organization as well as in the agency's. Invariably each restructuring inflicted certain transfigurations on the agency–client relationship.

The organizational structure adopted by agencies and clients in global campaigns

Having examined the agency–client relationship and viewing this as mainly client-led, we turn to the client–agency organizational structure adopted for global campaigns, to give better service to international clients. Research findings depicted a more detailed version of an agency – client organizational structure for global campaigns, than the one depicted earlier in Figure 8.5.

Yet again the starting point was the client. In order to be able to supply the best service and satisfy their clients, agencies mirrored their client's organizational structure, as seen in Figure 8.6. It was possible then to envisage a more comprehensive structure both within clients and agencies, than was possible at the beginning of the study.

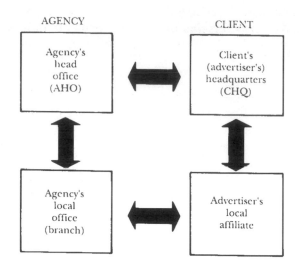

Figure 8.5 Simplistic depiction of agency – client organizational structure

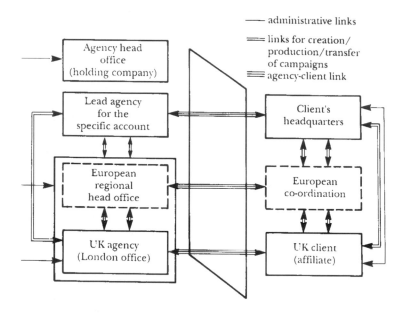

Source: Vardar, N. (1992) *Global Advertising: Rhyme or Reason?*, Paul Chapman, London

Figure 8.6 How agencies and clients organize themselves to conduct global advertising campaigns (the mirroring effect)

Figure 8.5 provides information on how agencies literally mirror the organizational set up of their clients. Agencies tried to match their customer's organizational structure to such an extent that if clients had a regional European co-ordination body, they would also form one within their own agencies.

In some accounts, this co-ordinating function would be under taken by the UK agency. In other cases, this would be technically within the same agency and perhaps operating even in the same building but independently – one as the UK agency and the other as the European regional co-ordinator. Which specific combination of possible organizational structures will be found for a particular account in an agency is determined by the client's specific organizational structure.

Links with the 'lead agency'

The nearest agency to the client's HQ would usually undertake the 'lead agency' role, which did not always coincide with the location of their official HQ. These 'lead agencies' were expected to handle the creation of campaigns, developing them from ad ideas and possibly producing or co-ordinating its production and then finally transferring the campaign to other local agencies that had the account in their own markets.

Throughout the campaign preparations there would be constant contact among the 'lead agency', 'European regional HQ' and the 'UK office'.

Furthermore, the 'lead agency' for account X might also be the local agency for account Y where client Y was based in a different country or town and the organizational structure for Y might be different from that required for client X. Thus, the agency closest to the client's HQ would be assigned the role of the 'lead agency' for that particular account.

Links with the official agency head offices

On the other hand, the agency's official HO where the holding company was based generally had administrative links with the European HO and individual agency branches.

These local offices reported to their holding company, mainly on financial issues and on meeting their annual targets. Other than that, these official AHO did not have any involvement in the creation of advertising campaigns that ran in local markets. Lead agencies were responsible and had the authority over campaign development. If the client's HQ was in the same city as the agency's HO, then the official AHOs became involved on the creative side.

The findings of this research did not yield any information as to the links formed between the official AHO and the 'lead agency' although these two roles were distinctly separated within agencies contacted.

The agency–client link

The third of type link found among agencies and clients while conducting global campaigns was the agency–client link. Again agencies restructured themselves so that their clients in each market, at each management level found their counterparts within the agency.

There were vertical lines of communication within both the client's organization and agency organization and horizontal lines of communication at the corresponding levels between the agency and the client. Each office kept in contact with its corresponding office. For example the UK agency never directly contacted the client's HQs. If it was required, they involved the lead agency or took the problem to the UK client, so that the client could handle it within its own organization.

Links within the client's organization

Finally links that were observed on the client side, with minor modifications. Three parties – HQ of the client, European co-ordination and the UK affiliate, each had administrative links and links for campaign development with each other. The client was not involved in the creation of the campaign. However, knowing their products and what is required for their brand, clients initiated the campaign. Therefore, within the client's organization, ideas were exchanged regarding a brief, product policy and all other relevant marketing mix elements.

Reasons behind the 'mirroring' effect

One of the major reasons was that these international clients were major world advertisers, devoting huge advertising budgets to their marketing activities worldwide.

One of the account executives stated that his client came within the top three or four of the agency's major worldwide accounts, with only 15 per cent of the client's total advertising expenditure. Yet this amount of advertising spending was probably a thousandth of the client's business. Therefore, the agency did not attempt to change the client's way of doing business, but rather tried to understand and work around the parameters established by the client.

Another reason for matching the client's organization within the agency was 'operational efficiency'. For example, if the client had divided itself as North and South Europe and if the agency had split Europe as Scandinavia, Central Europe and Mediterranean countries, responsibility would overlap, giving rise to further complications, e.g., 'Who would go to which meeting?' 'Who would be whose counterpart?' 'Who would communicate with whom?' These were the major practical reasons for setting up a similar organization to that of the client.

Probably another less rational reason, although equally important was securing the smooth conduct of business between parties and showing goodwill and courtesy to the client in meeting their requirements.

We wanted to find predictor variables that would enable us to identify campaigns that could be successfully transferred from one country to another. As a result of this we came up with some preconditions for running smooth global campaigns.

One of the these requirements was to make sure that the agency exactly reflected the client's organization from senior to junior management levels, extending over HQs as well as local affiliates.

The matching of organizational structures between the agency and the client was one of the preconditions for successful global campaign transfers across borders.

Furthermore, agency and client relationships never became static and both parties experienced continuous change. However, clients were always the initiators of any reorganizational change to take place. If clients underwent organizational change, then their agencies would automatically reorganize themselves to match their client's structure.

There were three links identified in agency-client organizations while conducting global advertising, which were:

- Administrative links between the agency HO and the local UK office (such as reporting on financial issues).
- Links for creation/production transfer of campaigns between the UK agency and the agency assigned to the role of the 'lead agency' for the specific account. Lead agencies were appointed depending on the proximity of a local agency, within the international network, the client's HQ. Lead agencies had considerable flow of input to other local offices on the creative side of a global campaign. Administrative links and links for creation/production transfer of campaigns were also replicated on the client's side at each corresponding level.
- The third link was the agency–client link. Clients had their 'shadows' in their agencies at each seniority level, with matching responsibilities and titles.

Miracle (1966, 87) suggests that as no two companies are alike, companies should choose an agency 'that most nearly meets its own particular requirements'. However, findings of this research indicated that in the past 30 years, international agencies have become flexible and very much client-led, most probably as a result of fierce competition faced in the international advertising arena. Therefore, agencies choose to adopt a method of adapting their own organizational structure to suit the needs of each individual client, by mirroring the client's organizational set up within their own agencies.

The findings of the Vardar–Paliwoda study may also be useful in assessing a brand's readiness for 1992 with regard to advertising activities.

Until now, it has been left to the discretion of the individual company whether or not to mount an international or global campaign. However, quite soon that freedom of choice will be regulated and shaped by the EU. Therefore, the findings of this research could also be applied by agencies in preparing their brands an integrated EU, in addition to other intra-agency controls they might have devised themselves.

Media availability

The ability to standardize a campaign internationally presupposes the availability of suitable media.

Television is by far the most important media internationally. Yet two-thirds of Western Europe may be said to be under-served in terms of programme choice, with government controlling the number of television channels, amount of broadcasting hours, and availability of advertising. No indigenous commercial television exists as yet in Sweden, although it receives commercial television from its neighbours including Norway and Denmark. Television reception, like radio, often extends beyond its intended market coverage, which means that markets which do not allow the establishment of an indigenous or local station, but are unable to jam or block signals from a neighbouring transmitter, do in effect have a commercial station.

However, satellite television holds the greatest promise for the future although it does present problems not only for advertisers and their clients in terms of standardization but for governments in terms of regulation. Note that the World Administrative Radio Conference (1977) assigned five satellite channels to every country in the world.

Pan-European research: readership data

There is generally no shortage of media data. The problem such as it exists is that surveys are restrictive, certainly national in character and usually sponsored by the publishers. Apart from the question of objectivity, there is a lack of verification for readership and circulation figures claimed. There is little complementarity as each uses a quite different means of sampling, and this non-standardized research methodology means that this plethora of existing national research material offers little insight into readership segments across nations.

All sorts of problems arise in the study of the individual media in each of these countries. Benelux, for example, is not a country but a region incorporating Belgium, Netherlands and

Luxembourg and with Flemish as well as French speakers. There are certain patterns of buying newspapers or magazines which are regional or national. There is the question too, of literacy levels and to a lesser extent of production both of which affect the demand and supply of print media.

Since 1980, various initiatives have been undertaken to arrive at surveys which examine readership segments across nations and these include:

1. *1980 European Business Readership Survey (EBRS).* A postal survey of men and women covering seventeen countries and including senior management in medium and large sized companies.

2. *Pan European Survey (PES)* (Fourteen countries surveyed, not just top management). It identifies men and women of high status. This sample identifies a universe of 3,755,000 businessmen and a total universe of 6,258,333.

The use of international publications like these can help advertisers establish an international image. For most products, national media have had to be used to provide the range, frequency and level of coverage thought to be required for success.

Advertising standardization versus local adaptation

The technology for standardization including satellite television is now available but local tastes will still influence whether products will be successful or not. Food is often held to be the most culture-bound product. It is arguable whether this extends also to soft drinks but Coca-Cola's canned diet drinks did not have the success in Britain that was expected from US experience, not from lack of advertising but due to the British habit of drinking tea and coffee during the day and not canned drinks, as in the USA. With younger generations being weaned on Coke and Pepsi, this may well change, however, within the course of a generation. Another strategy to penetrate this market was developed between Nestlé who makes Nescafé coffee and Nestea instant tea, and Coca-Cola to offer tea and coffee through vending machines.

Although there may be an international youth segment which knows no frontiers, young people also have different national attitudes towards advertising. This does not prevent them, though from identifying with their international superstars of music, television and cinema nor dressing nor seeking to behave like them.

There is little chance of a brand achieving a coherent international image when there is fragmentation in the market response. Secondly, as we have seen, not all media are universally available nor to the same degree. Worldwide advertising messages have to be suited to the best available media. A verbose TV commercial is unlikely to travel, on grounds of language alone. Marstellers estimate that an English language ad runs 15 per cent longer in French and 50 per cent longer in German, sometimes creating unforeseen difficulties in translating one print ad into several languages. Nevertheless, a multinational such a Kodak is now starting to regionalize its advertising in Europe.

To summarize, the media is seen then as the following.

Newspapers

Both national and international, e.g., *International Herald Tribune*, printed in Paris; the *Financial Times* now printed in London, Frankfurt, New York, Paris, Tokyo, Stockholm, Los Angeles, Leeds, Madrid and Hong Kong and the *Wall Street Journal* has had a European edition for a few years now but its circulation is less than a third that of the *Tribune*. Behind the *Wall Street Journal* is the first national US newspaper, the tabloid *USA Today*. Few countries resemble Britain in respect of its national dailies however, and it is more usual to find local or regional newspapers abroad. In France, for example, the pattern seems to be to buy a national daily in the morning and the regional paper in the evening. Of course another more recent entrant in this market was the launch of *The European* in May 1990 by the late Robert Maxwell. This has achieved a circulation of 153,000, approximately one-third of which are to be found in the UK. Although paraded as the first newspaper of the European Union it fails to present its readers with much of the hard news to be found in the more serious quality national dailies or periodicals such as the *Economist*. Its lower quality reporting, insufficient depth of coverage and lack of editorial policy place *The European* at a disadvantage with respect to the competition bidding for the European business person readership market. As a weekly it also finds itself in competition with the highly respected magazines such as *The Economist, Business Week, Time* and *Newsweek*. It is a question, though, whether the consumer perceives *The European* to be a newspaper or weekly magazine. It is an important question affecting its positioning.

Periodicals

These include business and financial periodicals such as *Business Week; Economist; Euromoney;*

Fortune; International Management; L'Express International and general magazines including *National Geographic; Newsweek; Time; Paris Match International;* and *Scientific American.* Many of these appeal to the same market segment across national boundaries. There are others also including certain international women's magazines, e.g, *Cosmopolitan, Elle* and various specialized interest and trade and technical publications which because of their very esoteric nature command only a small but dedicated readership. In-flight magazines may be seen as another way to target the business audience.

The cinema

A declining medium in western countries for a number of years because of home video recorders, but still very important in India, for example. Problems with this type of media are over the control of choice of cinema and the specific feature film which you wish your advertisement to accompany, and so this leads to lack of control over targeting, and quality of likely audience.

Increasingly, cinema makes use of international advertisements such as those prepared by Coca-Cola in their famous 'I'd love to teach the world to sing' advertisement. Not that this was an international advertisement as much as a blatantly US advertisement for a conspicuously US consumer product that has held a vast international market precisely on those

grounds. For many years, the advertising industry has held this advertisement as an example of global advertising. The true effectiveness of this particular advertisement could, however, only be judged by recall tests of the person in the street paired alongside the advertising executive. Both may have recall but for different reasons.

Television

There are few markets today which do not receive television. More than half the world's households have at least one. The role of advertising in television will vary more from country to country although it has elevated numerous 'rock' stars to the status of global commodities in the pursuit of the youth market. Exciting developments are taking place here which will retain television as the prime medium such as the developments of programming for certain identifiable niches, e.g., Nashville country and western music; religions, including Islamic programming; ethnic and special interests including science fiction. Targeting like this makes it easier for advertisers to reach their chosen audience. Within Europe there are two broadening systems in operation. PAL and SECAM exist in 95 per cent of Europe's households and plans for more direct-broadcast satellites will cover 44 million people in France, 55 million in Germany and 22 million in Scandinavia.

Exhibit 8.7   Stations losing their focus

It is a only decade since the concept of pan-European channels became a reality but the advertising world is already questioning whether they have a future. The problem, say advertising agencies, is that no one really knows how many people are watching. As a result, advertising revenue could begin to dry up. And if that happened, some of the channels could go off the air.

So far the sector, which includes European Business News, NBC Super Channel, Eurosport, Euronews and MTV Europe, rakes in only around $300 million from advertisers, according to Jane Perry, media research director of the European Advertising Agencies Association (EAAA). That is a drop in the ocean of European television advertising spend which totals $24 billion. And it is no secret in the industry that many of the channels are losing a lot of money.

That has not stopped their expansion. There are now 25 channels which regard the whole of Europe as being their market, according to a

report from the international research group IP. Their potential reach can be enormous given the growing number of multi-channel homes in Europe connected to cable or satellite. Eurosport reaches 67 million homes, MTV Europe can be viewed in 54 million households and NBC Super Channel can be accessed by 39 million homes. But how many are actually tuning in is unclear.

The EAAA is pushing international channels to create the sort of reliable data used by national television stations.

Audience research is the life blood of all media, and hardly any has been done on pan-European channels. Last year did see the first and second wave of the European Media Survey (EMS), which unfortunately for the international European channels showed that most, apart from Eurosport, lost some of their audience.

However, EMS is not enough, said Perry. EMS uses telephone interviews to map pan-European viewing habits, not the device traditionally used for

→ **Exhibit 8.7** *continued*

television research – 'people meters' or set-top boxes that track viewing. Only then can advertisers really know who they are reaching, how many and whether they are getting value for money.

Only people meters, said Perry, can provide the right sort of information. 'The problem with telephone interviews is that it is difficult to get realistic data. The results can be superficial.' However, Frances Whitehead, communications director at EBN, firmly supports EMS. 'EMS is very worthwhile,' she said.

Those advertisers which do use pan-European channels are relying on 'gut feeling', said Perry. 'They see these channels in hotels when travelling, so they assume the audience is people like themselves.' As a result, commercials tend to be for airlines and hotels. Derek Bowden, chief executive at Saatchi & Saatchi Europe, said: 'We use existing research plus common sense and gut feel. Good research will help those channels pick up advertising. The EAAA is right to push the issue.'

Graham Hutton, European media director at another international agency group Ammirati Puris Lintas, likens the pan-European channels' position to that of the international press 25 years ago. 'Until *The Economist* and The *Financial Times* began a businessmen's readership survey, there was no knowledge of what they were reading,' he said. Once that data was uncovered, print

advertising aimed at the affluent business executive began to take off.

Without a similar effort from international television, the channels will never be taken seriously, said Hutton. 'You can't have a great medium unless you can prove it. Unless you can prove it, there is a danger of becoming a figment of people's imagination.'

The future for some international channels is bleak, said Perry. 'Clients will start looking for justification. There is increasing concern. They are losing out on advertising. They are getting less money than they would have if they had decent data. The money spent on pan-European channels has grown quite dramatically, but it will grow less strongly without audience data,' she said. The problem is compounded by the fact that a significant amount of viewing is 'out-of-home', in hotels or offices where people meters are not installed, said Perry. However, she said that to get the extra income, the channels will have to spend. 'It will not be cheap,' said Perry.

One solution, said Hutton, could be the pooling of resources. 'It's expensive to do research. If three or four channels came together, they could promote themselves.' Without it, he said, 'as a generic medium, it will not be taken seriously'.

Source: The European, 16 22 January 1997, p. 22

Again national and international advertisements are being used because of origination costs. Multinationals, particularly, reap the benefits of such economies with video recorded adverts. On the negative side, the adverts are usually very US in style and fail to have as high a degree of impact on a British audience as on an US one. New developments are taking place in satellite television broadcasting which are likely to increase the number of television channels. The first Pan-European satellite television channel, SKY, is broadcasting from London, making use of a low-power 20 watt solar EC51 satellite. This satellite's 'footprint' covers Europe but because its signals are coded they have to be decoded at the other end. This is being done by means of linking up with existing television cable networks. One point which must be emphasized then is its precision because of this cable link. It is possible to state exactly who is receiving this signal and where.

The owners of News International have invested heavily in a two-part strategy. The first objective is to maximize potential existing cable

links. A lower-powered satellite, as at present, would otherwise require the viewer to purchase a large dish in order to receive its signal. Using existing cable networks means that the channel is able to start life with a ready-made audience. The second objective is to use a high-power satellite which will be a Direct Broadcasting Satellite (DBS) which will require only a small dish so cabling will not be necessary to receive SKY Channel.

Developments in private subscriber cable television will create opportunities to target directly at selected market segments only; teletext services operated by the television companies including the new faster retrieval of Fastext provide free computer databank information on a variety of subjects including programme titles. Viewdata services such as Prestel operated by British Telecom which connects the television by telephone to a central computer and transmits pages of computer text back to the television screen at home, allows the viewer to interrogate the computer, order goods and withdraw, deposit or ask questions of his bank or building society account.

Yet the outright winner in the application of this technology has been the French PTT in their development of the Minitel system which has more than 60 per cent penetration of households in France.

Radio

Availability differs considerably. This may be regional, national or international. In Britain, commercial radio is regional; only the BBC, which does not allow commercial advertising, is national. Across Europe there is the mighty Radio Luxembourg, which broadcasts a strong signal across Western Europe and is a commercial station broadcasting in several languages. In general, though, fewer listen to radio except for certain hours of the day and for certain programmes. Audiences are selective.

Posters

Outdoor hoardings appear to be found everywhere including the former communist countries. The former communist countries of Eastern Europe now have posters in abundance. Trams (streetcars) and buses are like mobile painted posters.

Leaflets

These may be black and white, or colour, with or without photograph. This form of advertising is dependent on the local sophistication of the printing industry and this requires local organization.

Point-of-sale materials

These should be localized for the market concerned and are dependent on prevailing customs as well as average sales and storage area of retail outlets.

Direct mail

Again, this is a localized form of advertising. The tendency may be not to use mail but the telephone. Mail may be slow and unreliable. People may not be used to receiving mail other than official letters which are usually bad news. There may be no special commercial mailings rates which would also make this method expensive and the response slow. Note that mail charges are now being compared across countries and so it is fairly common now for companies to send their overseas mail in bulk to Belgium for sorting and forwarding.

Trade fairs and exhibitions

These are international in scope and seem expensive relative to the short duration of the fair concerned, although governments usually support first-time exhibitors. It is up to the company to decide the relevance, size and quality of the anticipated audience relative to its target audience. There are high costs of space, stand construction, and manning.

In addition, we could add transport advertising; outdoor advertising at sports grounds including football matches; and neon signs and local attitudes towards their use. Against this listing, a few questions have to be set such as prevailing literacy levels. This would rule out printed advertising messages and would influence advertising more towards the spoken word on radio and on television. Reception coverage of television and radio may be open to some doubt, as may the reliability of circulation figures paraded for foreign newspapers and periodicals, unless there is a counterpart for the Audit Bureau of Circulation (ABC) which conducts an independent audit of magazines sold and therefore confirms circulation figures.

As countries differ, so must the way of putting the message across. The best approach is to 'preserve some covert multinationalization in the campaign but to add a deft touch that is distinctly French or British or Italian'. A study of a select group of multinationals operating in Western Europe found that there was a high degree of standardization in over 70 per cent of these enterprises. Companies sought standardization without sacrificing the benefits of local entrepreneurship.

Pattern standardization is a more planned, flexible form of standardization. The overall theme and individual components of a campaign are designed originally for use in multiple markets, developed to provide a uniformity in direction but not in detail. A pre-planned effort is made to develop an overall corporate advertising strategy and to provide some of the benefits attributed to standardizations while permitting local flexibility in response to individual market differences.

The main objectives in standardizing include:

1. To present a worldwide corporate image through media that are becoming increasingly international.
2. To reduce production and creative costs through economies of scale.
3. To reduce message confusion where there is media overlap or country-to-country consumer mobility.

One television film could be used in 25 or so markets. Also there is media overlap on the

Issues	Sensitive countries
Advertising to children	Canada, Scandinavia, USA, Greece, West Germany, Austria, Holland (toothbrush symbol in confectionery ads)
Class action by consumer associations	EC Commission, USA.
Comparative advertising	EC Commission (encouragement), France (relaxation), Philippines (ban), USA (encouragement)
Consumer protection in general	EC Commission, Scandinavia, UN organizations, USA.
Corrective ads	USA, EC Commission.
Feminine hygiene commercials (mandatory prior screening)	Canada (British).
Food, drugs, and cosmetics commercials (mandatory prior screening)	Canada, Mexico, Austria, Netherlands, Switzerland, West Germany.
Infant formula promotion	World Health Organization/UNICEF.
Reversal of the burden of proof on the advertiser	EC Commission, Scandinavia, USA.
Sexism in advertising	Canada, Netherlands, Scandinavia, UK, USA.
Use of foreign languages in advertisements	France, Mexico, Quebec Province.
Use of foreign materials, themes and illustrations	Korea, Moslem countries, Peru, Philippines.
Wording used in food and drug ads	Belgium, EC Commission, USA.
Cigarette advertising	Luxembourg, UK, Italy, Spain, Switzerland, Canada.
Alcohol advertising	Netherlands, Portugal, Spain, Switzerland, Canada.

Table 8.12   Issues in advertising and the countries where they are particularly sensitive

Source: Boddewyn, J. J. (1981) The global spread of advertising regulations. *MSU Business Topics*, Spring, 5–13

Exhibit 8.8 . Germany bans Benetton ads

Frankfurt – The German appeals court yesterday landed Benetton SA in legal hot water by ruling against the Italian clothing company's shock advertising campaign, saying it exploited people's pity for commercial gain.

The ruling by the federal court of justice, which confirms an earlier decision by a lower court in Frankfurt, is the latest in a series of controversies surrounding the company's advertising and business practices in Germany. Benetton said yesterday it would consider appealing to Germany's constitutional court over the matter.

The court decision covered three advertisements featuring a duck trapped in an oil slick, overworked South American children and a human body on which the words 'HIV positive' were stamped. The case was brought by the centre against unfair competition, an industry-supported body, against Benetton and Gruner+Jahr, publisher of Stern magazine.

The publishing company said it was likely to appeal against the decision on the grounds that it infringed freedom of opinion and expression. Stern carried the advertisements in 1992.

In its judgment, the court said 'Anyone who exploits feelings of pity in such an intensive way for commercial purposes, as in the advertisements subject to complaint, violates competition law.'

It said the picture with the 'HIV positive' words offended against the dignity of people infected with the HIV virus.

A Benetton spokeswoman said future advertisements were likely to feature less controversial work.

Source: Financial Post, 7 July 1995, p. 13

continent as, for example, among Dutch/Belgian/ French/German channels. Multinationals tend to rely heavily on home-country agencies with overseas branches.

Greater standardization is likely in the future.

Substantiating advertising claims

Firstly, countries where false advertising claims will not be entertained and substantiations may be sought. Clearance is mandatory for all commercials in France, Australia, Finland and the UK, and for Canada in relation to advertising to children. Self-regulatory bodies exist in at least 14 countries including Denmark, Norway, UK, Spain, Sweden, and Venezuela.

Product restrictions

If the product is considered immoral, unsafe, or unhealthy, its promotion is likely to be restricted. Thus most countries ban or severely limit the advertising of cigarettes, alcoholic beverages, lotteries and pharmaceuticals because their use, misuse or overuse is considered undesirable.

Balancing information and emotional appeal

Slogans like 'Things go better with Coke' allow people to imagine themselves in new situations. Are they being sold the sizzle or the steak? The concept or the product? The backlash over the

Table 8.13   Advertising regulations and response to these regulations

Key regulatory factors	Major regulatory developments	Suggested business responses
Consumer protection (for example, against untruthful, unfair, misleading ads).	Prior substantiation of advertising claims is becoming the norm.	More self-regulation by industry.
Protection for competitors (for example, against the misuse of comparative and co-operative advertising).	Growing product restrictions affect the advertising of them.	Collaboration with consumer organizations. Greater self-discipline by advertisers.
Environment protection (for example, against outdoor advertising).	More informative ads are in order. Advertising language is being restricted.	Expanded lobbying and public advocacy.
Civil rights protection (for example, against sexist ads).	Vulnerable groups such as children are becoming the target of advertising regulations.	Revised marketing and promotion policies.
Religion (for example, against the advertising of contraceptives).	More groups and people can now sue advertisers.	
Standards of taste and decency (for example, against sexy ads).	Penalties are getting stiffer.	
Nationalism (for example, against the use of foreign languages, themes, and illustrations).		

Source: Boddewyn, J. J. 1981 The global spread of advertising regulations. *MSU Business Topics*, Spring, 5–13; *Marketing*, 16 August 1983, 52

Exhibit 8.9   Ford workers angry as blacks are whited out

When Henry Ford launched his Model T automobile, he told customers they could have in any colour they liked – as long as it was black.

Mr Ford's comments will be seen as bitterly ironic by British workers who were photographed to launch the 'Everything we do is driven by you' advertising campaign in 1991.

Five members of ethnic minorities were invited to appear in the picture to show the racial mix of Ford's workforce at Dagenham, but in an 'ethnic-cleansed' version of the photograph last year, the black and brown faces had been mysteriously replaced by white ones.

Four of the five workers still working at Dagenham have since registered their anger over what they perceive as blatant racism.

→ Exhibit 8.9 *continued*

Bill Morris, general secretary of the Transport and General Workers' Union, yesterday condemned the incident as 'deeply offensive'. He said: 'This is an appalling situation which reveals the depths of racist attitudes in our society.'

He said the union had elicited fulsome apologies from management and a £1,500 cheque for each of the workers, in compensation for their hurt feelings. 'We shall be equally vigorous in tackling racism in future, wherever it surfaces.'

The dramatic transformation in the picture was first noticed by Noel Sinclair, a worker at Ford's Dagenham plant, when he walked into a showroom in Essex.

Mr Sinclair took the new brochure back to the paint, trim and assembly department at the Essex plant and showed four of his friends, who had readily agreed to pose.

Douglas Sinclair, a 56-year-old black man who has worked at the plant for 30 years, said his body remained in the picture, but a white, bespectacled face had appeared on top of it.

'My body was there, dressed in my overalls, the rings on my fingers were still there, but I had glasses on and a white face. It was embarrassing.

People at work started to come up to me and call me "Two Face".'

Patricia Marquis said she felt 'humiliated and angry' when she saw that her face had aged 20 years, that she had put on 10 lb and turned white.

'I wanted an explanation from them. They had changed my face for God's sake – what on earth did they think they were doing?' Keith Thomas, 40, who saw his face and arms replaced with those of a white man, immediately thought it was racist.' Why didn't they just use a different picture? It was a racist act, quite clearly.'

The TGWU branch at the plant had considerable difficulty containing anger over the incident, and hundreds of workers walked out three weeks ago, causing an estimated £2.8m worth of lost production.

Management said the 'mistake' had been made by Ogilvy & Mather, the advertising agency, which vehemently denies any racist intent.

The new picture, with the white faces, had been issued for a Ford promotion in Poland because the original photograph 'did not portray the ethnic mix' in Eastern Europe.

Source: *The Independent,* 21 February, 1996

Exhibit 8.10   Ford compensates four black workers after advert blunder

Ford Motor Company has apologised to four of its black assembly workers and paid them compensation after white faces were superimposed on their features in a nationwide advertising campaign.

Embarrassed Ford executives withdrew posters and scrapped thousands of copies of a booklet with the all-white line-up on its front cover – destined for showrooms across Britain.

Ford blamed the public relations fiasco on an error by Ogilvy & Mather, the advertising agency, but said no racial offence was intended. Ford has sent a cheque for £1,500 each to the three men and one woman to compensate them for any distress. A review of all the group's advertising and promotional material has been ordered.

The four workers were among 25 from Ford's Dagenham plant in Essex who posed in 1991 for a promotional picture. The negatives were later altered for a marketing campaign in Poland. Ford said: 'The modification was made because the UK version obviously did not portray the ethnic mix in Poland.'

When a picture featuring employees was required to promote the current Ford Credit Options programme in the UK, the Polish version of the picture was used, instead of the original.

Mr James Page, a director of Ogilvy & Mather, said in a letter to Ford: 'Unfortunately, we are unable to determine exactly who made this mistake as it is now 18 months since the negative was supplied.' Ogilvy & Mather said last night: 'Clearly our internal administration let us down and I believe this was a genuine mistake. It was certainly not a malicious or racist action.'

The four workers concerned – Mr George Pinto, Mr Douglas Sinclair, Mr Keith Thomas and Miss Patricia Marquis – complained to a TGWU transport union representative after being alerted by a colleague.

Ford said: 'When the mistake was discovered, immediate action was taken to withdraw the brochure containing the picture. The reason for the picture being altered was investigated and we explained fully what had happened to the employees involved and the trade unions.'

Mr Steve Hart, TGWU union representative

→

➤ ## Exhibit 8.10 *continued*

at Dagenham, said: 'It was an appalling incident, deeply hurtful and offensive. Lessons will have to be learnt. Ford were equally as appalled at what happened as we were'.

'The first campaign accurately reflected the make-up of the workforce at the plant. All the good that was done by that is wiped away by this kind of thing.'

Mr Bill Morris, general secretary of the

TGWU, said: 'The changes were deeply offensive to the people concerned, and to the Ford workforce as a whole. We welcome Ford management's regret over this incident, and the fact that equal opportunities training is to be given to advertising agencies used by the company in future.'

Source: Financial Times, 21 February 1996

---

new Coke formulation tends to show how consumers confuse the two. The advertiser seeks to move the audience from past awareness and interest to evaluation, trial and adoption. Comparative advertising is supported by the EU and the US administration because it is more informative, identifying and contrasting brands.

Use of language

The US and the EU are considering the legitimacy of words such as 'health', 'homemade',

and 'natural', and 'organic' when applied to food. The USA does not allow 'cough remedies' but 'cough suppressants'. French xenophobia prohibits totally the use of English words which have almost successfully passed into the French language such as 'cash and carry', 'jumbo jet', 'supermarket', etc. French law now forbids the use of English in French advertising as does Quebec Provincial legislation in Canada. These new products and concepts need now to be translated into French in order to find a market in France. Bilingual Canada is facing similar difficulties where most products appear with labels in French and English.

Exhibit 8.11   Admen watch their language

Not all the barriers to European trade have fallen with the creation of the single market. There was the problem with the Toyota MR2 in France. Pronounced in French, the name MR2 translates as 'shitty'. The cereal Bran Buds translates into Swedish as 'burnt farmers'. It should be obvious why Pschitt (a French soft drink), Bum crisps from Spain and Super Piss (a Finnish de-icer) have not been launched in Britain.

The problems of translation are only one reason why the single market has not resulted in very much single European advertising. A survey at the turn of the year found that four out of five of the biggest European advertisers had already centralized their marketing. But only one in 10 was already using pan-European advertising.

Nevertheless, the process is increasing. From Captain Birdseye selling fish fingers to Sharon Stone selling Pirelli tires, from housewives testifying to the cleaning qualities of washing-powder to Bertie Bassett selling Licorice Allsorts, the sales messages of the major advertisers are being addressed to as many countries at once as possible.

John Shannon, chairman of Grey Europe, says: 'International networks like ours are increas-

ingly being invited to pitch not just on a single country basis but on a pan-European basis. It's usually associated with a client who wants to centralize his marketing and advertising, and seeks economies, not the least of which is not wishing to duplicate creative work.'

There is still a difference between what advertisers profess in presentations and what they actually do. Tom Blackwell, deputy chairman of the marketing consultancy Interbrand, says: 'Agencies have been espousing the message of 'think global, act local' in order to promote their international networks because there are megabucks in supporting the international brands.' Richard Zambuni, deputy managing director of the brand development company Craton, Lodge and Knight, worked on packages for a brand of insect repellent in the mid-1980s. Each local marketing manager had a say in the process, so that the insect displayed on the pack varied from country to country. In Britain it was a bluebottle, elsewhere it was an ant, a mosquito or some other pest. The local chiefs even insisted on variations of color and positioning of an arrow emblem.

'The basic concept was very similar, but everybody wanted to make his mark. These days it

→ Exhibit 8.11 *continued*

wouldn't be tolerated,' he says. High values are set on a brand name which is consistent worldwide, like Coca-Cola, Nescafe or Marlboro. As a result, national heads have much less of a say than they used to. Zambuni's company has just worked on the relaunch of a Shell motor oil in which a single name – Helix – has replaced local variants in France, Germany and Italy. The design is also consistent.

Of course, some products transfer more easily than others. Recent years have seen a pan-European market develop for products like mineral water, pasta and confectionery. Almost anywhere you go in Europe, instant coffee is dominated by 'Eurobrands' like Nescafe, and detergent by the brands owned by Unilever, Procter & Gamble and Henkel.

CDP Europe tested 120 food and drink advertisements on a cross-section of consumers from six countries. The aim was to assess the advertisements for likability, desire to taste, and so on. Responses varied so much that the recommendation was that whatever could be done locally, should be, and where possible ads should identify a particular country.

The most liked? A British advertisement for the National Dairy Council: it would be difficult to get less pan-European than this ad's dancing milk bottles.

Source: Tim Westcott, *Calgary Herald*, 7 November 1993, p. E10

Table 8.14   U.S. corrective advertising cases

Company	Product	Claim	Order
R. J. Reynolds (1997)	Camel cigarettes	Joe Camel cartoon encouraging children to smoke cigarettes	Limit Joe Camel ads to adult locations, require a public education campaign and disclose confidential marketing data about Camel cigarettes. Further corrective advertising also likely.
Ashland Inc. (1997)	Valvoline Teflon containing TM8 engine treatment	Unsubstantiated claims about performance. Test claims false and misleading	Consent agreement with the FTC imposes constraints on future advertising claims but does not constitute an admission of a law violation.

Vulnerable groups

The unwritten convention that is generally adhered to is that it is unfair to advertise to the young, old, poor, sick, recently bereaved, and ignorant and this is generally observed.

Legal action

The traditional view that only injured parties can sue is now being changed within the European Community on the grounds that everyone has an interest in having false, unfair, and misleading advertising stopped before damage can be done. A draft EU directive would allow customers and competitors as well as their legitimate associations, to start legal action against unfair or misleading advertising.

Penalties

In settling a suit brought by the US Federal Trade Commission (FTC), the STP Corporation – a company in the main producing oil additives was ordered to spend $200,000 to place notices in 35 newspapers and 11 magazines with an estimated readership of 78 million. The notices stated that tests conducted by STP cannot be relied on to support its claim that its product reduces oil consumption.

Table 8.15   Wilkie, McNeill, Mazis' conclusions on corrective advertising

1. The FTC is empowered to order corrective advertising as a remedy against deceptive advertising campaigns.
2. There are important legal constraints as to when and in what manner the FTC can employ this remedy form.
3. Corrective advertising holds the potential to yield beneficial effects for consumers.
4. Corrective advertising appears to hold the potential to affect the sales and/or image of the advertised brand.
5. There is little evidence of a systematic FTC program for corrective advertising:
    *   bursts of case activity have been followed by long periods of inactivity.
    *   philosophical and personnel changes occurred throughout the 1970s and early 1980s at both the staff and Commissioner levels.
    *   past orders have used a wide range of requirements for corrective advertising.
6. Consent negotiations between FTC staff members and company representatives have played a key role in the exact requirements in almost every case to date.
7. Consumer effectiveness of corrective advertising has not been the primary concern of the orders issued to date.
8. In communication terms, past corrective advertising orders against major advertisers appear to have been weak.
9. In terms of consumer impacts, the major corrective advertising orders appear *not* to have been successful in remedying consumer misimpressions across the marketplace.
10. If corrective advertising is to continue as an FTC remedy, some changes in the form of the orders will be required.

Source: Wilkie, W. L., McNeil, D. L., and Mazis, M. B. (1988) Marketing's scarlet letter: the theory and practice of corrective advertising In *Promotional Management: Issues and Perspectives*, Govoni, N., Eng, R., and Golpe, M., Prentice Hall, Englewood Cliffs, NJ.

An EU draft directive on misleading and unfair advertising would permit courts to issue injunctions to cease and desist 'even without proof of intention or neglect or of actual prejudice.' Courts would be allowed to require publication of a corrective statement and of the court decision as well as to impose penalties taking into account the extent of the damage (this is already the case in France and the USA).

Develop self-discipline

Some companies have their own code of ethics, and in general these would suggest that perhaps there are less untruths to be found in industry and commerce than in personal classified advertisements for house and car sales, or armed services recruiting campaigns and supportive literature.

Finally, the last word on multinational standardization and regulation must go to George M. Black, Chairman of J. Walter Thompson's Frankfurt office, 'If I were to make a film for Europe-wide distribution, by the time we went through all the rules governing national advertising, we would be left with a poster.'

Revision questions

1. Why are there relatively so few global brands? Can we expect to see more in future?
2. Promotion has been said to be an umbrella term – what then does it include?
3. What are the advantages of trade fairs and exhibitions?
4. What is the appeal of public relations?
5. What does sales promotion consist of?
6. How do you define advertising?
7. How do brand names wear out? Can you supply an example?
8. What is the effect of 'noise' in the communications model?
9. To what extent does the innovation diffusion cycle aid understanding of the advertising task?
10. Listing country populations and per capita GNP figures is the same as listing the top markets worldwide, or not?
11. What significance can be derived from comparing total advertising billings in the US and Japan?
12. What is the role of the 'lead agency' in global advertising campaigns?
13. What is the 'mirroring effect'?
14. Examine advertising expenditures by

country and by media, what inferences do you draw?

15. How does the Pan European Readership Research Survey aid in making international advertising decisions?
16. Make the case for total advertising standardization versus local adaptation.
17. Examine the two exhibits on Ford advertising in Poland. Summarize in your own words what took place and how the situation could have been avoided.
18. Describe the products for which advertising is restricted. Do the restrictions apply also to the Internet?
19. How is corrective advertising pursued in the US and the EU?
20. Outline the constraints on language in advertising. Are they satisfactory in your opinion?

References

Boddewyn, J. J. (1987) International advertisers face government hurdles. *Marketing News*, 8 May, 20–21, 26.

Boddewyn, J. J. (1992) *Global Perspectives on Advertising Self-Regulation*, Quorum Books, Westport, Conn.

Brit, S. H. (1968) Are so called successful advertising companies really successful? *Journal of Advertising Research.*, June, 3–9.

Buzzell, Roy (1968) Can you standardize multinational marketing? *Harvard Business Review*, November-December, 102–113.

Douglas, S. P., and Wind, Y. (1987) The myth of globalisation. *Columbia Journal of World Business*, Winter, 19–29.

Eechambadi, N. V. (1994) 'Does Advertising Work?', *The McKinsey Quarterly*, No. 3, 117–129.

Ehrenberg, A. S. C. (1992), 'Comments on how Advertising Works', *Marketing and Research Today*, August, 167–169.

Elderfield, A. (1990) 'The Network Solution to Pan-European Promotion', *Business Marketing Digest*, **15** (3), 3rd Quarter, 51–58.

Gates, S. R., and Egelhoff W. G. (1986) Centralisation in headquarters-subsidiary relationships. *Journal of International Business Studies*, Summer, 77–92.

Govoni, N., Eng, R., and Galper, M. (1988) *Promotional Management: Issues and Perspectives*, Prentice-Hall, Englewood Cliffs, New Jersey.

Gruber, U. (1995) 'The Role of Multilingual Copy Adaptation in International Advertising', in Paliwoda, S. J. and Ryans Jr, J. K., *International Marketing Reader*, Routledge, London.

Hagel III, J. and Eisenmann, T. R. (1994) 'Navigating the Multimedia Landscape', *The McKinsey Quarterly*, No. 3, 39–55.

Hawkins, S. (1983) How to understand your partner's cultural baggage. *International Management Europe*, September, 48–57.

Jain, S. C. (1989) Standardisation of international marketing strategy: some research hypotheses. *Journal of Marketing*, **53**, 70–79.

Keegan, W. J. (1995) 'Global Product Management: Strategic Alternatives', in Paliwoda, S. J. and Ryans Jr, J. K., *International Marketing Reader*, Routledge, London.

Killough, J. (1978) Improved payoffs from transnational advertising, *Harvard Business Review*, July-August, 102–110.

Klein, P. R. (1991) 'Global Advertising: Does Research Find a Cross-Cultural Effect', *Applied Marketing Research*, **31**(1), 17–26.

Lilien, G. (1982) A descriptive model of the trade show budgeting decision process. *Industrial Marketing Management*, 12 February, 25–29.

Macrae, C. (1991) *World Class Brands*, Addison-Wesley, Wokingham, Berkshire.

Martenson, R. (1987) Is standardisation of marketing feasible in culture-bound industries? A European case study. *International Marketing Review*, Autumn, 7–17.

Peebles, D. M., Ryans, J. K., and Vernon, I. R. A New Perspective on Advertising Standardisation. *Journal of Marketing*, **22** (1), 28–34.

Rau, I. A., and Peeble, J. F. Standardisation of marketing strategy by multinationals. *International Marketing Review*, Autumn, 18–28.

Rogers, E. M. (1962) *Diffusion of Innovations*, New York, Free Press.

Rosen, B. N., Boddewyn, J. J., and Louis, E. A. (1989) US brands abroad: an empirical study on global boundary. *International Marketing Review*, **6** (1), 7–19.

Rosson, P., and Seringhaus, R. (1989) Business Performance of International Trade Fairs. In *Dimensions of International Business no. 2*, Carlton University School of Business, International Business Study Group, IBSG Occasional Paper V, June.

Ryans Jr., J. K. and Ratz, D. G. (1987) Advertising standardisation: a re-examination. *International Journal of Advertising*, **6**, 145–148.

Ryans Jr., J. K., and Ratz, D. G. (1987) Why standardize? *International Journal of Advertising*, **6**, 145–158.

Sandler, D. M. and Shani, D. (1992) 'Brand Globally but Advertise Locally? An Empirical Investigation', *International Marketing Review*, **9**(4), 18–31.

Schofield, B. (1994) 'Building and Rebuilding a Global Company', *The McKinsey Quarterly*, No. 2, 37–45.

Schwoerer, J. (1987) Measuring advertising effectiveness: emergence of an international standard? *European Research*, **15** (1), 40–51.

Szymanski, D. M., Bharadwaj, S. G. and Varadarajan, P. R. (1993) 'Standardization versus Adaptation of International Marketing Strategy: An Empirical Investigation', *Journal of Marketing*, October, **57**(4), 1–17.

Terpstra, V., and Yu, M. C (1988) Determinants of foreign investment of US advertising agencies. *Journal of International Business Studies*, Spring, 33–46.

Vardar, N. (1989) Management of international advertising: involvement of foreign headquarters in US subsidiaries and agencies. Unpublished Ph.D. thesis, Manchester School of Management, University of Manchester.

Vardar, N. (1995) 'Media Burst in a Euroasian Country: a Blessing or a Burden?' in Paliwoda, S. J. and Ryans Jr, J. K. (1995) *International Marketing Reader*, Routledge, London.

West, D. C. and Paliwoda, S. J. (1996a) 'Advertising Client-Agency Relationships: the Decision Making Structure of Clients', *European Journal of Marketing*, **30**(8), 19–36.

West, D. C. and Paliwoda, S. J. (1996b) 'Advertising Adoption in a Developing Market Economy: the Case of Poland', *International Marketing Review*, **1**(4), 82–101.

Wiechmann, U. E., and Lewis, G. P. (1979) Problems that plague multinational markets. *Harvard Business Review*, July-August, 118–24.

World Advertising Trends 1997 NTC Publications Ltd, Henley-on-Thames, Oxon.

Yip, G. S. and Madsen, T. L. (1996) 'Global Account Management: The New Frontier in Relationship Management', *International Marketing Review*, **13**(3), 24–42.

Web sites

AC Nielsen
http://www.nielsen.ca

Advertising and Marketing on the Internet
http://www.yahoo.com/
Business_and_Economy/Marketing/

American Marketing Association
http://www.ama.org/

AT & T Business Network – free site
http://www.bnet.att.com

Australian Tourist Commission
http://www.aussie.net.au

BBC
http://www.bbc.co.uk

Better Business Bureau
http://www.bbb.org/

The Body Shop
http://www.the-body-shop.com

Brand Naming & Brandtest Market Research
http://www.brandinst.com

British Library
http://portico.bl.uk

BSE (Mad Cow Disease)
http://www.bmj.com/bmj/bse.html

Business Site of the Day
http://www.bizniz.com/eurocool/

Businesses on the Internet
http://www.yahoo.com/
Business_and_Economy/Corporations/

Business to Business Marketing Exchange
http://www.btob.wfu.edu/b2b.html

C – Span : Cable Television on the Web
http://www.c-span.org

Cahners Manufacturing Marketplace: US manufacturers, distributors, products, news and hot links
http://www.manufacturing.net

Canadian Business InfoWorld
http://csclub.uwaterloo.ca/u/
nckwan/.html/directory

Canadian Advertising Rates & Data
http://www.cardmedia.com

Canadian Green Page
http://www.cdngreenpage.com

Canadian Newspaper Marketing Bureau
http://www.nmb.ca

Canadian WWW Central Index
http://www.csr.ists.ca/w3can/
Welcome.html

CBS Television
http://www.cbs.com/

Chanukah on the Net
http://www.jewishpost.com/
jewishpost/chanukah

Chartered Institute of Marketing
http://www.cim.co.uk

China Online Service – links to websites and information sources in China
http://www.gcinfo.com/main.html

Chinese Language Web Directory – What Site!
Http://www.whatsite.com

Chivas Regal Scotch Whisky

Christmas Traditions in France and in Canada
http://www.culture.fr/culture/noel/
angl/noel.htm

CIA Publications
http://www.odc.gov/cia/
    publications/pus.html

City.net – covers 4,300 destinations
http://www.city.net

Conferences, Conventions &
    Exhibitions – Global Listings
http://www.traders.co.uk/
    media_marketing/cce/cce.htm

CNN Interactive
http://www.cnn.com/

Commerce Business Daily
gopher:cscns.com
Choose: Internet Express Gopher by Subject
    Business-Commerce Business
    Daily-Softshare

Commercenet
www.commerce.net

Commercial Use of the Internet
http://pass.wayne.edu/business.html

Consumer Information Center
http://www.pueblo.gsa.gov/

Diners Club – Global weather, currency
    conversions, language translations, dealing
    with stress
http://www.dinersclub.com

Disney Channel – fun and games with a hidden
    educational agenda
http://www.disneychannel.co.uk

Disneyworld
http://www.disney.com/DisneyWorld/

Electric eye Multimedia
http://www.ideaguy.com

Electronic Marketing Home Page
http://www.america.net/~scotth/
    mktsite.htm

Europages
http://www.europages.com

Europe – Business Monitor
http://www.businessmonitor.co.uk

Europe – see Yellowweb Europe and Europages

European Electronic Information Market
http://www2.echo.lu

European Union – Citizen's First
http://www.eu.com

Fashion Café

Find it Fast
http://www.webcom.com/~tbrown/find-
    page.html

Frankfurt International Fair
http://www.messefrankfurt.de/

Geek Site of the Day
http://www.owlnet.rice.edu/~indigo.gstod/
    index.html

Glaxo-Wellcome
http://www.glaxowellcome.co.uk

Global Economic Forum
http://www.ms.com/GEFdata/digests/
    960129-mon.html

Global Internet News Agency
www.gina.com

Global Trade Center
http://wwwtradezone.com/tz/

Greenpeace International
http://www.greenpeace.org/

Holiday Inn
http://www.holiday-inn.com

Hotel & Travel Index On-Line
http://www.traveler.net/htio

Institute of Canadian Advertising

Insurance News Network
http://www.insure.com/

Internet Business Center
http://www.tig.com/IBC

Internet Marketing List Archives
http://www.popco.com/hyper/
    inet-marketing/

Internet Public Library
http://ipl.sils.umich.edu/

Internet Society
http://info.isoc.org/home.html

Internet Sleuth
http://www.intbc.com/sleuth/

Institute of Public Relations
http://www.ipr.press.net/

Internet Address Finder
www.iaf.net

International Internet Marketing
www.clark.net/pub/granered/iim.html

International Internet Name Registry
http://www.netnames.com

Irn-Bru (famous Scottish soft drink)
http://www.irn-bru.co.uk

Japan Web Servers
http://www.ntt.jp/SQUARE/
    www-in-JP.html

Japan: What's New in Japan
http://www.ntt.jp/WHATSNEW/

Japan Information Network
http://jin.jcic.or.jp/navi/category_1.html

JETRO (The Japanese External Trade
    Organization)
http://www.jetro.go.jp/index.html

Land's End – the famous clothing catalogue
    company
http://www.landsend.com/

Levi's – includes an online game called 'Riveted'
http://www.eu.levi.com/inner-
    seam/eu/vol2/iss3/game/intro.nhtml

Levi's 501 jeans
http://www.levi.com/menu

Magazine Publishers of America
http://www.ima.org/members/
    mmm02.html

Malls of Canada: The world's largest shopping
    malls
http:///www.canadamalls.com/provider/

MasterCard International
http://www.mastercard.com

Microsoft/NBC
http://www.msnbc.com

National Readership Surveys
http://www.nrs.co.uk

Newspage
http://www.newspage.com

Nielsen Media Research
http://www.nielsenmedia.com

Royal Family
http://www.neosoft.com/~dlgates/uk/
    ukspecific.html?pix_windsors.

Royalty – an entertainment
http://www.royalnetwork.com

NEC Corporation, Overseas Advertising
    Division, Tokyo
http://www.nec.co.jp/just_imagine/

Packaging Waste Legislation – the Sequoia
    Group
http://ourworld.compuserve.com/
    homepages/SeQuoia

Plain English Campaign
http://www.demon.co.uk/plainenglish

The Press Association
http://www.pa.press.net

Pointcast Network
http://www.pointcast.com

Pointcast Network Canada
http://www.pointcast.ca

Ragu pasta sauces
http://www.eat.com

Santa's Home Page
http://www.north-pole.org

Saturn – the idiosyncratic GM subsidiary, its
    cars and advance information
http://www.saturncars.com/

Save Your Marriage: nearest flowers,
    on-the-way champagne, restaurant, plus
    directions
http://www.zip2.com

Scottish Virtual Memorial Garden
http://www.hebrides.com

Scottish Tourist Board
http://www.holiday.scotland.net

Sellafield: how a nuclear plant uses PR.
http://www.bnfl.com

Smart Business Supersite
http://www.smartbiz.com/

Sony
http://www.sony.com/

The European Business Directory
http://www.europages.com/g/home.html

The Scotsman
http://www.scotsman.com

The Times
http://www.the-times.co.uk

The White House Home Page
http://www.whitehouse.gov/

Tracking time spent on-line
http://tucows.cableint.net/softime.html

Trade Compass
http://www.tradecompass.com

TradePort – extensive information on
    international business
http://www.tradeport.org

UPS Online
http://www.ups.com

Wall Street Journal Interactive Edition
http://www.update.wsj.com/

Wall Street Net
http://www.netresource.com/wsn/

Scotch Malt Whisky – Laphroaig
http://www.laphroaig.com

Scotch Malt Whisky – Glenmorangie
http://www.glenmorangie.com

Virtual Birmingham – information on 25,000
   Birmingham businesses
http://www.virtualbirmingham.co.uk

Virtual Cemetery – Scottish Hebridean
   Memorial Garden
http://www.hebrides.com

Virtual Job Fair
http://www.vjf.com/

Virtual Reference Desk
http://thorplus.lib.purdue.edu/reference/ind
   ex.html

Virtual Safari
http://www.tower.org/disease/animals.html

Virtual Shopping Malls
http://www.itl.net/shopping/index.html

Virtual Vineyards
http://www.virtualvin.com/

Visa Expo
http://wwwvisa.com

Wells Fargo
http://www.wellsfargo.com

Winter Web Wonderland
http://banzai.neosoft.com/citylink/xmas

World Bank
http://www.worldbank.org/

World Factbook
gopher: gopher.aecom.yu.edu

World Wide Web Virtual Library
http://W3.org

WorldClass Supersite
http://web.idirect.com/~tiger

WWW Yellow Pages
www.cba.uh.edu/ylowpges/ylowpges.html.

Yahoo: National Yahoos: Canada, France,
   Germany, Japan, UK, Ireland.
Metros: Chicago, Los Angeles, New York, San
   Francisco Bay Area, My Town

Yahoo Reuters
http://www.yahoo.co.uk/News

Yelloweb Europe
http://www.yweb.com/

CHAPTER 9

International marketing planning: reviewing, appraising and implementing

Planning is a word which has fallen greatly out of fashion. It has become a pejorative word and come to be associated with the worst excesses and failures of communism and of state planning, equivalent to a bureaucracy created for analysis but not for decision making. If we turn to Henry Mintzberg, one of the finest management thinkers of our day, we find him saying (Mintzberg, 1994) that planning is about future thinking, about controlling the future, about co-ordinating activities, that it is about decision-making that is integrated, that it is a formalized procedure to produce an articulated result in the form of an integrated system of decisions. Formalization of planning means to decompose, to articulate and especially to rationalize the processes by which decisions are made and integrated in organizations. Organizations both develop plans for the future and evolve patterns out of their past, so one can be called an intended strategy, the other a realized strategy. Intentions that are fully realized can be called deliberate strategies. However, Mintzberg points out forcefully that few strategies can be purely deliberate and few can be purely emergent, as one suggests no learning, the other, no control. All real-world strategies, Mintzberg points out, need to mix these in some way, to attempt to control without stopping the learning process.

Hamel and Prahalad (1994) in their book, *Competing for the Future*, wrote:

We are standing on the verge, and for some it will be the precipice, of a revolution as profound as that which gave birth to modern industry. It will be the environmental revolution, the genetic revolution, the materials revolution, the digital revolution, and, most of all, the information revolution. Entirely new industries, now in their gestation phase, will soon be born. Such prenatal industries include microrobotics – miniature robots built from atomic particles that could, among other things, unclog sclerotic arteries; machine translation – telephone switches and other devices that will provide real-time translation between people conversing in different languages; digital highways into the home that will offer instant access to the world's store of knowledge and entertainment; urban underground automated distribution systems that will reduce traffic congestion; 'virtual' meeting rooms that will save people the wear and tear of air travel; biomimetic materials that will duplicate the wondrous properties of materials found in the living world; satellite-based personal communicators that will allow one to 'phone home' from anywhere on the planet; machines capable of emotion, inference, and learning that will interact with human beings in entirely new ways; and bioremediation – custom designed organisms – that will help clear up the earth's environment. Existing industries – education, health care, transportation, banking, publishing, telecommunications, pharmaceuticals, retailing and others – will be profoundly transformed. Many of these mega-opportunities represent billions of dollars in potential future revenues. Each of these opportunities is also inherently global. No single nation or region is likely to control all the technologies and skills required to turn these opportunities into reality. Markets will emerge at different speeds around the world, and any firm hoping to establish a leadership role will have to collaborate with and learn from leading-edge customers, technology providers, and suppliers, wherever they're located. Global distribution reach will be necessary to capture the rewards of leadership and fully amortize associated investments. The future is now.

The international marketing plan

Strategic market planning is a process which logically we would expect to find taking place at all levels in the corporate organization. Unfortunately the evidence which exists shows that companies exercise planning more in the domestic sales organization than in the international. As an activity, planning should encompass all the factors which have been dealt with separately in this book so far, dealing with the marketing mix variables and the consideration of environments. If there is lack of appreciation and understanding of planning and consequent lack of control, it is because top management motivation is lacking in knowledge of what to do next. A positive approach is required of international marketing planning, planning to make things happen. As John Lennon observed, 'Life is what is happening when you are busy making plans.' Analysis and planning on their own are sterile activities.

International marketing cannot succeed without the active support and commitment of top management, yet market research, as applied to foreign markets, is secondary to subjective judgement and lacks the commitment of both the time and resources devoted to domestic market research. Consequently, international marketing planning is pursued at a much lower level and with much less commitment of resource than domestic marketing planning. With international marketing planning, the purpose, form and methodology employed differs according to company size, organization structure and length of involvement in international business activities. In its simplest form, international marketing planning as such may consist of no more than a sales budget or allocation handed to country managers by corporate management. Equally, it may also be complex, recognizing the higher-ordered interdependencies created by a global perspective of a truly multinational corporation. It has been argued, in fact, that co-ordinated plans and strategies are the hallmarks of the truly global company (Hulbert, 1980), indeed part of what we may call the organizational culture. (See Denison, 1996.)

Mike Wilson, in *The Management of Marketing*, identifies the following main elements of marketing plans.

- A statement of basic assumptions with regard to long- and short-term economic, technological, social and political developments.
- A review of past sales and profit performance of the company's major products by markets and geographic areas.
- An analysis of external opportunities and threats by markets and products.
- An analysis of the company's and competitors' strengths and weaknesses in facilities, products, finance, customer acceptance, distribution, personnel, pricing, advertising, sales promotion, etc. This analysis will often include assessments of indirect competition.
- A statement of long-term objectives (marketing, financial, growth, etc.), and the strategies for achieving them.

- A statement of the objectives and strategies for the next year with a detailed breakdown in units and revenue for each product, each market, each geographical area, and each unit of the company's marketing force.
- A programme schedule which is carefully co-ordinated with the budgets for the units involved and which shows the sequence of all marketing activities for each product in each market and geographic area so that public relations, advertising, product publicity, sales promotion, and field selling can be co-ordinated.
- Statements of objectives for each of the following years similar to the statements for the next year but less detailed.
- A summary of how the company intends to capitalize on its opportunities and correct its weaknesses; key priorities, etc.

Cain (1970) sees international marketing planning as having three levels:

1. *Operational planning level.* Shorter range (one-and three-year) planning is the responsibility of each overseas operating unit. The format in general follows that of US divisions and is supplied by the headquarters' planning staff. Plans include sales, profit and cash-flow projections by product line, market share, capital requirements, etc. Although plans are integrated at regional levels, individual unit plans are forwarded intact to New York headquarters.
2. *Strategic planning level.* Operating units – most of which are national in scope – are asked to plan ahead on a longer term basis for new products which might be developed from within or acquired. Headquarters deliberately provide only very general guidelines as to how far afield a local operation might explore. This is done to encourage the local managers to stretch their outlook. However, the scope normally is confined to the unit's country of operation, and plans are subject to review at headquarters.
3. *Corporate planning level.* Worldwide plans are developed at international headquarters, tied closely to overall corporate objectives and plans. This planning takes two forms:

    A. protective planning
    B. opportunity planning

Protective planning is strategic and long-range in character, anticipating worldwide changes in markets and business conditions relating to the present scope of operation. On the other hand, 'opportunity planning' is directed toward seeking new business directions for growth and diversification.

Overall, corporate expectations of planning are that it must:

- Minimize the negative consequences of a variety of adverse exogenous and endogenous conditions.
- Balance the available corporate resources against the set of global opportunities and alternatives.
- Co-ordinate and integrate the activities of a necessarily decentralized organization.
- Create a framework for a communication system which ensures that all parts of the organization are striving towards the same set of overall objectives and in doing so are using policies which are beneficial for the corporation as a whole rather than just individual parts of it.

Shruptine and Toyne (1981) argue that multinationals should concentrate on standardizing the process of planning rather than standardizing their marketing strategies. Planning is a decentralized activity not because of the geographic dispersion of the individual company units or because their individual legal status frequency provides them with a high degree of autonomy, but because differences in local operating conditions demand a local response.

Selectivity and distortion can, however, enter into the environment surveillance process via the data-gathering behaviour of the organization. Perceptual bias can enter the process at the stage of interpreting or evaluating the data, often performed by someone other than the data gatherer. Perceptual bias also occurs at the data transmission linkage between the data gatherers and the interpreters and between interpreters and users. A lingering doubt remains as to whether data gathers tend to

ignore data which is more qualitative than quantitative in nature, and so less easily verifiable.

The task facing a head office then is to ensure conformity within a set of overall objectives, performance criteria and company-wide policies to eliminate or at least minimize intra-company effects and inefficiencies. In many multinationals this situation has led to the institution of two distinctly separate long-range planning cycles which can be referred to as 'bottom-up' and 'top-down' planning. 'Top-down' planning may be a particularly appropriate approach when subsidiary managers around the world are not very familiar with the concepts and practices of long-range planning. 'Bottom-up' may be particularly relevant where local conditions are sufficiently different to necessitate a local plan. Here there is management recognition of the local subsidiary manager as an expert in the corporate planning cycle. In many cases, however, locational decisions seem to evolve from the culmination of a series of apparently unrelated events rather than a specific plan. There are three broad sets of factors to consider here.

1. Country-related variables that characterize the business conditions in a certain country or region in terms of the political, economic, legal, competitive and tax situation, the market potential, cost and availability of manpower, local capital, and required supplies.

2. Product-related characteristics such as a product's typical life cycle, the degree of technical sophistication, and economies of scale that are associated with its production, the relative importance of transportation costs, etc.

3. Company-related variables which take into account such characteristics as a firm's size and its experience in international operations and policies as an expression of the firm's management philosophy.

Table 9.1 International marketing planning matrix

	Marketing planning variables					
International decisions	Diagnosis of situation	SWOT analysis	Objectives	Sales vol. cost/profit forecasts	Marketing programme	Marketing budgets
A. Commitment decision						
B. Country selection						
C. Mode of entry						
D. Marketing strategy						
E. Marketing organization						

Source: Becker, H., and Thorelli, H. B. (1990) Strategic planning in international marketing. In *International Marketing Strategy*. 3rd edn, Hans B. Thorelli, S. Tamer Cavusgil (Ed.) Pergamon, Oxford

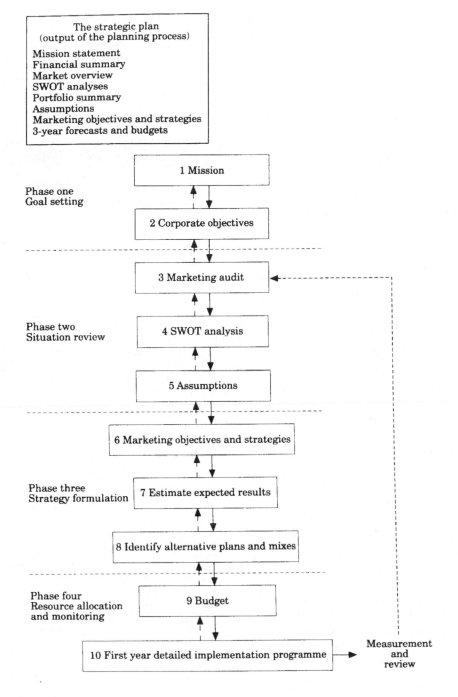

The strategic plan
(output of the planning process)

Mission statement
Financial summary
Market overview
SWOT analyses
Portfolio summary
Assumptions
Marketing objectives and strategies
3-year forecasts and budgets

Phase one
Goal setting

1 Mission

2 Corporate objectives

3 Marketing audit

Phase two
Situation review

4 SWOT analysis

5 Assumptions

6 Marketing objectives and strategies

Phase three
Strategy formulation

7 Estimate expected results

8 Identify alternative plans and mixes

Phase four
Resource allocation
and monitoring

9 Budget

10 First year detailed implementation programme

Measurement
and
review

Source: McDonald (1995)

Figure 9.1   The marketing planning process

Managerial decision making will result in specific marketing programmes on a global basis, with differentiated marketing programmes. This differentiation is in respect of both budget allocations and specific emphasis on marketing mix elements. The annual operating plan is the basis of planning in virtually all multinational subsidiaries. For most it is the starting point for longer term planning, typically for a five-year period. In the majority of cases, long-term planning is an exercise in extrapolation and very few companies practise strategic market planning.

Marketing programmes should be based on the concept of global segmentation. Unlike differentiating markets on a purely demographic or geographic basis, a segmentation study of urban dwellers across different countries may reveal greater similarities than a similar study conducted across the same country. The most viable and profitable segmentation basis is the examination of underlying factors which determine buyer demand. These factors can be broadly classified as *buyer expectations* and *buying climate*. The first is based on culture, social stratification, and family structure. The second refers to the specific situation in which consumers make decisions to buy and consume goods and services. It includes the economic, demographic, and physical settings in which buyers go about choosing and consuming products and services. It is based on

- financial factors (disposable personal income, asset holdings, etc.),
- geographical factors (temperature, humidity and altitude, tropical v temperate climate, etc.), and
- demographic factors (size of family, age distributions of family members, life cycle of family, etc.)

Exhibit 9.1   Portrait of the world

Four major types of consumers dominate the world, and their purchase decisions are heavily influenced by the wealth of their nations, according to a survey by Roper Starch Worldwide Inc., Mamaroneck, N.Y.

'As the world becomes closer due to technological advances in transportation and telecommunications, and with multinational companies expanding worldwide, increasingly there is great interest in whether individuals in different parts of the world are more alike than different,' said Thomas A. W. Miller, senior vice president of Roper Starch Worldwide.

The company conducted a series of studies on global consumer trends throughout March and April. Survey results are projectible to 1.97 billion adults worldwide, the company said.

The firm defined four major shopping styles of consumers. Whether driven by price, quality, or brand, consumers are heavily influenced by whether their homeland is a developed or developing nation.

1. 'Deal makers': 29 per cent of 37,743 repondents from 40 countries concentrate on the process of buying. This is a well-educated group, median age 32, with average affluence and employment.
2. 'Price seekers': 27 per cent place primary value on the product. This group has the highest proportion of retirees, the lowest education level, skews female, and has an average level of affluence.
3. 'Brand loyalists': 23 per cent of the respondents, and the least affluent. The group is mostly male, median age 36, who hold average education and employment.
4. 'Luxury innovators': 21 per cent seek new, prestigious brands and are the most educated and affluent shoppers, with the highest proportion of executives and other professionals. The group is mostly male with a median age of 32.

In the U.S., 37 per cent are deal makers, 36 per cent price seekers, 17 per cent luxury innovators, and 11 per cent brand loyalists. Deal makers

also predominate in Asia, Latin America, and the Middle East. Price seekers predominate in Europe and Japan.

'Price seekers exist mainly in competitive, developed markets like Europe and Japan,' said Miller, 'where shoppers generally cannot haggle or negotiate. Deal makers are more often in developing markets that have less brand competition and a tradition of bazaars and open air markets, where the process of buying is half the fun. The U.S. straddles the two styles because of our more heterogeneous culture and also because shoppers can bargain at many retail outlets and even large category-killer stores.'

Sixty-seven per cent of the respondents 'strongly agreed' that 'the most important thing about a brand is that it gives good value for the money,' and 66 per cent said, 'I feel really satisfied with myself, even excited, when I get a really good deal.' Thirty-nine per cent said, 'I spend a lot of time researching brands before making a major purchase,' and 'once I find a brand that satisfies me, I usually don't experiment with new ones,' said 43 per cent.

Another report in the series found that 61 per cent of consumers worldwide credited businesses with very or fairly often being creative and entertaining with advertising. Other positive effects of marketing drew less response. Sponsoring worthwhile events was recognized by 45 per cent, giving accurate information in advertising was acknowledged by 38 per cent, and respecting consumer's intelligence registered with 30 per cent.

Worldwide, majorities contended that businesses often exaggerate products' health benefits, persuade children to buy things they don't need, and exaggerate product sizes with excessive packaging.

North Americans were the biggest fans as well as the biggest critics of advertisers. Residents of Russia and the Ukraine were exceptionally negative. Twenty-three per cent of the latter said advertising is creative and entertaining, 10 per cent said it respects consumers' intelligence, and 9 per cent said it provides good information and that businesses often sponsor worthwhile events.

→

➤ Exhibit 9.1 *continued*

'Russians have not been exposed to advertising until recently,' Miller said. 'Russian advertising at this stage does not appear to be particularly creative. In addition, much of the old "advertising" was state-sponsored propaganda, leading the public to become cynical and disbelieve advertising. This is a challenging marketing climate for advertisers, but there is good reason to think that Russians may be particularly receptive to new, creative styles of marketing and advertising.'

Western Europeans were the strongest believers that businesses often persuade children to buy unnecessary items and exaggerate health benefits. Asian consumers, though, were least critical about children being conned into purchases. Miller said overall positive feelings about advertising in Asia are due to strong economic growth in the area.

Another study in the series indicated that the U.S. is considered a global leader of pop culture, with the best jeans, movies, TV shows, and cigarettes in the world. Japan ranked highest for technological goods and moderately priced cars. Germany had the best reputation for luxury cars and beer. Respondents who said they felt 'very' or 'rather positive' toward the U.S. totaled 67 per cent; toward Japan, 69 per cent; and toward Germany, 68 per cent.

Only 59 per cent of Asians liked Americans, fewer than citizens of other countries, and only 53 per cent of North Americans felt positive toward Japan, the lowest response for that country. But 63 per cent of North Americans held Germany in high regard, perhaps because they feel less resentment about foreign trade with Germany.

'With an economy increasingly global in scope, competition between the economic superpowers, most notably America, Japan, and Germany, is keen,' said Miller. 'Yet this survey indicates that in the eyes of consumers worldwide, for a variety of goods, only a handful of countries can be counted as the best producers.'

North Americans, however, had a considerably higher opinion of American products than did the rest of the world. Half or more of North Americans surveyed said that the U.S. makes the best of six of the 12 items asked about, including luxury cars, moderately priced cars, home electronics, cameras, perfumes, and chocolates.

Good news for the toothpaste industry: 95 per cent of those surveyed brush their teeth daily. Other activities that majorities worldwide engage in include reading a newspaper, listening to the radio, taking a shower, and washing their hair. The daily lives of North Americans and ex-Soviets differed the most.

Residents of Russia and the Ukraine were least likely to engage in a majority of the activities asked about, such as using a computer at home or at work, reading a magazine, eating at a restaurant, or making an international phone call. Of the 29 activities, they shunned 21.

In another portion of the research, 15 social problems were presented. Forty-nine per cent of the respondents said crime and lawlessness were their top concerns. Thirty-seven per cent said inflation and high prices, and 36 per cent said recession and unemployment occupied their thoughts most. Relatively few people were worried about terrorism (7 per cent), relations between racial and ethnic groups (6 per cent), religious extremism/fundamentalism (5 per cent), immigration (5 per cent), relations with foreign countries (3 per cent), or aid to poor countries in the Third World (3 per cent).

Seventy-four per cent of Russians and Ukrainians were worried about crime and lawlessness, the highest percentage worldwide. They also were most troubled about inflation and high prices (60 per cent), and 'having enough money to live right and pay bills' (45 per cent). Fewer Russians than other people worldwide worry about drug abuse (4 per cent), educational quality (4 per cent), or AIDS (3 per cent). Latin and North Americans are most worried about AIDS, 34 per cent and 33 per cent of the respondents, respectively.

Western Europeans (51 per cent) are most concerned about recession and unemployment. The recession in West Germany resulting from the integration of East Germany, as well as recessionary climates in other countries, may help explain widespread concerns. Corporate restructuring due to European integration and greater availability of cheap labor from Eastern Europe has made residents of Western Europe fear for their jobs. Western Europeans (18 per cent) are less concerned about inflation and high prices than people anywhere else in the world.

In a survey cosponsored by The Discovery Channel, Roper Starch Worldwide found that people around the globe watched an average of 2.7 hours of TV each day, with an average of a dozen channels at their disposal. Movies, news programs, and comedies are the kinds of shows that most people wanted to see more of on TV. Soap operas, children's programs, and religious programs were of least interest.

Far fewer North Americans than the global average were interested in seeing more of every type of show asked about, likely due to the abundance of selections they have already. In North

➡

→ Exhibit 9.1 *continued*

America, people get the largest selection of programs by far, with 27 channels. Russians and Ukrainians have the smallest selections, just four.

Residents of the Middle East are more interested than anyone else in the world about almost every type of program. They receive an average of 11 channels, but they watch much more TV. Sixty-nine per cent of Middle Easterners want more reli-

gious programs, 56 per cent want more police shows, 47 per cent want more children's shows, 45 per cent want more cartoons, and 43 per cent want more music videos. The group is least likely to be interested in full-length movies, the No. 1 choice among other people throughout the world.

Source: Marketing News, 28 August 1995, p. 20

In addition to difficulties often encountered in gathering information within the host country, there can sometimes be delays in the communication of information within the multinational. If there is difficulty in communicating relevant information from one subsidiary to another, or from a domestic product division to an overseas subsidiary, the planning activity within that subsidiary can be severely disrupted. It is not unusual for a subsidiary to be given a new product to introduce without adequate information on how that same product may have fared on launch elsewhere. It is even more common to find careless requests for information which emerge from head offices. Educating home-office personnel to the realities of subsidiary life may help, but companies must also pay more attention to the planning of intra-company communication flows. Procedures often need streamlining and more careful information management should result in a communication flow better co-ordinated to subsidiary needs. Similarly, there may be excessive emphasis by head office on short-term sales and product results. In either situation, strategic planning is

neglected to the longer term detriment of the company involved.

Again, culture has a role to play here. The work by Williamson (1975) is particularly interesting for we adopt value orientations which we have learned. The degree to which people align themselves on the following six paired variables helps identify these values:

1. Egalitarian or elitist.
2. Laying emphasis on accomplishment or inherited attributes.
3. Expecting material or non-material rewards.
4. Evaluating individuals or product in terms of objective norms or subjective standards.
5. Focusing on the distinctiveness of the parts (intensiveness) rather than the general characteristics of the whole (extensiveness).
6. Oriented towards personal or group gain.

A problem-solving orientation appears most commonly in a culture that has strong egalitarian, material, and individual value orientations. Individuals compete for, and win, status and material rewards on the basis of performance. Rewards for performance may

---

Table 9.2 Information used for marketing planning by nationality of subsidiary

Source of information	Proportion of firms using			
	American	European	Japanese	All firms
Distributors	43%	38%	33%	40%
Sales force	75%	71%	83%	74%
Management of other subsidiaries	39%	54%	50%	47%
Marketing research dept.	57%	71%	0%	57%
Historical data	75%	79%	33%	72%
Trade sources	29%	29%	50%	31%
Commercial suppliers	36%	8%	33%	24%
Official sources	39%	58%	50%	48%
Home Office	14%	38%	17%	24%
Number of firms	(28)	(24)	(6)	(58)

Source: Hulbert, J. W., Brandt, W. K. and Richers, R. (1980) Marketing planning in the multinational subsidiary: practices and problems. *Journal of Marketing*, **44**, 10

take the form of increased status, wealth or both. In North America, positional rewards limited to title rather than increased salary are viewed as almost no rewards at all, whereas in Britain they are still respected. Promotional information which supports products in culturally differentiated markets must also be individualized. Cultural values will strongly influence meaningful associations. They will control the types of product claims people are predisposed to entertain or consider plausible; they will influence the basis on which claims may be rendered verifiable but to admit the relevance of cultural values is not enough; management must assess the significance of cultural attitudes and not just take into account 'comparative curiosities like polygamy and cannibalism, or merely study such consumer habits as the frequency with which people change their clothes'. Table 9.2 examines the differences in information used for marketing planning by nationality of subsidiary while Table 9.3 examines the relative importance of data sources for five environmental domains.

As to the conditions under which planning has failed, a study by Ringbakk (1976) into corporate planning failures of 300 companies in Europe and America revealed ten reasons:

- Planning is not integrated into the total management system.
- Only some levels of management are involved in the process.
- Responsibility for planning is vested solely in planning staff.
- Management expects plans to be realized exactly as planned.
- Too much detail is attempted.
- Management fails to implement the plan.
- Extrapolation and financial projections are confused with planning.
- Inadequate information inputs.
- Too much emphasis is placed on only one aspect of planning.

- The different dimensions of planning are not understood.

However, it must be remembered that this is related to corporate strategic planning rather than international marketing planning which is inherently more difficult again because of the extra variables to be considered.

Turning specifically to international marketing planning, the four most prevalent problems adjudged by Cain (1970) for planning in the international arena may be said to relate to:

1. *Failure to 'take off'.* This may be due to distance, language, management climate, diversity and other factors unique to individual companies.
2. *Lack of acceptance by management.* It has been difficult for US companies to get overseas managers – whether nationals or Americans – to accept or use planning. This is often experienced when plans have originated solely at home base and do not reflect the 'real world' of the manager. As with planning anywhere, 'textbook' plans are doomed to failure.
3. *Quality of planning.* In many companies, foreign operating units have not yet attained the same quality of planning as their domestic counterparts. One reason for this is that planning data are neither as accurate nor as reliable as companies would wish.
4. *Lack of co-operation* among international units.

One of the accepted objectives of planning on an international scale is to realize synergistic benefits among various independent operations. While international planners must, and do, think synergistically, management abroad is inclined to think parochially.

With regard to the current practice of international marketing planning in the multinational corporation, Sheth (1977) argued the following.

Table 9.3 Relative importance of data sources for the five environmental domains (combined US and European samples)

Domains	Outside services	Outside experts	Home Office staff	Home Office top management	Business unit top management
Social	1.84	1.11	2.41	2.80	2.27
Political	1.80	1.32	2.31	2.82	1.96
Ecological	1.77	1.51	2.49	2.06	2.27
Economic	1.67	1.65	2.86	2.60	2.07
Technological	1.47	1.58	2.79	2.30	2.46

Source: O'Connell, J. J., and Zimmerman, J. W. (1979) Scanning the international environment. *California Management Review,* **22** (2), 19

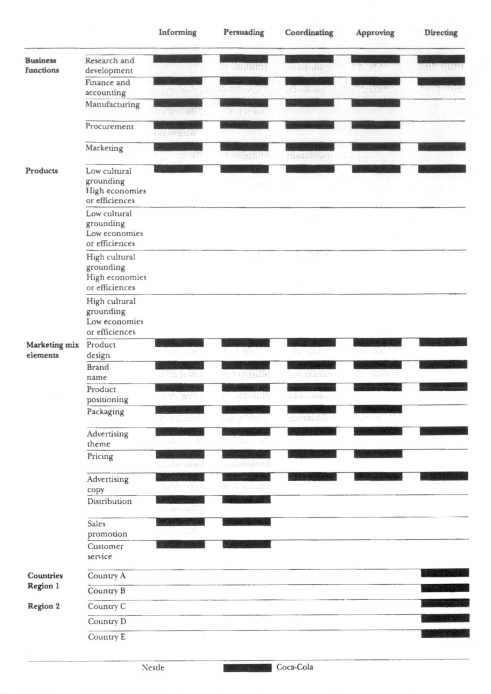

Source: Quelch, J. A., and Hoff, E. J. (1986) Customising global marketing. *Harvard Business Review*, May – June, 59 – 68

Figure 9.2   Global marketing planning matrix: how to get there

1.   There is no systematic and continuous assessment of buyer needs and expectations in the current practice of most corporations. Most of the marketing research is after-the-event: to find out whether a new concept or product developed by R & D will be acceptable to the customers. A continuous research effort to systematically monitor the current and changing needs of the market place is required.

2.   Present practice is to perform marketing research on a country-to-country basis. In addition, most multinational business decisions are centred around the question of whether the company should extend its strategic programmes to new countries or adjust it to suit local conditions. While such a practice was probably quite appropriate in previous times, and may continue to be useful even today for exporting or trading companies, it is myopic in the long run. It is not difficult to trace a number of failures in multinational activities directly to this practice. A systematic and continuous worldwide

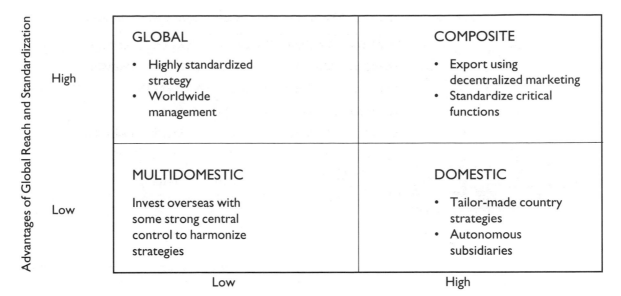

Figure 9.3   Strategies for globalizing markets

assessment of buyer needs and expectations is likely to point out that:

- potential markets are mostly in the metropolitan areas especially in the less developed countries,
- clustering metropolitan areas both within and between countries is more meaningful from a marketing viewpoint, and
- we shall probably find greater similarity between metropolitan areas across countries than within countries.

3   The assessment of customer needs and expectations should be based on data collected at the micro level, namely the household or business unit.

The focus on customer needs is a more enduring concept and tends to avoid the myopic tendency which a company is likely to fall into as its products become mature in their life cycle.

The limits of standardization

Quelch and Hoff (1986) consider four functions with regard to the appropriate degree of standardization or adaption:

- *Business functions* from marketing and finance to research and development.
- *Products.* Variables such as economies of scale and whether the product may be in any way regarded as culture-bound are important here.
- *Marketing mix elements.* Few companies use the same marketing programme worldwide.

- *Countries.* Small markets may more willingly accept a standard programme than large markets with strong management teams.

It is not to be seen as an either/or proposition but as an approach that may fall somewhere between the two ends of a wide spectrum. As Quelch and Hoff point out: 'The big issue today is not whether to go global but how to tailor the global marketing concept to fit each business.'

Taking the example of Coca-Cola and of Nestle, Quelch and Hoff identify five points at which headquarters can intervene with regard to three major problems: inconsistent brand identities; limited product focus; and slow new product launches. Persuasion can take the form of specialist headquarters staff visiting the subsidiaries 'not as critics but as coaches' so building trust while disseminating information about new methods and techniques. A matrix organization will mean headquarters shares responsibility and authority for programming. Co-ordination can take place with local subsidiaries working to headquarters approval or on their own working with certain agreed guidelines. While it is relatively easy to delegate authority it is not possible to direct motivation. This stimulus and encouragement is very necessary but difficult to build into an organizational plan, other than in ensuring that local subsidiaries have a degree of autonomy in their decision making and a mix of global and local brands.

In this respect Ohmae (1990) usefully points to the difference existing between Japanese and other Western multinational companies. The Japanese multinational is much more of a 'listening post' in that foreign market. The Japanese organizational structure is designed to transfer resources to critical areas. Ohmae (1990) also points to the function division of labour among headquarters, regional headquarters and country management emphasizing how many important functions can be effectively delegated to regional headquarters within the Triad, as in Figure 9.4.

Market concentration or market spreading?

A landmark study was *Concentration on Key Markets*, undertaken by the British Export Trade Research Organization (BETRO) and published by the British Overseas Trade Board (BOTB) in 1975. The basic objective of this study was to establish among exporting companies the markets in which they were successful out of all the export markets in which they were represented. Reviewing the allocation of company resources to these export markets, the overall recommendation was made that companies should concentrate on those markets which accounted for the bulk of their current export sales.

The BETRO study claimed a representative sample of 25 per cent of all British exporters, broken down into the following groups.

- One-third selling to less than 30 countries: exporting some 75–80 per cent of their output in the range then £10 million or more (1975 values) yet with a surprisingly small salesforce of some two to four men.
- A further one-third sold to between 30 and 60 countries, but here the large number of countries included some seen as an insurance policy in case existing markets elsewhere turned sour.
- The final one-third were selling to between 60 and 180 countries but were suffering from the diffusion of total effort expended over so many markets which proved a poor utilization of resources for the company concerned.

The issues which the BETRO report addressed specifically were the following:

1. *Market spreading*: Is it right to dissipate the efforts of a small selling organization over 154 countries with relatively modest returns?
2. *Market concentration*: Would it be wise to have a fresh look at the ten countries taking 90 per cent of company exports and ask 'Which are the four or five where we stand the best chance of increasing substantially our market share?' and when the answer is found, to deploy there all the marketing and technical talent that the company can muster?

Behind this was the principle of 'reinforcing success', and fighting against overextending the company resources. Nevertheless, the resources in finance and manpower required to develop a prosperous export business are surprisingly modest; they are well within the reach of the small company employing no more than 100 people. Advantages of market concentration building upon this principle of 'reinforcing success' included:

- A span of control especially when conditions become tough.
- Greater market knowledge in total and to a wider spread of people within the organization.
- Ability to identify the best markets and concentrate on them solely.
- The belief shared by 80 per cent of respondents that exports will grow faster than domestic sales in the next four to five years.

Inexperience in exporting was no more a barrier to success than was size. As the BETRO report stated: as far as newcomers to exporting are concerned, it can be stated with a fair measure of certainty that they can achieve just as good or even better results by never selling to more than ten countries as other companies who sell to 160.

There were in fact particular advantages of the small operation:

1. It needs a smaller organization with fewer staff and lower overheads.
2. It can acquire more detailed knowledge and a better understanding of agents' and distributors' capabilities. The small company has a chance to get to know them personally through close contact and so it has better knowledge of their needs and market requirements. This is primary information quite different from secondary, published sources of information. Here there was the ability to know what competitors were doing and how to adapt to market conditions.
3. Products may be sold less on price than on other factors such as:
   - reliability of delivery
   - after-sales service including technical support and spare parts
   - credit and discount terms
   - brand loyalty among customers
   - manufacturer's image within the trade and among customers

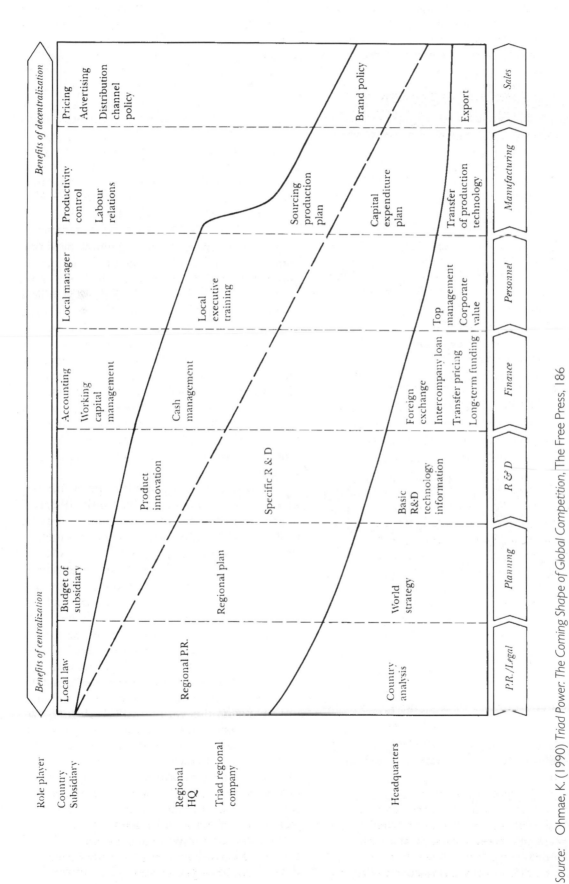

Source: Ohmae, K. (1990) *Triad Power: The Coming Shape of Global Competition*, The Free Press, 186

Figure 9.4 The centralization – decentralization spectrum

- ability to establish whether competition is primarily on price, quality, design, etc.

4. No potential distractions at least from various sources, as is the case with large organizations. The organization is structured instead for maximum effectiveness.

5. Concentration will lead to a rise in sales if a decision to concentrate is made during a period of boom and long delivery dates, and a company can gain a lot of goodwill by giving better delivery to its most important key markets. In periods of declining sales a 'concentrating' company will be in a better position to secure orders than those trading in a haphazard manner (even in a depression, when many companies lose market shares, some do gain a bigger share. This is more likely to be the company that knows its market and can seize the opportunity rather than others whose contacts are more superficial).

The recommendation for all companies irrespective of size is to:

- Concentrate scarce resources of talent, effort, and cash on a few markets.
- Invest manpower in export markets on a par with home markets.
- Maintain frequent personal contact with overseas customers.
- Invest in areas geared towards export growth.
- Undertake, as continuing company policy, comparative cost studies of home and export activities.

While this theory attracted interest and was meticulously followed by many, it has in fact proved disastrous for some, particularly those smaller more vulnerable exporting companies who now concentrated their effort on key markets. In many of these markets, the ability to consume was less in doubt than the ability to pay and so many companies have been brought to bankruptcy. Concentration proved to be little other than putting all your eggs in one basket. When disaster struck, everything was lost. The issue of market spreading or market concentration will not go away and is still being debated, see Fenwick and Amine (1979), Cooper and Kleinschmidt (1985), Lee and Young (1990) and Katsikeas and Leonidou (1996).

Planning and Third World markets

Third World markets are notably dissimilar. Basically, these fall into the following categories:

1. High-volume, low-value raw material exporters but with infrastructural base.

2. High-volume, low-value raw material exporters with little infrastructural base.

3. Low-volume, low-value traditional exporters but with infrastructural base.

4. Least developed nations.

It is not possible to segment on the basis of being single commodity exporters as this would apply to many in the first three categories. There are therefore those in category 2 above, such as Saudi Arabia, with little infrastructure but with new-found wealth and so able to make a quantum leap by buying in expertise from abroad to provide education and technical services wherever necessary.

Political risk is one of the most obvious dangers to international business. 'Political risk is the likelihood that political forces will cause drastic changes in a country's business environment that affect the profit and other goals of a particular business enterprise'. Risk of this kind may apply to an industry as a whole or to one company in particular. The most frequently encountered risk arises from political forces hostile towards foreign enterprise for philosophical reasons that diverge sharply from prevailing government policies. Other risks are social unrest and disorder; the private vested interests of local business groups; recent or impending independence; new international alliances; and armed conflicts or terrorism. Less predictable, and political only in the sense that it is a tool of politicians, is the exposure of corruption or scandal. This is often linked to a government official who might well have provided influence for a foreign firm.

Market access is another problem and investment has taken place by multinationals is in the past in order to produce goods within the protection of tariff walls. Market access may be restricted by the local government. Alternatively, for those choosing to enter there may be the attendant benefits of supplying a captive market, further protected from the entry of foreign competition. This has enticed some multinationals in the automobile industry for example to make investments which otherwise would not have appeared quite so attractive.

Market access implies not only entering the country and meeting the standard tariff and duty barriers, the various so-called 'invisible' tariff barriers relating perhaps to areas as diverse as health and safety but providing also for distribution to the final consumer. There may in fact be more similarity between city dwellers across nations than between nationals themselves. Marketing must identify this where it exists and make full use of this advantage.

Capital is not always the missing factor and this is why we began with a classification of developing countries. For oil-rich countries with new-found wealth the new problem is one of learning how to manage wealth after years of planning for poverty. Income from the oil industry may be seen too, as in the Boston Consultancy Group (BCG) product portfolio matrix, in terms of a 'cash cow' to be used and milked for cash to produce new 'stars' high in relative market share in high-growth markets. To diversify, technology and management are both required, and marketing is subsumed within these, as partly a social act, partly a technical science. To cite Drucker (1980):

Marketing is generally the most neglected area in the economic life of developing countries. It is manufacturing or construction which occupies the greatest attention in these countries. Its effectiveness as an engine of economic development with special emphasis on its ability to develop rapidly much-needed entrepreneurial and management skills needs hardly any elaboration. Because it provides a systematic discipline in a vital area of economic activity it fills one of the greatest needs of a developing economy . . . Marketing occupies a critical role in respect to underdeveloped 'growth' countries. Indeed, marketing is the most important 'multiplier' of such development. It is in itself in every one of these areas the least developed, the most backward part of the economic system. It is development above all others, that makes possible economic integration and the fullest utilisation of whatever assets and productive capacity an economy already possesses. It mobilises latent economic energy. It contributes to the greatest needs: that for the rapid development of entrepreneurs and managers, and at the same time it may be the easiest area of managerial work to get going . . . it is the most systematised, and therefore the most learnable and the most teachable of all areas of business management and entrepreneurship.

Marketing therefore has a special niche in the area of technology transfer from North to South or East to West and this becomes noticeable with the number of contractual arrangements including management contracts, which allow for manufacture under licence in a given country but for the licensor himself to buy back a given quantity of output. In this way, the host country is able to deal with shortcomings in marketing knowledge and lack of contact with, and general experience of, free world markets.

Capital has diverse roles to play. Establishing within the host nation perhaps as a joint venture with a local partner may enable the joint venture to take advantage of its new local identity to compete for local contracts and for local finance. Multinational subsidiaries worldwide export under the terms and assurances of national export credit guarantees departments – ECGD in the UK, Coface in France, Hermes in Germany, Eximbank in the USA, although the regulations vary as to whether these subsidiaries

can then compete for local export finance and the degree also to which they can also source from outside the country on a contract awarded government-backed export finance. The host government seeks greater self-reliance through import substitution; industrialization including not just production but a research and development facility as well; and a burgeoning export-intensive activity which will employ and train its national workforce and help its national balance of payments. Control arises via taxes, exchange control, and export/import licences. The very size and nature of projects being mooted by national governments as national priority projects make it possible only for global companies to enter the competition with tenders.

All of the world's 100 largest multinational corporations, ranked by size of their assets abroad, compared with those at home, were based in rich countries. This was one of the findings to emerge from the World Investment Report 1996, published by UNCTAD. For the global company, the criteria include profitability, long-term economic and political stability; necessary market size; reassurance of fulfilment of contracts; available skilled workforce which is non-unionized; a co-operative governmental attitude; and the ability to repatriate earnings back to the home country in the form of profits; management fees; royalties on production of sales under licence; loans, and leasing of plant and equipment. Difficulties arise here because the subsidiary is after all only one part of the global corporation and may be subject to head office rulings which do not take into account its best interest or continued viability in the foreign market. This may also engender conflict.

The pressure remains on the foreign subsidiary as to whom it recognizes as its master. It is partly for this reason that the issue of staffing is also important. Many multinationals which are deemed to be ethnocentric in their orientation because of a strong home-country orientation evidenced by the nationality of their foreign top management may in fact only be acting in their best interests as they perceive it. Alternatively, those with a polycentric orientation who have appointed local nationals as managers may therefore be seen to be storing up trouble for themselves, putting local nationals in the position of serving either foreign head office or national government interests. In practice, the situation is not quite so anxiety-ridden as may be depicted but presents one aspect of the dilemma involved in staffing foreign subsidiaries.

Some countries allow the MNEs to make the bidding for investments. Others have reserved for themselves the right to develop by themselves certain economic sectors. This is true of Mexico, Brazil, India, Venezuela, Nigeria and Indonesia but it is also true that these countries have a relatively high average income compared to the least developed nations.

Competition in developing countries is usually minimal and so the greater risk of competition arises from the potential threat of entry by a Western competitor. This is one way in which a local host government may maintain leverage on a multinational subsidiary. Where an investment is large, though, there may well be governmental undertaking to exclude further outside competition and grant certain exclusivity of supply to governmental departments, etc.

The situation which is most often depicted is one where the multinational subsidiary is faced with certain demands by the host government. Increasingly, though, because of the extraterritorial reach of UK legislation and US

administration, a multinational subsidiary may find itself subjected, as we have found earlier, to demands by the host government and by the home government as well. Figure 9.5 summarizes the situation – the home government may exercise some control over the issue of lines of credit; subsidies; grants; tax rebates and tax 'holidays'; export/import licences; pending and proposed company, employee, and union legislation; and finally, levels of taxation itself.

The US Government is still the home of most of the world's global companies and as such its power and ability to influence cannot be ignored. Although technically 'ultra vires' (acting outside of its legal jurisdiction) the USA has consistently sought to maintain controls and standards over US subsidiaries abroad to a similar degree as back home in the USA. This extraterritorial reach of US legislation has then to be taken into consideration.

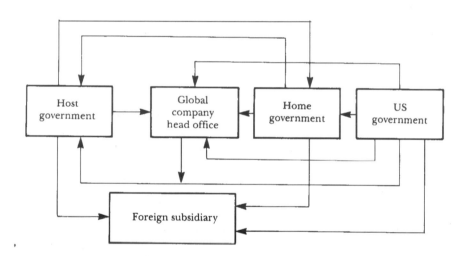

Figure 9.5   Direct pressures on a foreign subsidiary

Exhibit 9.2   Fighting for foreign friends

Last month's announcement that the Korean electronics LG group was to make the largest-ever inward investment in Europe by building a massive new factory in Newport led to a major political row.

While no one disputed that the 6,100 new jobs were seriously good news for South Wales, other areas of Britain shouted 'foul', claiming that the Welsh Development Agency had handed out too much public money to the private business.

It was, perhaps, a case of understandable jealousy. But other areas have also had their shares of success in attracting new jobs. The Government's achievement in obtaining inward invest-

ment may be one of its most enduring, and endearing, legacies.

Persuading businesses to invest in the UK requires a team effort, which is headed by the Invest in Britain Bureau, part of the Department of Trade and Industry. At a more local level, negotiation is conducted by a regional development organisation, such as the Welsh Development Agency.

Inward investment rests more on getting the practical details right than in handing over public money – though Ireland has made itself an attractive competitor by setting corporation tax for incomers at 10 per cent. One of the factors attracting LG was the provision of the right type of

➡

→ Exhibit 9.2 *continued*

land by Newport Council and the Welsh Development Agency. Specialist training is to be provided by local universities and by Gwent Training and Enterprise Council.

A similar situation is described by Siemens UK, part of the German electronics group, which is building a £1.1bn semiconductor plant on Tyneside. Although it is receiving a government grant of £30m, this is small beer in the total package and much less significant than the local infrastructure.

One of the most important factors for Siemens was that the clay subsoil will act as a damper to provide a vibration-free site. The utility provision was also vital, particularly the plentiful supply of clean water, a good electricity supply and cheap and excellent modern telecommunications facilities. The corporation needs to conduct regular video-conferences, and the ISDN standard cable connections provided by Tele West were important.

Good road, air and rail infrastructure made Tyneside an accessible site. Britain's high-quality utilities and good transport infrastructure are repeatedly quoted as key factors in attracting inward investment against East European competition.

North Tyneside Council laid on staff who could act as guides to key Siemens personnel, showing them around the area and advising them about schools and homes. It established a 21-day fast-track planning process to ensure the factory was given speedy approval, and established an effective liaison system between planners and building control officers and Siemens.

The TEC and local universities are providing training and retraining courses. The plentiful local labour – which is flexible and used to working night shifts without expecting high pay – was also important.

John Raine, chief executive of Derbyshire County Council, says that providing a warm welcome to a potential investor such as Toyota, which now has a factory in Derby, is essential. 'We hope they felt swayed by the good reception from the local authority and the local community,' he says.

The council undertook a comprehensive geological survey to assure Toyota that the site was appropriate for its use.

Although the help that Derbyshire gave Toyota to attract the new factory was criticised in 1989 – it led to a ruling by the European Commission that £4m had to be repaid to the council because it undercharged for service roads – the result has been more than 2,000 new, long-term jobs in the area and the establishment of a highly respected local employer.

Other regions have had similar successes, but a study produced earlier this year by Ernst & Young found that, in general, local authorities need to target their attempts to capture inward investment more carefully. Too many are wasting money on ineffectual advertising when they should be building contacts and visiting key people.

David Rees, partner for relocation and advisory services at Ernst & Young, explains: 'Some local authorities have been very successful in raising their profile . . . but to do so they have had to spend significant amounts of money.

'With 70 per cent of local authorities surveyed spending less than £50,000 on promotion, the extent to which they can compete is limited.'

Once a major corporation locates in the UK, a virtuous circle can be created. LG's Newport plant is expected to generate a further 9,000 jobs in dependent suppliers. Siemens decided to locate in the UK partly because it was becoming the company's third largest market – not least because of other multinationals with British factories.

And a recent study by the PACEC consultancy found that the superior management practices adopted by the big corporations, particularly those of the Far East, were having a beneficial knock-on effect on British industry. British firms improve their management skills when they come into contact with the world's industrial giants.

Source: The Independent, Section Two, 7 August 1996

Responses to irregular payments (did someone say bribery or corruption?)

It was IBM who coined the phrase 'corporate citizenship' when they stated that their aim was to be a good citizen in each country in which they were represented. Few organizations are of the global size of a corporation such as IBM, nor have the immediate visibility of such a large corporation and hence the need to produce a state-ment on corporate ethics. Many multinationals do, however, produce a leaflet on their corporate policy and business ethics.

Ethics do enter into the question of international business. Again, the extraterritoriality of US legislation, such as the Foreign Corrupt Practices Act of 1977, is making the issue more problematic. The Act prohibits companies from engaging in 'questionable payments', with penalties ranging from a million dollars for each corporate offence to $10,000 per offender and up to five years in prison. This Act affects not only US companies but also multinational corporations with representation in the USA. Therefore it is open to the USA to pursue a British or German multinational for what may be interpreted as irregular payments or inducements to trade in perhaps let us say an African country through its US representative base. The Act requires companies with securities registered under the Securities and Exchange Act of 1934 to keep books, records and accounts that in reasonable detail accurately and fairly reflect the disposition of their assets. Yet the Act does allow for certain 'grease' payments. In practice, few actions have been brought since the Act was passed and these have been resolved through negotiated settlements. There has been little opportunity therefore to test this Act in the courts.

The practice of business is not uniform the world over, and although shareholders or members of the public in an industrialized Western country may be shocked to hear that one of their largest companies has been active in what they interpret as being bribery and corruption, these terms of trading will almost certainly not have the same emotive appeal in the host country concerned. Payments for example made as 'dash', a

fairly innocuous but generally almost standard payment in Nigeria, to ensure that the bureaucracy will deal with an application, are legitimate under the US Foreign Corrupt Practices Act which therefore does not recognize this as bribery but as 'grease'. The African term is 'dash', the US term 'grease', but it is not bribery or corruption. It ensures that papers on a crowded desk will be moved from the bottom of the pile to the top of the pile for action. In bureaucratically infested countries this may be a common means of expediting business. Other non-payment forms of persuasion include nepotism which exists to varying degrees throughout the world.

There is no country in the world which openly welcomes bribery and corruption. It is seen as a social sin. Certain countries such as the CIS have heavy penalties for anyone found guilty under such a charge.

The crucial variables to consider here are the gifts, the timing of the exchange process and the relationship created. Cultural barriers are difficult to surmount and all actions have to be viewed; actions and the degree to which corporate outcomes have been influenced by inducements of one kind or another; changing what may otherwise have been the natural

Table 9.4   Some of the common international terminology for small-scale irregular payments

Baksheesh	In Turkey, Egypt, India and other Eastern countries a gratuity or gift of alms.
Mordida	A Spanish word meaning 'little bite' found in Mexico.
Jeito	Found in Brazil, means a favour rather than a transfer of money.
Dash	Used in Africa; quite commonly encountered.
Grease	Also 'facilitating payments'. Refers to legal and permitted payments of modest sums to foreign officials for speedy action of their normal duties.
Kumshaw	South-East Asia term for bribe.

Source: Adapted from Axtell, R. E. (1990) *Do's and Taboos Around the World*, © Parker Pen Company 1990. John Wiley & Sons

Table 9.5 Why do irregular payments continue to exist?

Home country perspective	*Host country perspective*
1. Price of doing business in certain countries.	1. Easy money.
2. Established practice impossible to circumvent.	2. Political involvement in decision making.
3. Governmental pressure.	3. Token of appreciation.
4. Creation of favourable public relations.	4. Friendly gesture.
5. Increasing competition worldwide.	5. Commission.
6. Pressure to achieve results.	6. Pressure for vendors.
7. In final analysis, Swiss bank secrecy.	

Source: Jain, S. C. (1979) What happened to the marketing man when his international promotion payoffs became bribes? In *International Marketing: Managerial Perspectives*, (Jain, S. C., and Tucker, L. N., Jr.) CBI Publishing Company Inc., Boston, MA.

outcome of events. As Jain (1979) points out there are five different possible courses of action for dealing with questionable payments: regulatory; legislative; diplomatic; code of conduct; and corporate action. However, governmental attitudes to this question vary quite enormously. In the USA, aside from the Foreign Corrupt Practices Act, the SEC will seek detailed information on previously unreported legal, business and financial activities of a company which may be considered material information from an investor's point of view. The SEC does not however define which may constitute material information to an investor. Elsewhere, France, Germany, Japan, Britain and Italy do allow for 'special expenses' abroad which qualify them for tax deductions. The regulations, however, are not explicit. The tax deduction is made easier where the payments are made to foreign nationals abroad to gain export business as existing laws may prescribe such payments by home-based to individuals within the national frontiers of the home country. What may be seen to be double standards is lessened to a degree by the fact that these companies are complying with the laws of the countries in which they operate.

Table 9.6 Major types of bribes

1.	Facilitating payments	Often termed 'grease', these are small amounts of payment in cash or kind to expedite documentation or to continue with the metaphor 'lubricate the administrative machine'.
2.	Middleman commissions	Those are individuals appointed in an ad-hoc manner to formulate sales 'in a non-routine manner, and payment to them of excessive allowances and commissions which are not commensurate with the normal commercial services they perform'. Often part or all of the commission may be deposited in a bank in a third country.
3.	Political contributions	Contributions which take the form of extortion since they are in violation of local law and practice. Also payments which while not illegal are specifically made with the intent of winning favours directly or indirectly.
4.	Cash disbursements	Cash payments made to important people through slush funds or in a third country for a number of different reasons which will promote the company's advantage.

Source: Jain, S. C. (1979) What happened to the marketing man when his international promotion payoffs became bribes? In *International Marketing: Managerial Perspectives* (Jain, S. C., and Tucker, L. N., Jr.), CBI Publishing Company Inc., Boston MA.

Exhibit 9.3 British banks balks at bribes

London. Standard Chartered PLC, a London-based international bank, will withdraw from countries where unethical behavior, such as bribery, is a prerequisite for doing business, John McFarlane, a bank director, said yesterday.

McFarlane's remarks followed a disclosure that the bank is investigating allegations that executives from its bullion arm may have paid commissions to officials in the Philippines and Malaysia to obtain business.

He said he had no comment to make on a report that the bank was also investigating the disappearance of US$10,000 in gold coins, allegedly given by the division to a Malaysian minister as a 'trade sample.'

'We cannot allow any one business to risk the reputation of the bank. We have also made it clear [to managers] that we will not tolerate another control failure,' said McFarlane, whose bank operates in 57 countries.

Two senior executives were dismissed by Standard as a result of the bank's investigation into expense claims in its Mocatta bullion arm.

The bank has suffered from a series of mishaps in Asia including a scandal in the Bombay securities market, which required a provision of £269 million ($578 million) against possible losses in 1996, and involvement in share support schemes in Hong Kong.

British government officials said yesterday they were concerned the move by Standard Chartered would further damage already strained relations between Britain and Malaysia. Malaysia earlier this year banned all British companies from bidding for Malaysian government contracts after British officials complained of widespread bribery demands.

Source: The Financial Post, 20 July 1994

Exhibit 9.4   How to bribe an official with the law's blessing

The bribery of foreign public officials by European executives is likely to remain legal until at least the end of the century.

The Organisation for Economic Co-operation and Development (OECD) is trying to outlaw corrupt payments – which in many European countries qualify for tax privileges. Delegates to a working party meeting in Paris next week are optimistic that an agreement can be reached.

But any consensus between representatives of the 31 countries expected to attend the meeting will have to be sanctioned at ministerial level at a meeting in May. Then it will be a matter of committing any agreement to national legislation.

Mark Pieth, chairman of the OECD working party, who is professor of law at the University of Basel in Switzerland, said he was hopeful that the combating of bribery would have a worldwide effect by the end of 1999. Until then the payment of 'commissions' to win contracts in foreign countries remains beyond the bounds of national law in most EU countries.

In Germany, France, Spain, Italy and the Netherlands, for instance, such payments are tax-deductible although in most cases the recipient of the bribe has to be named.

The revenue department in France operates a quota system of claims for deductions on unidentified bribes.

The OECD is committed to outlawing the practice, which is widespread in the electricity, construction and infrastructure sectors, but has been divided over an appropriate method.

Japan and the US are understood to be among the countries favouring an OECD recommendation which would then require individual countries to issue their own legislation. Such a method was adopted by the OECD in 1990 to counter money-laundering.

However, Carel Mohn, programme officer responsible for Germany at Transparency International, a Berlin-based anti-corruption agency, said France and Germany, which has been pushing strict anti-corruption laws in its parliament though only at the domestic level, wanted an OECD convention which would require signatories from all the countries to a more rigid and binding legal treaty.

But negotiations towards agreeing such a document are likely to miss the May deadline for ministerial action.

Mohn said: 'It would be a nightmare of long-drawn out negotiations if Germany pushes for a formal treaty.'

Delegates are hopeful that Germany and France can be persuaded to support a soft law approach from the OECD.

Source: The European, 6–12 February 1997

In 1981, Reardon (Axtell, 1990) conducted a study of international gift-giving practices on behalf of the Parker Pen Company. A telephone survey was conducted of 200 international business executives, producing ninety-seven responses. Responses indicated that gifts were typically distinctively American, useful, of conversational value, personalized or given with the recipient's personal preferences in mind, more often than not brand name items and below $26 in cost. These are intended courtesy gifts and approximately one-third of them carried a logo. There has to be separation between what is seen as a gift from what may be viewed as a bribe. Axtell (1990) quotes a Fortune 500 vice president of personnel as saying: 'If there is no compromise of business or personal interests by either party in the exchange, it is a gift'. Rarely though is giving an act of disinterested generosity. Many weary and experienced businessmen have been heard to exclaim over the years that there is no such thing as a 'free' lunch! This is at a low level but nevertheless isolates one aspect of the difficulty. Again, to cite Axtell (1990), he in turn quotes a corporate spokesman as saying:

'No business problem gets solved by simply throwing money at it and that includes what to give the client!' A lavish present can cause more lasting embarrassment than a modest one and in the mind of the recipient be a constant reminder of a duty to be performed. This then becomes unacceptable even where some local form of irregular payments is held to be the practice.

The question of corporate ethics in confronting such a practice abroad which is not in itself illegal is another matter. A three-step process by which a matter may be termed 'material' or 'misleading' and the issue of moral responsibility are outlined in Figure 9.6 which sees this issue as involving both internal and external dissent (Loeb and Cory, 1989).

'Whistleblowing' is to be seen therefore rather as a process than an event. Much thought and consultation should therefore be taken before going public to establish whether the general welfare of society is likely to be maintained or improved by public awareness.

This situation is less likely to occur when there is a system in place designed to prevent the very occurrence of such incidents but equipped

<table>
</table>

> ## Exhibit 9.5   America Online cuts Russians off over card fraud
>
> America Online, the world's largest provider of online services, has cut off access to computer users in Russia after fraudsters used numbers from stolen credit cards to enter its network and the wider Internet without paying.
>
> The company's unprecedented step – the first time AOL has blocked off an entire country – underlines the risks western companies face in granting credit to customers in Russia and some other east European countries. Fraud and non-payment have been so widespread that some mobile telephone companies call in customers when bills reach a set level.
>
> The online service, which has 7m customers worldwide, said fewer than 2,000 users in Russia were affected by its move. It acknowledged, however, that the incident might delay efforts to reach a broader audience there.
>
> The fraud was detected in early December when AOL noticed a surge in new traffic, dialling into access points set up in 40 Russian cities to give travelling customers connections at local call prices. On examination, the new customers appeared to have obtained valid credit card numbers – probably on the active underground market in Moscow – to establish fraudulent accounts.
>
> As do most online services, AOL allows new customers to register simply by dialling through a personal computer modem and entering a name and credit card details. No document-ary proof is required.
>
> AOL usually stops accounts only after the owners of stolen or misused credit card numbers call to complain about charges for services they did not request – but that may be a month or so after the fraud.
>
> It is a loophole not confined to Russia, but Ms Tatiana Gau, vice-president of integrity assurance at AOL, said: 'We have not encountered it previously in other markets.'
>
> Though AOL cut off access on December 14, it faces unquantified bills from the telecommunications companies that carried the electronic data from AOL's local access points to its network.
>
> *Source: Financial Times, 9 January 1997, p. 13*

to deal with such an incident, if and when it should arise. It is worth looking at an example of a corporate code of ethics. Provided for employees rather than the public, the corporate code of ethics seeks to forestall problems which may arise by instituting a code of practice to be implemented every day of the year with appropriate reporting procedures rather than as a set of emergency procedures when crises arise. Taking the example of Esso, known also as Imperial Oil in Canada, and as Exxon elsewhere, the tone is set in the opening foreword by the Chairman and Chief Executive Officer, Arden R.Haynes:

In all its actions, Imperial Oil is dedicated to the principle of ethical leadership. This calls on all of us individually, and as a company, to adhere to the highest of ethical standards, which surpass the letter of the law and embrace open and honest dealings in all of our relationships. It means capturing the high moral ground and standing on it.

It is perhaps not ideal to just select from such a document but it does Esso no discredit to extract that part of their code which deals with gifts and entertainment.

Employees are expected to take actions and make decisions based on an impartial and objective assessment of the facts of each situation, free from the influence of gifts and similar favours that might adversely affect judgment.

Similarly, the company must avoid both the fact and appearance of improperly influencing relationships with the organizations and individuals with whom it deals. Therefore, employees should think carefully about the implications before either accepting or giving a gift in their capacity as representatives of Imperial Oil, no matter how modest the gift or benefit may appear to be.

It is company policy to discourage the receiving of gifts or entertainment by employees from persons outside Imperial Oil and to discourage the giving of gifts or entertainment by employees on behalf of Imperial Oil to persons outside the company. Such practices are permissible only where they involve items of moderate value and conform to the following *basic principles*:

- they are infrequent
- they legitimately serve a definite business purpose
- they are appropriate to the business responsibilities of the individuals
- they are within limits of reciprocation as a normal business expense.

These principles are also contravened if the action involves the giving or receiving of gifts or entertainment by an employee's immediate family member.

In no case are employees permitted to give or receive gifts of cash, commissions, loans, shares in profit, securities or the equivalent of any of these things.

Employees should neither give nor receive gifts of more than a nominal value without the knowledge of managers who have the authority to provide consent. The level deemed to be of nominal value for gifts is $25 or less.

Employees may give or receive entertainment

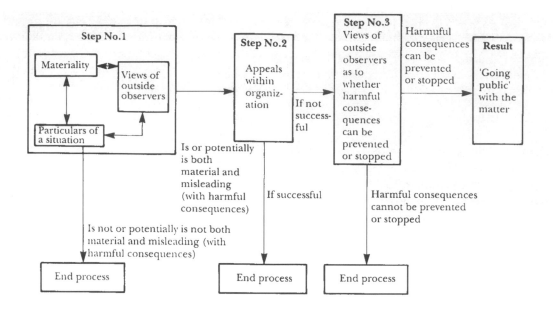

Source: Loeb, S.C., and Cary, S.N. (1989) Whistleblowing and management accounting: an approach. *Journal of Business Ethics,* **8**, 903–916

Figure 9.6

(dining or an amusement, sporting or recreational event) if the circumstances conform to the requirements set out in the statement of basic principles.

If you suspect that undue favouritism is being sought from you, it should be reported to your supervisor.

If you have any doubts, about the company's policy on gifts, honoraria and other benefits, a procedural memorandum is available from division or department management.

There should be no gaps or loopholes in a corporate code of ethics which is designed to protect the individual employee as well as the institution. Nevertheless, an ethics checklist is also provided as a further safety net:

Is it legal?
Am I making or proposing a decision that breaks the law or runs contrary to a company policy?

Is it fair?
Will my decision disadvantage or perhaps even bring harm to anyone – colleagues, customers, suppliers, the community? Or is it a decision that will make those affected by it feel they have been treated fairly in the long run as well as the short term?

Can I defend it?
If I had to justify my decision to my family, the media or the directors, would I feel embarrassed and uncomfortable? Or could I explain my decision with pride, believing that in making my decision I have done the right thing?

In 1976, the OECD adopted guidelines for multinational corporation behaviour as well as host country behaviour as part of a broader understanding on various investment issues. The OECD ministers have signed a *Declaration on International Investment and Multinational Enterprises*, which includes several interrelated elements.

- A reaffirmation by OECD members that a liberal international investment climate is in the common interest of the industrial nations.
- An agreement that they should give equal treatment to foreign controlled and national enterprises.
- A decision to co-operate to avoid 'beggar thy neighbour' actions, pulling or pushing particular investments in or out of their jurisdictions.
- A set of voluntary guidelines, defining standards for good business conduct which the ministers collectively recommended to transnational enterprises operating in their territories.
- A consultative process under each of the above elements of the investment agreement.

However, it carried no sanctions for violators. Similarly, the International Chamber of Commerce (ICC) based in Paris had its report *Extortion and Bribery in Business Transactions* ratified by its Council but could only hope that it would be adopted widely on a voluntary basis by companies and countries.

The UN has had two parts of its organization working on this problem. The Commission on Transnational Corporations finalized a code on transnational corporations but socialist and Third World member states of the UN worked to ensure that this applied to privately owned multinationals and not state companies. The other UN organization involved is the Committee on International Agreement on Illicit Payments. This would involve (Kirpalani, 1984) all members states bringing under its national law criminal penalties to cover

The soliciting, demanding, accepting or receiving, directly or indirectly, by a public official of any payment, gift or other advantage, or undue consideration for performing or refraining from the performance of his duties in connection with an international commercial transaction.

Organizational development to meet market needs

The intention here is not to study organization *per se* but to look inquisitively at the way in which the company operating internationally modifies its organizational structure to accommodate market dynamics including competition affecting product and service offerings as well as changes in consumer tastes. This will be the path along which transactions take place between the firm and its customers. Literature on the subject of multinational organization development has in the past questioned whether structure influenced strategy and vice versa. Let us state now that it is transactional considerations, not technology nor deregulation that are typically decisive in determining which mode of organization will be optimal in a given set of circumstances. Organizational deficiencies have meant that companies were unable to respond at precisely the right time to changes in market dynamics. Presently these changes are aimed at creating regional trading blocs.

Related issues are the level and quality of communication between the head office and not just the subsidiary as is often supposed, but what amounts increasingly to an international portfolio of different investments from wholly owned to joint venture to licensing or franchising and consortium marketing. Williamson (1975) traces the chronology of these changes which have been taking place. In the beginning there were markets, and progressively more refined forms of internal organization have successively evolved. First, peer groups, then simple hierarchies, and finally the vertically integrated firm in which a compound hierarchy exists.

In the quest to optimize resources, close monitoring has to take place with regard to the level of interaction between head office and its subsidiaries and affiliates. There is no single correct solution. The choice of organizational form must be situational, i.e. that which best suits the company concerned given the characteristics of the industry, the product range, customer characteristics, and national markets in which it is trading. Each company finds its own solution. There is no 'industry' solution either for some companies have changed their corporate structure more than once as has BP and the BBC for example, from a product structure to a regional structure and back again. Another point to bear in mind is that over time no variables hold constant. Companies divest themselves of certain product lines or subsidiaries or else acquire by takeover, merger, and slow or gradual build-up of own market presence.

Corporate organization has therefore to take into account a certain degree of flexibility for growth and product extension. Against this, there are often governmental barriers inhibiting foreign direct investment for example, or pressure – explicit as well as implicit – towards industrial co-operation and contractual joint ventures. There may well be variations to the trading environment peculiar to one particular trading region. Governments may impose political and philosophical strictures on the forms of organization which it will countenance within its own jurisdiction. Some designed to ensure a degree of local ownership; some designed to give a degree of local ownership of foreign subsidiaries to trusted political allies. The question of corporate culture – whether the firm is ethnocentric (home country orientation), polycentric (host country orientation), regiocentric (regional orientation), or geocentric (world orientation) – can also pose a barrier as this will influence the degree of freedom granted to the subsidiaries and affiliates in their reporting procedures to head office. An ethnocentric-oriented company attaches little value to international sales whereas a polycentric orientation means that each country subsidiary has independence of action. It is only with a regiocentric or geocentric orientation that the company starts to think of integrated marketing strategies.

As Figure 9.7 shows, there are five main groups of international company organization.

Type A – the direct type

The most senior staff of the company have a direct relationship with the foreign subsidiary. Multinationals such as the Swedish SKF ball-bearing company have traditionally been organized along these functional lines which

Degree of centralization	Organization type				
	A (direct)	B (geographical)	C (product)	D (matrix)	E (project)
High					
Medium					
Low					

The shaded squares are the most common

Source: Brooke, M. Z. (1984) *Centralization and Autonomy: A Study in Organization Behaviour,* Holt-Rinehart-Winston

Figure 9.7   Organization types

transcend national boundaries. This means that home-based functional managers are responsible for functional activities internationally.

Type B – the geographical type

This relationship is mediated through local managers who may have international, regional or national titles. The company sees more diversity in its markets than its products and so may choose to group area and technical specialists under this geographical grouping.

Type C – the product type

Product group managers have direct control over the subsidiaries operating in their product area. Standardization is ensured but at the cost of duplication of many head office services and a loss of coordination over subsidiary activities.

Type D – the matrix type

The matrix organization in which the subsidiary managers report along both the product group, and geographical lines, sometimes even functional lines as well. A country manager at head office is responsible for channelling all communication between head office and the subsidiary abroad. On the one hand, this creates the benefit of belongingness for the foreign subsidiary but there may be first too much communication between head office and subsidiary to make this feasible.

Theoretically, a matrix organization should have created responsiveness, efficiency within the organization and the creation of direct reporting channels of communication. However, Bartlett and Ghoshal (1989) report on the companies which experimented with this form of organization and found it to have failed them. These companies include Dow Chemical and Citibank.

Type E – the project type

The application to the total organization of the project organization devised for large-scale assembly operations like aircraft building. The company is organized into a series of project groups which bring together staff drawn from any relevant functional area and are constantly changing.

Type F – the mixed structure

The mixed structure is one which is made up partly of a product division and of an international division. Lack of co-ordination can have serious effects on any firm. Here, in Figure 9.10 product A has two divisions while product B has one. If co-ordination is not achieved, the costs can be serious. International division is responsible here for communications between the two product A divisions.

In general, the B type (geographical) is more frequently decentralized; the C type (product) more usually centralized; the E type (project) almost always centralized; while A (direct) and D (matrix) may be either.

Williamson (1975) refers to the issue of vertical specialization along product lines as the unitary form of organization or the U-form enterprise. Williamson summarizes the difficulties that the large U-form enterprise experiences in terms of indecomposability, incommensurability, non-operational goal specification, and the confounding of strategic and operating decisions. Incommensurability makes it difficult to specify the goals of the functional divisions in ways which clearly contribute to higher level enterprise objectives. Indecomposability makes it necessary to attempt more extensive co-ordination among the parts; for a given span of control, this naturally results in a greater loss of control between hierarchical levels. Moreover, to the extent that efforts at co-ordination break down

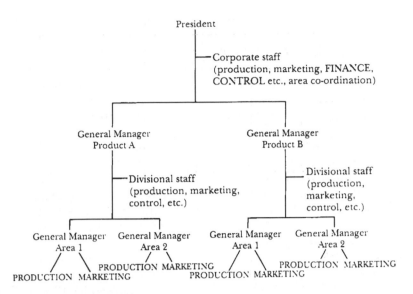

Note: The function in capital letters indicates operating responsibility. Those in lower case indicate mainly advisory and co-ordinating roles.

Source: Stopford, M., and Wells, L. T. (1972) *Managing the Multinational Enterprise*, Basic Books, New York

Figure 9.8   Geographical organization

and the individual parts suboptimize, the strategic interconnectedness between them virtually assures that spillover costs will be substantial.

The inherent weakness in the centralized and functionally departmentalized operating company becomes critical only when the administrative load on the senior executives increases to such an extent that they are unable to handle their entrepreneurial responsibilities efficiently. Unable to identify meaningfully with, or con-

tribute to, the realization of global goals, managers in each of the functional parts attend to what they perceive to be operational subgoals instead.

Williamson's six-way classification scheme for company organization

1.   *Unitary (U-form).* This is the traditional functionally organized enterprise. Williamson

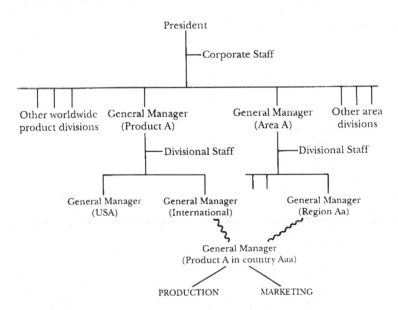

Note: A straight line indicates reporting relationships where responsibility is not shared. A zig-zag line represents reporting relationships where responsibility is shared

Source: Stopford, M., and Wells, L. T. (1972) *Managing the Multinational Enterprise*, Basic Books, New York

Figure 9.9   Product organization

makes an important contribution in acknowledging the importance of human factors
when approaching the problems of economic
organization. In addition, Williamson focuses
also on transactions and on uncertainty. It is
still the appropriate structure in most small
to lower middle-sized firms organized along
functional lines, e.g. sales, finance, manufacturing. Some medium-sized firms in which
intercommunications are especially rich may
continue to find this the appropriate structure. A variant on this structure occasionally
appears if that enterprise is of U-form character but the firm has become diversified to a
slight degree and the incidental parts are of
proven semi-autonomous standing. Unless
such diversification accounts for at least one-
third of the firm's value-added, such a functionally organized firm will be assigned to the
U-form category.

2. *Holding company (H-form).* This is the divisionalized enterprise for which the requisite internal control apparatus has not been provided.
The divisions are often affiliated with the
parent company through a subsidiary relationship. The divisions enjoy a high degree of
autonomy under a weak executive structure.

3. *Multidivisional (M-form).* This is the divisionalized enterprise adopted by General Motors
and DuPont in which a separation of operations from strategic decision-making is provided, and for which the requisite internal
control apparatus has been assembled and is
systematically employed. General managers
are concerned with strategic decisions including resource allocation. This separation from
operating duties and technical decisions is
important and designed to give freedom of
action. To perform the high-level planning
and control functions, the general management cannot become over-involved in operating matters.

4. *Transitional multidivisional (M-form).* This is the
M-form enterprise that is in the process of
adjustment. Organizational learning may be
involved or newly acquired parts may not yet
have been brought into a regular divisionalized relationship in the parent enterprise.

5. *Corrupted multidivisional (M-form).* The
M-form enterprise is a multidivisional structure for which the requisite central apparatus
has been provided but in which the general
management has become extensively
involved in operating affairs. The appropriate
distance relation is thus missing, with the
result that M-form performance, in the long
run, cannot reliably be expressed.

6. *Mixed (X-form).* Conceivably a divisionalized
enterprise will have a mixed form in which
some divisions will be essentially of the holding company variety, others will be M-form,
and still others will be under the close supervision of the general management. Whether
a mixed form is likely to be viable over the
long run is perhaps to be doubted. Some
'exceptions' might, however, survive simply
as a matter of chance. The X-form classification might thus be included for completeness
purposes and as a reminder that organizational survival is jointly a function of natural

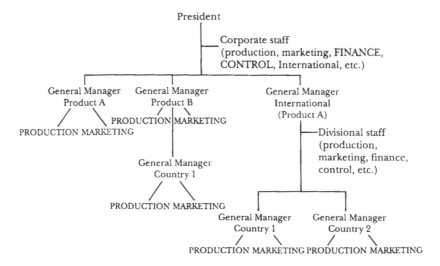

Note: The functions in capital letters indicate operating responsibility, those in lower case, mainly advisory or
co-ordinating roles

Source: Stopford, M., and Wells, L. T. (1972) *Managing the Multinational Enterprise,* Basic Books, New York

Fig. 9.10 Matrix organization

and chance processes. In the long run the rational structures should thrive but deviant cases will appear and occasionally persist.

The multidivision structure (M-form), requires an elite staff to assist general management in strategic decision-making responsibilities, including control. Relieved of operating duties and tactical decisions, a general executive is less likely to reflect the position of just one part of the whole. The characteristics and advantages of the M-form innovation is summarized by Williamson in the following way:

1. The responsibility for operating decisions is assigned to essentially self-contained operating divisions or quasi firms.
2. The elite staff attached to the general office performs both advisory and auditing functions. Both have the effect of securing greater control over operating decision behaviour.
3. The general office is principally concerned with strategic decisions, inviting planning, appraisal, and control, including the allocation of resources among the competing operating divisions.
4. The separation of the general office from operations provides general office executives with the psychological commitment to be concerned with the overall performance of the organization rather than become absorbed in the affairs of the functional parts.
5. The resulting structure displays both rationality and synergy: the whole is greater, more effective, more efficient, than the sum of the parts.

Table 9.7   Key problems identified by headquarters executives

	Rank (out of 182)	Score (in per cent)		Rank (out of 182)	Score (in per cent)
Lack of qualified international personnel			There is too much bureaucracy in the oganization	5	55
Getting qualified international personnel is difficult	1	73	Too much paperwork has to be sent to headquarters	6	54
It is difficult to find qualified local managers for the subsidiaries	1	73	Headquarters staff and subsidiary management differ about which problems are important	17	46
The company can't find enough capable people who are willing to move to different countries	15	60	Headquarters tries to control its subsidiaries too tightly	22	45
There isn't enough manpower at headquarters to make the necessary visits to local operations	22	57	*Excessive financial and marketing constraints*		
Lack of strategic thinking and long-range planning at the subsidiary level			The emphasis on short-term financial performance is an obstacle to the development of long-term marketing strategies for local markets	1	65
Subsidiary managers are preoccupied with purely operational problems and don't think enough about long-range strategy	3	71	The subsidiary must increase sales to meet corporate profit objectives even though it operates with many marketing constraints imposed by headquarters	7	50
Subsidiary managers don't do a good job of analysing and forecasting their business	5	65	Headquarters expects a profit return each year without investing more money in the local company	10	49
There is too much emphasis in the subsidiary on short-term financial performance. This is an obstacle to the development of long-term marketing strategies	13	61	*Insufficient participation of subsidiaries in product decisions*		
			The subsidiary is too dependent on headquarters for new product development	13	47
Lack of marketing expertise at the subsidiary level			Headquarters is unresponsive to the subsidiaries' request for product modifications	22	45
The company lacks marketing			New products are developed		

competence at the subsidiary level	4	69
The subsidiaries don't give their advertising agencies proper direction	8	63
The company doesn't understand consumers in the countries where it operates	8	63
Many subsidiaries don't gather enough marketing intelligence	17	59
The subsidiary does a poor job of defining targets for its product marketing	20	58

Excessive headquarters control procedures

Reaching a decision takes too long because we must get approval from headquarters	2	58
There is a communications gap between headquarters and the subsidiaries	31	51
The subsidiaries provide headquarters with too little feedback	33	50

Insufficient utilization of multinational marketing experience

The company is a national company with international business; there is too much focus on domestic operations	25	56
Subsidiary managers don't benefit from marketing experience at headquarters and vice versa	28	53
The company does not take advantage of its experience with product introductions in one country for use in other countries	36	49
The company lacks central co-ordination of its marketing efforts	45	46

Restricted headquarters control of the subsidiaries

The headquarters staff is too small to exercise the proper control over the subsidiaries	8	63
Subsidiary managers resist direction from headquarters	17	59
Subsidiaries have profit responsibility and therefore resist any restraints on their decision-making authority	36	48

Insensitivity of headquarters to local market differences

Headquarters management feels that what works in one market should also work in other markets	2	58
centrally and are not geared to the specific needs of the local market	22	45
Domestic operations have priority in product and resource allocation; subsidiaries rank second	31	43

Too little relevant communication between headquarters and the subsidiaries

The subsidiaries don't inform headquarters about their problems until the last minute	5	65
The subsidiaries do not get enough consulting service from headquarters	13	61
Headquarters makes decisions without thorough knowledge of marketing conditions in the subsidiary's country	12	48
Marketing strategies developed at headquarters don't reflect the fact that the subsidiary's position may be significantly different in its market	13	47
The attempt to standardize marketing programmes across borders neglects the fact that our company has different market shares and market acceptance in each country	27	44

Shortage of useful information from headquarters

The company doesn't have a good training programme for its international managers	7	50
New product information doesn't come from headquarters often enough	22	45
The company has an inadequate procedure for sharing information among its subsidiaries	27	44
There is very little cross-fertilization with respect to ideas and problem solving among functional groups within the company	27	44

Lack of multinational orientation at headquarters

Headquarters is too home-country oriented	17	46
Headquarters managers are not truly multinational personnel	17	46

Source: Weichmann, U. E., and Pringle, L. T. (1979) Problems that plague multinational marketers, *Harvard Business Review*, **July–August**

Divisionalization

Operating decisions are no longer taken at the top but are resolved at the divisional level, which relieves the communication load. Strategic decisions are reserved for the general office which reduces partisan political input into the resource allocation process. The internal auditing and control techniques which the parent office has access to, serve to overcome information-impactedness conditions and permit fine tuning to be exercised over the operating parts. Cash flows in the M-form firm are not automatically returned to their sources but are instead exposed to an internal competition. The usual criterion is the rate of return on invested capital. This assignment of cash flows to high-yield uses is the most fundamental attribute of the M-form enterprise.

Optimum divisionalization thus involves:

1. The identification of separable economic activities within the firm.
2. According quasi autonomous standing, usually of a profit-centre nature to each.
3. Monitoring the efficiency performance of each division.
4. Awarding incentives.
5. Allocating cash flows to high yield uses.
6. Strategic planning.

The general management of the M-form organization usually requires the support of a specialized staff to discharge these functions effectively. The performance potential in divisionalized firms frequently goes unrealized because general management 'either continue to be overly responsive to operating problems – that is, non-strategic but interventionist – or reduce the size of the corporate office to a minimum level at which no capacity exists for strategic and structural decision making'.

Hierarchy in the organizational framework

With regard to the hierarchy, which he points to as an alternative contracting mode to the market but subject to size and transactional limits, Williamson points to the affirmative ways in which hierarchy affects each of the factors in the organizational framework:

Bounded rationality
This refers to human behaviour that is 'intendedly rational but only limitedly so'. Hierarchy extends the bounds of rationality by permitting the specialization of decision making and economizing on communication expense.

Opportunism
Hierarchy permits additional incentive and control techniques to be brought to bear in a more selective manner, thereby serving to curb small-numbers opportunism.

Uncertainty
Interdependent units are allowed to adapt to unforeseen contingencies in a co-ordinated way and furthermore hierarchy serves to absorb uncertainty.

Small numbers
Small-numbers bargaining indeterminacies can be resolved by decree.

Information impactedness
This arises when true underlying circumstances relevant to a transaction or set of transactions, are known to one or more parties but cannot be costlessly discerned by or displayed for others. Hierarchy extends the constitutional powers to perform an audit, thereby narrowing, prospectively at least, the information gap between autonomous agents.

Atmosphere
As compared with market modes of exchange, hierarchy provides, for some purposes at least, a less calculative exchange atmosphere.

It is interesting next to compare Ouchi's *Theory Z* alongside Williamson's writings on hierarchy. Ouchi's *Theory Z* companies were those which had developed naturally in the USA but with many characteristics similar to firms in Japan. Theory Z organizations do have hierarchical modes of control and so do not rely entirely on the self-direction of the workforce. Nevertheless, self-direction does replace hierarchical direction to a great extent, which enhances commitment, loyalty and motivation.

Ouchi differentiates between a hierarchy or bureaucracy and type Z, in that the Z organizations have achieved a high state of consistency in their internal culture. They are, according to Ouchi, most aptly described as 'clans' in that they are intimate associations of people engaged in economic activity but tied together through a variety of bonds. Clans are distinct from hierarchies and from markets which are the other two fundamental social mechanisms through which transactions between individuals can be governed. In a market, each individual is in fact asked to pursue selfish interests. In a clan, each individual is also effectively told to do just what the other person wants. In the latter case, however, the socialization of all to a common good is so complete and the capacity of the system to measure the subtleties of contributions in the long run is so exact, that individuals will naturally seek to do that which is in the common good. Despite its remarkable properties, the clan organizational form in industry possesses a few potentially disabling weaknesses. A clan always tends to develop xenophobia, a fear of outsiders. At the extreme, Theory Z companies will express the 'not invented here' (NIH) mentality – 'We have most of the top people in the field so why should we?' The trouble comes if the company starts to slip. They will not know it since they have no external point of comparison. Building an organization, is, says Ouchi, not like building a house but more like building a marriage. An organization constantly in the process of development will degenerate without attention.

A Theory Z culture has a distinct set of values – among them long-term employment, trust, and close personal relationships. No area or facet of a Z company is untouched by that culture, from its strategies to its personnel – even its products are shaped by those values. Corporate cultures are not easily changed. Significant corporate cultural change may take between six and fifteen years according to one source, but according to Ouchi, it takes two years to persuade managers but ten to fifteen years to allow for this new work ethic to percolate through an organization at every level. Theory Z is to be distinguished from Theory X and Theory Y management approaches outlined by McGregor (1960). Nevertheless there are some clear parallels to be drawn. Theory X management assumes people are fundamentally lazy, irresponsible and need constantly to be watched. Management is centralized and authoritarian and both rewards and punishment are clearly detailed. On the other hand, Theory Y management assume people to be responsible individuals who need support and encouragement. Theory Z management, which we are discussing here, places more emphasis on a consensual participative decision-making process which makes co-workers feel part of a team. The Japanese organization emphasizing collective decision making, collective responsibility, and a concern for the whole.

In most businesses, strategic tensions are created by balancing the economic and political imperatives for the multinational managers to work with a variety of hybrid structures. Whether organized by area or product the hierarchy dominates. The hierarchy determines:

1. The nature of the information that managers collect and use, or their 'world view'. In a geographical structure this may be information that is relevant to national portfolios of diverse businesses; while in a product structure it may be information that is relevant to business portfolios consisting of diverse countries.
2. The way managers decide to compete – on a local for local basis (geographical structure) or by global rationalization (product organization).
3. The people who have the power to commit strategic resources (area managers or product managers).
4. The basis for administrative procedures, such as career progression (across businesses in a geographical organization or within a business across geographical organizations).

If one understood the hierarchy, one could understand the organization, its capabilities, and limitations. However, as global corporations are frequently complex organizations rather than 'pure' in product, functional, or geographical structure, then the following four orientations may usefully be considered, as by suitably modifying them, strategic direction can be altered.

1. *Cognitive orientation* or the perception of the 'relevant environment' by individual managers within the organization. The relevant environment of a business is constructed of an understanding of the key competitors, the competitive structure and the forces that are likely to mould the pattern of evolution of that business. We have to recognize that in a complex organization, different types of managers (area, product, or functional) and managers at different levels can have different perceptions of the relative environment. In other words, their cognitive orientations can be very different.
2. *Strategic orientation*, or the competitive posture and methods of competition that the various groups of managers are willing to adopt. If the various managers have different cognitive orientations, then they will have different perceptions of the appropriate strategic orientation to cope with the threats or to exploit the opportunities inherent in their different world views.
3. *Power orientation* or the locus of power among managers in the organization to commit resources – financial, technological, and managerial – to pursue a strategy.
4. *Administrative orientation*, or the orientation of support systems such as the accounting

system and the personnel system. Accounting data, for example, may be consolidated along product lines or along national subsidiary lines.

The mechanisms which managers in the hybrid or matrix structure can use to influence these four orientations include:

- Data management mechanisms.

- Manager management mechanisms – power to assign managers to key positions.
- Conflict resolution systems – mechanisms to resolve conflict including decision responsibility assignments are necessary.

These mechanisms can exist within four strategic control situations: fragmented, dependent, autonomous or integrated.

Exhibit 9.6 The sum of its European parts

The stampede of South Korean companies into Europe is gathering pace. Daewoo is poised to take over Thomson's consumer electronics business. Hyundai is to build a £2.4bn chip factory in Scotland. Samsung is in talks to buy Fokker, the Dutch aircraft-maker.

While the motives of the Koreans have been much discussed, another question is more elusive. The range of their investments is enormous, from microchips to earthmoving equipment. In many of those markets, only a handful of European manufacturers still compete. Why can companies from the other side of the world hope to succeed where the locals have failed?

Just this question is raised by Samsung, the biggest of the Korean conglomerates. In 1990, Samsung manufactured very little in Europe. It now makes semiconductors and computer monitors, microwave ovens, refrigerators, TV sets and VCRs, excavators, watches and cameras. Its future plans include air-conditioning equipment and vacuum cleaners, and perhaps personal computers and mobile phones.

In the past six years, Samsung's strategy has changed radically. At the outset its investments were driven by the threat of anti-dumping measures from the EU. By 1993, however, it had drawn up a European master plan. This forms part of a group-wide strategy which lays down that by the end of the decade, for instance, 70 per cent of Samsung's global production in electronics should be outside Korea.

Talking to Samsung executives in Europe, certain aspects of the plan recur. First comes brute volume of production. Mr Sang-Jin Park, president of the Spanish operation, says: 'Our starting point [in 1990] was rapid quantitative growth, to achieve scale economies. From this year, we aim at qualitative growth.'

With that comes a heavy emphasis on vertical integration. Samsung's biggest single strength is in manufacturing technology. It therefore aims to control most, if not all, of the elements of production.

The quantitative targets are punishing. Sam-

sung's Wynyard plant, on Teesside in the UK, will make just under 1m computer monitors this year. Next year's target is 1.6m to 2m. Its excavator plant in North Yorkshire will make 350 units this year. The target by the end of the century is 1,500.

Samsung supplies 10 per cent of the European market from its Berlin TV picture tube factory. By the end of the century it aims at 15 per cent. At its Barcelona plant, where it makes VCRs, 1996 sales of $330m are planned to double by the next century.

At this point, certain clichés about the Korean conglomerates come to mind: that they are obsessed with volume at the expense of profit, that they rely on cheap finance, and that their chief concern is to copy each other.

Samsung executives do not deny taking a long-term view of profitability. However, they insist that profit targets are set down from the outset. Mr In Kim, president of the Berlin operation, says that when the business was bought in 1993 from the Treuhand, the East German liquidating authority, the aim was to achieve a post-tax profit within three years. In the event, growth in the eastern European market for TV sets has proved disappointing, and the target has shifted. 'But if we had thought we'd lose money in the future', he says, 'we wouldn't have come here.'

As for finance, Korean interest rates are much higher than they used to be. Samsung says its European investments start life with an average of 30 per cent equity funding from the Korean parent. The rest is funded locally.

On the charge of copying Korean rivals, Samsung is politely dismissive. Mr Shin-Jae Kim, director of European strategy, says 'we used to study our Korean competitors' moves in great detail, but not any more. We don't rate Hyundai and Daewoo as the competition. Our aim is to be a global company. The companies we try to compete with are above their level, such as Sony and Philips.'

The central question remains: how can Samsung, with its vastly different cultural background, make a success of running businesses across

→ Exhibit 9.6 *continued*

Europe? More specifically, what kind of management structures does it put in place in its European operations?

Across Europe, Korean and local managers agree on one point. The aim is to produce a synthesis: a mixed style of management, taking the best from both sides. Mr In Kim says: 'In Korea, when we work on a project, we ask how well the

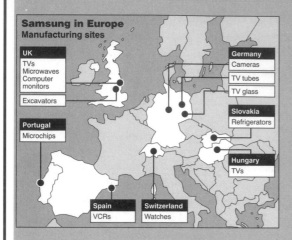

team is working. Here [in Berlin], individual ability is much higher, so the approach is more individual. Each concept has its strong and weak points.'

One weak point, it seems, is Korea's traditional autocratic approach to management. Mr John Harkness, plant director of the North Yorkshire excavator factory, says: 'Samsung is a huge company, with a huge bureaucracy: and yes, it's Korean. In the past its tendency was autocratic, but that's something the company is aware of and has discussed openly.' In particular, he says, the Korean approach of vast plants run by management hierarchies is ruled out. Instead, the management structure is flat, and authority devolved.

At the Wynyard electronics plant on Teesside, there is no executive car parking, and management and workers share the same cafeteria. Everyone clocks in, including the Scottish managing director, Mr Danny O'Brien. There are no trade unions.

Creating an indigenous management style is important for another reason. As part of its objective of moving production from Korea, Samsung has ambitious targets for making its European operations self-sufficient.

An important motive is the need to respond fast to market changes. Mr O'Brien says: 'It takes 45 to 50 days to move product from Korea. The response of the supply chain is critical to our success. The supply chain is also the biggest single element of our cost.'

In the master plan, self-sufficiency comes in three distinct phases: people, materials and technology. Wynyard has 1,200 employees. Only 17 are Koreans, and the number is falling. For materials, Wynyard's colour TV manufacture takes 75 per cent of its supplies from Europe. For microwave ovens and computer monitors, the figure is only between 25 per cent and 30 per cent, but is due to climb to between 75 per cent and 80 per cent in the next 24 months.

Next comes self-sufficiency in technology and design. Wynyard, Mr O'Brien says, already has its own TV technology. In microwave ovens and computer monitors, it has engineering capability. The design of microwave ovens and computer monitors still comes from Korea, but will be transferred to the UK in the next 24 months to 36 months. In TVs, the mechanical design of the chassis is already UK-based, and electronics design will be transferred next year.

This all sounds perfectly logical. But what about Europe's notoriously high labour costs? In the extreme case of Germany, where Samsung's two main plants are in the former communist east, this is clearly an issue. In Berlin, total wage costs are $27 (£17.40) per hour. In Barcelona, the figure is between $13 and $14, and in Wynyard, $9 to $10. In Samsung's Korean operations the average figure is $10, and in Malaysia it is $3.

In Berlin, some of this is offset by productivity. According to Mr Kim, the plant produces 20 TV picture tubes per head for Korea's 15 and Malaysia's 10.

Quality still lags behind. Yield rates are at only 90 per cent of Korean levels. However, Mr Kim says, three years ago they were at only 70 per cent, and he aims to match Korea within two years.

In Spain, the picture is markedly better. The Barcelona plant claims to have the highest productivity in VCR manufacture anywhere in the Samsung group – some 5 per cent to 7 per cent higher than the nearest competitor. The defect rate of about 3 per cent is apparently similar to Korean levels. But then, the Barcelona plant began life as a green-field site, as did Wynyard. The Berlin factory is more typical in one important respect: it was bought on the cheap, as a concern that was in effect bankrupt. So was the German TV glass factory in Brandenburg. The Rollei camera business, bought last year, had been bankrupt in the 1980s. Fokker, which it hopes to buy, went bust in March. Even the North Yorkshire factory now housing the excavator business was bought from the receiver.

→

→ Exhibit 9.6 *continued*

On the same principle, Daewoo is buying Thomson's lossmaking consumer electronics business. In other words, Koreans work on the explicit assumption that they can succeed where Europeans have failed. It all sounds uncomfortably like arrogance; but it is in everyone's interests that they should be right.

Source: Financial Times, 21 October 1996

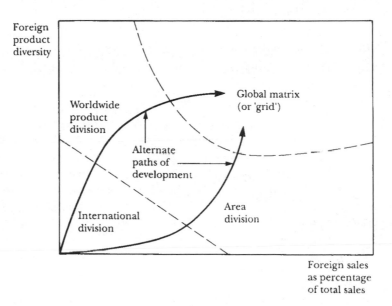

Source: Bartlett, C. and Ghoshal, S. (1989) *Managing Across Borders: The Transnational Solution,* Hutchinson, London

Figure 9.11   Stopford and Wells' international structure stages model

Table 9.8   Organizational characteristics of the transnational

Organizational characteristics	Multinational	Global	International	Transnational
Configuration of assets and capabilities	Decentralized and nationally self-sufficient	Centralized and globally scaled	Sources of core competencies centralized, others decentralized	Dispersed, interdependent, and specialized
Role of overseas operations	Sensing and exploiting local opportunities	Implementing parent company strategies	Adapting and leveraging parent company competencies	Differentiated contributions by national units to integrated worldwide operations
Development and diffusion of knowledge	Knowledge developed and retained within each unit	Knowledge developed and retained at the centre	Knowledge developed at the centre and transferred to overseas units	Knowledge developed jointly and shared worldwide

Source: Bartlett, Ghoshal, 1989

Alternative organizational patterns

The demise of the international division is detailed in Chapter 2 but thinking on the international division, and influences such as Stopford and Wells, have had a very profound and lasting effect long beyond the usefulness of the theory itself. Bartlett and Ghoshal (1989) point to the need for global integration and efficiency and to develop and diffuse worldwide innovations inter-

nationally. They differentiate between multinational, global and international companies before advocating the arrival of the transnational corporation. Similar to Perlemutter's classification above, the multinational as seen by Bartlett and Ghoshal has established itself through a local presence in many markets arising from a sensitivity and responsiveness to national differences. The global corporation has established cost advantages for itself through centralized global scale operations while the international company

Exhibit 9.7 Outline of a model of good marketing practice

The organization's policy and objectives for product/service quality are defined and documented. It ensures that the policy and objectives are understood, implemented and maintained at all levels in the organization through regular monitoring and reviewing by a member of staff with defined responsibility for ensuring that the requirements of product/service quality are implemented and maintained. Records of such reviews and their training implications are maintained. The responsibility and authority of all staff who manage and perform activities affecting the quality of customer service provision is defined and measured against agreed targets.

Marketing plans exist covering a defined period and relating to a stated business strategy. The organization can show how inputs from other areas of the business contribute to the development of the marketing plan. It can show that a level of qualified staff exists with clearly defined responsibilities for implementing those plans. The planning process and its related procedures are documented.

The training needs of marketing and sales/service staff are regularly identified and steps taken to provide appropriate training. The performance of marketing and sales/service staff is measured against agreed objectives. The duties of marketing and sales/service staff are clearly delineated within the overall management of the organization with defined lines of authority and communication.

Market requirements and potential are defined as a result of continually identifying and re-assessing the needs and preferences of existing customers and comparing and contrasting them with those of potential customers who deal with competitors. The organization has procedures to control the various elements of service design so that specified customer requirements are met.

Marketing audits are regularly performed as an integral part of the marketing planning cycle. The auditing process is documented.

The organization clearly defines and documents its marketing and sales objectives and strategies. It

takes steps to ensure that they are understood, agreed and implemented by contributory departments. The marketing plan defines objectives, strategies and plans for each target market sector and details resource requirements for the mix including pricing, promotion, service and distribution.

Procedures exist to protect customer data and information. The process for implementing after sales service or customer support programmes is defined, monitored and regularly reviewed by management. A procedure exists for handling and assessing customer complaints which prevents recurrence. Customers are regularly informed of progress relating to their requests, comments and complaints.

The organization ensures that purchased products or services conform to specified requirements. It also ensures that sales agents, external field forces and telephone sales operations conform to specified requirements and codes of practice.

Performance against marketing plans is measured and reviewed at appropriate intervals by management and appropriate corrective action taken where necessary. All departments that contribute to the formulation of marketing plans, or have responsibility for implementing aspects of them are involved in setting out plans for managing any organizational changes that may ensue.

A process of continuous information monitoring and feedback of customer experience and expectations is maintained via a customer database. Regular steps are taken to measure the organization's performance, and that of its competitors, along a defined set of customer requirements. Such information is collated and analysed for review by operational management. It is also collected for the broader market environment and for the activities of direct and indirect competitors and any other influential group. The process which is used to gather and report such information is defined and documented and its development resourced.

Source: Brownlie (1993)

has been able to exploit parent company knowledge through worldwide diffusion and adaptation.

Relevant control systems

The Boston Consulting Group (BCG) product portfolio matrix

It is a commonplace to raise questions such as 'Where are we now?' 'Where do we want to go?' 'How do we get there?' It is infernally difficult, however, to answer these questions, particularly as to which business the company sees itself being in. In one particular example, it was found that substandard gas pipes could also be used as scaffolding and so this opened up a new market for an existing product. Other existing products are finding new applications with the development of North Sea oil which, as an industry, has spawned many new developments of its own in welding, pipes, drilling, and construction.

A study of the market would be expected to examine sales trends: previous forecasts in rela-tion to performance; assessment of the general market situation and competitive environ-ment; problems and opportunities envisaged in the marketplace; planning assumptions and constraints. A distillation of this data combines with company strengths and weaknesses and is then moulded by corporate policy and the corporate view of the direction the company should take, so as to set marketing objectives in realistic terms, e.g., sales volume in money terms and in units, and market share in percentages.

The BCG product portfolio matrix has attracted a lot of attention among managers because it seeks to compartmentalize the company's entire product range into a 2×2 matrix where the respective axes are relative market share and market growth. The theories underpinning the BCG product portfolio matrix include the product life cycle hypothesis; the experience curve effect whereby each doubling of production volume will produce attendant cost savings of 25–30 per cent; and the correlation between relative market share and profitability which BCG emphasize strongly.

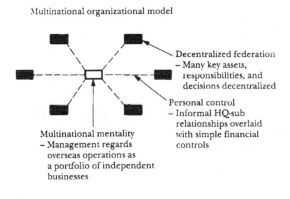

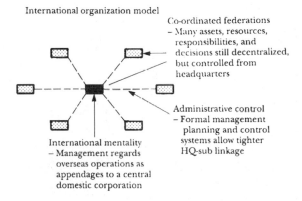

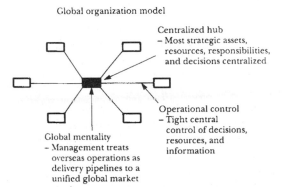

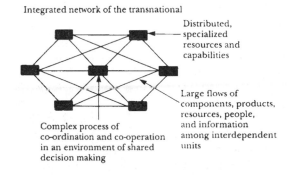

Source: Bartlett, C., and Ghoshal, S. (1989) *Managing Across Borders: The Transnational Solution*, Hutchinson, London

Figure 9.12

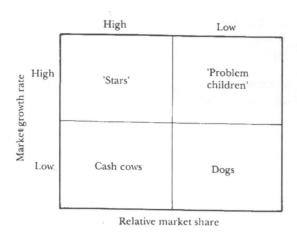

Figure 9.13   BCG business portfolio matrix – implications for investment

BCG makes an important distinction between actual market share and relative market share. Relative market share means a particular manufacturer's product market share relative to that manufacturer's largest competitor. Two companies may have the same actual market share but BCG would argue that there was a difference in the competitive position between two companies if one had a relative market share of 5 per cent and the other 15 per cent. A general rule is that relative market share would be deemed 'high' if in excess of 10 per cent. An example of market growth is that of word processors which grew at a rate of 34 per cent in 1984.

Next, to the technology employed (see Figure 9.13). BCG recognize only 'high' and 'low' on the two axes, market growth and relative market share. Where the company has a relatively high market share and is in a high growth market, this product would be a 'star'. This is a rising product in a buoyant market. The situation where there is a low-growth market but the company has a high market share is a 'cash cow'. Note that each cell has strategic implications. Cash cows are to be 'milked' to produce the cash to finance future 'stars'. Next, the situation where the company is enjoying relatively low market share in a buoyant growing market – this is termed a 'problem child', and is a suitable case for treatment. There is something wrong then with this present product offering in its current cost per unit, its packaging, or presentation and so a product in this category should be closely scrutinized and hopefully will, on relaunch, re-establish itself in the market place as a 'star'. On no account should 'problem children' be allowed to continue without some form of investigation taking place first. Finally, there is the least enviable situation of all, a low growth market and a relatively low market share which is a category the company should pull itself out of immediately. This is the 'dog'. Unfortunately, for the British, 'dogs' are to be put down, there is never any stay of execution for a 'dog'.

The ramifications for investment that are implicit in the product portfolio matrix are seen in Figure 9.13 while the possible outcomes are depicted in Figure 9.14 which shows a success sequence pattern and Figure 9.15 which shows a disaster sequence pattern. As well as watching product sales, the company should also be keeping a close watch on those products consuming,

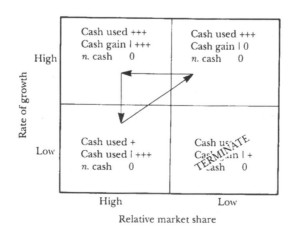

Figure 9.14   BCG business portfolio matrix – success sequence

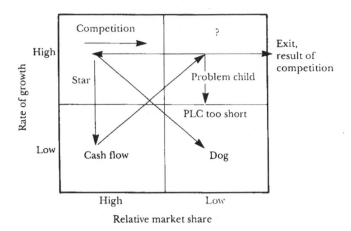

Figure 9.15   BCG business portfolio matrix – disaster sequence

rather than generating, funds although there are definitional problems. McNamee (1985) has pointed out how BMW of Germany would be a 'dog' company if its relative market share were relative to all motor cars produced and its marketing segment was the 'motoring public'. However, if BMW's market segment is regarded as fast, high quality, prestigious saloon cars, then its relative market share appears much higher.

The product portfolio matrix has a number of failings, however. The company's own financial resources may not be adequate to pursue market share. Also, if competitors use the same technique of market analysis, they may well follow the same strategy. Other problems arise as well in the unit of measure adopted for the matrix and so any consequent interpretation. As in the BMW example above, is the product market to be defined in broad or narrow product or need terms? Focusing on the total product market and just on the part of the market served by the company, will produce different results. So, too, will the definition of the market depending on whether it is seen as local, national or international. Narrow definitions will exclude longer term conceptual issues of a larger market. Again, focusing only on the market served may lead the company to overlook a significant opportunity or a competitive threat from the unserved portion of the market. Employing several alternative definitions varying product and market segments will help get around this problem (Day, 1977). However, there is a further problem with the matrix in that it may confuse slow growth for decline, for example, as it has only one model of the product life cycle and its stages in its formulation. The definition of market share can also be manipulated by managers who are in turn evaluated by this system. While providing a useful synthesis, it is a fallacy to treat all business as being similar. Day (1977) points also to a number of factors beyond share and market growth which may have a greater bearing on the attractiveness of a product market or business, including:

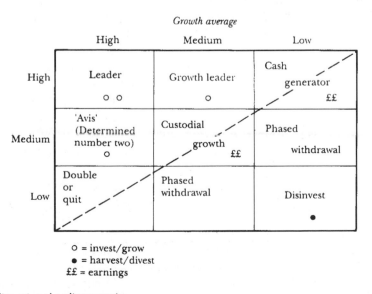

o = invest/grow
● = harvest/divest
££ = earnings

Figure 9.16   Shell directional policy matrix

- contribution rate
- barriers to entry
- cyclicality of sales
- rate of capacity utilization
- sensitivity of sales to changes in prices, promotional activities
- extent of 'captive' business
- nature of technology (maturity, stability, and complexity)
- availability of production and process opportunities
- social, legal, governmental and union pressures and opportunities.

There is perhaps too rigid a compression into only four cells and this is what gave rise to the Shell or General Electric directional policy matrix (see Figure 9.16). This recognizes that products may actually be on the fence between 'dog' and 'cash cow' or any two categories. Besides this, there was, too, the fact that there was room in the market for the company that either could not be number one or wished only to be number two, due perhaps to size or technological capability, etc

If the market is growing it may be relatively easy to acquire market share, but in a static or declining market, market share can only be bought at the expense of competitors who are likely to retaliate perhaps with price reductions, thereby jeopardizing the market for all concerned.

The matrix is as viable in an international context as in a domestic one, the only reservation being that governments may take notice of 'cash cows' being milked in their particular country to finance some 'stars' being nurtured in an overseas freeport. In the same way as Wells and Vernon showed how the PLC theory could be used for international markets, the same is true here of the BCG matrix. It has the same roots after all in the PLC theory but the experience curve emphasizes product unit cost advantages, and relative market share serves to emphasize this commercial advantage under the BCG guidelines. Whereas the PLC offered a postmortem rationalization for US investments, the BCG offers strategic alternatives as a result of the datagathering exercise, e.g., market segment concentration, market share holding, harvesting (taking the cash), and termination.

PIMS database

PIMS is an acronym for 'profit impact on marketing strategy'. Based in the Strategic Planning Institute, Cambridge, Massachusetts, PIMS has a database of 1,800 subscribers who are mainly US though it has subsidiary branches now throughout Europe, including London. For a subscription of several thousand dollars per annum, subscribers do not receive any 'omnibus' study or industry or product report. Instead, what they receive for their money is the ability to interrogate that database with a number of 'what if' questions. The subscriber inserts some key data about his company into the computer which then searches its memory for a similar company. The computer would then be able to respond to a question about the likely effect of a 4 per cent price increase, or to reveal trends, or to explain market phenomena.

PIMS does not predict the future. It tells instead what happened in highly similar circumstances based on millions of facts submitted by member companies. PIMS is based entirely on real life not theory. Academics and researchers decry the fact that it has a long list of variables, in excess of 120, and so, in arriving at a given point there is the problem known to statisticians of multicollinearity; in other words, we cannot be sure which of the 120 plus variables was responsible for this situation. No two companies are after all identical, so this is a weakness. However, PIMS exists as a business tool for businessmen and as such it appears to be receiving wide acclaim. Even if it cannot explain all the answers it is getting sufficient of the answers right to satisfy the businessmen who are generally much less interested as to how a particular solution was arrived at, than the solution itself.

PIMS make the following generalizations based on their experience:

1. Higher profitability is accounted for by
   - lower capital intensity (investment)
   - high market share
   - high product quality.
2. High market position and high product quality:
   - are very profitable
   - can be used as substitutes for each other.
3. If market is weak
   - do not use high prices
   - do not do R&D, imitate other products instead.
4. If market position is strong increase R&D expenses.
5. If one's product is of low quality do not advertise it.
6. To be profitable
   - introduce new products at the bottom of recession (a most difficult theory to put into practice)
   - do not spend more than 10 cents of the sales dollar for marketing.

Revision questions

1. How does international marketing planning differ from ordinary domestic marketing planning?
2. What is the difference between operational planning and strategic planning?
3. What are the corporate expectations of planning?
4. How many phases or stages are there to the planning process as described by McDonald?
5. Should marketing programmes be based on the concept of global segmentation?
6. What are the three sets of factors which influence locational decisions?
7. If more companies are practising international segmentation then that makes the table by Hulbert, Brandt and Richers (1980) redundant. Do you feel that to be the case?
8. Why has corporate planning failed? Why does it have such a bad name?
9. What has Mintzberg to say on corporate planning?
10. What are the four most prevalent problems in international marketing as identified by Cain (1970)?
11. What are the limits of standardization?
12. Discuss where you stand on the issue of market concentration or market spreading.
13. What specific additional problems may be encountered when planning for Third World markets?
14. What is the role of marketing in North–South technology transfer?
15. Devise a plan of action as to how you would deal with 'irregular payments' within your company. Is it bribery and corruption or is it a matter of degree, and doing as the locals do?
16. What is 'whistleblowing'? What sanctions face the whistleblower?
17. What are the five main groups of organizational grouping?
18. What are some of the problems that plague multinational marketers?
19. What is 'bounded rationality'?
20. What are the organizational characteristics of the transnational? Is the transnational different from the multinational?

References

August, O. (1996) 'When lax laws rock the foundations of business', *The Times*, December 2.

Axtell, R. E. (1990) *Do's and Taboos Around the World*, John Wiley & Sons, New York.

Bartlett, C. A., and Ghoshal, S. (1989) *Managing Across Borders: The Transnational Solution*, Hutchinson Business Books, London.

Beck, P. J., and Maher, M. W. (1989) Competition, regulation and bribery. *Managerial and Decision Economics*, **10** (1), 1–12.

Blitz, J. (1996) 'Bill to protect corporate whistleblowers', *Financial Times*, February 14.

Brooke, M. Z. (1984) *Centralisation and Autonomy: A Study in Organisation Behaviour*, Holt-Rinehart-Winston, Eastbourne.

Brownlie, D. (1996) 'Marketing Audits and Auditing: Diagnosis through Intervention', *Journal of Marketing Management*, **12** (1–3), April, 99–112.

Brummer, A. (1996) 'Whistleblower is left in penalty zone', *Guardian: Saturday Notebook*, March 30.

Bush, T. (1996) 'How to avoid spies', *Financial Times*, December 13.

Cain, W. H. (1970) International planning: mission impossible? *Columbia Journal of World Business*, July–August, 53–60.

Chang, T. L. (1995) 'Formulating Adaptive Marketing Strategies in a Global Industry', *International Marketing Review*, **12** (6), 5–18.

Cooper, R. G., and Kleinschmidt, E. (1985) 'The Impact of Strategy on Export Sales Performance', *Journal of International Business Studies*, **16**, Spring, 37–56.

Damsell, K. (1996) 'Com-Net may not trade again for some time', *Financial Post*, November 6.

Day, G. S. (1977) Diagnosing the product portfolio. *Journal of Marketing*, April, 29–38.

Denison, D. R. (1996) 'What is the Difference between Organizational Culture and Organizational Climate? A Native's Point of View on a Decade of Paradigm Wars', *Academy of Management Review*, **21** (3), 619–654.

Doz, Y. L., and Prahalad, C. K. Headquarters influence and strategic control in MNCs. *Sloan Management Review*, Fall, 15–29.

Drucker, P. F. (1980) Marketing and economic development. *International Marketing Strategy* (Thorelli, H. and Becker, H.) Pergamon, Oxford, 392.

Economist (1988) Business bribes: on the take, 19 November, 21–24.

Fadiman, J. A. (1986) A traveller's guide to gifts and bribes. *Harvard Business Review*, **64**, 122–126, 130–136.

Fenwick, I., and Amine, L. (1979) 'Export Performance and Export Policy: Evidence from the UK Clothing Industry', *Journal of the Operational Research Society*, **30** (8), 747–754.

The Financial Post (1994) 'British Bank balks at Bribes', July 20, p. 6.

Financial Times (1997) 'America Online cuts Russians off over Card Fraud', January 9, p. 13.

Gillespie, K. (1987) Middle East response to the US Foreign Corrupt Practices Act. *California Management Review*, Summer, 9–30.

Glover, T. (1996) 'The 24 Hour Working Day', *Information Strategy*, **1** (2), November, 49–51.

Gosling, P. (1996) 'Fighting for Foreign Friends', *The Independent*, Section 2, August 7, p. 17.

Hamel, G., and Prahalad, C. K. (1994) *Competing for the Future: Breakthrough Strategies for Seizing Control of your Industry and Creating the Markets of Tomorrow*, Harvard Business School Press, Boston, Mass.

H. B. Thorelli, Tamer Cavusgil, S. (1990) *International Marketing Strategy*, 3rd edn, Pergamon, Oxford.

Haynes, A. R. (1990) *Our corporate ethics*. Esso Imperial Oil, Toronto, Ontario, March.

Hulbert, J. M., Brandt, W. K., and Richers, R. (1980) Marketing planning in the multinational subsidiary: practices and problems. *Journal of Marketing*, **44**, 7–15.

ICC (International Chamber of Commerce (1977) *Extortion and Bribery in Business Transactions: Report adopted by the 131ˢᵗ Session of the Council of the ICC*, 29 March.

Jackson, T. (1996) 'The Sum of its European Parts: how Samsung has adapted the Korean approach to its new markets', *Financial Times*, October 21, p. 12.

Jacoby, N. H. N. (1977) *Bribery and Extortion in World Business: a Study of Corporate Political Payments Abroad*, Macmillan.

Jain, S. C. (1979) What happened to the marketing man when his international promotion payoffs became bribes? In *International Marketing: Managerial Perspectives*.

Katsikeas, C. S., and Leonidou, L. (1996) 'Export Market Expansion Strategy: Differences between Market Concentration and Market Spreading', *Journal of Marketing Management*, **12** (1–3), April, 113–134.

Lee, C. S., and Yang, Y. S. (1990) 'Impact of Export Market Expansion Strategy on Export Performance', *International Marketing Review*, **7** (4), 41–51.

Loeb, S. E., and Cory, S. N. (1989) Whistle-blowing and management accounting: an approach. *Journal of Business Ethics*, **8**, 903–916.

Matthias, P. (1996) 'Out of the Shadows', *Financial Post*, 9 December.

Mayerowitz, S. A. (1987) Treading the line between 'grease' and bribery. *Business Marketing*, **72** (1), 92–94.

McDonald, M. (1996) 'Strategic Marketing Planning: Theory, Practice and Research Agendas', *Journal of Marketing Management*, **12** (1–3), April, 5–27.

McGregor, D. (1960) *The Human Side of Enterprise*, McGraw-Hill, New York.

McNamee, P. M. (1985) *Tools and Techniques for Strategic Management*, Pergamon, Oxford.

Mintzberg, H. (1994) *The Rise and Fall of Strategic Planning*, The Free Press, New York.

O'Connell, J. J., and Zimmerman, J. W. (1979) Scanning the international environment. *California Management Reviews*, **XXII** (2).

Ohmae, K. (1990) *Triad Parer: The Cunning Shape of Global Competition*, The Free Press.

Ouchi, W. (1981) *Theory Z: How American Business Can Meet The Japanese Challenge*, Addison-Wesley, London.

Pisani, R. L. (1987) What is the price of security abroad? *Security Management*, **30** (2), 44–49.

Prahalad, C. K., and Doz, Y. L. (1981) An approach to strategic control in MNCs. *Sloan Management Review*, Summer, 5–13.

Pringle, P. (1996) 'Marlboro men offer America pipe of peace', *The Observer*, May 19.

Quelch, J. A., and Holt, E. J. (1986) 'Customising global marketing', *Harvard Business Review*, May–June, 59–68.

Ringbakk, K. A. (1976) Strategic planning in a turbulent international environment. *Long-Range Planning*, **9**, 2–11.

Robock, S. H., and Simmonds, K. (1983) *International Business and Multinational Enterprises*, Irwin, 3rd edn, p. 342.

Schechter, B. (1996) 'Group launched to expose unethical deals', *Financial Post*, November 18.

Schollhammer, J. (1972) Long-range planning in multinational firms. *Columbia Journal of World Business*, September–October, 79–86.

Shermach, K. (1995) 'Portrait of the World', *Marketing News*, August 28, p. 20.

Sheth, J. N. (1977) A market-oriented strategy of long-range planning for multinational corporations. *European Research*, January, 3–12.

Shruptine, K. F., and Toyne, B. (1981) International marketing planning: a standardised process. *Journal of International Marketing*, **1** (1), 16–28.

Sommers, Montrose and Kernan, J. (1967) Why products flourish here, fizzle there. *Columbia Journal of World Business*, March–April, 89–97.

Stapleton, J., and Thomas, M. J. (1997) *How to prepare a Marketing Plan*, 5th edn, Gower, Aldershot, Hants.

Stokes, R., and Lee, Y. (1996) 'Made in Korea, driven by ambition', *Scotland on Sunday*, July 28, p. 5.

Stopford, J. M., and Wells, L. T. Jr (1972) *Managing the Multinational Enterprise: Organization of the Firm and Ownership of the Subsidiaries*, Basic Books Inc., New York.

Stopford, J. M. (1980) *Growth and Organizational Change in the Multinational Firm*, Arno Press, New York.

Wall, M. (1996) 'Nolan Spotlight on Murky Quangoland', *Mail on Sunday: Financial Mail* (Analysis), May 12.

Wiechmann, U. E., and Pringle, L. G. (1979) Problems that plague multinational marketers. *Harvard Business Review*, July–August, 118–124.

Williamson, O. E. (1975) *Markets and Hierarchies: Analysis and Antitrust Implications*, Macmillan – The Free Press, New York.

Wilson, M. (1980) *The Management of Marketing*, Gower, Aldershot, Hants.

Web sites

International Marketing Review, Contents vol 10 no 1; Impact of Marketing Strategy
http://www.mcb.co.uk/services/contents/liblink/webpages/h 036010001.

International Tax Planning and Asset Protection Packages
http://www.marcade.com/p1 taxpac.html

Creative Planning International
http://pages.prodigy.com/creativeplanning/

International Planning Studies
http://www.carfax.co.uk/ips-ad.htm

Micro Planning International
http://www.microplanning.com/plan/AboutMPI.html

International Development Planning
http://www.planning.gatech.edu/acsp/special/internat.htm

Tax Planning International
http://www.bna.com/hub/bna/busintl/f.TPI.html

International Centre for Planning Research
http://info.cf.ac.uk/uwcc/cplan/page_4.html

International Estate Planning
http://www.macfaq.com/vendor/software/1237.html

Planning and Negotiations International
http://www.fcc.gov/Bureaus/International/WWW/p&ndinfo.html

Expertise Area Project Management
http://www.edu.fi/foy/1 exproj.htm

Planning Sciences International Ltd
http://www.busintel.com/ggentium.htm

International Planning Resources
http://www.lib.berkeley.edu/ENVI/cityintl.html

IPD Associates Inc.
http://www.nh-cbi.com/IPD/description.html

Journal of International Marketing
http://aaup.pupress.princeton.edu:70/CGI/cgi-bin/hfs.cgi/66/mich_state/jim.ctl

International Mission Planning for Space
http://sgra.jpl.nasa.gov/mosaic_v0.0/Papers_dir/500_dir/506.html

Information Technologies International
http://www.pcmd.com/iti

CHAPTER 10

Marketing in Europe

Wandering between two worlds, one dead,
The other powerless to be born

Matthew Arnold,
The Grande Chartreuse, 1.79

Europe, the seat of what we pretentiously call civilization, would have been completely overtaken in terms of economic significance were it not for the economic and productivity gains being achieved in recent years through unification. Western Europe has re-created itself effectively by means of the European Union. At the same time, political changes have meant that what was the Soviet Empire is now no more. There are now in fact many different Europes: Northern (Nordic), Southern (Mediterranean),

Exhibit 10.1

BUILDING Europe TOGETHER

1957-1997 TREATIES OF ROME   40 YEARS OF PEACE AND COOPERATION

THE EUROPEAN UNION

Table 10.1 The market to be served	
Eastern Europe	124 m
Russia	148 m
Ukraine	52 m
The Baltics	8 m
	332 m
Western Europe	357 m

Central and Eastern (the former communist states) and Western Europe (now uniting the countries of the Community and of EFTA). In this present chapter, we will concern ourselves with Western Europe – The European Union, and with Central and Eastern Europe, notably the former communist states, now seeking membership of the EU and of NATO, its former enemy. Europe has come full circle.

Background

To substitute for age-old rivalries the merging of essential interests; to create, by establishing an economic Community, the basis for broader and deeper community among people long divided by bloody conflict; and to lay the foundations for institutions which will give direction to a destiny henceforward shared

Preamble to the European Coal and Steel Community, Treaty of Paris, 1951.

Between 1957 and 1997 the European Community grew in size and changed in nature as its membership increased to 15; and the Commis-

sion became more of a legal entity in its own right as individual member states edged closer towards the full economic integration of a free trade area without frontiers that was the overriding aim of its founding fathers.

The economic reality of a common market was given further impetus with the European Monetary System first devised in 1979, and the concerted effort by all member states to create by 1992, a single unified market for goods and services. To this end, the Single European Act was agreed and signed by the governments of all member states. Europe, after perhaps decades of economic sluggishness, had once again become an exciting place to live. Political developments shook Eastern Europe apart in 1989, created a unified Germany in 1990, a Single European Market in 1992 and brought into being the Maastricht Treaty in 1993 which strengthened the Community further, preparing the way economic and monetary union (EMU) and a single currency and also by giving extra power to the European Parliament. The Maastricht Treaty introduced a common foreign and security

Figure 10.1

policy and co-operation in justice and police affairs. Henceforth, the term 'European Union' has been used to describe the wider framework in which all these activities now take place. As reflected in the following statistics, the European Union is now a redoubtable force in world trade and is preparing for the possible membership of certain Central European states by the year 2000.

The size of the market is large and without frontiers and with standardization of controls on patents, trademarks and general business practices, this economic bloc is now the largest single trading bloc in the world, accounting for approximately 40 per cent of global trade. With a total market size of more than 325 million people, it outnumbers the USA, although it has nine official languages as opposed to one. With a total land area less than 2 per cent of the total world size, the EU accounts for 7 per cent of global population but this is expected to decline to 4 per cent by 2020. An unequal importance in global trade therefore relative to its land size or population. The potential cost savings through standardization are great and may soon show the EUs current 38 per cent of global trade to be an acute understatement of the position.

The Single European Act was a major amendment to the Treaty of Rome. It was ratified by all national parliaments and provided impetus to a 'Europeanization' which was dreamt of by the founding fathers of the Union, and it also changed the institutions of the EU. The European Parliamentary elections of June 1989 gave the electorate in each country the opportunity to vote on the movement towards ever closer union of the peoples of Europe. It also appointed 518 members of parliament of a higher calibre than before to a European Parliament that had been given new powers. To understand these changes, a study of the background is necessary.

Historical background

Many noble attempts were made in the years immediately after the Second World War to create alliances which would make war a thing of the past. However, the refusal by the FSU to remove itself from the lands which it had just liberated from Nazi Germany inevitably soured this atmosphere and created the two political blocs of Europe, East and West, which then led to the creation in 1948 of the Brussels Treaty Organization, which was the forerunner of the North Atlantic Treaty Organization (NATO), to meet an immediate need for the defence of democracy. Also in 1948, there was the creation of the Organization for European Economic Co-operation (OEEC), the immediate predecessor of

the OECD and in 1949 the Council of Europe. However, by this time, the regional European-wide organization of the United Nations: the Economic Commission for Europe (established in 1947 for the purpose of economic reconstruction in Europe) had already been rendered inoperable by the now very real division of two camps within Europe: East and West and the onset of a Cold War between them.

Economic integration began properly in 1951 with the establishment of the European Coal and Steel Community (ECSC). Initiated by the French, it sought to end the historic rivalry between France and Germany, who shared the coal of the Saar Valley and the steel of the Ruhr Valley; and to make war between the two nations not only 'unthinkable but materially impossible'. The plan was to create, by the removal of trade barriers, a common market in coal, iron and steel, with free access to all members: West Germany, France, Italy, Holland, Belgium and Luxembourg. This was, therefore the creation of a grouping to be known for years thereafter as 'The Six'. The European Community came into being on 1 January 1958 with the Treaty of Rome which established it. This called for:

- a free trade area eliminating internal trade barriers,
- a customs union creating a common external tariff,
- a common market with free movement of the factors of production, and
- an economic union aiming at a unification of monetary and fiscal policy.

Common policies were also to be established in agriculture and transport. It also established the European Social Fund (ESF) and the European Investment Bank (EIB). A common commercial policy was also a declared aim, to make special and separate trading arrangements for the former colonial territories which were still underdeveloped.

Assuming that there is a spectrum of international integration (Holland, 1980), with at one end of the scale the independent national economy and at the other, the economy which has become so completely integrated that it amounts in practice to a region of another wider economy, between these extremes are five main stages of integration including:

1. A free trade area in which internal tariffs are abolished but countries' previous tariffs *vis-à-vis* other countries are maintained.
2. A customs union where a common external tariff on products is established, in addition to internal tariff abolition.

THE EUROPEAN UNION

NON-CONTINENTAL AND OVERSEAS TERRITORIES OF MEMBER STATES

Açores

Madeira

Canarias

Guadeloupe

Martinique

Guyane

Réunion

Suomi-Finland

Sverige

Danmark

Deutschland

Nederland

Belgique-België

Luxembourg

Österreich

Italia

Ελλάς-Ellas

Ireland-Éire

United Kingdom

France

España

Portugal

BASIC STATISTICS OF THE EUROPEAN UNION AND ITS FIFTEEN MEMBER STATES: COMPARISON BETWEEN THE EUROPEAN UNION (EUR 15), THE UNITED STATES AND JAPAN

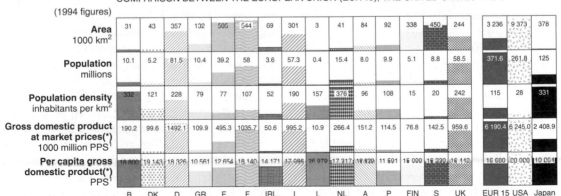

(1994 figures)

	B	DK	D	GR	E	F	IRL	I	L	NL	A	P	FIN	S	UK	EUR 15	USA	Japan
Area 1000 km²	31	43	357	132	505	544	69	301	3	41	84	92	338	450	244	3 236	9 373	378
Population millions	10.1	5.2	81.5	10.4	39.2	58	3.6	57.3	0.4	15.4	8.0	9.9	5.1	8.8	58.5	371.6	261.8	125
Population density inhabitants per km²	332	121	228	79	77	107	52	190	157	376	96	108	15	20	242	115	28	331
Gross domestic product at market prices(*) 1000 million PPS[1]	190.2	99.6	1492.1	109.9	495.3	1035.7	50.6	995.2	10.9	266.4	151.2	114.5	76.8	142.5	959.6	6 190.4	6 245.0	2 408.9
Per capita gross domestic product(*) PPS[1]	18 800	19 143	18 326	10 561	12 654	18 140	14 171	17 986	26 979	17 317	18 920	11 591	15 090	16 220	16 110	16 600	00 000	10 001

(*) Estimate

Source: Eurostat

([1])PPS = Purchasing power standard – a common unit representing an identical volume of goods and services for each country.

1 PPS = BFR 40.1; DM 2.225; DKR 9.365; PTA 130.5; FF 7.122; UKL 0.6942; DRA 211; 1 649.0 LIT; IRL 0.6865; LFR 43.02; HFL 2.284; ESC 127; ÖS 14.97; SKR 10.64; FMK 6.61; USD 1.08; YEN 194.79.

Figure 10.2

3. A common market in which restrictions to the movement of labour and capital between member states are abolished.
4. An economic union in which some national policies are harmonized in spheres other than tariffs, or labour and capital movements, but remain administered by the constituent member states.
5. Economic federalism in which certain key policies are administered by a central federal authority, rather than by the member states, and in which the previously independent national currencies are merged in a single common currency (or, on a weaker definition, bound in rigid and nominally invariable exchange ratios).

The period 1958–69 was a so-called transitional period but by this time, while the mechanism was still suffering from a number of imperfections it had also enjoyed its successes. Thus, in 1970 members voted for the Union to have a source of income of its own. The first enlargement took place in 1973 with the UK, Ireland and Denmark. Greece then joined in 1981 and Portugal and Spain became members with effect from 1 January 1986. On 3 October 1990, Germany was unified once again. On 7 February 1992 the Maastricht Treaty was signed which set up the European Union and on 2 May 1992 there was the signing of the treaty in Oporto setting up the European Economic Area. The European Union was established on 1 November 1993 with the entry into force of the Maastricht Treaty. On 1 January 1994 the European Economic Area was established but on 24 June 1994 treaties of accession to the European Union were signed by Austria, Finland, Norway and Sweden and on 1 January 1995, Austria, Finland and Sweden joined the European Union making it a union of 15 states. Norway continued to remain outside the Union after yet another failure to achieve ratification through a national referendum.

Each new member has on accession been given a number of years to make the transition to full membership of the EU, this transition meaning the dismantling of trade ties and tariff barriers. However, some of the outstanding applications are problematic. The economic status of the Central and East European countries applying now for membership is way below the poorest member nation. There are other tensions as well, Turkey has been waiting for years to have her membership considered as the first Muslim country to join but its non-Christian status poses a problem for German Christian Democrat politicians. At the same time, Turkey is witnessing a fast track procedure

being applied to its Central and East European neighbouring states.

The Union comprises of three separate legal entities:

*   The European Coal and Steel Community (ECSC).
*   The European Economic Community (EEC or Common Market).
*   The European Atomic Energy Community (Euratom).

It is administered and controlled by institutions common to all three: Parliament, Council of Members; Commission; Court of Justice and Court of Auditors. An Economic and Social Committee acts in an advisory capacity.

Changes resulting from the Single European Act have given Parliament the power to review certain Council decisions. Yet the Parliament is still in Strasbourg, the Members with their offices and the Commission in Brussels and their constituencies back home in their member country. Parliament has been given new powers so as to give a second reading to all legislation. Instead of being simply a 'rubber stamp' for the Commission, Parliament has the right to amend or reject proposed legislation put before it. The Council of Members also works on a slightly different basis in that now a majority is necessary rather than unanimity. This serves to streamline the functioning of the EU as a whole.

Economic size and potential of the Community

The Community has conspicuously failed so far to reduce the inequalities among its present members. Unemployment remains unacceptably high in peripheral areas. The second expansion of the EU meant taking in countries where the average GDP per head is not much over half that in the Community in general, though at purchasing parities rather more. This means any serious policy commitment on equalization of incomes requires transfers from north to south.

In population, Greece, Spain and Portugal added 21 per cent to the population of the Nine while in 1973 the UK, Denmark and Ireland added 33 per cent to the then Community of Six. However, Greece, Spain and Portugal brought no Commonwealth and fewer cheap food complications. At the same time it has to be recognized that their accession into membership comes in time of recession rather than boom, and that these three countries are poorer and therefore likely to be more onerous partners than the UK, Denmark and Ireland. Greece, Spain and

Portugal are highly competitive in traditional industries, extending in the case of Spain to steel and ships as well as textiles and leather goods. Spain and Greece are at an important stage in their industrial growth when they need to move from reliance on the traditional industries, such as textiles, to more advanced ones influenced by product innovation and specialization. Spain, which is in many ways comparable to Italy with a timelag of a few years, is well advanced in this direction, but is still relatively weak in capital goods and more complex chemicals, let alone the high technology area. Greece has much further to go; and there is general agreement that for Portugal the distance may be too great to cover without substantial aid and time. Meanwhile, Hungary, Poland, Czech Republic and Slovakia signed a treaty with the EU in December 1991 making them associate members of the Community and creating the opportunity for full membership within ten years.

Nevertheless, there are problems pending over:

- *Migrant labour*, given income differentials between the member states.
- *Agriculture* with the Mediterranean region including many underprivileged areas. There is the problem of a present wine surplus added to the fact that Spain is, too, a major wine producer. In fruit and vegetables, it is likely also that Spain and Greece will make inroads into this market which has been the preserve of Italy, France and Holland. There is, too, the question as to where Germany may buy its bananas.
- *Finance.* One could view the southern enlargement as a useful way of forcing a rich Europe to transfer large sums to the poorer states on its periphery but the unification of Germany has diverted attention away from these desirable objectives. Internally, the new Germany is trying to rebuild the economy of the newly acquired Six East German *lander* and without Germany's participation there is little likelihood of a redistribution of wealth within the Community. With regard to finance, there are a number of unknowns such as whether the problem of the Community Budget will resolve itself or whether there will be a radical realignment of the CAP but these problems have been swept aside for the moment as the pace quickens towards the unification of the Single European Market.
- *Foreign policy.* An EU policy requires uniformity and conformity. It will require all members to discipline themselves towards the aim of European unity. There will be little scope for opportunistic foreign policy on behalf of just one member state. The EU is a legal person able to conclude agreements with governments and international associations in its own right.

Exhibit 10.2   Washed up and wrung out

Twenty-five years ago, one in 50 Britons worked in the textiles and clothing industry, the largest and most concentrated in the world. The decline since then has been spectacular: a stream of bankruptcies, plant closures and redundancies.

Yet, the sector has clung on. Indeed, it still employs more than 400,000 people. Even more surprisingly, it remains the UK's fifth largest manufacturing activity.

On the stock market, though, it has been nearly annihilated. Textiles and clothing companies were the worst performing sector last year and now account for less than 0.3 per cent of the total market value of London shares.

Part of the reason is that some companies have ceased to exist and part is because the largest of the survivors, which dominate the stock market sector, have performed so badly for so long. Size offers few economies of scale in this business. And although a handful of companies have managed to buck the declining trend, they tend to be small, privately-owned and nimble.

Profit margins of around 5 per cent of sales may not look too bad. But the return on capital of the major quoted companies has been running at below 6 per cent on average – less than the return on gilts, which carry no risk. And periodic write-offs appear endemic. It hardly adds up to an appealing investment proposition.

Why are the former giants struggling? There are several explanations: one is that the economics of today's textile business do not favour large, high-cost concerns based in industrialised nations and run by highly-paid professional managers. These companies cannot compete on price with cheap-labour, bulk-producing rivals based in the emerging economies. Nor can they compete with their smaller European rivals when it comes to design flair and flexibility.

Another is that the one major retailer which has stayed loyal to its British suppliers, Marks & Spencer, is driving an increasingly hard bargain.

The European textile industry is dominated by small, private businesses these days. The fact that Britain still retains a large number of sizeable quoted companies is, essentially, an anomaly: many

→ **Exhibit 10.2** *continued*

are relics of its industrial past, unwilling to steer a new course despite changing economic circumstances.

In this regard, the most significant feature has been the proliferation of competitors in countries with low labour costs. These are more than 20 times higher in the UK than in Bangladesh, Pakistan, India, Sri Lanka, Indonesia or China. And, in textiles and clothing, labour can account for up to 30 per cent of total costs.

There is no hope of closing this gap in costs through economies of scale, since the industry requires very little capital. To flourish in the UK, producers need to play to different strengths – and their key advantage is proximity to their market.

Clothing retailers do most of their ordering months in advance. But, to re-order rapidly, it is far more convenient to use a nearby producer than one based thousands of miles away.

Sophisticated computer systems let local manufacturers know a particular garment has been sold as soon as their retailer customers log it past the cash till. The signal allows them both to send new stock to the customer promptly and to divert their own production to whatever lines are selling well.

Moreover, UK manufacturers are much better placed than those elsewhere to keep track of the nation's tastes in fashion, casual wear and working clothes. And they can also benefit from the country's strong tradition of good design schools and courses, which turn out a new crop of talent each year.

Add these advantages together and the blueprint for success is for a firm to concentrate on producing small runs, quickly, and with an inherent design premium. Of these factors, design comes first, be it as Speedo swimwear or a Burberry mac or a cashmere jumper. In Britain, as elsewhere, the future belongs to the small, nippy firms already dominant on the Continent.

The main reason the UK still has large, traditional textile companies is Marks & Spencer. But although St Michael is their saviour, some are beginning to feel he drives too hard a bargain.

Nowhere else in the world is a retailer as powerful, or as crucial to a particular sector, as the UK's leading high street clothing chain. M&S accounts for one-third of knitwear sales in Britain and a higher proportion still for other clothing, such as underwear. Most of the rest, sold by rivals, is imported from low-cost countries.

But where M&S has for years been given credit for aiding the survival of a UK production base, there are those who now charge it with distorting, and even crippling, its supplier industry.

Because it pays its bills so quickly, suppliers can slash their working capital, boost their stock turn and lift their return on capital. In recent times, though, it has become more and more inflexible over the prices it is willing to pay. In the past two years, this has been particularly hard for suppliers who have faced steep price rises for their raw materials.

Different M&S suppliers have found different answers to the price squeeze. Courtaulds Textiles, for instance, has gained leverage in the price negotiations by boosting its own size. The company, which is M&S's largest supplier, houses a clutch of otherwise unrelated businesses.

Others have moved their production sites offshore, heading for low-cost zones on the European fringes. Certainly, this cuts costs – but not to the level of competitors based entirely in such regions, and perhaps at the expense of other competitive advantages such as quality and speed of response.

Textiles offer no certainties to the private investor. Since the sector is in structural decline, spotting winners requires an eye for the extraordinary. But some of the smaller, more innovative companies do look interesting.

It is harder to be enthusiastic about the large, household name businesses. Some analysts argue that the sector looks modestly valued on yardsticks such as price/earnings ratios and dividend yields. Others warn that the industry has plenty to be modest about.

Source: Financial Times

Marketing by population concentration: the 'Golden Triangle'

Over three-fifths of the Community population and of its GNP are found in a comparatively small area outlined in Figure 10.3, which is some five to six times better off than some outlying areas of the Community. This is obviously of interest to companies geared towards the mass market. Most important languages within the EU are English and French. Radio Luxembourg broadcasts in both of these languages plus others as well, to an audience which encompasses nearly all the inhabitants of the most populous and wealthy conurbations forming the 'Golden Triangle'. Most of this region is now also covered by satellite television increasing the

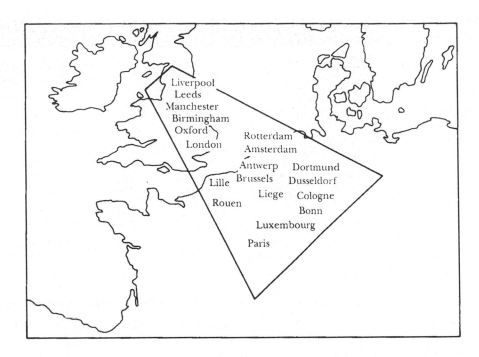

Source: Drew, J. (1983) *Doing Business in the European Community*, 2nd edn, Butterworths, London, p. 83

Figure 10.3   The Golden Triangle of the EC

possibilities for standardization of advertising even further, provided the member states and their peoples will accept it.

From a British perspective, this so-called Golden Triangle could well be challenged for including within it Leeds, Liverpool, Manchester and Birmingham, all of which are industrial cities which have 'peaked', most noticeably Liverpool. The most affluent areas are in London and the South of England. Hence the talk of a North/South divide within Britain. Liverpool has had very high levels of unemployment relative to any other city since the mid-1970s. Its industrial base has been much eroded as has its port which now only handles a fraction of the tonnage which it used to know. Leeds and Manchester are slightly different. Both have suffered from the slump in the world textile trade while Birmingham, being more dependent on the automobile industry, has perhaps suffered slightly less than the rest of this group, all of whom are struggling manfully to recover from a recession with declining industries.

Regional variation within the Community

The free movement of capital, goods, services and individuals within the Community will have some regional implications. Doubtless there will be a reallocation of resources within the Community as a result, some resources being diverted from one region to another while still new ones are created. There are some important implications here.

The disparity between the regions is not only self-evident but has come to the attention of the EU. The Single European Act commits the Community to a policy of cohesion and convergence towards the regions. The European Regional Development Fund (ERDF) founded in 1975 received new powers towards that end on 1 January 1989. Previously, as much as two-thirds of the Community budget went on agricultural subsidies. The other area of EU funding is the Social Fund.

All households which have less than 50 per cent of the equivalent mean national expenditure are considered to be below the poverty line. In 1988 this then meant 18 million households or just under 52 million people, three-quarters of whom lived in Germany, Italy, France and the UK, although the real divide is between Northern and Southern Europe. In Northern Europe fewer than one household in ten is disadvantaged whereas the number is one is five in Greece, Italy and Portugal (Eurostat, 1995). Regional assistance is therefore important in the realization of a single market and so to this end there are four structural funds which have been created.

European Union social policy

There are specific rights built into the Treaty of Rome, notably the fundamental right for

Community workers to live and work in the Member State of their choice, to improve their social protection and to help the unemployed retrain for jobs. The Community therefore created the European Social Fund to promote the geographical and occupational mobility of workers and the 1989 Community Charter of Fundamental Social Rights for Workers, known as the Social Charter, which has 12 principles:

1. The right to work in the EU country of one's choice.
2. The freedom to choose an occupation and the right to a fair wage.
3. The right to improved living and working conditions.
4. The right to social protection under prevailing national systems.
5. The right to freedom of association and collective bargaining.

6. The right to vocational training.
7. The right of men and women to equal treatment.
8. The right of workers to information, consultation and participation.
9. The right to health protection and safety at work.
10. The protection of children and adolescents.
11. A decent standard of living for older people.
12. Improved social and professional integration for disabled people.

The European Social Fund is the main Community tool for developing human resources and improving the workings of the labour market throughout the Community.

European Union regional policy

Levels of economic development, living standards and unemployment vary enormously

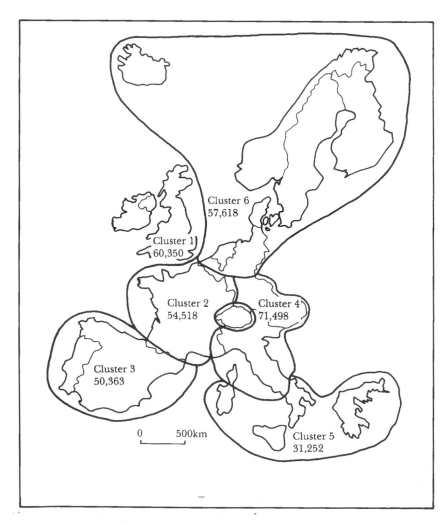

Note: Figures are for 1990 and in 000's of people.
Source: Ryans, J. K., and Rau, P. A. (1990) *Marketing Strategies for New Europe: A North American Perspective on 1992*, American Marketing Association, Chicago

Figure 10.4   The six clusters and their population (based on EU of 12)

across the European Community. The Community is pledged to reducing regional disparities in the longer term and so not surprisingly then, the Community's regional policy now accounts for more than a third of its budget. The European Investment Bank channels support through four main structural funds: the European Social Fund (ESF), which concentrates on vocational training and unemployment; the European Regional Development Fund (ERDF), which assists particularly poor regions by focusing on encouraging investment, infrastructure and small businesses; the European Agricultural Guidance and Guarantee Fund (EAGGF), which provides financing for farmers and area adapting to new forms of agriculture or developing new forms of industry; the Financial Instrument for Fisheries

Guidance (FIFG), which helps coastal towns affected by the decline of the fishing industry. A fine example of economic restructuring is provided by examining Ireland's membership of the EU and how through EU transfers and resultant high productivity gains, Ireland's economy has been able to overtake the UK economy (according to 1997 OECD but not EU statistics).

Decision-making bodies

These are the European Commission; European Parliament; Economic and Social Committee; Council of Members and European Court of Justice. The Commission is divided into 23 Directorate-Generals which are headed by 20 Commissioners.

Table 10.2   The six clusters and their characteristics

Cluster 1: UK and Ireland
* Northeastern Europe
* Average income ($11,450)
* Age profiles average of EC
* Common language (English)

Cluster 2: Central and Northern France, Southern Belgium, Central Germany, and Luxembourg
* Central Europe
* Average income ($15,470)
* Low proportion of middle-aged people and high proportion of older people
* French and German languages

Cluster 3: Spain and Portugal
* Southwestern Europe
* Young population
* Lower than average income ($6,530)
* Spanish and Portuguese languages

Cluster 4: Southern Germany, Northern Italy, Southeastern France (and Austria if it joins)
* Central Europe
* High proportion of middle-aged people
* Higher than average income ($16,740)
* German, French, and Italian languages

Cluster 5: Greece and Southern Italy
* Southeastern Europe
* Lower than average income ($7,610)
* Young population
* Greek and Italian languages

Cluster 6: Denmark, Northern Germany, The Netherlands, and Northern Belgium (and Switzerland, Iceland, Sweden, Norway, Finland if they join)
* Northern Europe and Switzerland
* Very high income ($19,420)
* High proportion of middle-aged people
* Multilingual: Scandinavian, French, Italian, and German languages

Note: Instead of viewing this as one market with a single area of affluence and relative degrees of poverty, Ryans and Rau (1990) identify six consumer clusters within this Community, each of which transcends national boundaries.
Source: Ryans, J. K., and Rau, P. A. (1990) *Marketing Strategies for the New Europe: A North American Perspective on 1992.* American Marketing Association, Chicago

In addition, there are said to be 2,000 committees, sub-committees and working parties. In normal practice, the Commission would also consult where appropriate with COPA, the grouping of agricultural organizations and with UNICE, the industrial association.

Commissioners are appointed by the member governments for a once-renewable four-year term, and are resident in Brussels. The main duty with which they are entrusted is to make proposals for Community action to the Council of Ministers. The President and Vice-President are chosen from among the 20 and hold their offices for four-year renewable terms. The UK, Germany, France, Spain and Italy each nominate two Commissioners while the other states nominate one each.

Each Commissioner is responsible for a portfolio, although some will carry more than one portfolio. Each has a private office (cabinet) to which he makes the appointments. Invariably, the members appointed are of the same nationality as the Commissioner. His deputy is known as the *chef du cabinet*. Beneath the Commissioner, there will be one or more Director General – similar to the permanent head of a ministry – who is responsible for a broad policy area, and he will, in turn, have below him, Directors and Heads of Division. The need for Commissioners to be impartial at all times is enshrined in the Treaty of Rome, Article 157, which requires that Commissioners 'shall neither seek nor take instruction from any Government or from any other body.' However, as the Commission staff only employs 11,000 (including translators, interpreters and some 2,600 in the separate scientific and technological Joint Research Centre) as against perhaps 20,000 for a British Ministry it is not hard to see that the Commission can only hope to be effective if the governmental departments of its member states agree to administer its policies. If the Commissioners approve of the draft directive drawn up by a Directorate-General, after any necessary amendments, it is then proposed by the Commission as a draft directive to the Council of Ministers. This gives member states, through the Council of Ministers, the final say on whether the directive becomes law or not. It can, however, take years before legislation is accepted and becomes law. Curiously, the Single European Act gave an impetus to the Commission to resolve 286 obstacles to the proposed Single Market.

The Council of Ministers consists of a minister from each member-state government, and the ministers change according to the subjects on the agenda and the Council meeting taking place, e.g., Agricultural Council; Social Affairs Council where the appropriate number from each member state would be present. Ministers represent the interests of their own governments, but try to arrive at agreements which are in the Community interest.

The Council of Ministers meets only for a certain number of days in a year, and are not resident in Brussels. Each member state takes a six-month turn to chair Council meetings, a national minister of foreign affairs being President of the Council during that period. There is a small

---

Exhibit 10.3   Suggested business EuroEnglish

The European Union Commissioners have announced that agreement has been reached to adopt English as the preferred language for European communications, rather than German, which was the other possibility. As part of the negotiations, Her Majesty's Government conceded that English spelling had some room for improvement and has accepted a five-year phased plan for what will be known as EuroEnglish (Euro for short).

In the first year, 's' will be used instead of the soft 'c'. Sertainly, sivil servants will resieve this news with joy. Also, the hard 'c' will be replaced with a 'k'. Not only will this klear up konfusion, but typewriters kan have one less letter.

There will be growing publik enthusiasm in the sekond year, when the troublesome 'ph' will be replaced by 'f'. This will make words like 'fotograf' 20 per cent shorter.

In the third year, publik akseptanse of the new spelling kan be expekted to reach the stage where more komplikated changes are possible. Governments will enkorage the removal of double letters, which have always ben a deterent to akurate speling. Also, al wil agre that the horible mes of silent 'e's in the languag is disgrasful, and they would go.

By the fourth year, peopl wil be reseptiv to steps such as replasing 'th' by 'z' and 'w' by 'v'.

During ze fifz year, ze unesesary 'o' kan be dropd from vords kontaining 'ou', and similar changes vud of kors be aplid to ozer kombinations of leters. After zis fifz yer, ve vil hav a reli sensibl riten styl. Zer vilbe no mor trubls or difikultis and evrirvun vil find it ezi tu understand ech ozer.

Ze drem vil finali kum tru.

(Alleged source: Internet Daily News, Brussels)

Exhibit 10.4 EU legislation from start to finish (directives and regulations)

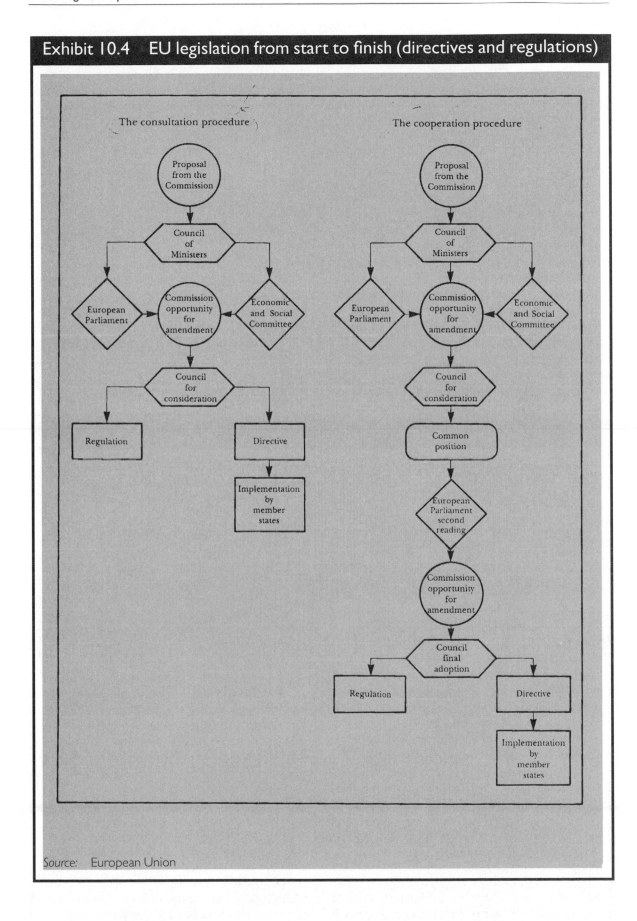

Source: European Union

permanent staff in Brussels but the main preparatory work is undertaken by the ambassadors and their embassy staff.

The ambassadors or representatives act as a link between the member countries and the Community. They meet in the Committee of Permanent Representatives known as COREPER. Over time, COREPER has become an important entity in its own right. The staff of COREPER are made up of civil servants seconded from their own government and experts. They service working parties, prepare agendas, and try to agree non-contentious proposals so that when the ministers attend much has already been agreed and only matters still in dispute need to be negotiated.

The European Council is a meeting of the heads of government and takes place three times per year. Contentious issues which have not been resolved at the Council of Ministers are discussed in the European Council. At the end of each Council, a communiqué is issued giving the broad outlines of what has been agreed. Scope

for progress exists as the heads of governments are often also heads of state in certain cases. If the political will also exists for agreement to take place, then the Council is capable of meeting this challenge. Margaret Thatcher when in power tested the efficacy of this system on more than one occasion over the issue of British payments to the EU budget and the nature of European unity whether federal with sovereign governments or a full economic and monetary union with significant sovereign powers to be transferred to Brussels.

The Court of Justice is the ultimate interpreter of the treaties on which the EU is based and the final arbiter of disputes concerning secondary legislation whenever there is a query or disagreement about the meaning of a particular regulation, directive, or decision. Its rulings are binding and take precedence over the decisions of national courts. Each member state is represented by a judge. It is situated in Luxembourg with a staff of 460 and is totally different from the European Court of Human Rights in

Exhibit 10.5   Brussels loses battle over car spare parts

The European Commission yesterday lost its long battle to reduce the dominance of big car manufacturers in the European market for car spare parts.

A Commission proposal that independent part manufacturers be allowed to reproduce freely car spares such as bumpers, windscreens, door panels and lamps, provided they pay a 'fair and reasonable' royalty to the car manufacturers, was dropped from a directive aimed at harmonising national laws on the protection of designs.

Ministers from member states rejected the proposal, following fierce lobbying by the car industry which enjoys a monopoly on the reproduction of spare parts in some member states and a dominant position in most.

'The council has missed a chance to set a clear standard which would apply for the whole territory of the Union and ensure the proper functioning of the single market in the field of designs,' Mr Mario Monti, single market commissioner, said. The consequence of yesterday's decision is that it will be up to member states to decide how far to liberalise the market for car repair parts.

This means independent suppliers in countries such as Britain, which liberalised the market for spares several years ago, will not be able to sell their products in countries such as France, where the market is almost entirely the preserve of car manufacturers.

Representatives of spare parts makers,

furious about the decision, said the outcome of yesterday's meeting would not even preserve the status quo; it would allow countries which at present permit some competition to extend the monopoly of car producers.

'The Council's decision excludes spare body parts from the benefits of the single market,' said ECAR, the body representing independent producers and insurance companies.

'Once again, the council has shown a cynical disregard for the interests of consumers and small and medium-sized enterprises which are no match when pitted against the protectionist demands of Europe's corporate interests.'

Car manufacturers argue it is only fair they receive protection against the reproduction of car spare parts, the design of which requires much time and investment. They also say that allowing them exclusive rights of reproduction sets higher safety standards.

In countries where a monopoly exists, consumers have to return to the manufacturer to replace a smashed wing mirror or broken window. In Britain, any independent supplier can do the job.

The UK voted in favour of the general proposal but a government official said yesterday the UK shared the Commission's regret that the council was unable to agree harmonised provisions relating to the repair of spare parts.

Source: Financial Times, 14 March 1997

Strasbourg which is part of the Council of Europe. It arose out of the European Coal and Steel Community (ECSC) but now has a much wider brief. There are 11 judges, each appointed for six years. Hearings are in public but deliberations are in secret. A judge can only be removed by the unanimous vote of his colleagues to the effect that he is no longer capable of carrying out his duties. A quorum consists of seven judges; there must be an odd number sitting and decisions are reached by simple majority. The Court produces its own reports containing the basic facts of the case, the summing up by the Advocate-General, and the judgement. Companies on whom the Commission has imposed fines may appeal to the Court. The Court also gives preliminary rulings for the benefit of national courts. It may proceed against member states if a member state is not fulfilling its legal obligations. It reviews the legality of Community acts, and it settles disputes.

The European Court set a precedent in May 1985 when it gave a ruling against the Council of Ministers, finding them guilty of breaching the Treaty of Rome by failing to ensure freedom to provide transport services across the Community. The complaint has been made by the European Parliament supported by the Commission and it establishes for the first time that the Parliament can take the Council to court. It will be seen by parliamentarians as opening a new door to extending their influence over Community politics and policies. It was not an unqualified success, however. The Court did not support the contention of the European Parliament that the Council was at fault for failing to agree a common transport policy. The Court said that the Council had failed to take measures to comply with the Treaty of Rome which stipulated that freedom of services should be established within the twelve-year transitional period after the Treaty signature in 1957. It is a moral victory for the Parliament although impossible to enforce. The Council has been told that it is its duty to agree, but it can hardly be forced to do so. The Council therefore remains free to deal with most of the Commission's 14 pending specific training proposals as it pleases. The Court did not accept the view of Advocate-General Lenz that the Council had a duty to reach a decision on such proposals as the weights and measurements of heavy goods vehicles, co-ordination of taxation of such vehicles, and harmonization of social measures in inland shipping. Nor did the Court accept the Dutch Government's proposal that it should transform freedom of transport services from a Treaty objective into directly applicable law, enforceable in national courts.

The European Parliament was greatly strengthened by the Single Act which previously only voted on money. It now had power to initiate legislation: amend or reject legislation rather than just give opinions as before. It still does not have an executive dependent on it and its power applies to the Commission not the Council.

Exhibit 10.6   Airbus is the model which could set Europe flying high

Germany is again expected to help pull the European economy out of the doldrums. But if European governments put as much goodwill into common policy making as they do into aircraft making, their economies – and employment – would be quicker to benefit.

Exports are leading a recovery in Germany, but job creation lags way behind as employers prefer overtime to hiring new staff. Unemployment is especially severe in the eastern *Länder* at just less than 16 per cent of the workforce, compared with 10.8 per cent for the country as a whole.

With the construction boom over in the east of the country, long-term problems such as an ageing population and low productivity are again coming to the fore. In the early 1990s the east German economy grew at a heady pace of close to 10 per cent each year. Last year growth slowed to only 2 per cent, and stagnation or even recession beckon further down the road after the meagre growth of 1 per cent projected for this year.

This background makes it difficult to rescind the 'solidarity' tax surcharge that was re-introduced in 1995 to help rebuild the eastern *Länder*. But, with a general election due in 18 months, taxation and the fiscal constraints of the Maastricht monetary union criteria are beginning to cause considerable strain between Chancellor Helmut Kohl and his coalition partners.

At first the cost of re-uniting Germany was met through a borrowing spree on the markets rather than higher taxes. Partly as a result, Germany's deficit and debt ratios today remain outside the Maastricht criteria and little improvement is expected this year. If monetary union had already taken place, Germany would fall foul of the stringent terms of the budget stability pact agreed last month in Dublin, at its own instigation. Would Germany's partners in a single currency accept

➡

→ **Exhibit 10.6** *continued*

that, six years on, reunification was one of those 'exceptional circumstances' which allow a country to escape the pact's sanctions?

Beyond Germany's paradoxical predicament, this example also highlights the shortcomings of European economic policy making. All the European Union seems to manage to achieve, usually with much effort, is the occasional arrangement to reduce some of the damage which national currency, interest rate and budget policies may cause to other EU countries.

But proposals for a more positive type of joint policy action are typically met with extreme suspicion and reluctance. Those put forward by EU president Jacques Santer over jobs, or more recently by France over stronger fiscal co-ordination, are good examples. The Treaty of Rome was signed 40 years ago, but this is still a 'union' where governments prefer to go it alone because the benefits of stimulative policies at home may spill over to other member countries!

As we discuss below, France argues that after monetary union, policy co-ordination through a 'stability council' of finance ministers will be in order. It stresses the need to counterbalance both the monetary power of the independent European central bank and the US's dollar policies. This is the rhetoric. But Germany is recognising that a stability council can help to bring about the common political spirit that is needed if monetary union is to succeed in the long term. The proposal would be in keeping with the key rationale of European co-operation, whereby countries agree to common disciplines because they will become stronger as a whole.

As the US showed over the past decade, better and more dynamic co-ordination of credit and budget policies are effective weapons against stagnation and high unemployment. European governments could achieve the same result, but they seem content to agree on collective discipline, while stopping short of launching common initiatives and joint positive action. This is why the public ends up feeling that the rules, regulations and policies emanating from Brussels make them vulnerable instead of protecting them.

Against this dismal background the example of the Airbus civil aircraft consortium seems to show the way forward. Thanks to the stronger legal structure agreed on 13 January by its British, French, German and Spanish shareholders, Airbus will be better placed to face US competition in the global aircraft market. Why can this success story not be extended to wider areas of European business?

The Single European Act and the Maastricht treaty provide the legal basis for ambitious, joint structural programmes in vital areas that will shape the future of European industry. But the competition policies in the Treaty of Rome tend to stand in the way, giving governments convenient pretexts for inaction and avoidance.

Europe's founding fathers were right to stress the positive role of market competition during postwar reconstruction, when governments controlled most of Europe's economy. Today the need to ensure that no firm can secure an overly dominant position in the single market cannot be denied. But in the future there is an even greater need for positive European action and co-operation within the global market. Action and vision from political leaders are required if Europe is to take off as Airbus has.

Source: The European, 16–22 January 1997, p. 18

Until 1981 the European Parliament held one-third of its sessions in Luxembourg and two-thirds in Strasbourg, in Eastern France. In 1981, it decided to hold no more sessions in Luxembourg, and this was upheld by the Court of Justice. However, more than three-quarters of the Parliamentary secretariat of approximately 2,600 are based in Luxembourg which means that they have to travel between Luxembourg and Strasbourg regularly but in the longer term it is most likely that the European Parliament will be based in Brussels. The first direct elections to the European Parliament were held in June 1979 and every five years thereafter. It is the only directly elected institution of the Community. There are now 518 members of the European Parliament who control 18 important permanent commit-

tees which scrutinize Commission proposals and prepare reports. They have a consultative role in proposals emanating from the Commission and ultimately have the right to dismiss the government, i.e., the Commissioners, provided over half the members vote. They also have the right to request changes within the European Community budget allocation, and may even reject the budget as a whole. They vote on European laws sent from the Commission to the Council of Ministers and have the right to approve new members of the Community or new association agreements with outsiders.

The Economic and Social Committee is purely consultative. Its membership is appointed for four years. Its membership is wide:

producers; workers; farmers; merchants; the professions; universities; consumer organizations; transport operators; or any appropriate interest group. Its members are selected by the Council from lists submitted by member states.

No particular importance is assigned to its role. Its functions are more like an in-house opinion poll for the Council and Commission. Its decisions are reached in open debate in full sessions rather than by lobbying.

Exhibit 10.7 Single market double-speak

As European finance ministers meet in Dublin this week to hammer out a stability pact for a single currency, a critical audit carried out by officials in Brussels has revealed that the Single Market, a key cornerstone of European integration, is less than semi-operational almost four years after it was ushered in with a fanfare.

The 'four freedoms' – free movement of persons, goods, services and capital – are still held hostage to national protectionism, with Brussels blaming governments for not implementing Commission directives speedily enough as well as stalling on other key areas (see table below).

rushing to implement Single Market legislation. Some countries blame recent weak growth on the internal market while others, such as the UK, have used Europe's rules as a political weapon, claiming 'Brussels is stifling us'.

Hans-Dietrich Genscher, former German deputy chancellor, counters the sceptics: 'If the Single Market had not been in place, the effects of recession would have been more sharply felt.'

But, as far as Britain is concerned it appears to be doing well out of the Single Market. According to the Economist, Germany buys more British goods than the whole of the US; Holland takes

Free movement of persons

x Convention on the crossing of eternal frontiers – stalled by the UK – Spanish dispute over Gibraltar
x Trans-European networks to link all corners of the EU – many projects, postponed due to funding problems
✓ The right for citizens to work or study in any EU member state

Free movement of goods

x Definitive VAT regime – still being discussed
x Competition between similar goods from different member states should create lower uniform prices – important price differentials still exist in many cases
✓ EU legislation on product liability and safety to protect consumers

Free movement of services

✓ Citizens may now choose their insurance policies from across the EU
x Any company has the right to offer its services in any member state – complaints brought every year show national rules still get around this
x The cost of mailing a letter anywhere in the EU should be the same – newcomers Austria, Finland and Sweden are still not included

Free movement of capital

✓ Individuals may have a bank account in any EU country
x No bar to money transfers between member states – all legal limits are gone but the commission says bank charges are often prohibitive
✓ Consumers can borrow money anywhere in the EU

According to 'Eurostat' figures, the Single Market is only 43 per cent operational. 'It is still an imperfect reality, with numerous hurdles and obstacles that hinder intra-Community trade,' said Jose-Maria Cuevas, president of Spain's Confederation of Employers' Organisations.

In particular, issues such as public procurement and investment services have not been completely opened up. Also, ministers are accused of stalling plans to harmonise VAT rates as well as establishing a common European company statute and rolling back their borders.

After the first wave of enthusiasm in 1992, national governments have been highly selective in

more than China and the 'tiger economies' of the Far East; even Sweden's 'backing Britain' policy is more profitable than the whole of Latin America; while sales to the Irish are more than to Canada, Australia, New Zealand and South Africa combined.

Despite this, British industry is still sceptical about the Single Market's rewards: 62 per cent of companies replied 'It doesn't help us much' to a 1996 Commission survey.

Sure, there are problems. VAT rates are all over the place, ranging from 15 per cent – 25 per cent; most countries still apply 'local' manufacturing rules (sometimes for dubious safety reasons)

→ Exhibit 10.7 *continued*

that favour their own companies; hefty bank charges across the EU cut deep into tight profit margins; service industries in particular hit a brick wall when pursuing new horizons.

'Fudge' is the word when national governments think it necessary to protect their own. Cuevas cites German distribution companies that will only handle goods bound for the shops packed in 'special' reusable collapsible boxes (Ifco). This might sound admirable, until it turns out that Ifcos are exclusively produced in Germany.

Even the Danes have a lot of bottle as cans of McEwans are ruled out of order. According to the Association of European Producers of Steel for Packaging, Denmark has a long standing ban on steel and aluminium cans for beer and soft drinks. As a result, getting into Denmark's markets means separate packaging for many.

However, the European Commission – defender of the EU's Treaties – was itself reluctant to criticise a serious breach of Single Market rules. The French lorry blockade restricted the free movement of goods, people and services, with thousands of citizens and companies affected. Brussels's president, Jacques Santer, told journalists that this was a 'social issue', an internal problem for France to sort out. Under the Single Market rules however, the courts should look on damages claims favourably.

But Brussels has gone pro-active. Last week, it launched the £20m 'Citizens First' initiative. It is the brainchild of Brussels Commissioner Mario Monti. Currently, 80 per cent of people are ill-informed about their rights as EU citizens – in particular the right to travel, live and work unhindered in any EU member state.

'Public awareness of the internal market is the best way to improve this situation', says Monti. He wants to reverse the statistics by giving people the facts. This year he is concentrating on 'working in another country' and in 1997, the programme will also cover cross-border shopping and safety at work. Those countries helping him out with the big launch are laying on seminars, trade fares and exhibitions. Britain and Denmark are not participating in the Citizens First festivities, but the free services will be on offer.

As from now, there is a permanent 'information on demand' service. Any Scot with a query can dial Freefone 0800 581 591 for help and advice. Brussels also has one of Europe's biggest World Wide Web sights on the Europa Server *http://citizens.eu.imt*). Guides and fact sheets about working on the continent are also available – in English and Gaelic.

Source: Scotland on Sunday, 8 December 1996, p. 4

A market without frontiers

Colchester and Buchan (1990) have illustrated from their research which businesses are likely to be 'Euro-homogeneous' and which are likely to be 'national-distributive'. They differentiate first in terms of value-added. High value-added with either a company or a rich individual as customer means a product area can be branded and distributed across Europe without, as they say, an urgent need for local skills, local investment and local adaptation of the product. On the other hand, the cheaper the product, the closer to the customer, the more investment is required in local understanding, local product variation and local distribution.

Yet frontiers also provide obstacles to trafficking in drugs; they prevent undesirable aliens and others including rabid dogs from entering the country; they help to counter terrorism and collect taxes. National police forces do not have powers as yet to cross frontiers traditionally regarded as inviolate.

The frontiers will be down for those within the Community. The question then arises of treatment of those without. Fears have been expressed of a Fortress Europe if protectionism were to hold sway in the event of a recession. These fears are discussed later in considering the views of those entering the EU from outside.

Harmonization measures for internal trade

The significance of 1992 is seen in Table 10.3 creating a new market greater than the USA or Japan which would streamline the efficiency of what is already the world's single largest trading bloc.

The White Paper of June 1985 spelled out 286 actions required to complete the internal market. The White Paper then is like an eight year plan which was the intention of President Jacques Delors, that it would take the time of two full Commissions to complete the internal market i.e., eight years. Delors was reappointed for a second term of office and has been the only President as yet to receive that distinction. Proposals

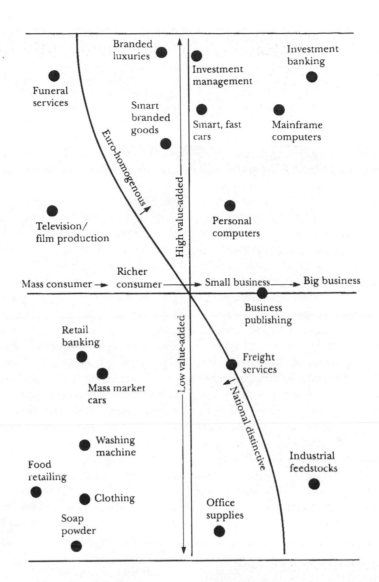

Source: Colchester, N., and Buchan, D. (1990) *Europower*, Economist Books and Random House, New York

Figure 10.5   The Colchester–Buchan diagram

had to be drafted in legal form to become Community law but had also to be ratified by the individual member states. The three broad headings under which the changes were required:

- physical barriers,
- technical barriers, and
- fiscal barriers.

The main incentive was not only standardization and simplification of trade procedures but to certain politicians the inherent appeal of free market forces to work within Europe. This had tangible benefits as Cecchini was to point to the actual costs of maintaining present systems with overladen bureaucracy. Cecchini pointed to the costs of administration as being 7.5 billion ECUs

Table 10.3   What the single market of 1992 created:

- Creation of European industrial standards
- Opening of public procurement markets
- Harmonization of company law
- Liberalization of services sector
- Freeing of capital movement
- Intellectual property law
- Approximation of indirect taxes
- Abolition of borders

(approximately = US $1). Freeing these markets of burdensome administration would mean savings for business and greater competition as well. Member governments were therefore given carte blanche to wield the axe at any expenditure of this kind and at the same time

receive widespread public acclaim for so doing. Another area was the potential price savings if price differentials were to be smoothed over the Community. Pharmaceuticals, telephones and motor vehicles were a few of the items selected for scrutiny.

Exhibit 10.8   EU hopes to put freight back on track

A shipment of steel coils bound from the Netherlands for Italy by train involves crossing three borders – into Germany, Switzerland and Italy. At each, there is a wait of several hours while customs and other paperwork is completed.

Incompatible signalling and power systems, differences in safety procedures and changes of crews and locomotives at each border reduce high-speed trains to a crawl.

A project for freight 'expresses' and European rail freight 'freeways' could provide the answer to the panoply of problems associated with moving goods by rail through Europe.

Some observers doubt whether Europe's fragmented railways can meet an ambitious timetable for rapid freight expresses by early next year. But executives from the railway companies

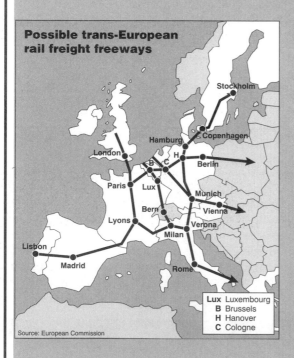

Possible trans-European rail freight freeways

Lux Luxembourg
B Brussels
H Hanover
C Cologne

Source: European Commission

believe it can be done and European transport ministers are expected in June to approve the first freeway between either Hamburg or Rotterdam and Milan.

The railways believe that by giving priority to freight on the freeways, simplifying border controls and establishing a uniform means of charging

for timetable 'slots', average speeds could be raised and rail could win back some of the market lost to road. Between 1970 and 1994 rail lost half of its freight market share, falling from 32 to 16 per cent of the total.

The European transport commissioner, Mr Neil Kinnock, who launched the freight freeways project last July, sees them as part of a revitalised European railway network which is commercially viable and no longer dependent on big government subsidies.

The Community of European Railways (CER), which groups European Union members, Norway and Switzerland, last week presented its proposals for implementing Mr Kinnock's plan, including a network of 16 freight routes. It suggested the creation of 'one-stop shops' to put together packages of prices, timetable 'slots' and service levels for customers.

The freeways would encourage shippers to move goods by rail, leaving road haulage to provide the short initial and final stages of the journey. This would benefit the environment and Europe's congested road network.

Combined transport or 'intermodal shipments' – involving road combined with rail movements of goods – are among the fastest growing areas of freight for many European railways. In France they account for 25 per cent of rail freight volumes while in the UK the opening of the Channel tunnel has made possible long-distance intermodal shipments to and from the Continent.

But formidable obstacles must be overcome. These include:

• The poor profitability of intermodal shipments. Intermodal transport is subsidised throughout Europe with, on average, journey lengths of 300km–500km necessary for even variable costs to be covered, according to Mr Helmut Draxler, director general of Austrian Railways and head of the CER's freeways project group.

Rail terminals require large and steady volumes of business to operate economically and there are relatively few routes where these conditions apply, warned

→ Exhibit 10.8 *continued*

Mr Stig Larsson, president of Swedish Railways.

The road haulage industry, with far lower infrastructure costs, sets the prices which rail must match. And while long-distance road haulage costs have fallen by 25 per cent in the past 25 years the cost of the short road movements to and from rail-heads have risen by 200 per cent, making intermodal shipments even less viable.

Many in the rail industry rest their hopes on a EU initiative to make all modes of transport, road as well as rail, bear the full costs, environmental and otherwise, of their activities.

But a study carried out for the European Conference of Ministers of Transport, which is meeting in Berlin this week, suggests the outcome may not be as favourable to rail because rail freight operators do not currently cover all their infrastructure costs.

- The deregulation of the European road haulage industry, which has brought down road haulage costs. Increases in the size of trucks allowed on Europe's roads, a move away from levying road taxes according to the distance travelled to a fixed charge

'vignette' and lax enforcement of violations such as overloading have all made life more difficult for rail.

- The insensitivity of many state-owned rail administrations to the concerns of freight customers. 'International links leave a lot to be desired,' said Mr Jacques Reinquin, logistics director in France for Hoechst, the German chemicals group. 'There needs to be more respect for timetables, and information to customers on the progress of shipments is insufficient.'

The automatic tracking of rail wagons, using lineside bar code readers or satellite positioning, is needed so that the railways and their customers know where a consignment is.

The US, where double-stacked container trains move cargoes over thousands of miles, is sometimes advanced as the model for European freight. But this ignores the shorter distances in Europe, the competition for timetable 'slots' with passenger services and the restrictions on double-stacking imposed by overhead rail power lines.

Source: Financial Times, 22 April 1997

Yet another but more contentious area is that of public procurement which Cecchini estimated as being worth 15 per cent of Community GDP in 1986. Discounting that portion which falls outside contracted procedures, Cecchini pointed to a sizeable market of 240–340 billion ECUs, equivalent to 7–10 per cent of Community GDP. Cost savings of 8–19 billion ECUs for the five countries surveyed in 1984: Belgium, France, Germany, Italy and the UK would arise from:

Table 10.4   A typology of costs – resulting from divergent standards and regulations

For companies
- duplication of product development
- loss of potential economies of manufacturing scale
- competitive weakness on world markets and vulnerability on European markets as companies operate from a narrow national base

For public authorities
- duplication of certification and testing costs
- not getting value for money in public purchasing, whose non-competitive nature is often reinforced by national standards and certification

For consumers
- direct costs borne by companies and governments means higher prices
- direct and larger losses due to industry's competitive weakness and inefficient structure

Source: Cecchini, P. (1988) The European Challenge: 1992 – The Benefits of a Single Market, Wildwood House, Aldershot, Hants.

1.   The static trade effect meaning public
      authorities buying from the cheaper (i.e.,
      foreign) suppliers (3–8 billion
      ECUs)
2.   The competition effect creating a downward
      pressure on prices charged by domestic firms
      in previously closed sectors to strive to com-
      pete with foreign companies entering the
      market (1–3 billion ECU).
3.   The restructuring effect. The longer run
      effect of economies of scale as industry re-
      organizes under the pressure of new competi-
      tive conditions (4–8 billion ECU). This saving
      is concentrated in certain high tech sectors
      such as computers, telecoms, and aerospace.

However, it would create a new European-wide
competitive environment and Cecchini looked
at the way in which this would affect key sectors
in the short and longer term.

Harmonization: the common commercial policy

In the period up to 1980 the Council of Ministers
had adopted about 136 directives relating to
industrial products and over 50 concerned with
foodstuffs. The industrial products include
motor vehicles (approx. 40); metrology, i.e. measuring equipment; cosmetics; solvents and other
dangerous substances; and electrical equipment. In the case of foodstuffs, directives govern
their labelling, durability, additives as well as
packaging (restriction on the use of PVC), presentation, advertising and composition. Additives have been subject to provisions specifying
maximum levels. Much had therefore been done
but there was still a long way to go since the
Commission had given this figure. It was
already a very time-consuming process. Also,
technological progress renders existing standards obsolescent and therefore renewed effort
has to be diverted into constantly bringing them
up to date. The Community was therefore forced
to adopt a speedier process in respect of agreeing
common standards.

The new policy introduced was that of
'mutual recognition'. In other words, if a product was safe for use or consumption in one member state it was held then to be safe for use or
consumption in all other member states of the
Community. At a stroke, this abolished the long
administrative delays and long complicated
quarrels over the agreement of community standards. Community standards were now the
standards agreed nationally. This proved to be a
popular move in that it expedited the transition
towards the Single Market. Politically it was

astute as it was expedient and it gave decision
making to member states.

However, although this meant that goods
lawfully produced or marketed in one state
should have access to all member states, there
were still:

•   health, safety and environmental protection
     barriers,
•   US and NATO barriers to intra-EU trade, and
•   limits to the portability of social security bene-
     fits, pensions, etc.

Controversies raged over the export of British
lamb and beef to France arising from the incidence of BSE or 'mad cow disease' in Britain.
Similarly German 'purity' laws on beer were
undermined when it became clear that British
beer could now be sold in Germany. Each
viewed the other as lax in a certain dimension
but now each member state's standards had to
be respected and in all Community markets.

Certification procedures also created problems. The definition of what is a British, French or
German car becomes more obscure once one
takes note of the multinational sourcing that takes
place in the automobile industry for example. The
British Association of Chambers of Commerce
allows for 'the last substantial stage of manufacture taking place in Britain' as sufficient to warrant the product in question being labelled of
British origin. This created real practical difficulties as well as legal difficulties. Taking the example of Nissan cars manufactured in Sunderland,
Britain – at what stage, if any, may these cars be
termed 'of British origin'? Measures such as percentage of value-added; and percentage of
volume of components sourced locally both give
different figures. At stake for Japanese manufacturers like Nissan is entry to the Community-
wide market. If the car is Japanese it may be
subject to voluntary restraint agreements as well
as Community external tariffs. If, on the other
hand, a Japanese car made in Britain is British
then exports to say France are of British cars
and quotas on voluntary restraint agreements
between France and Japan are unaffected. In view
of the importance of the economic stakes involved,
both France and Italy have fought vociferously to
block Japanese imports into the Community.

Single Administrative Document

Introduced into the UK on 1 January 1988, the
Single Administrative Document (SAD) replaced
literally hundreds of separate export, transit and
import forms which could now be computerized
and even carry an electronic signature.

In practice, whenever goods moved between EU member states three separate declarations were needed and these varied between states. SAD is a very necessary step towards substantial reform in intra-Community trade prior to 1992. SAD can be used as an export, transit and import declaration for any consignment moving within the Community. At the same time, a number of options for clearance were introduced which include the creation of Inland Clearance Depots (ICDs), facilities to clear goods at traders' own premises and simplified procedures for exports whereby goods may be cleared on the basis of minimum data with full declarations being provided subsequently. One innovation was the introduction of Customs Procedure Codes to identify the customs regime to and from which the goods are moving, e.g., warehousing, freeport, etc. SAD required seventeen acceptances to come into force. Now in force it will enable the collection of greater and better information than ever before to be placed. It is important to emphasize that the SAD was not a relaxation in controls but a change in paperwork. However, this very necessary change in administrative procedures will lead to greater efficiency in trade with and within the Community.

TARIC customs tariff

This new tariff came in alongside the SAD on 1 January 1988. Previously, the EU used a common customs tariff (CCT) to specify rates of customs duty and a separate but related system (NIMEXE) to collect trade statistics. Both are based on the Customs Cooperation Council Nomenclature (CCCN) which had become outdated.

A single goods description system has to satisfy the requirements of international trade. This means transport operators, governments and manufacturers. Inevitably, there will be pressures also for the ability of this system to accept computerization. A system has to meet a variety of different needs: to determine freight charges; collect customs duties; compute national production and international trade statistics and within industry, identify products. Technological development led to an ever increasing number of products being bundled into the 'other' category, as there was no specific category for them. As a result of these divergent pressures, the Customs Co-operation Council finally introduced after lengthy consultation with many international bodies, a Harmonized Commodity Description and Coding System. This system which came to be known as the Harmonized System was adopted on 14 June 1983.

The HS incorporates products which had not been invented when the CCCN had been developed. It also offered more detail than other systems. Nine thousand eight-digit headings of the CCCN are replaced by 14,000 eleven-digit headings. As a result of this new system, it is held to be easier to see whether goods are subject to quotas, tariff preferences; surveillance; countervailing duties; or anti-dumping duties to name but a few of the possible uses. It also introduced problems of reclassifying goods and products which may now with reclassification become liable for duty.

Patents, trademarks and standards

A European Patent Office was established in Munich in 1978. It is anticipated that a Community-wide patent will replace national patents before too long. Meanwhile, it should be noted that the Commission opposes the use of trademarks, patent licences and know-how agreements as a means of market protection. European standards are being established by the European Standards Organization CEN (European Committee for Standardization) and CENELEC (European Committee for Electro-Technical Standardization). These consist of over 160 committees presently dominated by French and German representatives. These standards are incorporated into national standards rather than being replaced by them. The German DIN organization (Deutsches Institut für Normung) is already the European leader. CEN and CENELEC are disappearing meanwhile under the weight of their own bureaucracy.

Competition policy within the EU

The foundation stone of the EU being free trade, it is not surprising then to find the Commission implacably opposed to all forms of cartel and collusion which 'have as their object or effect, the prevention, restriction or distortion of competition within the common market.'

Community competition rules are enshrined in Articles 85 and 86 of the Treaty of Rome which proscribe certain agreements, concerted practices and abuses of dominant positions which distort free trade in the Community. This applies to agreements which have as their object the restriction of competition as well as agreements which result in the restriction of competition. The removal of internal governmental restrictions that impede the free flow of goods, persons, services and capital is central to the Treaty of Rome which was to some extent superseded by the Single European Act.

In 1962, there were 18 national trading monopolies in the Community covering goods ranging from potassium, gunpowder and explosives to alcohol and tobacco. Partly by negotiation and partly by taking recalcitrant offenders to the European Court, the Commission has frequently achieved the objective laid down by the European Treaties, namely the abolition of discrimination between nationals of the member states in the procurement and marketing of goods. Despite recent advances, minor problems still exist, notably in the marketing of tobacco in Italy and France. In Greece, which joined the EU in 1981 the dismantling of state monopolies has been slow.

Yet for outsiders, it is different again. They fear that as these internal blockages disappear, the Community will reinstate them as a Community-wide move against foreign entrants. Internally, the only loophole is Article 36 which justifies restraints on trade provided it does not constitute a means of arbitrary discrimination or a disguised trade restriction where there are issues of public morality, public security, protection of health and life of humans, animals or plants; protection of national treasures possessing artistic, historical or archaeological value or the protection of industrial and commercial property. In a competition context the following are scrutinized very thoroughly:

1. *Market sharing agreements* which create protected markets, often in one member state. The Commission in 1969 banned a quinine cartel and imposed a fine, and in 1973 acted against a sugar cartel. At the beginning of 1989 there were 3,457 cases pending and they lack the resources to deal with them all.
2. *Price fixing agreements* such as the dyestuffs

cartel which controlled 80 per cent of the European market. Producers had agreed to raise their prices by the same amount and at virtually the same time. This was the first occasion when companies headquartered outside the EC were fined for their actions within its territories. In 1988, in the Wood Pulp Cases, the EC held that anticompetitive agreements by US firms operating in the USA to restrict direct sales into and within the Community will be subject to EC jurisdiction. In 1989 the EC imposed a total of ECU 60 million against cartels including 23 companies manufacturing thermoplastic products.

3. *Exclusive purchase agreements* to buy from specified manufacturers or importers, or exclusive supply agreements to sell to certain buyers. Such agreements, which have arisen in areas as diverse as records and heating equipment, are usually proscribed by the Commission as they create unfair advantage and act to distort free trade.
4. *Agreements on industrial and commercial property rights.* The exclusive use of patents, trademarks and works of art is not necessarily excluded from competition rules.
5. *Exclusive or selective distribution agreements.* Selective distribution arrangements are sometimes permitted if they improve the quality of the service provided. Discrimination against retailers for their pricing policies can be severely punished. However, it also encourages positive developments particularly with regard to co-operation between small and medium-sized firms. Escaping the general ban are the following types of agreement:

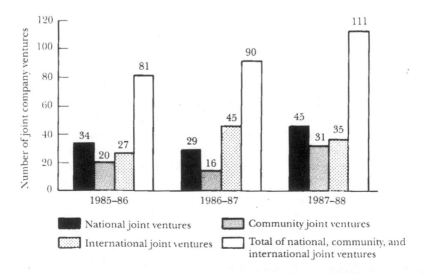

Source: Hufbauer, G. C. (1990) *Europe 1992: An American Perspective*, Brookings Institution, Washington, DC

Figure 10.6   Joint ventures in the European Community, 1985–88

- Exclusive representation contracts with trade representatives.
- Small-scale agreements, taking account of turnover and market share (which must not exceed 5 per cent of the total market in a substantial part of the Community or where the aggregate annual turnover of the companies in question amounts to less than 50 million ECUs. In these instances, the Commission will not intervene.
- Subcontracting agreements.
- Information exchanges between companies, joint studies and joint use of equipment.

Finally with regard to mergers, the position is less clear. The Commission is able to act only with respect to mergers which arise under the European Coal and Steel Treaty. The Commission did seek extra powers in this regard in 1973 and again in 1981, asking that the largest mergers be subjected to its scrutiny. The Commission also asked for the power to ban mergers which, in its view, pose a threat to effective competition in the Community. Yet cross European merger activity, like GEC-Siemens, could restructure many of the present European industries including retailing where Casino of France, Argyll of the UK, and Royal Ahold of Holland are to form a joint arrangement.

EU merger regulations seek surveillance over major mergers with a Community diversion, but provided the continued market share does not exceed 25 per cent, mergers will be allowed. The Community is more concerned with mergers in areas where the market share exceeds 30 per cent; the industry is already highly concentrated with significant entry barriers and price leadership is in the hands of a few powerful firms. An illustration is provided by the Commission's intervention in the British Airways' alliance with US Air even after the UK Monopolies and Mergers' Commission had given their approval. British Airways then had to expand opportunities for new competing carriers to obtain operating licences and at the same time hand over Heathrow slots so as to limit to some extent its market dominance.

Strategic alliances are likely to prove more important than mergers and hostile takeovers where Britain has accounted for more than 70 per cent of those to date, but are just as likely to be the focus of EU intervention as any of the other more traditional forms of market cooperation.

Common Agricultural Policy (CAP)

The objectives of the CAP, as detailed in Article 39 of the Treaty of Rome are:

- To increase agricultural productivity.
- To ensure a fair standard of living for the agricultural community.
- To stabilize markets
- To provide certainty of suppliers
- To ensure supplies to consumers at reasonable prices.

Approximately 70 per cent of the Community's total budget is accounted for by the CAP which did not come into operation until the 1960s. The most important prices fixed at Community level are:

1. Indicative or guide prices which are the expected prices for the producer.
2. Intervention price which is a lower price at which the Community is obliged to buy products from farmers, traders and co-operatives if they cannot be sold in the Community markets or be exported. When production exceeds demand there are surpluses, and in agricultural production, there are many such surpluses within the EC.

CAP also benefits the larger farmers since the more a farmer has to sell, the more he benefits from the revenue-enhancing effect of the policy. This created incentives for farmers to force up yields, expand consumption of inputs and develop intensive methods of farming, displacing labour. To reduce milk production, slaughter premiums were granted but this did not meet with success as the farmers collected the premiums and invested them in ever more productive dairy cattle.

Over the years, the Community has been trying to change towards a more viable farm size to improve the economics of its agricultural production and support schemes. The Mansholt Plan which was not adopted, was for a farm of 200–300 acres for wheat production, 40–60 cows for milk, 15–200 head of cattle for beef and veal production. Its aim was not to coerce but to create financial inducements to speed the adoption of the desired changes, particularly in regions with the worst structural problems.

Thanks to subsidies, the Community farm prices remain high by world market price levels, and guaranteed prices only stimulate further supplies thus exacerbating the situation further. The problem lies with CAP itself. Its objectives, as outlined above include terms which are outwardly agreeable but practically expensive to maintain. For example, providing certainty of supplies is usually a feature only of the public utilities: gas, water and electricity. To offer a 100 per cent level of service means inevitably that you have excess stocks by up to 10 per cent higher than anticipated demand. This obviously carries extra costs with it. As for the rest of its aims, it is open to question whether they are mutually exclusive, whether indeed it is possible to provide a fair standard of living, stabilize markets, ensure supplies at reasonable prices, all at the same time.

As previously noted, this accounted for two-thirds of the Community budget in the mid-1980s. Yet, in the move towards a Single European Market, no mention is being made of the CAP as the Community as a whole races to eliminate obstacles to trade according to the timetable it has set for itself.

A report by the National Consumer Council (NCC, 1988) found the CAP to be seriously deficient when measured against the following criteria:

* price which affects standard of living as well,
* quality and safety,
* access and choice,
* information and redress,
* efficiency and cost,
* equity, in the sense of resource allocation,
* transparency and accountability,
* representation.

The damning report by the NCC is worth citing

Prices are kept artificially high inside the EU, and destabilized outside the EU by the dumping of surpluses onto world markets. Despite claims to the contrary, the quality of food is not particularly enhanced by the policy and modern farming methods introduce health risks, are damaging to the environment, and reduce access to the countryside. While access to food supplies in toto have been guaranteed by the policy, the range of foods to which access is guaranteed has been unnecessarily restricted by EU regulations.

The policy does not measure up well on either efficiency or cost criteria: it is extremely expensive, highly bureaucratic and prone to fraud. In terms of equity it is a highly regressive policy for both consumers and producers – that is, it artificially inflates prices in a commodity which takes up a particularly high proportion of the budget of low-income families and regions, while giving most help to the larger, richer producers. The system completely lacks transparency: it is largely incomprehensible to all but a select few, and strategic moves involving large sums of money are often made behind closed doors, with consumers being scarcely represented at the vital moments of decision.

Exhibit 10.9   European Union and trade policy

Excluding intra-Community trade, the European Union accounts for 18.8 per cent of world exports, ahead of the United States and Japan both with 16 per cent. Since 1968, the Community has been a Customs Union with a common customs tariff for all its member states. The EU uses trade to support its close partners. It has signed preferential agreements, mainly with the Mediterranean, Central and East European and EFTA countries, granting advantages to these areas where its balance of payments is in surplus. The EU contributes to development aid by extending to countries in difficulties, the benefits of a system of generalized preferences (suspension of customs duties) which was set up in 1971 and recently revised. The EU has set up preference systems with the countries of Africa, Caribbean and Pacific.

The EU has strengthened its trade protection to shield Community industries from unfair practices by their competitors, by means of anti-dumping and anti-subsidy duties and safeguard clauses. The framework of the World Trade Organization, the 'trade barriers regulation' makes it possible to challenge any measures taken by third countries which are contrary to the rules of balanced trade. The EU has increased the efficacy of these measures by cutting the time limit for decisions and reforming the decision-making process, so that it will no longer be possible for a minority of countries to block the implementation of retaliatory measures. The EU's instruments for combating counterfeiting allow for copied or pirated goods to be stopped at the border. The EU has negotiated agreements and arrangements restricting imports of some sensitive products. Community preference – the fundamental principle of the Common Agricultural Policy – is also part of the European Trade Policy. When it comes to public procurement contracts, for example, preference is granted to bids by firms from within the European Union. All trade policy instruments are thus contributing alongside the other common policies to strengthening Europe's identity.

GATT negotiations allowed the EU to maintain its agricultural and audiovisual policies and win from its partners reductions in customs duties greater than those granted to them. The creation of the World Trade Organization makes it possible to ensure that the rapidly developing countries comply with all the rules of balanced trade in spheres such as intellectual property or the fight against dumping. The WTO discusses important issues such as the environment and workers' fundamental rights. It will have to put a stop to unilateral practices by any country. The EU and its member states have been playing a decisive role in this organization since it was set up on 1 January 1995.

Bankruptcy has threatened the future of the Community on several occasions, always as a result of the CAP policy of supporting agricultural prices at too high a level rather than stimulating structural reform. Several 'crisis' summit meetings of heads of state have taken place to try to control a runaway budget. On 2 February 1988 for the first time a legally binding ceiling was introduced for CAP price policy spending. Compensation was introduced for farmers who set aside arable land for at least five years. Longer term reform beyond budgeting stabilizers is required.

Questions as to representation of consumer interests were clearly raised by the NCC Report but not answered. To cite their report again:

We have concluded that consumers' interests are paid scant regard at all levels and stages of the decision-making process. At the national level, policy formation is dominated by the agricultural lobby and its sponsoring ministries. Where formal consultative committees exist, consumer representatives always form a small minority. At Community level, consumer interests have virtually no influence on policy formation. Agricultural policy proposals are formulated in the agriculture directorate (DGVI) – the sponsoring directorate of farmers – which works in virtual isolation from other directorates. It has established agricultural advisory committees but, again, consumer interests are in a small minority and, in any case, these committees are often not consulted early enough in the decision-making process to affect policy.

The 'Euro' currency

The Maastricht Treaty of 1992 established a single currency for all member currencies to be known as the 'Euro'. The timescale for introduction is from 1 January 1999 until 1 January 2002 when notes and coins denominated in Euros will begin to circulate alongside notes and coins in national currency. National currencies will be completely replaced by the Euro as of 1 July 2002. In the meanwhile, member states are expected to bring their economies closer together and four convergence criteria have been established:

- Member States must avoid excessive government deficits. Their performance is measured against two reference ratios: 3 per cent of GDP for the annual deficit and 60 per cent of GDP for the stock of government debt.
- Inflation should not exceed by more than 1.5

percentage points that of the three best performing Member States in terms of price stability in the previous year.
- The country's currency must have remained within the normal fluctuation margins of the European Monetary System (EMS) for at least two years.
- Long-term interest rates should not exceed by more than two percentage points the average of the three Member States with the lowest rates in the Union.

The significance of this initiative is immense. It signals a single monetary policy within a single economic market and therefore is a logical extension of the Single Market. Payments and transfers between member states will be quicker and cheaper as no actual monetary conversions are required. This will have important effects on costs for business as well as pricing since there will be none of the sudden exchange rate movements that have troubled weaker currencies in the past. All in the European Union will be able to share the benefits of a unified strong currency, which eliminates uncertainty and therefore currency speculation. As an international currency it may rival the dollar but the workings of the European Central Bank have yet to be fully assessed. It may well be that the Euro fails to deliver the strength of the Deutschmark and so may lead to a rush into dollars. However, as businesses within the EU will then trade in Euros there will be less need for member states to hold foreign reserves, much of which has traditionally been held in US dollars. There may well be a time in the future then when the European Central Banks seek to eliminate this dollar overhang and reduce their reserves in US dollars. This would have a strong effect on the US dollar, significantly weakening it against the Euro. Companies will be able to review their treasury operations and take advantage of the many cost saving opportunities presented. However, it has equally significant advantages for EU consumers as well who will be able to choose amongst suppliers from all across the European Union as prices will then be directly comparable. Competition will have received a further strong boost but once again the effect will largely be to increase critical mass required to compete, increase the size of the largest businesses and create further industrial concentration. Both inside the EU and for those outside the EU, the arrival of the Euro will be one of the most significant events of our lifetime. Further integration will undoubtedly follow.

Exhibit 10.10   What will happen on 1 January 1999?

In what areas do the countries wishing to join the Euro need to step in their efforts in order to fulfil the criteria?

Member States have made real progress towards economic convergence, but government deficits are still running too high. The situation as regards the other convergence criteria has improved considerably in recent years, especially for inflation, which has hit record lows (3.1% for the Union as a whole in 1995), and for long-term interest rates.

Is deficit reduction compatible with the fight against unemployment?

Deficit reduction is the only possible option if we are to lay the foundations for healthy economic growth, which is the necessary precondition for creating jobs and fighting unemployment in Europe.
    Economists agree that, given the globalization of the economy, allowing government deficits to

process of introducing the single currency in those countries which meet the convergence criteria laid down in the Treaty. In practical terms, the following arrangements will come into effect:

- the conversion rates of the participating currencies (both among themselves and against the Euro) will be irrevocably fixed;
- a single monetary policy will be framed and implemented by the European System of Central Banks (ESCB), composed of the central banks of the participating countries and the European Central Bank (ECB), to be set up in 1998. The ESCB will conduct its monetary and foreign exchange operations in Euros;
- the participating Member States will denominate their new public debt issues in Euros;
- financial markets will follow suit and use the

Budgetary convergence on the road to the Euro: how much have Member States achieved so far?

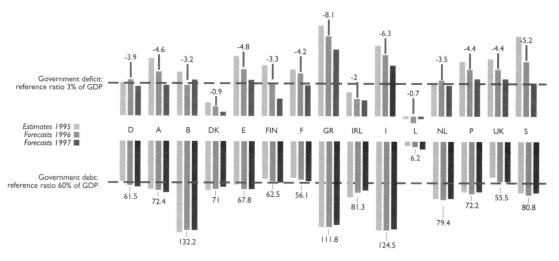

GOVERNMENT DEFICIT (% of GDP)

Government deficit: reference ratio 3% of GDP

Estimates 1995 ◼
Forecasts 1996 ◼
Forecasts 1997 ◼

Government debt: reference ratio 60% of GDP

GOVERNMENT DEBT (% of GDP)

grow is no longer a valid way of boosting economic activity. On the contrary, analysis of the economic performance of European countries over the last 25 years shows that unemployment falls – sometimes quite sharply – in countries which cut back their government deficits, as was the case, for example, in Denmark from 1982 to 1986 or as Ireland has done over the last decade.

What will happen on 1 January 1999?

1 January 1999 will mark the beginning of the

Euro, which will thus immediately take its place in the international monetary system.

Are the convergence criteria too strict?

No. The convergence objectives set by the Treaty on European Union are realistic, and this is true even of the one which is most difficult to achieve for most Member States, namely the government deficit criterion. The average deficit has declined substantially in Europe over the last two years, from 6.3 per cent of GDP in 1993 to 4.7 per cent

Exhibit 10.10 continued

Steps leading to the Euro

1 July 1990
Stage one of economic and monetary union begins. Capital movements in the EU Member States are fully liberalized (except where temporary derogations have been granted).

15 and 16 December 1995
Madrid European Council
- The name 'Euro' adopted for the single currency.
- Technical scenario for introduction of the Euro and timetable for change-over to the single currency in 1999 finalized (end of the process scheduled for 2002).

1 January 1999
Stage three of EMU begins.
- Council to fix irrevocably the conversion rates of the currencies of participating countries both among themselves and against the Euro.
- The Euro is to become a currency in its own right and the official ecu basket will cease to exist.
- Council regulation establishing the legal framework for introduction of the Euro is to enter into force.

1 January 1993
The single market is completed.

By 31 December 1996 at the latest
- The EMI to specify the regulatory, organizational and logistical framework for the European Central Bank (ECB) and the European System of Central Banks (ESCB).
- The Commission, Council and EMI to prepare the legislation on the ECB and ESCB and on the introduction of the single currency.

From 1 January 1999
- ESCB to frame and implement single monetary policy in Euros and conduct foreign exchange operations in Euros.
- Member States to issue new public debt securities in Euros.

1 November 1993
- The composition of the ecu basket is frozen.
- The Treaty on European Union signed in Maastricht enters into force.

Stage two of EMU begins.

As early as possible in 1998
The Heads of State or Government to decide which Member States will be the first to take part in the single currency, on the basis of the convergence criteria and in the light of economic data for 1997.

From 1 January 1999 to 1 January 2002 at the latest
- ESCB to exchange at par value currencies with irrevocably fixed conversion rates.
- ESCB and public authorities in Member States to monitor changeover developments in the banking and finance sectors and assist the whole of the economy to prepare for the changeover.

1 January 1994
- The European Monetary Institute (EMI) is set up in Frankfurt.
- Procedures for coordinating economic policies at European level are strengthened.
- Member States strive to combat 'excessive deficits' and to achieve economic convergence.

As soon as possible after that decision
- Member States to appoint Executive Board of the ECB.
- ECB and Council to set the date for introduction of Euro notes and coins.
- ESCB to start issuing banknotes in Euros.
- Council and Member States to start minting Euro coins.

1 January 2002 at the latest
- ESCB gradually to put Euro notes into circulation and withdraw national banknotes.
- Member States gradually to put Euro coins into circulation and withdraw national coins.
... The process comes to an end . . .

31 May 1995
The Commission adopts Green Paper on the single currency (reference scenario for the transition to the single currency).

Before 1 January 1999
Final preparation of the ECB and ESCB:
- Council to adopt legislation on the key for capital subscription, collection of statistical information, minimum reserves, consultation of the ECB, and fines and penalties which can be imposed on undertakings.
- ECB and ESCB to get ready for becoming operational: setting up the ECB, adopting the regulatory framework, testing the monetary policy framework, etc.

1 July 2002 at the latest
The changeover to the Euro is complete in all the participating Member States.

→ **Exhibit 10.10** *continued*

in 1995. The effort that still has to be made between now and the end of 1997 is therefore on a par with what has been achieved over the previous two-year period.

Entering the EC from the outside

The associate members of the Community: The Lomé Convention

The aid agreements currently in force between the Community and the 70 African (71 including South Africa), Caribbean and Pacific (ACP) countries are of a commercial and financial nature, granting the advantage of preferential access to Community markets. The Convention covers the following:

Trade co-operation
Practically all products from the ACP countries may be imported freely into the EU, but the arrangement is not reciprocal. ACP countries may charge import duties provided that they do not discriminate between member states.

Exhibit 10.11   ACP states 'need banana regime'

African, Caribbean and Pacific countries risk economic ruin if the European Union is forced to withdraw preferential access for their banana exports, the European Commission has warned.

The prediction is part of the Commission's latest offensive to defend the EU's controversial banana regime which gives ACP banana producers duty-free access. The arrangement has been challenged by the US in the World Trade Organisation.

The US challenge is a test case for the preferential trade terms the EU offers ACP countries under the Lomé convention. The WTO is due to issue an interim report on the case this week.

Although the Lomé special access arrangements were granted a waiver under the General Agreement on Tariffs and Trade (Gatt) in 1994, the US has maintained that the waiver was never intended to cover the EU banana regime.

The US says the regime is rigged to protect EU companies at the expense of Latin American groups. In addition, it says the arrangement does not benefit Lomé countries but has a negative impact on the economic and trade interests of Latin American producers. Washington cites as evidence the fact that the regulations have cut access of producers in Ecuador, Honduras, Guatemala and Mexico to the EU by 27 per cent.

In a blunt defence of the preferential terms, the Commission argues that banana export earnings are a 'critical component' of the economies of the ACP countries.

'The destruction of the Caribbean banana industry would provoke severe economic hardship and political instability in a region already struggling against deprivation,' says a Commission document distributed to EU member states.

The Commission points out that economies of scale and lower wage costs have driven down the cost of banana production in Latin American, making it impossible for smaller producers in the Caribbean to compete.

The Commission dismisses the contention that EU companies are benefiting at the expense of US and Latin American groups, pointing out that Del Monte and Dole, both US companies, have increased EU market share.

The paper also questions Washington's motive for launching the WTO challenge, as the US is not a big banana-producing country. The paper suggests the challenge is politically motivated pointing out that US interest was sparked by a complaint lodged by Chiquita Brands and the Hawaii Banana Industry Association.

Source: Financial Times, 18 March 1997

Financial and technical co-operation
The common unit of currency for conversion purposes is the ECU (European Currency Unit). Funds of nearly 6,000 million ECU were set aside for use up to 1985. (The financial details of Lomé 4 are discussed later in this chapter.) These funds were to finance investment projects by the ACP countries and will be managed jointly. Four major sectors share most of the aid: rural devel-opment, industrialization, economic infrastructure and social development. There is also provision for regional co-operation of two or more ACP countries and support for small and medium-sized firms.

Stabilization of export earnings
The STABEX system compensates ACP states for losses if the volume of exports in their most

important products falls below a certain level. The poorest countries do not have to repay the compensatory amounts, but other countries do if the situation improves. The scheme is intended to even out large deficit and surplus positions which have caused such wide price fluctuation that, in some instances, the rational planning of a developing economy has become almost impossible. A parallel system (SYSMIN) exists for the support of the ACP countries' key exports and aims at safeguarding mining production.

Industrial and agricultural co-operation

The intention is to grant aid to help ACP countries to develop and diversify their industrial production, in particular through the transfer of technology. This policy will raise the important question of the Community's obligation to buy the goods which the industries of the Third World produce. This will put pressure on Community industries, in particular very heavy pressure on labour-intensive, low-technology industries. It will accelerate their decline and push industry within the Community into higher technologies and more sophisticated service. Co-operation will be stepped up in areas such as new energy sources. Private investment will also be encouraged.

Institutions

The Lomé Agreement (which runs out in the year 2000) is implemented by a Council of Ministers aided by a Consultative Assembly of representatives of the ACP countries and the European Parliament. In each of the countries – totalling over 70 – there is a representative of the Community, whose task is to manage the operation of the Convention. Although at present only trade relations are involved, there is clearly present the germ of the idea of Community representatives acting more as ambassadors to the ACP countries. It could make individual embassies largely redundant in time.

The principal agreements between the Community and the Mediterranean countries are:

1. With Maghreb countries – Algeria, Morocco and Tunisia.
2. With the Mashreq countries – Egypt, Jordan, Syria and Lebanon.
3. The agreements with Israel, Cyprus, Malta and Turkey.

The commercial aspects of the agreements involve free access for industrial goods to the Community and concessions covering some agricultural products. The agreements are not reciprocal, although in the case of Israel there will be a free trade area for industrial products.

Arrangements have been made in the agreements to ensure that the nearly one million Maghreb workers in the Community benefit from the same pay and conditions of work as Community nationals. A Council of Ministers determines the policies behind the various treaties, but the negotiation and renegotiation of the treaties is the responsibility of the Commission.

There have been four Lomé agreements since 1975. The third Lomé agreement came into force 1 May 1986 for a five-year period. However, despite the elaborate structure created to encourage trade with the Community, Lomé has not been a success. Between 1975 and 1990 ACP exports to the EU declined from taking first 8 per cent of EU imports to 3.8 per cent of EU imports and within that, 90 per cent of these exports are represented by bulk commodities. Lomé is nevertheless important, it provided $9.4 billion in aid between 1985 and 1990. Measures exist for ACP exports to enter the EU quota and duty-free and there is a mechanism to stabilize the earnings of the ACP commodity exporters. Lomé 4 was signed in December 1989 for a ten-year period with a total package valued at ECU 10.7 billion.

However, despite these clear advantages, the Lomé conventions have not been successful and the ACP countries have perhaps even been less successful at penetrating the Community markets than any other group worldwide. Certainly, aid has not been co-ordinated and the ACP wished to be treated as a group rather than have differential rates of preferential treatment. During the period 1975–1990 liberalization of trade has meant also that perhaps even if the Lomé Convention did not exist, that 70 per cent of ACP exports would still enter duty-free (Laurie, 1990). This indicates competition and the lack of protection from third party suppliers as perhaps before. Over the years, too, the EU has expanded and its newer members including Spain and Greece have a significant financial interest in fruit and vegetables. Bananas and rum are two items produced by the ACP countries and subject to national quantitative restrictions. A longer term plan with certain guarantees and offering the opportunities for economic diversification through an aid package may prove to be highly beneficial.

Lomé 4 proposes some changes to previous arrangements. Firstly with regard to the rules of origin, the ACP share in value-added has been reduced to 45 per cent instead of 60 per cent. Next and most importantly, there have been changes to the Stabex system which started in 1985. Stabex accounts for 12 per cent of the European Development Fund. The conditions have changed in that payments made under Stabex do not now need to be repaid although in practice this was already the case. The Lomé 4 fund has been increased to ECU 1.5 billion to allow for bad years such as 1988 when the coffee and cocoa market prices experienced a severe downturn.

Longer term, marketing is the only way in which the ACP countries can hope to survive. Aid has not worked except to partially cushion some of the worst effects of commodity price crises. Focusing on developing new markets, improving production, improving general competitiveness and creating more awareness and efficiency through marketing systems is the only alternative to the bottomless purse expected of the Lomé Conventions.

Exhibit 10.12 Excluded from the Christian family

It began with a gaffe that has left several Christian Democrat members of the European Parliament uncharacteristically shy of press interviews.

That was succeeded by a diplomatically worded text, full of smooth phrases but ultimately reinforcing the same message. 'Neither we nor Turkey stand to gain by its incorporation into an integrated European Union.'

The blunt comments of leading European centre-right politicians at their 4 March summit in Brussels finally lifted the veil of ambiguity over Ankara's prospects of EU membership.

Gone were the justifiable arguments about Ankara's record of human rights' violations, dubious democratic credentials and occupation of north Cyprus. In their place was an icy realism.

President of the European People's Party Wilfried Martens said it was 'not acceptable' for Turkey to become a member of the EU. And president of the European Union of Christian Democrats Wim van Welzen said that the Union had cultural, humanitarian and Christian values different to Turkey's. Against a backdrop of other comments from Germany's Chancellor Helmut Kohl and Foreign Minister Klaus Kinkel, an unequivocal, some might say unsavoury, message was emerging. Turkey was – and would always be – unacceptable to the Union because it was an Islamic and not a Christian state.

The views expressed at the summit received backing from Helmut Kohl, José María Aznar, Jean-Luc Dehaene, Romano Prodi and Commission President Jacques Santer.

The remarks of Van Welzen and Martens were covered in detail by several European papers. Writing in the respected Dutch liberal daily *De Volkskrant*, Brussels editor Jos Klaassen accused the EU of hypocrisy. Right from the beginning, when Turkey first began to court what was then the Common Market, Brussels 'should have said that it did not believe Turkey belonged to the European family'.

The views expressed on 4 March fuelled a series of requests from journalists for interviews.

Yet these were not readily granted. By the end of March, Van Welzen's staff were referring all calls to Martens, explaining that Van Welzen was no expert on Turkey, but Martens was.

Yet Martens also seemed unwilling to engage in spontaneous discussion. Instead, he spoke on the 'sensitive' issue at the Bertelsmann Foundation in Kronberg on 18 March. Martens said in the speech that Turkey had three 'ambivalent features'. It sought recognition as a democracy yet retained 'some of the reflexes of an authoritarian empire'; it was 'both eastern and western, not easily perceived by us as belonging to our cultural context'; and it 'professes to be secular' yet remained 98 per cent Muslim, while also showing some tendencies of a return to Islam.

Martens argues that while it is in Europe's 'strategic interests' to maintain a good relationship with Turkey, it is not appropriate for it to join the EU.

Ankara wields growing influence in oil-rich Turkic-speaking countries across Soviet central Asia, while its pivotal position between China, Russia and Europe makes it vital to Europe's security interests.

Martens argues that the relationship with Turkey should be a positive one of 'genuine partnership', but he states: 'Turkey should preserve and develop its place within the European forum. Neither we nor Turkey stand to gain by its incorporation into an integrated EU.'

With June's European Council meeting in Amsterdam approaching, and the move to open the EU door to ten central and east European countries, including Cyprus, Martens calls for a constructive relationship.

Ankara, he says, should not be allowed to jeopardise their accession: 'The quality of our relations with Turkey is just as important as those we must develop with Russia.'

Cynics simply argue that this holds out towards both a similar ostracism. The problem of Turkey's identity is not new. A saying describes

→ Exhibit 10.12 *continued*

the dilemma: 'Turkey is a man running west on a train heading east.'

In his article, Jos Klaassen suggests that, because of Turkey's situation, Brussels may find it cannot sustain the exclusive policy indefinitely. 'When a new crisis threatens, perhaps Europe will once again develop an interest in Turkey.'

'The Turks were welcomed as members of the Council of Europe and Nato because of the Cold War.'

'No one should be surprised if Europe shortly resumes its flirtation with Turkey.'

Source: The European, 3–9 April 1997

Exhibit 10.13 Ten question on the European Union and world trade

1. Why is trade so important for the European Union?

A fundamental principle of the EU since its earliest days has been the promotion of free trade between its members. Encouraging trade by removing national legislative and customs barriers within the Union is a key way of increasing prosperity and raising living standards. The EU is the world's most important single market with 370 million inhabitants. It also accounts for over a fifth of total world trade in goods – more than any other trading group. Just as the union promotes trade within the borders of its 15 members, so it does with the rest of the world.

2. What are the general overall benefits and the specific advantages to business of encouraging international trade?

Trade is the lifeblood of an economy. The European Commission estimates that between 10 and 12 million jobs in the Union depend directly on exports. By reducing or abolishing the tariffs EU exporters have had to pay in the past, further sales will be encouraged, helping European business to compete on more equal terms with competitors around the world. Similarly, cutting back on time-consuming paperwork will reduce delays and costs. Estimates vary on the potential impact of the latest international agreement to boost world trade, negotiated in the Uruguay Round, but some predictions suggest it could add an extra ECU 180 billion of global income per year.

3. How do individuals benefit?

On a personal level, we benefit from a wide range of cheaper imports from around the world, stretching from clothing to food. Not only is this good for our pockets, but we enjoy a greater choice in what we can buy. More international trade means more EU exports, strengthening national economies and increasing the chances of creating new jobs.

4. What is the impact of increased trade on the environment?

Critics maintain that promoting trade may be detrimental to the environment as developing countries, in particular, try to encourage economic progress by subordinating long-term environmental needs to shorter term financial ones. The Uruguay Round took these anxieties into account and there are now international efforts to balance environmental concerns with the benefits of trade. Governments can still set tough environmental standards provided these are not used as an excuse to block trade.

5. Does freer trade bring any disadvantages?

Any moves that reduce tariff barriers and other hurdles faced by imports will inevitably have an impact on those companies and industrial sectors that have sheltered behind them. The new competition will lead to changes in what they produce and how they produce it. If tackled wisely, these changes will ensure greater efficiency and a more viable long-term future. In some areas, like agricultural production, the changes are already being introduced by internal EU reform programmes. While jobs may be squeezed in some areas, they will expand in others as a result of the new international rules.

6. How is world trade regulated?

Until January 1995, international trade rules introduced after the Second World War were regulated by the General Agreement on Tariffs and Trade, established in 1947 in Geneva, Switzerland. The GATT supervised the rules designed to avoid any repetition of the disastrous protectionist policies of the 1930s, and acted as a forum for settling trade disputes. At its outset, the GATT had just 23 members. When it became part of the new World Trade Organization in 1995, almost 130 countries had joined.

7. What was the Uruguay Round?

One of the GATT's roles was to encourage further moves towards removing trade barriers. These international negotiations took place in a series off 'rounds' of which the Uruguay Round, named after the country in which it was launched in 1986, was the most ambitious. It took seven

years to complete and included more countries —
over 125 — and trade areas than ever before.
These ranged from agriculture, textiles and clothing to banking, tourism and even international
telephone calls. It also provided for stronger copyright protection of artistic and literary work,
including computer programes.

8.   *What was the European Union's role in the
Uruguay Round negotiations?*
The 12 (now 15) members of the European Union
spoke as one in the Uruguay Round. The European Commission, which has responsibility for
negotiating the EU's external trade agreements,
did so on the basis of the strategies agreed within
the Union. By acting together under Commission
leadership, the individual members of the Union
were able to combine their strengths and face the
United States as equals across the negotiating
table. The lengthy process had another important
spin-off. It increased understanding between EU
countries and instilled new mutual confidence
going far beyond trade issues.

9.   *What is the World Trade Organization?*
The World Trade organization (WTO) came into
existence in Geneva on 1 January 1995, succeeding

and considerably enlarging the earlier role of the
GATT. It has a potential membership of over 150
countries and has five essential tasks. These involve
administering the new multilateral trade arrangements, acting as a forum for further negotiations,
settling disputes, overseeing national trade policies
and co-operating with other international bodies
on global economic policy making. It is not a 'free-
trade' body, rather one that operates a system of
rules dedicated to open, fair and undistorted competition. Its first, temporary, Director General was
former EU Commissioner Peter Sutherland. Its
second was former Italian diplomat and ex-senior
European Commission official, Renato Ruggiero.

10.   *How are international trade rules policed to stop
cheating?*
International trade rules are no use unless everyone respects them. The European Commission,
which is in charge of the Union's day to day trade
policy, has a number of defensive measures to protect its industries and farmers against illegal competition. WTO members also undertake not to
take unilateral action against each other and to try
to settle any trade disputes according to agreed
procedures in Geneva.

Japan and the EU

Japan . . . has been the object of sustained discrimination at the hands of the Community since its establishment.

(Ishikawa, 1990)

Japan looks at the Community as a community of member states and sees quite different
levels of treatment emanating from its member
states. Its worst scenario would be for the EU to
turn inward into Europe. An introspective Community may well lead to further protectionism
and fears then of a Fortress Europe. Britain,
which has attracted more direct investment
from Japan than any other country within the
EU, does not have the restrictions on products to
be found elsewhere in the Community. While
the Community strives for the removal of
national restrictions presently permissible
under Article 115 of the Treaty of Rome, it does
not rule out Community-wide restrictions in
areas considered to be sensitive and here it is
worth noting that the Community's external tariff ranges between 4 and 22 per cent.

In total Japanese trade with the world as a
whole, more than 1,000 products are subjected to
national quantitative restrictions. To emphasize
that Japanese restrictions belong more to the

past than the present, see Table 10.5. Within the
automobile industry, national restrictions are
plentiful. Fiat did have 60 per cent of the Italian
market whereas the Japanese had only 1 per
cent. In France, Japan was limited to 3 per cent of
the market; in Britain to 11 per cent under a voluntary export restraint agreement and so only in
Germany is there free trade. The Japanese cite
figures to show that they have 40 per cent market
share in Ireland, Finland, Greece and Norway;
and 30 per cent in Austria, Denmark and
Switzerland. However, none of these countries
has an automobile manufacturer.

The EU is worried that Japanese foreign
direct investment within the Community will
only aggravate existing excess capacity. The
issue of origin applicable to Japanese cars made
within the Community is another thorny problem. Britain was happy to certify that Nissan cars
made in Britain with a 60 per cent local content
were British. However, applying the label 'made
in Britain' would allow these cars entry into
other member states of the Community bypassing national quantitative restrictions presently
in force. The issue of how to measure local content and the level which may be required for certification purposes is difficult. Derek Barron,
former Chairman of Ford UK, recommended
that the level should be fixed at 80 per cent and

that this should not be measured as at present by ex-factory value which can introduce marketing costs and even profit. Only the actual cost of the product should be taken as a base. At first, France and Italy resisted but climbed down in April 1989; they establish 80 per cent local content as being a minimum requirement for acceptance of these Japanese cars as British. Japan's fears extend then into anti-dumping measures against what the Community has called 'screwdriver' assembly plants; fears of new rules of origin; and of the Community applying what it terms reciprocity in trade as viewed by the Community alone.

US and the EU

From a US viewpoint, the single market will have a bearing on:

1. US exports to the EU and indirectly to the third markets.
2. A unified Europe may turn protective towards high technology industries and grant

recognition' applies between member states except where there are issues of health, safety or the environment. The degree to which the EU will accept US certification and product testing is not clear.
6. Government procurement procedures are to be opened up. This raises some fears of favouritism for European companies and specific fears for the continuation of US exports of telecommunications equipment, for example.
7. Competition policy. The pursuit of an antitrust policy when vetting mergers and acquisitions by non-European companies is awaited with some trepidation.

The EU is the USA's largest export market. However, the US Administration are likely to concern themselves more with operating conditions within Europe rather than export opportunities to Europe which can fluctuate more wildly. Overall the US is favourable towards the changes taking place. Most of the disputes (80 per cent) have concerned agriculture and fish-

Table 10.5 Comparison of residual quantitative restrictions

Country	Agricultural and fisheries products		Manufacturers and minerals		Total	
	(1)	(2)	(1)	(2)	(1)	(2)
Japan	55	22	35	1	90	23
USA	1	1	4	6	5	7
West Germany	19	3	20	1	39	4
UK	19	1	6	2	25	3
France	39	19	35	27	74	46
Italy	12	3	8	5	20	8
Benelux	10	2	4	3	14	5
Denmark	62	5	2	0	64	5

Notes: (1) At the end of December 1979, (2) At the end of April 1987.

Source: GATT. Cited in Ishikawa, K. (1990) *Japan and the Challenge of Europe 1992*, Royal Institute of International Affairs, London

them preference over foreign competitors including the USA.
3. The issue of 'reciprocity' which has been raised many times, that in return for US companies being allowed to operate freely in the Community, the same might be given to European companies in the USA. This could lead to problems in protected areas such as US banking.
4. Quantitative restrictions are currently national in character. If applied in a unified manner across Europe, the EU could be seen to be championing trade protectionism.
5. Technical standards. The concept of 'mutual

eries and were caused by what were seen to be EU nontariff barriers and subsidies.

In terms of marketing-related issues, they strongly support the greater use of global and regional marketing strategies while at the same time there may be some stricter regulations then in force. Some greater difficulty is foreseen in finding EU-wide distributors though it is not identified as a major problem. It may well, however, prove to be a problem for those particularly small and medium size companies entering the market late. A physical presence was seen to be necessary although it is expected that the competitive environment will intensify. A single European location for distribution to all 15 European member states will then become feasible and will encourage development of Eurobrands; and mergers and acquisitions leading to further industry concentration. A 'Fortress Europe' scenario is quite likely resulting from the increased internal competition. Finding good European wide distribution may become a problem although standardization of market conditions will lessen the effect of cultural differences and limit the need for a 'nation-by-nation' approach to marketing across Western Europe. Finally, US companies will be able to exploit labour mobility, management transfer flexibility and an overall 'intra-European' managerial learning curve (Ryans and Rau, 1990).

Postscript

Significant measures have been taken to unify the internal markets of the Community and create common market conditions. Harmonization of taxation rates will have to take place or member states will face huge diversions of revenues and a good deal of tax-dodging besides. *The Economist*, for example, pointed to the anomalies of taxation and indicated how mail order by Mothercare of the UK of children's wear into France could be expected to be very successful if tax rates remain the same and Britain's remains at zero.

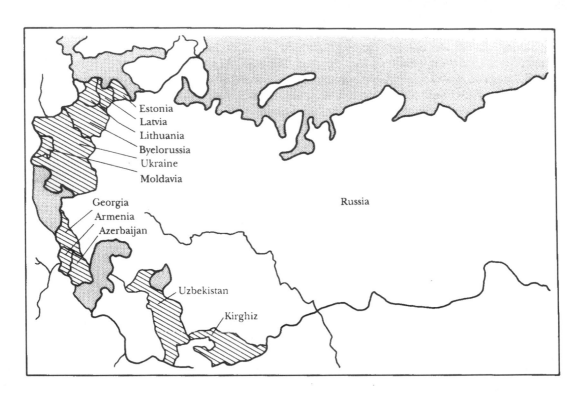

Figure 10.7   Commonwealth of Independence States

Area: 22,402,200 sq. km.
Republics
The Russian Federated
    Republic – 76.22%
Kazakhstan – 12.1%
The Ukraine – 2.7%
Turkmenia – 2.17%
Uzbekistan – 2%
Byelorussia – 0.93%
Kirghiz – 0.9%
Tadzhikistan – 0.64%
Azerbaijan – 0.4%
Georgia – 0.31%
Lithuania – 0.29%
Latvia – 0.28%
Estonia – 0.21%

Moldavia – 0.15%
Armenia – 0.13%
(The White Sea 0.4% and the Sea
    of Azov 0.17% are not formally
    included in any republic).
Population – 290 million
Nationalities – 120
Languages 130 (70 literary
    languages)
Religious communities – 1070
Largest nationalities
Russians – 145 million
Ukrainians – 53 million
Uzbeks – 13 million
Byelorussians – 9.7 million
Kazakhs – 7 million

Tatars – 6.5 million
Azerbaijanis – 6 million
Armenians – 4.5 million
Georgians – 3 million
Lithuanians – 3 million
Moldavians – 3.2 million
Tadzhiks – 3.2 million
Germans – 2 million
Kirghiz – 2 million
Jews – 1.8 million
Chuvashes – 1.8 million
Latvians – 1.5 million
Bashkirs – 1.5 million
Mordovians – 1.3 million
Poles – 1.3 million
Estonians – 1.1 million

However, Britain will still stay with imperial measures until the end of the decade. Alcoholic beverages will continue to use gills, and pints and petrol (gasoline) will continue to be priced per gallon. Even if current practice in filling stations (gas bars) is for prices to be displayed per gallon and per litre, pumps have been recording this in litres not gallons. In pubs and restaurants, it is quite different. Beer is dispensed in automatically controlled quantities of half and one pint and glasses by law must be stamped as accurately containing a half or one pint. To allow for beer froth, fill lines are indicated often on the outside of these glasses. In this area, metrication will be costly in the conversion. In other areas, such as confectionery and biscuits, the conversion is piecemeal and packages will be found currently on supermarket shelves stating either metric or imperial weights.

Many steps have already been taken e.g., EU passports and driving licences. There will be harmonization of the majority of existing anomalies but not all – Britain will still continue to drive on the left, but it is now connected to the rest of Europe as a result of the Channel Tunnel, which carries two rail tunnels and one service tunnel for security/safety, each 35 km long, crossing the Channel between Calais and Folkestone. With the French high speed train, the TGV, the distance between London and Paris has been reduced to three hours. This will lead both to creation and diversion of investment and resources to the new European gateways. The Channel Tunnel will put places like Dunkirk within easy reach of London, Paris, Brussels, Bonn, Luxembourg and the Hague and within easy reach of 80 million consumers: one-third of the population of the entire Community. A free warehousing system together with an Enterprise Zone 25 kms from the cross-channel tunnel will give Dunkirk a head start in the industrial relocation that is likely to take place.

European Economic Area (EEA)

At its inception, the merger of the EFTA and European Community created a new economic bloc with a single set of rules and a total population of over 380 million. The accession of Austria, Finland and Sweden to the European Union leaves only four countries linked to the Union only by the EEA agreement: Iceland, Liechtenstein, Norway and Switzerland. The EEA enshrined the 'four freedoms' on which the Community and Single Market of 1993 are founded: free movement of people, goods, services and capital.

Marketing in Central and Eastern Europe

Background to the political and economic changes

What was once is no more. What we have to realize is that we have a completely new situation since 1989 and all the old rules no longer apply. On the face of it we have two quite different scenarios being enacted. In Central Europe we have Hungary, Czech Republic and Poland now as members of the OECD and together with Slovenia trying to gain membership of both the European Union and of NATO. OECD is no longer just a club of the rich industrial nations and Central and Eastern Europe is no longer a grouping of Soviet satellites. The Soviet Empire has collapsed totally. It is a great irony that the democratization of Eastern Europe could only have been possible with the acquiescence of the leader of a totalitarian state.

In what was the Former Soviet Union, there is a quite different scenario where there is a Commonwealth of Independent States (CIS), an ad hoc, very loose, low profile organization lacking the will as well as the ability to hold together the now proudly independent republics. The largest independent republic is the Russian Federation (still the largest country in the world) accounting for the bulk of the population of the Former Soviet Union and most of its mineral wealth and resources. The Russian Federation includes a number of autonomous republics including Kabardino-Balkaria; North Ossetia; Checheno – Ingushetia; Dagestan; Klamykia; Mordovia; Chuvashia; and Mari-El. The Independent Republics include the Russian Federation: Latvia; Estonia; Lithuania; Byelorussia; Ukraine; Georgia; Moldavia; Armenia; Kazakhstan; Azerbaijan; Kirghiz; Uzbekhistan and Tadzhikistan. Some of these regions have a population which is mainly Muslim and therefore may ally themselves more with neighbouring Muslim countries than with any Russian central government. The bulk of the population previously belonging to the Former Soviet Union now lives within the Russian Federation, leaving 26 million (just less than the population of Canada) dispersed among the remaining republics.

The fall of the Berlin Wall led to the fall of the Soviet Empire. East Germany became part of the new unified Germany and the newly liberated Poland, Czech Republic, Slovakia and Hungary sought and gained associate membership of the European Union, further distancing them-

Exhibit 10.14   Post-communism: the gaps emerge

Technology gap
Giantism – Nowa Huta is typical
Redirection of substantial technological abilities as epitomised by Polytechnica Lodz

The productivity gap
Unproductive deployment of labour
We pretend to work, you pretend to pay us' syndrome.
Little purchasing power, low standards of living

Capital gap
Low investment quality
Low profitability
Foreign debt incurred in 1970s

Marketing gap
Centrally planned
Economies had *no* concept of markets nor of consumer sovereignty.

Environment gap
Ill-conceived industrial policy and no investment in

anti-pollution devices and disregard of civilian welfare

Infrastructure gap
Inefficient communication
Poor infrastructure

Motivation gap
Erosion of work ethic
Underemployment in the workplace
Failure to reward managers or to provide incentives

Management gap
Lack of a managerial class – feeling of professionalism among managers, largely absent.
Know-how fund

Legislative gap
Corporate law, tax law, capital market law, market procedures based on law – largely absent.

Democracy gap
Poland did not have democracy until 1989.

selves from their previous colonial masters and at the same time taking steps to ensure their continued independence. Eastern Europe was never one homogeneous region and the drive towards marketization of these previously centrally planned economies has created further marked differences. Again, one needs to think of segmentation. There is an array of different opportunities to be found within these economies but one strategy will not work for all. For one thing, these countries are all now truly independent and for another, they know it and want to be courted as independent states.

The differences still exist between Europe and the CIS in the way in which the reform movement got under way. In Central Europe, it has been a grass-roots bottom-up revolution whereas in the CIS the reform movement has been led from the top down. This is significant particularly when assessing the present state of the region. The power base in Eastern Europe is now with the people; in the CIS, it is with a President who is taking forever more and more power into the post of presidency. In the period immediately following the December 1991 events, Yeltsin as President of the Russian Federation has taken on many of the powers which were controlled by Gorbachev as Soviet President. It is similar to the French Revolutionary cry 'The King is Dead! Long live the King!' It is important to point out though that the Soviets have lived with Communism longer than the

rest of Eastern Europe and perhaps are more used to being directed, and like their East European compatriots, have seen many attempts at economic reform before. The secret to political life in the CIS republics is now once again in gauging the degree to which the leaders are serious about reform. Timing is of the essence and without commitment, these reforms will fail and yet it is the entire period since 1918 that has created this situation. Generations have been brought up to believe that they were taking part in a struggle that simply had class divisions between capitalist and worker. The CIS have less now to struggle for than their East European counterparts for while the East Europeans have realized their dreams of independence and are now cultivating a pride in themselves once more, the CIS have had this lifelong struggle which was their *raison d'être* and the excuse for generations of shortages, explained to them as being simply a vain pursuit. Heavy defence spending finally made the former Soviet Union crumble; the substitutions demanded to allow continued defence spending finally became unbearable even for the former Soviet Union.

In the aftermath of 1989 the path towards reconstruction is taking place with closer ties between East and West than for many generations. The Central European states are now much changed. Their leaders include many national leaders of resistance and reform who are wary of communism. Changes taking place in Eastern

Figure 10.8

Europe are to marketization and privatization of the state monolith. East Germany merged with West Germany as of October 1990, Poland abolished all central planning on 1 January 1990 and Czechoslovakia first changed its name to the CSFR then amicably split into two: the Czech and Slovak Federal Republics.

Only Bulgaria voted for the continuation of communism. Overall, these changes have been both sweeping and fundamental and must be seen as permanent.

Structural economic change

The path towards a free market economy is slow and painful. Despite its economic and productive potential, the traditional share of Central and

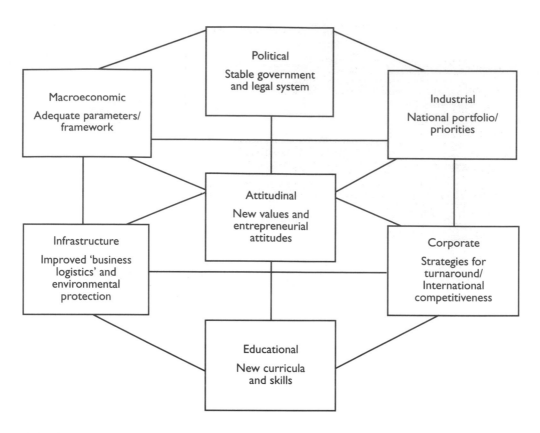

Figure 10.9   Turnaround of Eastern Europe
National Change programmes need several interrelated levels of action

Eastern Europe and the former Soviet Union in global trade was very low. It is a stark case of economic underachievement encouraged by the overt policies of successive politicians to maintain a steady status quo. All the Former Soviet satellites had been living with shortages for generations. All have been hard pushed to find the convertible currency to repay outstanding borrowings. This influenced Hungary and Poland, the two most indebted nations, to follow the lead of Romania in joining the IMF. Financial aid came with the proviso that economic restructuring had to take place and this followed in the wake of massive political changes also taking place. The CMEA or Comecon is now but a memory except to new voters who would only have been 11 years of age when the changes were occurring. The CoCom list of Western embargoed goods enforced by NATO was effective in enforcing the isolation of the then Eastern Bloc. The size of these markets, the fact that they were mainly virgin territory for Western goods and exhibited pent-up demand, made them attractive to many Western firms. However, from the outset, there were some irreconcilable differences. The Easterners looked to the product of democracy not the process and expected to act as consultants to incoming Westerners but Westerners looked to introduce their brands with their way of doing business. The market structure has been severely

shaken but not dismantled. Market reforms are being pursued with varying degrees of speed reflecting the varying degrees of personal conviction and priorities of the ministers involved as regards privatization of the economy.

Doing business in Central and Eastern Europe

The politicians may have changed, but not in all cases. For the most part they are born again 'free marketers' because they are adaptable politicians. Change has been espoused with different degrees of conviction and it also has to be recognized that across this entire region we are faced with national governments composed of many previous communists as the democratic vote has leaned towards the left. In addition, the civil service in each state has remained intact since the departure of the communists, meaning that the bureaucracy may not wish to operationalize change in every case.

*   The region is as diverse as ever. It has never been one market and is not now. At the forefront of market change and also leading in terms of Western investment into the region are Poland, Hungary, Czech Republic, Slovakia and Slovenia. The creation of a CEFTA or Central European Free Trade Area as a step-

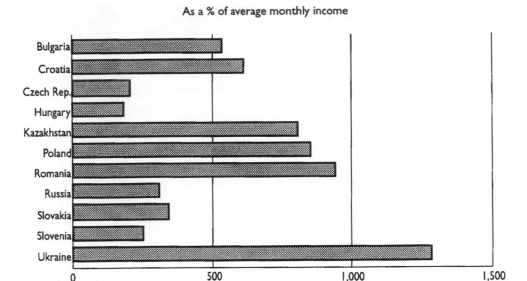

As a % of average monthly income

Source: Business Eastern Europe, July 25, 1994, p. 7.

Figure 10.10   Purchasing power in Eastern Europe

ping stone to preparing them on the way to membership of the EU has revitalized their economies and increased their internal trade substantially while also creating confidence with Western investors.

• The free market has arrived. The large state enterprise continues to act as a financial albatross on the backs of these fledgling economies but the bulk of the GDP earned is being found in the private sector.

• Privatization has been painfully slow in many cases and even in Poland which is more enlightened, a minister sought to reopen and renegotiate a deal once concluded. This was the reprehensible business practice to be found in communist times, and hopefully it will not be replicated elsewhere. It is a retrograde political step, which would appear to have been necessitated in this particular case by the onset of a coming general election and a minis-

Table 10.6   Central and Eastern European country rankings

(1 = best ranking, 5 = worst ranking)

	Business opportunities	Political risk	Credit ranking	Status of economy	Stability	Business infrastructure	TOTAL
Czech Rep.	2	1	1	3	1	2	10
Poland	1	2	2	3	2	2	12
Hungary	3	2	2	3	2	2	14
Slovenia	4	2	2	3	2	2	15
Estonia	4	2	3	3	2	2	16
Latvia	4	2	3	3	2	3	17
Lithuania	4	2	3	3	2	4	18
Bulgaria	3	3	4	3	3	3	19
Romania	2	3	4	3	3	4	19
Russia	1	4	4	3	5	3	20
Slovakia	4	3	3	4	3	3	20

Source: 'Emerging Markets Profiles', Ernst and Young, April 1995 in Business Europa, November/ December 1995, p. 27

Table 10.7 Selected CEER panel rankings of market attractiveness

		Av. Score	Last year's ranking	Econ. growth	Price stability	Global integration	Currency stability	Rule of law	Ease of portfolio investment	Productivity
1.	Czech Rep.	8.3	1	7.5	8.0	9.2	8.0	8.8	8.8	7.7
2.	Slovenia	8.2	2	6.7	8.3	9.2	8.2	8.5	6.8	9.0
3.	Poland	8.1	3	8.5	6.0	9.2	8.0	9.0	8.7	7.5
4.	Estonia	7.6	6	7.2	6.0	8.2	8.0	7.8	6.8	6.3
5.	Hungary	7.5	4	5.3	6.2	9.2	7.3	8.8	8.5	7.8
6.	Croatia	6.8	8	6.7	8.3	6.7	7.2	6.2	5.3	7.2
7.	Slovakia	6.7	5	6.8	8.3	7.2	7.5	6.7	6.3	6.7
8.	Latvia	6.5	7	5.2	6.3	7.5	6.8	7.5	5.8	5.8
9.	Lithuania	6.2	9	5.3	5.2	8.0	7.8	7.7	6.0	5.5
11.	Romania	5.1	10	6.5	4.0	5.8	3.7	5.2	4.8	4.2
12.	Russia	4.8	14	3.7	5.7	5.5	6.2	4.0	5.5	5.0
16.	Albania	3.5	13	5.8	7.0	3.4	5.0	4.8	1.4	2.8
18.	Ukraine	3.4	20	2.5	4.2	4.3	5.0	3.7	3.0	4.0
20.	Bulgaria	3.3	11	2.3	1.7	5.2	1.3	4.3	4.0	4.0

Note: Grades were given on a scale of 0 to 10, with 10 the highest score.

Source: *Wall Street Journal Europe, Central and East European Review,* December 1996–January 1997, p.10

ter belonging to a sleepy rural party. Note that the term 'privatisation' is translated only as 'ownership changes' in Polish and this has been a more accurate translation as the Treasury continues to assume responsibility for certain large state enterprises.

- The market is dynamic and competition is intense. Countries such as Poland allow semi-convertibility of their national currency, at least within Poland. This has been very reassuring to Western investors.
- Poland has become the economic tiger of Cen-

tral Europe with the highest economic growth rates in all of Europe for 1995 and 1996. This attracts further Western investment.

- Sheer market potential is still the main draw for foreign investors. Poland has a market of 39 million people, 98 per cent are ethnic Poles, mostly Catholic and half of them are under 40 years of age. Yet a further strategic reason for investing in Poland, say, would be the current and future access to the European Union. For investors in the Pacific Rim it would make sense if they did not already have

Table 10.8 Post-communism: not everyone has learnt their lesson

	Democracy	Economic performance	Internal stability	Relations with neighbours	Human rights	Outlook
Czech Rep.	4	4	5	4	4	√
Poland	4	5	4	5	4	√
Hungary	4	4	4	5	4	√
Slovenia	4	4	5	4	4	√
Estonia	4	5	3	2	3	√
Albania	2	3	3	3	2	√
Serbia-Montenegro	1	1	2	1	1	×
Bosnia-Herzegovina	2	1	1	1	2	×
Belarus	1	1	2	3	1	×
Azerbaijan	2	3	2	2	2	√
Georgia	2	2	2	2	2	√
Tajikistan	1	1	1	2	1	×

Key: 5 – Outstanding.
      4 – Suitable for EU/NATO membership.
      3 – Tolerable.
      2 – Worrisome.
      1 – Deplorable.

Source: *The World in 1997,* Economist Publications, London

Table 10.9   The grey spectrum

Registered	Unregistered	Illegal
'HIDDEN' ACTIVITIES INCLUDED IN OFFICIAL GDP		
• Construction of new houses • Growing/selling own produce • Production controlled by criminal groups	• Construction of new houses • Wages for work on small farms	• Theft of construction materials • Unpaid use of collective goods/services on private farms
GOODS AND SERVICES MISSING FROM OFFICIAL GDP		
• Unreported wages, entrepreneurial income • Final consumption reported as intermediate consumption, or as inputs for private firms (car, TV etc) • Barter	• Production of unregistered firms • Room, house letting • Paid housework, baby-sitting, secretarial work etc • Unrecorded deals between state firms	• Production of alcohol, drugs etc • Prostitution, illegal abortion • Unpaid use of phone, mail etc at workplace • Unpaid use of TV, electricity, water, transport etc
VALUE DIFFERENCES ON GOODS AND SERVICES		
• Tips • Extra payments for obtaining goods in short supply	• Trade margin on goods sold on street/in houses • Intellectual property infringements	• Smuggling • Trading stolen goods • Black market currency trading/private lending
INVISIBLE INCOMES		
• Purchase of state assets at very low prices • Extraordinary capital gains in privatization		• Theft of cars, durables • Tax evasion • Insurance fraud • Bribery, embezzlement, racketeering, gambling

Source: Arvay, J. and Dallago, B. IIASA, (1994), in *Business Central Europe*, **2** (8), February, 9

Exhibit 10.15   Warning to buyers of farms in eastern Europe

Agriculture in eastern Europe is still starved of capital and many farm businesses are crying out for western investment, the Oxford Farming Conference was told yesterday.

However, buyers face pitfalls as well as potentially large rewards, said Mr Jan Cermak, international business development manager for Adas, the UK agricultural advisory service.

'If we were to assume that the Klondike gold rush was orderly in comparison with the central and east European way of doing business, then we are probably not too far off reality,' he said.

Mr Cermak said the farming industry in the Czech Republic, Slovakia, Poland and Hungary would soon be very competitive – with the exception of the dairy sector, where production levels were still low.

East European agriculture offered a vision of life after the Common Agricultural Policy, he said. Subsidies in the Czech Republic amounted to less than 12 per cent of the value of production – compared with about 42 per cent in the European Union – and were often targeted at poorer hill farms.

'The region has seen the emergence of a very strong and dynamic corporate farming sector, where companies farm 1,500 to 3,500 hectares of rented land with economies of scale and considerable buying power,' Mr Cermak said.

Cereal growing in central Europe benefited from a warm climate, which meant grain driers only had to be used once every five or six years. Grain stores capable of holding 40,000 to 60,000 tonnes were dotted around the lowlands of the Elbe and Danube and were well-served by railways, he said.

> → Exhibit 10.15 *continued*
>
> Opportunities for foreign investment arose from the lack of local credit, because banks were still reluctant to lend to farmers, he said.
>
> The Dutch, Danes and Germans were already 'scouring the countryside looking for the opportunity to jam their boot in the door,' Mr Cermak told the conference.
>
> Potential UK buyers could apply for grants of up to £50,000 from the government under the Know-How Fund to determine the feasibility of an investment.
>
> Among the success stories, delegates were told, was that of one south of England farmer who bought 80 per cent of a farming company near Prague for no more than the cost of a second-hand Skoda car. However, another UK farmer had been stymied by a tenants' revolt on the land he was about to buy.
>
> Westerners had to be prepared for slow negotiations, potential partners reluctant to adopt new technology and production techniques, and sellers with 'grossly inflated ideas about valuation of assets'.
>
> *Source: Financial Times*, 9 January 1997

a base within the European Union to start to consider the lower costs and similar access enjoyed by the Central Europeans. Korea has become a large investor in Poland, Czech Republic and elsewhere now in Central Europe. Costs are lower, wages are about 10 per cent of corresponding German levels but productivity is lower.

- The infrastructure is still weak and these countries remain cash based economies which is good news for those in the cash and carry business, and the millions employed in the grey economy who do not pay tax. Over time, this will change but for the next six years at least this will continue.
- Banking and finance is weak, and few have bank accounts relative to the West. However, the potential for profitability is enormous if we then calculate on introducing the electronic ATM cash machines instead of bank branches. Poland is among the least banked nations in Europe with 91 bank branches per 1 million inhabitants, creating huge profitability potential if they then go over to introducing ATM machines. There is presently 350 ATMs installed in Poland but 6,000 are envisaged. Similarly, half a million have credit cards but the potential is to reach 4 million within four years. For VISA cards at the moment there are only 140,000 cardholders and they are using the cards as a debit card, not as a credit card.
- A combination of a grey economy and cash based economy means in effect that personal disposable incomes are much higher than declared and this together with a tradition of conspicuous consumption means that if people have money they will spend it, not save it. This is sufficient to fuel the current spending spree but not sustain it in the longer term, which will need the provision of consumer finance.
- Retailing in Poland is weak and the average store size is only 50 m² or smaller which explains why the British, Dutch, Germans and French are all eager to get into the market. It is because it constitutes virgin territory for these large established retailers and competition that is relatively easy for them to handle.
- Distribution was one of the very first problems that had to be addressed, and foreign entrants met this. Note that when Coca-Cola wanted to enter the Polish market they saturated the small shops with chilled drink cabinets so as to entice people to buy their product the way they like it to be served: chilled.
- Shortages no longer apply to this region. Everything is available at a price, including goods from designer shops.
- Communications have always been poor. There is still a cultural block in terms of sending pieces of mail. It is a throwback to communist times when the popular saying was: 'ink stains!'. In other words, do not commit yourself to anything, and especially not in writing. E-mail and the Internet are now accessible just about everywhere and the take-up is high. So, too, with cellular telephones which have allowed these economies to make a quantum leap from a situation of shortage to a situation of plenty thanks to satellite and cellular telephones being made available where landlines were still not present. In the previous regime, it was entirely possible to wait 13 years for installation of a telephone. Technology has circumvented the need for that infrastructural investment in landlines by developing alternative technologies. Thirty-eight per cent of households in Poland have a telephone compared with 93 per cent in the UK. However, penetration of cellular telephones is correspondingly higher.

- Commercial and industrial property and real estate prices are rising very quickly.
- Pensions in Poland are index linked and so it will be a matter of time before politicians choose to deal with this important issue of 9 million pensioners who consume 20 per cent of the national budget.
- The pattern of trading as well as the commodity structure of exports has changed very significantly, with 80 per cent of Polish exports now going to OECD countries. A similar effect has been noted amongst the other CEFTA members.
- The potential of the Eastern Bloc is being overlooked by the Central Europeans in their mad rush for membership of the European Union.
- New industries such as advertising are being created with Western investment. In Poland, advertising is now an industry with billings in excess of $800,000 yet in 1989 there was only one state advertising agency in each of these communist countries. However, advertising costs are rising quickly to meet Western levels and there is increasing indifference to advertising now, almost as a backlash against propaganda to which previous generations were subjected.
- Networking is very important because of the speed of change and the continual number of new entrants.
- Innovation is occurring in all sectors of the economy. New magazines and periodicals are appearing, new cable television channels, new commercial radio channels and new services are being offered.
- Legislation has been slow to respond to the new realities and so the legal system would appear to be no better than a patchwork quilt. Resort has been made to legislation in many cases prior to the entry of the communist system, dating back often to the 1930s and earlier. New legislation has been introduced to cover intellectual property and industrial property rights, which would severely impede foreign investment if they were not in place. New legislation covers foreign investment, acquisition and joint ventures but the system as a whole needs to be overhauled. It is interesting to note that what was once acceptable practice is now no longer tolerated. Previously when the government was partner to a car company it would ask for payment of the car to be made before delivery took place in a few years' time. Should the price increase before delivery then the customer had also to pay for all these increases as well. Such practices have now been outlawed in Poland. Again, where financial penalties are stated these are often now derisory and unfortunately can be ignored. Poland is now in the process of having a new constitution approved.
- Finance and banking is weak as previously mentioned and this is a disincentive to set up in business. Equally, lenders are now looking to the dynamic market in consumer durables and more lending is now being directed towards this sector than to business start-ups

Table 10.10   Key areas for investment

- Environmental clean-up, which includes treatment of effluents and airborne emissions and their future eradication.
- Consumer goods.
- Food production and distribution.
- Health care, in terms of health education and resources including buildings, equipment and pharmaceutical preparations.
- Transportation, where traditional subsidies have been ended, but infrastructural work needs to be undertaken to speed both passengers and freight.
- Packaging, where plastics have not been used to any great extent in the past and packaging as a part of product design is unknown.
- Communications.
- Services, such as financial services and banking.
- Retailing, which is generally backward in terms of merchandizing as well as display, customer service training, sales training and computerized sales systems including EFTPOS terminals.
- Tourism, where hotels are needed in many cities and towns. Budapest is well served now but Warsaw now needs some economy or budget hotels as most of its city centre hotels are now in the luxury class. This could create interesting additions for tour operators to add to their programmes of short-stay city breaks.

Source: Paliwoda, S. J. (1995), *Investing in Eastern Europe – Capitalizing on Emerging Markets*, Addision-Wesley/EIU Books, p.21

if for the simple reason that it is more profitable and less risky. However, for the national economies concerned it will have important effects if this becomes a trend.

- Market information is poor and market research although available is uncertain. There is no Dun and Bradstreet equivalent so finding out about borrowers is difficult, particularly as many have not been long in business themselves.
- Doing business is still time consuming and with the fragmentation of markets and the dynamics of the market it is difficult to identify the decision makers.
- Visible change can be seen at all levels of society. Change is here to stay. Massive office construction projects and residential areas are under way in capitals such as Poland's. Many such as PepsiCo, owners of Taco Bell, Pizza Hut and Kentucky Fried Chicken restaurants, are looking for similar locational opportunities across the region.

- Management is in short supply so there are some excellent openings at high salaries for expatriates, at least in the short term.

Postscript

Communism left behind a legacy of acceptable sub-optimization, a conducive environment in which underachievers could thrive. Expectations will take time to change but attitudes towards ownership, the private sector, and the selling of state assets are important for the present-day economy. Hayder and Kuras (1995) used the term 'Polish Bermuda Triangle' to depict a situation where investment opportunities were being lost to Western investors and to the Polish economy through three points of the triangle: frightened local management fearing for their own jobs, heavily unionized labour with political clout seeking written assurances and guarantees, and ignorant foreign investors

---

Exhibit 10.16   Russian tax police go to work with AK-47 rifles

'Do you want to live a normal life in a decent country where children are properly educated and your grandparents get their pensions on time?' the voice used to boom from the television screen. 'Then why don't you pay your taxes.'

But the tax authorities have just released a new advertisement – and this one has a more menacing tone: 'The tax police have guns,' intones a voice. 'And they know how to use them.'

Clearly, if Russians can't be persuaded to pay taxes – and a recent survey found 61 per cent believed tax evasion was not a crime – then coercion is the only option.

So the tax police have decided to parade a 500-man Swat (Special Weapons and Tactics) team before the cameras, brandishing AK-47 assault rifles, sniper rifles, tear gas, grenades, shotguns, bullet-proof body armour, heavy-duty saws and mountaineering equipment. These members of the Physical Protection Department assist the State Tax Police, guard tax offices and provide special protection for tax inspectors.

As this week's deadline to file tax returns passed, revenue service offices were inundated by queues of frightened citizens. The Federal Tax Service says it expects about five million people to file declarations, up by 100 per cent from last year. But according to one inspectorate covering northwest Moscow, there is a long way to go. Its figures show around 4,000 returns were filed in an area covering 700,000 adults. This year it has received just 1,000 more returns than last year.

Russia's massive unpaid tax bills are disingenuously cited by the government as an excuse for wage and pension arrears. It is also the main reason the International Monetary Fund suspends monthly loan payments. To many Russians, the idea of paying taxes is anathema. Olga Krutskikh, deputy director of Inspectorate No 15, explains that paying taxes won't become a part of life for Russians until people see the benefits.

'If people lived in normal apartments and rode on good public transport; if their children went to good schools and they always received salaries on time, they would understand the need to pay taxes,' she said.

Low and middle-income Russians believe, with some reason, that the country's rouble billionaires and firms with government contacts get away with paying nothing.

The aim of the tax drive is to destroy Russia's black economy, and according to Mikhail Polyakov, head of the Swat unit: 'The most difficult task is to kick the economic base out from under organised crime.' Honest entrepreneurs, however, complain equally justifiably that Russia's tax code is so complicated that it is impossible to abide by it and make a profit.

Being a tax official is not much fun. Last year the Swat team took 36 people under special protection during a period which saw 26 tax officials assassinated, 74 wounded in the line of duty and 41 subject to arson attacks.

→

→ **Exhibit 10.16** *continued*

Last December the head of one Moscow tax office was threatened and her son kidnapped. When the Swat team eventually found him, his face had been beaten beyond recognition.

On the other hand, the tax police are hardly irreproachable. Small deals with minor traders are commonly struck by officials who value their lives, but that is nothing to the shenanigans of those at the top.

A recent report found they have been building themselves luxurious apartments, illegally investing government money and helping themselves to budget funds to pay their own income tax bills.

An investigation into the State Tax Service by parliament's accounting chamber, printed in the weekly newspaper *Argumenti i Facti*, revealed that top tax officials had spent 6.6 billion roubles ($1.1 million) of taxpayers' money buying and renovating apartments.

It also accuses them of investing 'billions' of roubles in private banks and firms. The money for these illegal activities came from a 'social development fund' created to improve working conditions for tax service employees.

This was supposed to be financed from fines and back payments collected by the service. But since 1995, it has been paid for from the budget – in other words, Russia's taxpayers.

Last year half the fund was supposed to go to regions outside Moscow but got lost somewhere between the finance ministry and the State Tax Service. This left regional offices without money to pay rent or telephone bills. Tax officials had allegedly used the cash to pay their income taxes.

Source: The European, 3–9 April, 1997

unaware of local market conditions and demands. There is a growing demand for new products and services, a need and a realization that foreign investment is a requirement but political tensions are being created over tax breaks offered to multinationals in particular. Poland is now being seen as a strategic market able to command an interesting position between the old satellites of the FSU and those aspiring to the EU. It is therefore able to attract investment from the Far East as its new prominence offers geographical advantage and logistical opportunities. The old rules no longer apply. It is to be hoped that the legislators will apply perspicacity in devising the new ones.

There remain opportunities, particularly in the sectors listed in Table 10.10.

Revision questions
1. From what early origins did the European Union emerge?
2. What is EFTA? What is the EEA?
3. What is the present size and economic potential of the EU?
4. Describe the marketing opportunities created by the European Union.
5. Outline the potential for market segmentation within the EU.
6. Where is the Golden Triangle and what is its significance?
7. The EU is often parodied because of its desire to impose common standards. Is there a case for standardization as in the Common Commercial Policy?
8. Is the Common Agricultural Policy likely perhaps to bring down the EU?
9. Outline the position of countries outside the EU toward the enlargement of the EU, notably Japan and the US.
10. What is the Lomé Convention and does it appear to be effective?
11. How has 'dumping' come to be a political issue?
12. Name six of the gaps which existed after 1990 when Central and Eastern Europe moved towards democratic systems and free market economies.
13. The remains of what was the Soviet Empire are now independent countries in Central and Eastern Europe looking towards the EU for stability; the Russian Federation and the other independent republics. Name three in each category and state what their present-day objectives are.
14. What were the old problems which they faced and what are the new problems emerging?
15. What is the potential for trade and investment of the Central and East European region?
16. What is the significance of the grey economy to Western marketers?
17. Which entry methods would you recommend if asked to devise a strategy for Eastern Europe?
18. Where are the quantum leaps in development? What quantum leaps are being observed in Central and Eastern Europe and why should this be of interest to marketers?

19. Outline the implications for marketers of dealing in a cash-based economy.
20. What are the growth sectors to be found in Central and Eastern Europe generally?

References

Barnard, B. (1996) 'EU's old economic ties fraying: trade pact with former colonies lags global times', *Journal of Commerce and Commercial*, September 25, **409** (28816), 24C–25C.

Barnard, B. (1996) 'A Buyer's Market (global logistics services)', *Journal of Commerce and Commercial*, October 2, **410** (28821), 1C–3C.

Belkin, J. and Warshaw, J. (1996) 'Opportunities exist for US Insurers in EU Insurance Market', *Best's Review* – Life-Health Insurance Edition, June, **97** (2), 49–51.

Business International S. A. (Weekly Newsletter), *Business Eastern Europe*, London.

Caplen, B. (1996) 'Borderless World Wish', *Asian Business*, February, **32** (2), 55–56.

Carlson, G. S. (1995) 'US keeps watch over Canada – EU grain pact', *Feedstuffs*, December 4, **67** (50), 3–4.

Caudron, S. (1994) 'The Myth of the European Consumer', *Industry Week*, February 21, **243** (4), 28–33.

Cecchini, P. (1988) *The European Challenge: 1992 – The Benefits of a Single Market*, Wildwood House, Aldershot, Hants.

Colchester, N., and Buchan, D. (1990) *Europower*, Economist Books and Random House, New York.

East European Trade Council (EETC), London, monthly bulletin.

Eurostat (1995) *Europe in Figures*, Brussels and Luxembourg.

Ferguson, W. (1994) 'EU product and service standards (ISO 9000)', *Journal of Small Business Management*, October, **32** (4), 84–88.

Financial Times Survey, 'The Czech Republic', Friday December 6, 1996

Financial Times Survey (1997) 'Investing in Central and Eastern Europe', Friday April 11

Healey, N. M. (1995) *The Economics of the New Europe*, Routledge, London.

Hufbauer, G. C. (1990) *Europe 1992 – An American Perspective*, Brookings Institution, Washington DC.

Ishikawa, K. (1990) *Japan and the Challenge of 1992*, Pinter Publishers for Royal Institute of International Affairs, London.

James, C. (1996) 'Banana Exporters seek Support against US attack', *Journal of Commerce and Commercial*, December 18, **406** (28622), 5A–6A.

Jorn, K. (1996) 'The European Union and the Japanese Market', *Journal of Japanese Trade & Industry*, January–February, **15** (1), 20–24.

Laurie, S. (1990) Unequal partnership. *Banker*, January, 40–41.

Lohbeck, D. (1996) 'A Review of CE Marking', *Design News*, September 23, **51** (18), 212–213.

London Chamber of Commerce and Industry (1990) *Winning Business in Eastern Europe: A Guide to European Community Funding and Opportunities*, June.

Mellors, C., and Copperthwaite, N. (1990) *Regional Policy*, University of Bradford and Spicers European Policy Reports, Routledge, London.

Misser, F. (1996) 'A Farewell to Alms?' *African Business*, April, No. 209, 19–21.

Monti, M. (1996) *The Single Market and Tomorrow's Europe: A Progress Report from the European Commission*, Kogan Page, London.

Moscow Narodny Bank Ltd. (bi-monthly) *Press Bulletin*, London.

National Consumer Council (1988) *Consumers and the Common Agricultural Policy*, HMSO, London.

Paliwoda, S. J. (1991) Changing East-West trade patterns: implications for global tourism. *World Travel and Tourism Review*, **1**, CAB International, Wallingford, Oxon.

Paliwoda, S. J. (1995) 'A New Marketing Environment as Eastern Europe moves Westwards', in Paliwoda, S. J. and Ryans Jr., J. K. (1995), *International Marketing Reader*, Routledge, London.

Paliwoda, S. J. (1995) *Investing in Eastern Europe*, Addison-Wesley/EIU Books, London.

Paliwoda, S. J. (1996) 'Creating a Marketing Orientation in Transitional Economy Countries', William Davidson Institute Symposium, University of Michigan.

Paliwoda, S. J. (1997) 'Capitalizing on the Emergent Markets of Central and Eastern Europe', *European Business Journal*, No 2.

Paliwoda, S. J., and Liebrenz, M. L. (1984) Expectations and outcomes of multinational joint ventures in Eastern Europe. *European Journal of Marketing*. **18** (3).

Postal Direct Marketing Service (PDMS) 'Guide to Cross-Border Direct Marketing', draws on information from 11 European postal authorities, and includes details of a pan-European survey showing that 57 per cent of business exporters now use cross-border direct mail. There are explanations of how to get started, a nine step planning model, creative ideas and barriers to success and how to overcome them. The guide is free to businesses from: PDMS Information Centre, PO Box 132, DK-2800 Lyngby, Denmark.

Ryans Jr., J. K., and Rau, P. A. (1990) *Marketing Strategies for the New Europe: A North American Perspective on 1992*, American Marketing Association, Chicago.

Schmitt, B. (1995) 'Divisive Issues key to MSA (multilateral steel agreement)', *American Metal Market*, February 8, **103** (26), 1–3.

Shaw, J. (1996) *Law of the European Union*, Second Edition, Macmillan, Basingstoke, Hampshire.

Sherlock, J. (1995) 'A Single European Market?' in Paliwoda, S. J. and Ryans Jr, J. K. (1995), *International Marketing Reader*, Routledge, London.

Silva, M., and Sjögren. B. (1990) *Europe 1992 and the New World Power Game*, John Wiley & Sons, New York.

Taylor, C., and Press, A. (1988) *1992: The Facts and Challenges*, Ernst and Whinney for the Industrial Society, London.

Traffic Management (1994) 'Logistics Strategies for a "New Europe" ', August, **33** (8), 49A–52A

Transition Brief, Newsletter of the Centre for Cooperation with the Economies in Transition, OECD Secretariat, Paris.

Vermulst, E., and Waer, P. (1990) European Community rules of origin as commercial policy instruments? *Journal of World Trade*, **24** (3), 55–99.

Verrue, R. (1995) 'Economic Transition in Eastern Europe', *Management Accounting*, June, **73** (6), 6–7.

Web sites

Business Europa – business throughout Central and Eastern Europe
http://www.business–europa.co.uk

Business Information
http://www.businessmonitor.co.uk

Business Information Resources
http://sashimi.wwa.com/~notime/eotw/business_info.html

Business Information Server
http://www.dnb.com/

Business Site of the Day
http://www.bizniz.com/eurocool/

Business Statistics
gopher: University of Michigan:
una.hh.lib.umich.edu
Choose: ebb Current Business Statistics

Businesses on the Internet
http://www.yahoo.com/
Business_and_Economy/Corporations/

Business to Business Marketing Exchange
http://www.btob.wfu.edu/b2b.html

Christmas Traditions in France and in Canada
http://www.culture.fr/culture/noel/angl/noel.htm

CIA Publications
http://www.odc.gov/cia/publications/pus.html

Commerce Business Daily
gopher:cscns.com
Choose: Internet Express Gopher by Subject
Business-Commerce Business Daily-Softshare

Commercenet
http://www.commerce.net

Commercial Use of the Internet
http://pass.wayne.edu/business.html

CyberShop
http://www.cybershop.com

Czech Happenings
http://www.ios.com/~jirim/czech.html

Czech Republic: Business Monitor – Arthur Andersen, Czech Republic Index

Czech Republic general lists
http://www.cesnet.cz/html/cesnet/wwwservers.html

Czech Republic Government Information
http://www.czech.cz/

Czech Republic Subject Index
http://www.columbia.edu/cu/sipa/REGIONAL/ECE/czechrep.html

Department of Trade & Industry – Central Europe
http://www.dti.gov.uk/ots/centeuro

E-trade
http://wwwetrade.com

ECHO – European Commission Host Organisation
http://www2.echo.lu/echo/en/echodesc.html

EU Basics – general EU questions
http://eubasics.allmansland.com/general.html

Europa
http://europa.eu.int/welcome.html

Europages
http://www.europages.com

Europe – Business Monitor
http://www.businessmonitor.co.uk

Europe – see Yellowweb Europe and Europages

European Electronic Information Market
http://www2.echo.lu

European Information: The European
    Commission's Representative in the UK
http://www.cec.org.uk

European Union – Citizen's First
http://www.eu.com

European Union and the Internet
http://www.helsinki.fi/~aunesluo/
    eueng.html

Federal Express
http://www.fedex.com

France general lists
http://www.urec.fr/cgi-bin/list

France government information
http://www.ensmp.fr/industrie

Germany general lists
http://www.chemie.fu-berlin.de/
    outerspace/www-german.html

Germany – government information research
    and technology
http://www.dFin.de/bmbf/

Holiday Inn
http://www.holiday-inn.com

Hotel & Travel Index On-Line
http://www.traveler.net/htio

Hungary. Network
http://www.hungary.com

Hungary – American Chamber of Commerce
http://www.hungary.com/amcham/html

Hungary – A Soft Road to the Hungarian
    Economy
http://www.bekkoame.or.ip/~hyoko

The Hungarian Economy/MIT
http://iqsoft.hueconomy/index.html

Industry.net
http://www.industry.net

International Franchise Association

Internet Business Center
http://www.tig.com/IBC

Internet Marketing List Archives
http://www.popco.com/hyper/
    inet-marketing/

Internet Public Library
http://ipl.sils.umich.edu/

Internet Society
http://info.isoc.org/home.html

International Small Business Consortium
http://www.isbc.com

Lands' End – the famous clothing catalogue
    company
http://www.landsend.com

L.L.Bean
http://www.llbean.com

Los Angeles Times
http://www.latimes.com

Minitel
http://www.minitel.fr

National Readership Surveys
http://www.nrs.co.uk

Netmart
http://www.netmart.com

Nielsen Media Research
http://www.nielsenmedia.com

Political Risk Services
http://www.polrisk.com

Royal Family
http://www.neosoft.com/~dlgates/uk/
    ukspecific.html?pix_windsors.

Royalty – an entertainment
http://www.royalnetwork.com

News in Motion
http://www.newspaper.com

PC Daily News
http://www.zdnet.co.uk

Poland – Analysis: IT Weaknesses in Poland
http://gurukul.ucc.american.edu/MOGIT/
    sdiamon/weakpage.html

Poland BEMS Home Page
http://www.stat-usa.gov/bems/bemspol/
    bemspol.html

Poland – Business, Tourist and Cultural
    Information
http://www.wonet.com.pl

Poland Country Guide–Business in Poland
http://ciesin.ci.uw.edu.pl/poland/orbis/
    business.htm

Poland – Exploring Poland via the World Wide
    Web
http://jhunix.hcf.jhu.edu/~klism_jr/
    Poland.html

Poland: Historical Statistics
http://www.ssc.upenn.edu/~szyrmer/
    e95s/e95s.notes.histstat.html

Poland Home Page
http://users.aol.com/DAorlowska/home/
  poland.html

Poland – Warsaw – let yourself in!
http://www.explore-poland.pl/
  warsaw/guide/g101.htm

Poland – Warsaw Voice
http://www.contact.waw.pl/voi

Polish Home Page
http://info.fuw.edu.pl/pl/
  PolandHome.html

Polish Press Agency
http://www.pap.waw.pl/

Reebok
http://www.reebok.com

REESWeb – Russian & East European Studies
  Department of the University of Pittsburgh
http://www.pitt.edu/~cjp/rees.html

Russia
http://www.russia.net

Russian MBA Association
http://www.serve.com/mbafsu/

Scottish Tourist Board
http://www.holiday.scotland.net

Scotweb
http://www.scotweb.co.uk

Small Business Administration
http://www.sbaonline.sba.gov

Small Business Information
http://www.ro.com/small_business/
  homebased.html

Business Network International
http://www.bninet.com

Statistical Agencies on the Internet
http://www.science.gmu.edu/csi779/
  drope/govstats.html

Statistics UK
http://www.emap.com/cso

SunSITE Classic – Previous Best of the Web
  Award winner
http://sunsite.unc.edu/

The European Business Directory
http://www.europages.com/g/home.html

Trade Compass
http://www.tradecompass.com

TradePort – extensive information on
  international business
http://www.tradeport.org

Trade Statistics
http://www.census.gov/ftp/pub/
  foreign-trade/www/

TradeWave Galaxy – Public and commercial
  information and services
http://www.einet.net/galaxy.html

U.S. Fedworld
http://www.fedworld.gov

Scotch Malt Whisky – Laphroaig
http://www.laphroaig.com

Scotch Malt Whisky – Glenmorangie
http://www.glenmorangie.com

Scotland – Virtual Memorial Garden
http://www.hebrides.com

Stationery Office Web Site (for all EU
  publications)
http://www.the-stationery-office.co.uk/

US views on the EU: Country Report on
  Economic Policy and Trade Practices, U.S.
  State Dept.
gopher: UMSLVMA.UMSL.EDU:70/00/
  library/govdocs/CRPT0023

Virtual Cemetery – Scotland
http://www.hebrides.com

Virtual Shopping Malls
http://www.itl.net/shopping/index.html

Virtual Vineyards
http://www.virtualvin.com/

Winter Web Wonderland
http://banzai.neosoft.com/citylink/xmas

World Bank
http://www.worldbank.org/

World Factbook
gopher: gopher.aecom.yu.edu

World Health Organization
gopher: gopher.gsfc.nasa.gov

World Wide Web Virtual Library
http://W3.org

Yellow Pages website
http://www.yell.co.uk

Yelloweb Europe
http://www.yweb.com/

CHAPTER 11

Marketing in the Pacific Rim

Asia is not going to be civilized after the methods of the West. There is too much Asia and she is too old.
Rudyard Kipling, *Life's Handicap*, 'The Man Who Was' (1891)

APEC and the economic potential of the region

The 1995 statistics for GWP (Gross World Product) show the USA accounting for 22 per cent, Western Europe for 21 per cent and Japan for 8 per cent, reflecting again the pattern of the trading Triad discussed earlier. However, there is clear consensus amongst economic analysts that the future leadership of global trade belongs to Asia and particularly to the Pacific Rim. Europe has been able to achieve economic gains only through the benefits arising from economic harmonization measures developing out of the European Union, without which the old European nations would be quite different today and much poorer. What then is striking is that the organization which holds the promise to do the same for this region – APEC – in fact straddles more than one continent and has the potential at least to become the largest economic trading bloc in the world. APEC is an economic grouping of 18 countries which together account for more than half of all global economic activity. The timetable for APEC is loose with certain conditions to be met first by the richer developed economies by 2010 and by the remainder by 2020, so it is for the moment no more than a distant cloud on the horizon. Similarly, the ASEAN Free Trade Area is not scheduled to implement the Common Effective Preferential Tariff Scheme before 2003, and 2008 in the case of Vietnam.

Nevertheless, the impact is one that will provoke permanent change in global trade patterns. This was pointed out by the Canadian Deputy Minister for Foreign Affairs and International Trade:

The potential of the Asia-Pacific market is absolutely enormous. By the year 2000, the region will account for 60 per cent of the world's population; 50 per cent of the world's GDP and 40 per cent of global consumption. By 2020, seven of the top 10 economies in the world will be in Asia Pacific. And it is increasing its share of world merchandise trade – from about 37 per cent in 1983 to 48 per cent in 1995.

Source: Canada Export, January 1997.

This should in fact be considered alongside the eight Asian megatrends which Naisbitt states are changing the world:

1.   From Nation States to Networks.
2.   From Export-led to Consumer-driven.
3.   From Western influence to The Asian Way.
4.   From Government controlled to Market-driven.
5.   From Villages to Supercities.
6.   From Labour-Intensive to High Technology.
7.   From Male Dominance to Emergence of Women.
8.   From West to East.

The first half of this chapter examines China; the second half examines Japan.

China

China is one of the four major ancient countries of civilization and invented the compass, gunpowder, papermaking and printing. However, after the sixteenth century the development of China slowed greatly. After the Second World War and up to 1978, China entered a period of self-imposed isolation from the rest of the world. In 1978, China introduced the 'Open Door' policy on economic reform and since then the economy has grown very quickly. By the year 2000, China's import volume will be equivalent to one-seventh of the current global annual trade volume. China is still a communist country trying to embrace communism alongside the benefits of capitalism. It was Deng Xiaoping in 1982 who first presented the concept of one country but two systems. There are many seeming contradictions but in China there are none of the signs which were evident in the Former Soviet Union (FSU) before its collapse, such as the strong centralization. In fact, foreign trade corporations now exist in all provinces, SEZs' and most cities. Centralized control has decreased. Membership of the communist party in China is growing steadily and keeping pace with economic gains.

China is governed by the State Council, which is the executive of the National People's Congress (NPC). The Constitution of the People's Republic of China identifies six bodies: the National People's Congress, the President of the People's Republic of China, the State Council, the Central Military Commission, the Supreme People's Court and the Supreme People's Procuratorate. All of these are created by the first, the National People's Congress, and are responsible to it and its Steering Committee. The NPC is the highest tier of state power in the PRC.

Jiang Zemin is President of a country which includes seven free trade zones, 23 provinces (since China includes Taiwan in this definition), six autonomous regions (including Hong Kong) and three municipalities. All China is on Beijing time (GMT + 8 hours).

The Communist Party was founded on 1 July 1921 in Shanghai and came to power in 1949. China is presently enjoying high economic growth of around 10 per cent per annum over the past six years and the Ninth Five-Year Plan to the year 2000 outlines proposals for economic structural reform and national economic development. With such high economic growth, China is experiencing a phenomenon where its per capita GNP doubles every few years. Economic forecasts to 2010 show that this trend should continue. The statistics for GDP per capita show a figure of $2,300 US, which takes China out of the category of the poorest and puts it on track to overtake the USA within 30 years.

China is the world's most populous nation, although it is expected that it will be eclipsed by India early in the next millennium, around the year 2040. Population growth in China has been stemmed now to only 1.212 per cent. The Chinese population includes 56 ethnic groups of which the Han people account for 92 per cent. China is the third largest country in the world by size of landmass, after Russia and Canada. Eighty per cent of China's landmass is uninhabitable mountainous and desert regions, so the population lives in an area that measures 740,000 square miles, which is approximately the size of Mexico. The amount of land under cultivation continues to fall because of erosion and economic development. Since 1949, there has been a loss of 15 per cent and so China's biggest problem becomes one of feeding its ever-increasing population. However, economic growth over the past six years has been of the order of 9–10 per cent.

Currency

Until 1994, China operated a dual currency system whereby domestic companies traded in yuan while foreign transactions required Foreign Exchange Certificates which led in turn to three different exchange rates: the official rate, an alternative conversion rate for currency swaps between companies in a given province, and, finally, the black market rate. The situation now is much less complicated. In 1994, the FECs were phased out and the official rate and swap market rates were unified, effectively devaluing the yuan by 33 per cent.

The renminbi (international symbol 'RMB') is divided into 100 fen. Within China, the currency is also referred to as yuan. The RMB trades in a managed float. The currency is partly convertible and is projected to be fully convertible by the year 2000. Foreign companies no longer need to balance their imports with foreign earnings and convertibility ushers in new opportunities in the way of financing, as foreign currency loans now become conceivable. Convertibility will further support China's application for membership of the WTO.

Guanxi

The use of personal networks and drawing on relationships is important. Chinese society focuses on the importance of the family clan, spreading outwards from immediate family members. There is an unspoken sense of reciprocity and equity. Developing personal networks means that one enters into a two-way social relationship. The Chinese word 'guanxi' embodies this social responsibility which should be separated from the concept of 'schmoozing' as it is termed in North America where the purpose is simply to wine and dine in order to buy influence. Here, there is the difference between what we may call personal relationships and corporate relationships. Guanxi is an investment in personal relationships, not a fee for a service. It is important, though, for understanding how society functions.

Chinese communism and the fall of Soviet communism

Peter Drucker was perceptive in his comments on the fall of communism in the Soviet Bloc when he said:

Communism collapsed as an economic system. Instead of creating wealth, it created misery. Instead of creating economic quality it created a 'nomenclatura' of functionaries enjoying unprecedented economic privileges. But as a 'creed', Marxism collapsed

Table 11.1 Economic factors for key Pacific Rim nations			
Country	*Chief characteristic*	*Positive economic factors*	*Negative economic factors*
Hong Kong	The colony will return to China in 1997, will eventually become economically integrated with Southern China and the financial and trading centre for overseas Chinese. New infrastructure projects, such as the building of a new airport, are planned	Strategic location China's economic reforms Highly developed infrastructure Development of South China Economic Zone	High inflation Brain drain Rising labour and land costs Possible communist influence
Singapore	This is the business centre for ASEAN (Association of South East Asian Nations – Singapore, Malaysia, Indonesia, the Philippines, Thailand and Brunei). Singapore has many high-technology industries, is part of the growth triangle and the growth of local business groups has been encouraged	Political stability High-quality labour force Highly developed infrastructure ASEAN economic development Strategic location	Increasing labour and land costs Heavy dependence on foreign capital Rising labour and land costs Small domestic market
South Korea	Characterized by some relations with North Korea and the liberalization and opening of capital markets. Upgrading of industry and infrastructure developments is under way	Rising income levels and growing domestic demand Economic exchange with China and North Korea Superior bureaucracy High education levels	High inflation Weak technology base Inadequate infrastructure North Korea's political instability Inefficient industrial organization
Taiwan	Is part of the South China Economic Zone and has established relations with China. Taiwan is currently undergoing financial reform	Strong domestic demand Economic exchange and links with China Abundant funds High education levels	Uncertainty over political relationship with China Labour shortages Inadequate infrastructure Sluggish private investment
Malaysia	Undergoing economic development of private sector and development of supporting industries. Part of the Growth Triangle and enjoying growth of local business groups.	Political stability Proximity to Singapore Liberal policy on foreign investment Improving ties with other ASEAN countries	Labour shortages Weak infrastructure Heavy dependence on foreign capital Underdeveloped supporting industry Economic disparity between ethnic groups
Philippines	Here state-owned companies are being privatized, some progress in land reform has been made and former US military bases are being developed.	High-quality, cheap labour Good international relations Weakening Communist influence	Political instability Inconsistent government policies Inadequate infrastructure Heavy debt repayment burden Poverty in countryside
Thailand	This country is undergoing political democratization. Domestic markets are expanding, financial markets are being internationalized and developments in infrastructure are under way.	Rising income levels Expanding exports of industrial manufactured goods Rising economic exchange with Indo-China Plentiful natural resources and labour	Skilled labour shortages Overcrowding in Bangkok Worsening environment Underdeveloped supporting industry Income disparity

Indonesia	Part of the Growth Triangle and now enjoying post-Suharto leadership. Major developments in infrastructure are under way.	Relatively politically stable Plentiful natural resources and labour Financial support from industrial countries Large domestic market	Inadequate infrastructure Heavy debt burden Economic disparity between ethnic groups
China	Undergoing transition into a socialist market economy. State-owned enterprises are being reformed. Hong Kong is soon to be returned and there are developments in the infrastructure	Acceleration of reforms Vast domestic market Replacement of central planning with market mechanism Improving investment environment Rise in foreign direct investment	Low productivity in state-owned enterprises Fiscal deficits Inflation Population problem Income disparities between coastal and inland regions

Source: Kwan, C. H. (1996) *The Asian Economies in the 1990s, Economic Interdependence in the Asia Pacific Region*, International Journal of Retail and Distribution Management, **24**(11) 16–29

because it did not create the 'New Man'. Instead, it brought out and strengthened all the worst in the Old Adam: corruption, greed and lust for power; envy and mutual distrust; petty tyranny and secretiveness; lying, stealing, denunciation and, above all, cynicism. Communism, the system, had its heroes. But Marxism, the creed, did not have a single saint.

Peter F. Drucker, *Post Capitalist Society*, Butterworth-Heinemann, 1993.

However, the situation in China is quite different from the FSU and in *Asia Rising*, Jim Rohwer put forward the following reasons why China was different:

1. China was pulling itself back from hard-style communism after 30 years and not 70 years in the FSU.
2. Commercial habits were still strong therefore in China.
3. China, unlike the FSU, had never developed a strong central planning apparatus and decentralized decision making and resource allocation were still being practised.
4. China began its reforms in a state of rough macroeconomic balance. The currency was sound, prices stable and no foreign debt.
5. China had a robust grassroots economy.
6. As a nation, China's savings and investment record has been amongst the highest in the world.
7. Modern China has 60 per cent of the population in the workforce and there is a strong work ethic.
8. The Chinese Communist Party continues to grow in membership and has a centralized system of ranking, privileges and controls that closely follows the 2,000-year-old methods of the Chinese imperial bureaucracy. It is intrusive at all levels and requires only obedience, the ideological dimension of communism having been disproved long ago in China with the Cultural Revolution.

Exhibit 11.1   China 'could overtake US by 2020'

China's economy will be larger than that of the US by the year 2020, provided the present direction and momentum of economic reforms are maintained, a report* by Australia's Department of Foreign Affairs and Trade said yesterday.

Despite substantial progress, China's economy is still 'only about half way' in its transition from a centrally-planned to a market system, the report adds.

The 430-page study, China Embraces the Market, described as 'remarkable' the internationalisation of the Chinese economy, with the ratio of trade to gross national product growing from 10 per cent in 1978 to 36 per cent in 1996.

'China's increasing interdependence with the world's trade and investment systems is perhaps the most striking phenomenon of China's recent development,' the report, prepared by the department's East Asia analytical Unit, states.

China's economy was second only to that of the US in 1997, 'measured in terms of domestic purchasing power'. 'If the US maintains 3 per cent growth, its average over the past 15 to 20 years, and China grows at 7 per cent a year, slightly less than its post-1978 average, China's total domestic purchasing power will overtake that of the US by 2020.'

The purchasing power parity (PPP) measurement of an economy is increasingly favoured by

→ **Exhibit 11.1** *continued*

economists over the simple per capita gross domestic product formula. PPP refers to the capacity of a unit of local currency to buy a 'basket of goods and services', providing a standard to compare sizes of competing economies.

China's per capita income is still low, the report goes on, citing World Bank estimates of 350m people out of a population of 1.2bn living below China's poverty level of $1 a day.

Labour productivity is also extremely low, only about 10 per cent of that in the US and comparable to India's. 'This indicates both the economy's development needs and its growth potential, if it applies modern technologies in agriculture, industry and services. All these factors will produce immense trade and investment opportunities, with the need for significant capital flows into China.'

China's growing participation in the world economy saw it leap from 34th place in terms of two-way trade in 1978 to 10th in 1996, accounting for more than 3 per cent of world trade.

China had achieved its aim of quadrupling per capita GNP in 1995, five years ahead of the target year 2000. Between 1978 and 1994, state-owned enterprises' share of industrial output shrank from 78 to 34 per cent, excluding urban col-

lectives. This could be attributed to 'more efficient allocation of resources in most sectors as central planning had been replaced by a more market-oriented approach where international trade and investment have been significant. High savings, high investment and rapid expansion of the urban labour force provide the necessary capital and labour to underpin this growth.

'Long-term sustainability of economic growth will depend on continuing success in macro- and micro-economic reforms, accelerating structural change within agriculture and industry, and further integration into the world economy.'

The Communist party would keep power and stay committed to continued economic reform and integration into the world economy. 'Economic reform has delivered strong growth and tangible benefits.

'The leadership recognises the economy needs to maintain relatively rapid growth, to avoid widespread unemployment and possible social disruption.'

* *China Embraces the Market: Achievements, Constraints and Opportunities. East Asia Analytical Unit, Department of Foreign Affairs and Trade, Canberra, April 1997*

Source: *Financial Times*, 22 April 1997

Economic background to the world's largest market

The People's Republic of China (PRC) was established in 1949, but it chose to maintain an isolationist policy with the rest of the world until 1978 when it joined the United Nations and began to involve itself in world affairs. Since 1949, the important events have been the 'Great Leap Forward' in 1958, an early attempt to modernize China, but the border conflict with the USSR soured Sino – Soviet relations and led to them questioning the wholesale implementation of the Soviet Communist model. The Cultural Revolution, which isolated China from foreign influence, lasted from 1966 to the death of Mao in 1976. Since then, the Chinese Communist model has moved dramatically further from the Soviet model. Canada and China established diplomatic relations in 1970. In 1972 China signed a treaty with Japan, in 1975 with the EU, and in 1980 joined the IMF and the World Bank.

In 1978, economic reform started in China, well ahead of the FSU. This was designed to transform the country into a powerful modern socialist state, by means of the 'Four Moderniza-

tions' namely industry, agriculture, national defence, and science and technology, to quadruple its 1980 GNP by the year 2000. The 'Four Modernisations' are attributed to the late Deng Xiaoping, but had been advocated earlier, in 1975, by the late Premier Zhouen Lai, who lived in the shadow of Chairman Mao. The 'Open Door' resulted from the Sixth Five-Year Plan (1981–1985). It was the first published plan since the First Five-Year Plan (1953–1957). In 1984, there began the sale of stock in state-run companies. In 1985 the first Trademark Protection law and, in 1988 the Copyright Agency of China was established in Beijing, at the same time as the Shanghai Municipal Copyright Office. Also in 1988, the state monopoly on banking was broken with the first independent development bank.

With moves towards currency convertibility its role is less than before but countertrade is still likely to play a large role in this modernization programme, for China is an underdeveloped country and a market unlike other communist countries, partly due to its size, housing one-quarter of the world's population (which means more than one billion inhabitants, of whom 800 million are peasants), and partly to its politics which ensured its isolation from the rest of the world.

Arriving now with the intention to spend on industrial investments, China is being well received by world trading, banking and financial communities, yet per capita income in 1989 was $360. The Bank of China signed numerous agreements with leading banking institutions in the West and Japan for both private commercial credits and government backed export credits, although its foreign trade represents a very small share of its national income. China needs both to encourage exports and lower tariffs.

Foreign investment is being successfully drawn into the Special Economic Zones, such as Shenzen and the 14 coastal cities (or ETDZs) of which more later.

With the rise to power of Deng Xiaoping in December 1978, China underwent a series of changes. Firstly, in the political arena, many Chinese citizens who were alienated under former regimes were rehabilitated. Moves are taking place which, taken together, are very significant, for example: direct election of representatives at the country level; and a greater role for legislation, developing a basic criminal and civil code as well as laws relating to the operations of foreign firms in China. In the absence of commercial law, trade took place on trust. Secondly, intellectual liberalization is greater than before but not yet complete. The Communist Party adheres rigidly still to four basic tenets: the leadership of the party; the guiding role of Marxism, Leninism and Maoism; the maintenance of the 'people's democratic dictatorship' as China's form of government; and the pursuit of a socialist road to economic development. Thirdly, since 1958 there has been 're-adjustment' of the former Soviet model of development, which was transplanted wholesale into China in 1953. This rift widened with the border conflict with the USSR in 1960, but continued during the decade of the Cultural Revolution in the late 1960s, when a Chinese model of communism was being searched for, and on into the 1970s. Chinese communism has placed the political focus on the economy and not on the 'class' struggle.

Trading with a decentralizing planned economy

Since 1982, the pattern has been one of decentralization. The Ministry of Foreign Economic Relations and Trade (MOFERT) has had to share its authority with other ministries and provincial governments. This was designed to stimulate local involvement in foreign trade but has also created confusion over authority for necessary approvals. There is flexibility in the Chinese form of central planning which allows for the special treatment of the Special Economic Zones. Provided a proposed foreign investment is able to comply with the Five-Year Plan, the Open Door Policy encourages that investment. Whereas in the former Soviet model of central planning only state enterprises have the right to undertake foreign trade. In China there have been cases of joint ventures and, even wholly foreign-owned subsidiaries being allowed to undertake foreign trade. China, therefore, describes itself as a planned economy with market regulations. China seeks to maintain strong control only over those commodities which are essential to people's lives.

China needs an infusion of capital, technology and Western management expertise as it has a technology gap in most of its basic industries of up to ten years. To eliminate the black market in bonds, fully computerized stock exchanges were set up in Beijing, Shanghai, Shenyang, Wuhan, Guangzhou and Haikou. Originally this was to be a national stock and bond market. Shenzhen, which is a semi-official stock

Table 11.2 China at a glance		
	1989	*1994*
GNP US $ million	393,006	630,202
Population (thousand)	1,105,067	1,190,918
GNP per capita	360	530
Agriculture's share in GDP (%)	32	19
Life expectancy	70	69
Total fertility (per woman)	2.4	2.0
School enrolment (% of school age)	82	96
Illiteracy	31	27

Source: World Bank Atlas, 1990 and 1996, Washington DC, USA

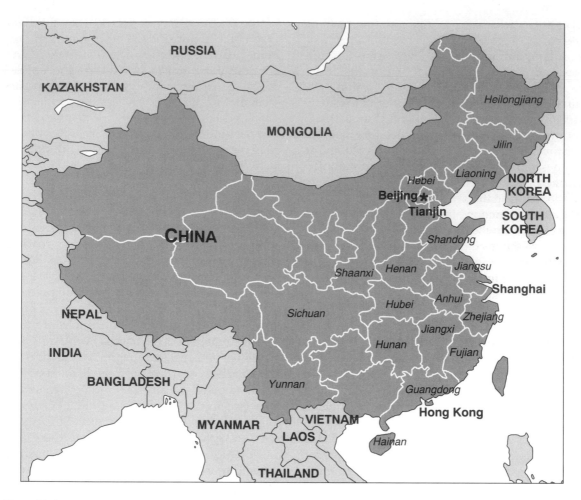

Figure 11.1

Table 11.3 Industrial output in 1995			
Product	*Output*	*Product*	*Output*
Chemical fibre	2.9 million tons	Cloth	21 billion metres
Sugar	5.656 million tons	Synthetic detergents	2.218 million tons
Energy production output (converting into standard fuel)	1.239 billion tons	Power output	1,000 billion
Kilowatt-hours ten nonferrous metals	4.25 million tons	Cement	450 million tons
Sulphuric acid	17.41 million tons	Soda ash	5.82 million tons
Farm chemicals (converting into 100%)	360,000 tons	Power equipment	16.82 million kilowatts
Integrated circuit	312.92 million pieces	Micro-electronic computers	403,000
Machine-made paper and paper board	24 million tons	Colour televisions	19.58 million
Steel	94 million tons	Timber	66.5 million cubic metres
Chemical fertilizer (converting into 100%)	24.5 million tons	Automobile	1.503 million
Program control	16.35 million lines	–	–

exchange, trades in stocks and bonds. The Shanghai exchange has the potential to become the most important for the international business and banking community.

China does have some industrially advanced regions but reforms are needed to increase the productivity of investments, meet the multiple objectives of a modernizing economy and the diversified needs of the people. The Chinese are still, though, a long way from a fully-fledged stock exchange. The number of companies trading on the stock exchange is increasing. There are restrictions on foreign companies operating in China which would hinder the development of the stock exchange, but there are deficiencies also in legislation and general regulations relating to securities, as well as in accounting practices. Furthermore, the volatility which can make a lucky speculator rich does not exist in the Chinese model. Beijing has ruled that the limit of fluctuation cannot exceed 0.5 per cent either way in any one business day. Still, there exists the problem of how to absorb the latent purchasing power that exists in China for which estimates vary as to how much is in free circulation among this population of approximately 1.2 billion people. The desire is to mop up this excess spending power and to divert this to some of the enterprises that urgently require funds. The problem, however, is still the state control planning system. When faced with rising levels of unemployment in 1989, Chinese leaders turned to one of the companies on the Shanghai exchange and ordered it to hire 2,400 employees from other failing enterprises. This kind of situation is not encountered in Western markets and would generally not be regarded as an 'off-the-balance-sheet' risk that may be encountered. The Chinese infrastructure is young and weak, and the integration of capitalism and communism is poorly defined, and so what emerges is a weak hybrid of a system unable to please anyone.

This new China has set lower industrial targets but higher targets for light industry which produces consumer goods. This is intended to absorb greater purchasing power and meet new consumer demands, as seen in declining sales of plain clothing, characteristic of the Maoist period, and the desire for more fashion. However, although productivity changes have been taking place, the share of old people in the population is rising alongside these other social trends. Whereas, previously, bicycles, sewing machines and watches have been most important, this has now changed to colour televisions, refrigerators, tape recorders, washing machines and cameras, in that order. Politically, there is no longer the need for China to be internally so self-reliant, and so, China's new leaders have greatly expanded trade with the West. Guangdong Province, close to Hong Kong, is now rivalling the performance of the 'Four Mini-Dragons': Singapore, Hong Kong, Taiwan and South Korea.

Exhibit 11.2 Plastic cards gain Chinese acceptance

In Asia, consumers tend to use cash – more than 92 per cent of sales transactions are conducted in cash and in China the proportion is even higher.

Such cultures promise 'unbelievable growth' to Mr Edmund Jensen, president and chief executive of Visa International, which has expanded exponentially in the region as Asian consumers convert in droves to credit and debit cards.

In an interview, he frequently repeats a favourite statistic: Visa transaction volumes have grown about 25 per cent a year for the past three years, while consumption levels have only grown approximately 5 per cent.

'Our growth has been displacing cash, not extending credit,' he says, explaining how Visa card transaction volume in Asia-Pacific grew to $171.8bn in the year to December 1996.

In China, Visa's volume grew to $59.3bn in 1996 and the number of Visa cards in issue rose to 11.9m, up 45 per cent on the previous year. Of those, the vast majority are debit cards, with credit cards numbering only a few thousand.

Visa describes current sales as 'a drop in the bucket' and this week the company is pushing further into the Chinese market with publicity-oriented initiatives.

Today, more than 100 Shanghai outlets will be authorised as Visa outlets, expanding the web of Chinese hotels, restaurants and shops now accepting plastic from the growing number of international tourists.

Yesterday, Visa launched its first affinity card with a cultural institution – the Shanghai Museum Dragon Affinity Card, a debit card issued as a partnership between the China Construction Bank and the Shanghai Museum, Shanghai's beacon of cultural regeneration.

At the beginning of this week, Visa announced the first Hong Kong dollar-based credit card, issued by the Guangdong Development Bank, adding to the only other international credit card issued in China – a US dollar card issued by Industrial and Commercial Bank of China.

→ Exhibit 11.2 *continued*

The credit cards are issued in foreign currency because until China introduces full currency convertibility, international credit cannot be authorised in Chinese yuan.

That is only one reason, though, for the sluggish development of the credit card business. Beijing has been concerned about fostering a credit boom in China's increasingly commercial culture and, as a result, ICBC has issued less than 3,000 credit cards.

Mr Dennis Goggin, president of Visa International Asia-Pacific, says: 'In most emerging markets, the government is very wary of starting out with an expansion of consumer credit. In China, they are not looking to grow that part of the economy and also there is no credit checking, no credit scoring, so the credit growth is very slow.'

Mr Jensen forecasts progress in the credit card business: 'Debit cards are growing very rapidly here and after the banks get that card base, they move into opening lines of credit for consumers.'

Visa's competitors – Mastercard and American Express – are equally excited by that prospect.

Visa, which has been in China for eight years, is trying to expand its presence by helping the People's Bank of China, the central bank, with its 'Golden Card Project', China's vision of a modern, electronic cashless payment system.

The project would catapult China to a level of cashless payment that surpasses that of many western economies. The Golden Card involves a chip card system intended to work as an 'electronic wallet', offering credit, debit and stored value for paying bills or making purchases over the Internet.

Mr Jensen believes China can 'leapfrog' Western countries, because it 'does not have the baggage of existing infrastructure'. His colleague, Mr Goggin, suggests such a leap is not only possible but likely, given the analogy with cellular telephones, which took off more quickly in Asia than in Europe, where people were already tied to land lines.

By 2003, the People's Bank forecasts that more than 200m payment cards will have been issued in China. Given that Visa has issued 550m cards after 25 years in the business, Mr Jensen suggests China's targets are 'ambitious', but 'three years ago, we were talking about a few million cards; now there are 40m, so 200m is attainable by 2003'.

Source: Financial Times, 8 April 1997

Exhibit 11.3   City grooms car giant for global conglomerate status

Something is cooking at the Shanghai Automobile Industry Corp (SAIC), the government-backed group which runs the most profitable joint venture in China.

First, it played white knight to two unprofitable listed companies, which are in businesses unrelated to its own.

Then, news emerged it was finalising talks to take over 20 per cent of Shanghai Dazhong Taxi, a well-run taxi-leasing listed company, from a government bureau.

Finally, during US Vice-President Al Gore's visit to China last week, it completed details for a US$1.57 billion joint venture with General Motors to make Buick cars.

Why all these corporate manoeuvres?

It is no secret the municipal government is giving SAIC all the backing it needs to help it leapfrog into the league of the world's top 500 companies by 2000.

The apparent strategy is to turn SAIC into a diversified conglomerate while retaining car production as its core business – a prudent ambition in view of China's application to join the World Trade Organisation.

While Shanghai Volkswagen, its money-churning car venture with Germany's Volkswagen group, has dominated the mainland car market with its Santana sedans, it faces increasingly stiff competition from other domestic manufacturers.

The competition will escalate when China joins the WTO within the next year or two, which will require Beijing to further cut tariff and non-tariff barriers for imports, including cars.

With less than two years to play with, SAIC is seeking to consolidate its leadership by joining GM to set up China's biggest car joint venture. Whether it will turn out to be a cash cow such as Shanghai Volkswagen is too early to tell.

At any rate, with two big car facilities within its fold, SAIC's leadership position will be hard to challenge. China would dearly love a domestic car producer capable of competing with foreign producers at home and abroad.

Still, it remains commercially imprudent to rely solely on one source, car sales, for income. So, it recently sought to diversify by taking over as controlling shareholder two manufacturers, Shanghai Video & Audio Electric and Shanghai Vacuum Electronic Devices.

➤ Exhibit 11.3 *continued*

One makes colour television sets, the other TV parts; both are in the red. It was puzzling why SAIC was keen to take them over, since it meant injecting money and management expertise into them.

Was SAIC asked to bail out the two to ward off unwanted attention from Sichuan Changhong, China's biggest and most profitable colour TV producer?

Changhong was said to be eyeing Shanghai Video and Shanghai Vacuum with the aim of expanding its position in Shanghai.

That reportedly got the Shanghai government worried that other Shanghai brands could be gobbled up.

There is talk the local government asked SAIC to step in because it did not want Shanghai Video and Shanghai Vacuum to be controlled by a successful domestic producer from another province.

Shanghai was the leader in home appliance production in the 80s, but gradually lost that position to areas with more nimble domestic producers.

SAIC may have done well in car production, but can it repeat the success in colour TV production?

Its plan to acquire 20 per cent of Shanghai Dazhong Taxi makes more sense. Dazhong buys its taxi fleet from SAIC's Volkswagen joint venture and needs money to upgrade the fleet.

The SAIC-Dazhong alliance will result in cost savings for the taxi operator, while the car producer will be able to diversify its income. It seems to be a 'win-win' alliance.

SAIC needs more such tie-ups and fewer politically directed deals to realise its ambition of playing in the global big league.

Source: South China Morning Post, 4 April 1997

Africa	1.4%
ASEAN	6.9%
Asia	58.6%
European Union	13.0%
Latin America	2.3%
North America	15.8%
Oceanic	2.0%

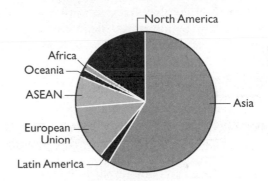

Source: China's Customs Statistics, November 1996

Figure 11.2   China's trade with the world

Exhibit 11.4   WTO entry vital for credibility, says report

Failure to accede to the World Trade Organisation will damage China's economic credibility and jeopardise its future development, according to a Japanese trade policy report.

The sixth annual report, prepared by the Ministry of International Trade and Industry, argued for China's early entry to the global trade body.

China, Taiwan and Russia are among 29 economies that have applied to join the WTO.

The report said prompt accession for China and Taiwan was important because it would promote expansion of global trade through further liberalisation of their trading regimes.

It would also bring them under a common set of rules and give them a common forum for multi-lateral dispute settlement.

'The accession will also promote further inte-

gration of China into the global economy,' the report said.

In Russia's case, it said accession would contribute to its economic development as well as strengthen the multi-lateral trading system.

The report said that if China should fail to accede to the WTO, it would 'seriously damage the credibility of the Chinese economy.

'Trade and investment from the rest of the world that are essential for its further development will also suffer.'

The report noted that keeping China outside the WTO 'no longer prevents it from playing a major role in the real global economy and it is becoming increasingly burdensome for the multi-lateral trading system.

'Besides the transitional period China may

➤

→ Exhibit 11.4 *continued*

require for each commitment, it is necessary that China makes clear its conviction to adhere to the WTO rules,' it said.

Restrictions on trading rights or the right to engage in imports and exports, which are restricted to 'licensed' companies and effectively ban foreign companies, should be eliminated.

China should provide a clear timetable for the elimination of import restrictions in a transparent manner.

Beijing also needed to address subsidies, trade-related aspects of investment measures, industrial policy measures and protection of intellectual property rights.

The report said high tariffs remained a concern, 'but of particular concern is China's commitment in the distribution sector, whose restriction may cause substantial barriers to trade'.

It noted that most-favoured nation status from the US 'makes WTO membership of far less significance to China than it would be otherwise, and is said to be one of the largest issues in the negotiations'.

China's share of world trade was 1.8 per cent in 1985, rising to 2.8 per cent in 1995.

The report said Taiwan's decision to accede to the WTO as a developed economy 'reflects its economic strength and competitiveness.

'Taiwan has also rapidly rectified aspects of its trade regime that were inconsistent with WTO rules,' it said.

Japan reached an agreement with Taiwan in February concerning bilateral negotiations on market access.

'For Taiwan, the significance of accession to the WTO will be particularly large,' the report said, adding that Taiwan's economy was 'highly dependent on foreign trade'.

'Having lost diplomatic relations with many countries, accession to the WTO, which guarantees reductions of barriers to its trade and the elimination of discriminatory treatment against it, will ensure further development of Taiwan's international trade,' it said.

China objects to Taiwan's accession before itself gaining admission.

China applied to rejoin the General Agreement on Tariffs and Trade (Gatt) in 1986, but the Tiananmen Square crackdown of 1989 put consideration of the application on hold until 1992.

It initially wanted to be a founding member of the WTO, which replaced Gatt in 1995, but there were large gaps between the level of conformity to WTO rules demanded by members and what China was prepared to concede.

In 1995, it reapplied for WTO membership.

China's application has taken more than a decade and has so far involved 22 working party sessions.

Momentum in negotiations picked up in late 1996 as the United States became more enthusiastic about holding talks with China. US objections had stymied attempts to gain accession.

Source: South China Morning Post, 1 April 1997

Table 11.4   Economic profile

	Population (million)	GNP (billion USD)	GNP/person PPP	Growth rate 1985–93
Japan	125	4321	21350	3.2
China	1197	630	2510	6.9
Hong Kong	6	126	23080	5.3
Rep. of Korea	44	366	10540	7.8
Indonesia	190	168	3690	6.0
Malaysia	19	69	8610	5.7
Philippines	66	63	2800	1.8
Singapore	3	65	21430	6.9
Thailand	59	130	6870	8.2
Vietnam	72	14	n.a.	n.a.
Bangladesh	118	27	1350	2.1
India	914	279	1290	2.9
Pakistan	126	56	2210	1.6
Sri Lanka	18	12	3150	2.8

Note: China now includes Hong Kong and in 1999, Macau. The figures have been presented to highlight differences in the economies.

Exhibit 11.5 Citic: The keeper of the keys to China

Beijing – Mr Wang Jun has sipped coffee socially with President Clinton, met Mr Morihiro Hosokawa informally when he was Japan's prime minister and chatted with Philippine President Fidel Ramos. He golfs with China's business elite and hobnobs with its political leaders.

And he frequents, and chairs, the pricey Capital Club, a dining spot perched at the top of one of Beijing's tallest buildings.

Mr Wang's key to this select company: his chairmanship of the China International Trust and Investment Corp, the most influential financial and industrial conglomerate in China.

Founded at the dawn of the late Deng Xiaoping's economic-reform era as the government's window onto the capitalist world, Citic today reflects China's emergence both as a major force in the global economy and as the ultimate potential market for foreign firms with merchandise or services to sell.

This week, while in Beijing to help patch up US-Chinese relations, US Vice-President Al Gore watched Boeing sign a deal to sell planes and General Motors agree to set up a new car-manufacturing plant. The size of the GM investment alone far exceeds an entire year's worth of foreign investment during the first years of Citic's existence.

Mirroring the explosive growth of China's economy, Citic has ballooned into a sophisticated US$23 billion (S$33 billion) conglomerate with massive holdings in Hongkong and substantial assets scattered throughout the world.

At the same time, because of its size and its impeccable connections, it is courted avidly by foreign companies eager to establish or expand operations aimed at China's 1.2 billion consumers.

Citic owns a steel mill in Delaware, forests in Washington state, and a meat-processing company and aluminum smelter in Australia. It owns one of China's largest banks and chunks of a myriad of ventures in China: satellites, bridges, power plants, accounting and law firms, pharmaceutical makers, department stores, auto plants and textile manufacturers.

It governs its own island – Daxie Island near Ningbo, south of Shanghai – which it plans to transform into a super-port. And its Hongkong affiliate is a major player in the close-knit Hongkong business world, providing political reassurance while muscling its way into bigger roles in the territory's main utility, telephone company and two major airlines.

Since the revelation that Mr Wang attended a Feb. 6, 1996, White House meeting for major Democratic Party contributors, some people in the Justice Department and Congress are wondering whether Citic's tentacles are reaching into American politics.

Access is a key part of Citic business, but it is usually the part Citic sells, rather than buys.

Business people in China say they believe Mr Wang's visit had more to do with American companies trying to cozy up to China than with the Chinese trying to gain influence in the United States. In an interview earlier this month, Mr Wang said his US trip was initiated by Lehman Brothers Inc, which is competing for a bigger role managing China's new stock and bond offerings.

As China's leading 'red chip' company, Citic is the most sought-after partner for 'blue chip' foreign firms seeking footholds in China. Its partners include Bechtel Group Inc., Coopers & Lybrand, Siemens AG, United Technologies Corp., Ciba-Geigy AG, Reynolds Metals Co. and Cable and Wireless PLC – to name a few.

For the princelings of the next generation, business rather than the military or politics has been the most alluring career.

Mr Wang studied at a Harbin engineering school, spent 10 years at ship-building plants, and served two years in the military. But he did not join the Chinese Communist Party until 1978, at the age of 39.

'It raised a lot of eyebrows,' Mr Wang said, 'but it's my personality. I don't like to follow orders of superiors.'

He joined Citic as soon as it was created.

Now, like many of China's emerging capitalists, he talks about assets and profit margins. He complains about high business taxes. He keeps a computer on his desk. He drives a blue BMW and keeps a golf club in the office.

With China awash in foreign investment – more than US$40 billion poured in last year – deal makers now seek Citic. One person who has knocked on its door is former US Secretary of State George Shultz, on behalf of his old engineering and construction firm Bechtel.

Mr Shultz and two Bechtel executives visited Rong Yiren, the first head of Citic, in Beijing on the day in March 1993 that he was named China's vice president. The upbeat Mr Rong proposed that Bechtel join Citic in building a superport on sparsely populated Daxie Island.

Later, Citic bought the island and won the right to issue permits and approvals, power normally reserved for local or provincial governments. Bechtel is the lead developer with plans for ports, warehouses, railroads, roads, water and electricity infrastructure.

→ **Exhibit 11.5** *continued*

Nowadays, Citic can be choosy about its investments. Two years ago, Mr Wang lamented that it was a shareholder in more than 200 Chinese enterprises, many of them flops. Overall, Citic's return on its domestic manufacturing investments was zero, he said in an interview.

Since then, the company has focused more on high technology, infrastructure and financial services. Among its projects: a deal with Siemens and Deutsche Bundespost Telekom to set up a phone service company in four cities to challenge the state telephone monopoly.

Citic has also been wheeling and dealing in Hongkong, where companies are looking for political cover before the return of the British colony to Chinese rule on July 1. Many leading Hongkong families and companies are suddenly ready to sell shares to Citic's Hongkong affiliate, Citic Pacific – often at bargain prices.

Citic Pacific is 26.5 per cent owned by Citic Hongkong, which is a wholly owned unit of the Chinese parent company. The chairman of Citic Pacific is Larry Yung, the son of former Citic chief Rong and now a high-profile member of Hongkong's business elite.

Earlier this year, Citic Pacific bought a 20 per cent stake in China Light & Power, the colony's largest electric utility. The Kadoorie family, one of Hongkong's oldest and richest families, which had rebuffed Citic's overtures in the past, agreed to reduce its stake in the utility to make room.

Citic Pacific has also increased its stake in Hongkong's flagship airline, Cathay Pacific, from 10 per cent to 25 per cent. Hongkong has not been the only place that Citic has ventured overseas in search of investment targets instead of investment funds. It also has substantial investments in the United States.

The Chinese central bank has criticised Citic, saying it has too many long-term investments and not enough liquid assets. The central bank, the Finance Ministry and a state economic-reform commission held discussions about Citic's strategy in November.

Analysts say that given Citic's advantages, its performance is weak. Mr Wang also said that three times last year, state auditors conducted 'massive investigations' of Citic's books to search for improprieties and bad loans but found nothing significant.

'An important lesson my father taught me is to be an upright person,' Mr Wang said.

Source: The Straits Times, 28 March 1997

Exhibit 11.6   US must do more to cut deficit: China

China yesterday defended its growing trade surplus with the United States, setting out its arguments in a White Paper released ahead of US Vice-President Al Gore's visit next week.

The 18-page document, released by the State Council, also tried to explain the factors for statistical differences of up to US$29 billion (S$41.47 billion) in yearly surplus figures computed by each side.

Vice-Minister Sun Zhenyu of the Ministry of Foreign Trade and Economic Co-operation (Moftec), speaking at a press conference yesterday, told the US to do more to increase its exports to China.

Hours before he spoke, trade figures released by the US on Thursday showed that China's trade surplus with the US totalled US$3.7 billion in January, climbing 40 per cent higher compared to the same month last year.

Several analysts have said that China's trade surplus with the US, now a festering issue, could become a big thorn in bilateral ties in the near future.

Recognising this, Mr Sun warned that the trade imbalance had 'become such a general concern to American people from all walks of life that failure to handle the issue properly could hold up the normal development of the economic and trade relations between the two countries'.

Saying that the US had to play its part to reduce the surplus, he urged US companies to be more competitive in the Chinese market.

More specifically, he said that Washington's reluctance to provide preferential loans to American firms eyeing projects in China had lost them contracts and opportunities. He also said that Washington should relax its restrictions on technology exports to China.

On its part, China would continue to open up its markets, lower tariffs, phase out non-tariff measures and send Chinese delegations to the US to explore technology, projects and products with US companies.

He said Chinese exports posed no threat to American production and jobs because the products sold were no longer produced in the US.

→ Exhibit 11.6 *continued*

Turning to statistical differences in trade figures compiled by each side, an issue which has simmered for several years, he said these arose from processing trade and transshipment.

According to China, its trade surplus with the US hit US$10.5 billion last year, while the US claims the figure to be US$39.5 billion.

The White Paper attributed the huge discrepancy to several factors including statistical methods and US policies, such as its rules for determining import sources.

The White Paper also outlined inroads made by American firms in areas such as banking and insurance, shipping, and retailing.

Source: The Straits Times, 22 March 1997

Market information

There is more readily available market information than ever which, while of significant progress, is still scant by Western standards.

Livingstone (1987) summed up the problems of conducting market research in China quite succinctly:

Not least, it is a closed society in the information sense, with advertising by poster or television relying on a blunderbuss effect rather than targeting; and where, as one student suggested, the only realistic manner of acquiring a sampling frame for local consumer market research would be to enlist the cooperation of the local police station, as the only source of information.

Westerners who wish to learn more of the opportunities available may contact:

- Foreign Trading Corporations (FTC)
- CITIC: China International Trust and Investment Corporation
- Leadership in specially designated areas: the SEZs and ETDZs.

As credit is presently squeezed, the means to attract foreign trade and investment will comprise chiefly of variants of joint ventures and countertrade. Access to the internal domestic Chinese market is still limited. Chinese consumers are generally more confident of the quality of imported goods, so the challenge is that of giving an imported-look to joint-venture products. As 99 per cent of the population speak only Chinese, but while the Chinese characters will remain the same, this entails a number of different dialects. Mandarin, based in the North, is the most common. To Westerners it creates confusion as to whether we use the term Beijing or Peking to refer to the same place. Ogilvy and Mather opened in Beijing in 1986 and have developed Chinese packaging for Maxwell House, Pond's, Seagrams, and Johnson and Johnson, among others (Fyock, 1990).

Intellectual property protection

China has a fairly recent but relatively comprehensive legal system to protect intellectual property. China is a member of WIPO, the Paris Convention, Madrid Arrangement, Berne Convention and other international treaties but still awaiting membership of the WTO.

China has bolstered its laws relating to intellectual property to include copyrights, patent rights, right of exclusive use of trademarks, monopoly of discovery, patent for invention and other proprietorial rights pertaining to scientific and technological knowledge.

The Patent Law came into force in 1985 and was amended in 1992 so as to offer 20-year protection from the date of application. The principle of granting patent application to the first registrant is the practice here. The Trademark Law was amended in 1993 to cover services as well as products and introduce penalties for infringement. The Law on Copyright came into force in 1991 and this covered audiovisual products and computer software as well as the more usual musical and artistic works. An anti unfair competition law passed into law in 1993 stated that trade must be based on the principle of voluntariness, equality, fairness, sincerity and credibility as well as on recognized business ethics. This introduced criminal offences covering many business situations including falsification of trademarks. There were 26 trademark agencies designated by the government in 1995 to act on behalf of foreign companies.

The Chinese market

Before 1978, private enterprise was not allowed. For Chinese nationals, there are three types of economic enterprise permitted in China – individual, collective and state. Economic reform allows farmers as well as industrial enterprises to sell their surplus or to swap their produce for other products. Industrial enterprises are being made responsible for their own profits and losses under the Assets Management Responsibility System. Unprofitable enterprises have been closed, or threatened with closure, while profitable ones have been allowed to retain a greater part of their net income to use for bonuses, benefits and new investments.

Exhibit 11.7   US retailer sued over label on imports

US textile manufacturers are to sue The Limited, a leading American retailer, for importing allegedly mislabelled clothing from China.

The American Textile Manufacturers' Institute yesterday accused The Limited and several retailing subsidiaries – including Victoria's Secret, Abercrombie & Fitch, and Lane Bryant, of importing clothing labelled as made in such locations as Hong Kong, knowing they were manufactured in China in order to avoid US quotas and duties.

The landmark case, which is intended to recover millions of dollars of lost customs duties owed on allegedly mislabelled products from China, is the first filed under the False Claims Act which allows private parties to bring civil actions on behalf of the government to recover losses incurred by fraud. The ATMI said the suit, if successful, could be a model for combatting customs fraud.

Mr Samuel Fried, general counsel of The Limited, said the company had not had time to review the charges but was committed to complying fully with the spirit and letter of all import rules.

The US Customs Service has prosecuted numerous cases of clothing from China shipped via a third country. China says its clothing exports amount to $13bn, but the total recorded by importers worldwide is $23.7bn.

If ATMI is able to prove mislabelling, performed with the knowledge of The Limited, the US is entitled to damages of more than 12 times the value of the imported merchandise. ATMI could collect 15–25 per cent of that. A clothing industry representative said ATMI had an even stronger motive for its law suit: disruption of clothing trade with Asia because several ATMI members had set up production in the Caribbean and Mexico.

ATMI said it sent investigators into China, who brought back photographs and documents which could prove that clothing allegedly produced in Hong Kong was made in factories in China.

It said, for example, that the Landale Garment Factory in Hong Kong was under contract to produce tens of thousands of pieces of clothing between January and June 1996 for one of The Limited's importers – Tarrant Apparel Group. But the factory, visited on 35–40 occasions, was not engaged in cutting fabric and had only a few workers operating a few sewing machines. Often the factory was idle.

Source: Financial Times, 10 April 1997

Enterprises have also been leased to individuals or groups under contracts.

Chinese society remains rooted around the concept of the commune which consists of a cluster of villages around a traditional market town with a population which varies between 15,000 and 50,000. These resemble large villages. Next down the scale is the co-operative and there may be eight or ten of these per brigade. However, even here change is taking place as responsibility shifts to smaller units and the family groups, the households classed as self-employed, which are so important for China's agricultural output. In total, six kinds of businesses are permitted under the individual enterprise form (Reader, 1984):

- Commercial – retailing items purchased wholesale from collective and state enterprises.
- Handicrafts – making and selling simple items such as toys or baskets or art works; some forms of art work, such as paintings, can only be sold to the state for resale by the state.
- Transportation – primarily 'pedicabs' or three-wheeled bicycles with a seat for one or two passengers.
- Repairing – shoe repair, bicycle repair, etc.
- Services – barbering, hairdressing, tailoring, etc.

- Food preparation – from street stands to small restaurants.

With the permission of the local AIC (Administration of Industry and Commerce), and through contracts approved by them, individual enterprises may hire up to five apprentices and up to two assistants. The reasons offered for this are to better serve the needs of consumers and to help alleviate the pressing problem of unemployment.

Keith and Kimberley (1983) interpret these changes in the Chinese system as follows.

1. The commune system should be seen in a historical perspective as a product of evolutionary adaptation and not as an immutable institution created during a heroic period of socialist construction.
2. Experimentation with alternative institutional arrangements has always been part of the Chinese style of rural development and thus, the recent innovations and experiments are consistent with past approaches to development problems.
3. There is an economic logic to the commune system that can best be understood when the household economy is regarded as the base of the system and the fourth tier of a four-tiered institutional hierarchy.

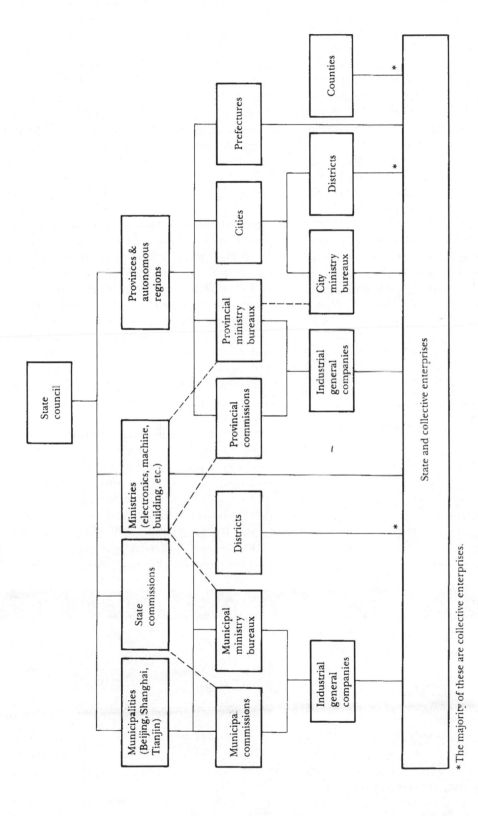

* The majority of these are collective enterprises.

Figure 11.3   China's state planning system

Source: Campbell, N. (1987) Enterprise autonomy in the Beijing municipality. In *Management Reforms in China* (Warner, M.), Frances Pinter, London

4. The essence of the new reforms is a shift of responsibility for crop cultivation from the production team to the household economy, but not to the private sector. This shift does not imply the imminent disbandment of the commune system, although in some circumstances the commune system could be severely weakened and even destroyed.

5. Some aspects of the new reforms, if not corrected, could lead to greater inequality, lower levels of capital accumulation and slower long run rates of growth of output, but these consequences are not inherent in the reforms.

6. Such evidence as exists indicates that the distribution of collective income in rural areas, including collective income originating in the household economy, continues to be relatively egalitarian.

7. Moreover, in the few cases where comparisons over time are possible, there is no evidence that the reforms have been associated with an increase in the degree of inequality at the local level.

China's party and state bureaucracies are in need of reform. Bureaucracy is being reduced with planned decentralization and the average age of officials is to be reduced while their expected level of education is increased. The present economic system is highly centralized with:

- decision-making confined to the leading central economic organs,
- highly centralized planning precludes the functioning of markets, and
- functioning of the economy depends mainly on administrative measures with little impetus from economic interests.

Much has to be done in the range, quality and design of these manufactured products. While in energy, China is beginning to experience shortages, although petroleum exported was only 12 per cent of output and coal exported was only 1 per cent of output, it does mean that there is little scope here for export expansion as things exist. Longer term, China's economic development will depend on export earnings from coal, steel, oil and petroleum-related commodities, but in the short term, will have to focus on tourism and consumer goods. Meanwhile, transportation remains a problem and harbour facilities are not sufficiently developed to serve an expansion of foreign trade.

Special Economic Zones (SEZ)

There are thirteen. The first was Shenzhen in the province of Guangdong (or Canton) in 1979. Since then, three further SEZs have been established in South China: Shataojiao in Shenzhen and Zhuhai in Guangdong, at Huli in the City of Xiamen in the province of Fujian. Further decentralization came about in 1984, making the conditions more favourable to foreign investment, and in 1988, Hainan Island acquired SEZ status at the same time as being promoted to being an autonomous province. The SEZ are able to accept foreign investment in virtually any area of economic activity of interest to China, including services as well as production. Since May 1990, foreigners are now able to engage in land development, and to install electric power and telephone services, and to operate these utilities in one of the designated investment zones. Technologically advanced investments benefit from a reduced level of taxation. The 13 zones include Dalian, Fuhan (in Shenzhen), Fuzhou, Guang-zhou, Hainan, Ningbo,

---

Exhibit 11.8 Harry Ramsden's expands in Asia

Fish and chips, that British contribution to world cuisine, are alive and well and expanding their presence in Asia.

The deep-fried slices of potato and battered fish have been repackaged and 'branded' for maximum marketing mileage.

'We have a unique concept – there's nobody else with a brand image in fish and chips,' John Barnes, chairman of Harry Ramsden's, said in Singapore, where the company has just opened a restaurant.

When the company's first outlet in the region opened in Hong Kong in 1992, Mr Barnes saw great potential.

'The reaction in Hong Kong, where two thirds of the customers are Chinese, says it all: there is an affection for British fish and chips done well in a larger than life concept,' he said.

If the Singapore venture proves successful, Malaysia, Indonesia and Thailand could follow.

With a plan to open 10 restaurants a year between now and 2000, there could be as many as 60 Harry Ramsden's open by the millennium from the present 25.

The three most recent were opened in the space of a week – in Oxford, England; Inverness, Scotland; and Singapore.

Source: *South China Morning Post*, 2 April 1997

Qingdao, Shanghai, Shantou, Shataojiao (in Shenzhen), Tianjin, Xiamen and Zhang jiagang.

Economic and Technical Development Zones (ETDZ)

Economic and Technical Development Zones were created in 1984. These comprise of the 13 open coastal cities and are now being termed China's new Gold Coast:

Dalian	Qinhuangdao
Qingdao	Yantai
Namtong	Lianyungang
Ningbo	Shanghai
Fuzhou	Wenzhou
Zhanjiang	Guangzhou
	Behai

Preferential administrative procedures and tax incentives would be made available to foreign investors within ETDZ boundaries provided that the economic activities, which they financed, qualified as high technology by Chinese standards or as production enterprises for export. For production enterprises, or scientific and technological research institutions, the ETDZ has much to commend it, but these are the limits within which the ETDZ is allowed to operate. Yet, there is the advantage here of location, unlike the four SEZs which are all located in South China. Regulation is on two levels, national and local, and applicable to the ETDZs themselves, but there is overlap and lack of definition of terms and direction.

Exhibit 11.9 Grand Met unit starts joint venture in China to make, sell spirits

Beijing – International Distillers & Vintners, a unit of Grand Metropolitan PLC of the U.K., has launched a joint venture that will make and sell whiskey, brandy and vodka in China, executives said.

The production venture, capitalized at $27 million, marks Grand Met's first sizable step into the mainland's massive food and drink market, said Grand Met Chairman George Bull.

Under the terms of agreement, IDV will hold a 67 per cent stake and provide technology and management to the venture. Its partner, Qufu Distillery of China's eastern Shandong province, has a 33 per cent interest and has promised to share its mainland distribution network, according to executives.

Mr Bull said IDV's drink business will lead Grand Met's 'step-by-step' approach to Chinese palates. 'We are very anxious to expand the program of sale of our brand of spirits.

Grand Met's only other attempt to crack the China market has been with its Haagen-Dazs ice cream stores, one of which opened in Shanghai last summer.

Grand Met now, however, is seeking franchising opportunities for Burger King, the world's second-largest hamburger chain.

Mr Bull disputed perceptions that Burger King has moved much slower than competitor McDonalds Corp. in tapping China's fast-food potential. Since acquiring Burger King in 1989, Grand Met's priority has been on revitalizing domestic sales, he said. 'Now the focus is moving overseas, and we're gathering our resources to move forward.'

Source: Asian Wall Street Journal, 19 March 1997

Table 11.5 General information on real use of foreign investment in China

Year(s)	Total (billion U.S. dollars)	Foreign loans (billion U.S. dollars)	Direct foreign investment (billion U.S. dollars)	Other foreign investment (million U.S. dollars)
1979–1983	14.438	11.755	1.802	881
1984	2.705	1.286	1.258	161
1986	7.258	5.014	1.874	370
1988	10.226	6.487	3.194	545
1990	10.289	6.534	3.487	268
1991	11.554	6.888	4.366	300
1992	19.202	7.911	11.007	284
1993	38.960	11.189	27.515	256
1994	43.213	9.267	33.767	179
1995	48.133	10.327	37.521	285

Source: The Internet, China Business Guide, June 1997

Table 11.6   Foreign direct investment in the PRC

	1979–89	1996
Total foreign direct investment		
Number of contracts	21,776	24,529
Amount contracted	$32.4 billion	$73.2 billion
Amount utilized*	$18.5 billion	$42.4 billion
US direct investment		
Number of contracts	959	3,023**
Amount contracted	$3.9 billion	$9.7 billion**
Amount utilized*	$1.7 billion	$3.8 billion**
US share of total contracted investment	12.2%	13.3%**

Source: PRC Ministry of Foreign Trade and Economic Cooperation, State Statistical Bureau (SSB)

* Includes utilized investment in material processing, compensation trade, and leasing arrangements.

** US investment figures for 1996 are US-China Business Council estimates based on straight-line projections of January–September 1996 SSB data.

Source: Kapp, R. A. (1997) 'The Legacy of Deng Xiaoping', *China Business Review*, March–April, 26–29

Each ETDZ has a sino-foreign joint venture management company managing it, which acts as the regulatory authority, but the question of jurisdiction enters into financing, for example. Investments in Shanghai of 30 million dollars require central Government authorization, but elsewhere the quota limit will be lower.

The ETDZ is able to levy a local income tax, usually around 10 per cent, but this is decided locally and so the coastal cities of China have to be compared with each other. Legislation changes in 1986 offered particular tax incentives to exporting companies and technologically advanced foreign companies. The services sector was, therefore, excluded. This may be because of Chinese disappointment with both the levels and the nature of foreign investments in the period 1979–1985, which was centred mainly on hotels and tourism with some Hong Kong investment in relatively unsophisticated technology (Larson, 1988). Yet, prior to 1985, China had no legislation in force relating to contracts with foreign parties. Two principles are important to note here. The first is that of 'equality and mutual benefit.' The other is of 'achieving unanimity through consultations.' These two principles are embedded in Chinese legislation.

ETDZs offer:

- preferential treatment,
- infrastructure and services,
- experienced management pro-sino-foreign joint ventures, and
- proximity to other foreign investing companies.

Chinese foreign investment

By the end of 1995, China had approved 258,000 foreign funded projects with the agreed invest-

ment reaching 395.7 billion US dollars and the real investment totalling 135.4 billion US dollars. Altogether more than 120,000 foreign funded enterprises had opened with a combined workforce of more than 16 million people.

Investing in a joint-venture project

China openly welcomes both equity and contractual forms of joint venture with its 'open door' policy on foreign investment. In 1979, the Government established the Foreign Investment Control Commission to scrutinize and approve all joint-venture agreements. The law on joint ventures requires foreign investors to abide by Chinese laws and decrees; second, it protects the rights and interests of foreign investors; and third, it emphasizes the need to accelerate the pace of China's 'Four Modernizations', which include the comprehensive modernization of industry, agriculture, national defence, and science and technology. Enterprises which are export-oriented receive a special priority. The foreign investor is expected to provide the advanced technology and equipment, while China contributes the necessary land and workforce. This means that ventures which are labour intensive are best suited to these conditions.

Arising from this law, the China International Trust and Investment Corporation was established. Known as CITIC, it operates under the control of the Chinese State Council, and can assist to contact various ministries, provincial and local administrations. CITIC is a holding company with its own bank and trading company, and is able to invest in a joint venture with a Western partner and to even issue its own bonds abroad.

Table 11.7   An investor's lexicon

Approval authority
Shenpi jiguan
   The organization that has the legal authorization to approve an activity involving a foreign investment enterprise. For example, the Ministry of Foreign Economic Relations and Trade or their local-level counterpart is the approval authority for foreign investment contracts.

Contractual joint venture (CJV)
Hezuo jingying qiye
   Contractual joint ventures can take two forms: 1) a limited liability entity with legal person status that closely resembles an equity joint venture; 2) a business partnership in which the parties cooperate as separate legal entities and carry out their respective contractual obligations without establishing a joint management entity. In either case, contractual joint ventures differ from equity joint ventures in two important respects: the forms of investment contributed by each party need not be in cash or in kind (e.g., labour and utilities have in some cases been allowed as contributions); and profits are shared based on a ratio specified in the contract, not necessarily according to investment contributions. Contractual joint ventures are also often called cooperative ventures or coproduction agreements.

Department in charge
Zhuguan bumen
   The department in charge of a joint venture is generally the Chinese partner's supervisory organization. For example, in a light industrial joint venture with a factory as the Chinese partner, the local light industrial bureau will usually be the department in charge of the joint venture. The department in charge has primarily administrative functions and acts as a channel for the joint venture's business with China's bureaucracy. For example, project proposals, joint venture contracts and feasibility studies, and advanced technology applications are first submitted to the department in charge, which then forwards them to the appropriate approval authorities.

Equity joint venture (EJV)
Hezi jingying qiye
   A limited liability corporation in which the Chinese and foreign partners jointly invest in and operate the corporation. Profits and risk are shared according to the percentage of equity held by each partner. Investment contributions may be in cash or in kind.

Foreign investment enterprise (FIE)
Waishang touzi qiye
   Term used to collectively refer to equity joint ventures, contractual joint ventures, and wholly foreign-owned enterprises. Does not include offshore oil investment contracts. Much of China's new investment legislation is being written to apply to these three types of projects.

Wholly foreign-owned enterprise (WFOE)
Waishang duzi qiye
   A limited liability entity solely owned and operated by a foreign investor. The foreign investor receives all profits and bears all risks.

Source: Zhang, S. X., and Snyder, J. L. (1988) The Five Ps. *China Business Review*, March–April

Table 11.8   Foreign investment enterprise (FIE) headaches

* Too many people involved in negotiations
* Unfamiliarity with international practice
* Aversion to risk
* Impractical goals
* Secrecy
* Diverse objectives
* High housing costs
* Labour issues
* Procurement problems

Source: Givant, N. (1990) Investing in Shanghai. *China Business Review*, March–April, 28–30

Table 11.9   Disincentives to invest
1. Historically inefficient allocation and use of natural human resources.
2. Inadequate infrastructure for absorbing and disseminating technology rapidly.
3. Inability to translate experiential laboratory or small-scale production successes into broader gains.
4. Inadequate management skills, training, discipline and problem-solving expertise.
5. Labour costs that have not been competitive with other Asian countries.
6. Lack of qualified scientific, engineering and technical personnel.
7. Absence of standardization in instrumentation and scientific manufacturing equipment.
8. Shortage of hard foreign currency and inability to generate foreign exchange through exports of high technology products due to substandard products.
9. Lack of uniform dissemination and enforcement of laws, rules and regulations.

Source: Chwang and Thurston (1987) 'Technology takes command: the policy of the People's Republic of China with respect to technology transfer and protection of intellectual property.' *The International Lawyer*, **21**, (Winter), 132. Cited in Larson, M. R. (1988) 'Exporting private enterprise to developing communist countries: a case study on China.' *Columbia Journal of World Business*, **23**, (Spring), 85

China's Ministry of Foreign Economic Relations and Trade (MOFERT) issued new rules on 22 October 1990 which state that joint ventures, other than in the following restricted categories, can now run indefinitely:

• service trades including hotels, apartments and offices, entertainment, restaurants, taxi services, photo development, mechanical maintenance, and consultancy,
• land development and real estate,
• resource exploration and extraction, and
• projects restricted by the state and projects for which state laws require a time limit.

The Eighth Five-Year Plan, while emphasizing agriculture, transportation, raw materials and energy as priority sectors, has lowered the growth rates that were written into the Seventh Plan (1986–90).

Establishing a joint venture in China is not particularly easy. Whereas in the past, foreign investors did put up with inefficient work practices, exorbitant overheads and cumbersome bureaucracy just to get established, there is now a different attitude among Western investors who see less appeal in China, and consequently, are taking a more pragmatic and tightly focused approach to Chinese market entry. Selwyn (1990) points to three trends taking place:

1. Foreign companies are driving harder bargains.
2. They are choosing their joint venture partners carefully.
3. They are seeking longer joint venture contracts to give them time to amortize start-up costs.

Issues over CoCom strategic export controls have yet to be lifted. This means that some technologies and some exports will not be allowed by the NATO-member countries, even if these same technologies may be available within the Pacific Basin itself.

There were 100 companies which had established trade relations with China by 1976, rising to 174 in 1980, and 182 in 1981. In terms of the often very necessary international trade agreements and protocols which facilitate international trade, China had concluded 88 of these in 1980 alone, and by the end of 1980 had signed foreign credit agreements totalling $20 billion, and more than 360 joint venture projects were set up with foreign funds amounting to $1.5 billion.

By 1995, China had approved 258,000 foreign funded projects. Ownership is determined by the proportionate percentage of capital committed. Management is by a board of directors appointed in proportion to the equity ownership of the participants. Joint ventures are expected to generate foreign exchange. Gross profits are taxed under the Joint Venture Income Tax Law at a rate of 30 per cent, plus a tax surcharge of 10 per cent, unless the entity is located in a designated economic zone in which case special tax incentives are granted (Larson, 1988).

Political interference in joint ventures increased following the Tiananmen events, and this was reflected in Chinese representation on mixed boards of control and also demands for paid political study for the workforce. Approvals were held up and bureaucratic delays worsened, not only between ministries but between the provinces and MOFERT. Accounts receivable were extended beyond 100 days and were dubbed 'unreceivables' by one Western general manager (*China Business Review*, 1990). Credit squeeze and inability to access investment capital posed another major obstacle. The retrenchment following the Tiananmen events also dated the very interesting study by Frankenstein and Chao (1988) of decision-making in the Chinese Foreign Trade Administration.

The negative impact of the events of Tiananmen in June 1989 are seen also in the levels of incoming foreign investment to China, although the time lag involved in these contracts from signature to official ratification made the situation look better than it in fact was, and so, although the investment conditions had not changed, the will of foreign investors had suddenly dissipated. That will has since revived, but China is showing itself to be more selective about the kinds of investment that it wants to bring in, emphasizing technology and export-intensity, and dragging its feet on investment proposals related to luxury goods.

Zhang and Snyder (1988), in a study of foreign investment projects in China, came up with a checklist that amounts to Five Ps: project, partner, pattern, profitability, and protection, each of which includes a number of variables.

Wholly Foreign-Owned Enterprises (WFOE)

Since 1 April 1986, it is possible for a wholly foreign-owned enterprise (WFOE) to be established outside, as well as within, a SEZ or ETDZ provided that it 'utilizes advanced technology and equipment, or exports all or a major portion of its products' (Larson, 1988). The ground rules are still to be defined, however, and so the SEZ or ETDZ seems safer against an assurance that the Government will not nationalize an enterprise 'except under special circumstances' as yet to be defined.

WFOEs have been the most controversial forms of foreign investment and their terms of incorporation remain unclear (Barale, 1990). Nevertheless, the number of WFOEs is increasing, some 423 such contracts were signed in the first six months of 1989. WFOEs are expected to show that they are self-sufficient, that their foreign exchange income meets their needs and exceeds their renminbi income. Where a WFOE involves $10 million or less, then the authority for approval lies with the provinces. A WFOE may not produce items for local sale that are restricted by the State, or manufacture export items that require export licences from MOFERT. The provinces and local authorities still report approvals to MOFERT. The five stages are:

1. A company interested in establishing a WFOE prepares a proposal stating the general purpose of the project, its products, planned production, registered capital and loans, intended market, and estimated size of facilities and number of employees.

2. If there is support from the department in charge of the industry, the foreign company is asked to prepare a feasibility study which will be examined alongside the project proposal by the State Planning Commission.

3. MOFERT approval, which is more legalistic in nature assessing the good financial standing of the company and power of attorney of the local representative.

4. Application to the local Administration of Industry and Commerce (AIC) for a business licence. This is then the completion of the

---

Table 11.10   Potential investor checklist

Project
- Is the proposed investment project compatible with Chinese planning goals?
- Does it fall into a priority sector of China's economy?

Partner
- Is the potential Chinese partner authorized to participate in foreign investment projects?
- Do other parties need to be involved in the transaction?
- What are the advantages and drawbacks to your potential partner?

Pattern
- What type of investment structure is best for the project?

Profitability
- What is the project's market and anticipated market share?
- What form will profits take?
- What are the restrictions on using and repatriating foreign exchange?

Protection
- What kind of protection does Chinese law provide this type of investment?
- How will disputes be resolved?

Source: Zhang, S. X., and Snyder, J. L. (1988) 'The Five Ps.', *China Business Review*, March–April

formal legal establishment. AIC may seek changes, particularly where there may be domestic sales of the WFOE's products.

5.   Tax registration must follow within 20 days. WFOEs are taxed at the rate of the Foreign Enterprise Income Tax Law rather than those of the Joint Venture Law.

Joint-venture dissolution

There is a lack of clarity in the existing Chinese legislation, but Article 102 of the Implementing Regulations to the 1979 Equity Joint Venture Law states six permissible bases for terminating an equity joint venture (Frisbie and Kay, 1990):

*   termination of contract duration,
*   inability to continue operations due to heavy losses,
*   inability to continue operations due to the failure of one of the parties to carry out its contractual obligations,
*   inability to continue operations due to heavy losses caused by force majeure,
*   inability to obtain the desired objectives of the operation and at the same time to see a future for development, and
*   occurrence of other reasons for dissolution prescribed by the contract and articles of association.

Very few joint ventures have been terminated relative to the number in operation. Aside from the expiry of contracts, where it may be noted that the average duration of joint ventures is between 11 and 15 years, a unanimous vote of the board of directors and approval of the government department that originally approved the joint venture contract – usually MOFERT – is also required. The decision has to be publicized in local newspapers to give creditors notice of intention to cease operations. The quite different philosophical approach of Chinese Government officials to Western accounting conventions will undoubtedly present problems in the evaluation of assets and liabilities, including obligations to the redundant workforce.

The future

In foreign policy, China has maintained its own independence, totally separate from, and often conflicting with, the former Soviet Union even in its communist days. Yet, politics are drawing China closer to full membership in the Pacific Basin. China now has responsibility for Hong Kong and Macao, and Taiwan has now dropped its vehement opposition to the PRC which will

increase the potential for trade. Enlargement of ASEAN to include Japan, China and Taiwan and activation of APEC would create a redoubtable force for trade.

Ironically, the USA was the prime mover in this region of the world before the economic rise of Japan, and had done much to foster economic integration within the region. Singapore, South Korea, Taiwan and Hong Kong are good success stories referred to as either Newly Industrialized Countries (NIC) or, more popularly, as the Four Mini Dragons.

Japan

Japan in the world economy

Japan is the second largest consumer market in the free world – very close in size to the now united Germany, but more than three times that of Great Britain.

The Gross National Product of Japan is the second largest in the industrialized world after the USA. It is more than three times as large as that of the UK and is expanding at a much faster rate than that of any other advanced industrialized country. Japan is a market of 112.6 million people and has an average growth rate of 0.3 per cent with a per capita income higher than that in the UK. Imports have been increasing fast but have not kept pace with Japan's exports.

Against a backcloth then of a static world market, the law of comparative 'disadvantage' holds sway over that of comparative advantage. In Japan, it has been particularly noted that the terminology of trade has taken on military overtones in the usage of such terms as 'trade war', for example. The USA now refers to the trade talks with Japan as being under the Structural Impediment Initiative. Talks have gone on now for decades without any real tangible results. Those talks with the USA now focus on rice, the distribution system and defence spending. However, Japan's production costs still remain relatively low and its productivity is improving.

Insatiable world demand for Japanese exports, combined with limited domestic imports, low inflation rates, an embarrassingly large trade surplus, and a fairly steady rate of GNP growth, have made Japan's record appear unavoidably good compared with that of any of its partners or competitors in the West. In 1988, the Japanese trade surplus with the EU was $22.8 billion, twice what it was just three years before.

Approximately 60 per cent of Japan's imports are fuels and raw materials, with only 27 per cent accounted for by manufactures. Japan, however, claims that its strategy has been to implement a domestic demand-oriented economy. Despite Japan's trading performance the yen is not an international currency and is artificial also in that it makes imports higher than they should actually be. One of the US demands is for Japan to do more to bolster and internationalize the yen. Ninety-seven per cent of Japanese imports and 60 per cent of exports are priced in US dollars. Pressures on high inflation and interest rates do not exist in Japan to the extent known in other Western economies.

Japan's very large trade surpluses have been a political agenda item for many years, but continue still to grow while Japan's trading partners in the West, including Britain and the USA, both accuse Japan of treating them as developing countries because of the imbalance in the value of the commodity composition of their bilateral trade flows. Japan imports fuel and raw materials and some beverages, while being a

world leader now in cars, computers and electronics, all high value-added export items, further worsening the trade imbalance.

The Japanese, despite their large investments in Europe, centred mainly in Britain, are mistrusted by both continental European industrialists and their governments, over a range of issues, including (Sasseen, 1989):

- the targeting of strategic industries,
- the low quality of investment and jobs,
- dependence on important components,
- lack of R&D facilities,
- lack of true integration into Europe, and
- the still closed Japanese market.

The Japanese respond by saying that they are investing in Europe in order to get around

Table 11.11

	1992	1993	1994	1995	1996
Exports from Japan	7,442(+10)	8,536(+14)	8,842(+4)	9,614(+9)	8,994(-6)
Exports to Japan	2,331(−1)	2,654(+19)	2,991(+13)	3,783(+26)	4,264(+13)
Deficits for the UK	5,211(+16)	5,883(+12)	5,850(−1)	5,831(0)	4,731(−17)

Source: Overseas Trade Statistics by CSO
(Million Pounds, % Change over previous year)

Exhibit 11.10 Canadian tomatoes in Japan

Selling high-quality food should be a straightforward proposition – get a good, fresh product into a consumer's hand at a fair price and the deal is done. Unfortunately, it's rarely that simple when the food product crosses an international boundary. Take the case of Canadian hot house tomato sales to Japan.

Back in 1987, Japanese food brokers approached British Columbia hot house tomato growers about importing Canadian tomatoes. But the importers and growers discovered that the Japanese authorities had banned imports of tomatoes from any country where tobacco blue mould exists.

Canadian tomato crops have never shown signs of blue mould infection, but tomatoes and tobacco are from the same plant family and that was enough for Japanese officials who were concerned about the potential for tomatoes being a pathway for tobacco blue mould.

But B. C. Hot House Foods Inc. and Agriculture and Agri-Food Canada weren't prepared to give up on such a potentially lucrative market. A

series of comprehensive tests were designed and carried out to prove beyond any doubt that tomatoes grown in Canada could not be carriers of the offending tobacco blue mould.

A review by Japanese scientists confirmed the results and in September of 1996, after almost a decade of experiments and negotiations, Japan removed the ban on seven tomato varieties, including one grown extensively in Canada. Trial shipments have already gone from B.C. and Ontario to Tokyo and Osaka stores. The first results are encouraging.

'They've got the money and we've got the premium product,' says Denton Hoffman from the Ontario Greenhouse Vegetable Growers' Association. 'It should be a marriage made in heaven.'

The future success of agri-food trade with Asia will be built by private industry and the Canadian government working as partners. In international trade, it's the best way to get the job done and the product sold.

Source: CYAP

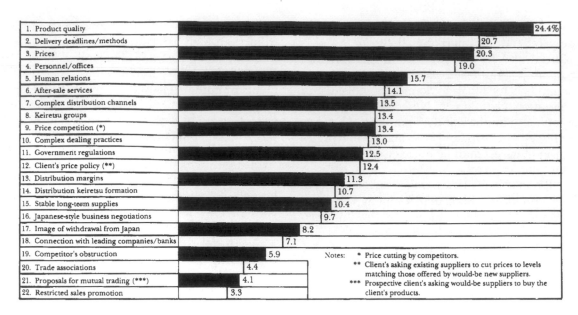

	%
1. Product quality	24.4%
2. Delivery deadlines/methods	20.7
3. Prices	20.3
4. Personnel/offices	19.0
5. Human relations	15.7
6. After-sale services	14.1
7. Complex distribution channels	13.5
8. Keiretsu groups	13.4
9. Price competition (*)	13.4
10. Complex dealing practices	13.0
11. Government regulations	12.5
12. Client's price policy (**)	12.4
13. Distribution margins	11.3
14. Distribution keiretsu formation	10.7
15. Stable long-term supplies	10.4
16. Japanese-style business negotiations	9.7
17. Image of withdrawal from Japan	8.2
18. Connection with leading companies/banks	7.1
19. Competitor's obstruction	5.9
20. Trade associations	4.4
21. Proposals for mutual trading (***)	4.1
22. Restricted sales promotion	3.3

Notes: * Price cutting by competitors.
  ** Client's asking existing suppliers to cut prices to levels matching those offered by would-be new suppliers.
  *** Prospective client's asking would-be suppliers to buy the client's products.

Source: Fujigane, Y., and Ennis, P. (1990) Keiretsu – what are they doing, where are they going? *Tokyo Business Today,* September, p. 29

Figure 11.4   Business problems Japan poses for foreign countries

the high yen, and the 'dumping' charges levied by the EU. This is true of Canon and Ricoh, to take but two examples. However, to take this investment into a proper perspective, the total amount is small compared, for example, to the US investment in Europe or Japanese investment in the Pacific Basin, which is 8.3 times that invested in Europe (Bruce, 1990). Only 2 per cent of the foreign money coming into Britain is from Japan, yet this investment is strategically placed in manufacturing and the electronics industry, and Britain accounts for more than one-third of Japanese investment in Europe. Given these facts and what he calls 'a spiral of disindustrialization', Fred Burton, of the University of Manchester, has argued for a more aggressive stance to be taken by the EC in trade with Japan, creating a European model of the Japanese MITI (Ministry of International Trade and Industry), and setting a clear policy line. Without this, Japan will emerge dominant over all of Europe. It is, perhaps, worth pointing out that a survey of Japanese citizens found their favourite words to be 'effort' and 'persistence' (Turpin, 1990).

Japan's export performance is due to:

1. *Stable prices.* First, the impact of an artificially low yen exchange rate on the price of its exports, then as the yen appreciated, the substitution of parts and components from offshore production plants in the Pacific Basin, and the growth of Japanese foreign direct investment generally.

2. *Slack domestic demand.* Holding down imports of raw materials and fuels as well as manufacturing goods, plus soft prices for imported energy.

3. *Interest rates.* The Ministry of Finance cannot lower interest rates because lowering interest rates would probably weaken the yen, thus making Japanese exports even more competitive and Japan's trade partners more unhappy. Western nations should continue to press for the internationalization of the yen, forcing yen export prices higher at least in the short term.

In the long term, Japan should continue to attract foreign direct investment (FDI). It presumably restricts FDI but the strength of the economy is to be seen in the lowest inflation rate of any major industrial country. Slowly, Japan is moving to the point where its own capital markets now play a significant role in the international financial system. The Tokyo Stock Exchange is now the largest in the world. Yet pressure continues to mount on Japan, which has taken steps since 1980 to revise its formerly very rigid exchange control laws.

Reasons for the Japanese moving into foreign markets

1. Satellite manufacture became profitable because of yen revaluation.

2.   Commercial and other services, required to support satellite manufacturing, increased the outflow from Japan.

3.   Strategic overseas investment in the extractive industries safeguards the supply of essential basic materials, e.g., copper, iron ore, bauxite, and coking coal.

Economic and social background

Japan consists of four main islands: Kyushu, Shikoku, the main island Honshu, and Hokkaido. Others lying to the south of Kyushu, such as Okinawa and others, were administered by the USA until May 1972.

The land mass is almost double the size of the UK, comprising 145,000 square miles (94,000 square miles in the UK). The country is mountainous and volcanic, with short fast-flowing unnavigable rivers.

The country is influenced by the Chinese who introduced their script into Japan in 400 AD. From the twelfth century, political power lay with the military rulers, the Shogun. The first European contact came in the sixteenth century from the Portuguese in 1542 at Tanegashima.

The Portuguese and Spanish brought Christianity which taught that people were equal before God and that God was all powerful and to be respected above all others, a philosophy which certainly did not appeal to the leading class of society at the time who saw in Christianity something that was revolutionary to their way of thinking and so could be highly disruptive. For this reason Japan lived in near isolation for some 260 years, trading only with the Dutch

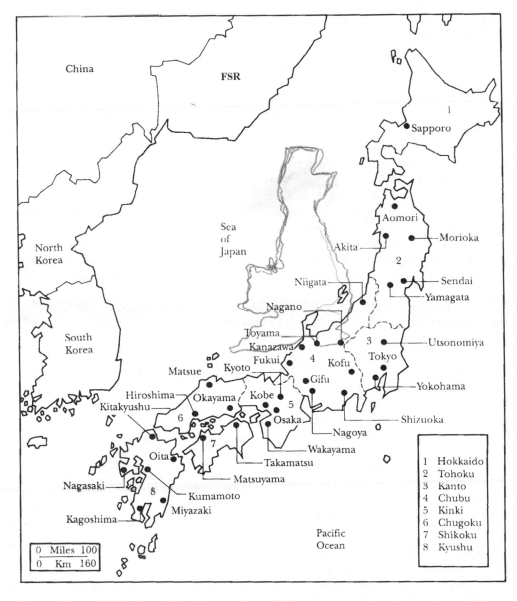

Source: Financial Times (1990) Special Supplement: Japan, 9 July

Figure 11.5   Map of Japan

through one small port as the Dutch did not try to spread Christianity. In a mirror image of what is taking place in our present time the US sent out an ambassador, Townsend Harris, in 1856 to convey the message to Japan that it must open up its market. This broke Japanese isolation. The overthrow of Tokugawa Shogun and restoration of the Emperor Meiji followed. The latter moved from the traditional imperial capital of Kydo to the Tokugawan Shogun's capital at Edo, which was renamed Tokyo, which means 'Eastern capital'.

Japan annexed Taiwan in 1884–85, and acquired Korea as a colony in 1911. It joined the Allies in the First World War, and has in the past shown a desire to dominate China. In 1941, Japan attacked the USA and later there was the US bombing of Hiroshima and Nagasaki, which ended the war for Japan. The Peace Treaty, which ended the occupation, was signed at San Francisco on 8 September 1951. Japan regained its independence in April 1952. Neither the USSR nor China was a party to this treaty.

Japan has since looked to the USA for security, as her largest market and supplier of foodstuffs. Relations with the FSU have for long been cool because of the Russian annexation of four small islands off Hokkaido at the end of the war. The FSU has also criticized the Japanese Treaty of Peace and Friendship with China as being 'anti-Russian' in nature. Previously Japan supported Taiwan but after the Nixon visit to China, Japan moved to recognize the People's Republic of China. Article 9 of the Japanese Constitution renounces war as a sovereign right and declares that war potential will never be maintained. There is a self-defence army, navy and air force, but the country spends a total of only 1 per cent of GNP on defence.

Religions are not mutually hostile nor mutually exclusive. For example, although Buddhism is the most common religion, there is a common practice of having a Shinto priest bless a new commercial enterprise. There is respect for religions, and more overlap between religions in Japan than would be found elsewhere. The main religions are:

Shinto

An indigenous religion which worships a deity as manifested in works of nature or man, which inspire feelings of awe or respect.

Buddhism

This was introduced from China in the sixth century. There are a number of different sects, but this is the most common religion now in Japan.

Christianity and new religions

Christianity is a minority religion. The Soka Gakkai or Value Adding Society combines the pursuit of material benefit with an intolerant form of Buddhism (Nicheren Shoshu Sect).

Coming to terms with Japanese growth

As perceived by Westerners, an aura of mysticism surrounds the East, and Westerners are

Table 11.12   Estimated number of Japanese rivals in selected industries

Air conditioners	13	Motorcycles	4
Audio equipment	24	Musical instruments	4
Automobiles	9	Personal computers	16
Cameras	15	Semiconductors	34
Car audio	12	Sewing machines	20
Carbon fibres	7	Shipbuilding**	33
Construction equipment	15*	Steel***	5
Copiers	14	Synthetic fibres	8
Facsimile machines	10	Television sets	15
Lift trucks	8	Truck and bus tyres	5
Machine tools	112	Trucks	11
Mainframe computers	6	Typewriters	14
Microwave equipment	5	Videocassette recorders	10

* The number of firms varies by product area. The smallest number, ten, produced bulldozers. Fifteen firms produced shovel trucks, truck cranes, and asphalt paving equipment. There are 20 companies in hydraulic excavators, a product area where Japan is particularly strong.

** Six firms had annual production in excess of 10,000 tons.

*** Number of integrated companies.

Source: Porter, M. E. (1990) *The Competitive Advantage of Nations*, Macmillan, London

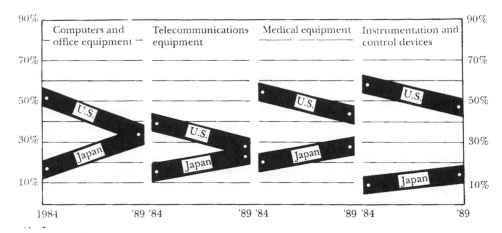

Source: Sako, M. (1989) Parntership between small and large firms: The case of Japan. In *Partnership Between Small and Large Firms*, Directorate for Enterprise of the Commission of the European Communities, Brussels, Graham and Trotman, London

Figure 11.6   Production structure of typical Japanese automaker as of 1981

unable to understand a religious reverence for the Japanese imperial family. The culture and value system is different in Japan from that practised in Britain. Nevertheless, there is the danger of unquestioning acceptance of Japanese invincibility, stemming perhaps from the unity of mind and body found in Japanese exports such as the martial arts, which in fact originated first in India then moved to China and then Japan.

Important societal changes are taking place. Japanese consumers are becoming accustomed to affluence and to finding, through travel, that Japanese goods are cheaper abroad than at home.

A rapidly growing proportion of Japan's population is over sixty-five, thus creating further opportunities for retirement and leisure as well as automation, roboticization, retraining and health care programmes. As a nation, Japan's strengths lie in innovation not invention, and not in labour cost either, for Japan is demanning heavily. Yet, as Martin Beresford (1981) noted in *Management Today*, October, pp. 60–66, 'much of Japan's success has resulted from just "doing things better"', i.e., applying quite unexotic technology steadily to improve product design or productivity in existing industries.

The Japanese have an organizational system, known as 'keiretsu', which is the engine behind their growth. These we shall deal with later, but it is important to note their history, centralization, family ties, cross-holdings, debt ties and managerial exchanges, also the closeness of banks to Japanese industry. Next, it pays to examine the Japanese strategy in entering Western markets. This has been said to resemble a cascading strategy pattern (Lorenz, 1981). They

enter into carefully selected small segments and then gradually move across the entire market. An examination of Japanese marketing strategies since the 1950s shows how, in numerous cases – transistor radios, televisions, cars, stereo, hi-fi – the Japanese have consistently used essentially the same strategy. The strategy is to launch a single product into the foreign market. This will be aimed at a small but well-defined market segment. Consequently, it does not arouse competitive reaction. Meanwhile, the gradual build-up of parts, maintenance, and after-sales is taking place. Once this has been done, the product range is extended, 'cascading' into the market with new lines of products.

Company size alone is not the reason for Japanese growth, as we shall see. While Japanese companies are large on a global comparison, over 80 per cent of the country's labour force of 34 million work in small or medium-size companies, which are just as dynamic and competitive as their larger counterparts.

Geographical distance, but more importantly, psychic distance, appear to be creating an advantage in favour of Japanese businessmen *vis-à-vis* UK businessmen where, by way of comparison:

An attitude born in the British Empire and corner-store tradition seems to prevail among many [British businessmen] of best doing business with people who think the same way as they do. One effect is this failure to realize that much good business can be done with countries with different economic systems – consequently there is defensiveness where there should be aggression.

Meanwhile, the Japanese hold continues to spread from electronics and motor vehicles to computers and telecommunications to numerically controlled machine tools, tractors and construction machinery.

From 1953 to 1973, Japan invested more per unit of added value than its major Western competitors, i.e., 24.2 per cent compared with 13.3 per cent for the UK, and taking base index as 100 for Japan in 1953, the 1973 figure for the UK is 40 (Boulton, Jenney, 1981). It must also be conceded that Japan has earned an outstanding reputation for its harmonious relationship between government and industry in backing innovation.

The most significant single item in Japanese export trade is the sale of computers and telecommunications equipment, followed by automobiles. In 1960, crude oil accounted for 28.7 per cent of Japan's imports. In 1985, crude and refined oil was responsible for 28.7 per cent of imports, followed by natural gas and oil products. By way of further comparison, the USA which developed the automobile industry at the turn of the century, sells too few cars to Japan to have them recorded in official statistics, but Japanese car imports into the USA in 1990 accounted for 21.5 per cent of Japanese imports. US auto manufacturers do not make right-hand drive cars for the Japanese market but ask dealers instead to make 'conversions'.

Nevertheless, Japanese industry has demanned wherever possible. Citing the case of the Japanese electronics industry, for example, as having multiplied its output 3.4 times between 1968 and 1978 while its exports increased 5.2 times, its production finally became 25 per cent larger than the combined production of West Germany, France, Italy and the UK. Again, there are colour television assembly lines nearly 70 per cent of which are now fully automated, lowering production times from six man hours to one and one-half, and reduced power consumption per 20-inch set from 325W in 1972 to 95W in 1977. A 1984 survey of 763 Japanese companies showed the proportion allocated to basic research to be an average 5.2 per cent of total outlay. While 117 firms replied that they spent over 20 per cent on basic research, 291 stated only 2 per cent. This survey

also showed heavy dependence on universities and research institutes, which does not happen in the Western world.

There was little Japanese investment in the EC in the 1960s, except for relatively insignificant areas like zips and stationery. In the 1970s this came to include ball bearings, colour televisions, chemicals, and synthetic fabrics. In the 1980s, Nissan and Honda began car production in Europe, and as Europe prepares for the Single Market this flow has increased.

The Sogo Shosha: Japanese international trading companies

In postwar Japan, the Sogo Shosha were divided up into many different and separate companies. Mitsui, then the largest (now it is Mitsubishi), was divided up into over 200 companies, but by 1959 it had reassembled, and now handles approximately 10 per cent of Japanese exports on its own. Mitsui is now the fourth largest US exporter after Boeing, General Motors and General Electric.

The nine big Sogo Shoshas account for an estimated 50–60 per cent of Japan's external trade. The Sogo Shosha have an impressive pedigree going back more than a hundred years. Their strength lies in their integration of trading, manufacturing, and banking affiliates. Mitsubishi is linked with Mitsubishi Bank; Mitsui with Mitsui Bank; Marubeni with Fuji; C. Itoh to Dai-Ichi Kangyo Bank. These banks rank among the largest in the world in asset terms. At the end of 1981, the nine major Sogo Shoshas had a total of approximately 57,000 personnel. Of these, about 23,900 (including 6,300 expatriate personnel) were working at a total of 1,044 overseas offices, including wholly owned affiliates and joint ventures.

It is usual to read of obituaries for the Sogo Shosha – only 20 per cent of Japan's domestic wholesale trade now goes via the top ten trading houses compared with a majority situation in early 1950. The threat derives from the increasing independence of Japanese car manufacturers and others; from Japanese banks lending directly

---

Table 11.13   The myths of the Japanese market

1. How Japanese distribution system is impenetrable.
2. Product testing and certification requirements make it impossible for foreign companies to enter Japan.
3. The Japanese will only buy Japanese products.
4. The Japanese will not work for a foreign company.

Source: Alden, V. Z. (1987) Who says you can't crack Japanese markets? *Harvard Business Review*, **65**, (1) 52–56

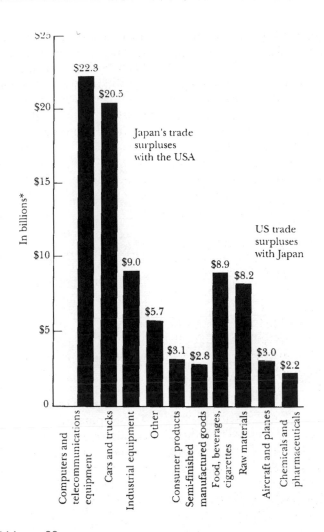

Source: *Fortune* (1991) 6 May, p. 39

Figure 11.7   US – Japanese trade and surpluses

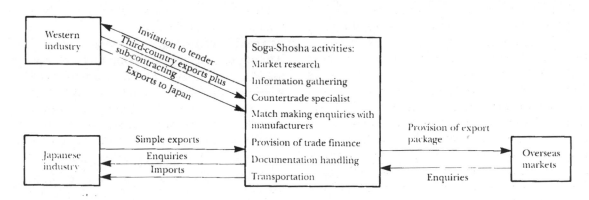

Source: Blenkhorn, D. L., and Noori, A. H. (1990) What it takes to supply Japanese OEMs. *Industrial Marketing Management,* **19,** 21–30

Figure 11.8   The Zaibatsu approach to OEM/supplier relationships

to the small company rather than via them; and from the fact also that gross profit margins for the traditional business of Sogo Shoshas is falling, signalling stagnant turnover and rising costs. Against this, it should be noted that the Sogo Shoshas are moving increasingly into third-country trade, acting as an intermediary for other Western companies, while at home they are being seen to be active in new investments, e.g., cable television and data communications.

Imports into Japan

Japan is said to still retain an ancient complex distribution system that has evolved from agricultural produce. This poses a problem for domestic as well as foreign companies. Japan has more wholesalers and retailers per capita than any other industrial nation. It is explained by the 'Keiretsu' system in which producers, importers, distributors, and retailers are all financially linked with each other, either directly or through a bank or Sogo Shosha. This results in close ties and bonds forged by mutual obligation and service.

Technically, all imports require licences under Article 52 of the Japan Foreign Exchange Law. However, most goods enter unrestricted and with nominal formality. This can be done under the Import Declaration Scheme (IDS) or under the import quota scheme. Under the Import Declaration Scheme, the only requirement is to report to the Ministry of International Trade and Industry (MITI) through foreign exchange banks on the remittance of payment abroad. Under the import quota scheme, certain goods are subject to a specific quantitative restriction. Under Articles 21 and 22 of GATT, the Japanese Government is allowed to restrict imports for security, public health, revenue or other reasons (including heavy aircraft, aircraft engines, explosives, arms, swords, tobacco products, and narcotics). Under this system, an importer must first obtain an Import Quota Allocation Certificate from MITI which entitles him to receive an import licence on application to an authorized foreign exchange bank. The size of import quotas are decided by the Japanese authorities on a global basis, but the amounts are not made public. Allocations are made to importers on the basis of their past performance, usually twice a year.

Tariffs

Except for certain raw materials, essential items of industrial equipment, antiques, and a few other manufactured goods, imports are liable to customs duties. Most are calculated as a of the value of the goods. Of the 2,576 headings in the Japanese Customs Tariff, 412 are duty free and these are mainly raw materials which represent almost 50 per cent by value of Japanese imports. The tariff rates then are:

* Basic Rate
* GATT Rate
* Temporary Rate (reviewed annually)
* Special Rate under Generalized Preferences

Japan's tariffs are on average lower than those of most industrialized countries, but 'non-tariff barriers' constitute a problem. Toyota produce a booklet to help foreign suppliers around the maze of bureaucracy which, combined with long distribution channels, can be a barrier to entry to the market. Import regulations include the following.

Duty assessment

This is on the basis of the declared CIF value. On this basis, the customs may increase the basis for assessment of duty in order to bring the CIF price up to the value which an independent buyer would have to pay, assuming he had no special relationship with the supplier. This 'arms length' concept is introduced here and is in fact a countervailing duty to ensure that imports do not gain over domestic products.

Duty is normally levied *ad valorem*. However, for wool and Scotch whisky, a specific duty may be levied solely on the basis of the quality.

Internal taxes

These operate, regardless of whether they are for domestic for foreign goods, from 5 per cent on cosmetics to 30 per cent on motor boats, etc., but there are also excise duties.

Import documentation

Certificates of origin are not required for goods for which conventional or beneficial rates of duty are claimed, such as goods entitled to MFN status. A declaration of origin in the commercial invoice is sufficient.

Transit and bond

Although there are no designated free ports as such, certain factories and warehouses have been designated for the processing in bond of imported materials and goods for ultimate re-export. These are of five types:

1.   Designated bonded area owned or administered by the Japanese Government, local public bodies, or Japan National Railways.
2.   Bonded sheds.
3.   Bonded warehouses.
4.   Bonded manufacturing warehouses.
5.   Bonded exhibition sites.

Storage for imported goods is for up to 24 months but may be extended. The total number of bonded facilities in Japan is 3,300, located in nine areas – Tokyo, Yokohama, Kobe, Osaka, Nagoya, Moji, Nagasaki, Naha and Hakodate. Each contains all forms of bonded facilities.

Table 11.14 The six big enterprise groups and their Shacho-kai (1 October 1983)

Group name / Shacho-kai name	Mitsubishi / Kinyō-kai	Mitsui / Nimoku-kai	Sumitomo / Hakushi-kai	Fuji / Fuyō-kai	Dai-Ichi / Sankin-kai	Sanwa / Sansui-kai
Main manufacturing corporations	Mitsubishi Chemical Industries Ltd; Mitsubishi Rayon Co.; Mitsubishi Steel Mfg Co.; Mitsubishi Heavy Industries; Mitsubishi Motor Industry; Mitsubishi Electric Corporation; Mitsubishi Oil Co.	Mitsui Toatsu Chemicals Inc.; Tōray Industries; Japan Steel Works; Mitsui Engineering and Shipbuilding Co., Ltd.; Toyota Motor Co.; Toshiba Co.	Sumitomo Chemical; Sumitomo Metal Industries; Sumitomo Heavy Industries, Ltd.; Nippon Electric Co.	Shōwa Denko K.K.; Tōyō Rayon Co., Ltd; Nippon Kōkan K.K.; Kubola Ltd; Nippon Seiko K.K.; Nissan Motor; Oki Electric Industry Co. Ltd.; Hitachi; Tōa Nenryō Kōgyō K.K.	Denki Kagaku Kogyo K.K.; Asahi Chemical Industries Co.; Kawasaki Steel Corporation; Kawasaki Heavy Industries; Ishikawajima-Harima Heavy Industries; Isuzu Motors, Ltd.; Fijitsu; Hitachi; Showa Oil Co.	Tokuyama Soga Co. Ltd; Unitika; Teijin; Kobe Steel; Hitachi Shipbuilding and Engineering Co.; Daihatsu Motor Co.; Sharp Corporation; Hitachi; Maruzen Oil Co.
Others	Nippon Kōgaku K.K.			Canon	Asahi Optical Company; Nippon Columbia Co.	
General trading company	Mitsubishi Corporation	Mitsui and Co.	Sumitomo Shōji Kaisha	Marubeni Corporation	C. Itoh and Co.	Nisshō-Iwai Co.

Source: Sumiya, T. (1984) *Kokka to kigyō*, pp. 82–83. Cited in: *Japanese Competition since 1945* (Morris-Suzuki, Tessa; Seiyama, Takuro, 1981), M. E. Sharpe Inc., Armonk, NY.

Table 11.15 Comparison of retail and wholesale business*			
	Japan	USA	UK
Number of retail stores	1.62m	1.5m	343,000
Number of wholesalers	437,000	376,000	95,000
Retailers per 10,000 people	132	65	61
Wholesalers per 10,000 people	36	16	17
Retailers per wholesaler	3.7	4.0	3.6

Note: As the Japanese data are for 1988 and the US and UK data are for 1982, this is an attempt to statistically camouflage important infrastructural differences in what is in the West – a highly dynamic industry in which Britain, in particular, excels and has taken the lead in retail merchandising style and excellence.

Source: Wagsty, S. (1989) Protection for small business. *Financial Times: Special Supplement – Japanese Industry*, 4 December, p. 3

Distribution in Japan

Japanese distribution is a particular problem for foreign companies seeking to enter Japan. Japanese trading companies have been accused (Foster, 1988) of taking on agencies for Western products in order to control their distribution while a decision is made about whether some associated manufacturing unit should bring out a duplicate. Other foreign companies, such as those in the automotive industry, are effectively trying to 'carry coal to Newcastle' in trying to penetrate the Japanese automotive market, as forty US auto parts manufacturers set out to do. Traditional market supply structures have to be taken into consideration. Also, pricing low will not secure a long-term advantage in Japan, whose buyer-seller relationships are traditionally close and secure. Nevertheless, TRW supply rack and pinion steering systems; Allied Signal supply turbo-chargers; Motorola supply car phones; Tenneco supply silencers (mufflers); and Champion supply spark plugs.

Often held to be a non-tariff barrier that blocks imports once they have been allowed into Japan, there are some significant changes taking place. First, the Japanese distribution system is very traditional, and it has the longest distribution channels in the world because of the system whereby manufacturers at the top, and all the intermediaries below, will have a cross-shareholding in each other. Inroads into this system have been made mainly by foreign companies creating new distribution systems as they enter Japan for the first time, such as Coca-Cola. Again, distribution systems in Japan have featured in the US trade talks with Japan under the banner of the Structural Impediments Initiative (SII). Yet, Japanese legislation, such as the Large Store Law, protects small retailers from predatory large stores.

Where bureaucracy gets in the way, there is usually also a way to circumvent it. For example, many companies have lured former civil servants as consultants, although this may often be seen to fall into a questionable 'grey area', as in the past with scandals over Lockheed payments to 'consultants'. Japanese former civil servants have to work one year then before joining the company as an adviser, then director, etc. Mitsubishi hired an adviser who is now Managing Director. At all times, creativity is required in dealing with the Japanese market. If, for example, it is not possible to get into the Defence Ministry, then perhaps contact Mitsubishi who is also a large defence supplier.

Perhaps another point to note also is that the Japanese distributor will look at annual sales, whereas a Western company may be more concerned with the immediate short-term results. Again, a Japanese importer may be more concerned with total sales volume than unit profitability, so here are some inherent differences in business approaches. While licensing has been popular in the past, and franchising is now very common, there is now the easing of restrictions on expanding large retail outlet chains in Japan, so there are increasing market opportunities and these could well be developed through joint ventures. In pharmaceuticals, Japan is the second largest market in the world and, with a rapidly ageing population, may soon overtake the USA. This question of distribution is a crucial one for all concerned.

Business America (1988) reports a few cases of US successes in bypassing the distribution system, such as American Natural Beverages Inc., marketing a natural soda with trendy packaging. Electrolux decided to bypass the existing distribution system and, with sales of more than $133 million, has obviously been successful in selling direct to the customer. Electrolux have since concluded an agreement with the Sharp Corporation to co-design, produce and distribute products (Berge, 1990). The stimulus to change the Japanese system is lacking and that really ought to come from Japanese consumers, who, as mentioned elsewhere in this chapter, are largely unrepresented. Fields (1989) points to this and the fact that the Japanese consumer does not realize that the continued existence of this antiquated distribution system is what keeps retail prices high internally.

Under pressure from the West, Japan has had to urge its salaried workers to spend money on imports. The Ministry of Posts and Telecommunications has initiated a mail order catalogue programme that allows Japanese consumers to order imported goods directly from foreign suppliers. Japan's imports of manufactured goods have, however, increased since 1986. *Takahide* (1988) reported that changes were taking place within the distribution system which were visible from:

1.   a decline in the number of stores,
2.   responses to changes in the marketplace,
3.   diversification, and
4.   introduction of point of sale and information systems.

Berkwitt (1986) outlines a description of Ohmori Co. Ltd., which is at the top of the three-tier distribution system in which primary wholesalers buy from manufacturers, who sell merchandise to the secondary wholesalers who, in turn, sell to the tertiary wholesalers who sell to the user.

Japanese expectations of suppliers

Total foreign direct investment in Japan is small relative to that which has been built up in the USA. Americans are ethnocentric, and carry a mental map of the world which amplifies the size of the USA from East to West and crowds out all other nations and continents. Japan is a foreign market for Westerners, but has had an economy which offers only limited Western

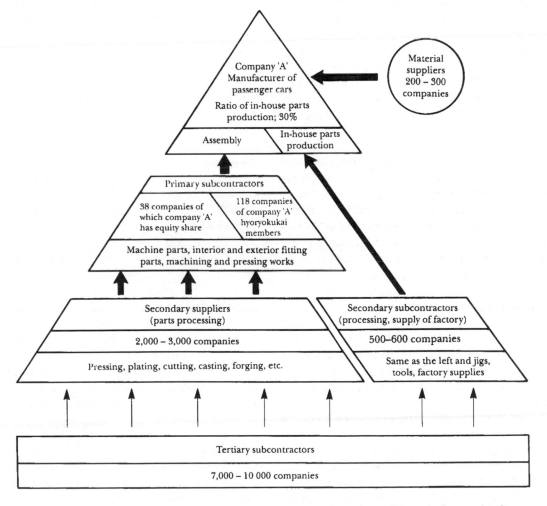

Source: Sako, M. (1989) Partnership between small and large firms: The case of Japan. In *Partnership Between Small and Large Firms*, Directorate for Enterprise of the Commission of the European Communities, Brussels, Graham and Trotman, London

Figure 11.9   Production structure of typical Japanese automaker as of 1981

Table 11.16 Subcontractors, companies that subcontract, and subcontractors' output

Industry	Sub-contractors		Companies that subcontract		Subcontractors' output		
	1976	1981	1976	1981	1976	1981	Growth rate 1981/1976
Total manufacturing	60.7	65.5	32.5	37.0	140,898	265,489	88.4
Foodstuffs	14.5	17.5	4.9	5.5	13,497	15,790	17.0
Textiles	84.5	84.9	24.4	26.5	11,863	15,868	33.8
Clothing and other textile goods	83.9	86.5	39.1	40.9	6,197	11,445	84.7
Wood, woodwork	42.9	48.9	17.7	20.3	5,795	7,297	25.9
Furniture, furnishings	41.2	51.6	30.7	34.9	4,643	8,155	75.6
Pulp, paper and paper products	44.8	51.6	36.3	42.9	2,218	3,559	60.5
Publishing, printing and others	50.8	59.0	57.4	65.7	3,586	8,723	143.3
Chemicals	37.1	38.5	27.7	27.12	2,717	4,258	56.7
Oil and coal products	27.0	38.9	19.1	17.1	111	281	153.2
Rubber products	61.1	71.8	37.3	40.2	1,252	3,341	166.9
Leather, leather products, furs	62.5	68.8	32.0	31.4	834	1,409	68.9
Ceramics	29.4	36.6	21.0	24.5	1,942	4,206	116.6
Steel	70.4	72.0	44.6	41.6	5,370	8,050	49.9
Non-ferrous metals	68.7	73.6	46.1	47.4	3,174	6,093	92.0
Metal products	74.8	78.6	40.3	44.5	19,584	40,423	106.4
Machinery	82.7	84.2	54.9	55.7	17,560	34,755	97.9
Electric machinery	82.3	85.3	55.1	57.9	16,674	35,036	110.1
Transportation machinery	86.2	87.7	45.5	48.8	13,779	25,791	86.5
Precision machinery	72.4	80.9	54.8	54.4	2,782	6,764	143.1
Other manufacturing	56.5	62.2	31.9	37.7	9,294	20,817	124.0

Note
Percentage of contractors

$$= \frac{\text{No. of small and medium subcontractors}}{\text{No. of small and medium manufacturers}} \times 100$$

Source: MITI: Small and Medium Enterprise Agency. 'Basic Survey on Industry' cited in Sako, M. (1989) Partnership between small and large firms: the case of Japan. In *Partnership Between Small and Large Firms* (ed. DG XXIII – Directorate for Enterprise of the Commission of the European Communities), Brussels, Graham and Trotman Ltd, London

access to its markets. Consequently, Japanese consumers, whose personal disposable incomes increased vastly throughout the 1980s and into the 1990s, are beginning now to experiment with non-traditional Western imports. Tariffs, non-tariffs and an idiosyncratic distribution system tell only part of the tale. The Japanese consumer is just not used to imports.

A useful starting point is made with the way in which Japanese business people view foreign companies. Notice how, in Figure 11.11, the perception of the degree of adaptation to Japanese business produces changes between those actually doing business with foreign firms and those who are not. The same is equally true of other criteria which score a low evaluation, including

delivery, after-sales service, product modification and development.

Taking this a stage further, Blenkhorn and Noori (1990) pinpointed nine criteria found to be crucial in the forming of relationships:

* *Well defined mandates, goals and objectives.* Teamwork and good communications evident.
* *Focussed customers.* Single sourcing with suppliers, close relations and close physical proximity.
* *Supplier aggressiveness.* Working on very low margins which creates the need for high productivity to maintain low cost structure.
* *User/producer interface* close in case of product development, general exchange of information.

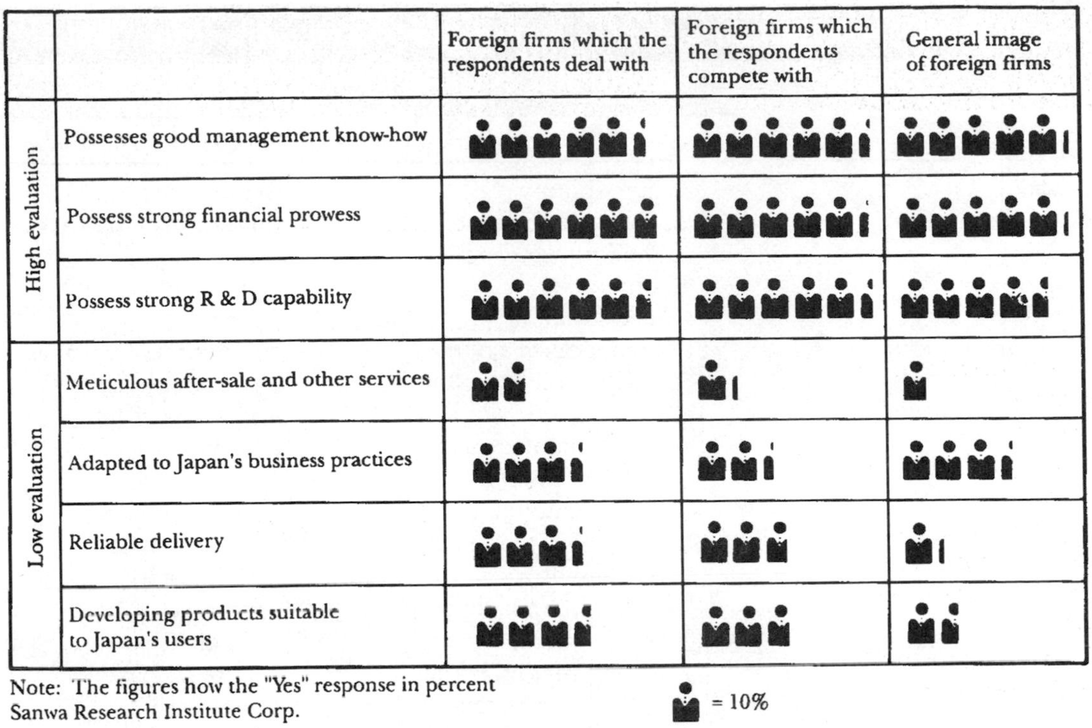

Foreign firms which the respondents deal with
Foreign firms which the respondents compete with
General image of foreign firms
High evaluation
Possesses good management know-how
Possess strong financial prowess
Possess strong R & D capability
Low evaluation
Meticulous after-sale and other services
Adapted to Japan's business practices
Reliable delivery
Developing products suitable to Japan's users
Note: The figures how the "Yes" response in percent
Sanwa Research Institute Corp.
= 10%

Source: *Tokyo Business Today* (1990) July, p. 27

Figure 11.10 How Japanese business people view foreign companies

First tier supplier
First tier supplier
First tier supplier
OEM
First tier supplier
First tier supplier
Second tier suppliers
Third tier supplier
Fourth tier supplier
Fifth tier supplier (home workers)

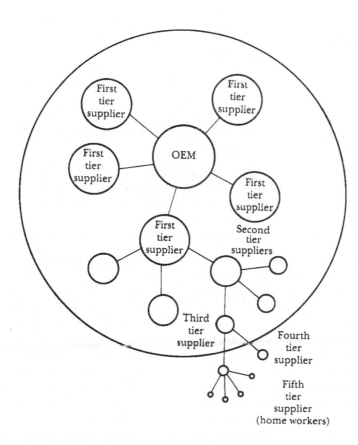

Source: Blenkhorn D. L., and Noori, A. H. (1990) What it takes to supply Japanese OEMs. *Industrial Marketing Management*, **19**, 21–30

Figure 11.11 The Zaibatsu approach to OEM/supplier relationships

| Table 11.17   A comparison of Japanese and North American suppliers |

Criterion	Attribute	
	Japan	North America
Quality	Part of the process	Monitored after production
JIT delivery	Not a new phenomenon: part of the total supply/delivery system	Imposed by external forces – customers or threat of competition from the Japanese
Process/equipment	Synchronized with their major customer(s) and suppliers	Firm specific centred rather entire system centred
Culture/people/attitude	Team playing, job enlargement, attempts to play down rank or hierarchy on job	Union centred them – us attitude
Innovative thinking	Mandatory to survive as auto assemblers demand innovative, cost saving solutions	Encouraged but historically not mandatory to survive as parts maker
Efficiency	Efficiency enhanced through manufacture of robots or modification of purchased equipment	Often look to external sources to increase efficiency
Competitiveness/price	Other Japanese firms seen as major competitors and in-house capability of auto assemblers	Offshore parts makers viewed as major competitors
User/producer interface	An ongoing R&D thrust with regular exchange of personnel	Often limited to the order at hand
Degree of computer linkage/ sophistication	The supplier/assembler interface perhaps is very similar in both Japan and North America	
	Extensive use of CAD/CAM in design engineering	Much less use of CAD/CAM
JIT necessity	Pressure to adopt came from the auto assemblers	
	Much more commonly utilized and understood	Being adopted by those suppliers that wish to remain suppliers
Design-to-cost criteria	Historically a common occurrence in the Japanese auto industry, but the rise in the yen has intensified its use	No data
Outsourcing	More outsourcing often offshore caused principally by increased value of the yen	More outsourcing precipitated by OEM's desire to reduce fixed costs
	More for both groups but for different reasons	

Source: Blenkhorn, D. L., and Noori, A. H. (1990) What it takes to supply Japanese OEM's. *Industrial Marketing Management*, **19**, 21–30

- *Selection of suppliers based on equipment compatibility.* Equipment capability and compatibility rated more important than price.
- *Zero defect policy* found everywhere in Japan.
- *Just-in-time (JIT) delivery*, reducing inventory costs and lowering per unit costs.
- *Encouragement of innovative thinking* between the firm and its suppliers. Working on designs together.
- *Culture, people and attitude.* Japanese societal norms play a large role in the expectations of manufacturer/supplier relationship.

A comparison, then, between the Japanese and the North American supplier performance

Table 11.18 The companies Toyota directly controls

	Shares owned by Toyota (%)
Toyota Automatic Loom Works, Ltd	23.1
Aichi Steel Works, Ltd.	21.2
Toyoda Machine Works, Ltd	21.0
Toyota Auto Body Co.	40.2
Toyota Tsusho Corp.	21.1
Aisin Seiki Co.	21.6
Nippondenso Co.	23.0
Toyota Boshoku Corp.	8.9
Kanto Auto Works, Ltd.	48.8
Toyota Gosei Co.	38.3
Hino Motors Ltd.	10.8
Daihatsu Motor Co.	14.1
Towa Real Estate Co.	49.0
Toyota Central Research and Development Laboratories Inc.	—

Source: Shimizu, Y., Tsutsui, M., Inaba, Y., and Umesawa, M. (1990) Production keiretsu: a new export from Japan. *Tokyo Business Today,* September, p. 30

levels is outlined in Table 11.16. Yet, although this explains part, it does not explain all. The Zaibatsu organizational relationship, whose manufacturers have a financial equity stake in their suppliers, and perhaps all the way down the distribution channel, has also to be considered. Blenkhorn and Noori (1990) chart this organizationally and describe these relationships as tiers in terms of closeness to the manufacturer. Tier 2 would be closest and may be directly controlled by the manufacturer, but likely to be a single source supplier until going through the tier. The organizational linkage with the manufacturer becomes weaker and the supplier itself also becomes smaller in size (see Figure 11.12).

The importance of these relationships becomes clearer when one realizes that Hitachi,

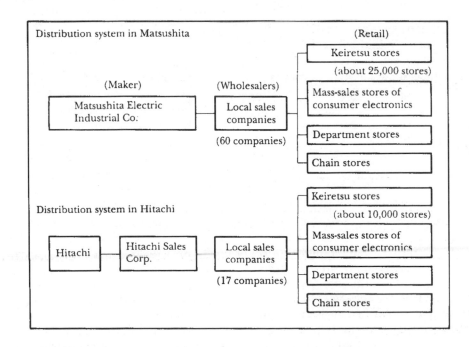

Source: Hara, E., Takito, H., and Umesawa, M. (1990) Distribution Keiretsu: Electronic stores rebel. *Tokyo Business Today,* September, p. 36

Figure 11.12

for example, has 800 affiliated companies and only in August of 1990 did it drop the word 'keiretsu' from its organizational chart. This name change comes at a time when the traditional 'keiretsu' system is coming under closer scrutiny as the USA argues that it lies at the heart of Japanese protectionism, as keiretsu group members purchase as much as possible from each other, thus limiting the potential for imports. Also, because of the recycled stock holdings, it becomes more difficult for foreign firms to acquire Japanese companies. The keiretsu have been traditionally strong in consumer electronics and in the automobile industry in Japan, though there is some evidence that this is now changing (Fujigane and Ennis, 1990).

There are three types of keiretsu:

1. Capital connected, including the former Zaibatsu, Mitsui, Mitsubishi, Simitomo, Fuji Group including firms from prewar Yasuda Zanbateu; bank-centred groups led by Dai-Ichi Kangyo (successor to Furakawa Zaibatsu); and Sanwa Bank.

2. Production keiretsu, mainly in the automotive industry, characterized by the vertical integration of manufactures and their suppliers. Toyota has an auto parts association, called 'Kyohokai', grouping 178 companies, and another in plant and equipment 'Eihokai' with 77 firms. Nissan has 'Takairakai' totalling 104 firms and participates in 'Shohokai', which has 70 companies, including Hitachi and Matsushita.

3. Sales distribution keiretsu, involving vertical integration of product distribution from factory to retail outlets, eg. Hitachi, Matsushita, but the number is declining. Matsushita has 25,000 retail shops; Toshiba, 12,500; Hitachi, 10,000; and Sanyo, 6,000. Product availability is limited to keiretsu stores which maintain prices at a high level.

The Japanese consumer

Japan's increasing affluence is also effecting societal change. Youth are now used to high technology products and express themselves through fashion rather than politics. More importantly, people are being freed from the old sex stereotyped roles. Traditionally, a housewife would be responsible for 80–90 per cent of the housework as well as for 80 per cent of the household's discretionary expenditure. As society changes and the individual's place within that society changes, it also has important implications for marketing because it means that the decision-making on products is shifting together perhaps with its usage. With increasing affluence, Japanese consumers are now developing expensive consumer tastes. Ohashi (1989) examined these changes from a marketing perspective and isolated seven factors across four generations or cohorts within Japanese society. Of major importance are four particular trends which emerge from this study:

1. The growing influence of women and their ability to express themselves within society. This will cause a break with the old values which tied women to housework.

2. From self-orientation to individualization. Self-expression through consumption will spread to future generations as well.

3. A new family concept. Traditionally cohesive, there will be the advent of separate nuclear family units with children on an equal footing as individuals with their parents.

4. Importance of the living space. Younger generations will demand better quality and more spacious housing than presently exists, and will model themselves on Western-style living and leisure activities.

As regards the mobilization and institutionalization of the Japanese consumer, this is presently very low level. The consumer in Japan is poorly represented. Imports are expensive despite the yen being high, and Japanese consumer goods can often be bought more cheaply abroad than within Japan itself, but Japanese consumer groups appear to be protectionist by nature (Aishikawa, 1990). There are four main groups:

1. *Cooperative consumers' societies* which are tied to a political party. Out of power political parties have much to gain from being seen to be championing the consumer cause, as has been the case with the Japan Communist party.

2. *Housewives' organizations* which involved themselves in joint purchasing from farms, price surveys, recycling, studying consumer projections, testing products and organizing cookery classes.

3. *Advocacy groups*, e.g. Consumer Union of Japan (EUJ) founded in 1969 and heavily influenced by the US consumer advocate, Ralph Nader. Lawsuits and publicity for bad products, and championing of new legislation, are part of its repertoire. It is unconnected with any political party.

4. *Expert groups*, e.g. lifestyle consultants, lawyers, consumer affairs experts. They become involved in broadening the liability base for product defects and prevention of fraudulent contracts for example.

Consumer groups believe generally that Japan must be self-sufficient in food as in the highly political area of rice. The consumer groups have failed to find a united voice on many of the issues now confronting Japanese society. Japanese consumers are unaware of the power of consumer associations in other parts of the world. They seem to believe that free competition is not in the best interests of the consumer, and that government legislation is necessary to ensure adequate consumer protection from manufacturing firms. Meanwhile, while quality, reliability and after-sales service are held to be important, European firms emerged in a Japanese survey as being ill-prepared and failing to gather enough information about the market before actually entering it. The lack or inadequacy of instructions in Japanese was the leading reason to emerge after price for not buying European (*Marketing*, 1987).

Japan, home of the Deming Prize for quality, is not infallible, however, as recent reports show. The need to cut costs because of a high yen, and the introduction of parts and components now manufactured in the Pacific Basin, are contributory factors to what appears to be a slippage in quality. Higher automation and more imported components may be significant factors, but the Japanese Government has intervened to ensure that this deterioration does not become a slide. JD Power and Associates of California, who regularly evaluate cars, stated that defects per 100 Japanese cars sold in the USA dropped from 131 in 1987 to 121 in 1989, and that was better than any US car maker's record (Neff, 1990). Nevertheless, *Tokyo Business Today* (1990) stated that seven recalls were made in 1989 and ten in the first five months of 1990, and clearly showed concern. While it is heartening to see the urgent concern of the Japanese industry and of the Government, there is also a need to introduce a system to resolve and redress the consumer for damages as a result of product defects.

Product testing for imports

With motor vehicles, individual units may be tested on arrival or they may be subject to an exhaustive test when import is first undertaken, after which a model is given 'type approval' which then permits further imports of that model without testing. Testing can take several months and cost 20,000–200,000 yen. (The Japanese also politely point out that test cars are often not in a saleable condition afterwards.) There are a number of Japanese safety and environmental protection regulations for vehicles.

In the case of pharmaceuticals, all drugs or medical devices imported into, or manufactured

in, Japan must be tested and then registered by the Ministry of Health and Welfare before being put on sale in Japan. The registration period is often lengthened to between six months and one year by regulations which require double blind testing of new products, ethical testing, and even supplying the authorities with vaccine serum in the case of new vaccines. These testing requirements also involve the exporter in costs which often reach several thousand pounds sterling. All importers of pharmaceuticals must be licensed by the Ministry of Health and Welfare to handle pharmaceuticals. This entails having at least one employee who is a registered pharmacist.

Electrical appliances have to be tested by the Japan Electrical Testing Laboratory and can take from one to three months. Gas appliances must be tested and approved by the Japan Gas Appliance Inspection Association before they can be sold in Japan.

Processed cheese is subject to an import quota and so the Japanese authorities may, in cases of doubt, test imports of natural cheeses in order to check that they are not processed ones, in spite of the fact that natural cheese is not on the import quota. In the case of natural cheeses, it is possible to avoid such testing provided the consignment is accompanied by an official public analyst's certificate to the effect that the import in question is a natural cheese.

Market prospects for exports to Japan

The prospects for exports to Japan are outwardly good but direct exports are difficult. In high value areas, such as cars or microelectronics, Japan exports at least four times as much as it imports.

1. Distance and resulting high costs where there is a ratio of high bulk to value on exports.
2. Tariffs and certain non-tariff barriers estimated to number 258 in all, including the designation of scheduled air traffic.
3. Distribution – in Japan this is said to be the major reason for the Western failure to infiltrate the Japanese market. This is often more difficult than entering Japan (Shimaguchi and Lazer, 1979; Czinkota, 1985). This is seen as a non-tariff barrier because of the high number of small firms, doubtless aided by the retention in Japan of retail price maintenance. There are 300,000 wholesaling firms (Tonja) who keep on selling to each other and atomistic competition among its 1.6m retailers. A particular point to note is that retailers and

Table 11.19   Ten golden rules for trading profitably with the Japanese
1. Do your homework first. Don't assume that the Japanese are just another customer – they're not.
2. Get your board's commitment. Selling to Japan isn't cheap, especially now.
3. Don't give up easily, even when all appears lost. If you persevere, and you have a reliable product and quality standard, you will sell eventually.
4. Behave in a low-key style. Stay unassuming, don't force your sales pitch. Aim to build bridges, not conquer them.
5. Keep your nerve. Don't take fright if the Japanese field a massive team against you. The more they bring to the meeting, the more you are probably respected.
6. Be patient but prepared. The Japanese take a long time to make a decision but, once it's made, seek action quickly. Use the long gestation time to prepare your ground, because that's what the Japanese are doing.
7. Beware of Japanese innocence. They may appear unworldly – they're not. Commercially they are both shrewd and clever, and you will need your wits about you. Once they have reached an agreement with you, they are loyal and honourable.
8. Relate your strengths to Japanese needs. Try to see your product from your Japanese customer's position. If you do, you will drive a better deal.
9. Protect your technology. Japanese companies work in closer harmony than British companies. Don't let your technology be ripped off.
10. Involve the whole company. Make sure your team know what is expected of them from Japanese buyers and inspectors. Good all-round performance means you are better placed for the next business, even though your price might not be the lowest.

Source: Dale, I. (1988). Cited in Hard Sell in Japan. *Management Today*, (Foster, G.) September, 99

wholesalers demand a lot from manufacturers. This has the following effects:

- Necessitating substantial capital investment by the manufacturer.
- Limited freedom on pricing, given that only wholesale selling prices can be determined by the manufacturer.
- Frequent price changes are best avoided, partly due to the depth of the distribution channel. A Japanese manufacturer summarized it thus: 'We cannot consider our growth without our dealers' growth, and our dealers' growth cannot be considered without ours.' This perspective engenders harmony but inhibits change taking place.
- Rebates (traditional in the Japanese food business) – the largest rebates may be higher than the normal margins allowed.
- Supply (prompt delivery is essential).
- Promotional assistance and budgeting are required.
- Sales – frequent personal visits to customers at all levels are most important.
- Training support for education, management, technical staff is required.

4. Royalties for manufacture under licence. Quick approval is usually granted. Previously licensing was the only method of entering Japan.
5. Capital investment in a joint venture manufacturing arrangement.

From the British perspective, Japan is the number one market for worsted cloth, number two for quality knitwear and number three for Scotch whisky, although this has been dropping from 3 million cases p.a. to 2.5 million. Parallel exporting has done some damage to established brand pricing and image. The overall picture which emerges, though, is of a commodity trade pattern with British exports to Japan being quite unlike Japanese imports into Britain, gauged either in overall value or unit value, as well as technological input.

Advertising in Japan

Advertising is seen to be creative rather than a sales tool. Bert Marsh of Young and Rubicam defined three main types of advertising in Japan: follow-the-leader, use of celebrities, and use of mood. The key to sales is distribution not advertising. Following the competition is not particularly frowned on. Celebrities are often used to position a product. Since Americans are considered to be great coffee drinkers, then it follows that US actors are in demand for coffee commercials. The actor's image is important to the positioning of the product. Direct confrontation or 'knocking copy' is not used. Mood is very extensively used, depicting perhaps the beauties of nature, and only at the very end of the commercial, introducing the product in question. To Westerners, this is not effective advertising, but to the Japanese, this form of advertising adds to

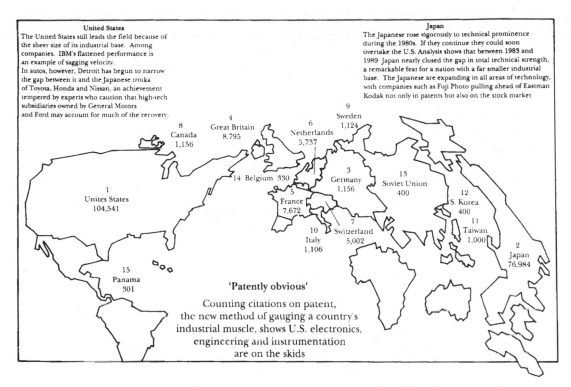

United States
The United States still leads the field because of
the sheer size of its industrial base. Among
companies, IBM's flattened performance is
an example of sagging velocity.
In autos, however, Detroit has begun to narrow
the gap between it and the Japanese troika
of Toyota, Honda and Nissan, an achievement
tempered by experts who caution that high-tech
subsidiaries owned by General Motors
and Ford may account for much of the recovery.

Japan
The Japanese rose vigorously to technical prominence
during the 1980s. If they continue they could soon
overtake the U.S. Analysis shows that between 1983 and
1989 Japan nearly closed the gap in total technical strength,
a remarkable feat for a nation with a far smaller industrial
base. The Japanese are expanding in all areas of technology,
with companies such as Fuji Photo pulling ahead of Eastman
Kodak not only in patents but also on the stock market

9
Sweden
1,124

4
Great Britain
8.795

6
Netherlands
5,737

8
Canada
1,156

14 Belgium 330

3
Germany
1,156

13
Soviet Union
400

1
Unites States
104,541

5
France
7,672

12
S. Korea
400

11
Taiwan
1,000

7
Switzerland
5,002

10
Italy
1,106

2
Japan
76,984

15
Panama
301

'Patently obvious'

Counting citations on patent,
the new method of gauging a country's
industrial muscle, shows U.S. electronics,
engineering and instrumentation
are on the skids

Source: The Globe and Mail (1991) Toronto, 8 June, p. D5

Figure 11.13

the image of the company. Commercial films are left to the film producer rather than the agency and different agencies may be used for different media. Advertising is still secondary to good distribution in effecting sales in Japan.

Proctor and Gamble, despite being a very successful global company, foundered in Japan because of their inability to read the market. Price discounting alienated the wholesalers and retailers, and raised questions in the consumer's minds about the quality of the product. Advertising for brands, such as 'Cheers' and 'Camay', were of a hard sell with customer testimonials and were soundly disliked. 'Cheers' advertisements were liked the least on Japanese television. Proctor and Gamble introduced disposable nappies (diapers) to the Japanese market, but fell from 90 per cent of the market to 15 per cent between 1981 and 1986 as a result of Japanese competition with an improved product. Proctor and Gamble lost, also, because they focused advertising on the brand and not the company. With Ariel they are preparing a formulation for the Japanese market to allow for short cycles, cold water and small machines, adapting to market needs at last (Trachtenberg, 1986).

Innovation and product development

As Figure 11.14 shows, Japan is a major global player in industrial innovation. The days when Japan simply absorbed technology from other

countries and improved on it are long gone. Japan creates its own innovations and has all the resources needed to carry this through, including skills, engineering base and strong financial structure. New products, particularly in electronics, come from Japan and consumers in Britain or the USA now seek out Japanese products over domestic competitors. It raises again the question of whether a locally US or British made Japanese product can claim the country of origin of its host country, a very complicated issue now before GATT's Uruguay round. In the USA, there is an Auto Parts Advisory Committee, an industry group which advises the US Department of Commerce. They estimated only 20 per cent and not 48 per cent of the Honda Accord was domestically produced (Holden, 1991). However, to take another source, Taylor (1991), writing in *Fortune*, states 75 per cent of the Honda Accord is US domestic content. Within this 75 per cent, however, most of the US parts come from Honda's own factories or other Japanese suppliers in the USA, leaving around one-quarter of the domestic parts to be sourced by traditional US producers.

Trademarks and industrial property rights

The Department of Trade recommends that the registration of trademarks be considered by any company seriously intending to do business in Japan, as it is relatively simple and inexpensive. Inventions should also be protected, although the processes are more complicated. For companies with a large range of designs, the protection of all of them could be very expensive and they might consider protecting only those designs which have greater potential in Japan. The Japanese classification is different from that in use in most European countries and makes no provision for service marks, but this is changing to conform with international classifications.

For application for registration to be successful, the inventions and designs must not have been known publicly or worked publicly in Japan; nor should they have been described in publications circulated in Japan or in any other country prior to the application. The first person to apply for registration of a patent or trademark obtains the right. Unlike the UK and some other countries, proof of prior use does not confer priority rights. The Japanese Unfair Competition Prevention has given some protection to unregistered designs and trademarks provided that they are 'well known' to Japanese consumers or dealers of the products concerned. However, under the Paris Convention for the Protection of Industrial Property to which both the UK and Japan are signatories, an application made in one of the signatory countries is treated as if it were made at the same time in other signatory countries, provided that the application claiming priority under the Convention is made in those other countries within 12 months of the first application in the case of inventions, and within six months in the case of designs and trademarks.

Doe (1988) cites a Nihon Keizai Shimbun report that two-thirds of major Japanese companies had been hurt by violations of their intellectual property rights, and that the pressure was now on to try to resolve a situation where patent violation cases in Japan were now steadily increasing. NEC Corporations sued Seiko for trying to sell an NEC compatible personal computer although Seiko eventually replaced the operating system software in question. Many other comparable products have since appeared. Doe (1988) cites also the case of two company employees who were convicted in criminal court of embezzlement for using a computer program from their old job in their new job. Yet, an important underlying assumption is that the Japanese tend to view improvements as new inventions in their patent laws and that may extend to software. If there is a 25 per cent improvement, then it is a new invention, and the same may happen in software. Doe (1988) points out also that Japanese law tends to be more concerned with the larger issues of user rights

and the greater social good, than with simply the rights of the individual creator, believing that it is selfish and antisocial to keep to oneself that which everyone else needs.

Japan and the UK did not become parties to the Trademark Registration Treaty which was floated in August 1980 but failed. It would have meant that to register a trademark in the signatory nations designated by the application filing one application to the UN World Intellectual Property Organization (WIPO). Unless the government of a designated country refuses to register it within 15 months of the publication by WIPO, it automatically becomes registered in that country. Applications are published by WIPO as soon as they are filed. It is not necessary to use the trademark in order to register it, but it will cease to be protected it if is not used within three years of registration.

Licensing

British companies have been slower than others to enter into licensing in Japan. Of 1,755 agreements (with a duration of more than one year) in 1978, the number of agreements entered into by UK companies was 135, compared with 870 for the USA, 186 for West Germany, and 206 for France. A study reported in the *Globe and Mail* (1991) showed that this situation has not materially changed.

Foreign investment in Japan

Tokyo Business Today (1990, July) produced a ranking of the top 300 foreign-owned companies and affiliated firms. It may be worth noting that the ranking included companies in which there was a foreign equity, participation of more than 20 per cent, and so covered strategic investments made by foreign companies in Japanese companies, as well as joint equity ventures, such as the No. 2 listing of Matsushita and Philips, and the No. 1 listing of the wholly owned IBM subsidiary, IBM Japan. The report was based on information provided by the National Tax Administration Agency as corporate financial information was not freely available in all cases.

Foreign direct investment

Well over 1,000 foreign investors have already established a direct stake in Japanese industry. The MITI study of 1979 showed that half of these were US companies and there were only seventy-seven UK companies with a stake of less than 20 per cent in equity in Japanese companies. Other findings included:

- Fifty-two per cent of all foreign investors in Japanese firms were in manufacturing industry with a particularly heavy preponderance in the chemical and general machinery section.
- Of a total of 655 foreign-affiliated manufacturing corporations in Japan, 42 per cent (273 corporations) are 50 per cent foreign-owned; 26 per cent (172 corporations) are less than 50 per cent foreign-owned; 32 per cent (210 corporations) are more than 50 per cent foreign-owned.
- Although foreign-affiliated Japanese firms were responsible for only 2.2 per cent of total sales of all Japanese enterprises in 1977, their share of certain business sectors has been increasing steadily and average profitability is consistently greater than domestic Japanese enterprises.

McDonalds

Joint ventures

Until the early 1970s wholly owned subsidiaries were discouraged. It was much easier to establish with 50 per cent or less of the equity. Measures in 1973 and 1975 allowed foreign investment of up to 100 per cent by new enterprises, but still controlled certain activities (e.g., nuclear energy, power, light and gas supply, manufacture of aircraft, arms and explosives), and restricted other activities (e.g., agriculture, forestry and fishing, petroleum and mining, leather and leather products manufacture). Even so, approval was automatic up to an ownership level of less than 10 per cent for a single foreign investor and less than 25 per cent for all foreign investors (15 per cent in the case of fisheries), provided that no one designated by the foreign investors was proposed as a director of the new company. Approval was also automatic for foreign ownership of 50 per cent in a new enterprise in the mining industry.

The amended law on foreign exchange and foreign trade control came into effect in 1980, introducing a prior reporting procedure, with in-depth examination of foreign investments confined to the restricted industries. Joint ventures still remain popular because they use the Japanese company's existing distribution network and leave personnel problems to the Japanese partner. However, the partners must agree on marketing methods, pricing policy, and definition of export areas. Joint ventures have tended to move away from distribution towards semi-processing to supply local manufacturing capacity. Provisions of the Anti-Monopoly Law and Fair Trade Commission should be given close examination in relation to each stage of an expanding joint venture. The majority of investments receive clearance from the Bank of Japan in two weeks. Remittance of profit or capital requires the permission of the Bank of Japan, but no difficulties should normally be encountered over this. Tax on the income of branches follows the same general lines as that on joint ventures or wholly owned subsidiaries.

Strategic business alliances: a better alternative to protectionism

Much of the response of the Western industrialized nations has been spent in terms of debating the merits and demerits of protectionism. The Japanese have been embarrassingly successful in their global trade of technologies which they have originally imported and developed themselves. One such example in machine tools is Fujitsu Fanuc, which controls half the world's market for numerically controlled machine tools, although they did not invent them. Another is the House of Fraser decision to open a

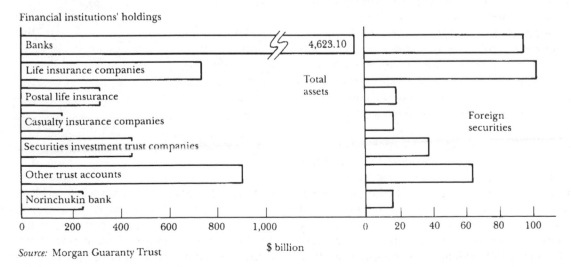

Financial institutions' holdings

Source: Morgan Guaranty Trust

$ billion

Source: Financial Times (1990) 15 March

Figure 11.14

Table 11.20 The world's ten largest banks, 1982, 1986					
1982			*1986*		
1.	Citicorp	USA	1.	Dai-Ichi Kangyo Bank	Japan
2.	Bankamerica Corp.	USA	2.	Fuji Bank	Japan
3.	Banque Nationale de Paris	France	3.	Sumitomo Bank	Japan
4.	Crédit Agricole	France	4.	Mitsubishi Bank	Japan
5.	Crédit Lyonnais	France	5.	Sanwa Bank	Japan
6.	Barclays Group	Britain	6.	Citicorp	USA
7.	National Westminster	Britain	7.	Norinchukin Bank	Japan
8.	Dai-Ichi Kangyo Bank	Japan	8.	Industrial Bank of Japan	Japan
9.	Société Générale	Japan	9.	Crédit Agricole	France
10.	Fuji Bank	Japan	10.	Banque Nationale de Paris	France

Source: Burstein, D. (1990) *Yen! Japan's New Financial Empire and its Threat to America,* Fawcett Columbine, New York

Harrods shop within Tokyo's giant Mitsukoshi store. Marks & Spencer Plc faced initial success with their range of products in 50 Daiei stores, but then sales peaked and thought had to be given as to how to increase sales to the consumer. M & S have developed St Michael boutiques in Japan with the Daiei chain and are now seeking to move up-market. Such cases of startling Japanese export success are found alongside domestic non-tariff barriers and a domestic currency which defies international pressure for revaluation. This has led to the creation of a trade ombudsman to handle complaints concerning imports. It remains to be seen whether this is simply a delaying tactic or a sincere response. As things stand, each and every official Japanese movement – whether Cabinet changes or an economic mission of the leading Japanese industrialists to Europe – is scrutinized for meaning, while in such areas as car exports, the Japanese are asked to exercise what is termed 'voluntary restraint'. By restricting the Japanese manufacturers to approximately 11 per cent of the British market, shiploads can be planned to the point where a Japanese car sold on the UK market is new – because of the voluntary quota – while a British car, because of having stockpiles of unsold inventory, will generally be at least 15 months old at the time of sale. British protectionism in this case has turned to Japanese disadvantage.

Consider next the argument for co-operation, part of the official Japanese response to reduce the EC deficit with Japan of 10.7 billion dollars. Industrial co-operation is a phenomenon born of our times. Market development costs plus the size of market required to ensure a return on investment have led to the bringing together of industrial producers in a number of different areas, the most highly publicized of which has been the Honda Rover agreement.

Outlining the basis for an agreement – to ensure a community of interests and like benefits, and to define the respective duties of either party – is an essential prerequisite. A case study investigation of two Japanese factories matched with one British factory and one US, found that the implications for public policy were:

1.   Direct investment of Japanese companies is not likely to have an immediate or substantial effect on local development.
2.   Once Japanese multinationals establish their factories, they are less likely to shift their operations to some other region.
3.   New investment in modernization and automation of production will not be able to make domestic companies competitive against Japanese.
4.   A licensing agreement with, or takeover by, the Japanese would not be effective measures to revive competitiveness of the domestic industry.

In so far as Britain is concerned, the possible avenues for Japanese participation in British manufacturing industry have been reduced to joint venture or acquisition with public anxiety over the Japanese challenge to European industry, as in the case of Nissan, for example, in Britain.

The car industry is such that negotiations are constantly taking place over possible joint ventures and industrial co-operation on the development of engines and gear-boxes. A close association with Honda may, therefore, blossom into a more permanent relationship, as has happened with industrial co-operation ventures elsewhere. Meanwhile, a test case in Italy has already established the Honda-Rover to be a British car, by virtue of the last substantial part of production, amounting in this case to 60 per cent by volume or 70 per cent by price.

Another example of co-operation is that between ICL with Fujitsu. This venture provided for co-operation in marketing, technology and semiconductor purchasing. ICL, in return for agreeing to market Fujitsu computers, received early access to the Japanese group's computer technology. Under this deal, ICL also purchased substantial quantities of microchips. For ICL, it presented an opportunity to re- structure and complete its product range without overreaching its already thin resources. For Fujitsu, there was the obvious advantage of market access, technology sharing and exports. This has since led to a majority Fujitsu stake in ICL.

In other industries, such as industrial robotics, petrochemicals, and telecommunications, agreements have been signed between Hitachi and GEC; ICI and Mitsui Petrochemical; Hitachi and Thomson; and Fujitsu and Siemens. TI and Fairchild are establishing semi-conductor plants in Japan.

The potential for industrial co-operation

Yet further possibilities present themselves if one considers the importance of the Japanese Sogo-Shoshas, the trading houses, with their worldwide network of offices and speciality in Eurodollar lending. Mr Ikeda of Marubeni Corporation, the fourth largest Japanese trading company, has gone on record (Keizam Koho Center, 1986) as having 17 per cent of his corporation's turnover in the form of 'third-country' trade.

While a recession lasts and while interest rates in the West are double those prevailing in Japan, reasons abound for inertia among Western nations. Interest rate differentials provoke massive international monetary displacements. Japan, again peculiarly with a large amount of savings deposits, is relatively insulated from such shocks. By way of comparison, Britain, with its network of building societies, would appear to be investing its savings in unproductive investments.

The first advantage of the Japanese then is in capital and, secondly, in their dominance of the technologies which they have acquired and developed. For meaningful co-operation to develop, there has to be a mutually profitable exchange. At the moment, there is the universal impression of the Japanese being interested only in selling, not buying. Given a more outward-looking breadth of perspective, opportunities for Anglo-Japanese co-operation exist in the following areas.

Ongoing research and development and technology improvements
Already this is taking place as we have seen in computers, but scope exists to do likewise in other sectors of electronics or automotive engineering, an area in which the UK is particularly skilled.

Marketing and distribution in third markets
This is under way with Honda-Rover in continental Europe.

Joint entry into third markets
This was hinted at as a possible means of developing Anglo-Japanese trade and reducing a trade imbalance. Presently, this does not exist but could certainly do so.

Co-production and specialization of production
Co-operation is true of Honda-Rover. Specialization is also included but to a lesser degree as this particular agreement is of a shorter nature to that of the ICL-Fujitsu co-operation where there is clearer product line specialization taking place over time.

Financial services
Those on offer suggest a certain synergy with those of our own institutions. As yet this remains to be developed, although banking institutions are finding Japan to be an attractive site for location, given that Tokyo has emerged as a world financial centre, above London and New York.

The West have had their request sustained for an ombudsman for Japanese foreign trade in view of the complex Japanese administrative blocks, and major non-tariff barriers (57 non-tariff barriers, including import inspection, guarantees, testing, etc.). Tariffs were reduced on 323 items, including chocolate, biscuits, agricultural tractors and tobacco as of April 1983. Simplification and improvement of import inspection procedures, and the strengthening of the Office of the Trade Ombudsman, are also being sought.

Pressures on the Japanese financial system

Pressures for change in the Japanese financial system arise due to the following.

1. *Plentiful supply of capital.* Japan is awash in capital and exports it. Japan was the largest single supplier of savings for the world in 1984, but since then OPEC is no longer a source of new cash. Japanese banks now dominate world banking.
2. *Domestic dissent.* Affluent savers want higher yields, corporate borrowers want more choice, and the strongest banks and brokerage houses are chafing under restrictions unlike those found in any other major market.
3. *Impatient foreigners.* The patience of foreign banks and businessmen with Japan's closed

capital markets has run out. Unless some reciprocal privileges are offered soon, they are threatening to hold up the expansion of Japanese banks in their markets. 'Reciprocity' is now a key issue in all international trade talks.

Japan has been inching its way towards financial liberalization since it passed a major revision of its Foreign Exchange Law in 1980. The revision abolished formal controls that enabled the Government to regulate all foreign-currency transactions by Japanese residents. In theory, the new law allowed a free flow of funds in and out of Japan, but in practice the Government used administrative guidance with its banks to make sure they restricted flows.

If capital flows were free, a huge rush of money would quickly leave Japan at current interest rates. In the short term, the yen would weaken, but Japanese interest rates set by the market would then go up and capital would flow back into Japan. Unfortunately, the yen would be stronger than it is and Japanese companies would have to compete on the same basis with the same finance costs as Western companies.

The services sector

Growth of the service sector, together with the appearance of new electronics industries, has served to keep the Japanese economy moving during the past few years, while traditional pillars of the economic system have been crumbling (investment in services sector more than doubled that of either the auto or steel industries). However, the new 'soft' industries, as they have been called by Government ministers, have brought problems as well. According to the Finance Ministry, which created the term 'softnomics' (in a book on the Japanese economy issued in early 1983), the new trend means first and foremost that the Government has become seriously short of information about what is happening in the economy.

Service sector companies, as well as many of the small high-technology companies, as the major users of robots and numerically-controlled machines, tend to be small enough not to attract the attention of Japanese tax authorities and they are unlikely to be invited to become members of the various industry associations through which Japanese economic ministers keep in touch with different sectors of the economy.

A further problem posed by the growth of the new soft sectors is that of statistical definition. Japan's Industrial Taxation Index, which

generally has been regarded as a key economic indicator, is based overwhelmingly on the product of the traditional 'hard' industries. A new industrial production index, which makes due allowances for soft sectors of the economy, is seen as an urgent necessity by the Ministry of Finance and is, in fact, in the process of preparation.

Services require less, but more frequent, investment than steel or shipyards. Thus, the questions arise as to whether they are more stable and whether it is possible to plan the necessary investment cycles more accurately than has been possible with other industries.

Revision questions

1. What is APEC? What is ASEAN? How do they differ?
2. What was the significance of the 'Open Door' policy and when does it date from?
3. How large is China's landmass? What is the size of its population?
4. What is 'Guanxi'?
5. Explain the differences between Russian communism and Chinese communism.
6. What is the significance of the open coastal cities?
7. What are the special economic zones (SEZ's)?
8. Is there a role for countertrade in China today?
9. What features of Chinese society should a Western marketer consider prior to market entry?
10. Comment on Livingstone's remark about the feasibility of market research in China.
11. What are the attractions of a joint venture?
12. What is the attraction of Japan as a consumer market?
13. Why have the Japanese been traditionally slow in moving production and investment overseas?
14. Compare Porter's 1990 estimates of the number of Japanese rivals in selected industries with the position today.
15. What changes have been taking place in the Fortune 500 listings?
16. What is the role of the Sogo Shosha?
17. Explain the meaning of 'kaizen' and 'zaibatsu'.
18. Is internal distribution in Japan still a barrier to free trade?
19. Offer reasons as to why Japan should have so many subcontractors.
20. What is the source of the Japanese competitive advantage – financing or fully integrated enterprises?

References

Argy, V., and Stein, L. (1997) *The Japanese Economy*, Macmillan Press, London.

Anglo-Japanese Economic Institute (1988) *Why Britain? Japanese Business Reasons for Investing in the UK*, London.

Ayala, J., and Lai, R. (1996) 'China's Consumer market: A Huge Opportunity to Fail?' *McKinsey Quarterly*, No. 3, 56–71.

Barale, L. A. (1990) Wholly foreign owned enterprises: changing policy, changing attitudes. *China Business Review*, January–February, 30–35.

Berkwitt, G. J. (1986) Japan's three-tiered distribution. *Industrial Distribution*, **75** (7), 53–57.

Blenkhorn, D. L., and Noori, A. H. (1990) What it takes to supply Japanese OEM's. *Industrial Marketing Management*, **19**, 21–30.

Brahm, L. J. (1996) *China as No. 1: The New Superpower takes Centre Stage*, Butterworth-Heinemann Asia, Singapore.

Brahm, L. J., and Daoran, L. (1996) *The Business Guide to China*, Butterworth-Heinemann Asia, Singapore.

Bruce, L. (1990) Special report: Japan, coming of age. *International Management*, February, 46–57.

Burton, F. N. (1989) 'Trade Friction between Europe and Japan: The Need for a European Consensus', Working Paper, Manchester School of Management, University of Manchester Institute of Science and Technology, February.

Business International Asia/Pacific Ltd., *Business China*, twice monthly report on China, Hong Kong.

Chen, M. (1995) *Asian Management Systems: Chinese, Japanese and Korean Styles of Business*, Thunderbird/Routledge Series in International Management, London and New York.

China Business Review (1990) Two years of troubles, November–December, 32–37.

de Mente, B. (1990) *Japanese Etiquette and Ethics in Business*, 5th edn, NTC Business Books, Lincolnwood, ILL.

de Mente, B. (1990) *How to do Business with the Japanese*, NTC Business Books, Lincolnwood, ILL.

de Mente, B. (1990) *Chinese Etiquette and Ethics in Business: A Penetrating Analysis of the Morals and Values that Shape the Chinese Business Personality*, NTC Publishing Group, Lincolnwood, Chicago.

Denny, D. C. (1989) Can you do market research in China? *China Business Review*, May–June, 36–46.

Dibb, S. (1996) 'The Impact of the Changing Marketing Environment in the Pacific Rim: Four Case Studies', *International Journal of Retail and Distribution Management*, **24** (11), 16–29.

Drifte, R. (1990) *Japan's Foreign Policy*, Routledge, London.

Economist, 'Ready to face the World? A Survey of China', March 8, pp. 1–27.

Edwards, R., and Skully, M. (1996) *ASEAN Business Trade & Development*, Butterworth-Heinemann Asia, Singapore.

Far Eastern Economic Review (1996) 50th Anniversary Review, October.

Fields, G. (1989) The Japanese distribution system: myths and realities. *Tokyo Business Today*, July, 57–59.

Foster, G. (1988) Hard sell in Japan. *Management Today*, September, 94–99.

Frankenstein, J., and Chao, C. N. (1988) Decision-making in the Chinese Foreign Trade Administration: a preliminary survey. *Columbia Journal of World Business*, Fall, 35–40.

Frisbie, J., and Kay, D. B. (1990) Joint venture dissolution: few legal guidelines make contract language the key. *China Business Review*, November–December, 42–45.

Fujigane, Y., and Ennis, P. (1990) Keiretsu – what they are doing: where they are heading? *Tokyo Business Today*, September, 26–30.

Fureng, D. (1983) Some problems concerning China's strategy in foreign economic relations. *International Social; Science Journal*, (97), 455–566.

Fyock, D. A. (1990) Packaging an image: China's enterprises are struggling to adapt public relations to a socialist society. *China Business Review*, September–October, 20–22.

Gillespie, R. E., and Ruwart, S. E. (1989) Hainan: facts, figures and fantasies. *China Business Review*, January–February, 20–30.

Givant, N. (1990) Investing in Shanghai: since Tiananmen, city officials have taken a more intrinsic approach to foreign projects. *China Business Review*, March–April, 28–39.

Griffin, Keith, and Griffin, Kimberley (1983) Institutional change and income distribution in the Chinese countryside. *Oxford Bulletin of Economics and Statistics*, **45** (3), 223–248.

Hara, E., Takito, H., and Umesawa, M. (1990) Keiretsu: what they are doing, where they are heading? *Tokyo Business Today*, September, 26–36.

Harding, H. (1984) The transformation of China. *Brookings Review*, Spring, 3–7.

Harwit, E. (1990) China's elusive panda: the controversial new auto manufacturer looks to succeed where others have stalled. *China Business Review*, July–August, 47–47.

Horsley, J. P. (1989) Foreign investment incentives in Hainan. *China Business Review*, January–February, 31.34.

Hu, Z., and Khan, M. S. (1997) 'Why is China Growing so Fast?' Economic Issues #8, International Monetary Fund, Washington DC.

Ishikawa, K. (1990) *Japan and the Challenge of Europe 1992*, Pinter Publishing for Royal Institute of International Affairs, London.

JMA Management News, Japan Management Association, Tokyo and Malibu, California quarterly.

Johanson, J. K. (1986) Japanese marketing failures. *International Marketing Review*, Autumn, 33–46.

Johanson, J. K., and Nonaka, I. (1996) *Relentless: The Japanese Way of Marketing*, Butterworth-Heinemann, Oxford.

Kang, T. W. (1990) *Gaishi: The Foreign Company in Japan*, Harper Collins, USA.

Keegan, W. J. (1984) International competition: the Japanese challenge. *Journal of International Business Studies*, **15** (Winter), 189–193.

Keizan Koho Center (Japan Institute for Social and Economic Affairs) (1984) KKC Brief No. 15, January, *Sogo Shoshas Spearhead a Growth Area – Third Country Trade*.

Kelly, L. R. (1994) 'Doing Business in China: The Dragon Gathers Speed', *Prism*, First Quarter, 31–49.

Kotler, P., Fahey, L., and Jatusripitak, S. (1985) *The New Competition – What Theory Z Didn't Tell You About – Marketing*, Prentice-Hall.

Larson, M. R. (1988) Exporting private enterprise to developing communist countries: A case study on China. *Columbia Journal of World Business*, Spring, 79–89.

Leong, S. M., Ang, S. H., and Tan, C. T. (1996) *Marketing Insights for the Asia Pacific*, Asia Pacific Marketing Federation and Heinemann Southeast Asia, Singapore.

Lieberthal, K., and Prahalad, C. K. (1989) Maintaining a consistent China strategy. *China Business Review*, March–April, 47–49.

Lim, L. Y. C., and Stoltenberg, C. D. (1990) Becoming a region: Southeast Asia's economic integration presents opportunities for U.S. companies active in China. *China Business Review*, May–June, 24–32.

Lim, W.-S. (1990) Pragmatic partners: Stable trade and expanding investments link China and Singapore. *China Business Review*, July – August, 22–29.

Livingstone, J. M. (1987) The marketing concept in China – a qualified acceptance. In *Management Reforms in China* (Warner, M.), Frances Pinter, London.

Lorenz, C. (1981) How Japan 'cascades' through Western markets. *Financial Times*, 9 November.

Luo, Y., and Chen, M. (1997) 'Does Guanxi influence firm performance?' *Asia Pacific Journal of Management*, **14**, 1–16.

Macleod, R. (1988) *China: How to do Business with the Chinese* , Bantam Books, Toronto and New York.

MacMurray, T., and Woetzel, J. (1994) 'The Challenge facing China's State Owned Enterprises', *McKinsey Quarterly*, No. 2, 61–74.

Naisbitt, J. (1996) *Megatrends Asia*, Nicholas Brealey Publishing, London.

Neff, R. (1990) Now Japan is getting jumpy about quality. *Business Week*, 5 March, 40–44.

Nishikawa, K. (1990) Are Japanese products full of defects? *Tokyo Business Today*, August, 50–53.

Nishikawa, K. (1990) Why Japanese consumer groups oppose market opening measures. *Tokyo Business Today*, March, 40–43.

Noguchi, A. (1990) Pharmaceutical giants flex their muscle. *Tokyo Business Today*, March, 36–38.

Ohashi, T. (1989) Marketing in Japan in the 1990s: homing in on the holonic consumer. *Marketing and Research Today*, November, 220–229.

Ohbora, T., Oishi, K., and Yamanashi, H. (1994) 'The Emperor's New Stores', *McKinsey Quarterly*, No. 2, 75–82.

Overholt, W. H. (1994) 'China's High Road to Economic Development', *McKinsey Quarterly*, No. 1, 124–139.

Pearson, M. (1990) Party and politics in joint ventures. *China Business Review*, November–December, 38–40.

Porter, M. E. (1990) *The Comparative Advantage of Nations*, Macmillan, London.

Pye, L. (1982) *Chinese Commercial Negotiating Style*, Oelgeschlager, Gunn & Hain Publishers Inc., Cambridge, MS.

Reader, J. A. (1984) Entrepreneurship in the People's Republic of China. *Columbia Journal of World Business*, Fall, 43–51.

Reid, D. McH. (1995) 'Critical Success Factors in Japanese Consumer Products Market: Guidance for Foreign MNCs', *The International Executive*, **37** (6), 555–581.

Rohwer, J. (1995) *Asia Rising: Why America will Prosper as Asia's Economies Boom*, A Touchstone Book published by Simon & Schuster, New York.

Sako, M. (1989) Partnership between small and large firms: the case of Japan. In *Partnership Between Small and Large Firms*, (ed. D. G. XXIII – Directorate for Enterprise of the Commission of the European Communities), Brussels, published by Graham and Trotman Ltd., London.

Saludo, R. (1997) 'Eye of the Beholder: Is the US Media Demonizing China? The answer isn't a simple "yes" or "no"', *Asiaweek*, April 4, 22–25.

Sasseen, J. (1989) The rising sun over Europe: why Japan's latest thrusts into Britain and the Continent are causing alarm. *International Management*, July/August, 14.20.

Schlossberg, H. (1990) Japan market hardly closed to US firms. *Marketing News*, 9 July, pp. 1–2.

Seligman, S. D. (1989) *Dealing with the Chinese: A Practical Guide to Business Etiquette in the People's Republic Today*, Warner Books, New York.

Selwyn, M. (1990) China: where the tough get going. *Asian Business*, **26** (11), 54–57.

Shimaguchi, M., and Lazer, W. (1979) Japanese distributions channels, invisible barriers to market entry. *MSU Business Topics*, Winter.

Shimizu, Y., Tsutsui, M., Inaba, Y., and Umesawa, M. (1990) Production Keiretsu: a new export from Japan. *Tokyo Business Today*, September, 30.

Shiotani, T. (1988) Outline of Japanese distribution system. *Business Japan*, August, 89–97.

Simon, D. F. (1990) Shanghai's lure for high-tech investors. *China Business Review*, March–April, 44–49.

The World Bank Atlas 1990, World Bank, Washington, DC.

Tokyo Business Today (1990) A ranking of the most profitable foreign firms in Japan, July, 46–51.

Trachtenberg, J. A. (1986) They didn't listen to anybody. *Forbes*, 15 December, pp. 168, 169.

Turpin, D. (1990) Persistence and the competitiveness of the Japanese firm. In *The World Competitiveness Report, 1990*, (IMD) Geneva.

Wagsty, S. (1990) Japanese financial markets. *Financial Times, Special Supplement*, 15 March.

Walters, P. G. P., and Zhu, M. (1995) 'International Marketing in Chinese Enterprises: Some Evidence from the PRC', *Management International Review*, **35**(3), 265–279.

Warner, M. (1987) *Management Reforms in China*.

Weil, M. (1990) China's exports: on the edge. *China Business Review*, January–February, 36–43.

Westwood, R. I., and Posner, B. Z. (1997) 'Managerial Values across Cultures: Australia, Hong Kong and the United States', *Asia Pacific Journal of Management*, **14**, 31–66.

Wilkinson, E. (1990) *Japan Versus the West*, Penguin Books, London.

Woodward, K. (1991) Tianjin comes of age. *China Business Review*, January–February, 20–25.

Yi, X. B. (1990) *Marketing to China: One Billion New Customers*, NTC Publishing Group, Lincolnwood, Chicago.

Zhang, S. X., and Snyder, J. L. (1988) The Five Ps. *China Business Review*, March–April, 14–18.

Web sites

APEC – Asia Pacific Economic Cooperation
http://www.apecsec.org.sg/apecpnewg.html
http://www.iijnet.or.jp/vj/p-asia/g-info/S1-J.html

APEC – Home Page of the Asia Pacific Economic Cooperation Secretariat
http://www.apecsec.org.sg/apecnet.html

ASEAN and Pacific Studies
http://merlion.iseas.ac.sg/asean.html

Asia – The Datafile: magazine on the Internet in Asia
http:///www.dataphile.com.hk

Asia Internet Directory
http://www.asia-inc.com/aid/indexhtml

AsiaOne – East Asian and Western Pacific destinations plus Turkey
http://www.web3.asia1.com.sg/tnp/jourrney/travel/travel.html

Asia Online
http://asia-online.com/

Asia Pacific Business and Marketing Resources
gopher: hoshi.cic.sffu.ca
Choose: David See_Chai Lam Centre for International Communication–Asia Pacific Business & Marketing Resources

Asia Pacific Management Forum
http://www.mcb.co.uk/apmorum/nethome.htm

Asia Pages – online business, consumer and tourist information
http://www.asiapages.com.sg

Asia Trade
http://www.asiatrade.com/index.html

Asian Business
http://web3.asia1.com.sg/timesnet/

Asian Institute of Technology's Asia Info Page
http://emailhost.ait.ac.th/Asia/asia.html

Asian Sources Online:product, supplier, country – ASM Group
http://www.asiansources.com

Associated Press news wire
http://www.csmonitor.com/headlines/apfeed/apfeed.html

AT & T India Horizons
http://www.att.com/indiahorizons/home.html

Australia general lists
http://www.csu.edu.au/links/ozweb.html

Australia Online
http://australia-online.com

Australian Government Information Sources
http://www.nla.gov.au/oz/gov.html

Australian Tourist Commission
http://www.aussie.net.au

Southeast Asian Information:
http://www.channelA.com/
http://www.asia1.com.sg/htmlBank
    of America: Global Capital Markets Group
http://www.bofa.com/capmkts4.html

BEMs – Big Emerging Markets (US
    Classification)
http://www.stat-usa.gov/itabems.html

BradyNet Inc
http://www.Bradynet.com/m-local.html

Brainstorm Business Forum – home of CBI,
    Chambers of Commerce, Best Practice
http://www.brainstorm.co.uk

Business Information
www.businessmonitor.co.uk

Business Information Resources
http://sashimi.wwa.com/~notime/eotw/
    business_info.html

Business Information Server
http://www.dnb.com/

Business Opportunity Search Engine
http://www.cashquest.com

The Business Page International
http://www.sgn.com/4sale.html

Business Plan Generator
http://www.tripod.com/planet/toybox/
    business_plan

Business Site of the Day
http://www.bizniz.com/eurocool/

Business Statistics
gopher: University of Michigan: una.hh.lib.
    umich.edu
Choose: ebb Current Business Statistics

Businesses on the Internet
http://www.yahoo.com/Business_and_Econ-
    omy/Corporations/

Business to Business Marketing Exchange
http://www.btob.wfu.edu/b2b.html

Business Week online edition
http://www.businessweek.com

China Online Service – links to websites and
    information sources in China
http://www.gcinfo.com/main.html

China Garment Enterprise Association (200
    Member Companies across China)
http://www.sh.com/custom/cgea.htm

China Homepage
http://www.ihep.ac.cn/china.html

China Internet Company

Chinese Language Web Directory – What Site!
http://www.whatsite.com

CIA Publications
http://www.odci.gov/cia/publications/
    pubs.html

CNN Interactive
http://www.cnn.com/

Commerce Business Daily
gopher:cscns.com
Choose: Internet Express Gopher by Subject
            Business-Commerce Business Daily-
            Softshare

Commercenet
www.commerce.net

Commercial Use of the Internet
http://pass.wayne.edu/business.html

CultureFinder
http://www.culturefinder.com/
    index.htm

Currency Conversion Information – Olsen and
    Associates 164 Currency Converter, Zurich,
    Switzerland
http://www.olsen.ch/cgi-bin/exmenu/

Currency Converter
http://bin.gnn.com/cgi-bin/gnn/currency

Dictionaries
http://www.onelook.com

DigiCrime
http://www.digicrime.com/

Diners Club – Global weather, currency conver-
    sions, language translations, dealing with
    stress
http://www.dinersclub.com

Distance calculator
http://www.indo.com/distance

Encyclopedia
http://clever.net/cam/encylpedia.html

Encyclopedia Mythica
http://www.pantheon.org/mythica

EWR (Early Warning Report): Chokepoints for
    World Trade
http://www.subscriptions.com/beacon/
    mapchokepoints.html

Export – Import Pathfinder
http://mickey.queens.lib.ny.us/guides/
export_i.html

ExportNet – Export Today Matchmaking service
http://www.exporttoday.com

Financenter
http://www.financenter.com/

Find it Fast
http://www.webcom.com/~tbrown/
findpage.html

Flags of all Nations
http://www.wave.net/upg/immigration/
flags.html

Foreign Exchange Rates
http://www.dna.Ith.se/cgi-bin/kurt/rates/

Foreign Exchange Rates
http://www.asia 1.com.sg/cgi-bin/bt/
multi. p1

Foreign Language fonts
http://wwfonts.com

Foreign Language Lessons for Travellers
http://www.travlang.com/languages

Global Change Research Information
documents and publications
http://www.gcrio.org/docpub.html

Global Economic Forum
http://www.ms.com/GEFdata/digests/
960129-mon.html

Global Interactive Business Directory
http://wwwpronett.com

Global Internet News Agency
www.gina.com

Global Trade Center
http://wwwtradezone.com/tz/

Hong Kong
http://www.hongkong.org.

Hong Kong Business Directory
http://www.hkdir.com.hk

Hoover's Business Resources
http://pathfinder.com/money/hoovers

Hotel & Travel Index On-Line
http://www.traveler.net/hito

Human Rights Web
http://www.traveller.com/~hrweb/
hrweb.html

International Financial Encyclopedia
http://www.euro.net/innovation/
Finance_Base/Fin_encyc.html

International Franchise Association

Internet Business Center
http://www.tig.com/IBC

Internet Marketing List Archives
http://www.popco.com/hyper/
inet-marketing/

Internet Public Library
http://ipl.sils.umich.edu/

Internet Sleuth
http://www.intbc.com/sleuth/

Importing and Exporting
Usenet: alt.business.import-export

Inc. Online
http://www.inc.com

Infomarket – gathers finance and business
related links:
http://www.fe.msk.ru/infomarket/
ewelcome.html

International Business Forum
http://www.ibf.com

International Business Practices Guide

University of Missouri St Louis
gopher: umslvma.umsl.edu
Choose: The Library
Government Information
International Business

International Business Resources on the WWW
http://ciber.bus.msu.edu/busres.htm

International Chamber of Commerce, Paris
http://www.iccbo.org

Internet Address Finder
www.iaf.net

International Internet Marketing
www.clark.net/pub/granered/iim.html

Internet Export Resources
http://web.ukonlin.co.uk/Members/
jim.haa,ill/contens.htm

Japan Web Servers
http://www.ntt.jp/SQUARE/www-in-
JP.html

Japan: What's New in Japan
http://www.ntt.jp/WHATSNEW/

Japan Information Network
http://jin.jcic.or.jp/navi/category_1.html

Japanese conversation basics
http://www.wsu.edu:8080/~tsonobe/japan

JETRO (The Japanese External Trade
Organisation)
http://www.jetro.go.jp/index.html

Mapquest
http://www.mapquest.com/

MasterCard International
http://www.mastercard.com

NBS – Marketing Resources
http://www.nbs.ntu.ac.uk/sites/
mktglink.htm

News of the Day
http://www.dnai.com/~vox/news/
newspage.html

Nijenrode Business webserver – Economic data,
statistical data, trends per country
http://www.nijenrode.nl/nbr/trends

Orientation – Hong Kong based multi-language
Web index
http://www.orientation.com

PC Webopaedia Lite Version 1.5
http://www.sandybay.com/pc~web/
download.html

Political Risk Services
http://www.polrisk.com

Qantas Airways Ltd
http://wwwanzac.com/qantas/qantas.htm

Thomas Ho's favourite Electronic Commerce
WWW Resources
http://www.engr.iupui.edu/~ho/interests/
commmenu.html

New Zealand Government Web Pages
http://www.govt.nz/

New Zealand Information
http://manuka.lincoln.ac.nz/libr/nz

News in Motion
http://www.newspaper.com

Newsgroup for Importing and Exporting
news:alt.business.import-export

Next Online – some of Australia's best Internet
with links to Australia's Net Directory
http://www.next.com.au

The Press Association
http://www.pa.press.net

Pointcast Network
http://www.pointcast.com

Pointcast Network Canada
http://www.pointcast.ca

Regional Information Guides by Price Waterhouse
http://www.i-trade.com/infsrc/pw

Securities Exchange Commission corporate
filings database

http://edgar.stern.nyu.edu/EDGAR/
toolsNT.shtml??

Singapore Web Servers
http://www.w3.org/hypertext/
DataSources/WWW/sg.html

Singapore – Straits Times Interactive
http://www.asia 1.com.sg/straitstimes

SilverPlatter World: a worldwide library of
electronic information
http://www.silverplatter.com/

Singapore Info Web
http://www.technet.sg/InfoWEB/
welcome.html

Slang Dictionary
http://www.blender.com/blender
1.1/digest/popspeak/popspeak 1.html

South China Morning Post
http://www.scmp.om/cdcom

Statistical Agencies on the Internet
http://www.science.gmu.edu/csi
779/drope/govstats.html

Swissair
http://www.swissair.com

The Economist
http://www.economist.com

Trade Compass
http://www.tradecompass.com

TradePort – extensive information on international business
http://www.tradeport.org

Trade Statistics
http://www.census.gov/ftp/pub/
foreign-trade/www/

Trade Wave Galaxy – Public and commercial
information and services
http://www.einet.net/galaxy.html

Translations Service
http://www.globalink.com/home.html

UNCTAD (UN Conference on Trade and
Development)
http://www.unicc.org/unctad/en/
enhome.htm

United Nations Development Program:
sustainable human development
http://www.undp.org/

US Dept. of Commerce
http://www.doc.gov/
CommerceHomePage.html

Fedworld
www.fedworld.gov

US National Trade Data Bank
http://www.stat-usa.gov/BEN/Services/ntdbhome.html

US News & World Report Online
http://www.usnews.com

US Patent and Trademark Office
http://www.uspto.gov/

US Trademark Library
http://www.micropat.com

USA – Economic Bulletin Board
gopher://una.hh.lib.umich.edu/11/ebb

Wall Street Journal Interactive Edition
http://www.update.wsj.com/

Wall Street Net
http://www.netsource.com/wsn/

Web Page for Global Business
http://www.seattleu.edu/~parker/homepage.html

Web Sites for International Information:
http://www.ustr.gov/
http://www.i-trade.com/

http://www.stat-usa.gov/BEN/subject/trade.html
http://www.itaiep.doc.gov/

Virtual Reference Desk
http://thorplus.lib.purdue.edu/reference/index.html

Visa Expo
http://wwwvisa.com

World Bank
http://www.worldbank.org/

World Factbook
http://www.odci.gov/cia/publications/95fact/index.html

World Wide Web Virtual Library
http://W3.org

WTO (World Trade Organization): Agreement Establishing the WTO:
http://www.soton.ac.uk/~nukop/data/fullrecs/1660.htm

WTO
http://www.unicc.org//wto/Welcome.html

WWW Yellow Pages
www.cba.uh.edu/ylowpges/ylowpges.html.

Index

Buyer credit, 265

C factors, 42, 73
Cabotage, 289
Campaign transferability, 327–32
Canada, 9, 87, 230, 465
    language in, 195–6, 344
    see also North America
CAP (Common agricultural policy), 68, 415–17
Capacity, production, 17, 118, 131
Capital, 22
    in joint ventures, 170
    shortages, 364–5, 428
Car industry:
    in China, 450–1
    in Egypt, 63–4
    and European Union disputes, 62, 63, 260
    Ford, 162–3, 212–13
    market for, 57
    origin of parts and assembly, 153–4
    and parallel importing, 302–3
    spare parts market, 404
    strategic business alliances in, 164, 165
Car ownership data, 85
Caribbean countries, 420–2
Cartels, 283
Cascading strategy, Japan's, 191, 469
Cash disbursements, 369
    see also Irregular payments
CBI (Confederation of British Industry), 119
CCC (Customs Cooperation Council), 152
CDs, price challenge to, 283
CEN (European Committee for Standardization), 413
CENELEC (European Committee for Electro-
    Technical Standardization), 413
Central and Eastern Europe, 427–37
    applications for European Union, 396
    buyback in, 278
    political background, 75, 393, 427–9
    tripartite ventures in, 174
    see also Czech Republic; Former Soviet Union;
        Poland; Romania; Russia
Centralization, 43, 363, 374
Ceylon *see* Sri Lanka
Channel Tunnel, 427
Children and advertising, 328, 341
China International Trust and Investment Corp
    (Citic), 453–4, 460
China, People's Republic of, 442–64
    brand piracy in, 236
    car industry in, 450–1
    Citic in, 453–4, 460
    currency in, 443
    Economic and Technical Development Zones
        (ETDZ), 459–60
    economy of, 445–7, 449
    financial services in, 447, 449
    foreign investment in, 459–60
    Gucci in, 189–90
    Hong Kong, 259, 444
    L'Oreal's expansion in, 169
    market in, 455–8
    and the origins of tea, 240, 241
    politics in, 443, 445, 447

    Tiananmen Square events, 75, 462–3
    Special Economic Zones (SEZ) in, 458–9
    trade surplus with US, 454–5
    and the WTO, 61, 451–2
    see also Pacific Rim
CIF (cost, insurance, freight), 87, 294
Cinema, 338
CIP (carriage and insurance paid), 266, 294
CIRFS (man-made fibres producers), 68
CIS (Commonwealth of Independent States), 426,
    427, 428
Citic (China International Trust and Investment
    Corp), 453–4, 460
Clearing account, bilateral trading, 277
CMR Convention 1956 (road transport), 291
Coca-Cola, 220
    advertising campaign, 338
    bottle, 198–9, 232
    branding, 329, 332
    as franchise operation, 141
    parallel exporting of, 259
Cognitive dissonance, 323
Colchester-Buchan diagrams, 408, 409
Commission for International Trade Law
    (UNCITRAL), 55–6
Commissioners:European Union, 402
Committee on Origin, 152
Committee of Permanent Representatives
    (COREPER), 404
Committee for the Simplification of International
    Trade Procedures (SITPRO), 119, 293
Common agricultural policy (CAP), 68, 415–17
Common commercial policy, 412
Commonwealth of Independent States (CIS), 426,
    427, 428
Communications, 22, 313, 320–3
    in Eastern Europe, 434
    as export barrier, 107
    and language, 195–8
    see also Internet; Language
Communism in China, 443, 445, 447, 456, 458
Compaq computers, 299
Comparative advertising, 327–8, 341, 344
Compensation trading, 278
Competition, 16–17, 22
    costs of, 43
    five forces of, 57
    impact of multinationals, 18
    new, 188–9, 191
    perfect, 252
    within European Union, 413–15
Competitiveness, 17, 57
    global, 10–11
    national, 4–8
    and value chains, 84
Compliance strategies, 47–8
Concentration *see* Market concentration
Concentration on Key Markets (BETRO), 362
Conciliation, 55
Confederation of British Industry (CBI), 119
Consensus Arrangement, 265
Consensus, the (credit group), 69
Consignment Account, 272
Consortia, exporting, 116–18, 127

480 +